# Microcomputer Buses and Links

# Microcomputer Buses and Links

**D. Del Corso**
*Dipartimento di Elettronica, Politecnico di Torino, Italy*

**H. Kirrmann**
*Brown Boveri Research Center, Baden, Switzerland*

**J. D. Nicoud**
*Swiss Federal Institute of Technology, Lausanne, Switzerland*

1986

ACADEMIC PRESS
*Harcourt Brace Jovanovich, Publishers*
London   Orlando   San Diego   New York   Austin
Boston   Sydney   Tokyo   Toronto

ACADEMIC PRESS INC. (LONDON) LTD
24-28 Oval Road
London NW1

*US edition published by*
ACADEMIC PRESS INC.
Orlando, Florida 32887

Copyright © 1986 by
ACADEMIC PRESS INC. (LONDON) LTD

*All Rights Reserved*
No part of this book may be reproduced in any form, by photostat, microfilm or any other means, without written permission from the publishers

*British Library Cataloguing in Publication Data*
Del Corso, D.
 Microcomputer buses and links.
 1. Computer networks
 I. Title  II. Kirrmann, H.
 III. Nicoud, J. D.
 004.6   TK5105.5
 ISBN 0-12-209040-3

Printed in Great Britain by J. W. Arrowsmith Ltd, Bristol

# PREFACE

Microcomputers are still evolving rapidly. Sixteen-bit processors have REPLACED 8-bit processors for most professional applications, and are about to be replaced by 32-bit processors. Multiprocessor systems will assume major importance in the near future, when the mechanisms for efficient task scheduling and error recovery are better understood, and when "standard" buses support clusters of microprocessors. Local networks will interconnect hundreds of systems, and will be interconnected together with open systems; they will provide users WITH variety and quality of services never before reached.

This book is intended for design engineers who want to understand the hardware aspects of microcomputer systems at the bus and I/O interface level. A systematic approach has been followed in order to provide a clear understanding of the concepts associated with all buses, and to indicate the practical solutions implemented by manufacturers. The book can hence be considered as a design guide, more with the purpose of helping the reader to understand the principles of existing buses and links than with the objective to encourage him to design new buses. A strong effort must be made in this field to avoid the proliferation of "standards", trying to concentrate on a few of the existing ones and learning to live with their weakpoints if necessary.

The book is organized into ten chapters. The first one is an introduction which provides the motivation for the detailed bus analysis given in Chapters 2 to 7. Chapters 8 and 9 approach the difficult art of interface design. Chapter 10 presents a survey of serial buses and networks. RS-232 is covered in some detail, due to its use and misuse within the microprocessor industry.

The protocol aspects of Local Networks are not covered in this book. Only the physical layers of local area networks are explained in Chapter 10 for completeness and for comparison with parallel buses and links, more within the scope of short distance serial buses than of long haul networks. This field will expand very rapidly; the principles covered here will remain as a basis for understanding in the field.

The appendix provides a summary of the principal links and backplane buses, to allow easy comparison of their major features, and to provide a good preparation for studying the full documentation of the selected buses or links.

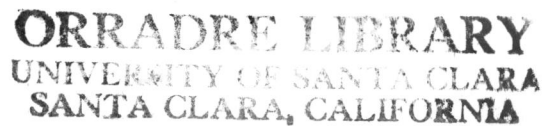

The reading of this book requires a minimum knowledge of the field. Engineers with practical experience and students will obtain the greatest benefit from its structured approach, made by authors who are both experienced engineers and pedagogues. An index specifies the places where important terms are defined in italics and used in a context which helps in understanding them. References to the most important books and papers are given between brackets.

Many qualified and helpful people have contributed directly or indirectly to the work and understanding of the authors. A subgroup of the European Distributed Intelligence Study Group (EDISG) worked on buses since 1977, looking for an efficient replacement for the CAMAC system. The IEEE-P896 committee started a similar project in 1979. It refined the specifications and carried out several redesign phases until an acceptable solution was found. That sometimes painful bus acceptance procedure was very helpful in understanding the basic issues of bus design. Many disagreements regarding the final solution arose due to different basic options, and frequently it was long after the dust had settled, that the effective reasons for disagreement were understood.

The material accumulated due to the work of the P896 group, chaired from 1978 to 1982 by Andrew Allison and since 1983 by Paul Borrill, has been very useful in the preparation of this book, even if for many reasons we have not been able to describe all the details. Probably, if all the information had been available to the participants of P896 from the beginning, more fruitful discussions would have taken place, due to a better understanding of the basic issues and the use of a common terminology.

We would also like to thank our supporting organizations, which have taken care of our occasional travel expenses and have helped us to write this book. The team at Lausanne has been very responsive in improving the tools which allowed the printing of this text, and the draughtsmen are to be congratulated on their fine work.

Many corrections and suggestions have been provided by Hermann Schmid, Ferdynand Wagner, Frederick Edwards and Steffen Bartschat. This has greatly improved our text, and both the authors and readers thank them. Last but not least, our wives and secretaries have been very cooperative and patient with us; we have appreciated their support very much.

DDC HK JDN<br>
October 1985

# CONTENTS

1. **INTRODUCTION** — 1
   - 1.1 INTERCONNECTION SCHEMES — 1
     - 1.1.1 Microprocessor System — 2
     - 1.1.2 Types of interconnections — 3
   - 1.2 DESIGN CHOICES — 5
     - 1.2.1 Physical and electrical specification — 5
     - 1.2.2 Serial versus parallel links — 6
     - 1.2.3 Point-to-point versus bused connections — 7
     - 1.2.4 Multiple sources and multiple destinations — 9
     - 1.2.5 Single-master and multiple-master systems — 10
     - 1.2.6 Conclusion and classification — 10

2. **PRINCIPLE OF OPERATIONS** — 13
   - 2.1 LOGIC ELEMENTS AND NOTATIONS — 13
     - 2.1.1 Terminology — 13
     - 2.1.2 Numbers — 14
     - 2.1.3 Signals — 15
     - 2.1.4 Logic equations — 16
     - 2.1.5 State and timing diagrams — 17
     - 2.1.6 Combinatorial logic elements — 18
     - 2.1.7 Flip-flops — 21
     - 2.1.8 Registers — 22
     - 2.1.9 The metastable state — 24
     - 2.1.10 Block diagrams — 26
   - 2.2 TECHNOLOGICAL CONSTRAINTS — 27
     - 2.2.1 Characteristics of transmission media — 27
     - 2.2.2 Free-space transmission — 28
     - 2.2.3 Wire transmission — 29
     - 2.2.4 Optical fibers — 31
     - 2.2.5 Multi-wire media — 32
     - 2.2.6 Transmission lines — 35
     - 2.2.7 Line driving techniques — 36
     - 2.2.8 Bus drivers and receivers — 37
     - 2.2.9 Features of parallel buses — 39
   - 2.3 STANDARDIZATION AND OSI MODEL — 39
     - 2.3.1 Hierarchical modular decomposition — 40
     - 2.3.2 Functional decomposition in communications — 41
     - 2.3.3 The OSI Reference Model — 46
     - 2.3.4 Wrapping — 50
     - 2.3.5 Use of the OSI-RM to standardize buses — 51
     - 2.3.6 Consequences of interface design — 53
     - 2.3.7 A discussion of the OSI Reference Model — 53
     - 2.3.8 Standardization process — 54
     - 2.3.9 Requirement and functional description — 55

## 3 POINT-TO-POINT TRANSFERS 57
### 3.1 ACTIONS 57
3.1.1 Elementary operations of an information transfer 57
3.1.2 Mapping of actions into signals and lines 58
### 3.2 CYCLES 59
3.2.1 Sequencing of actions 59
3.2.2 Fully interlocked sequences 64
### 3.3 SOURCE/DESTINATION PROTOCOLS 64
3.3.1 Source-activated protocol 66
3.3.2 Destination-activated protocol 67
3.3.3 Example: the Centronics protocol 68
3.3.4 Example: remote A/D reading 68
### 3.4 READ/WRITE PROTOCOLS 69
3.4.1 Commander and responder 69
3.4.2 Example: data transfer in a microprocessor system 70
3.4.3 Masters and slaves 71
### 3.5 BIDIRECTIONAL LINKS 72
3.5.1 Readpulse/writepulse protocol 73
3.5.2 Example: MULTIBUS 1 transfers 73
3.5.3 Advanced read/write protocol 74
3.5.4 Example: FASTBUS transfers 75
3.5.5 Valid/request protocol 76
3.5.6 Lines versus logic 76
### 3.6 SYNCHRONIZATION OF THE ACTION SEQUENCE 77
3.6.1 Handshaken cycles 77
3.6.2 Example: Q-BUS DATI and DATO cycles 80
3.6.3 Synchronous cycles 80
3.6.4 Example: control signals of static RAMs 83
3.6.5 Semi-synchronous cycles 85
3.6.6 Single-line handshake 88
3.6.7 Speed comparison of protocols 88
3.6.8 Clocked interfaces and protocols 89
3.6.9 Example: the Z80 memory protocol 90
### 3.7 PROTOCOL CONVERSION 90
3.7.1 Layered protocol conversion 91
3.7.2 Conversion of the action encoding 91
3.7.3 Example: interface of memory devices 92
3.7.4 Synchronous units on a handshaken bus 93
3.7.5 Synchronous units on a semi-synchronous bus 94
3.7.6 Semi-synchronous units on a handshaken bus 95
3.7.7 Example: microprocessor interface with a handshaken bus 96
3.7.8 Summary of conversion possibilities 97

Contents ix

## 4 SINGLE-MASTER BUSES 99
### 4.1 ADDRESSING TECHNIQUES 99
- 4.1.1 Graphical representation 99
- 4.1.2 The slave selection process 100
- 4.1.3 Decoded selection 100
- 4.1.4 Coded selection 101
- 4.1.5 Mixed selection 104
- 4.1.6 Incomplete selection 105
- 4.1.7 Geographical selection 106

### 4.2 ADDRESS/DATA PROTOCOLS 109
- 4.2.1 Handshaken addressing 109
- 4.2.2 Microcycle protocol 110
- 4.2.3 Merged protocol 113
- 4.2.4 Mixed synchronization 114

### 4.3 MULTIPLEXED BUSES 117
- 4.3.1 Multiplexed protocols 117
- 4.3.2 Examples of multiplexed buses 118
- 4.3.3 Performance of multiplexed buses 120
- 4.3.4 Pipelining of operations 122

### 4.4 MULTIPLE TRANSFER CYCLES 123
- 4.4.1 Read-modify-write 123
- 4.4.2 Read-after-write 124
- 4.4.3 Block transfer 125

## 5 MULTIPLE-MASTER BUSES 127
### 5.1 RESOURCE SHARING 127
- 5.1.1 Resource allocation techniques 128
- 5.1.2 Model of the exclusive access system 130
- 5.1.3 Sequential token passing 132
- 5.1.4 Switch-on-demand token passing 134
- 5.1.5 Multiple access by collision detection 136

### 5.2 EXCLUSIVE ACCESS BY ARBITRATION 138
- 5.2.1 FIFO resource handling 138
- 5.2.2 Fixed priority arbiters 139
- 5.2.3 Variable-priority arbiters 140

### 5.3 ARBITRATION CIRCUITS 143
- 5.3.1 Arbitration structures 143
- 5.3.2 Basic priority circuits 144
- 5.3.3 Daisy chain arbiters 146
- 5.3.4 The linear self-selection arbiter 148
- 5.3.5 The coded self-selection arbiter 150
- 5.3.6 Mixed arbitration techniques 153

|   |   |   |   |   |
|---|---|---|---|---|
| | 5.4 | THE SYNCHRONIZATION PROBLEM | | 154 |
| | | 5.4.1 | The basic exclusion mechanism | 154 |
| | | 5.4.2 | Fair access logic | 156 |
| | | 5.4.3 | Output synchronization | 158 |
| | | 5.4.4 | Sequencing of allocation operations | 160 |
| 6 | SPECIAL PROTOCOLS | | | 163 |
| | 6.1 | INTERRUPTS | | 163 |
| | | 6.1.1 | Requirements of an interrupt system | 164 |
| | | 6.1.2 | Handling of multiple interrupts | 166 |
| | | 6.1.3 | Centralized interrupt controller | 167 |
| | | 6.1.4 | Daisy chain distributed interrupt controller | 168 |
| | | 6.1.5 | Self-selection distributed interrupt controller | 171 |
| | | 6.1.6 | Mixed interrupt control systems | 172 |
| | 6.2 | SPECIAL TRANSFER CYCLES | | 173 |
| | | 6.2.1 | Split cycles | 173 |
| | 6.3 | EXTENDED PROTOCOLS | | 174 |
| | | 6.3.1 | N-partner handshake | 174 |
| | | 6.3.2 | An example of N-partner protocol: IEC 625 | 178 |
| | | 6.3.3 | The Enable/Disable technique | 179 |
| | | 6.3.4 | Generalization of the Enable/Disable technique | 180 |
| | | 6.3.5 | Bus supervisors | 182 |
| 7 | ERROR HANDLING | | | 183 |
| | 7.1 | DEFINITIONS | | 183 |
| | | 7.1.1 | Error sources and effects | 183 |
| | | 7.1.2 | Fault tolerance | 185 |
| | | 7.1.3 | Coding theory | 187 |
| | 7.2 | ERROR DETECTION AND CORRECTION IN SMALL DATA ITEMS | | 191 |
| | | 7.2.1 | Parity | 191 |
| | | 7.2.2 | Longitudinal parity | 192 |
| | | 7.2.3 | Single error correction | 193 |
| | | 7.2.4 | Single error correction, double error detection | 197 |
| | | 7.2.5 | Efficiency of SEC and DED | 200 |
| | 7.3 | ERROR DETECTION IN LONG MESSAGES | | 201 |
| | | 7.3.1 | Checksum | 201 |
| | | 7.3.2 | Cyclic Redundancy Check | 202 |
| 8 | CHARACTERISTICS OF BUS LINES | | | 207 |
| | 8.1 | METHODS AND TOOLS | | 207 |
| | 8.2 | IDEAL TRANSMISSION LINE BEHAVIOUR | | 209 |
| | | 8.2.1 | An experiment | 209 |
| | | 8.2.2 | Behaviour at switch-on ($0 \leq t < t_{pd}$) | 210 |
| | | 8.2.3 | First reflection ($t = t_{pd}$) | 212 |
| | | 8.2.4 | Return to sender ($t = 2 \cdot t_{pd}$) | 214 |
| | | 8.2.5 | Matching the line | 215 |

| | | | |
|---|---|---|---|
| 8.3 | WAVE PROPERTIES | | 216 |
| | 8.3.1 | Linear model | 216 |
| | 8.3.2 | Trapezoidal waves | 217 |
| | 8.3.3 | Frequency-dependent losses | 219 |
| | 8.3.4 | Non-linear elements | 219 |
| 8.4 | TRANSMISSION LINE PARAMETERS | | 220 |
| | 8.4.1 | Model of a transmission line | 220 |
| | 8.4.2 | Characteristic impedance | 221 |
| | 8.4.3 | Propagation speed | 222 |
| | 8.4.4 | Numerical values | 223 |
| | 8.4.5 | Loading a line | 228 |
| 8.5 | LATTICE DIAGRAM | | 230 |
| | 8.5.1 | Homogeneous line with termination | 230 |
| | 8.5.2 | Line with discontinuities | 233 |
| | 8.5.3 | Driving a line from the middle | 237 |
| | 8.5.4 | Wired-OR glitches | 238 |
| 8.6 | BERGERON'S DIAGRAM | | 240 |
| | 8.6.1 | The wave equations | 240 |
| | 8.6.2 | The terminations | 241 |
| | 8.6.3 | Quiescent state | 243 |
| | 8.6.4 | Turn-on | 243 |
| | 8.6.5 | Forward and backward waves | 243 |
| | 8.6.6 | Timing diagram | 244 |
| 8.7 | NON-LINEAR DRIVERS | | 245 |
| | 8.7.1 | Open-collector driver | 245 |
| | 8.7.2 | Three-state driver | 247 |
| | 8.7.3 | Receiver characteristic | 250 |
| | 8.7.4 | Reflections and the operating region | 251 |
| | 8.7.5 | Open-collector vs. three-state drivers | 254 |
| 8.8 | TERMINATIONS | | 257 |
| | 8.8.1 | Parallel termination | 257 |
| | 8.8.2 | Series termination | 257 |
| | 8.8.3 | Bus termination | 258 |
| 8.9 | CROSSTALK | | 261 |
| | 8.9.1 | Definitions | 261 |
| | 8.9.2 | Calculating crosstalk | 263 |
| | 8.9.3 | Reducing crosstalk by line arrangement | 267 |
| 9 | INTERFACE DESIGN | | 271 |
| 9.1 | SYSTEM DECOMPOSITION | | 271 |
| | 9.1.1 | Single processor bus system | 272 |
| | 9.1.2 | Dedicated buses | 272 |
| | 9.1.3 | Multiprocessor bus systems | 273 |

| | | | |
|---|---|---|---|
| 9.2 | | SYNCHRONIZATION TECHNIQUES | 274 |
| | 9.2.1 | Asynchronous approach | 274 |
| | 9.2.2 | Synchronous approach | 274 |
| | 9.2.3 | Synchronization of non-synchronous data | 275 |
| | 9.2.4 | Synchronization design | 276 |
| 9.3 | | BUS INTERFACE | 277 |
| | 9.3.1 | Master and slave | 277 |
| | 9.3.2 | Transfer handshake | 278 |
| | 9.3.3 | Asynchronous implementation | 281 |
| | 9.3.4 | Synchronous implementation | 282 |
| | 9.3.5 | Complete transfer sequence | 285 |
| | 9.3.6 | Arbitration | 286 |
| | 9.3.7 | Selection | 288 |
| | 9.3.8 | Interrupt request | 289 |
| 9.4 | | DATA MULTIPLEXING AND ALIGNMENT | 289 |
| | 9.4.1 | Multiplexing | 290 |
| | 9.4.2 | Driver arrangement | 291 |
| | 9.4.3 | Address space | 291 |
| | 9.4.4 | Straight and justified buses | 291 |
| | 9.4.5 | Complex devices and bus drivers | 293 |
| | 9.4.6 | Big endian and little endian | 295 |
| 9.5 | | LOGIC DESIGN AND IMPLEMENTATION | 296 |
| | 9.5.1 | Component selection | 297 |
| | 9.5.2 | Timing analysis | 298 |
| | 9.5.3 | Board layout | 299 |
| | 9.5.4 | Backplane and connectors | 299 |
| | 9.5.5 | Conclusion | 299 |
| **10 SERIAL LINKS** | | | **301** |
| 10.1 | | SERIALIZATION OF INFORMATION | 301 |
| | 10.1.1 | Bit transfers and synchronization | 302 |
| | 10.1.2 | Character transfer and synchronization | 303 |
| | 10.1.3 | Message transfer and synchronization | 304 |
| | 10.1.4 | System organization | 305 |
| 10.2 | | MODULATIONS TECHNIQUES | 305 |
| | 10.2.1 | Principles of modulation/demodulation | 306 |
| | 10.2.2 | Capacity and bandwidth | 307 |
| | 10.2.3 | Encoding/decoding schemes | 308 |
| | 10.2.4 | Implicit clock schemes | 309 |
| | 10.2.5 | Self-clocking schemes | 312 |
| | 10.2.6 | Special encodings | 314 |
| | 10.2.7 | Comparison | 316 |

| | | | |
|---|---|---|---|
| 10.3 | IMPLEMENTATION OF SERIAL SCHEMES | | 317 |
| | 10.3.1 Transfer of parallel data | | 317 |
| | 10.3.2 Source controlled full serial transfer | | 318 |
| | 10.3.3 Destination controlled full serial transfer | | 319 |
| | 10.3.4 Distributed clock | | 320 |
| | 10.3.5 Bidirectional transfers | | 320 |
| | 10.3.6 Example: NOVRAM circuit control | | 321 |
| | 10.3.7 Two-line transfers | | 322 |
| | 10.3.8 One-line transfers | | 323 |
| | 10.3.9 Asynchronous transfers | | 323 |
| | 10.3.10 Example: SIMSER transfers | | 325 |
| | 10.3.11 Character oriented protocols | | 325 |
| | 10.3.12 Bit oriented protocols | | 327 |
| | 10.3.13 Protocol conversion | | 328 |
| 10.4 | RS-232-LIKE LINKS | | 328 |
| | 10.4.1 DTE and DCE | | 328 |
| | 10.4.2 Modem control | | 329 |
| | 10.4.3 RS-232 connectors and conventions | | 330 |
| | 10.4.4 RS-232-like data transfers | | 331 |
| | 10.4.5 DTE to DTE direct transfers | | 333 |
| | 10.4.6 RS-232 control signals | | 335 |
| | 10.4.7 Null-modems and Null-DTE | | 337 |
| | 10.4.8 Extension cables | | 339 |
| | 10.4.9 Not connected lines | | 340 |
| 10.5 | OTHER SERIAL STANDARDS | | 340 |
| | 10.5.1 RS-423/V10 electrical specifications | | 341 |
| | 10.5.2 RS-422/V11 electrical specifications | | 341 |
| | 10.5.3 Current loop | | 342 |
| | 10.5.4 X20 and X21 recommendations | | 343 |
| | 10.5.5 Serial interface S5/8 | | 344 |
| 10.6 | MULTIPLE ACCESS SERIAL BUSES | | 347 |
| | 10.6.1 Access mechanism | | 348 |
| | 10.6.2 Polling | | 348 |
| | 10.6.3 Token passing | | 349 |
| | 10.6.4 Pure broadcast (Aloha) | | 349 |
| | 10.6.5 Carrier sense | | 349 |
| | 10.6.6 Collision detection | | 351 |
| | 10.6.7 Immediate acknowledge | | 351 |
| | 10.6.8 Collision arbitration | | 352 |
| | 10.6.9 Example: the COBUS network | | 352 |
| | 10.6.10 Example: the $I^2C$ network | | 354 |
| | 10.6.11 Efficiency comparison | | 355 |

| | 10.7 | NETWORK | 356 |
|---|---|---|---|
| | | 10.7.1 Topology and technology | 356 |
| | | 10.7.2 PABX and ISDN | 357 |
| | | 10.7.3 Metropolitan networks | 357 |
| | | 10.7.4 Ring architectures | 357 |
| | | 10.7.5 Twisted pair buses | 358 |
| | | 10.7.6 Coaxial cable buses | 358 |
| | | 10.7.7 Broadband networks | 359 |
| | | 10.7.8 Fiber optic networks | 360 |
| | | 10.7.9 Radio waves | 360 |
| | | 10.7.10 The 802 family of standards | 361 |
| | | 10.7.11 Hierarchy | 363 |
| **11** | **APPENDIX** | | **365** |
| | 11.1 | PARALLEL LINKS | 366 |
| | | 11.1.1 Centronics-Epson | 366 |
| | | 11.1.2 HP-IB, IEEE 488 or IEC 625 | 367 |
| | | 11.1.3 SCSI | 368 |
| | | 11.1.4 Floppy interface | 369 |
| | | 11.1.5 Disk interface ST506/412 | 370 |
| | 11.2 | SERIAL LINKS | 371 |
| | | 11.2.1 RS 232 or V 24 / V 28 | 371 |
| | | 11.2.2 X 20 with DIN-66 258 connector | 372 |
| | | 11.2.3 X 21 with ISO-4903 connector | 373 |
| | | 11.2.4 S 5/8 | 374 |
| | 11.3 | BACKPLANE BUSES | 375 |
| | | 11.3.1 IEEE P 961 (STD-bus) | 376 |
| | | 11.3.2 MUBUS | 378 |
| | | 11.3.3 IEEE P 1000 (STE-bus) | 380 |
| | | 11.3.4 IEEE 696 (S-100) | 382 |
| | | 11.3.5 IEEE 796 (Multibus 1) and AMS-M | 384 |
| | | 11.3.6 G64 and G96 | 386 |
| | | 11.3.7 Q-BUS | 388 |
| | | 11.3.8 M3BUS | 390 |
| | | 11.3.9 IEEE P 1014 (VME) | 392 |
| | | 11.3.10 NUBUS | 394 |
| | | 11.3.11 MULTIBUS II iPSP | 396 |
| | | 11.3.12 IEEE P 896 (Futurebus) | 398 |
| | **REFERENCES** | | **401** |
| | **INDEX** | | **409** |

# 1 INTRODUCTION

A data processing system is composed of many interconnected modules. There are many different types of modules, varying from functional sub-units inside integrated circuits to boards, racks, and cabinets. Different types of connections between the modules, such as narrow aluminium strips on silicon, copper tracks and wires, optical fibers, or radio links, are used. There are some design problems that are common to all of these interconnection subsystems; others are related only to specific systems. Special techniques have been developed to describe the structure and the behaviour of the connections and, for some of them, widely accepted abstract models have been developed.

This introduction is an overview of the various techniques used to exchange information between different subsystems; it discusses the various requirements, shows some often used description techniques and taxonomies, and points out the constraints which must be considered in the design of an interconnection system. The details of these topics and of each protocol are the core subject of this book and are analysed in full detail in the following chapters.

## 1.1 INTERCONNECTION SCHEMES

This section will discuss the need for, and 'the existence of different types of interconnections. This variety corresponds to different factors such as distance, speed and cost. A list of features which classify each interconnection structure is also given. Other general introduction to interconnection techniques can be found in [BOR80], [GUS84], [WAR81a,b,c].

### 1.1.1 Microprocessor System

Let us consider, as a first example, the organization of a simple data processing system, shown in figure 1.1a. The CPU (Central Processing Unit) reads instructions and data from the memory, performs operations on them, and exchanges information with the external world through some input/output interface. All these operations are supported by an internal communication structure called a SYSTEM BUS. This bus could be a printed circuit which interconnects the various boards, as shown in figure 1.1b, or it could be completely hidden inside the integrated device, as in single-chip microcomputers.

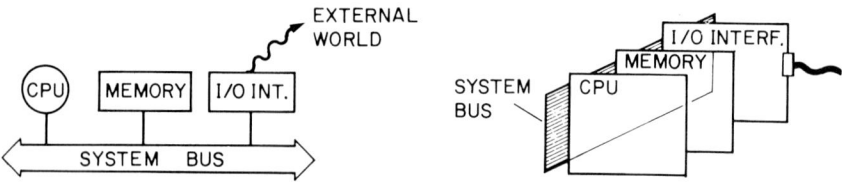

Fig. 1.1  Organization of a microprocessor system

In order to read an instruction, the CPU (Central Processing Unit) selects a memory cell by sending an address on the bus; it then receives the data using the same bus again.

This describes the READ operation. The inverse operation, that is, entering data into memory, is called WRITE. Data can also be exchanged with the external world by writing (or reading) to interface registers rather than to memory.

The most simple machines carry out these operations without any feedback; it is assumed that data is transmitted at the correct time, and that everything is going the right way. A better technique utilizes an ACKNOWLEDGE operation where the memory notifies the CPU that data is available (in read operations), or that data has been stored (in write operations). This is termed a cycle-by-cycle HANDSHAKE, because there is an acknowledgement of each elementary operation. The same concept can be applied to streams of data, where, for example, a printer sends special control characters to the CPU in order to inform it that its buffer is almost full. This is an example of a higher level acknowledgement.

Another example of an information transfer in this simple system is the INTERRUPT mechanism. A peripheral can request the attention of the CPU by sending an interrupt signal. Because, in many cases, all interrupt requests are "ORed" (collected via an OR function) to a single input pin on the CPU, this operation must be followed by other transfers in order to identify the peripheral which has issued the interrupt.

### 1.1.2 Types of interconnections

We can now look at the complete organization of a complex processing system in more detail. As shown in figure 1.2, we find many types of interconnections here. The metallized paths between the MOS *(Metal Oxide Semiconductor)* devices inside an integrated circuit (1) can be considered of the most elementary level. The *ICs (Integrated Circuits)* are connected using printed conductors which make up a circuit board (2), and boards are connected by means of a backplane bus (3). Inside the backplane itself we can identify sets of lines used as independent communication structures, such as the interrupt bus (4). Some basic operations of these interconnections have already been outlined in the previous section.

Looking again at figure 1.2, we find that many external units are also tied to the processing system by means of a wide range of interconnection subsystems. A video terminal uses an RS-232/V24 serial line (5); a mass-memory unit exchanges information through some parallel interface as SCSI (6); a printer uses a simple parallel interface of the "Centronics" type (7). If programmable instruments are used, the most common interconnection technique is the IEC 625 (also known as IEEE 488) bus (8).

A remote digital volt meter can be read by the computer via a custom parallel interface (9). Another special interface is used to bring data to external display panels (10). A single wire can enable a computer to detect the activation of at least one of many independent emergency pushbuttons (11). Finally, many computers can be connected to communicate with each other on a Local Area Network such as Ethernet (12) or through telephone lines.

All the information exchanges carried out in the systems shown in figures 1.1 and 1.2 must follow well-defined rules in order to perform properly. This set of rules is called the *PROTOCOL* of the connection system. The following sections show why different protocols are required by analysing the main features of each interconnection technique.

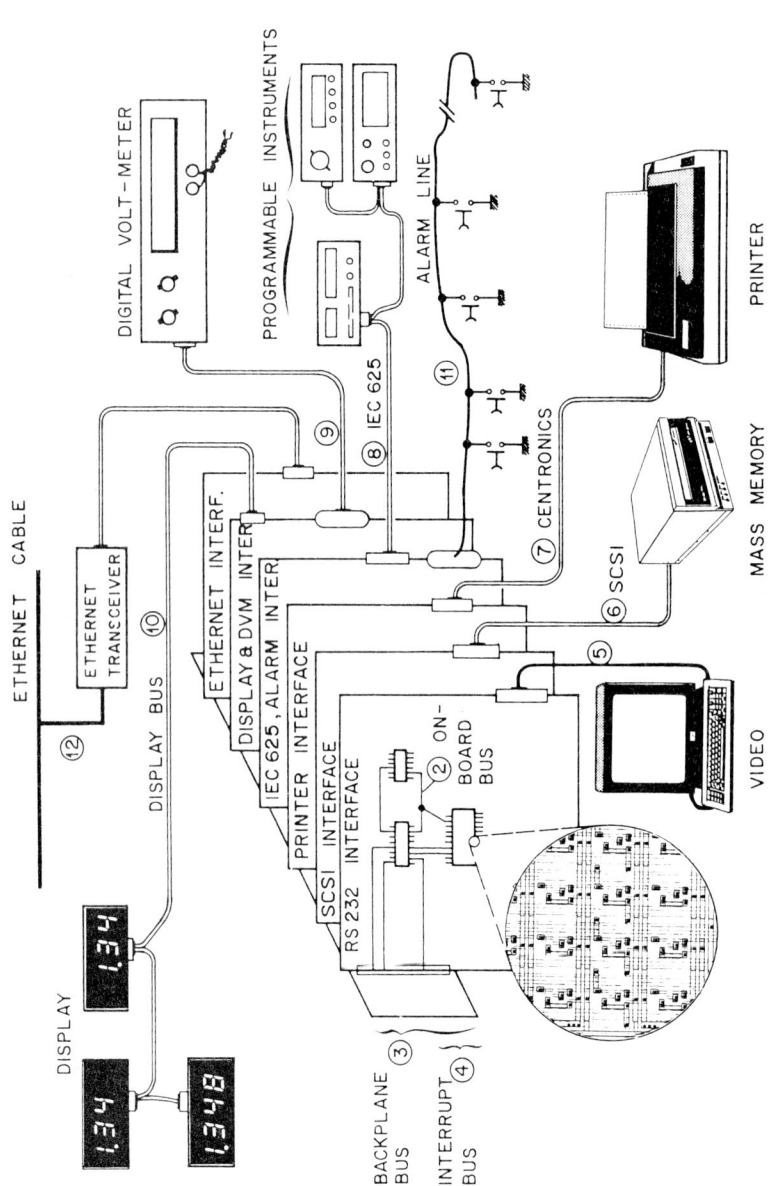

Fig. 1.2  Examples of a hierarchical set of interconnections

## 1.2 DESIGN CHOICES

Faced with the different possibilities of interconnections, the designer has to choose the best solution. This section will survey briefly the major design choices, that will be detailed in the next sections.

### 1.2.1 Physical and electrical specification

The first and most obvious difference among the connection structures shown in figure 1.2 is the use of different connectors, such as direct connectors to printed circuits on the backplane (3), "DB-25" male and female plugs in RS-232 (5), flat cable connectors, etc. Their actual shape depends on the number of wires, environmental factors inside or outside the cabinet (shielding, waterproofing ...), and cost and reliability constraints. The connector is part of the connection specifications. A good choice is extremely important, because it ensures the fulfilment of reliability requirements.

Another characteristic of an interconnection link is the type of signal used to transmit information and control. In most cases, they are represented by LOW and HIGH electrical levels; in the Ethernet link (12), more complex shapes are generated by using the Manchester encoding technique, as shown in figure 1.3. The voltage levels of the low and high levels must also be specified: most connections in figure 1.2 work with standard TTL levels, while RS-232 uses +12 V and -12 V for higher noise immunity.

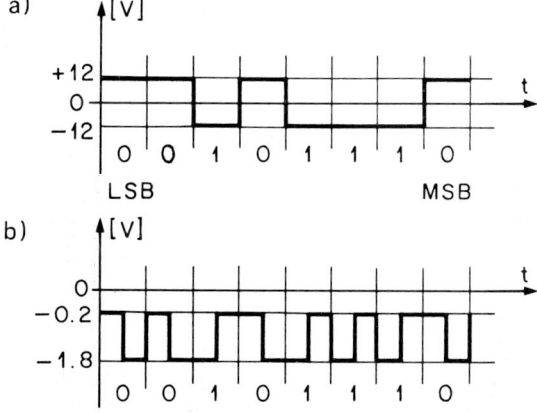

Fig. 1.3 Encoding for serial transmissions
 a) PCM-NRZ (used in RS 232)
 b) Manchester (used in Ethernet)

## 1.2.2 Serial versus parallel links

One feature that distinguishes the various interconnections of figures 1.1 and 1.2 is the physical structure of the link itself. When only a few wires or a single coaxial cable is used, the information must be serialized and is thus transmitted one bit at a time, as shown in figure 1.4.

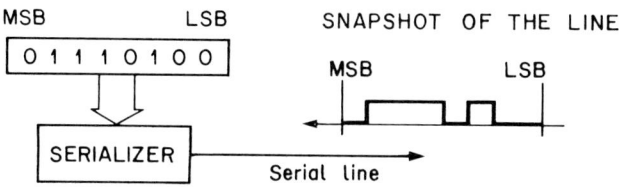

*Fig. 1.4 Serial transmission of information*

We find two such SERIAL LINKS in figure 1.2: RS-232 and Ethernet. RS-232 is the standard connection for modems and is also used with peripherals such as video terminals, printers and others. It contains actually two serial links, one going from the computer to the terminal, and the other going in the opposite direction. Ethernet is a Local Area Network (LAN), and it is used to transfer information at high speed in both directions between many stations.

Another communication technique utilizes many wires which enable the computer to send many bits of information at the same time, as shown in figure 1.5. In this case, we speak of a PARALLEL LINK. All the connection structures in figure 1.2, except RS-232 and Ethernet, follow this approach. A parallel communication structure is faster and requires a simpler interface than a serial one; on the other hand, the serial link uses fewer wires. Thus, serial lines are better for medium to long distance communications, while parallel links are used to achieve higher speed or very simple interfaces.

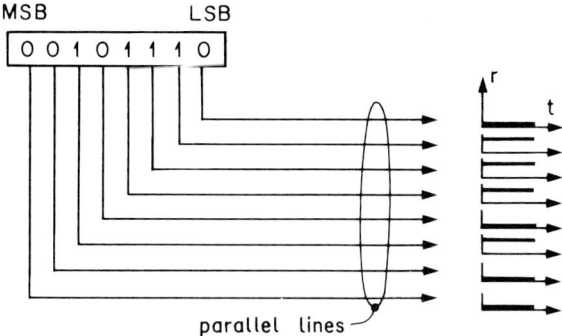

*Fig. 1.5 Parallel transmission of information*

### 1.2.3 Point-to-point versus bused connections

The simplest connection subsystem is the POINT-TO-POINT link, which allows the exchange of information between only two units. The structure of a point-to-point link is shown in figure 1.6. In the large system of figure 1.2 we can identify at least three examples of point-to-point connections:

- the RS-232 serial line between the computer and the video terminal (4)
- the parallel Centronics printer cable (6)
- the computer-DVM (Digital Volt-Meter) connection (8).

These point-to-point interconnections have different structures; the RS-232 is a serial link, while the others are parallel. The Centronics and the DVM interfaces transmit information in one direction only: from the computer and to the computer, respectively. The complete RS-232 interface is bidirectional, transmitting data in both directions.

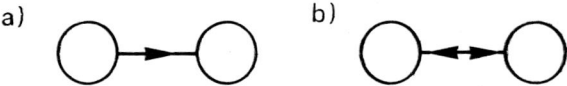

*Fig. 1.6 Point-to-point link*
  *a) Unidirectional*
  *b) Bidirectional*

The terms SIMPLEX, DUPLEX and HALF DUPLEX are also used to indicate point-to-point links able to transfer information in only one direction, in both directions at the same time, or in both directions at different times, respectively (section 10.4.2).

The other connections in the figure use the same physical link to exchange information among many units. The usual structure of these connections is the BUS, as shown in figure 1.7. We call these BUSED MULTIPOINT or MULTIDROP systems. The advantage of a bus is that it requires fewer wires and fewer interfaces than a set of point-to-point links.

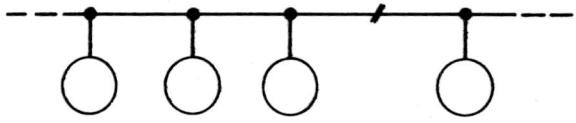

*Fig. 1.7 Multidrop link*

We can identify many multidrop connections in figure 1.2:

- the backplane bus, which carries the information between the boards (3)
- the SCSI link between the computer and the mass memory system (6)
- the IEC 625 bus which interconnects many programmable instruments (8)
- the display panel interface (10)
- the emergency line, which collects various inputs from many switches (11)
- the Ethernet serial bus (12).

An additionnal parameter which classifies the interconnection systems is the *TOPOLOGY*. Other structures, such as the star, ring and connected network, shown in figure 1.8, can be used. These systems, however, can be regarded as either a set of point-to-point links or as a bus which passes through all units.

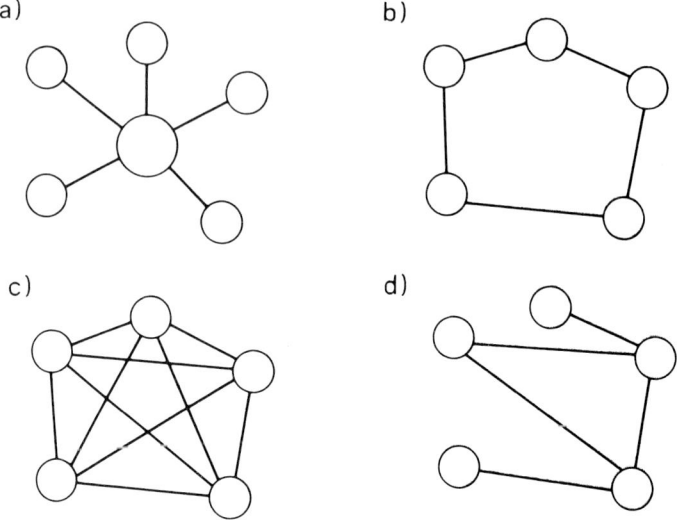

Fig. 1.8  Connection topologies
 a) Star
 b) Ring
 c) Fully connected network
 d) Partially connected network

## 1.2.4 Multiple sources and multiple destinations

A multidrop connection can be used to transfer information from a single source to a well-defined module, selected among those tied to the bus. This technique is utilized, for instance, in the display-panel interface (10) of figure 1.2 : the computer must send each character to a well-defined panel. This operation requires a selection procedure which identifies the units which must receive the information. This selection procedure is called ADDRESSING (figure 1.9a).

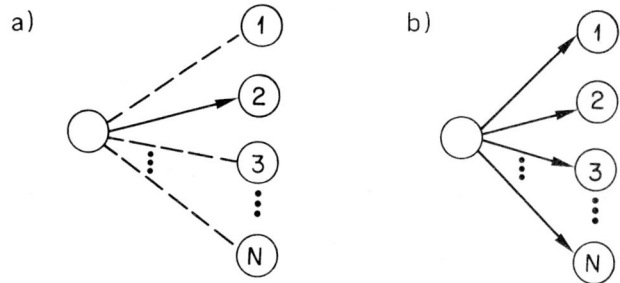

*Fig. 1.9 Types of operation*
  *a) Addressed transfer: the information goes to module 2 only*
  *b) Broadcast: the information goes to all modules*

On the other hand, some special commands, such as "display off" or "lamp test", must be sent directly to all display modules, without any addressing operation. An operation which transfers data to many units during a single cycle is called a BROADCAST (figure 1.10b).

We can also perform the inverse operation, that is, we can collect information through the bus from many sources at the same time. For instance, the emergency line (11) shown in figure 1.2 is activated by the contact closure of any switch tied to it, and the interrupt bus of the backplane (4) collects interrupts from many sources and sends them to the interrupt control logic on the CPU board. In both cases, we may have a single source or many sources active at the same time. The operation of collecting information from many sources is called a BROADCALL. The units which use the link at the same time in a broadcall may send fully equivalent information, such as the closure of alarm switches, thus they would not be required to identify themselves. On the other hand, if their data is not equivalent, further operations which identify the source will be needed. In the interrupt bus, the source is identified by a vector transmitted on the bus itself. In this last case a proper mechanism must select the highest priority interrupting device, which is enabled to transmit the interrupt vector.

The second classification parameter, then, is the type of transfers allowed in the multidrop. The above examples show that some protocols include a mechanism to select the source and/or the destination, while others allow broadcast and broadcall transfers.

### 1.2.5 Single-master and multiple-master systems

Let us suppose that a certain unit has control of a bus; it starts the operations on the bus, selects the other partner, and carries on the information transfer. This unit is called the *MASTER*; the other units are the *SLAVES*. A bus can be organized around a single master or have multiple-master capability. In the example of figure 1.2, single-master buses are:

- the computer-display bus (10); all transactions are handled by the computer, which is the only master in this link
- the IEC 625 instrumentation bus (8); here too, only one device, the computer, has control of the bus
- the SCSI link (6); the computer is the master also of this bus.

Buses with multiple-mastership are:

- the backplane bus (3): if the system has Direct Memory Access (DMA) capability, or if it is a multiprocessor, many units are able to control the bus
- the Ethernet coaxial bus (12); operations on the Ethernet can be initiated and controlled by any station.

If multiple mastership is allowed, the link protocol must include a procedure to grant the bus to only one requester at a time. This procedure is called *ARBITRATION*.

### 1.2.6 Conclusion and classification

The previous sections identified some of the parameters which allow us to describe and classify interconnection structures. We can now say, for instance, that the SCSI and IEC 625 connections are parallel buses, which allow bidirectional information transfers, and support single mastership. Even with these common features, they have different connectors, different protocols and different performance. RS-232 is a connection composed of two unidirectional serial point-to-point links, uses non-TTL electrical levels, etc. All of the structures shown in figure 1.2 can be described in this way, but it is extremely difficult to define a unique framework to classify all of the possible interconnection techniques. Some attempts in this direction can be found in [THUR79], [LEVY78], [DELC79] and [PATZ80].

# 1 Introduction

The physical specifications of an interconnection identify the type of connector, the number of wires used, and their sizes. At the electrical level, we can determine the values of voltages and currents used to carry the information (e.g. TTL levels, or +/-12 V for RS-232). The link can be serial or parallel, and have a point-to-point or a bus connection topology. Other degrees of freedom include the synchronization technique and other features of the protocol.

This summary is not exhaustive and other possible system configurations are not discussed in this short introduction. The purpose of this section is only to show the variety of choices. Each interconnection structure has specific protocol requirements, which will be discussed in the following chapters.

An example of complex interconnection struture which uses different types of buses is described in [BUR79]. More sophisticated design problems are analysed in [TOR77]. A review of interconnection possibilities for multiple processor systems as in [JEN76].

# 2 PRINCIPLE OF OPERATIONS

A top-down approach for analysing bus operations would start from the ISO Model and detail the elements afterwards. A bottom-up approach has been prefered here. Some well known concepts and the terminology are presented, then the technological constraints which limit and influence the design are emphasised, and finally the layering and standardization problems are considered.

## 2.1 LOGIC ELEMENTS AND NOTATIONS

This section introduces the most important basic notions and terminology which are related to the representation of the information and to the implementation of the interfaces. A good preliminary knowledge of logic circuits is required from the reader. The purpose of this section is to define the notations and symbols that will be used throughout this book.

### 2.1.1 Terminology

The computer vocabulary is diverse and not yet settled. The situation is worse in non-English languages, where a strange mixing of original English terms, deformed English terms, and correct native language terms occur. Due to the slowness of the terminology standardization committees, the difficulty of the concepts, and the large number of books written with different sets of notations and vocabulary, it is difficult to select notations that will please everybody. The terminology and notations used in this book are believed to follow the best microcomputer industry practice. The book's terminology has been strongly influenced by the IEEE group on Terminology for Interface Standards [LANG81].

## 2.1.2 Numbers

All data handled by computers are coded in binary form. A *BIT* (b) is a piece of information, which can take one of two values, e.g. 0 and 1. A set of 4 ordered bits is a *NIBBLE*; it allows the encoding of 16 elementary pieces of information. A set of 8 ordered bits is a *BYTE* (B); it allows the encoding of 256 elementary pieces of information.

Larger sets of bits are usually multiples of 8 bits. The term *WORD* is frequently used to define a set of bits which may have a precise meaning in a given environment (PDP11: 16 bits, VAX: 32 bits). In this book, WORD will be used only to define a set of bits without a given size. Some frequently occurring sizes have the following names:

- a set of 16 ordered bits is a *DOUBLET*
- a set of 24 ordered bits is a *TRIPLET*
- a set of 32 ordered bits is a *QUADLET* or a *QUAD*
- a set of 64 ordered bits is an *OCTUPLET* or a *BIQUAD*
- a set of 80 ordered bits is a *DECUPLET*
- a set of 128 ordered bits is a *QUADQUAD*
- a set of any number of bits or bytes is a *BLOCK OF DATA* or *MESSAGE*

A *REGISTER* is composed of a set of cells which stores a word. Usually, a reserved name is given to the register. A *MEMORY LOCATION* is identical to a register. Memory locations are usually numbered, although user defined names may be associated with them.

A number of locations (usually of byte size) equal to $2^{10}$ = 1024 is named a *KILO* (K). One can notice the usage of the upper case K to distinguish the power of two from the usual power of ten. A Kb is a kilobit and a KB is a kilobyte (1024 bytes), but 1 kB is 1000 bytes. Similarly, $2^{20}$ = 1048576 is named a *MEGA* (M) (bits or bytes).

The bits in a word form a *BINARY NUMBER*. The left-most bit is the *MSB* (Most Significant Bit). The right-most bit is the *LSB* (Least Significant Bit).

Binary numbers are frequently translated into their *HEXADECIMAL* equivalent : each group of 4 digits is translated into the corresponding hexadecimal digit 0 to F. Binary numbers are here preceded by B´, hexadecimal numbers by H´. For instance, B´0011010110110010 = H´35B2.

The DECIMAL system is used to count bits in a word, to define the size of certain elements, to number devices, and to measure time. The hexadecimal system is used to number memory locations and to express the binary content of a register or a location. By default, a number like 1101 is a decimal. In order to avoid any confusion, it is recommended that also the decimal numbering system be specified by writing D´1101.

## 2.1.3 Signals

A digital system can assume a finite number of STATES. Each state is defined by a combination of values of some LOGICAL VARIABLES, also named BOOLEAN VARIABLES. A SIGNAL allows us to observe, that is, to communicate to another system, the state of the system, that is the value of logical variables. We consider here only LOGICAL SIGNALS which can take two values and are associated with a boolean variable. These two values are named TRUE and FALSE, which is synonymous to ACTIVE and NOT ACTIVE, ASSERTED and NEGATED, respectively.

The name of a signal should be as explicit as possible, and preferably short. It should clearly define the action that corresponds to the signal. For instance, "DIRECTION" is not a good name. "DIROUT" or "WRITE" are better names, if there is a clear "in-out" or "read-write" direction in the system.

A signal may encode an action in several ways:
- its active static level (figure 2.1a)
- its non-active static level (figure 2.1b)
- its positive non-active to active dynamic transition (figure 2.1c)
- its negative active to non-active dynamic transition (figure 2.1d)
- its duration (figure 2.1e)

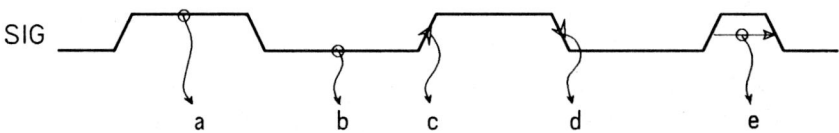

Fig. 2.1  Static, dynamic and pulse encoding action of a signal

Signals are represented by means of specific values of physical quantities (voltage, current, light). This allows us to transmit and sense logical variables on conductive media (wires, optical fibers). We shall focus on electrical levels carried by the link wires; they are called LINES or BUS SIGNAL LINES. The two levels are named HIGH and LOW, high corresponding to the higher positive voltage or current. We shall abstain from using the symbols "1" and "0" to indicate the logic levels, in order to avoid the confusion between logic symbols and electrical levels.

The physical states which correspond to the active and non-active states must accept error margins. For instance, with TTL (Transistor Transistor Logic) technology [TTL84], electrical voltages between 0 V and 0.8 V are named $V_{IL}$ (Voltage In Low) and correspond to a non-active level on this line; voltages between 2.4 V and 5 V are named $V_{IH}$ (Voltage In High) and correspond to an active level on this line. The no-man's land between these two levels must be crossed quickly, that is, in a few ns, when using TTL technology. With the ECL (Emitter Coupled Logic) [BLO82], $V_{IL}$ is specified as below -1.6 V and $V_{IH}$ above -0.8 V.

The correspondence between the action, the signal name, the line level, the drawn representation and the viewing of electrical levels on the scope must be clearly defined; at each step, an inversion is possible. This inversion is, indicated by a name change, e.g. a WRITE signal is encoded into a READ line, or by a trailing star, e.g. a WRITE signal is encoded into a WRITE* line. Other notations for an inverted signal use an overline or a slash (see section 2.1.4).

In the last example, the line WRITE* is ACTIVE-LOW: the WRITE action is performed when the line is at its LOW level. Active-low lines are often used with TTL, because the default level (HIGH) is associated with a logic state in which no action is performed.

### 2.1.4 Logic equations

As explained earlier, a signal is given a name according to the function performed. If, due to the implementation, the signal is active low, it will be written with a horizontal overhead bar, or with a prefix or a postfix / (slash). A postfix * (star) is also widely used, mostly for the backplane bus lines.

Direct signal:    SIG
Inverted signal:  $\overline{SIG}$, /SIG, SIG/ or SIG*

A logic function is expressed by an equation. Logical NOT, OR and AND are represented by the / (slash or inverting prefix), + (plus sign), and the * (star sign), respectively. Due to the possible confusion about the double definition of the star sign, and for improved legibility, a space must surround the + and * signs used to indicate explicitly the OR and AND operations. Parentheses can be used for complex expressions.

SELECT    = SIG * /GATE + /(DECO * TEST)
          AND   NOT  OR  NOT     AND

The implementation of a function is derived from the logic equations, which can take different forms according to different needs. The implementations can be achieved using gates, PROMs (Programmable Read Only Memory), PLAs (Programmable Logic Arrays) or PALs (Programmable Array Logic) [FLET80]. State machines can be implemented using REGISTER, that is, gates and registers, or PROMs, PLAs or PALs which include a register [MMI84].

## 2.1.5  State and timing diagrams

The evolution of a system in response to the change of external conditions can be represented by a STATE DIAGRAM, which shows all the possible states of the system. Each STATE is represented by a "bubble" with arcs emanating from it. These arcs are associated with a logical expression which, when true, enables the state change (figure 2.2). The state diagram can be used for synchronous, asynchronous and mixed systems. In the case of asynchronous systems, only one variable is allowed to change at a given time. In synchronous systems, the input status must by synchronized. The state diagram can be easily converted into a truth table, from which the combinatorial system of a state machine can be designed. The optimization of sequential systems is difficult, however, due to the many factors that influence them.

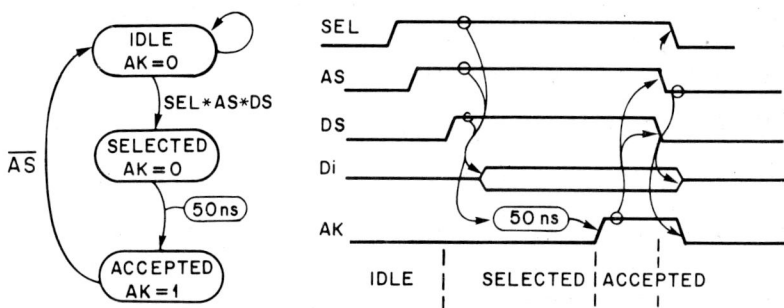

Fig. 2.2  Typical state and timing diagram

A TIMING DIAGRAM can be efficiently used to represent the evolution of a system, and it is better suited to show the detailed sequence of a set of signals. A timing diagram resembles what can be seen on the oscilloscope's screen, and thus it should be drawn with correct timing proportions to make the verification easier (figure 2.3).

Timing diagrams (figure 2.3), although functional, can also be utilized to represent physical and timing constraints and attract the attention of the designer to propagation delays, the difference between three-state and open collector signals, synchronization problems, etc. Arrows and other adequate drawing conventions, as shown in previous figures, will help make timing diagrams a very powerful way of describing a sequence of actions or the evolution of a protocol.

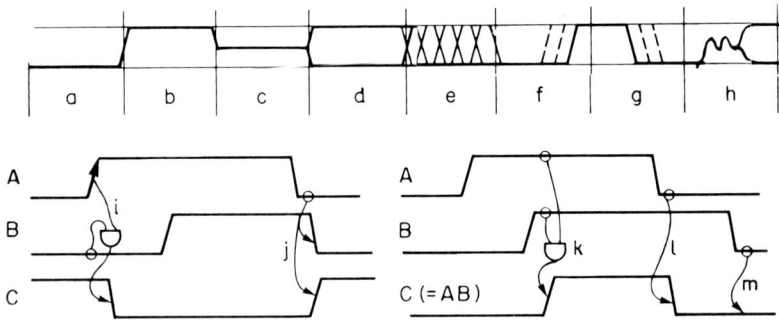

Fig. 2.3  Timing diagram conventions
  a) low signal (state 0)
  b) high signal (state 1)
  c) floating three-state signal or undriven bus level
  d) steady signal or bus status
  e) signal changing in any direction (undefined)
  f) signal changing from low to high
  g) signal changing from high to low
  h) signal with undefined metastable state
  i) positive transition of signal A and inactive value of signal B cause signal C to be deasserted
  j) non-active state of signal A deasserts signal B and C
  k) the logical AND of signal A and B asserts signal C
  l) non-active state of signal A deasserts C
  m) non-active state of signal A would also deassert C or maintain it at zero

## 2.1.6 Combinatorial logic elements

A *DIGITAL SYSTEM* has several inputs and outputs which are logical signals. A logical system can be broken down into several interconnected subsystems. This partitioning is usually stopped at the *GATE* level. The set of basic gates is shown in figure 2.4.

Functionally, the four basic gates *NOT*, *AND*, *OR* and *XOR* allow a complete description of any functions to be performed. Because inverted signals are frequently used, each gate has two symbols,

## 2 Principle of Operations

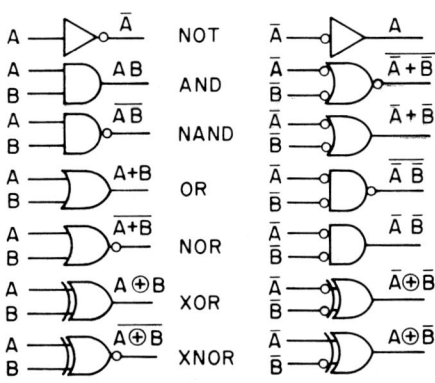

Fig. 2.4  Gates

according to de Morgan's Theorem [FLET80]. The consistent usage of inverting circles simplifies the utilization and verification of logic diagrams.

The output of a logic element is usually in the totem-pole form, with only one transistor active at any time, as shown in figure 2.5a. OPEN COLLECTOR outputs are only half active, because they have only one active state, which is usually state low. A pull-up resistor must be used to obtain state high as in figure 2.5b.

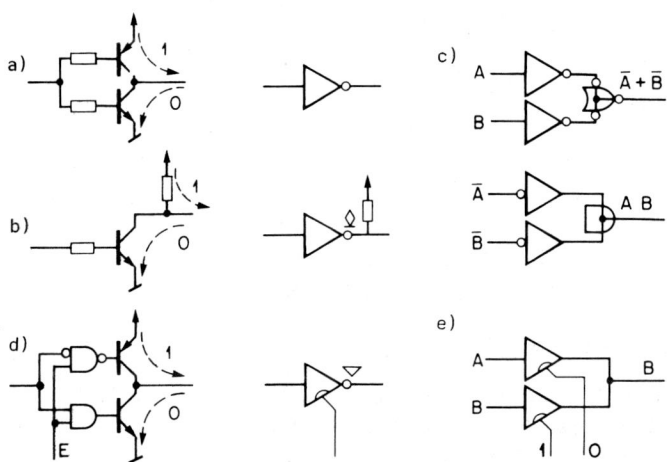

Fig. 2.5  Totem-pole (a), open collector (b,c) and three-state outputs (d,e)

When the output corresponds to an inverted signal, it is logically and physically ACTIVE LOW. A logical OR function is performed when several active-low outputs are connected together as in figure 2.6c. This is named WIRED OR. Due to de Morgan's Theorem, the same circuit without inversion, that is, with active-high levels, performs also the WIRED AND function as in figure 2.6c.

THREE-STATE gates have an additional control signal which enables the output, thus generating on the output a third floating state as in figure 2.5d. Three-state outputs can be connected together if only one output is active and all the others are three-stated as in figure 2.5e.

Special symbols emphasize the special nature of the outputs or the control inputs of logic elements. These symbols are borrowed from the 1972 IEC notations, and help with the legibility and understanding of the schematics. The other IEC symbols are not as clear and not yet accepted by manufacturers. Thus, MIL-STD 806b symbols are used when available.

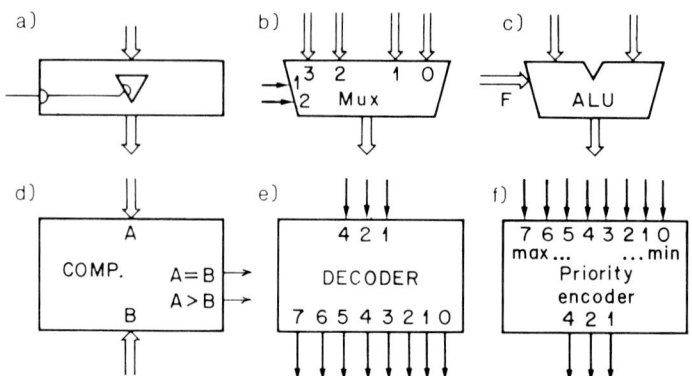

*Fig. 2.6 Complex combinational logic elements*

More complex logic elements are given in figure 2.7. The functions performed are suggested by their names. Logic equations or truth tables can completely describe their functions. The major devices are listed below:

a) A *BUFFER* controls the transfer of, and regenerates, signals
b) A *MULTIPLEXER* selects one of two or more inputs
c) An *ALU* (Arithmetic and Logic Unit) performs 2- and 1-operand operations (ADD, XOR, NOT, etc.) on binary numbers
d) A *COMPARATOR* compares two operands for signed and unsigned magnitude
e) A *DECODER* has one output active, which is defined by the selection of the input word

f) A *PRIORITY ENCODER* defines the address of an active input (with a known priority if several inputs are active).

## 2.1.7 Flip-flops

*FLIP-FLOPS* are simple logic networks with two steady states. Their simplest form is the *R-S FLIP-FLOP* built from two gates as in figure 2.7a. Flip-flops are preferably drawn as in figure 2.7b. Their operation may be represented by the timing diagram of figure 2.7c. Signal S "sets" the flip-flop (activates the output), while signal R "resets" it. The input state S=1 R=1 is usually not allowed, since the two outputs Q, $\bar{Q}$ would not be complementary and would have a state which might depend on the flip-flop's implementation as in figure 2.7a.

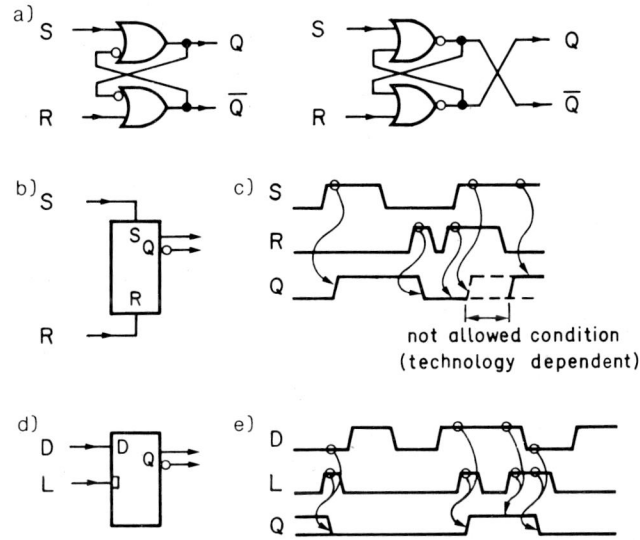

*Fig. 2.7 Static flip-flops*

The *LATCH* copies the input D to the output Q as long as the input L (Load) is active, as in figure 2.7d. The output is "frozen" when the "Load" input is inactive.

R-S flip-flops and latches are named *STATIC FLIP-FLOPS* since the states of the input signals immediately influence the output.

*DYNAMIC FLIP-FLOPS* have at least one input signal which performs an action when asserted or deasserted (dynamic action). This action is said to be *EDGE-TRIGGERED* and may depend on static inputs.

The D FLIP-FLOP copies the state of the D input during the positive clock edge as in figure 2.8a. This function is similar to the latch (figure 2.8d), but shows significant differences.

The J-K FLIP-FLOP (figure 2.8b) toggles according to the J and K input value. Thus, it can be utilized to build a counter (figure 2.8c).

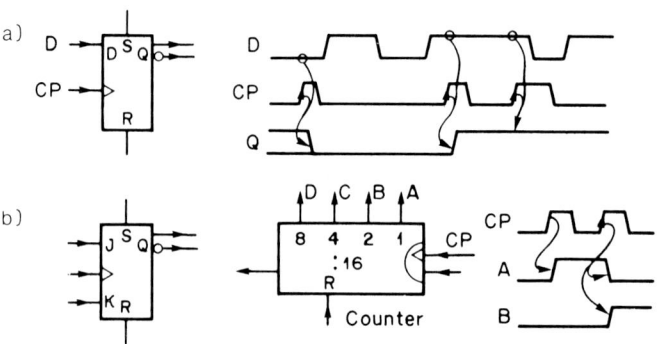

*Fig. 2.8 Dynamic flip-flop and counters*

Static (level-triggered) or dynamic (edge-triggered) actions may set or reset a flip-flop. Static actions may be used if the commands are exclusive, as in the first part of figure 2.9a. If only one of the actions is edge-triggered, a D or J-K flip-flop may be used, as shown in figure 2.9b. A DUAL FLIP-FLOP is required if both set and reset actions are edge-triggered, as shown in figure 2.9c. This flip-flop is not available as a standard component, but is easily built using two D or J-K flip-flops.

## 2.1.8 Registers

PARALLEL REGISTERS are either static (built with the latches of figure 2.7;), and named LATCHES (figure 2.10a) or dynamic (built with the edge-triggered flip-flops of figure 2.8) and named EDGE-TRIGGERED REGISTERS (figure 2.10b). In many cases, both latches and edge-triggered registers can be used for the same function, with a proper design.

The outputs of most registers can be three-stated, as shown in figure 2.10c). This timing diagram is valid both for a latch and for an edge-triggered register, except during the edge triggering (vs. the static action) of the LOAD signal.

## 2 Principle of Operations

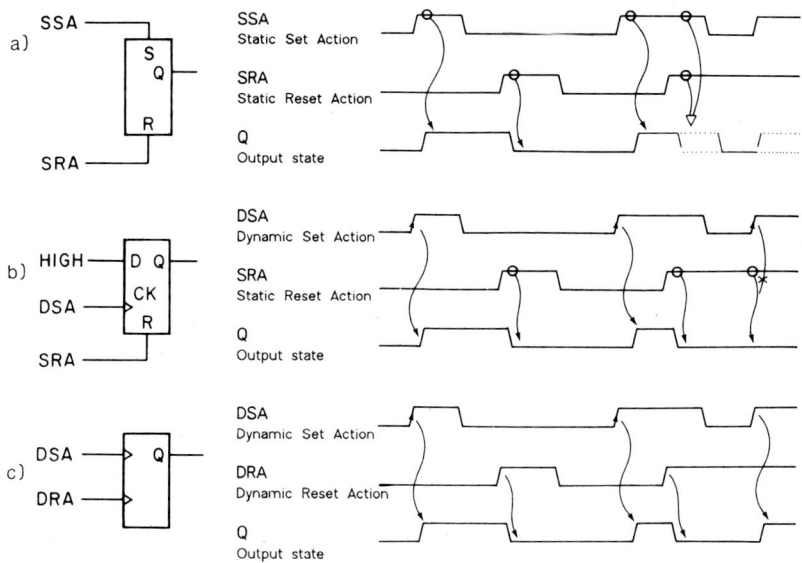

*Fig. 2.9 Static and dynamic actions on the state of a flip-flop*

SHIFT REGISTERS are used to shift data loaded in parallel or serially (figure 2.10d). They can convert serially entered data to parallel data, and the reverse (figure 2.10e).

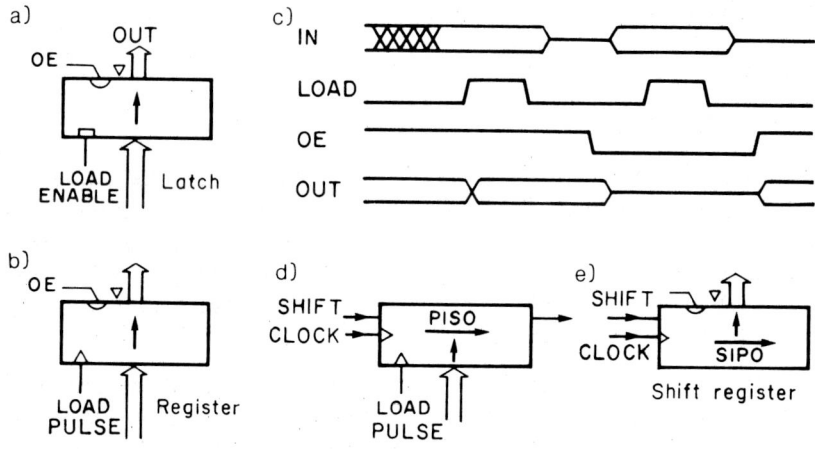

*Fig. 2.10 Parallel and serial registers*

Parallel registers are sometimes named *PIPO* (*Parallel-in Parallel-Out*) and serial registers named *PISO* (*Parallel-In Serial-Out*) or *SIPO* (*Serial-In Parallel-Out*).

A *STATE MACHINE* is a combination of an edge-triggered register, which holds the present state, and a combinatorial circuit which defines its future state and the outputs according to the present state and its inputs [FLET80]; it is a general model for all sequential opeations.

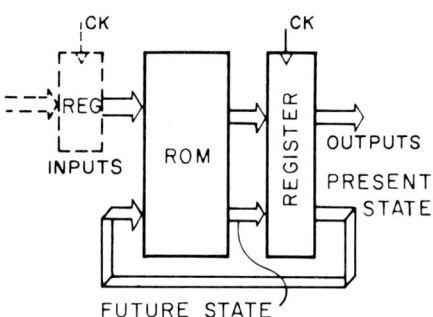

*Fig. 2.11 Finite state machine*

## 2.1.9 The metastable state

A flip-flop has a predictable future state only if the manufacturer's specifications are followed. For instance, in the case of a D flip-flop, the D input must be stable at a time $t_{set-up}$ before the clock is allowed to change, and must remain in the same state a time $t_{hold}$ afterwards, as shown in figure 2.12. At these conditions, the manufacturer guarantees a maximum amount of time $t_{prop}$ needed to reach the new state.

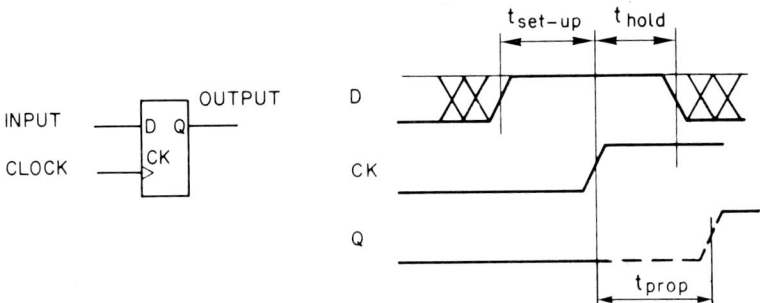

*Fig. 2.12 Timing specifications for a D flip-flop*

# 2 Principle of Operations

These manufacturer's specifications are only achievable in a synchronous circuit, when the timing relationship of D and CK can be determined. If the flip-flop is used as a synchronizer, i.e. to sample an asynchronous input D with the clock CK, then no relationship between D and CK can be guaranteed. This situation occurs, for instance, in a microprocessor when it is sampling external signals such as the interrupt request, or during arbitration.

When the set-up and hold times are not respected, there are cases (in a rather narrow time frame around the clock edge, which depends on the flip-flop technology) where the output Q hesitates. It is called the *INSTABLE STATE*, more frequently improperly named *METASTABLE STATE*. The physical motivations of this behaviour are analysed in [CHAN72], [STO82], [SAM82], [MARI81] and [MEA80]. There is an instable equilibrium point, similar to what would happen if a golf ball were rolled over a bell-shaped obstacle (figure 2.13).

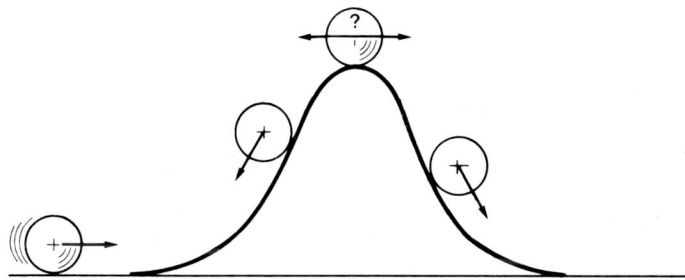

*Fig. 2.13 Instable state*

If the push is strong enough, the ball will pass; if it is not strong enough, the ball will fall back; but if the ball has just the right amount of energy, the ball will remain on top of the obstacle, until some disturbance changes its status.

Flip-flops behave in a similar way. No upper bound of their decision time may be given, only probabilities may be provided, and most manufacturers do not document this behaviour. For instance, for a given flip-flop and a given amount of time in which the input D changes, a decision may be made in 90% of the cases within 10 ns, in 99% of the cases within 20 ns. The probability of bad synchronization within 100 ns is much higher than the probability of failure, in the range of $10^{-6}$. Significant differences in reliability may be observed between different flip-flops, depending on the technology used and the internal structure.

Thus, after each synchronization, the logic must wait until the probability of a late toggling is sufficiently low. Double synchronization is recommended, which can be achieved by cascading two flip-flops which have a common clock to sample the inputs (figure 2.14).

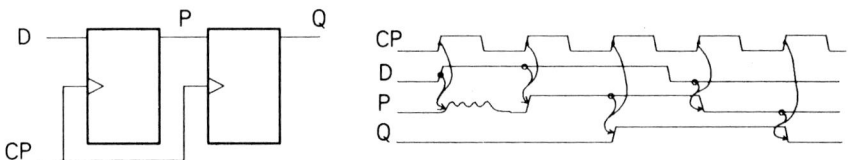

*Fig. 2.14 Double synchronization*

### 2.1.10 Block diagrams

The data flow between the elements of a system is best shown with a BLOCK DIAGRAM. Address and data buses are represented by wide tracks, their widths being roughly proportional to the number of lines. A bus looks in this way like a flat cable and follows the same bending rules. The least significant bit-line is always the right-most or up-most line.

Control lines are drawn as individual lines, or as a separate bus. As an example, figure 2.15 shows a typical block diagram for a 16-bit microprocessor system.

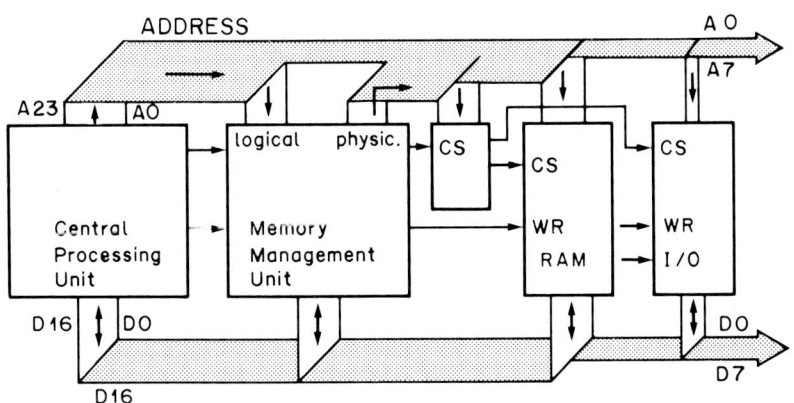

*Fig. 2.15 Example of a block diagram of a microcomputer*

## 2.2 TECHNOLOGICAL CONSTRAINTS

This section will sum up some technological constraints in the design of serial and parallel buses. A more detailed analysis will be presented in Chapter 8.

### 2.2.1 Characteristics of transmission media

The physical medium has a large influence on communications. Among the important factors are the bandwidth of the communication channel, the number of parallel channels, the propagation delays, the useful transmission distance, the capability to BROADCAST (multiple receivers) and BROADCALL (multiple simultaneous responders), and the medium's behaviour during simultaneous accesses (see section 11.6).

Generally, the information is conveyed by an electromagnetic wave, but sometimes, sonic waves are used. In a FREE-SPACE propagation, the air or the "ether" is used as a medium, and the transmission can be either omnidirectional or direct.

GUIDED TRANSMISSIONS comprise a wave guided by a physical conductor, such as a waveguide, an optical fiber, or a coaxial cable. In a guided transmission, the power of the transmitter is very low, usually less than 1W, compared to about 100 W for a directed microwave link. In a guided transmission, LOSSES occur at the TAPs or points where the receivers are connected; hence, their number is limited.

A transmission medium has a limited BANDWIDTH which limits the rate at which data can be transmitted. This bandwidth is a function of the travelling mode of the wave and of the dielectric and magnetic properties of the medium.

The PROPAGATION DELAY is the time needed by a wave to travel from the transmitter to the farthest receiver. The speed of the wave in a medium is always lower than the speed the wave would have in vacuum. Typically, optical or electrical waves travel at about 60% of the speed of light in a vacuum. In a printed circuit board, signals travel at about half the speed of the light, that is only 15 cm per nanosecond.

A propagating wave is subject to ATTENUATION: it looses energy and may need to be amplified and regenerated by repeaters, which themselves add propagation delays. This limits the economically feasible distance the link may span.

No medium is completely homogeneous. Changes in the transmission properties of the medium are called DISCONTINUITIES. They cause REFLECTIONS of the wave at points like connectors and taps, and especially at the end, when the medium is bounded. The reflected waves will cause signal distortions unless they are properly absorbed. The absorption of reflections is, however, only practical in guided transmissions. In free-space propagation, reflections cannot be suppressed, but directional receivers can obviate them.

INTERFERENCES often called EMI (Electro-Magnetic Interferences) are waves generated by external sources which distort the signal wave if the transmission medium is not properly shielded.

CROSSTALK is an interference which results from the interaction between the waves of two parallel media. The coupling between the two lines can be inductive, capacitive or ohmic. The shielding against parallel conductors is more difficult to achieve than against external interferences. Better solutions have been introduced, such as flat cables twisted on most of their length.

The GROUNDING problem affects all electrical signal transmissions. The transmission of an electrical signal implies a SIGNAL RETURN LINE, or GROUND. This ground must be connected to EARTH for safety reasons; since the earth is a good conductor, current loops may appear on the signal return line, which add erroneous voltages to the signals.

For protection against electromagnetic interferences, a SHIELD, consisting of a Faraday's cage around the conductor, is used. Depending on the kind of interferences that are expected, the shield must be grounded at one end only (low frequency interferences) or at both ends (HF interferences) or, even better, at several places.

A figure of merit of a transmission medium is known as the SPEED BY DISTANCE product or CD. It is the product of the available bandwidth C multiplied by the useful distance D.

## 2.2.2 Free-space transmission

Transmission of information using propagation through free space (air, "ether") may be OMNIDIRECTIONAL or DIRECTIONAL. Omnidirectional transmission makes use of a very large medium in order to reach receivers scattered over a large geographical region, either because there are many receivers, as in a commercial radio broadcast, or because their location is unknown within that region.

Omnidirectional transmissions require large amounts of power and sensitive receivers, since the wave power decreases with the square of the radius of reception. Furthermore, omnidirectional transmissions result in a wasteful use of the available spectrum, since simultaneous transmissions on the same wavelength cannot occur inside the same transmission range.

Optical and sound transmissions are used in household appliances such as TV or toy telecontrols. Some terminals are attached to the computer via an infra-red free-space transmission system. An optical free-space transmission is achieved using a powerful light emitting diode (LED) and a sensitive receiving diode or photo-transistor, operating at infra-red wavelengths. This method is suitable for low data rates and short distances, but is not very reliable.

Directional transmissions make a better use of the available spectrum and use less transmission power, at the expense of reaching a reduced geographical region. Microwave and satellite radio transmissions can be considered as being directional if the antenna beam is narrow enough.

### 2.2.3 Wire transmission

One of the oldest transmission mediums is the *TWISTED PAIR* shown in figure 2.16, which is largely used in telephone communications.

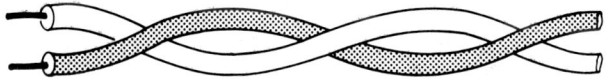

*Fig. 2.16 Twisted wire pair*

The twisting of the wires provides some shielding against interferences. The signal on a twisted pair is preferably transmitted as a voltage difference from one conductor with respect to the other. This is called a *DIFFERENTIAL, SYMMETRIC* or *BALANCED* transmission. Transmissions of up to 10 Mb/s are possible. A group of wire pairs may be shielded as a whole to reduce interferences, but crosstalk between adjacent pairs is not reduced by this shielding.

Another well known medium is the *COAXIAL CABLE*. It can span a distance of several kilometres and provide a higher bandwidth than twisted pairs and better shielding against interferences. Its attenuation is frequency dependent and in the order of 30 dB/100 m at 500 MHz. Since the conductor is completely enclosed in the shield, there are virtually no low-frequency interferences; a second ground shield is often used against high-frequency interferences. A detailed view of a coaxial cable is shown in figure 2.17.

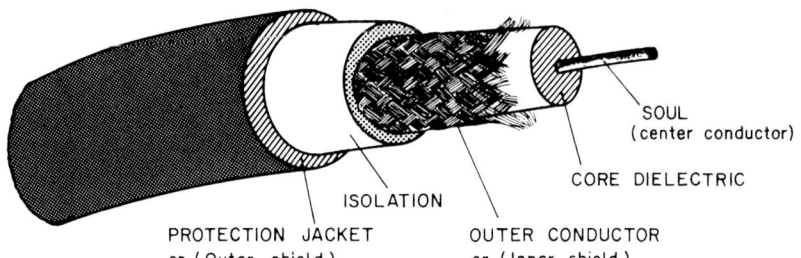

*Fig. 2.17 Coaxial cable*

The bandwidth of a coaxial cable can be as high as 1 GHz and it allows the transmission of information in a *FREQUENCY MULTIPLEX* mode, that is, with several information channels, each transmitting at a different frequency, such as different stations in radio or TV broadcasting. The information is modulated on a carrier, and the dedicated channels can function totally in parallel. They can be assigned to speech, video and digital transmissions. Such frequency multiplexing of several medium-rate channels is known as a *BROADBAND* communication, as opposed to a *BASEBAND* communication, in which there is only one channel, but a high data transmission rate. Broadband cables use the field-proven technology of cable TV, while baseband cables use more expensive equipment which is better adapted to rough environments.

Although the broadband communication method allows the parallel transmission of information over different channels, the sum of the bandwidths of the individual channels cannot exceed the bandwidth of a baseband transmission which uses the same medium, so there is no net throughput gain.

Coaxial cables can be tapped for broadcast and broadcall. Taps in coaxial cables are more expensive than in a twisted pair, especially in broadband cables. In this last case, the transmission is essentially unidirectional (the wave should always travel in the same direction), due to the repeaters.

Broadband cable connectors are standard UHF connectors such as those used for TV sets. Baseband cables use quite costly axial connectors, since they usually have a double shielding.

## 2.2.4 Optical fibers

Optical fibers can also be considered as electromagnetic wave guides. They exhibit characteristics similar to coaxial cables. Their bandwidth is very high (above 1 GHz) and their CD is impressive ($10^{13}$). The attenuation is below the values found in electrical cables (1 dB/km). They can therefore span larger distances without repeaters and are practically immune to interferences and crosstalk. Additionally, optical fibers do not have grounding problems and have small diameters. Optical fibers guide light using reflections under a shallow angle, as shown in figure 2.18.

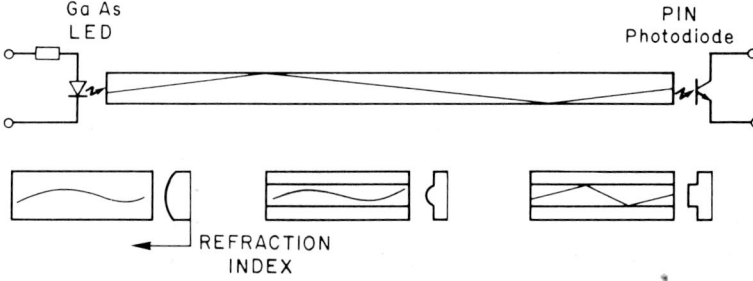

Fig. 2.18 Transmission of light in an optical fiber

This reflection occurs on the skin due to a change in the refraction coefficient between the centre of the fiber and the periphery. Three kinds of optical fiber are shown in figure 2.18; they differ in the manner in which their refraction indexes change. Some fibers have an abrupt change, while others have a continuous change from the centre to the periphery. One should recall that the optical fiber is extremely transparent; only about half of the light is lost in a distance of 1 km. However, this minimum loss can only be achieved within a very narrow range of wavelengths, more specifically, those to which the fiber and its transmitter are tuned.

Optical cables and connectors are very expensive. The lifetime of an emitting diode is relatively small, and its output power decreases with time. Also, optical fibers are difficult to splice and tap, because each tap causes a strong discontinuity and a loss of light, which limits the transmission distance. For these reasons, optical fibers are used mainly as point-to-point links with only one transmitter and one receiver, and not as buses.

## 2.2.5 Multi-wire media

The throughput of information can be increased by providing several physical channels which carry the information in parallel. In order to implement a parallel connection, one could choose, for instance, a group of twisted pairs of coaxial cables, but this would be very difficult to arrange mechanically.

FLAT CABLES are a better solution. They consist of several parallel conductors (8 to 96) embedded in an insulating material (plastic). Since the distance between these individual conductors is standardized, the cable can be easily pressed into a connector, using an appropriate tool, to establish a contact for every conductor in one operation (figure 2.19). Connectors can also be inserted at different places to build a multi-drop cable.

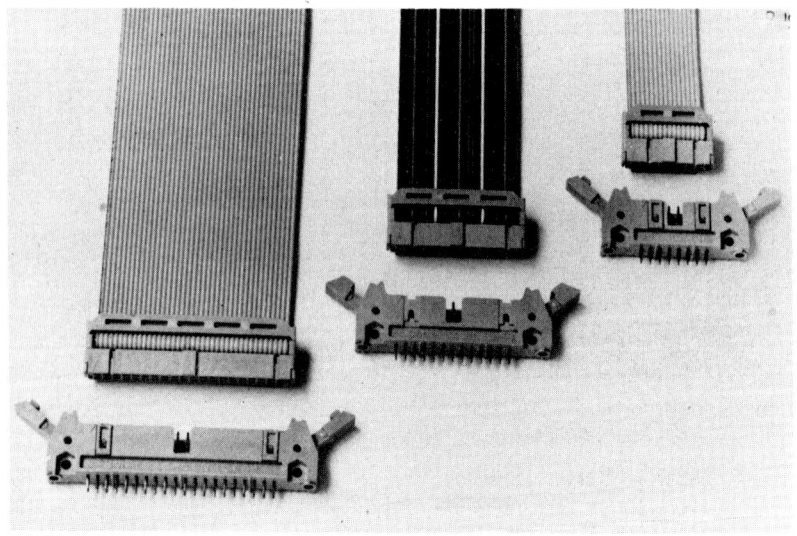

Fig. 2.19 Flat cable and connector

Flat cables are used extensively to connect boards and subsystems (e.g. printers or disk drives interfaces). Their length is, however, limited to a few metres. Flat cables are a poor electric medium: crosstalk is high since there is no shielding between the conductors. The occurrence of crosstalk could be reduced by connecting every second conductor to ground, but then one would lose half of the available conductors. One side of the flat cable is often covered with a conductive material in order to shield against interferences.

In connections where distances are short and the bandwidth of the signal is high, such as between a CPU and a memory, a large number of parallel wires is used. Computer boards are typically connected to each other by 60 to 120 conductors. Older machines, and some very high-speed computers such as the CRAY-XMP, use wire-wrap connectors for each board, where each individual pin is connected using twisted pairs. This is a very expensive method of connecting boards; a more popular solution is the utilization of a BACKPLANE BUS, which is formed by a printed circuit motherboard on which the connectors of the different boards are placed at regular intervals. The conductors are etched into the printed circuit board as shown in figure 2.20.

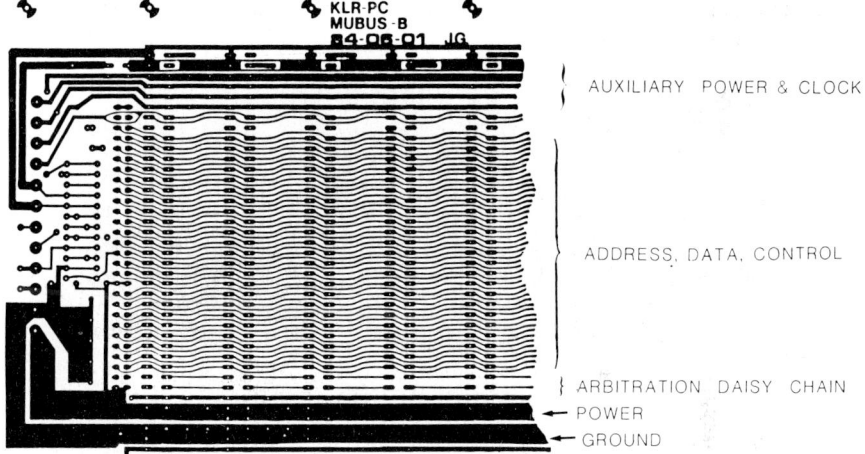

Fig. 2.20 Typical etch pattern of a backplane bus

Backplane buses are similar to flat cables in that crosstalk between adjacent lines is high and shielding against interferences is poor. Due to the presence of numerous connectors which may or may not have a board inserted in them, the characteristics of the transmission line are highly variable and the transmission cannot be optimized for all cases. Shielding against interferences and the reduction of crosstalk are achieved by using a ground plane, which can be implemented on the opposite face of the backplane or on a separate layer.

Backplane buses also carry power to the boards. For this reason, they need high current conductors which are provided by using wide tracks or additional layers. In high-performance buses, for example, up to six layers are used.

The connectors of parallel buses have an electrical, but also a mechanical role in that they contribute to the mechanical mounting of the boards. Female EDGE CONNECTORS or DIRECT CONNECTORS, for example, receive a male part formed by the edge of the printed circuit board which is inserted into the connector. The edge contacts are galvanically plated with gold in order to reduce corrosion. Direct connectors, shown in figure 2.21, are commonly used with most of the parallel buses found in the U.S. on low cost commercial hardware.

*Fig. 2.21 Edge connector*

INDIRECT CONNECTORS or TWO-PART CONNECTORS are formed by two parts; one part contains the pins, the other the sockets. One part is mounted on the backplane (generally the socket), while the other is placed on the board, as shown in figure 2.22.

The most popular indirect connectors have been standardized by the German Standard Institute DIN and later by the IEC. DIN 41612 C defines a family of connectors containing up to 3 rows of 32 pins each, which, incidentally, is the most popular bus connector in Europe. These connectors have an advantage in that the mechanical alignment of the board and the socket is solved by the connector, and thus does not affect board manufacturing much. The reliability of the indirect connector's contacts is higher than those of the edge connector. Indirect connectors also have a higher pin density of 96 pins over 70 mm, while typical edge connectors can offer only about 64 pins over the same distance. They are currently displacing the direct connector.

2 Principle of Operations                                              35

*Fig. 2.22 Indirect connector*

## 2.2.6 Transmission lines

A *TRANSMISSION LINE* is a piece of conductor to which transmitters and receivers are connected, either at both ends of the line (point-to-point connections), or along the line (bus connections), as in figure 2.23.

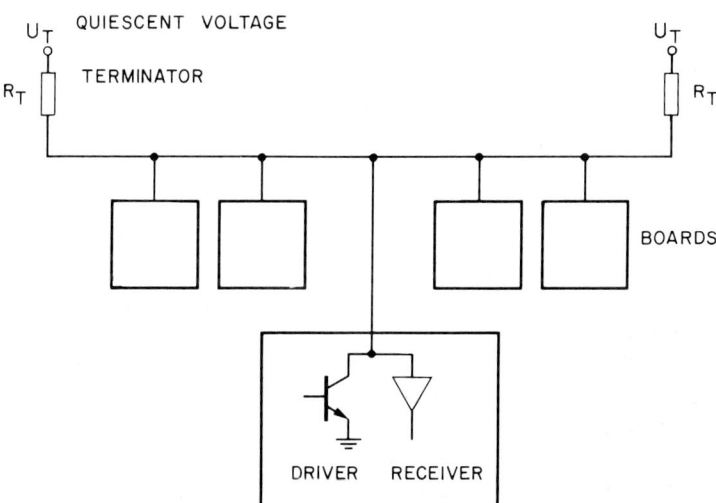

*Fig. 2.23 A bus line with several transmitters and receivers*

When a transmitter is turned on, the resulting change in voltage and current propagates as a wave from the driver towards the ends of the line. When the wave reaches one end of the line, it is reflected, and this return wave now interferes with the original wave (Chapter 8). Thus, these reflections may cause the false triggering of receivers. Therefore, in order to reduce reflections, a line must be terminated by an absorbing resistance or TERMINATOR.

This terminator often has the additional purpose of providing the quiescent voltage $U_T$ of the bus line, meaning that it fixes the voltage of the line when no transmitter is active.

The value of the termination resistance depends on the characteristic impedance of the medium, that is, on the dielectric properties and especially on its capacitive load. More details are given in chapitre 8.

### 2.2.7 Line driving techniques

The signal on a conductor is generated by a circuit named a TRANSMITTER or DRIVER. When the signal voltage is referenced to ground, the transmission is said to be ASYMMETRIC (figure 2.24a). This allows the use of one common ground for several signal lines. Only one amplifier is needed to drive each signal line. Note the use of terminators, the two return lines, which reduce crosstalk, and external shield against the interferences shown in figure 2.24.

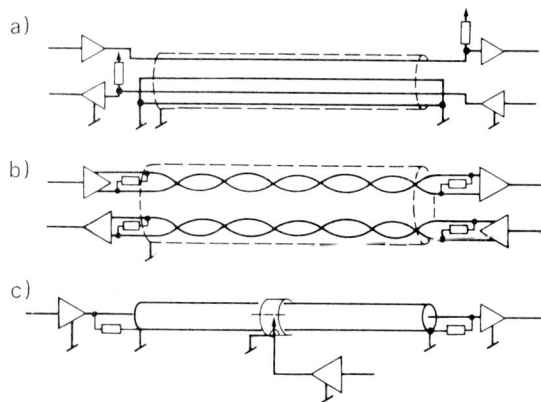

*Fig. 2.24 Asymmetric and differential transmission*

A symmetric or differential transmission eliminates the common return/ground by transmitting two signals of opposite voltages over a pair of wires, as in figure 2.24b. The reduced noise levels in this transmission result in reduced voltage swings and therefore longer transmission distances.

Finally, figure 2.24c shows how a coaxial cable is driven: either from one end through point-to-point links or through taps in the middle. Note that a driver in the middle still has to drive a load equal to half of the termination resistance.

A great variety of voltage levels are used to transmit information on lines. Standard computer buses make *BINARY* transmissions, meaning that the receivers can distinguish only 2 voltage levels, called "Low" and "High", respectively. The receivers must then have thresholds which are adapted to the driver's output swing (figure 2.25).

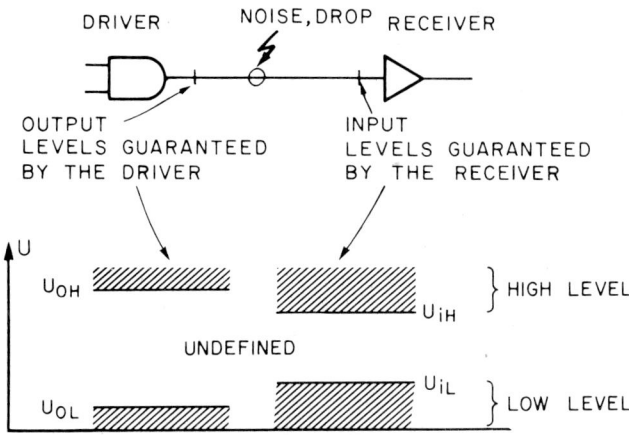

*Fig. 2.25 TTL driver and receiver levels*

*TERNARY* information transfers are also often found. They provide a reference voltage which indicates "no transfer" or a special marking.

Serial buses using twisted pairs utilize high voltage swings in order to overcome the expected high environmental noise. Buses using coaxial cables work with lower levels and less power. For instance, Ethernet operates with −0.225V (high level) and −1.825V (low level). These levels are compatible with the ECL levels.

## 2.2.8 Bus drivers and receivers

We will now focus our attention on the binary transmitters used in most parallel buses. Normal gates (section 2.1.6) do not match the electrical characteristics of twisted or coaxial cables correctly. Thus, drivers either of the three-state or the open collector type have to be used, which can provide a higher output current.

The three-state design is the standard choice for parallel buses, implemented by backplanes or flat cables. Optimized TTL three-state drivers are available in octal packages; they are cheap and have propagation delays of less than 10 ns. In parallel buses, where several three-state drivers are connected to the same line, only one driver should be active at a time. If several drivers are activated, an electrical collision occurs, the state of the line is undefined and the drivers may be damaged.

Open collector drivers are only half-active (section 2.1.6). They can only pull the line low. A pull-up resistor maintains the line in the high state when no driver is active. This pull-up resistor can be used as the terminator of the line at the same time. Since open collector drivers have only one active state (the low state), two or more drivers can control the same line simultaneously. The result of a collision in a transmission using open collector drivers is that the line will go low if any driver pulls it low, independent of any driver which would let the line go high.

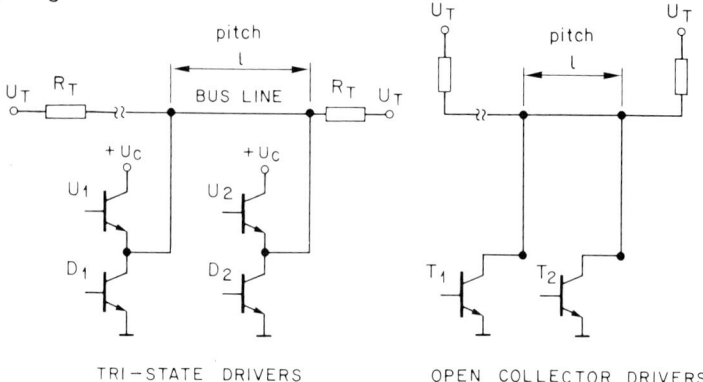

TRI-STATE DRIVERS         OPEN COLLECTOR DRIVERS

*Fig. 2.26 Tri-state and open collector drivers*

Open collector drivers are preferred for some high-speed buses where the current requirements are high, mainly because they are more reliable than three-state drivers, since they dissipate less power (half of the power is dissipated in the external termination/pull-up resistor, and not on the chip). Recently, some specialized open collector drivers have been manufactured which reduce the occurrence of crosstalk by shaping the signal properly. These devices exhibit only a small bus load, but they do not use TTL-levels.

*RECEIVER* circuits operate generally with levels similar to the TTL logic. They do not use the same internal logic design; the input stage is optimized to reduce the input current and the capacitive loading. The *HYSTERESIS* effect of certain receivers is a very useful feature which helps reduce the effects of noise, although this effect varies with temperature. Common Schmitt trigger TTL inputs exhibit a hysteresis of about 200 mV.

Manufacturers have also developed integrated circuits which are adapted to the transmission lines with matched drivers and receivers, called TRANSCEIVERS, including both open collector and tri-state drivers.

### 2.2.9 Features of parallel buses

Parallel buses are rather short: they vary in length between 10 cm and 5 m. The propagation delay is low comparing to serial buses, having a value of about 20 ns for a fully loaded backplane of 50 cm, i.e. when all possible transmitters and receivers are connected. This property provides for an efficient mutual synchronization between two devices on the bus. Furthermore, it permits efficient read operations: the master can request the slave to send data and will receive it within the same bus cycle.

The propagation delay along the bus is not a big problem; the large number of parallel lines, however, is. The power dissipation of an interface can be quite high since a large number of transmitters are operated in parallel. Currents in the range of 20 mA to 48 mA, and more recently, to 64 mA or 100 mA are quite common. If 32 lines switch at the same time, the current on the ground conductor could exceed 3 A. More will be mentioned on the subject of line adaptation and glitches in Chapter 8.

## 2.3 STANDARDIZATION AND OSI MODEL

Computers and communication systems are complex and difficult to understand and specify. One description method which has become popular consists of the functional decomposition of a system and its layering into levels of abstraction. This decomposition is achieved by dividing a complex system into understandable parts, which are themselves complex objects, but whose external description is simple. This method has already been clearly described in the work of the French philosopher Descartes (1596 - 1650).

The description of a communication system in terms of a layered architecture has become common since the ISO (International Standard Organization) published its "Open System Interconnection Reference Model" (OSI-RM) [FOLT83]. This model was inspired by long-haul communications over telephone networks. In a modified form, this scheme is also useful in describing and specifying most local networks, links and parallel buses. The following paragraphs will explain some of the basic issues in the description and standardization of communication systems. It will also describe layering, explain how it is used to standardize buses and links, and point out its limitations.

## 2.3.1 Hierarchical modular decomposition

A decomposition can be either modular or functional. MODULAR DECOMPOSITION is the decomposition of a structure into several different physical parts, which are further decomposed into subparts. FUNCTIONAL DECOMPOSITION is the decomposition of a structure into functions, which are themselves implemented by other functions, but not necessarily on a different part.

As an illustration of a modular decomposition, we will attempt to describe a car. An alphabetic list of some 10000 parts would be indigestible. We thus tend to decompose the car in terms of large and complex objects, such as wheels, doors, cabin, transmission, motor, etc., which are themselves composed of simpler objects, such as a piston, carburetter, starter, plug, etc.

We can fully describe the car in terms of a collection of complex objects, all of which have about the same complexity. These objects and their interaction form a LEVEL OF ABSTRACTION. The level of abstraction is not a natural property of the car: it depends on the view of the person which makes the description. But, in general, it

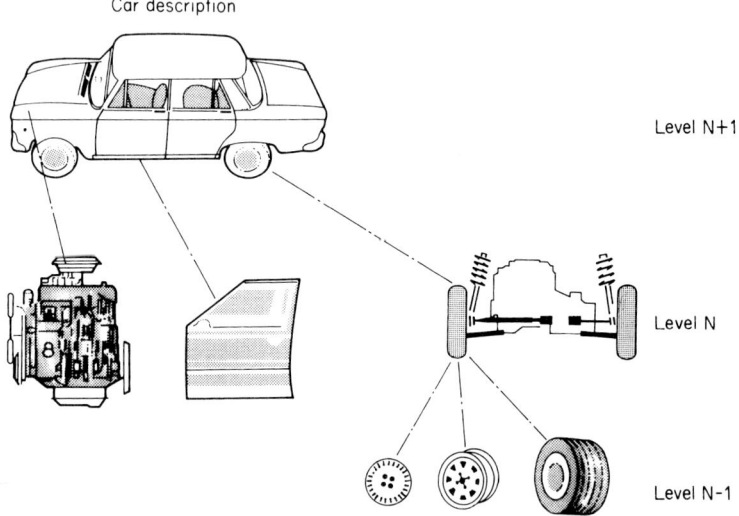

Fig. 2.27 Modular decomposition of a car

makes little sense to mix high-level objects like the motor and low-level objects like a screw into the same description. Figure 2.27 shows how a car is decomposed into elementary parts.

Once the interaction of the abstract objects have been described at a higher level, one can go into more detail and describe the objects themselves. The description of the individual objects follows the same rules as above for the whole car. After having described the car in general, we can now describe the motor, consisting of several lower-level objects such as the carburetter, rod, piston, housing, etc. These objects conform to a lower level of abstraction.

We can continue this game and define objects such as screws or washers, and even lower levels of objects until we reach the level of "atomic" parts, which we decide not to decompose further. The collection of all the atomic objects forms the lowest level of abstraction.

Thus, a car can be described at different levels of abstraction, which form a hierarchy, going from an abstract, high level description to a more concrete and detailed description. The objects of each level are described using lower level objects, which form the next lower abstraction level, and these objects are described by more fundamental objects until we reach a satisfying level of abstraction consisting of atomic parts which are not easily divided any further. Every hierarchy is based on a unidirectional relationship. The transition from one level to the next is given here by the relation "is composed of". Interestingly, the high-level object "car" may itself become an atomic object when dealing with higher-level functions such as road traffic or environmental impact.

## 2.3.2 Functional decomposition in communications

Let us take a telephone communications network to aid in the illustration of a functional decomposition. As in the above example of the car, a communication system consists of several parts. We could now do the same exercise, and decompose the network into exchanges, links and telephone sets, the telephone sets into screws and bolts, etc... but this is not our goal here.

We are not interested in the question "What are the parts of the telephone system?", but in the question "What is the service the telephone network provides?". And, as we describe each service, we will ask the same question again under the assumption that a service is implemented by one or many other services.

Consider two people using a telephone : the objects we deal with at this level of abstraction are the people and the existence of a telephone link between them (figure 2.28).

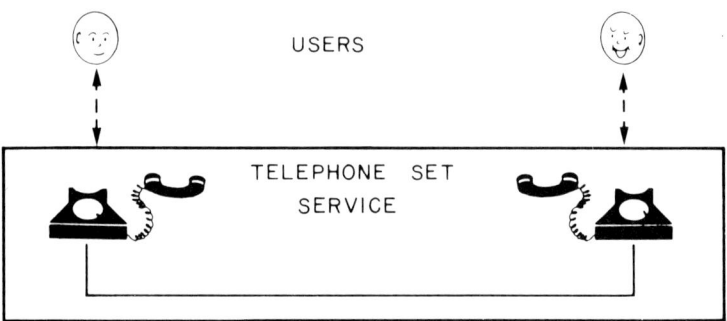

Fig. 2.28 Two people telephoning

With this level, we distinguish two people, or PEER ENTITIES which communicate by using a TRANSPORT SERVICE. The conversation obeys a collection of established rules of diplomacy, which any polite person should follow, which is called the PROTOCOL. For instance, the call begins with a phase of SESSION ESTABLISHMENT, such as saying "Hello" and one's own name, checking if the partner is the intended one, and so on. Especially in Europe, it may be necessary to agree on which language to speak: this is the NEGOTIATION phase, in which the parties agree on certain parts of the protocol. The call terminates with a SESSION TERMINATION in which the parties agree to cease the call.

During the conversation, it may be necessary to correct some transmission errors by asking the partner to repeat a sentence or to spell a word: this is the ERROR CONTROL. It may also be necessary to CONTROL the FLOW of information, if for instance one partner speaks too fast while the other is trying to write down part of the conversation. Finally, the conversation also consists of USER DATA, which is the actual information the two people exchange.

Thus, a conversation consists on the one hand of PROTOCOL INFORMATION and on the other of USER DATA. The meaning of the user data, and such facts that the people are, say, John and Mary, and that Mary invites John to dinner, do not belong to this abstraction level, but to some higher level. In order to perform this communication, these people use the SERVICE of the telephone. At this level of abstraction, we are not interested in how the telephone works as long as it provides the service of communication.

2 Principle of Operations                                             43

In reality, though, people do not speak directly to their counterpart, or peer entity, but to their telephone set. The interaction of the person and the telephone service is called the *INTERFACE* or *ACCESS*. Both terms are synonyms in the OSI terminology, but since the first term is somewhat related to a hardware device, we prefer the more general term of "access".

A person accesses the telephone network by lifting the receiver, dialing and speaking, while the network responds with ringing, dial tones, busy tones, error messages ("this number not available any more"), clicks, noises, tax pulses and, eventually, with the voice of the counterpart. The information interchanged between the person and her telephone consists of two parts : on the one hand the information intended for the counterpart and, on the other hand, the information exchanged to control the telephone service.

Conceptually, there are two kinds of communication, depending on one's point of view. There is a *HORIZONTAL COMMUNICATION* which occurs within the same layer and makes an abstraction of the transport system. The information transported horizontally is called the *PEER DATA*. It consists of both useful and protocol data.

Then there is a *VERTICAL COMMUNICATION* which takes place between an entity and the transport system at the same site. The information exchanged vertically consists of the previously seen peer data, which is renamed *INTERFACE DATA*, in addition to the information which controls the transport system, but which is not transmitted further, called the *INTERFACE CONTROL*, as shown in figure 2.29.

The horizontal communication is only conceptual, while the vertical communication is the one which physically takes place.

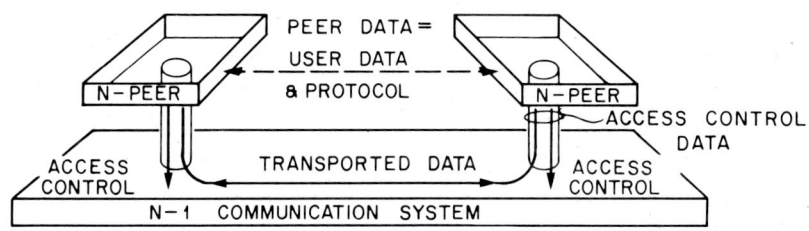

*Fig. 2.29 Service, protocol and interface (one layer)*

In figure 2.30, only two peer entities are shown, but the concepts can apply equally to conference calls with N-peer entities. Only two peer entities were chosen in order not to overload the drawings. The concept of peer entities is basic to the decomposition of a communication system. Any communication system is reduced to a set of peer entities and a communication medium between them. Now, the communication system, in our case the telephone, has been described by the SERVICES it provides, and by the ACCESS PROCEDURES (operating instructions) which are required to use these services. The description of the access service answers two separate questions: "what service does the communication system provide", and "how do I use it". Once the answers to these two questions are known, a communication may take place. The telephone system is then reduced to a black box the user does not need to know about.

Now, let us go one step deeper into the abstraction. The engineer, being a restless enquirer, is interested in something more: "how does such a telephone service work?". The next lower level of abstraction will describe how the telephone service is provided. The telephone system is, of course, quite complex and consists of many objects such as telephone sets, exchanges, transmission lines, multiplexers, etc. The telephone system itself can also be described as a set of peer entities (the telephone sets) which use a common transmission system (the lines and the exchanges) as shown in figure 2.30.

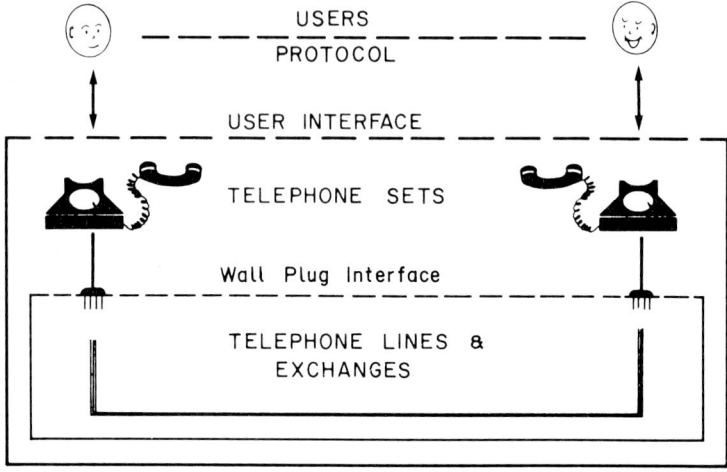

*Fig. 2.30 Telephone set layer (two layers)*

The peer entity "telephone sets" communicate conceptually with each other by means of a protocol invisible to the user. For instance, if one telephone set receives the number of another, the bell should ring at the other location, without any necessary interventions by the user at that location.

# 2 Principle of Operations

The telephone sets have an interface to the communication system, which is the wall plug. This interface is standardized, at least within the same company or the telephone company. The mechanical dimensions of the plug, the electrical levels, the dialing, the ringing, the taxation pulses, and the frequency band of the voice signals are all standardized. This allows a common interface to the telephone exchange and also the interchangeability of the telephone sets. The same exercise can now be continued with the telephone exchange. When the peer users are connected to different telephone exchanges, the exchanges act as peer entities to transmit the voice from one user to the other (figure 2.31). They use the services of the long-haul communication network. The interface between the exchange is also standardized, and obeys the rules set up by international organizations.

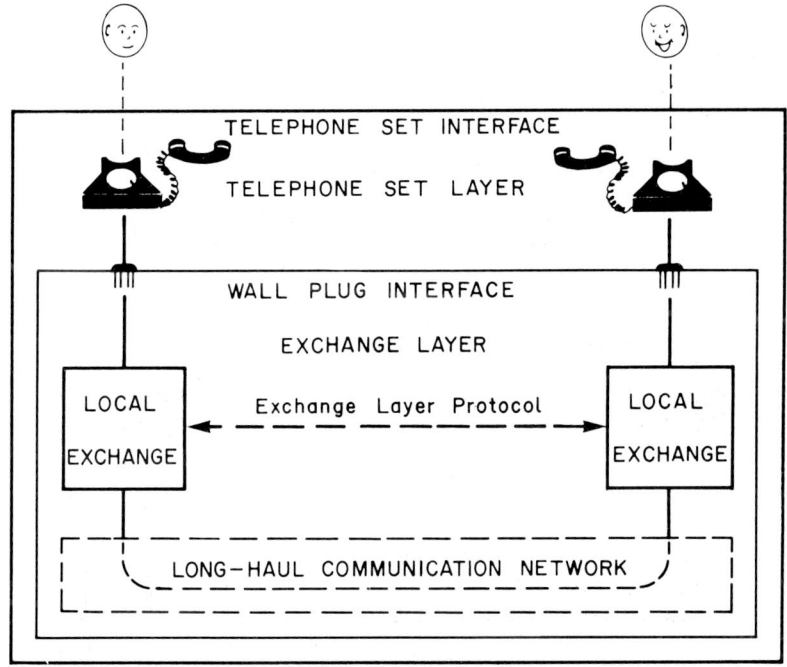

Fig. 2.31 Exchange layer (three layers)

This layering will stop when no further peer entities are recognizable. In an intercom, for instance, there is no exchange layer. If both users are connected to the same local exchange, there is no long-haul link. The full hierarchy which results is shown in figure 2.32.

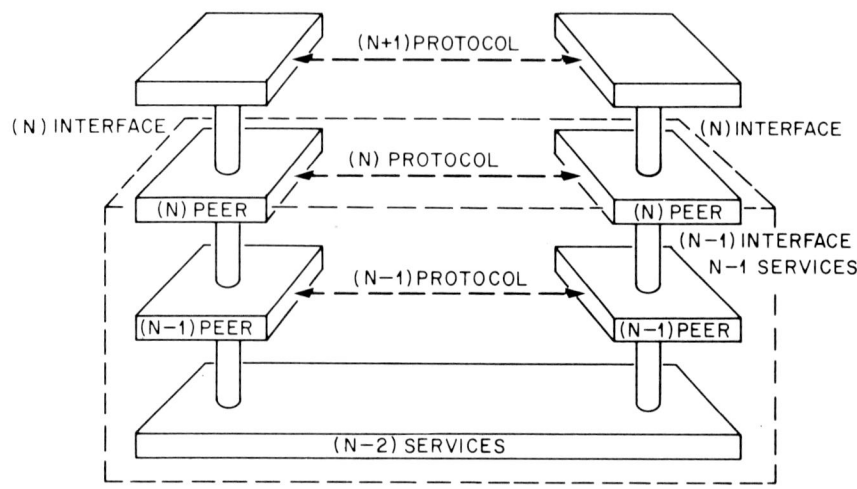

*Fig. 2.32 (N+1) layer hierarchy*

## 2.3.3 The OSI Reference Model

The OSI-RM (Open System Interconnection Reference Model) [FOLT83][DAY83] is a framework for the description of a communication system. It has been standardized by ISO and CCITT (see section 2.3.8). It is not a description of a particular system, but a "description of a description". It cannot, for instance, be implemented, but it defines a standard guideline on how to decompose a communication system. The OSI-RM (as defined above) uses the functional description of a communication system by utilizing the layering concept described above:

- A communication system can be described by a hierarchy of layers
- At each layer, interacting peer entities which use a common communication service are visible
- The description of these peer entities and their interaction defines the abstraction layer (N). The description of the interaction of these peer entitites is called the PROTOCOL at layer N or (N) PROTOCOL
- The (N) protocol is realized by exchanging "horizontal" information between the (N) Peer Entities. This "horizontal" information within the (N) layer consists of "user data" which is the useful data, and of "protocol data" which the (N) Peer Entities exchange to coordinate their activity. Protocol and user data are transmitted by messages called PDU (Protocol Data Units) at layer N or (N) PDU

## 2 Principle of Operations

- The Peer Entities of the (N) layer implement the protocol by using the services available at that site of a lower communication layer (N-1)
- Each layer (N) provides a set of services for the layer (N+1) above it and uses itself the services of layer (N-1) below it, except for the bottom layer, which implements the actual communication and cannot be subdivided into any more peer entities
- All services and access procedures of a layer (N) form its (N) interface. The (N) interface describes a collection of services and how to use them
- In order to use the services of layer (N-1), a peer entity of layer (N) calls the access procedures of layer (N-1). To be able to do so, layer (N) must interchange information with layer (N-1). This information is the ACCESS DATA
- The information flowing "vertically" accross the interface between layers (N) and (N+1) at the same site consists of "interface control information", which is used to coordinate the communication between layer (N) and (N-1) and of the INTERFACE DATA, which is the data this layer should transmit to the peer layer or receive from it. Interface control and interface data are transmitted by messages called IDU (Interface Data Units) at layer N-1 or (N-1) IDU

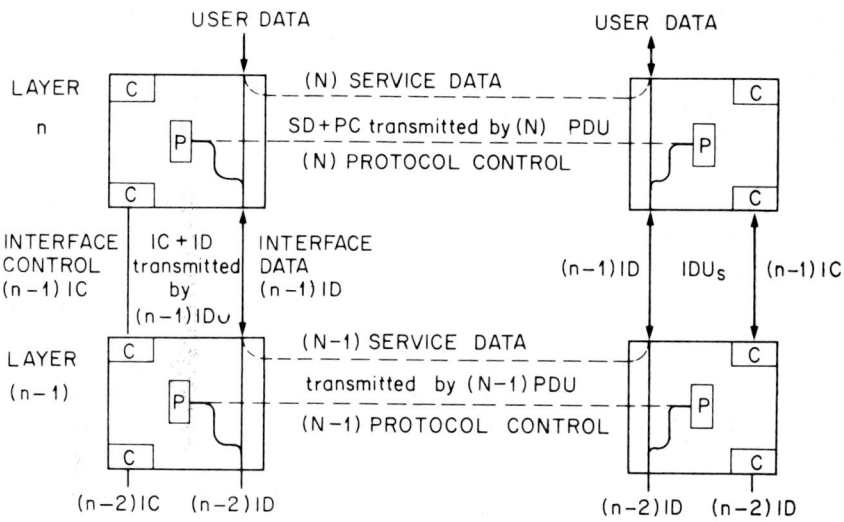

Fig. 2.33 Layered model of a communication system (PC = Protocol Control, PDU = Protocol Data Unit, ID = Interface Data, IC = Interface Control, IDU = Interface Data Unit)

- The service data is the data transmitted between (N-1) Entities on behalf of the (N) layer. It is semantically identical to the (N-1) IDU and the (N) PDU, but the format may differ. Service data are transmitted by messages called *SDU (Service Data Units)* or (N-1) SDU. For instance, what is conceptually one single (N) PDU may be transmitted by several consecutive (N-1) SDU. The service data of the upper layer is identical to the user data
- The implementation of a layer (N) is not specified. It is only assumed that the implementation of layer (N) uses the communication services of a lower layer (N-1) if it needs them.

The OSI model consists of 7 levels called layers. The lower layers have been defined accurately and have been implemented in several applications, while the higher levels are not as easily defined and distinguished. Each layer consists of a set of peer entities which communicate by using a suitable "horizontal" protocol and are located at different sites. The OSI-RM unfortunately uses the word "system" to refer to a site. Each layer implements a set of services which are used by the layer above it through *SAP (Service Access Points)*, which define the vertical interface. SAPs roughly correspond to procedure calls. These layers are shown in figure 2.34.

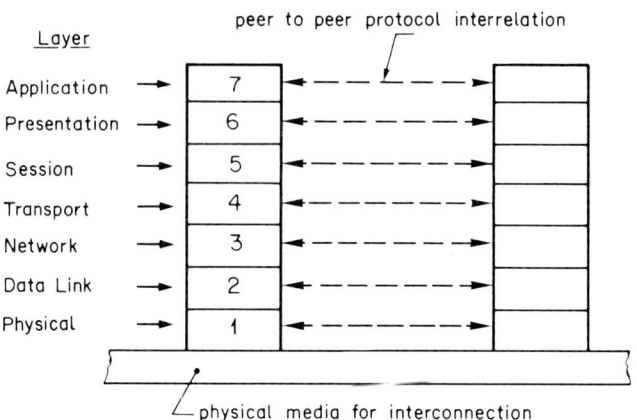

*Fig. 2.34 The OSI reference model*

Here is a short description of each of the OSI layers:

1) The PHYSICAL LAYER is the bottom layer, which does not contain any peer entities. It defines the mechanical and electrical characteristics of the communication medium. For instance, it specifies the type of cable (coaxial, twisted pair..), its mechanical and electrical characteristics (characteristic impedance, coating, etc.).

the electrical levels on the cable, and the connector type. The function of this layer is to physically transmit one basic item of information. By basic item we mean a single bit in a serial bus or a single word (8, 16 or 32 bit) in a parallel bus. The layer is not concerned with the meaning of this information. RS232 (V24) is a typical example of a specification for this layer.

2) The *DATA LINK LAYER* uses the services of the physical layer to send a succession of bits, called a *MESSAGE* using serial buses, and a *TRANSACTION* using parallel buses. A message contains typically the address of the destination or the source or both; the protocol information contains the useful data and a redundant piece of data for error detection.

HDLC is a typical example of a data link layer protocol. Figure 2.35 shows the frame format of an HDLC message.

| FLAG<br>01111110 | ADDRESS<br>8bit | CONTROL<br>8bit | INFORMATION<br>n bit | ERROR DETECTION<br>16bit CRC | FLAG<br>01111110 |
|---|---|---|---|---|---|

*Fig. 2.35 HDLC frame*

Since the physical link is considered unreliable, the data link layer adds an error detection code or, in some cases, an error correction code to the message. Since the peer entities only have a limited buffer space for messages, the data link layer implements a flow control. Dedicated messages or part of the data message header tell the source that the destination cannot receive any further messages or that it is ready to receive them again.

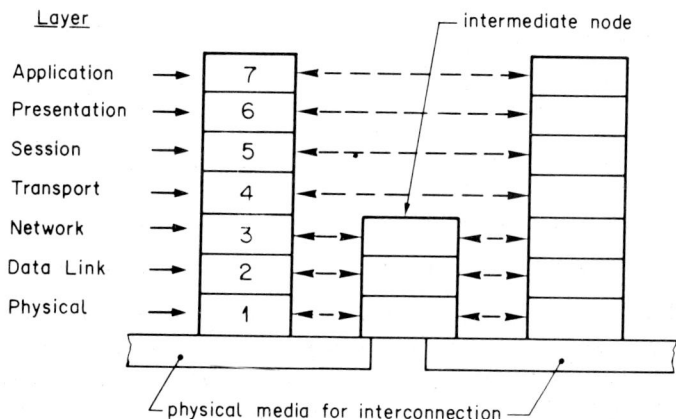

*Fig. 2.36 OSI-RM with a relay site*

3) The *NETWORK LAYER* uses the services of the data link layer to perform networking functions. When a network layer exists, a node may have the additional function of a RELAY SITE to relay messages for which it is not the final destination. This situation is typical in a telephone exchange: a node often has to relay messages between two remote exchanges. If the function of a site is to only relay messages (repeater), the network layer is the site's upper-most layer, as shown in figure 2.36.

4) The *TRANSPORT LAYER* is responsible for the transport of a message of arbitrary length, such as a file. If it is too long, it must be cut into packets which are transmitted sequentially. The transport layer is responsible for the decomposition of the lengthy messages into packets, and for the reconstruction of the original message at the destination, taking into account that certain packets may have been lost, duplicated, or have arrived out of order because they travelled through different paths in the network.

5) The *SESSION LAYER* is concerned with the establishment of the communication between the users, accounting, authorization, and in particular, with the negotiation phase, in which the parties agree on certain parts of the protocol. The work on the definition of this layer and the following is still in progress as of 1985.

6) The *PRESENTATION LAYER* is the user's interface to the network. It should present to the user a sight of the peer entity which is independent of the type of computer used.

7) The *APPLICATION LAYER* is the user's program. The OSI model makes no assumptions about this layer.

## 2.3.4 Wrapping

When information passes from layer (N) to the next lower layer (N-1), it is *WRAPPED* with the protocol information of layer (N-1). Layer (N-2) adds its own protocol information, and so on. The useful information must be unwrapped as it passes to the higher layer.

This is similar to what happens to a letter: The useful content is first fitted into a standard form (company paper, standard header, usual greetings, etc.). Then the letter is put into an envelope, and covered with information for the postal transfer (destination address and sender address for error recovery) and put into the post office box. The letter is sorted and put into a postal bag which is labelled with the service information of the post office. After sorting, the postal bags are put into a town destination crate and loaded in the railway truck, which is itself labelled with the service data of the railroad or truck company. At the destination, the letter is successively unwrapped until the receiver finally reads it.

In a typical digital communication, the user data is wrapped with a header indicating the destination and the source, some management information such as sequence numbers, and a trailer with a checksum for error detection. At the link layer, synchronization headers and synchronization bits are added. At the physical layer, the individual bits are encoded, modulated and transmitted. This wrapping is referred to as DATA ENCAPSULATION (figure 2.37).

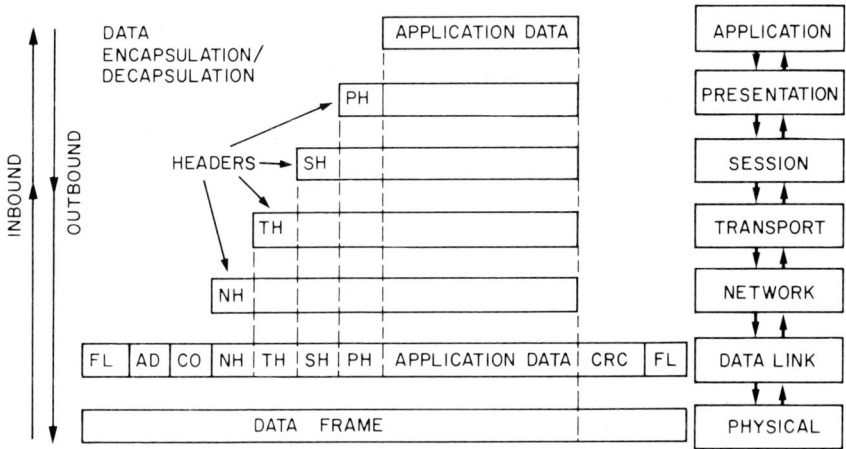

*Fig. 2.37 Wrapping the information*

There is often more protocol information than useful data. Consider the extreme case of a remote terminal session between a personal computer and a remote data base, acting as peer entities over a network in communication similar to X-25 [DOLL78]. In the dialogue, the data base prompts the user "Shall I continue?". The user responds with a "Y". This character is formed into a message, possibly extended by some service information. Level 2 (HLDC) adds a flag, an 8-bit address for the exchange, an 8-bit control field with the sequence number of the last received message and for this reply, adds 1's where needed and finally adds a CRC. Level 1 will modulate this information over the carrier. In total, this makes about 60 bits just to say "yes".

### 2.3.5 Use of the OSI-RM to standardize buses

The concept of the OSI-RM, not the OSI-RM itself, has proven to be an adequate help to the specification and design of serial and parallel buses. This will be illustrated by two examples.

The Ethernet specification is structured in a way similar to the OSI Model: The "blue book" [DIX80] describes two layers: a "physical layer" and a "data link layer", each of which are actually split in two.

The physical layer specifies the physical connections: the cable type and marking, the connector type, the tap type for the main cable and the connection cable between the transceiver and the controller. It also describes the electrical signal levels on the cables. Somewhat above these descriptions (but conceptually within the physical layer), the Manchester encoding (section 10.2.5) of a single bit and the collision mechanism is described.

The data link layer is subdivided into two sublayers, the data encapsulation layer and the link management layer.

The link management layer provides the services of transmitting an already formed frame (i.e. a message with header, address and CRC) and to ability to receive such a frame (without decoding its content). To achieve this, it uses the services of the physical layer to access the medium (and possibly back-off because of a collision). It does not check the validity of the message and the only service information it gives is an "excessive collision number".

Work is in progress to define the higher levels of Ethernet. It should be noted that the Ethernet designers do not adhere to the strict hierarchy of the OSI model. They allow layers to be bypassed.

The layering concept can be adapted equally well to the standardization parallel buses.

Starting at the bottom, we can define a *PHYSICAL* level in which the mechanical dimensions and the pin-out of the connectors are defined. An higher *ELECTRICAL* level specifies the electrical characteristics of drivers, receivers, and of the backplane (impedance, terminators, etc.). The layers above this level are not defined by electrical levels any more, rather with logical signals. The next layer defines elementary *ACTIONS*, grouped to perform the transfer of simple items of information (*CYCLE level*); the interpretation of this information is not relevant at this level.

At the next stage, cycles are grouped to form complete *TRANSACTIONS*, which include arbitration, addressing and data transfer. Above this level, the *APPLICATION* layer consists of processor instructions which make use of the bus facility to transfer data, without knowing the operation of a bus in detail. A good example of layered specification for a parallel bus is P896 [P89683].

## 2.3.6 Consequences of interface design

It is interesting to note that the speed of the logic is a function of the depth of the layer of the reference model. Structured layering is thus not only important for the description of the bus and for the understanding of its function, but also for its implementation. Actually, the separation of a communication operation into modules which implement different layers yields a very efficient interface structure. For instance, it is wise to separate the parts which implement the physical layer from all others, because these are high-current, high-speed parts using a different technology from the rest (ECL-like for Ethernet, special trapezoidal drivers for IEEE 896). Then, the control of the bus can be segregated: it is conveniently implemented by a high-speed state machine (sequencer), e.g. in TTL-Fast logic family, and receives its instructions from a lower speed sequencer, e.g. in CMOS logic family, which implements the link layer. The distance from the physical layer is inversely proportional to the speed of the communication. Standard microprocessors are able to manage the protocol at the highest layers.

## 2.3.7 A discussion of the OSI Reference Model

The OSI Reference Model has received wide publicity. It has also awakened undue expectations and raised unfair criticisms. The OSI-RM has, for the first time, clearly defined the elements of a complex communication system. It has separated the issues of protocol, service and interface, and introduced the notion of peer entities. It is a framework for all works in the field.

On the other hand, the OSI model has a very rigid structure: it supposes that all layers and all interfaces are implemented. For each layer, both the upper interface and the lower interface are specified. There is practically no freedom in between, which can have disastrous effects on efficiency. In fact, it is not clear why a peer entity is necessary for each level. If this assumption were followed in the telephone system, then a person with a dial disk telephone would be unable to communicate with a PCM telephone, since the PCM telephone would lack some intermediate levels. Thus, the freedom to skip the interface of layers which need not be implemented should exist. The specification of both interfaces only makes sense if each layer corresponds to a physical device which is plug-compatible, that is, completely interchangeable with another. This fact is considered by some designers who try to implement an OSI-RM-like architecture, such as X25.

The OSI-reference model is not concerned with all the functions that are necessary in order to realize a layer, but only defines which communication functions a level should use. It is, therefore, natural that the level of description becomes more and more abstract as one proceeds toward describing the highest layers.

### 2.3.8 Standardization process

Standardization is the difficult task of defining common interfaces between parts which work together to perform a specified function. The acceptance of a standard by a wide community of users is an even more complicated issue, which is beyond the power of the engineer. Numerous international bodies, among them the *ISO (International Organization for Standardization)*, the *IEC (International Electrotechnical Committee)*, the *CCITT (Comité Consultatif International des Télégraphes et Téléphones)*, as well as national organisations such as the *IEEE (Institute of Electrical and Electronics Engineers)*, the *ANSI (American National Standards Institute)*, the *EIA (Electronic Industry Association)*, the *ECMA (European Computer Manufacturers Association)*, the *DIN (Deutsche Industrie Normen)*, the *AFNOR (Association Française de NORmalisation)*, the *CEI (Comitado Eletrotecnico Italiano)*, the *SEV (Schweizerischer Elektrotechniker Verein)*, the *BSO (British Standard Organization)* and others have produced standards for computer parts such as sockets, board sizes, buses, communication systems, tape formats, etc. A list of the most popular standards in computer communication can be found in the Appendix.

A standard should guarantee that parts of different design and manufacture will be compatible electrically, mechanically, functionally, etc., that is, work together. The *DEPTH* of the standard is the degree of compatibility, which extends from the requirement of "does no harm when connected together" to the more restrictive case of "plug-compatibility", which states that any product that complies with one given standard can totally replace any other which also obeys this standard. Computer products are rather complex parts, however, which provide many distinct functions. Standardization can apply to all functions, or only to a subset of them. For instance, the ANSI X3.64 1977 standard for terminals standardizes such functions as "position cursor", or "erase to end of screen". Most terminals on the market, in fact, provide additional functions which are not ANSI, such as "fill screen with E" (for diagnostics). Of course, programs which make use of these special functions are not compatible and must thus be rewritten for each new terminal. The much-heralded term of *UPWARD COMPATIBILITY* or *DOWNWARD COMPATIBILITY* only means that a product with a higher functionality retains, as a subset of its functionality, a set of standardized functions. This product is only compatible so long as it does not make use of its higher functionality, thus the basic choice is between efficiency, functionality and standardization.

Standardization does not only apply to the interchangeable products on the market, but also to any technical activity within the same firm, which involves the cooperation of different designers. Most standards are, in fact, in-house standards, which sometimes become standardized nationally later.

## 2.3.9 Requirement and functional description

Standardization requires a strict DESCRIPTION of the different parts and of their interaction. A standard is formulated in a way which leaves little or no room for ambiguities. Such a careful description is called a SPECIFICATION. Like any description, a specification is done in a particular language: either plain English, a mechanical drawing, electrical schematics, a state machine, a PASCAL program, or any language on which different people can agree. In order to put an emphasis on the fact that the description language itself is free of ambiguities, some people like to speak of a FORMAL SPECIFICATION. The proof that the formulation itself is consistent is called a VALIDATION. The proof that a specification is free of contradictions or ambiguities and reflects the intention of the designer is an interesting research subject called a VERIFICATION. A validation can be compared to the syntax check done by a compiler, while a verification is the debugging that follows later.

A description always responds to a specific question, for instance: "what is the object used for?", "what does the object do?", "how is the object used? or "how is the object built?". Ideally, a standard should only specify the external function and the use of an object, without specifying what the object is or how it is manufactured. This leaves the largest amount of room for the engineer's creativity.

One could standardize a window, for instance, by specifying the composition of the glass, its thickness, its cooking process and the handling of its surface. This is called the IMPLEMENTATION SPECIFICATION, which states what the object is. On the other hand, one can also specify that the window must be transparent and be able to withstand the impact of a stone weighing 1 kg falling from a height of 1 m. This is called the REQUIREMENT SPECIFICATION, which responds to the question: "what does the object do?" or "what service does this object provide?".

The requirement specification, which is a set of requirements, obviously leaves more room for technological improvements than the implementation specification, which is a set of solutions. Current standards mix implementation and requirement specifications. The distinction is often blurred, since one can formulate the requirements so as to imply a solution, or because the requirements are too complicated to describe otherwise. For instance, the same bus driver can be specified once as an implementation specification and once as a requirement specification :

Implementation specification (what IS it?): "the driver shall be a 74S38"

Requirement specification (what DOES it do?): "the driver shall be open collector or open-drain, active low, and able to sink at least 48 mA at 0.4 V in the "low" state over the full industrial temperature range, with a leakage current of less than 400 $\mu$A when in the high state. The capacitive load due to this driver shall be less than 20 pF. The propagation time shall be less than 10 ns".

A particular problem of standardization is that the people which standardize usually have a solution or a product in mind. They will tend to narrow down the requirements so as to imply only a single possible solution, namely the one they already know. This is in some way more forgivable than the opposite approach, which is, to state requirements without knowing whether any product is able to meet them.

Thus, the STANDARD should state all the specifications that an object must meet, but no more than strictly necessary.

# 3 POINT-TO-POINT TRANSFERS

An information transfer is effected when a piece of information is correctly moved between separate parts of a system. This procedure is carried out using a sequence of more elementary operations, such as the enabling of drivers, the strobing of registers, etc.

As a first step, we shall consider in this chapter the transfer of information between two units only. Two problems are addressed: the first is how to translate a behavioural description of an operation sequence into link control signals. The second is how to synchronize the operations carried out by the two communicating units.

## 3.1 ACTIONS

The information transfer process can be described as a sequence of elementary *ACTION*s, that is, logic operations which cannot be divided further into simpler ones. We usually verify these transfer operations by looking at some electrical signals on a scope. This section introduces the relations between the pure logical description (based on actions), and the implementation (utilizing voltage levels on wires) of a transfer protocol.

### 3.1.1 Elementary operations of an information transfer

The most simple and straightforward type of information transfer is the *POINT-TO-POINT* connection, already outlined in section 1.1. A point-to-point transfer involves only two units and moves the information in one direction, as shown in figure 3.1.

The modules that participate in a point-to-point transfer are:
- a *SOURCE* unit, which initially owns the information;
- a *DESTINATION* unit, which receives the information after the transfer operation.

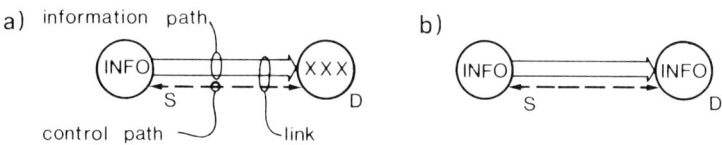

*Fig. 3.1 Point-to-point transfer*
  *a) before the transfer operation*
  *b) after the transfer operation*

Generally, the destination unit contains a register in order to keep the information stable after the transfer operation. It can also use the information immediately, without storing it, for instance, in an address decoder.

The two units are connected by a *LINK*, which is the actual structure that is carrying out the process of information exchange. The link is both a logical and a physical entity; the physical link consists of interconnecting devices such as drivers, wires, backplane conductors and receivers. The *PROTOCOL* of the link specifies the sequence of elementary actions which correctly transfers the information.

The link can be divided into two parts, as shown in figure 3.1:
- An *INFORMATION PATH* which carries the transferred information. An arrow, oriented from the source towards the destination, explicitly shows the direction of the information flow.
- A *CONTROL PATH* which controls the operation of the information path; the control can flow either from the source to the destination and/or vice-versa, according to the specific protocol.

The transfer of a single item of information requires a coordinated sequence of elementary actions on both the information and the control paths. The specification of this sequence is the first step toward defining the protocol of the link.

## 3.1.2 Mapping of actions into signals and lines

Let us repeat some of the more important definitions already outlined in section 2.1.3. The activation of each elementary action of the protocol is associated with a state (or change of state) of a boolean variable. These variables are called *SIGNALS*. A signal (that is,

# 3 Point-to-point Transfers

a boolean variable) can be either *TRUE* or *FALSE*. The words *ACTIVE/NOT ACTIVE*, with the same meaning of true/false, respectively, can also be used.

The first step is to represent signals by means of specific values of physical quantities (voltage, current, light). This allows us to transmit and sense logical variables on conductive media (wires, optical fibers). We shall focus on electrical levels carried by the link wires; they are called *LINES* or *BUS SIGNALS*.

The execution of an elementary action is therefore explicitly expressed as a voltage or current value or change of value, and the two values of a boolean signal are associated with two levels of voltage or current. The most positive electrical level is called the *HIGH* level, the other being the *LOW* level.

The names of signals and lines are related as much as possible to the actions associated with them. The name of a signal or of a line may contain a trailing asterisk (*) as a negation indicator. Adding or removing an asterisk will invert the correspondence between logical and electrical values.

A one-by-one correspondence between actions and wires is not mandatory. For instance, $2^N$ mutually exclusive actions can be encoded into N wires. This possibility generates the many different protocols for information transfer. It will be shown in Chapter 10 that serial buses encode both control actions and information on a single wire.

It must also be pointed out that many actions can be multiplexed on the same line at different times. Since this multiplexing requires the use of clocks or qualifiers to define the time slots, the actions, in this case, are actually encoded into the multiplexed line plus clock and/or qualifiers. Multiplexed protocols for parallel buses are discussed in section 4.3.

## 3.2 CYCLES

A *CYCLE* is the complete sequence of elementary actions that transfer an item of information from the source unit to the destination. This section describes two different approaches building up these sequences.

### 3.2.1 Sequencing of actions

To transfer a single element of information, the source must place it on the information lines of the link and notify the destination that these lines carry the new valid data. This sequence of operations is shown in figure 3.3: a VALID line directly carries the VALID signal.

The destination module uses the VALID signal to store the information in a register or to start other processes related with the information received, such as the selection of a memory cell.

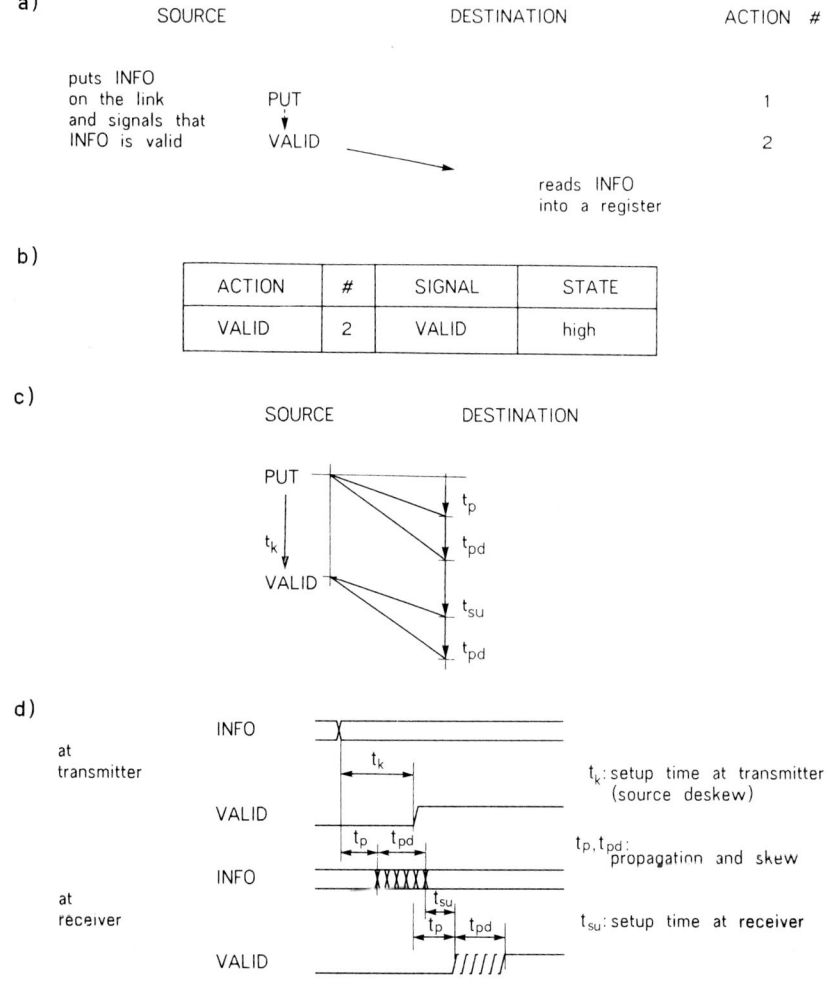

Fig. 3.2  Transfer of a single item of information
  a) Action flow
  b) Action encoding
  c) Action flow with skew effects
  d) Timing diagram

# 3 Point-to-point Transfers

We need the VALID signal when an encoded information is carried by many lines, because the voltage levels settle to the final value at different times. This phenomenon, called *SKEWING*, is caused by the difference in electrical characteristics of registers, drivers, wires and receivers. The VALID signal defines a time reference for the settling of all information lines.

The effects of skewing are shown in figure 3.2c and 3.2d. In this example, the VALID action can start only after a *SOURCE DESKEWING* delay $t_k$, which guarantees a specified set-up time at the destination.

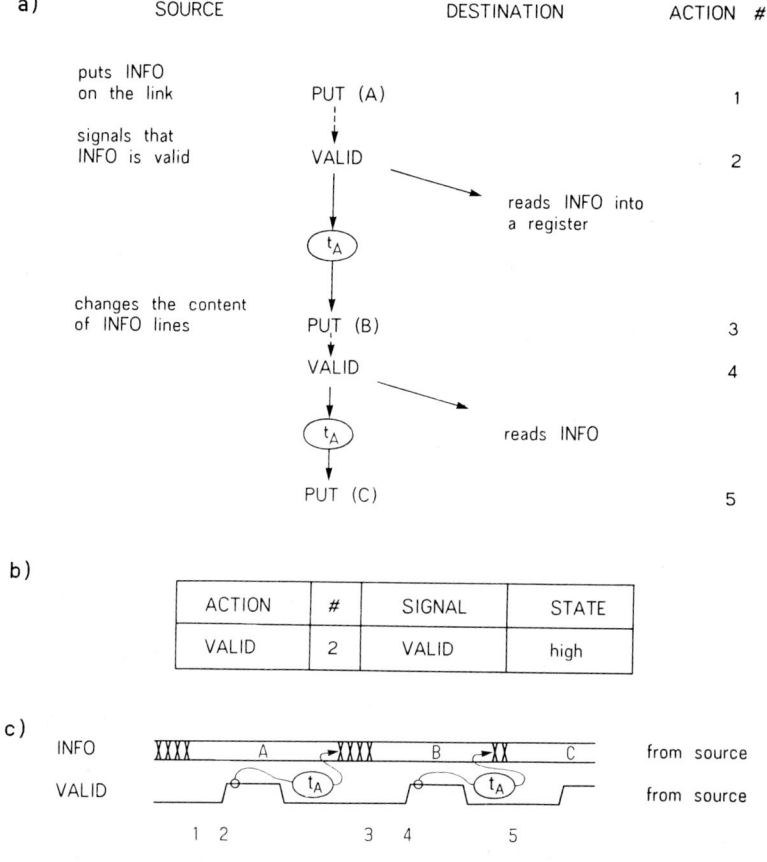

*Fig. 3.3 Synchronous multiple transfer*
  *a) Action sequence*
  *b) Action encoding*
  *c) Timing diagram*

In most cases, a link is not used for a single transfer, and therefore the sequence of operations described above must be followed by other similar cycles. Before changing or removing the information, the source must verify that it has been correctly stored or used in another way. Therefore, in order to correctly perform these operations, the link control logic must know when the next cycle can start. Two basic approaches exist:

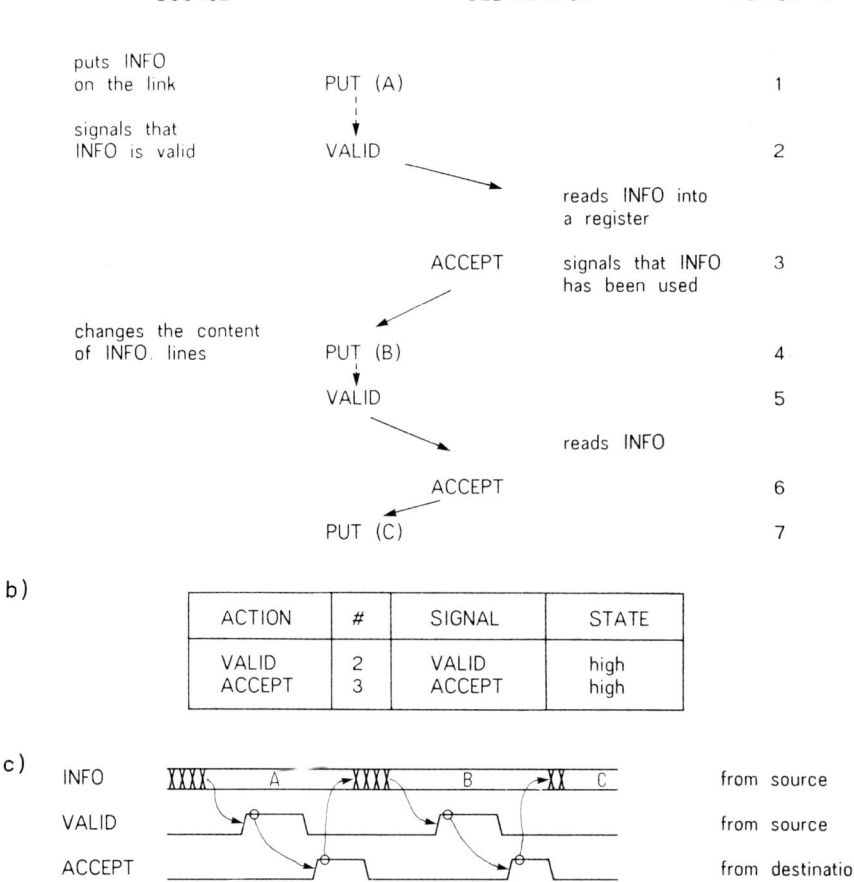

Fig. 3.4  Handshaken multiple transfer
  a) Action sequence
  b) Action encoding
  c) Timing diagram

- The control logic assumes that the information has been used within a fixed time $t_A$, and after this time it changes the information and starts a new cycle. Since, in this case, the source has complete control of the timing and thus synchronizes the link to its speed, this transfer technique is called SYNCHRONOUS.
- A new action is inserted into the cycle; it means "information has been used and is no longer needed", and is called the ACCEPT action. This action is activated by the destination and changes the timing of the cycle, which is now synchronized by cooperation between the source and the destination modules. This cycle is called HANDSHAKEN.

The action flow and the timing diagrams for these operations are given respectively in figures 3.3; and 3.4.

The synchronous protocol of figure 3.3; uses a fixed delay, represented by the time $t_A$ from VALID to the changing of information, during which the information is guaranteed stable. When the ACCEPT action is included in the cycle, as in figure 3.4, this delay is replaced by the waiting of a response from the other unit.

In the handshaken cycle, the action activated by the two modules is interleaved and both the source and the destination cannot proceed in the sequence if the other module has not responded to the previous action. This procedure incorporates the most elementary HANDSHAKE. HANDSHAKEN CYCLES are also often called ASYNCHRONOUS. Since the latter has a completely different meaning in serial protocols, we use "handshaken" to specify asynchronous parallel protocols.

a)

| ACTION | # | SIGNAL | STATE |
|---|---|---|---|
| VALID | 2 | VALID | low-to-high |
| (dummy edge) | N | VALID | high-to-low |
| ACCEPT | 3 | ACCEPT | low-to-high |
| (dummy edge) | M | ACCEPT | high-to-low |

b)

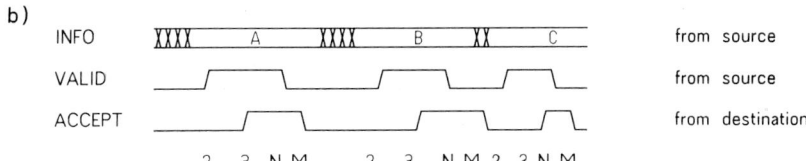

*Fig. 3.5 Interlocked edge-activated handshake*
  *a) Action encoding*
  *b) Timing diagram*

## 3.2.2 Fully interlocked sequences

Let us again consider the action sequence of figure 3.4. The starting conditions must be the same for each cycle (VALID and ACCEPT low in this example); therefore, when actions are encoded into signal transitions, we must also insert some "dummy" edges in order to recover the correct level for the next cycle. Figure 3.5 shows the same action sequence of figure 3.4b with edge encoding of actions and the recovery edges.

The level changes marked with N and M are not associated with an action, and therefore they have no meaning. We can, however, exploit this possibility to insert two more actions into the sequence:

- NOTVALID (from source module): specifies that the information is no longer valid and will be changed;
- READY (from destination module): specifies that the unit is ready for a new cycle.

A cycle that also includes these actions is said to have *FULL INTERLOCK* or *FULLY HANDSHAKEN* control. The action sequence and the timing diagram for fully interlocked multiple information transfers are shown in figure 3.6.

It must be pointed out that in this control sequence a module performs an action only if the other one has activated the preceding protocol action. In this way, both units have some control in the sequence of operations, and the transfer timing is synchronized by the cooperation of the two units.

## 3.3 SOURCE/DESTINATION PROTOCOLS

In the timing diagram shown in figure 3.6, one can identify two different types of cycles, clearly shown by the frames W and R in figure 3.7.

Both cycles are complete because each signal returns, at the end of the frame, to the same logic level it had at the beginning. In the frame W, the first action comes from the source module, hence we shall call this cycle *SOURCE-ACTIVATED*. In the frame R the first action comes from the destination unit and, therefore, this cycle will be called *DESTINATION-ACTIVATED*.

3 Point-to-point Transfers                                                            65

a)
| SOURCE | DESTINATION | ACTION # |

puts INFO on
the link and      PUT (A)
signals that         ↓
INFO is valid     VALID                                                           1

                           → ACCEPT    reads INFO and
                                       signals that INFO          2
                                       has been used

signals that INFO  ←
are not valid     NOTVALID                                                        3

                           → READY     new INFO
                                       can be received            4

                  PUT (B)
                     ↓
                  VALID                                                           5

                           → ACCEPT                                               6

                  NOTVAL                                                          7

                           → READY                                                8

                  PUT (C)
                     ↓
                  VALID                                                           9

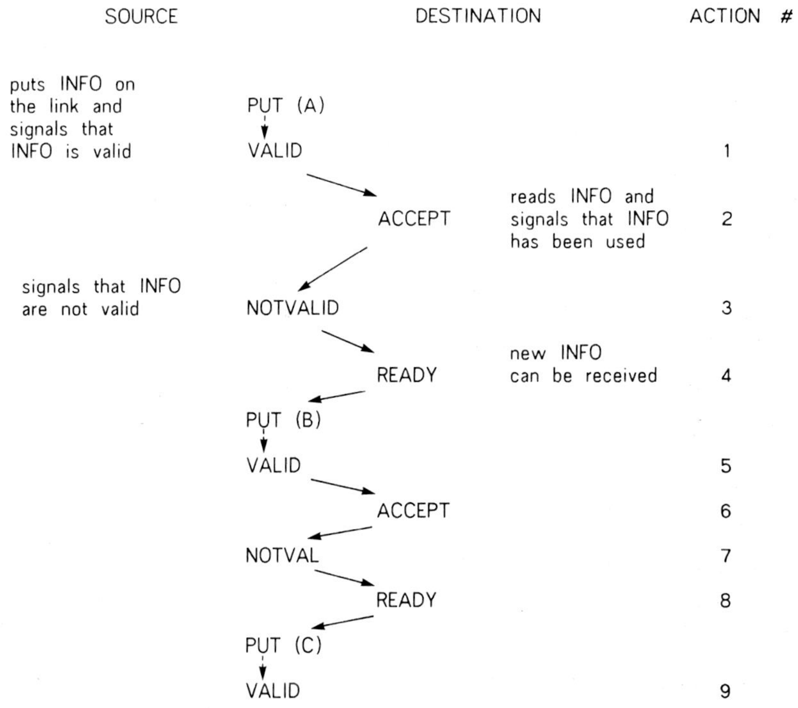

b)

| ACTION | # | SIGNAL | STATE |
|---|---|---|---|
| VALID | 1 | VALID | low-to-high |
| NOTVAL | 3 | VALID | high-to-low |
| ACCEPT | 2 | ACCEPT | low-to-high |
| READY | 4 | ACCEPT | high-to-low |

c)
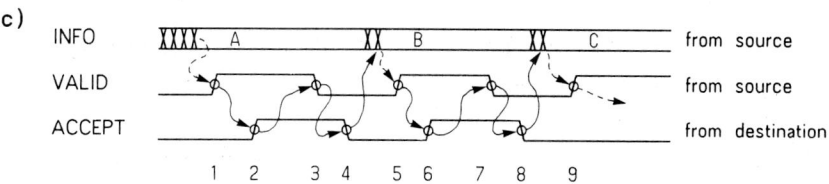

*Fig. 3.6  Fully interlocked 4-action handshake*
   *a) Action sequence*
   *b) Action encoding*
   *c) Timing diagram*

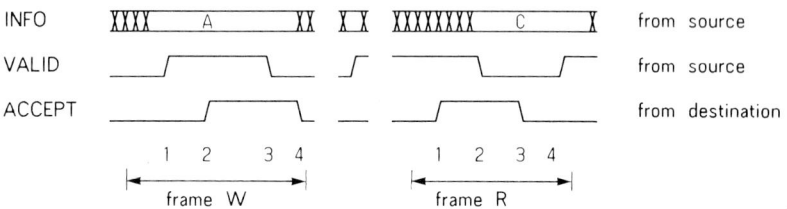

*Fig. 3.7 The two basic types of information transfer*

## 3.3.1 Source-activated protocol

The action flow for the cycle specified by frame W of figure 3.7 is repeated in figure 3.8. This cycle starts when the source module sends the information towards the destination. The sequence of elementary operation is as follows :

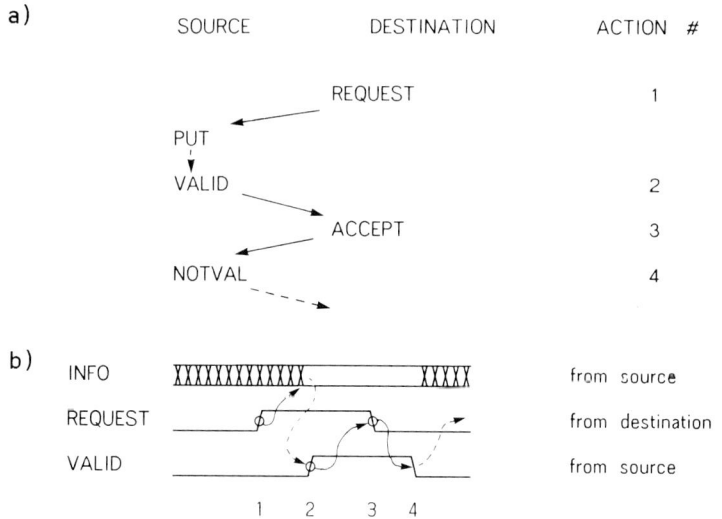

*Fig. 3.8 Source-activated cycle*
 *a) Action sequence*
 *b) Timing diagram*

- Action 1: the control action VALID notifies the destination that new information is available on the link. The destination senses VALID and starts the process of using the information, that is, either stores it in a register or decodes it into other signals
- Action 2: the destination does not need the information any more and signals it to the source by means of the ACCEPT action
- Action 3: INFO is no longer valid and will be changed
- Action 4: the destination is ready for a new cycle.

### 3.3.2 Destination-activated protocol

In the action sequence of the frame R, the first action can also be interpreted as a request for new INFO, and therefore it will from now on be called *REQUEST*. The action sequence and the timing diagrams for this cycle are given in figure 3.9.

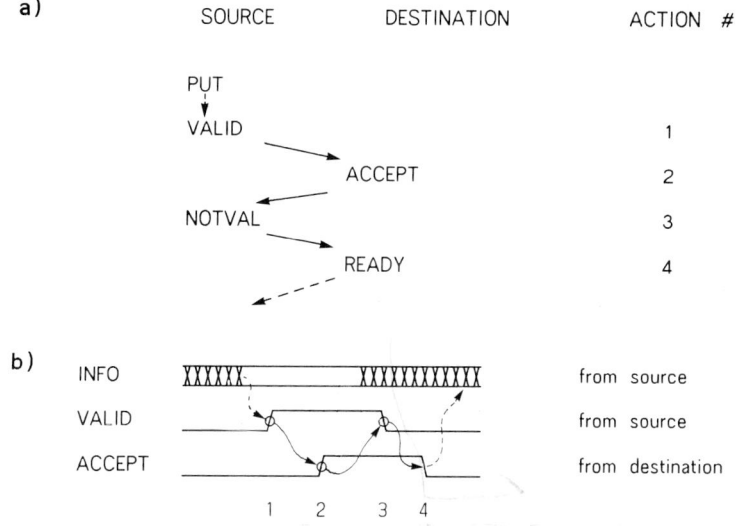

Fig. 3.9  Destination-activated cycle
  a) Action sequence
  b) Timing diagram

The first action (1) is an information REQUEST from the destination towards the source. In response to the request, the source prepares the information. Then, the source module puts the information on the link and signals that it is valid (2). From this point on, the sequence will be the same as that for source-activated transfers. The only difference is that here, the NOTVAL action, besides saying that the information is no longer valid and is being removed, is also used to notify the destination that a new request can be made.

### 3.3.3 Example: the Centronics protocol

An interface to a simple printer is a typical example of a transfer that uses a source-activated handshaken protocol, because data is sent by the computer to the printer. Information is transferred using 8-bit characters, and Centronics seems now to be the de-facto standard. A complete description of the Centronics interface is the Appendix; the transfer protocol and the action encoding are shown in figure 3.10.

a)

| ACTION | SIGNAL | STATE |
|--------|--------|-------|
| VALID  | DSTB*  | low   |
| READY  | BUSY or ACK* | low<br>high-to-low |

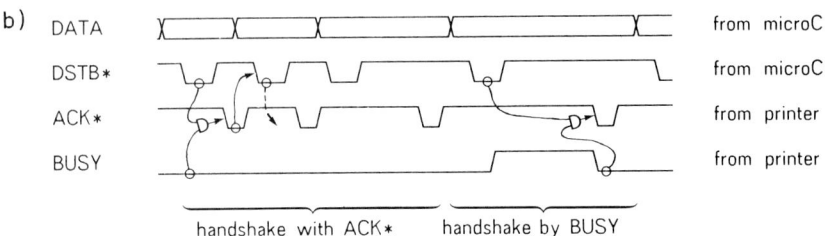

*Fig. 3.10 Centronics protocol*
  *a) Action encoding*
  *b) Timing diagram*

We can compare the signals of figure 3.10 with those of figure 3.9. The actions ACCEPT and READY are now encoded in the two lines ACK* and BUSY, rather than in the two edges of the same bus signal. The information transfer is blocked by either ACK* being always low or by BUSY being high. The ACK* and BUSY signals have some redundancy; BUSY means that ACK will be delayed, but an interface can use both or only one and still work with a correct handshake.

### 3.3.4 Example: remote A/D reading

The interface between an Analog-to-Digital (A/D) converter and a computer is an example of destination-activated protocol. The A/D converter starts the translation of the analog input signal into a binary pattern when it receives the Conversion Start command (CVST). After some time, the conversion is complete and the digital data at the

output can be read through the interface. As soon as the correct data
are available, the A/D raises a Conversion Complete (CC) bit, the
processor reads the data, and a new conversion can be started.

For the information transfer protocol, CVST represents the
REQUEST action of the destination, and CC the VALID response from
the source. A protocol to transfer correctly information from the A/D
to a destination register is shown in figure 3.11.

a)

| ACTION | SIGNAL | STATE |
|---|---|---|
| REQUEST | CVST | low-to-high |
| ACCEPTED | CVST | high-to-low |
| VALID | CC | high |
| NOTVALID | CC | low |

b)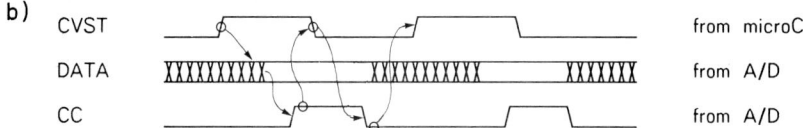

Fig. 3.11 Transfer protocol to read data from an A/D
converter
 a) Action encoding
 b) Timing diagram

## 3.4 READ/WRITE PROTOCOLS

The source-activated and destination-activated protocols described
in section 3.3 can also be analysed from a slightly different point of
view: one can focus on the direction of the control flow rather than
on the direction of the information flow. We can thus define different
TYPEs of communicating units and new ROLEs for them. It will be
shown how this approach is better suited for the usual organization of
processing systems.

### 3.4.1 Commander and responder

Let us call COMMANDER the module that activates the first action
of the cycle. The other unit will be called RESPONDER. As shown in
figure 3.12, the source activated cycle can be seen as a transfer
from the commander to the responder, while the destination-activated
cycle is a transfer from the responder to the commander. These cycles
are respectively called WRITE (write to responder), and READ (read
from responder).

In each operation, each module assumes a SOURCE/DESTINATION role for the information transfer, and a COMMANDER/RESPONDER role for the flow of control signals:

- in the WRITE cycles the COMMANDER acts as the SOURCE of the information, and the RESPONDER is the DESTINATION of the information
- in the READ cycles the RESPONDER acts as the SOURCE of the information, and the COMMANDER is the DESTINATION of the information.

The protocols that allow the exchange of the source/destination roles between the commander and the responder, thus enabling us to perform both read and write cycles between a pair of units, are called READ-WRITE PROTOCOLS.

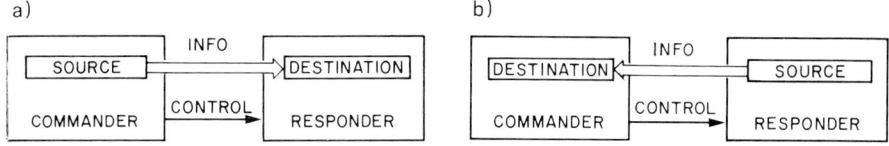

Fig. 3.12 Two types of information transfer
    a) Write operation
    b) Read operation

A description using as its basis commander and responder units matches the usual architecture of processing systems. Namely, the CPU (or a DMA controller) is the commander, while usually memory or I/O registers are the responder. Data transfers are called READ or WRITE according to the direction of the information flow.

### 3.4.2 Example: data transfer in a microprocessor system

Following the approach of the previous paragraph, we can define a model for the single transfer operation in a modular microprocessor system. These machines consist of some modules (CPU, memory, I/O interfaces) tied to the same link: the local bus. Any transfer will occur between one register of the CPU and another external register.

If we only look at the data transfer between these two registers, we can directly use the protocols defined above. Since all the operations on the bus are under control of the CPU, this module is the commander. Memory cells and I/O registers can become the responder; figure 3.13 shows two examples:

- execution of an output (OUT) instruction: this instruction causes a data transfer from the accumulator to an output register. The commander (the CPU) acts as the source of the data, so the operation is a write
- instruction fetch: this consists of a data transfer from a memory cell to the instruction register of the CPU. The commander (CPU) is now a destination and the cycle is a read.

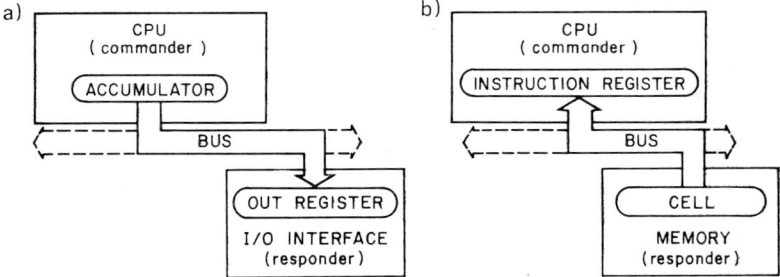

*Fig. 3.13 Model of input/output data transfers in a microprocessor system*
  *a) Execution of an OUT instruction*
  *b) Fetch of a one-word instruction*

## 3.4.3 Masters and slaves

In the example of figure 3.13 we can identify two different types of modules:

- Those modules that can act as commanders in a transfer operation (that is they can initiate a transaction) are called MASTERs
- Those modules that cannot initiate a transaction, but only participate in it after having been requested by a commander, can only be responders and are called SLAVEs.

In a typical microprocessor system, the master modules are the CPU and the DMA controllers, while the slaves are the memory and I/O interfaces. In many cases, a single logical slave, such as the memory, is distributed through many boards (physical modules). Since each of them has its own interface with the system bus, we shall consider these units as different slaves.

From the definition, one can see that being a master or a slave is not a variable role temporarily assumed by modules, but a specific property of the module itself. In other words, a module is designed to be either a master or a slave (or both, in some special cases).

The number of masters and slaves that are connected by the same link defines the type of protocol that can be used. The source-destination protocols described in this chapter can be directly used when one master and one slave are the only modules connected to a link. In this case they always act as the commander and the responder, respectively. The protocols for systems with a single master and many slaves are described in Chapter 4. The more general case of multiple-master systems will be analysed in Chapter 5.

## 3.5 BIDIRECTIONAL LINKS

In a READ-WRITE protocol, the exchange of the source-destination roles reverses the direction of the information flow between the commander and the responder. The transfer protocol can use two separate paths in the two directions, one for read cycles and the other for write cycles. The first version of S100 bus, for instance, used in Altair microcomputers, followed this approach.

When a single link supports both types of cycles it is called BIDIRECTIONAL. In a bidirectional link, the control signals must also

a)

| | ACTION | # | SIGNAL | STATE |
|---|---|---|---|---|
| WRITE cycle | VALID | 1 | WRITEPULSE | low-to-high |
| | NOTVAL | 3 | WRITEPULSE | high-to-low |
| | ACCEPT | 2 | ACKNOW. | low-to-high |
| | READY | 4 | ACKNOW. | high-to-low |
| READ cycle | REQUEST | 5 | READPULSE | low-to-high |
| | ACCEPT | 7 | READPULSE | high-to-low |
| | VALID | 6 | ACKNOW. | low-to-high |
| | NOTVAL | 8 | ACKNOW. | high-to-low |

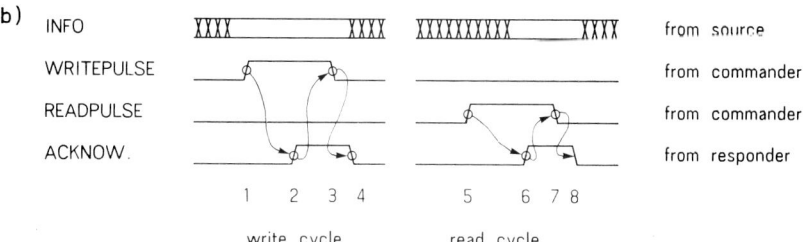

*Fig. 3.14 Readpulse/writepulse protocol*
  *a) Action encoding*
  *b) Timing diagram*

# 3 Point-to-point Transfers

specify the direction of the information transfer, that is, the role (source or destination) of each module. This information will be encoded in the set of control signals together with the other protocol actions.

In the following paragraphs we shall describe some possibilities for the implementation of read-write bidirectional protocols. In all cases here described, the action sequence of read and write cycles is asynchronous and follows the basic flow of figures 3.8 and 3.9.

## 3.5.1 Readpulse/writepulse protocol

An example of a complete encoding of the actions for a readpulse-writepulse protocol is shown in figure 3.14, together with the corresponding timing diagram. The commander uses the signals WRITEPULSE and READPULSE, in write and read cycles, respectively, and the responder uses an ACKNOWLEDGE for the handshake. It must be pointed out that this last signal encodes different actions in the read and write cycles.

## 3.5.2 Example: MULTIBUS 1 transfers

The IEEE 796 backplane bus (also known as MULTIBUS 1, see Appendix), uses a readpulse-writepulse protocol for data transfer

a)

| | ACTION | # | SIGNAL | STATE |
|---|---|---|---|---|
| WRITE cycle | VALID | 1 | MWTC/ | high-to-low |
| | NOTVAL | 3 | MWTC/ | low-to-high |
| | ACCEPT | 2 | XACK/ | high-to-low |
| | READY | 4 | XACK/ | low-to-high |
| READ cycle | REQUEST | 5 | MRTC/ | high-to-low |
| | ACCEPT | 7 | MRTC/ | low-to-high |
| | VALID | 6 | XACK/ | high-to-low |
| | NOTVAL | 8 | XACK/ | low-to-high |

b)

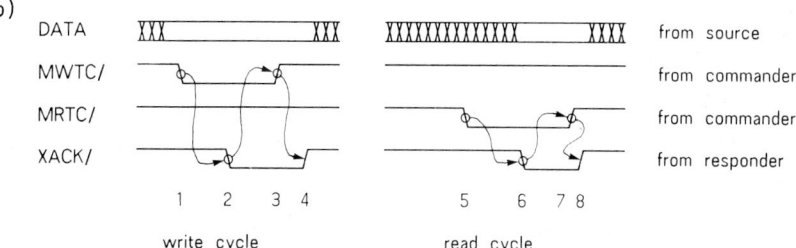

Fig. 3.15 MULTIBUS 1 memory write and read cycles
    a) Action encoding
    b) Timing diagram

between various boards. Four lines are used, two for memory and two for I/O transfers, plus a handshake signal. The action encoding and the timing of Multibus read and write transfers are shown in figure 3.15. A trailing slash (/) is used as a negation indicator, according to INTEL's MULTIBUS 1 specifications.

### 3.5.3 Advanced read/write protocol

We can also use a separate signal which specifies the type of operation (read or write). If this signal is active, for instance during read cycles, it will be called READ. Since it must be valid at the very beginning of the cycle, this technique is called ADVANCED READ (or ADVANCED WRITE, if a write-active signal is used). A STROBE signal completes the encoding of the actions ruled by the commander, and the responder still uses only the ACKNOWLEDGE.

In this protocol, each action is encoded into a pair of signals: READ and STROBE or READ and ACKNOW. The action encoding and a timing diagram of an advanced read protocol are shown in figure 3.16.

a)

| ACTION | | # | SIGNAL | STATE |
|---|---|---|---|---|
| WRITE cycle (READ low) | VALID | 1 | STROBE | low-to-high |
| | NOTVAL | 3 | STROBE | high-to-low |
| | ACCEPT | 2 | ACKNOW. | low-to-high |
| | READY | 4 | ACKNOW. | high-to-low |
| READ cycle (READ high) | REQUEST | 5 | STROBE | low-to-high |
| | ACCEPT | 7 | STROBE | high-to-low |
| | VALID | 6 | ACKNOW. | low-to-high |
| | NOTVAL | 8 | ACKNOW. | high-to-low |

b)

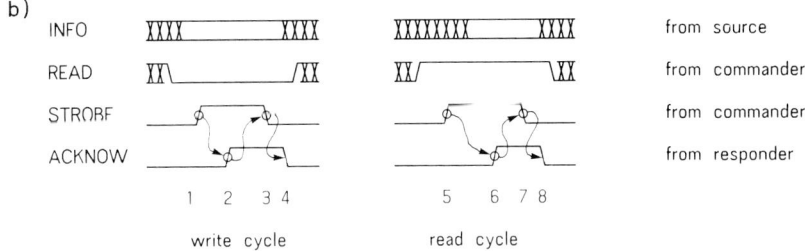

*Fig. 3.16 Advanced read protocol*
  *a) Action encoding*
  *b) Timing diagram*

### 3.5.4 Example: FASTBUS transfers

FASTBUS [FAST81] is a standard defined by the US Nuclear Instrumentation and Measurement Committee to be used in large data acquisition and processing systems. This standard was created to support the heavy requirements of nuclear applications. The complete FASTBUS protocol is quite complex, but we shall consider here only the transfer of single data from or to memory. For these operations, FASTBUS uses a handshaken advanced-read protocol.

At the beginning of a cycle, a RD signal defines the direction of the transfer (read or write). A Data Strobe (DS) is used as a data request in read operations and as a strobe pulse for write transfers. The handshake signal is the Data Acknowledge (DK). The action encoding and timing diagram of FASTBUS single-data transfer cycles is shown in figure 3.17. Bus lines are not inverted because the logic used is ECL (active-high drivers).

a)

|  | ACTION | # | SIGNAL | STATE |
|---|---|---|---|---|
| WRITE cycle (RD low) | VALID | 1 | DS | low-to-high |
|  | NOTVAL | 3 | DS | high-to-low |
|  | ACCEPT | 2 | DK | low-to-high |
|  | READY | 4 | DK | high-to-low |
| READ cycle (RD high) | REQUEST | 5 | DS | low-to-high |
|  | ACCEPT | 7 | DS | high-to-low |
|  | VALID | 6 | DK | low-to-high |
|  | NOTVAL | 8 | DK | high-to-low |

b)
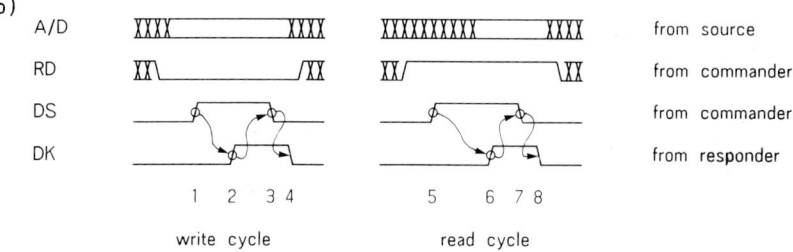

*Fig. 3.17 FASTBUS data transfer protocol*
 *a) Action encoding*
 *b) Timing diagram*

## 3.5.5 Valid/request protocol

Another example of action encoding for R/W protocol is shown in figure 3.18. Here, the information on the direction of the transfer is encoded in the sequencing of signals, that is, in the time position of edges. The signals used by this protocol are VALID and REQUEST, respectively issued by the source and the destination, as in section 3.3.1 et 3.3.2.

a)

|  | ACTION | # | SIGNAL | STATE |
|---|---|---|---|---|
| WRITE cycle | VALID | 1 | VALID | low-to-high |
|  | NOTVAL | 3 | VALID | high-to-low |
|  | ACCEPT | 2 | REQUEST | low-to-high |
|  | READY | 4 | REQUEST | high-to-low |
| READ cycle | REQUEST | 5 | REQUEST | low-to-high |
|  | ACCEPT | 7 | REQUEST | high-to-low |
|  | VALID | 6 | VALID | low-to-high |
|  | NOTVAL | 8 | VALID | high-to-low |

b)
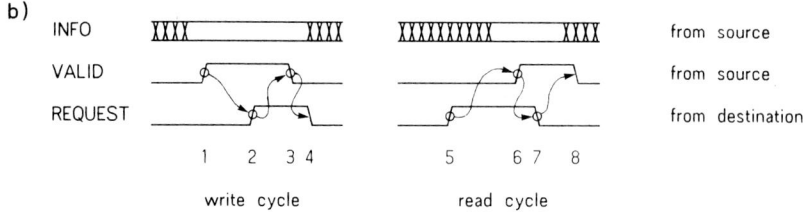

Fig. 3.18 Valid/request protocol
   a) Action encoding
   b) Timing diagram

It must be pointed out that in this protocol the read and write cycles are distinguished by the signal activation sequence. Namely, if VALID is active before REQUEST, the cycle will be a write, while if REQUEST becomes active first, the cycle is a read.

## 3.5.6 Lines versus logic

In the valid/request protocol, the read/write information is encoded into the time domain, that is, into the sequence of edges. Any interface with a link that follows this protocol must use flip-flops in order to store the current state. On the other hand, in the protocols shown in section 3.5.1 and 3.5.3, the read/write

3 Point-to-point Transfers    77

information can be decoded from the protocol signals using only combinatorial logic. The valid/request protocol uses only two control lines (both other examples need three lines for a full handshake), at the expense of a more complex interface.

## 3.6 SYNCHRONIZATION OF THE ACTION SEQUENCE

The action sequence of a protocol must run at a speed that is compatible with the interfaces of the modules. Some possibilities have already been described in section 3.2. We shall now analyse in more detail the constraints on speed and the techniques used to guarantee the compatibility of modules with different timing requirements. The first step is to classify the protocols according to the technique used to synchronize the action sequences of the commander and responder.

### 3.6.1 Handshaken cycles

Let us again consider the interlocked action flow shown in figure 3.19. With this protocol, each module only proceeds in the sequence if its partner has performed a well-defined action. This means that in the handshaked transfer, each item of information must be acknowledged before the next item can be transferred. This interlock mechanism is explicitly shown by the cause-effect arrows in the timing diagram. This chain of arrows shows that a module must complete the operations belonging to the previous action before activating the next one.

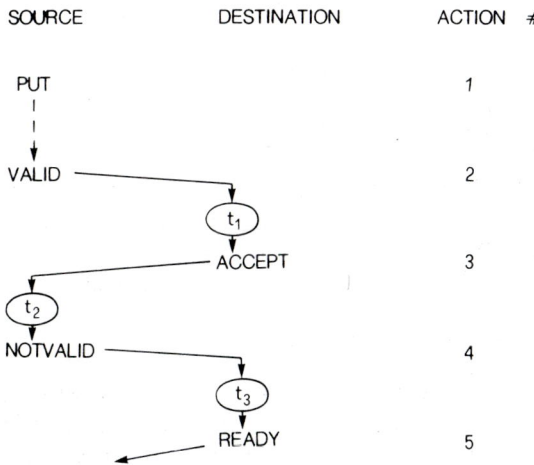

*Fig. 3.19 Interlocked action sequence: write cycle*

As an example, figure 3.20 shows the interlock of actions in a READPULSE/WRITEPULSE protocol with actions encoded into the signal edges. The time elapsed from the cause (starting action of the arrow) to the effect (next action) depends on the module responsible for the activation of the next action, which can therefore insert a delay of arbitrary length in the sequence. The module which has control of each delay is explicitly shown by the arrow labels in the timing diagram of figure 3.20. Dotted arrows are associated with action pairs that are executed by the same module (e.g. PUT/VALID, see figure 3.19). There is no handshake associated with these operations.

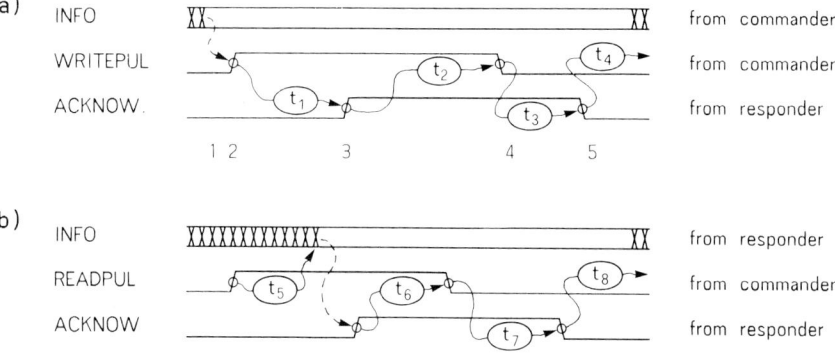

Fig. 3.20 Handshaken cycles with explict indication of the cause-effect relationship
  a) Write operation
  b) Read operation

This interlock in the action sequence allows us to change the speed of the operations in order to comply with the timing requirements of each module. For instance, in the cycles of figure 3.20:

- $t_1$: the responder inserts this delay into the write cycles before an ACCEPT (ACKNOW rising edge). When the information is entered into a register, $t_1$ allows the generation of an internal strobe signal with the proper set-up, width, and hold times, or the decoding of the information, taking care of the required propagation delays
- $t_5$: the responder inserts this delay into the read cycles before a VALID (ACKNOW rising edge), in order to prepare the information. For instance, if the responder were a memory cell, $t_5$ would depend on the access time of the memory device

3 Point-to-point Transfers

- $t_6$: the commander can insert this delay before an ACCEPT (READPUL falling edge), in order to use (store, decode) the information. We must remember that when data is stored into a register of the CPU, it must remain stable for some time before and after the internal register strobe pulse
- $t_7$: the responder is ready for a new REQUEST. The associated delay must consider the buffer disable time, the precharge time of dynamic RAMs, etc.

In some cases, a delay depends only on the propagation time of the link and on the response time of the first link interface layer. Let us consider, for instance, the delay $t_2$ in the write cycle shown in figure 3.20a. The writepulse can be removed immediately after the acknowledge; thus, no internal delay is usually associated with these actions inside the commander module.

Each delay is controlled by the module, which must complete some internal operations before going to the next step. The interlocked procedure can thus guarantee that no overrun will occur, and that the

a)

| | ACTION | # | SIGNAL | STATE |
|---|---|---|---|---|
| DATO cycle (WRITE op.) | VALID | 1 | DOUT | low-to-high |
| | NOTVAL | 3 | DOUT | high-to-low |
| | ACCEPT | 2 | RPLY | low-to-high |
| | READY | 4 | RPLY | high-to-low |
| DATI cycle (READ op.) | REQUEST | 5 | DIN | low-to-high |
| | ACCEPT | 7 | DIN | high-to-low |
| | VALID | 6 | RPLY | low-to-high |
| | NOTVAL | 8 | RPLY | high-to-low |

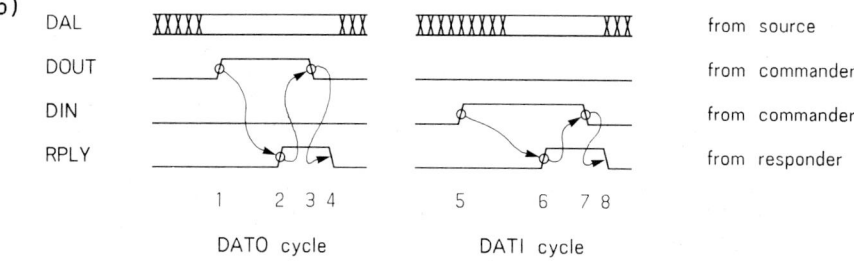

b)

Fig. 3.21 Q-BUS write (DATO) and read (DATI) cycles
 a) Action encoding
 b) Timing diagram

timing of the information transfer will be correct. As shown in figure 3.20, there is no interlock associated with the action pair PUT/VALID (1 and 2 in the figure). Thus, the PUT action will no longer be shown, because it is not relevant to the protocol control structure.

### 3.6.2 Example: Q-BUS DATI and DATO cycles

The Q-BUS (see Appendix) is the system bus used in the DEC LSI-11 processor family. The subset of signals which controls the data transfer is an example of a handshaken Readpulse/Writepulse protocol. The read and write operations in Q-BUS, performed respectively by DATI and DATO cycles, are shown in figure 3.21.

### 3.6.3 Synchronous cycles

The information transfer procedure can be changed if more constraints are imposed on the two modules. In a write cycle, for instance, the ACCEPT action is no longer needed, if the speed of the destination is fixed and known to the source. The action sequence of figure 3.19 becomes that of figure 3.22: the interlock subsequence VALID-ACCEPT-NOTVAL is replaced by the sequence VALID-delay($t_A$)-NOTVAL. The destination does not participate in this part of the sequence: all the actions are carried out by the source, and so there is no handshake (and no interlock) in this part of the protocol. Since the ACCEPT action is not transmitted on the link, data must be used within the fixed time $t_A$. In this case, the information transfer can be verified by higher protocol layers (e.g. by means of another transfer in the opposite direction).

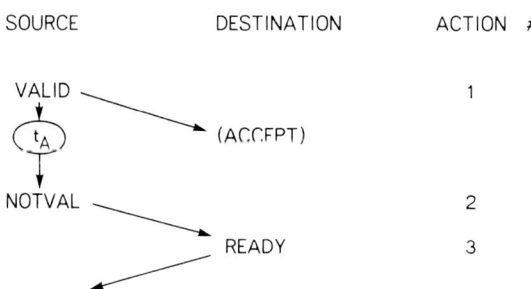

*Fig. 3.22 Action sequence of a write cycle without ACCEPT action*

Even though the explicit READY action from the destination is maintained, a signal going from the destination towards the source will still be required to encode this action. If the READY action is replaced by another fixed delay, as shown in figure 3.23a, the timing depends only on the two fixed delays $t_A$ and $t_B$, defined by the commander upon knowledge of the responders speed of action. This line can be removed, and the cycle is therefore called SYNCHRONOUS.

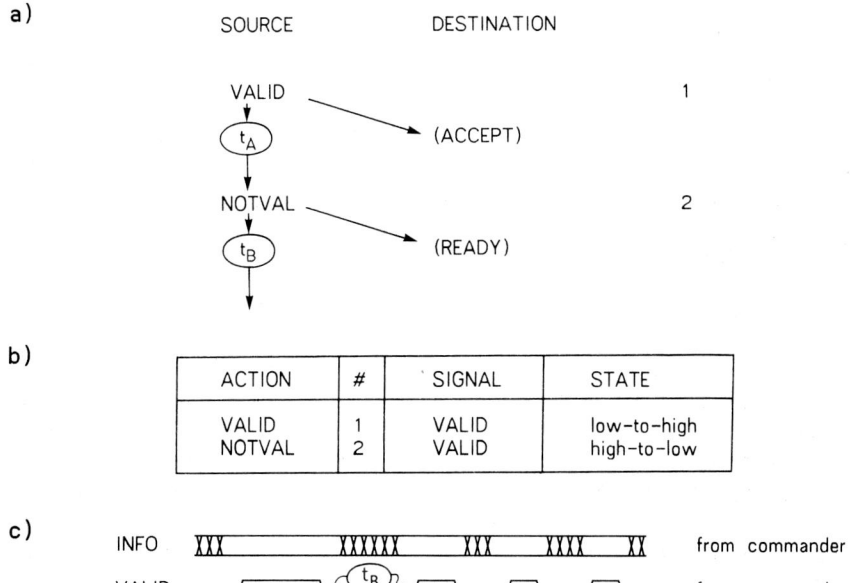

Fig. 3.23 Synchronous write cycle
  a) Action sequence
  b) Action encoding
  c) Timing diagram

The synchronous cycle starts when the information is validated by the source (1). The destination must use, that is, either store or decode, this information within the delay $t_A$ (implicit ACCEPT). On the falling edge of VALID (2), the source informs the destination that the information is no longer valid. The destination must be ready for a new cycle within the delay $t_B$ (implicit READY).

The two actions activated by the source are encoded into the VALID signal; the control structure of this protocol uses a single line, as shown in figure 3.23c.

The same technique can be used in read cycles; the action sequence, the signal encoding, and the timing diagram of a synchronous read protocol are shown in figure 3.24.

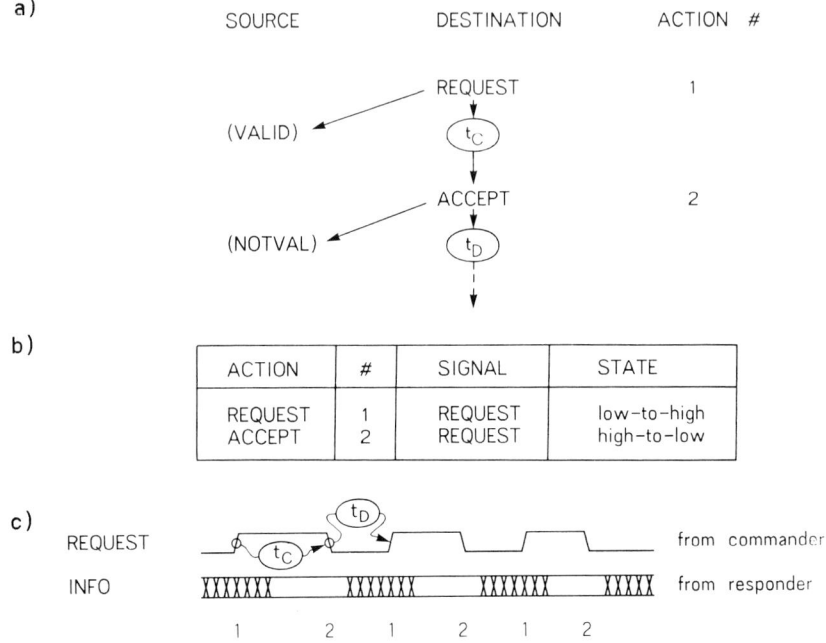

Fig. 3.24 Synchronous read cycle
 a) Action sequence
 b) Action encoding
 c) Timing diagram

The other bidirectional handshake read/write protocols described in section 3.5 can also be modified into the synchronous ones by removing the signals that encode the actions activated by the responder. For the advanced read/write and the readpulse/writepulse protocol, the ACKNOWLEDGE signal is deleted. The valid/request protocol described in section 3.5.5 becomes synchronous by deleting REQUEST in write cycles, and VALID in read cycles. These changes are shown in figure 3.25. The dotted lines show the signals that have been removed and replaced by assumptions on the speed of the destination.

The readpulse/writepulse and the valid/request protocols now look exactly the same. This occurs because the ones with the original handshake are different only in the encoding of the actions activated by the responder. When these actions are removed, the two protocols become identical, with only difference being the name of lines.

# 3 Point-to-point Transfers

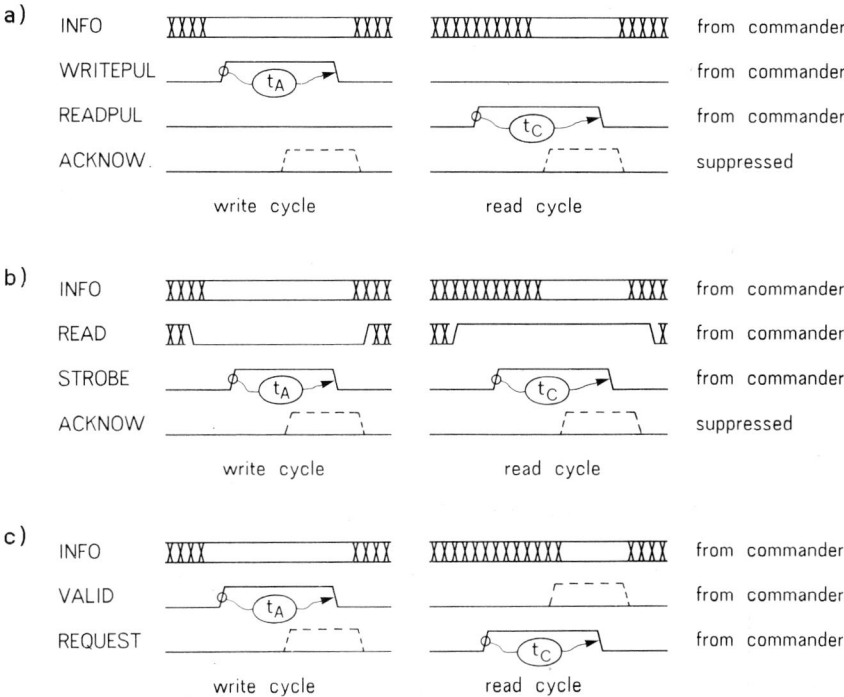

Fig. 3.25 Synchronous protocols
   a) Readpulse/writepulse
   b) Advanced read
   c) Valid/request

## 3.6.4 Example: control signals of static RAMs

In most cases, static memories respond to synchronous protocols. They are responders, and the commander must provide the proper delays in the control sequence that fit the timing requirements specified in the device specifications. For instance, let us consider a RAM chip which uses an advanced read protocol, as described in section 3.5.3. The control signals are a Chip Enable (CE) and a Write Enable (WE). In read cycles, valid data is available (VALID action) following an access time from the activation of CE (REQUEST action); in write cycles, data must be valid for the write time, that is, until the ACCEPT action is completed. The complete timing of this memory is shown in figure 3.26.

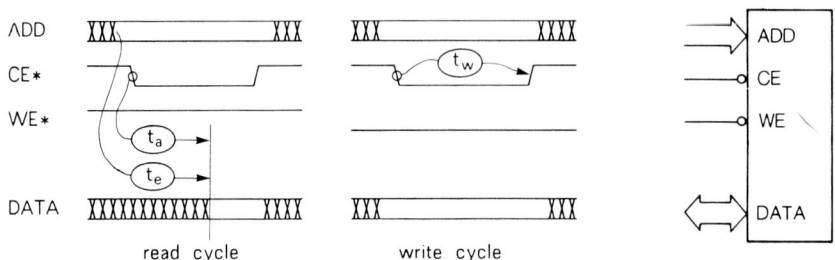

Fig. 3.26 Static memory, advanced read protocol
$t_a$: access time from address settled
$t_e$: access time from chip enabled
$t_w$: write time

Other devices follow different protocols; let us consider, for instance, the usual organization of byte-wide RAMs. These chips are controlled by a Chip Select (CS), a Write command (WR) and an Output Enable (OE); the Chip Select may be considered a general enable, and the other two signals implement a readpulse/writepulse protocol. In read cycles, data is valid within specified delays from addressing, chip select, and out enable. The REQUEST action is encoded in these control signals, but, due to the different paths inside the chip, the timing specifications are not the same for all signals. An example of timing specifications for a static RAM with this protocol is shown in figure 3.27.

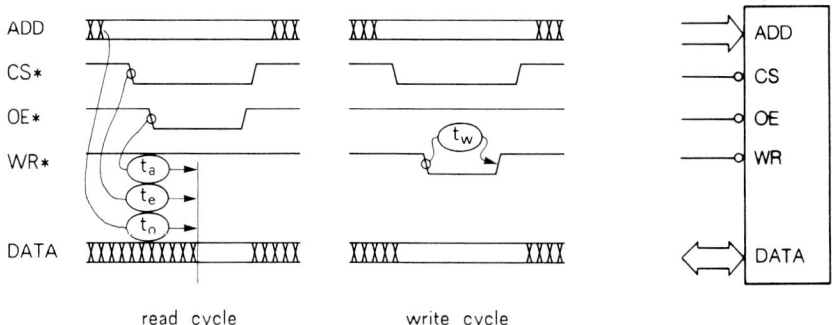

Fig. 3.27 Static memory, readpulse/writepulse protocol
$t_a$: access time from address settled
$t_e$: access time from chip enabled
$t_o$: access time from out enabled
$t_w$: write time

## 3.6.5 Semi-synchronous cycles

The synchronous protocol with no possibility of change, described in the previous section, is simple, but too rigid for many applications. On the other hand, the handshake protocol described in section 3.6.1 fits any timing requirement, but uses a higher number of control lines and requires more complex interfaces in the responder modules. An intermediate possibility is to define a protocol that runs synchronously by default, but becomes handshaken when there is an explicit request to change the timing. These protocols are called SEMI-SYNCHRONOUS.

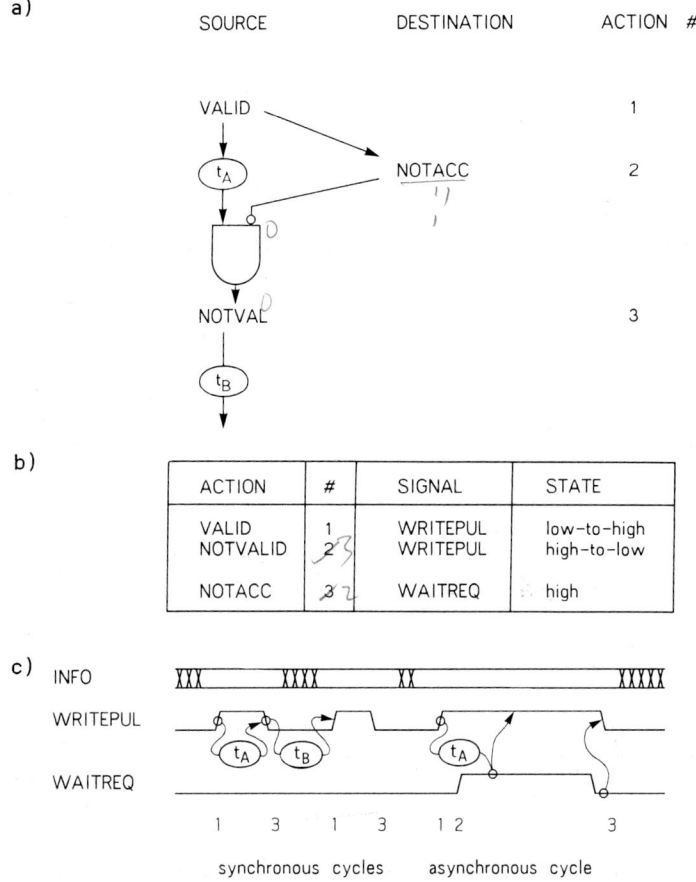

*Fig. 3.28 Semi-synchronous write cycles*
 *a) Action sequence*
 *b) Action encoding*
 *c) Timing diagram*

The action sequence of a semi-synchronous protocol is derived from the synchronous one, with the addition of a lock condition to the simple delay. The next action starts only if a blocking action from the responder is not active.

An example of a semi-synchronous write cycle is shown in figure 3.28. With action 1, the source notifies the destination that the information is valid. From this time, the source waits for the delay $t_A$, then checks if the NOTACC (Not Accepted) action has been activated. When the delay $t_A$ has expired and NOTACC is not valid, the action sequence at the source continues with the NOTVAL action. The timing of semi-synchronous write cycles for a readpulse/writepulse protocol with the NOTACC action encoded into a WAIT signal is shown in figure 3.28c.

a)

|  | ACTION | SIGNAL | STATE |
|---|---|---|---|
| write cycle | NOTACC | WAITREQ | high |
| read cycle | NOTVAL | WAITREQ | high |

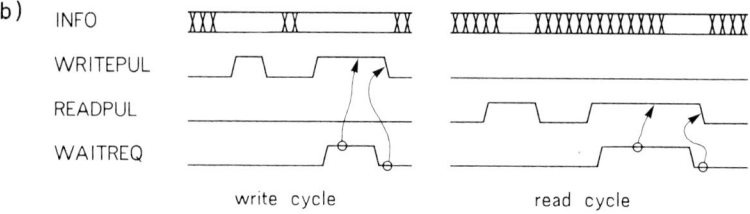

Fig. 3.29 Readpulse/writepulse semi-synchronous protocol
 a) Action encoding
 b) Timing diagram

Figure 3.28c shows two synchronous (WAIT is not used) and one semi-synchronous (WAIT is used) operation. Since the WAIT signal is sampled after the delay $t_A$ from VALID, the two above-mentioned conditions, that is, "delay expired" and the value of NOTACC, are checked by a single operation. If WAIT is active, the cycle is stopped and WAIT is sampled again; as soon as WAIT is not active, the cycle continues. The cycle is slowed down only when required, and thus, when WAIT is not active, the action sequence is carried out in a minimal amount of time.

The same technique can be used in read cycles: the execution of the synchronous action sequence can be conditioned by a NOTVAL action from the source. The timing diagram of semi-synchronous read and write cycles with a readpulse/writepulse protocol is shown in figure 3.29. The two actions NOTACC and NOTVAL are both encoded into the WAIT signal during the write and read cycles, respectively.

The main advantage of this technique is that, in a system where all units work at the same speed, the WAIT signal is never used, and thus, the protocol handling circuitry on the responder modules can be very simple. Only the slower units have to handle WAIT signals and

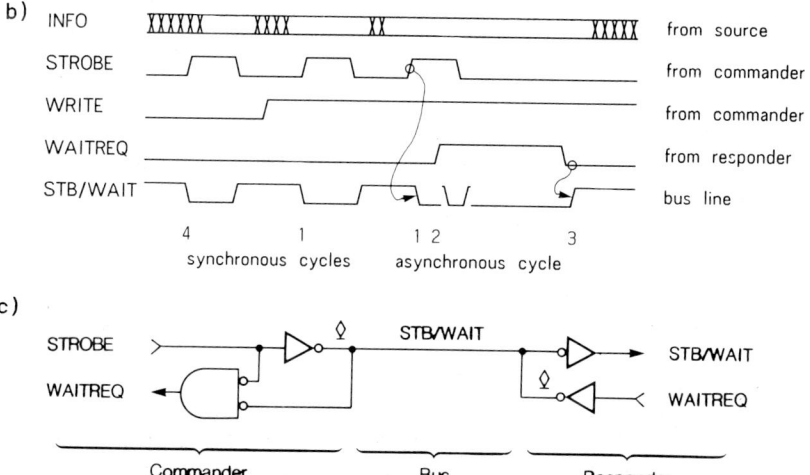

*Fig. 3.30 Single-line handshake*
  *a) Action encoding*
  *b) Timing diagram*
  *c) Interface logic*

are therefore more complex. The drawback is that, since the interlock is removed, the source cannot verify the presence of the destination and the correctness of the operation.

It must also be pointed out that the destination, when required, must activate the WAIT signal within a predefined time related to $t_A$. This constraint creates an inconsistency in the protocol: slower units, that is, those that should use WAIT, must react within a fixed amount of time. Thus, at least some part of the interface of these units must be fast enough.

### 3.6.6 Single-line handshake

With the semi-synchronous protocol, the VALID and WAIT signals can be encoded into a single bus line using wired-OR logic. This technique is shown in figure 3.30; an active-low STB/WAIT line is forced to low level by the STROBE signal from the commander (it corresponds to the VALID action in write cycles, and to REQUEST in read), or by the WAIT signal issued by the responder (this corresponds to the NOTACC and NOTVAL actions respectively).

At the end of the STROBE pulse the commander tests the STB/WAIT line; if it is high the action sequence continues at full speed. If the line is still low it means that the responder has activated the WAIT signal, and the cycle is slowed down. We find here the same timing constraint of the two-wire semi-synchronous handshake: the WAIT signal must be activated before the end of STROBE (this corresponds to the delay $t_A$ in figure 3.28).

### 3.6.7 Speed comparison of protocols

The synchronous and semi-synchronous protocols can only use two actions per cycle (VALID, NOTVAL), while the full handshaken protocol needs four of them (VALID, ACCEPT, NOTVAL, NOTACC). Each action is associated with a level change in a link control line; a level change on a bus line requires time to slew, to settle, and to propagate. From this point of view, the synchronous protocols seem faster because they use only two edges, but this analysis is correct only if the source speed always matches the maximum speed of the destination. As a general rule, a synchronous protocol must be designed to fit the requirements of the slowest unit; the delays inserted by the commander will be the same for accesses to fast and slow slaves. Interlocked protocols use 4 edges but can go faster, because there is no fixed delay in the action sequence, and each unit runs at maximum allowable speed.

# 3 Point-to-point Transfers

Semi-synchronous protocols have speed performance and constraints similar to those of the synchronous ones, due to the fixed delays in the action sequence. A comparison between two specific synchronous/asynchronous protocols is given in [BOR84]. Faster protocols, which use as few as only one edge per cycle, are discussed in section 6.2.3.

## 3.6.8 Clocked interfaces and protocols

A processing logic is usually synchronized by a clock; the timing of the transfer operations is therefore related to this clock, which also times the protocol actions. For instance, this happens in all microprocessors where the link interface is integrated into the processing logic.

Thus, when synchronous and semi-synchronous protocols are used in a clocked system, the delays are related to the clock period rather than being continuously variable. In this case, inputs, such as WAIT, are sampled by an edge of the clock, and thus the timing can be modified only by finite steps of one clock period.

The difference with respect to the semi-synchronous not-clocked prototocol described in the previous section is shown in figure 3.31. In the not-clocked (asynchronous) protocol, the sequence of operations continues as soon as the WAIT signal becomes not active; in the clocked one, nothing happens until the next edge of the clock is encountered. A handshake protocol can be clocked in the following manner: the acknowledge signal is sampled by the clock edges and here, too, the action sequencing is timed by the clock.

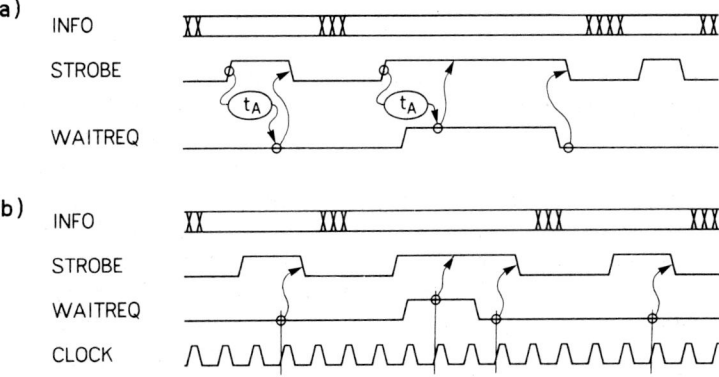

Fig. 3.31 Comparison of semi-synchronous advanced read protocols
 a) Asynchronous
 b) Clocked

The clock synchronization may act at different levels. If the clock is used only in the sequential machines which control the interfaces, we speak of CLOCKED INTERFACES. In this case, the processing units may also run on the same clock, or with different clocks. If the clocks are independent (that is, they may have any phase relationship), care must be taken in order to avoid metastability problems at the interface between logic blocks which run on different clocks (Chapter 9). If all of the system, that is, both processing logic and interfaces, is timed by the same clock, there is no synchronization problem, and we can speak of CLOCKED PROTOCOL.

### 3.6.9 Example: the Z80 memory protocol

The Z80 microprocessor and many others use a semi-synchronous readpulse/writepulse clocked interface for all transactions on the data bus. Figure 3.32 shows Z80 memory write cycles. The state changes of control signals are specified from the clock edge; we can also verify that the handshake line (WAIT*) is sampled on the same edge.

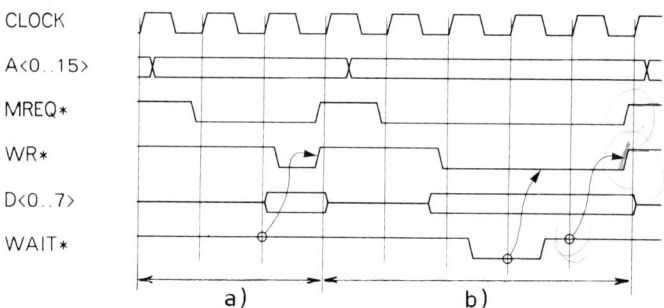

Fig. 3.32 Z80 protocol for memory write
  a) Full speed cycle
  b) Slowed down cycle

## 3.7 PROTOCOL CONVERSION

When the units used to build up a system follow different protocols, the control signals of each interface must be adapted to the unique protocol used by the interconnection link. The same problem occurs when the information is moved to different link levels, from the memory chips, for instance, to the system bus.

## 3.7.1 Layered protocol conversion

Two types of protocol conversion can be identified: the first changes the action encoding and the second modifies the synchronization of actions. A protocol conversion that changes the synchronization of the action sequence needs flip-flops or delays. The following paragraphs show some examples for the most common cases of protocol conversion.

In all cases, the protocol translation is performed by an interface layer added to the existing module. As shown in figure 3.33, this creates a new functional module, which follows the rules of a different protocol.

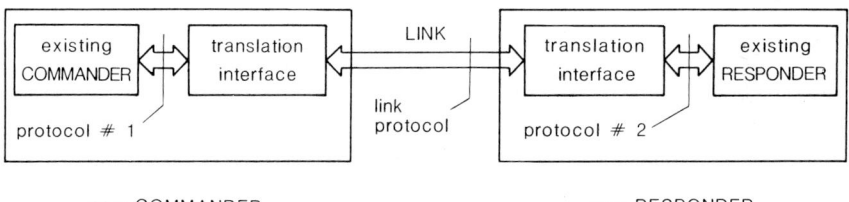

*Fig. 3.33 Layered protocol conversion*

## 3.7.2 Conversion of the action encoding

In order to connect two interfaces that follow the same action sequence (e.g. both are synchronous or fully interlocked), but use different action-to-signal mapping (e.g. one interface uses an advanced read/write protocol, and the other a readpulse/writepulse), one must modify the correspondence between actions and signals. This process requires only combinatorial logic that translates one set of control

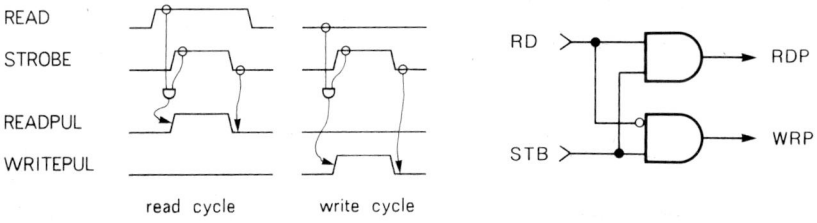

*Fig. 3.34 Conversion of the advanced read protocol into readpulse/writepulse*

signals into the other. The advanced read protocol can be converted into the readpulse/writepulse protocol with two gates, as shown in figure 3.34.

The inverse process, that is, going from readpulse/writepulse to advanced read, is more complex. Namely, the readpulse/writepulse protocol issues the read/write information together with the two pulses, while the advanced read protocol requires that the READ signal is already settled before the strobe pulse STROBE is initiated. The translation interface must wait for the activation of the READPULSE or WRITEPULSE in order to discriminate between read and write cycles. If the cycle is a read, the READ signal must be activated first, and the STROBE pulse must be sent later. If the cycle is a write, the strobe pulse can be sent directly since the read signal must be kept not-active. An example of a circuit which executes this translation is shown in figure 3.35. The delays $t_1$ and $t_2$ guarantee the set-up and hold times of READ towards STROBE.

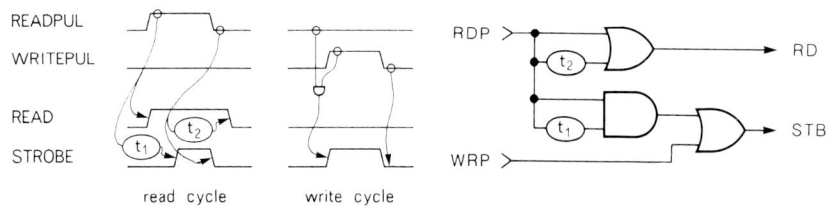

Fig. 3.35 Conversion from readpulse/writepulse into advanced read

This last example points out the main limitation of a protocol conversion that performs only a change in action encoding: it follows from the causality principle, that when translating from protocol A to protocol B, the signals of protocol B cannot precede those of protocol A, which carry the same information. If the order of operations must be modified, the translation process must thus delay some actions in order to build the desired sequence.

### 3.7.3 Example: interface of memory devices

A translation of action encoding is often required between microprocessors and memory. Two examples are given in figure 3.36, namely the interface between a readpulse/writepulse microprocessor (Z80) and an advanced read memory, and its inverse: an advanced read micro (MC6800) linked to a writepulse/readpulse memory. Due to the problems mentioned in the previous section, the former must use a delay.

# 3 Point-to-point Transfers

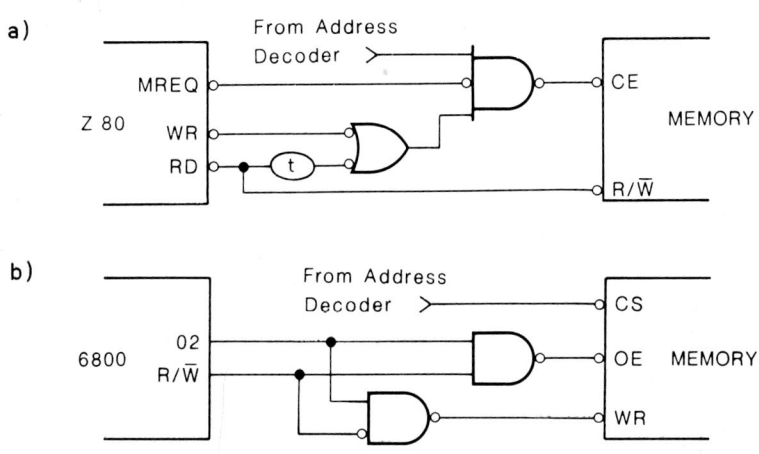

*Fig. 3.36 Examples of interfaces between micros and memories*
  *a) Connection of a static memory to a Z80*
  *b) Connection of a static memory to a MC6800*

## 3.7.4 Synchronous units on a handshaken bus

As a first example of a protocol conversion we shall examine the connection of a synchronous responder to a handshaken link. This may correspond, for instance, to the interface of a memory chip to a bus which uses a handshake signal ACKNOW that carries the actions ACCEPT/READY (write cycles) or VALID/NOTVAL (read cycles). These actions are not defined for a synchronous responder, and must thus be generated in the protocol translation interface. figure 3.37 shows how to obtain the acknowledge signal during the write cycle: since the VALID action is encoded in the rising edge of WRITEPUL, one can simply delay it in order to get the acknowledge. In read cycles, the acknowledge is obtained using a similar scheme, eventually with a different delay.

It must be pointed out that the inverse process is not allowed. Handshaken responders cannot be interfaced to a synchronous link, unless an acceptable upper bound to the responder's reply time is defined. Namely, the link assumes that the sequence proceeds within fixed time slots, while the handshaken responder inserts an unconstrained delay between the VALID (or REQUEST, in read cycles),

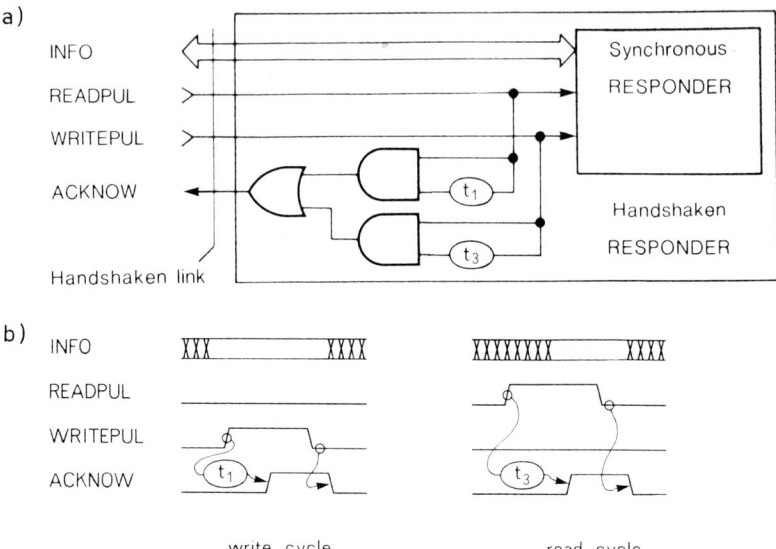

*Fig. 3.37 Interface of a synchronous responder to a handshaken link*
*a) Logic structure*
*b) Timing diagram*

and the ACCEPT (or VALID) actions. For this reason, purely synchronous links are used only when all the modules of the system are designed together.

These conversion schemes are actually the first step in the design of handshaken memory boards using standard synchronous memory chips.

### 3.7.5 Synchronous units on a semi-synchronous bus

When a synchronous responder is tied to a semi-synchronous link, the response actions NOTACC and NOTVAL must only be generated if the responder has to slow down the action sequence on the bus, that is, if the time required to accept (write cycles) or to prepare (read cycles) the information is respectively greater than $t_A$ in figure 3.23 or $t_C$ in figure 3.24. A block diagram of the interface logic for the connection of a "slow" synchronous responder to a semi-synchronous link is shown in figure 3.38.

3 Point-to-point Transfers

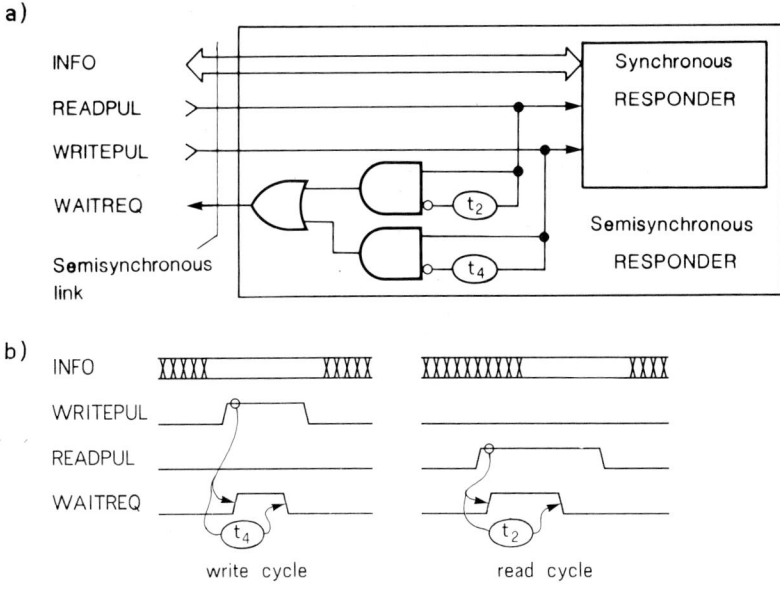

Fig. 3.38 Interface of a synchronous responder to a
semi-synchronous link
a) Logic structure
b) Timing diagram

### 3.7.6 Semi-synchronous units on a handshaken bus

Similar techniques can be applied also to commander modules; figure 3.39 shows how to convert a semi-synchronous commander into a handshaken one. In this case, we need a storage element, that is, a flip-flop, to distingush the "ACKNOW not yet active" at the beginning of the cycle from the state "ACKNOW no longer active" at the end.

The flip-flop must be forced to assume the reset state at power on or to unlock the commander when no responder sends the acknowledge, e.g. by means of a time-out circuit.

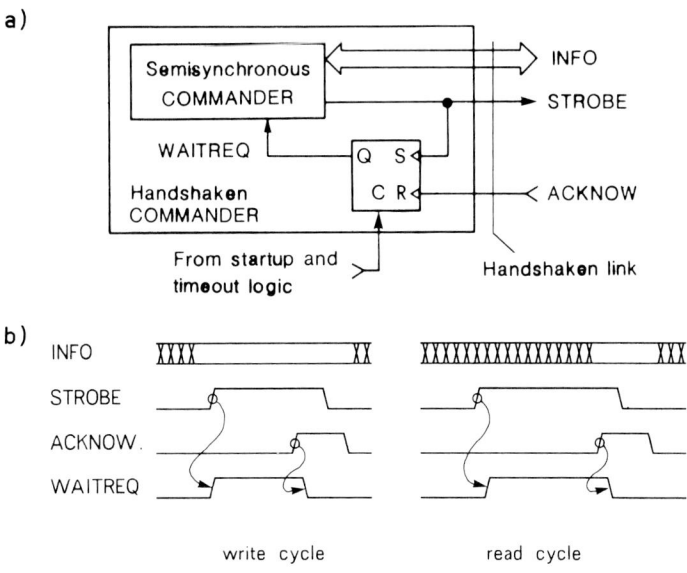

Fig. 3.39 Interface of a semi-synchronous commander to a handshaken link
a) Logic structure
b) Timing diagram

### 3.7.7 Example: microprocessor interface with a handshaken bus

Almost all 8-bit microprocessors follow a clocked semi-synchronous protocol, as described in sections 3.6.5 and 3.6.8. Their protocol can be easily converted into a handshaken one, which is often used on the system bus by means of the technique shown in figure 3.39. Due to the limitations of the clocked processor interface, the timing can change only in discrete steps of one clock period.

Some devices, such as the Motorola 6800, follow a clocked synchronous protocol, and do not accept a WAITREQ signal. In this case, the only possibility to achieve a delay is to halt the clock, as shown in figure 3.40. This clock stretching technique is sometimes used also with semi-synchronous microprocessors, because it allows the insertion of delays shorter than one clock period.

3 Point-to-point Transfers

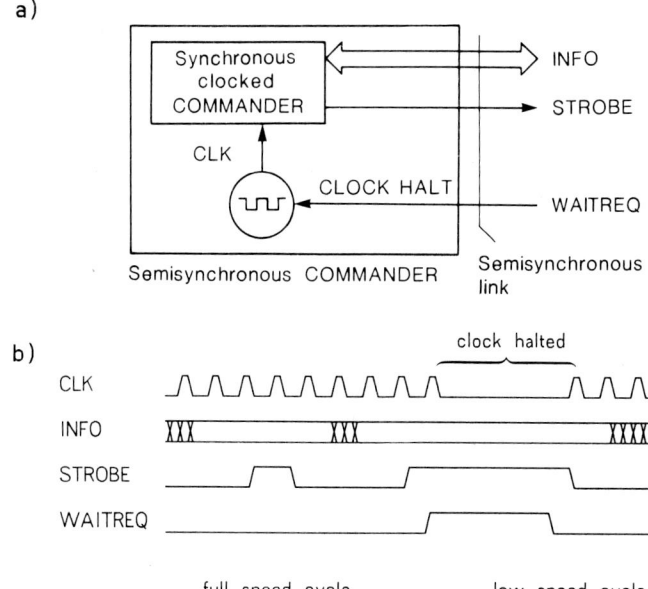

Fig. 3.40 Conversion of a clocked synchronous protocol into a handshaken one
 a) Logic structure
 b) Timing diagram

### 3.7.8 Summary of conversion possibilities

The previous sections showed that the translation of one particular protocol into a different one can be easily carried out in most cases, with some restrictions only for synchronous modules. For instance, a synchronous commander must run at a fixed speed, and can exchange information only with responders which are fast enough for its requirements. A synchronous responder can be easily connected to slower commanders, or to any commander which can be slowed down by a handshake.

As a general rule, responders can always go at a slower speed and, therefore, they can be easily interfaced with links which are handshaken or semi-synchronous. Only when the link is synchronous, must the speed of commanders and responders match; that is, the slowest responder must be faster than the fastest commander. The feasible protocol conversion and the requirements for module matching are summarized in figure 3.41.

a)

| COMMANDER | LINK | CONSTRAINTS |
|---|---|---|
| handshaken | handshaken<br>semisynchronous<br>synchronous | no<br>speed<br>constraint |
| semisynchronous | handshaken<br>semisynchronous<br>synchronous | no<br>speed<br>constraint |
| synchronous | handshaken<br>semisynchronous<br>synchronous | commander<br>slower<br>than link |

b)

| LINK | RESPONDER | CONSTRAINTS |
|---|---|---|
| handshaken | handshaken<br>semisynchronous<br>synchronous | no<br>speed<br>constraint |
| semisymchronous | handshaken<br>semisynchronous<br>synchronous | no<br>speed<br>constraint |
| synchronous | handshaken<br>semisynchronous<br>synchronous | responder<br>faster<br>than link |

*Fig. 3.41 Summary of protocol conversions*
  *a) Connection of a commander to a link*
  *b) Connection of a responder to a link*

# 4 SINGLE-MASTER BUSES

The main benefit of the bus connection topology is that the exchange of information between many units is possible using a single physical link. With the bus organization, there is no restriction on the number or type of modules that are connected to the same link, provided that electrical and mechanical constraints are fulfilled.

When more than a single master/slave pair is tied to the same bus, we must insert protocol operations in order to identify the units involved in each information transfer. As a first step towards the most general case, we shall examine in this section systems in which only one master and many slaves are tied to the link.

## 4.1 ADDRESSING TECHNIQUES

In a single-master bussed system, the responder is selected by means of an information exchange on the bus itself. This information can be transferred using different techniques: the identity of the responder can be mapped into a single bit within a word, into multiple bits, or can depend on the position of the module in the backplane. All these possibilities are discussed in this section.

### 4.1.1 Graphical representation

The definitions of system units given in section 3.4.1 are still valid:
- a COMMANDER is the master which is actually in charge of handling the information transfers on the bus;
- a RESPONDER is a slave which, when requested by a commander, participates in one or more information transfers.

Usually, the information transfer involves one commander and one responder, that is, only two units. In some special cases, however, many responders can exchange information with the same commander in a single transfer cycle. This possibility will be analysed in section 6.3. Masters, slaves, commanders and responders are graphically represented in figure 4.1.

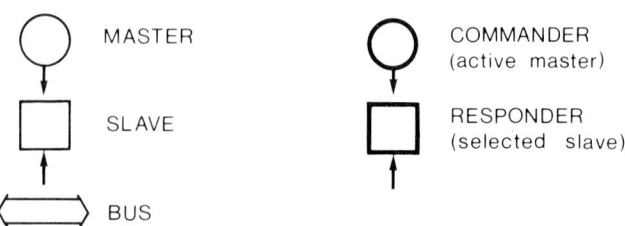

Fig. 4.1   Graphical representation of bus modules

### 4.1.2   The slave selection process

The organization of a single-master, multiple-slave system is shown in figure 4.2a. In this structure, the commander is already identified, while the responder must be selected among the slaves. The process of selecting one responder out of many slaves is called ADDRESSING. The addressing operation causes an evolution of the multiple-slave system as shown in figure 4.2b.

After this process, a logical point-to-point connection between the commander and the responder is set up, and the point-to-point protocols described in Chapter 3 can be used to exchange information in a subsequent data transfer cycle.

### 4.1.3   Decoded selection

The most elementary selection technique is the use of an independent SELECT signal to identify each responder. Slave #A is selected when the signal $SELECT_A$ is active. This technique is called DECODED or LINEAR addressing; the action sequence can be made synchronous or handshaken with any one of the techniques already described in section 3.6.

A block diagram and the action flow of a synchronous decoded addressing system is shown in figure 4.3. The cycle starts with the activation of a $SELECT_A$ signal; after a delay $t_A$ the master continues with the other transfer operations. At the end of the transaction the SELECT signal can return to the not-active state.

4 Single-master Buses                                                                 101

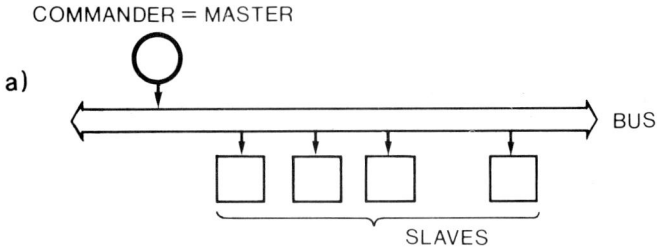

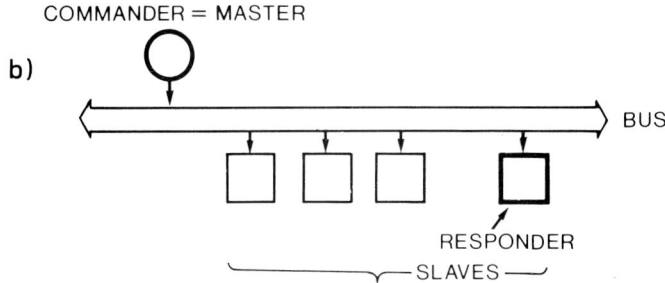

*Fig. 4.2  Organization of a single-master system and the slave selection process*
  *a) Before the selection*
  *b) After the selection*

The cycle can be made handshaken by replacing the delay $t_A$ with an ADDACCEPT action from the responder. The address handshake is often mixed with data handshake, and this case is discussed in section 4.2.1; in order to keep matters simple, we shall only consider synchronous addressing procedures here.

The use of a separate selection signal for each slave requires a set of point-to-point lines, that is, a star connection, with the master at the centre. These lines are not bussed, and their number increases according to the number of elementary slaves. Therefore, this kind of topology is not the best choice for bus-based structures, where each line is tied to all modules. The linear addressing technique is actually used only to select a very small number of slaves.

### 4.1.4 Coded selection

In order to reduce the number of bus lines required for the selection, we could encode the signals which identify the slaves. After the encoding, the set of N identifiers would be replaced by an M-bit word, where $N = 2^M$. This word is the ADDRESS; the technique is called CODED (or ENCODED) ADDRESSING, and the slave #A is selected when ADDRESS = <address of A>

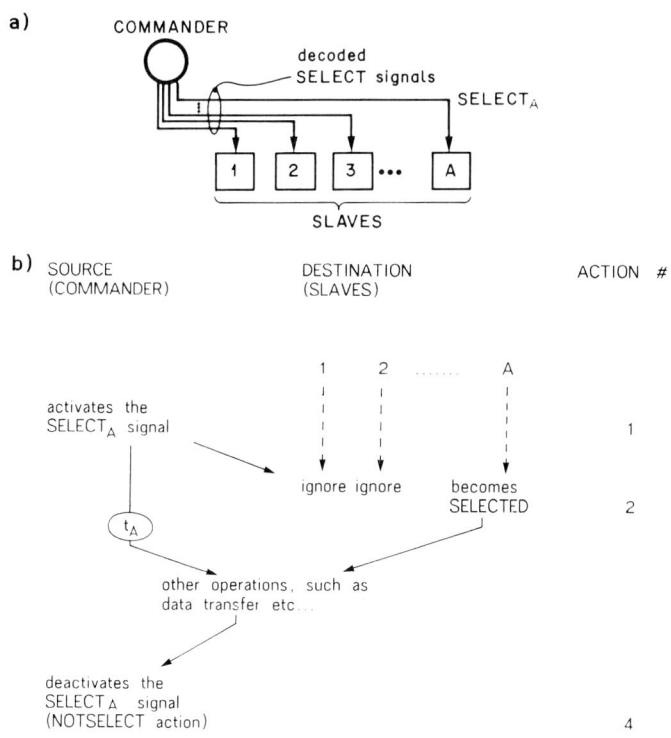

Fig. 4.3 Synchronous decoded addressing cycle
 a) Block diagram
 b) Action sequence

As detailed in section 3.2.1, when a piece of data is encoded, it must also be validated when stabilized by a separate timing signal. We shall call this signal Address Valid (ADDVAL). A block diagram and the action sequence of the coded slave selection technique are shown in figure 4.4.

4 Single-master Buses                                                          103

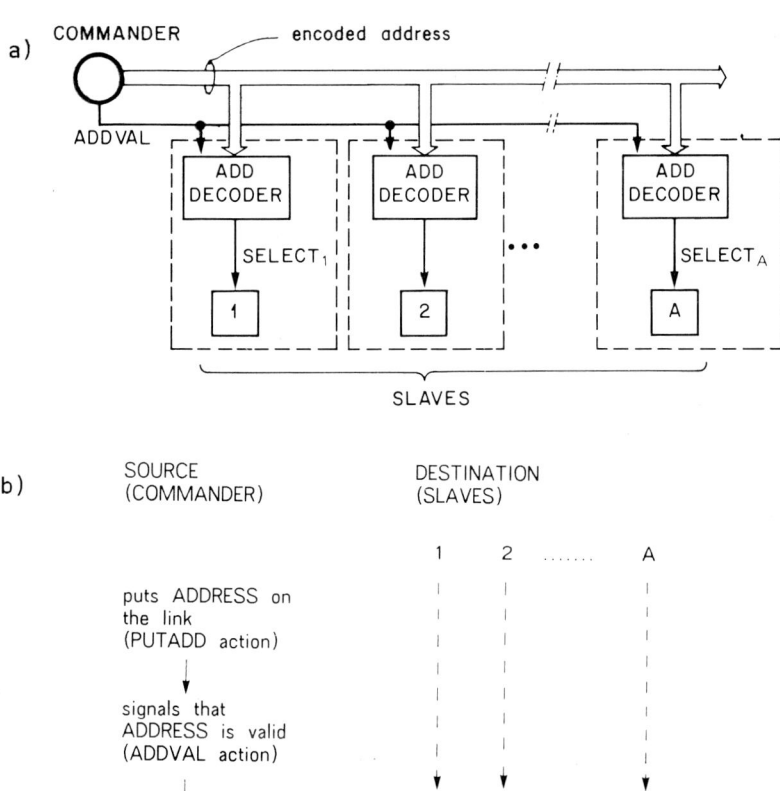

*Fig. 4.4 Encoded selection of the responder*
  *a) Block diagram*
  *b) Action sequence*

The sequence of elementary actions for a handshaken selection cycle with an encoded address shown in figure 4.4b is similar to the sequence of figure 4.3b. The decoded SELECT action has been replaced by PUTADD and ADDVALID.

Encoded addressing allows the selection of one particular unit out of many using a rather small number of lines; it is therefore always used in integrated devices in order to reduce the number of I/O connections.

### 4.1.5 Mixed selection

The linear and the coded selection techniques are often used together. Let us consider, for instance, the block diagram of a memory board, shown in figure 4.5.

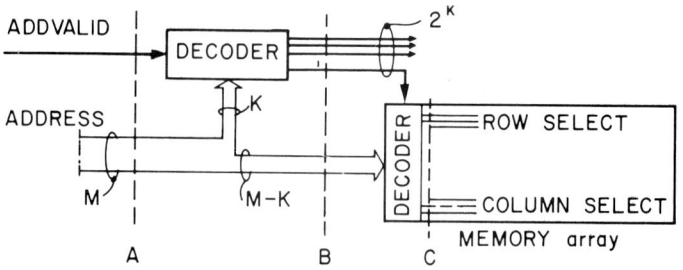

*Fig. 4.5 Mixing of linear and coded selections in a memory board*

We can see that in section A, the set of selection signals consists of an M-bit coded address and of a validation. On the other hand, in section B the address has been partially decoded, and the signal set consists of M minus K bits of address (still encoded), plus $2^K$ selection signals. Going further inside memory devices, we can find a section C, behind the on-chip address decoders, where the selection signals consist of two fully decoded sets, the row select and the column select, respectively. We can speak in this case of MIXED ADDRESSING. It must be pointed out that the separate ADDVAL signal is required only for fully encoded addresses, while it is merged into the decoded select commands in sections B and C.

Two separate validation signals are often used to distinguish two independent address spaces. For instance, microprocessors like the Z80 provide separate I/O and memory spaces by means of the two validation strobes MEMREQ and IOREQ. This is actually another example of mixed selection.

A translation from a coded into a linear selection scheme is always easily performed using a simple decoder. The inverse process, that is, encoding a linear set of selection signals into an address word and a validation, can be achieved using the circuit shown in figure 4.6. To guarantee deskew, a delay must be inserted into the conversion logic, as discussed in section 3.2.7.

## 4 Single-master Buses

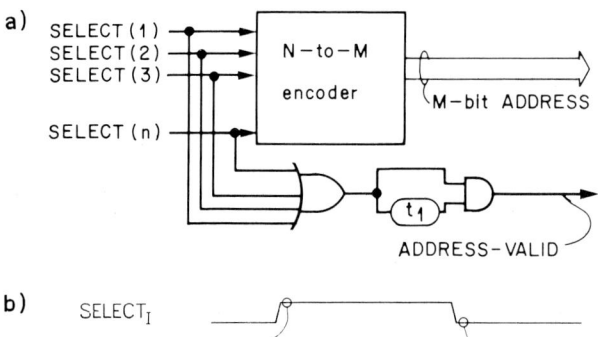

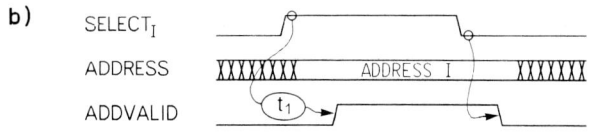

*Fig. 4.6 Conversion from a decoded to an encoded address*
*a) Block diagram*
*b) Timing diagram*

### 4.1.6 Incomplete selection

Some simplified selection techniques are often used to save decoding circuitry at the expense of some restrictions on the address space mapping.

Let us consider, for instance, a microprocessor system with an address space of 64 kbytes, used for an application where only 16 kbytes of memory are required. We assume also that the memory is organized into banks of 4 kbytes each, thus, four such banks make up the full 16k memory space. Inside each bank, 12 bits (ADD <0..11>) are used to identify the single memory cell ($2^{12}$ = 4k), and the remaining 4 (ADD<12..15>) must be used for the selection of banks. Since there are only 4 banks to select, we could use only two bits, as shown in figure 4.7a. In this case, we speak of an *INCOMPLETE* selection, because the address information is not completely used. Another possibility to save decoding logic is to use directly some bits of the coded address word as linear selection flags, in order to identify blocks of slave units, as shown in figure 4.7b. Since in this last case the values of bank addresses follow a geometric sequence (1, 2, 4, 8....), we shall call this technique a *GEOMETRIC* selection.

Using incomplete addressing, the two unused bits correspond to "don't care" conditions in the address word, and thus the group of 4 banks is replicated 4 times, as shown in figure 4.8a. Using geometric selection, addresses with two or more 1s are not legal; following the

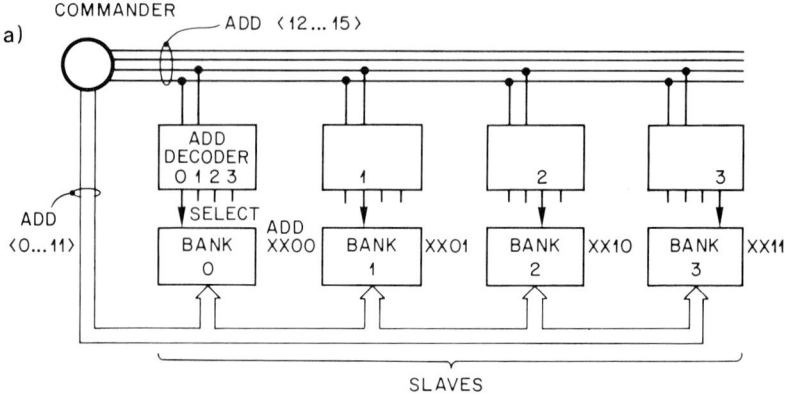

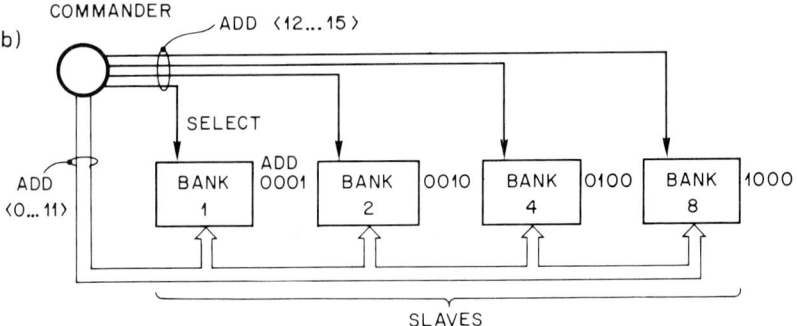

Fig. 4.7 Simplified selection logic
a) Incomplete addressing
b) Geometric addressing

previous example, codes like 0011, 0101, etc., on ADD<12..15> are forbidden because they would select two (or more) banks at the same time. The memory map is shown in figure 4.8b.

Due to the above-mentioned constraints, the incomplete and the geometric selections are only used in systems designed for a fixed configuration, without the possibility of change or of an extension of the slave map.

### 4.1.7 Geographical selection

The term GEOGRAPHICAL addressing defines a selection technique which activates the slave units according to their specific position in the backplane. The slave identifier, in this case, is no longer bound to the module itself, but to each bus connector on the motherboard.

4 Single-master Buses                                                                    107

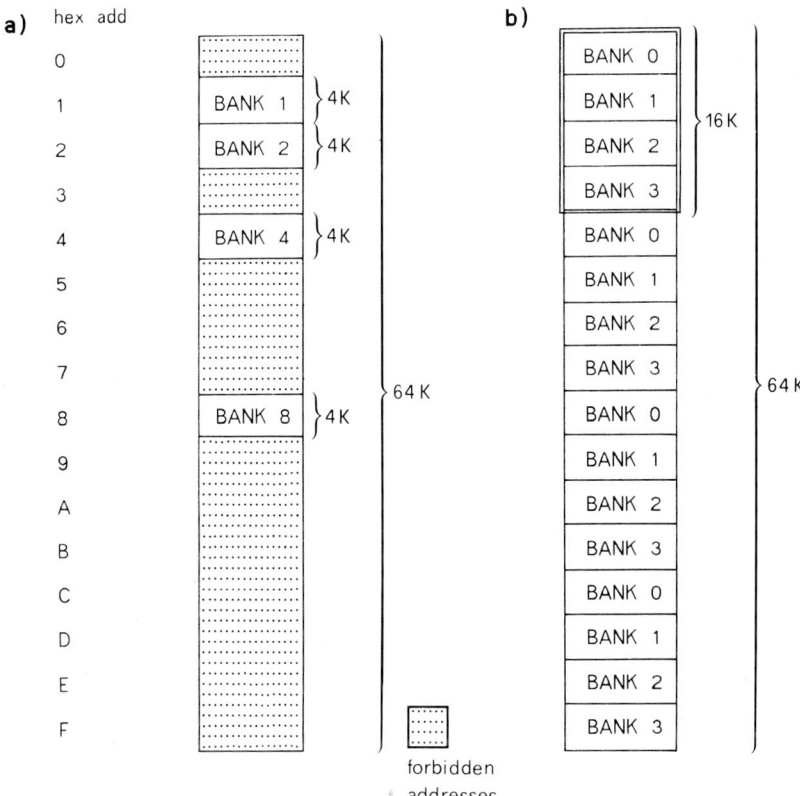

*Fig. 4.8  Address maps for simplified selection*
  *a) Incomplete addressing*
  *b) Geometric addressing*

The geographical addressing always requires a special layout of the backplane, that is, either a set of star-connected lines, or some custom wiring on the connectors, as shown in figure 4.9. One can also use special mechanical arrangements, such as an address preset switch on the card, positioned by tabs on the connector. Using geographical addressing, the module identifier cannot be set by jumpers or switches placed on the board itself.

As for other cases, we can identify two basic techniques :
- **LINEAR GEOGRAPHICAL ADDRESSING**: a set of point-to-point lines carries the SELECT signals from the master connector to the various slave connectors, as shown in figure 4.9a. The backplane cannot be homogeneous since one connector has special wiring for the master.

- **CODED GEOGRAPHICAL ADDRESSING**: a position identifier is hardwired onto each connector and is sensed and used by on-board selection circuitry, as shown in figure 4.9b.

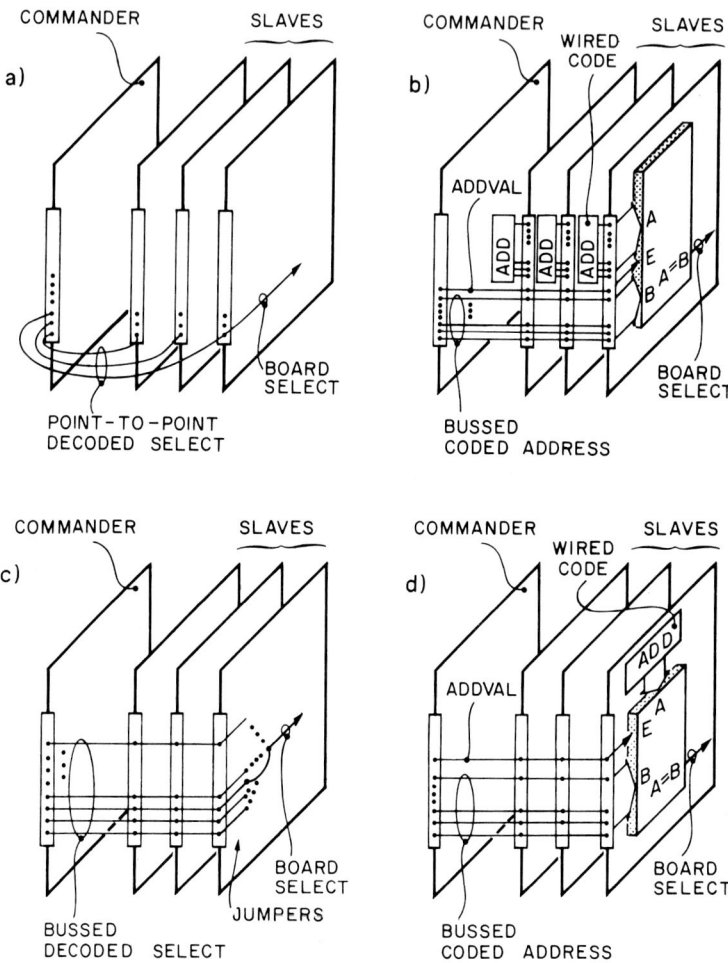

Fig. 4.9  Backplane organization for geographical and logical addressing
  a) Decoded geographical
  b) Encoded geographical
  c) Decoded logical
  d) Encoded logical

4 Single-master Buses    109

Both the linear logical (section 4.1.3) and the linear geographical addressing modes use a set of decoded select signals, but the module identification techniques and the backplane structures are different. As shown in figure 4.9, in both cases, each SELECT line comes from a separate pin on the master. For decoded logical addressing, these lines go to different pins on the slave connectors, and the address can be selected by jumpers on the module itself. For decoded geographical addressing, all the SELECT lines go to the same pin on the slave units; the address depends only on the module position and cannot be modified by changes on the module board. Some of the buses listed in Appendix allow geographical selection, as detailed in the comparison table.

## 4.2 ADDRESS/DATA PROTOCOLS

As already discussed with point-to-point transfers, there are many choices for the organization of a complete transaction. First of all, different techniques can be used to synchronize the address and the data cycle. Then, these cycles can be either considered as two independent information transfers, or merged into a unique operation. These two basic techniques are analysed in the following sections and will be used as a reference to describe some more complex protocols.

### 4.2.1  Handshaken addressing

The responder selection operation is actually a write operation, and can be synchronized by adding an ADDACCEPT or an ADDNOTACC action to the control structure in order to obtain a handshaken (section 3.6.1) or a semi-synchronous (section 3.6.5) action flow, respectively, as shown in figure 4.10.

Since many slaves are connected to the same bus, the signals which carry the handshake actions may come from many sources. In order to avoid the presence of a set of point-to-point lines, all the handshake signals are encoded on a single line, using the wired-OR technique mentioned in section 2.1.6.

The basic addressing protocols presented here are handshaken, since this is the most reliable and complete protocol. As explained in section 3.6.3, one can make them synchronous by replacing the interlock with a delay. Some of the most common synchronization techniques for a complete transaction are discussed in section 4.2.4.

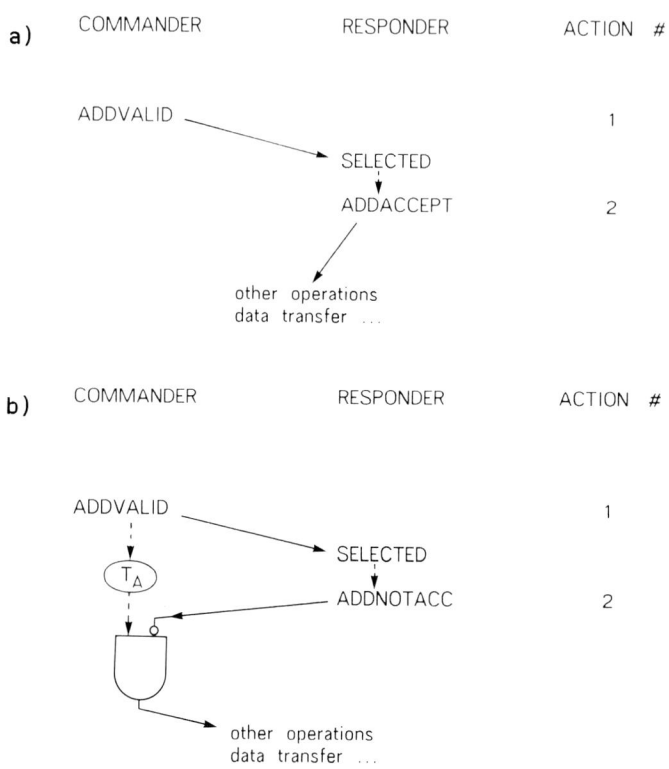

Fig. 4.10 Action flows of the addressing operation
a) Handshaken
b) Semi-synchronous

## 4.2.2 Microcycle protocol

When the address and data transfers are handled as two self-standing cycles with separate control structures, we shall speak of a *MICROCYCLE* protocol. The complete transaction is actually broken into two operations, and each cycle follows an independent action flow. An example of complete action sequences for write and read operations with a handshaken microcycle protocol is shown in figure 4.11. The action subsequences 1-2-3-4 and 5-6-7-8 correspond to a handshaken write (the selection cycle), and to a handshaken write or read (the data cycle), respectively.

# 4 Single-master Buses

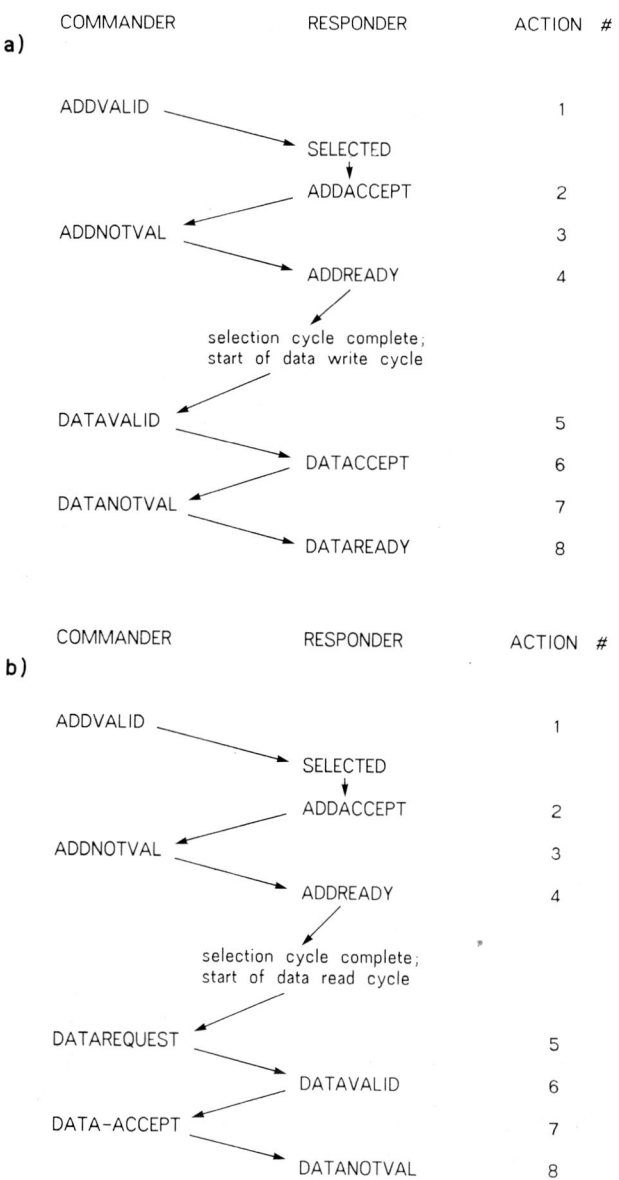

Fig. 4.11 Action flow of a complete address/data transaction with microcycle handshaken protocol
  a) Data write cycle
  b) Data read cycle

An example of action encoding using an advanced read protocol for the data cycle is given in figure 4.12, together with the timing diagram.

a)

| ACTION | | # | SIGNAL | STATE |
|---|---|---|---|---|
| write operation (READ = 0) | ADDVALID | 1 | ADDSTB | low-to-high |
| | ADDNOTVAL | 3 | ADDSTB | high-to-low |
| | ADDACCEPT | 2 | ADDACK | low-to-high |
| | ADDREADDY | 4 | ADDACK | high-to-low |
| | DATAVALID | 5 | DATASTB | low-to-high |
| | DATANOTVAL | 7 | DATASTB | high-to-low |
| | DATACCEPT | 6 | DATACK | low-to-high |
| | DATAREADY | 8 | DATACK | high-to-low |
| READ operation (READ = 1) | (the actions of the address cycle are encoded as for write operation) | | | |
| | DATAREQUEST | 5 | DATASTB | low-to-high |
| | DATACCEPT | 7 | DATASTB | high-to-low |
| | DATAVALID | 6 | DATACK | low-to-high |
| | DATANOTVAL | 8 | DATACK | high-to-low |

b)

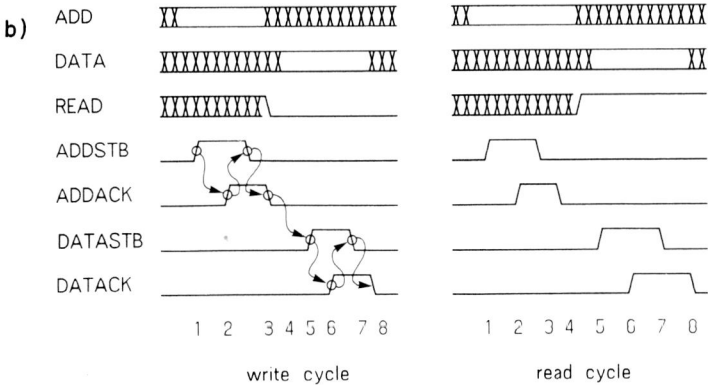

*Fig. 4.12 Complete address/data transaction with microcycle handshaken protocol*
*a) Action encoding*
*b) Timing diagram*

## 4.2.3 Merged protocol

Another protocol technique is to interleave the actions of the two cycles and thus to make a sort of "transfer handshake": the addressing cycle cannot be closed (ADDNOTVAL active) until the data transfer is completed (DATANOTVAL active). In this case, the action sequences for the selection and the address cycles are mixed together, and we speak of MERGED protocol. The action sequence of an address/data merged protocol is shown in figure 4.13.

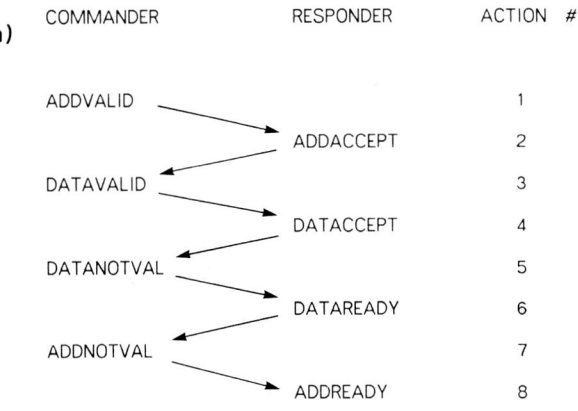

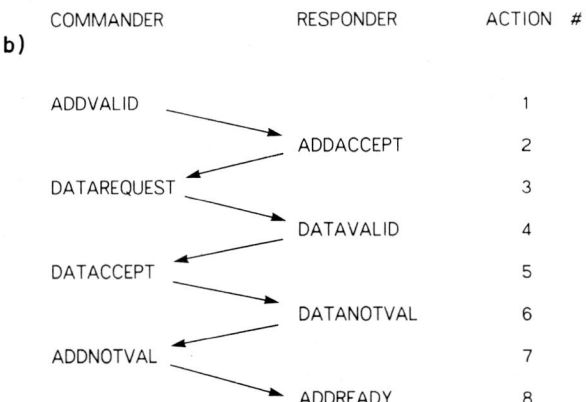

Fig. 4.13 Action flow for a complete address/data transaction with merged handshaken protocol
 a) Data write cycle
 b) Data read cycle

In this example, the action subsequence 1-2-7-8 corresponds to a handshaken write cycle that transfers the address from the commander to a selected responder with full handshake. The subsequence 3-4-5-6 (data transfer) corresponds to a handshaken write and a handshaken read, respectively.

For this protocol, we can keep the same action-signal encoding already used for the microcycle protocol (see figure 4.12), and thus obtain the timing diagram of figure 4.14.

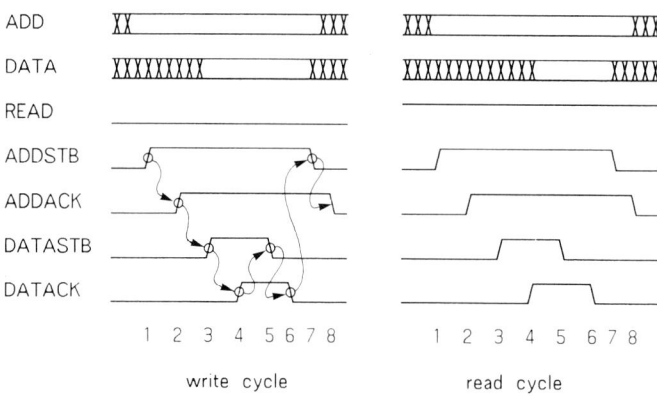

*Fig. 4.14 Timing diagram of write and read transactions with handshaken merged protocol*

### 4.2.4 Mixed synchronization

Since a transaction contains two operations (selection and data transfer), and each operation can be synchronous, semi-synchronous or handshaken, there are, in principle, 9 choices for protocol synchronization. We shall, however, examine in detail only two techniques, which correspond to widely used simplifications of the microcycle and merged protocols.

A first technique to simplify the transaction protocol is to use a single line for the address and the data acknowledge. It corresponds to merging the ADDACC with the DATACC during write cycles, and with the DATAVALID during read cycles. The action flows and the timing diagram of read and write transactions with merged protocol and single acknowledge are shown in figure 4.15. We can verify that we still have an interlock between commander and responder operations.

4 Single-master Buses    115

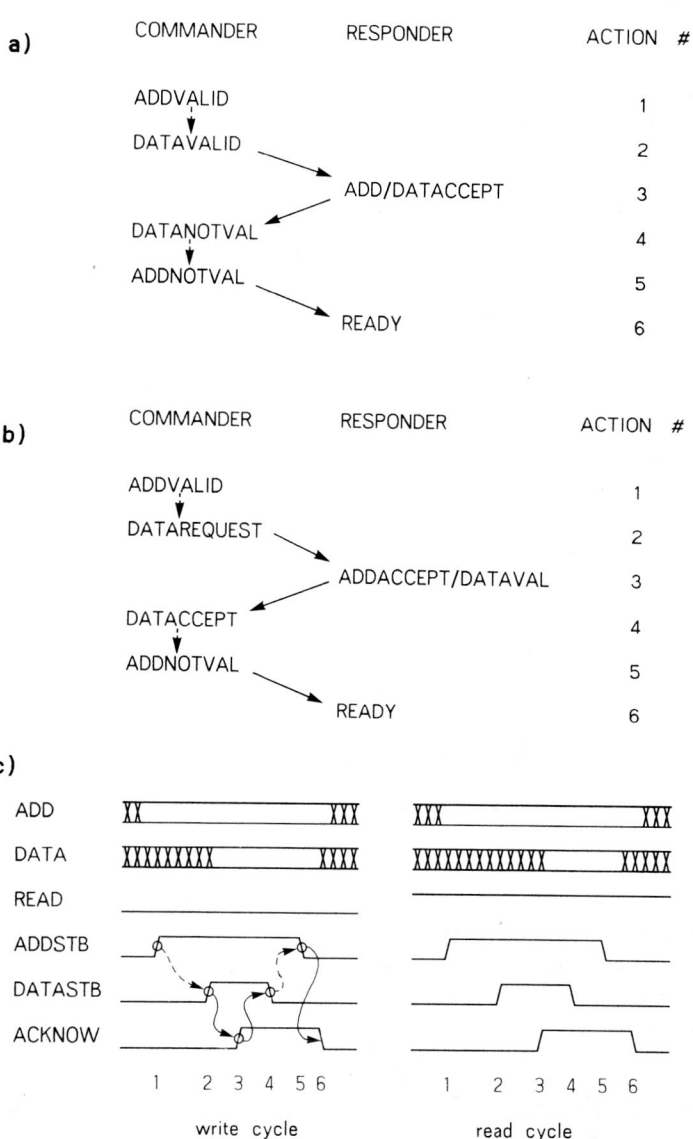

Fig. 4.15 Transactions with merged protocol, single acknowledge
   a) Action flow
   b) Timing diagram

The single acknowledge is used, for instance, in VME and in MULTIBUS (see list of signals for these buses in Appendix). The latter actually also merges ADDVAL/DATAVAL and ADDVAL/DATAREQ.

Using microcycle protocols we often find a synchronous address cycle followed by a semi-synchronous or a handshaken data cycle. The slave selection logic in this case must be fast enough to catch the address within the fixed time imposed by the commander. The former approach is followed by some microprocessors (e.g. Intl 8086, Zilog 8000), the latter by the M3 backplane bus [DELC81], [CON83]. The timing diagrams for these two cases are shown in figure 4.16.

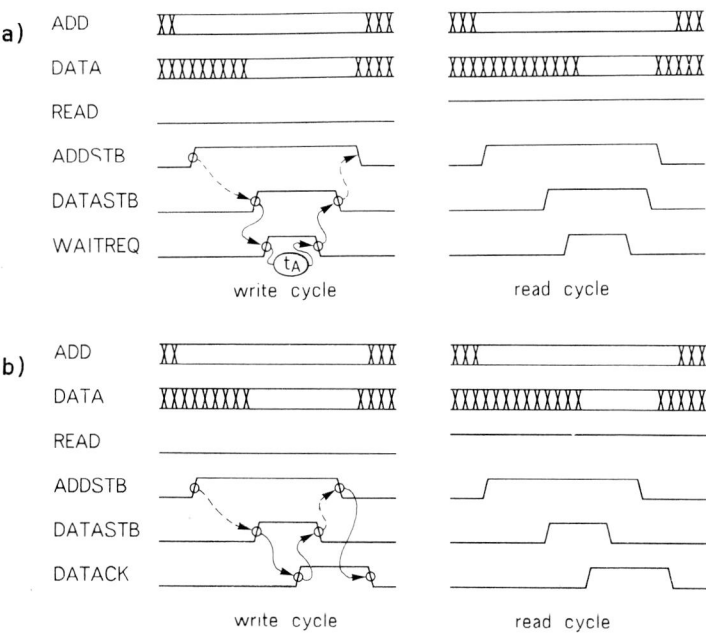

Fig. 4.16 Transactions with microcycle protocol, synchronous address cycle
  a) Semi-synchronous data cycle
  b) Handshaken data cycle

## 4.3 MULTIPLEXED BUSES

It can be seen from figure 4.13 that the information which represents address and data must stay on the ADDRESS and DATA lines, respectively, for a small percentage of the time only. An obvious possibility is to use a unique set of lines to transfer both types of information, using the time-multiplex technique. Also, because the control lines are used only when the corresponding information field is active, even some control signals can be multiplexed. Multiplexing adds a new degree of freedom to information transfer protocols. In order to point out all the choices, we shall first examine the organization of a *MULTIPLEXED BUS* from a rather general point of view, and then show how actual implementations fit into the whole frame.

### 4.3.1 Multiplexed protocols

From figure 4.13, it can be seen that it is possible to put address and data directly on to the same set of lines at different times; we thus obtain multiplexed ADDRESS/DATA cycles, as shown in figure 4.17.

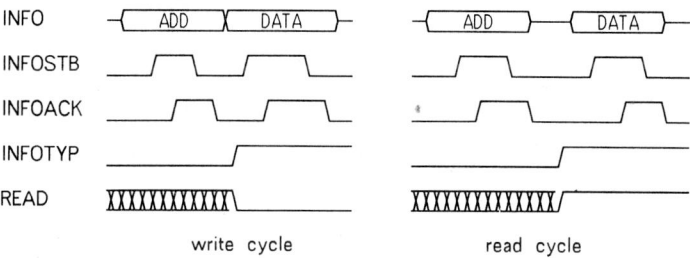

*Fig. 4.17 Timing diagram of write and read transactions with multiplexing of address and data; handshaken microcycle protocol*

This simple ADDRESS/DATA multiplexing is only one out of many possibilities of multiplexing techniques. The main guideline is that the packets of information to be exchanged on a bus are organized in many different ways using two degrees of freedom: space and time. When the information bits are spread over a set of separate lines we speak of *PARALLEL BUS* and *PARALLEL TRANSFER*. The opposite possibility is to time-multiplex the bits on a single line; in this case we speak of *SERIAL BUS* and *SERIAL TRANSFER* techniques.

When a set of lines is shared by different types of information, the control signals must also specify the type available in the current cycle, such as ADDRESS or DATA in the previous example. There are two basic choices that influence this operation: using separate sets of control signals, as shown in figure 4.17, or using a unique set of control signals, and thus qualifying the type of information by means of another line.

This last technique actually involves a multiplexing of the control signals. The timing diagram of figure 4.18 shows the same operations as in figure 4.17 with a different action encoding: the same line carries the strobe pulse for both address and data, and another line carries the acknowledge for both. A third line qualifies the type of information being exchanged.

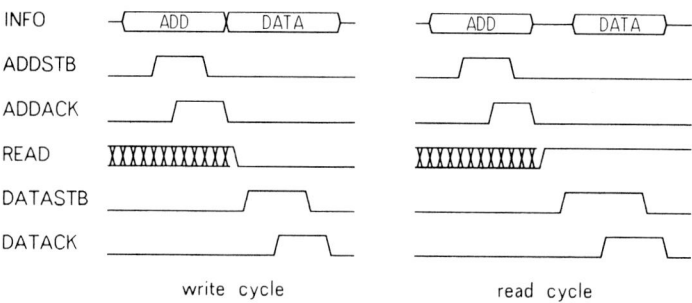

*Fig. 4.18 Timing diagram of write and read transactions with multiplexing of both information and control signals*

The number of separate control sets or of qualifiers depends on how many different types of information are transmitted on the same lines. As an example, figure 4.19 shows the various possibilities of controlling the flow of a 24-bit address and 16-bit data on an 8-bit information bus. The sequence of information packets is the same in all of these examples.

### 4.3.2 Examples of multiplexed buses

8-bit microprocessors need 16 bits of address and 8 bits of data. Owing to the constraints of a 40-pin package, the possible elimination of 8 lines would be appreciated, and several multiplexing schemes are used for this purpose, as shown by the examples in figure 4.20. The fully multiplexed scheme of figure 4.20d is interesting only with 16 or 32-bit micros.

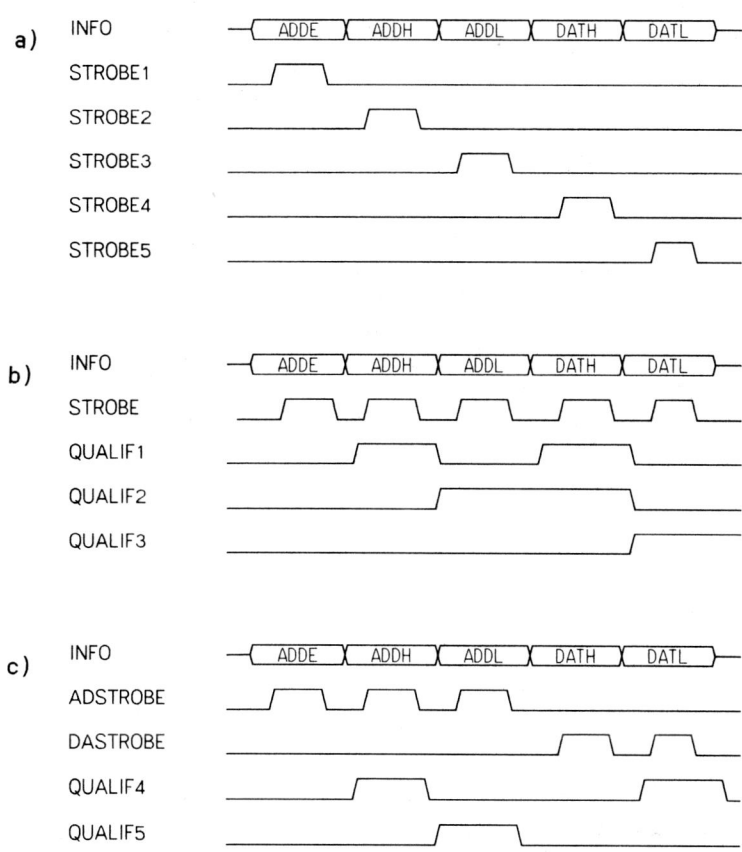

Fig. 4.19 Different encoding of strobes and qualifiers in a multiplexed bus
  a) Fully decoded strobes
  b) Single strobe, encoded qualifiers
  c) Separate address and data strobes, and encoded qualifiers

On the 8080, data is multiplexed with cycle status; the 8085 mixes data with the low address byte; the 1802 multiplexes high and low address bytes, the NS32032 and the P896 mix all address and data bits. In any case, the first time slot is used for the address or other selection information (e.g. status); data is actually needed (or available) only after the addressing operation, and thus they are issued (or received) during the second time slot. When only addresses are multiplexed (e.g. the 1802), the most significant part is sent first, because it has to be used by the module decoding logic.

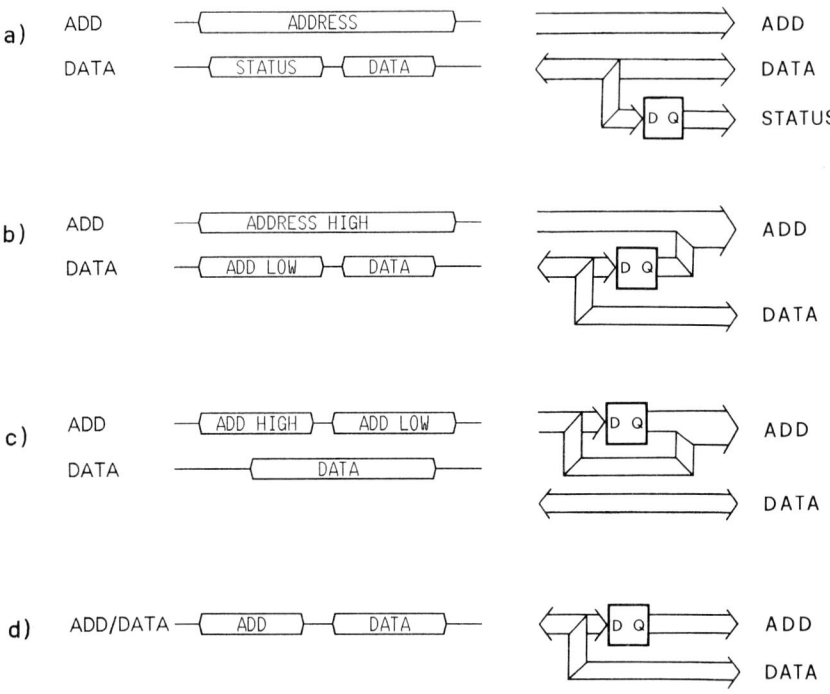

Fig. 4.20 Examples of multiplexed buses
  a) Intel 8080
  b) Intel 8085
  c) RCA 1802
  d) National 32032

### 4.3.3 Performance of multiplexed buses

When the information is time-multiplexed, the designer saves bus lines, but the complete transfer operation requires more time. We shall analyse briefly the impact of multiplexing on the information throughput of a bus. In order to compare the various possibilities, we must first define some parameters related to the global amount of information which can be transferred. If we do not consider the bus control structure, these parameters are:

- The bus width W: the number of lines that can be used simultaneously to transfer information.
- The bus bandwidth C: the number of cycles supported per time unit.
- The bus throughput T: the global amount of information that can be transferred per time unit.

When each cycle transfers W bits and there is no time wasted between cycles, the throughput can be written as:

$$T = C \cdot W$$

The choice of C and W affects the design and the cost of a bus. In order to increase W, the designer must add lines to the bus; actually, this means that his design must include larger (or denser)

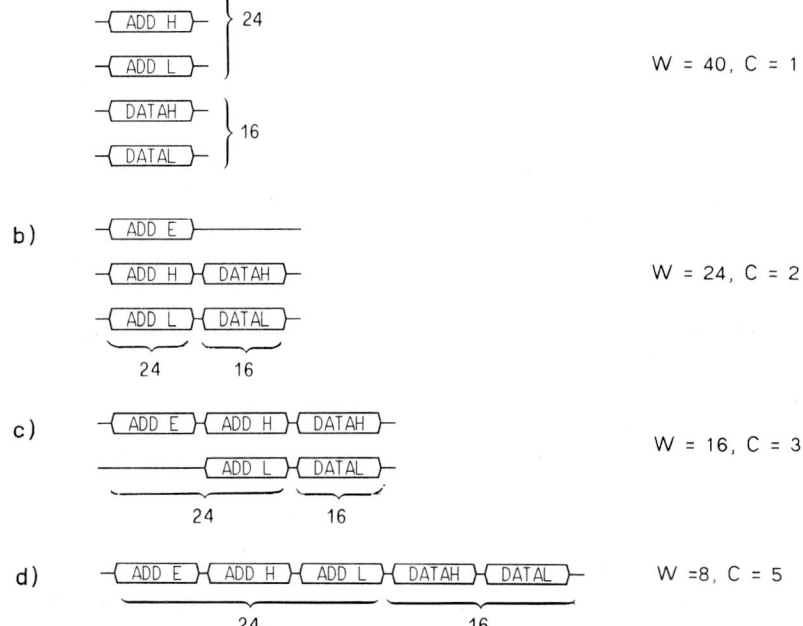

Fig. 4.21 Possible organizations of a transaction with 24 address bits and 16 data bits
   a) Fully parallel
   b) ADD/DATA multiplexing
   c) Word multiplexing
   d) Byte multiplexing

connectors and backplanes, and more bus-buffer ICs (drivers and receivers), which also implies a higher power consumption. On the other hand, the bandwidth C can be enhanced only by increasing the speed of the signals. This again is expensive, because it requires faster logic (that is, more power), and more sophisticated design and implementation techniques.

To point out an example of bus structures with different performance, we can consider some possible organizations of the bus in a system that uses 24-bit addresses and 16-bit data. Four different space/time choices are shown in figure 4.21.

If all the buses used in this example have the same bandwidth, the complete address/data transaction requires a time proportional to the number of cycles C. With this assumption, the throughput of each bus is proportional to W, unless there is some cycle that does not use the full width of the bus. If $I_T$ is the information actually transferred in a transaction, we can define a "utilization factor" U as:

$$U = \frac{I_T}{W \cdot C}$$

If we consider again the example of figure 4.21, where the information transferred consists of an address and a data field, the utilization factor obtained is:

$$U = \frac{W_{ADD} + W_{DATA}}{W_{BUS} \cdot C}$$

which equals, for the four different organizations shown in the example of figure 4.21:

a) $U = 1$   b) $U = 0.83$   c) $U = 0.83$   d) $U = 1$

We can therefore verify that choices b) and c) do not exploit the most optimal bus throughput.

### 4.3.4 Pipelining of operations

The first approach to increase the throughput of a bus is to use the full width of address and data. However, if we keep the usual sequence of operation (addressing, data transfer, new addressing, ...) its performance would be almost the same as that of a multiplexed bus, because address lines are not used during data transfer and vice versa. The solution to increasing the throughput is to perform some operations concurrently; the addressing and the data transfer of the same transaction must be sequential, but we can transfer data output and the next address during the same time slot.

In this way, the operations are both *PIPELINED* and multiplexed; the available bandwidth is exploited optimally, because all lines are used in all time slots. An example of address/data pipelined transfer is shown in figure 4.22.

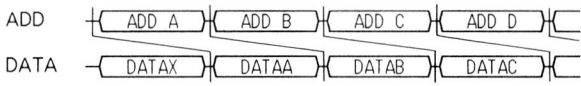

*Fig. 4.22 Pipelined operations on a multiplexed bus*

When the bus commander is a microprocessor, the pipelining of operations requires pre-fetch and queueing capability, because the new address must be available before the end of the current instruction. This technique is used, for instance, in the Intel iAPX 286 system.

## 4.4 MULTIPLE TRANSFER CYCLES

Besides the addressing and transfer of single data items, there are other types of information transfer. This section discusses the features of these cycles, their protocol requirements, and shows how they still rely on the elementary operations defined in Chapter 3.

### 4.4.1 Read-modify-write

A *READ-MODIFY-WRITE* cycle (RMW) consists of a double access to a slave with a single addressing operation. The first access reads a memory cell, the second one writes the same cell. The RMW operation can be used, for instance, to test the value of a register (memory or I/O) and to change it without re-addressing the same register. An example of a complete RMW cycle is given in figure 4.23.

Since there is only one addressing operation, a single master is responsible for the whole sequence of operations, which is inherently *INDIVISIBLE*. Indivisible RMW accesses are required to handle hardware semaphores (also called *LOCKVARIABLE*) in multiple-processor systems [DIJK65]. If a processor uses only single read and single write accesses, indivisibility must be guaranteed using other tricks such as a lock flag which inhibits new accesses to the slave, or by locking the bus arbitration system, or by special hardware on the semaphore memory [CIVE80].

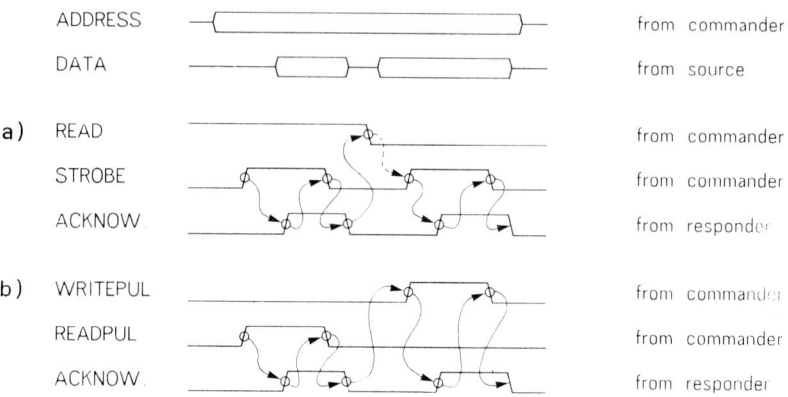

*Fig. 4.23 Read-Modify-Write cycle (data transfer only)*
  *a) Advanced read protocol*
  *b) Readpulse/writepulse protocol*

## 4.4.2 Read-after-write

A READ-AFTER-WRITE access (RAW) has the same structure as the RMW: a single addressing cycle which brackets a write and a read operation. The RAW can be used to verify that information has been correctly stored, or to read back results from fast processing peripherals; e.g. one can write the operand in a square root circuit, and read the result within the same RAW cycle. While the RMW is a true enhancement of system functionality, because it allows the implementation of hardware semaphores, the result of RAW is only an increase in performance. An example of a RAW cycle is given in figure 4.24.

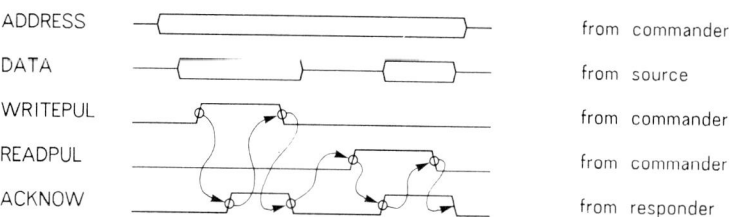

*Fig. 4.24 Read-After-Write cycle (readpulse/writepulse protocol)*

4 Single-master Buses                                              125

## 4.4.3  Block transfer

In a *BLOCK TRANSFER* many read or write operations are executed for a sequence of adjacent memory locations, but only the first address is transmitted by the commander, as shown in figure 4.25.

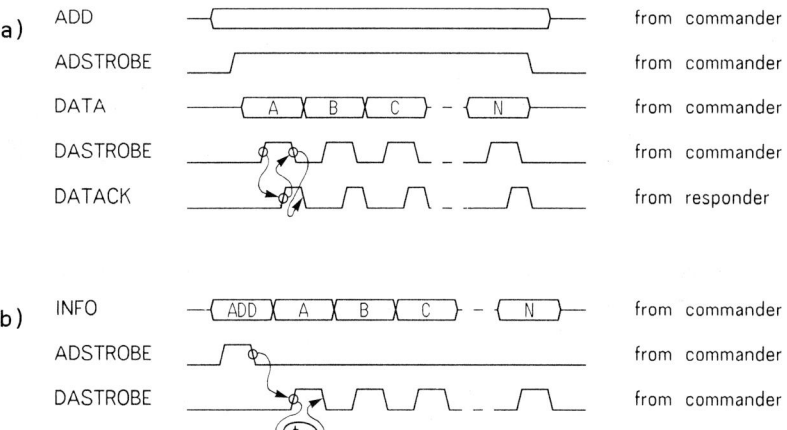

*Fig. 4.25 Examples of block transfer*
  *a) Merged address/data handshaken protocol*
  *b) Multiplexed microcycle synchronous protocol*

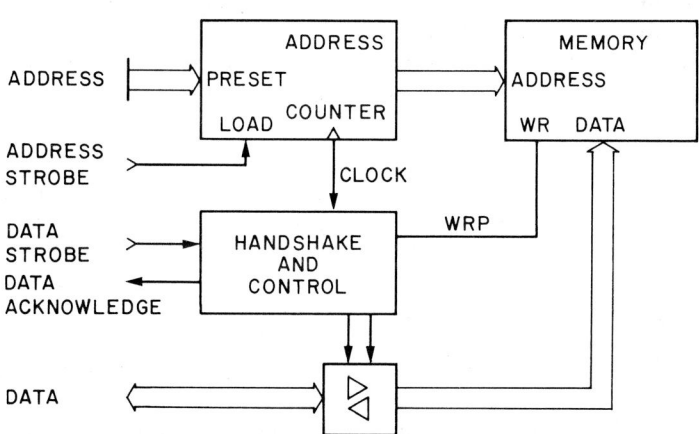

*Fig. 4.26 Simplified block diagram of a memory interface which handles block-write operations*

Since only the starting address is transmitted on the bus, the source and the destination units must have independent address pointers to access the group of cells which are transferred. An example of the interface logic for block transfer is given in figure 4.27.

The block transfers have definite speed benefits, especially in multiplexed buses, because they allow the transfer of N data words with N + 1 cycles, compared with the 2N cycles required with single-data operations.

Further increases in speed can be obtained with the modified handshake shown in figure 4.27. All transitions of the VALID and of the ACKNOWLEDGE signals are used, and the bandwidth of these signals is half that in figure 4.26, for the same throughput. This technique is used in FASTBUS and in P896.

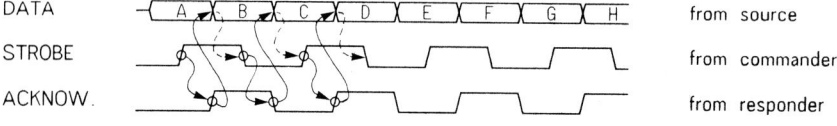

*Fig. 4.27 Modified handshake for high speed block transfer*

# 5 MULTIPLE-MASTER BUSES

A *MULTIPLE-MASTER BUS* is a communication structure with which one can connect many units (masters and slaves) which are all able to use the bus and to perform independent information transfers. But, since the bus is a single resource which can carry only one information packet at a time, only one master at a time may have control of the bus, that is, act as a commander. To guarantee this condition, the protocol of multiple master buses must include a sequence of operations which selects a unique commander.

This chapter describes the various methods that can be used for the selection of the commander in bus-based systems. The bus assignment is considered here as a specific case of resource sharing. Since we are now describing communication structures, the considered resource is a bus, and the resource requesters are the master units. Similar techniques are used for the assignment of the resource CPU to one of many interrupting peripherals which request service (as discussed in Chapter 6) and, in other cases, for the handling of a single-resource in a multiple-user environment.

## 5.1 RESOURCE SHARING

A good example of resource sharing is a discussion within a group of people. There is no problem as long as only one person at a time wants to say something. If many people have something to say, only one at a time may actually speak, because otherwise, the mixing of words would make the conversation very difficult to understand. In order to avoid a garbled conversation, people use elementary courtesy rules (wait until the current speaker has finished, ask if somebody else wants to speak), or abide by the decision of a single person who assigns the right to speak to only one person in the group at a time.

In any case, only one of the requesters at a time is allowed to have control of the air, which is the resource used as a transmission media for the voice.

The same problem occurs in communication structures. Many units (masters) may have simultaneous requests for the bus; if many of these requesters use the bus at the same time, no correct information transfer can be performed. This section will describe the various techniques which can be used to share correctly a communication resource between many requesters.

### 5.1.1 Resource allocation techniques

We can model the resource/requester system for communication structures as in figure 5.1. No information exchange can be performed until an ALLOCATOR gives EXCLUSIVE ACCESS of the communication structure to a single master. Figure 5.1 shows the logical structure of the allocation system; its actual implementation may seem quite different because the allocator is composed of various sub-units which are either centralized in a single module or distributed among the modules. The allocation can also be executed by an algorithm which is executed locally by each requester, based on some common variables. These are only different implementations, however, which will be analysed in sections 5.3 and 5.4; all the allocation systems must work as a single logic entity, and one is required for each shared resource.

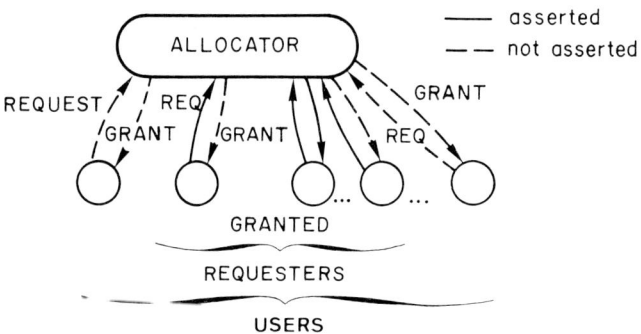

Fig. 5.1 Logic structure of the allocator

Allocation comes into play whenever several clients request the use of a unique service or resource. This is called a CONTENTION. The allocator should grant the resource to one and only one of the requesters. In multimaster parallel buses, the resource is the bus itself and the requesters are all the masters which need the bus to transmit

# 5 Multiple-master Buses

their data. If the resource is used by more than one requester at a time, a so-called COLLISION will occur. In a communication system, a collision may lead to completely unpredictable results and may even cause damage to the circuits. In some buses, collisions are legal during some part of the information transfer, as a means to achieve an exclusive access.

As shown in figure 5.1, each user that needs the resource sends a REQUEST to the allocator. One of them will receive the right (called a GRANT) to use the resource; the unit which is allowed to use the resource is GRANTED (in a bus-based system, for example, we say that the commander is granted the use of the bus, or that the bus is granted to the commander).

Let us consider, as a first example, a system where a resource can be requested by only two users. In this simple case, we can assign the resource to one user by default, and then switch it to the other user when requested. This is called DEFAULT ASSIGNMENT: the allocator is actually part of the default user. When it receives a request from the other user, it issues the grant to this requester; when the request is removed, the default user receives the resource again for its use. Using this technique, the allocator thus only needs to ensure that the resource is switched at the right time.

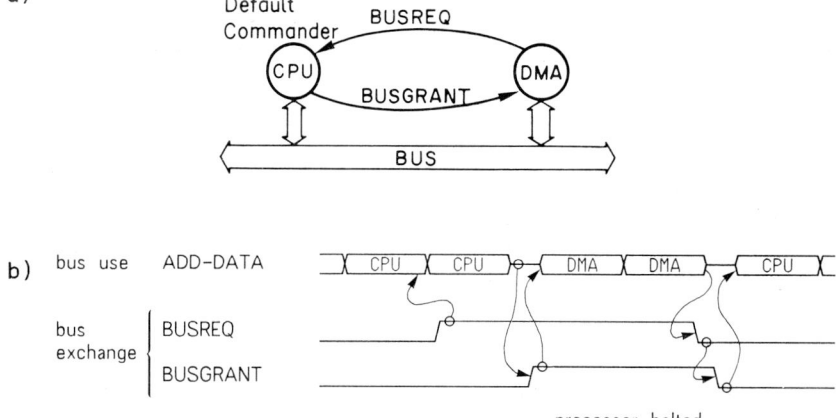

*Fig. 5.2   CPU bus exchange sequence*
  *a) Block diagram*
  *b) Timing diagram*

This structure is typically used for the CPU local bus in simple microprocessor systems; the CPU has control of this bus by default, but releases it after a request from another master (e.g. the DMA controller). In order to avoid collisions or incomplete transfers, the request is honoured only at the end of each bus transaction. An example of a bus exchange using this technique is shown in figure 5.2.

We could still use the default assignment technique when there are three or more users that can request a resource: one requester would keep the resource by default, and the others would request it when required. However, an exclusive access structure as described in the following sections would become mandatory in order to discriminate between the two or more requests of non-default users.

### 5.1.2 Model of the exclusive access system

The N-way allocation may follow complex rules and is handled, in most cases, by a hierarchy of sub-units. A more detailed view of the exclusive access process is given in figure 5.3.

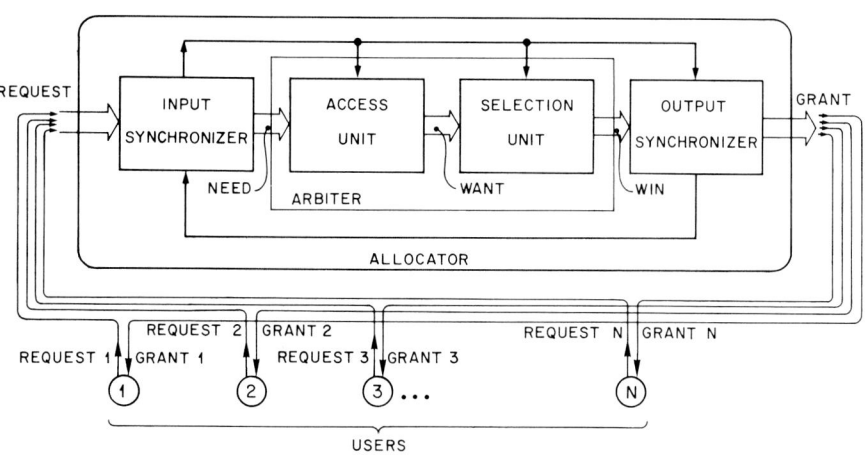

*Fig. 5.3 Complete model of an exclusive access system*

Since the requests may come from asynchronous masters or may be asynchronous because of propagation delays, the first unit, the INPUT SYNCHRONIZER, provides a time reference for the following blocks. It basically prevents the arrival of new requests while the arbitration logic is making a decision. This function is discussed in more detail in section 5.4.1.

After this, an ARBITRER selects the user which will be served in the next access cycle. This subsystem is composed of an ACCESS UNIT, which orders the requests in a way that corresponds to the service sequence. This order may be based on the arrival time, on the identity of the requesters, or both, as defined by the ACCESS POLICY of the system. The access scheme also defines the temporal behaviour of the allocator, or, more precisely, the access policy gives some information on how long a device will wait for the resource.

The second part of the arbiter is a SELECTION unit, which picks the WANT (request) on the top of the service queue and activates the corresponding WIN output (resource). Complete arbitration circuits (that is including the access and the selection units) are described in section 5.3. The resource (the bus) may be assigned to a new requester only after the previous user has completed its operations. Grants must therefore be synchronized with the activities performed on the resource: this job is accomplished by an OUTPUT SYNCHRONIZER, which somehow knows the state (BUSY or AVAILABLE) of the resource. More details on output synchronization are given in section 5.4.2. The various exclusive access techniques correspond to different types of behaviour associated with the model shown in figure 5.3. The basic choices are:

- The resource requests bypass the arbitration logic and go directly to the output synchronizer. The access starts with a resource occupation phase; if many users are occupying the resource, a collision is detected, the bus released and, in order to avoid any loss of information, the transfer is re-attempted. If no collision is detected within a defined amount of time, meaning that only a single user wants to use the bus, this particular user is finally granted the bus. This is called COLLISION DETECTION: the basic technique is described in section 5.1.5; since it is used mainly in serial buses, more details are given in Chapter 10.

- The allocator does not know the identity of the requesters or, even, does not know at all that some requests are pending. Therefore, the resource can be assigned only by routing the grant through all possible requesters. The grant is carried by a TOKEN; this technique is called TOKEN PASSING and is described in sections 5.1.3 and 5.1.4. This basic mechanism can be used with any allocation technique with only minor variations, using D flip-flops or other registers to switch the grants only at well-defined times, as shown in figure 5.4a. In most cases, these registers can be clocked directly by the BUSY signal. In a distributed arbiter, the synchronization logic is divided into single flip-flops placed on each unit, as shown in figure 5.4b.

- Each user has an independent request signal, which goes to the allocator which can thus identify active requesters. After the input synchronization, the arbiter (access and selection units) makes a decision on which request to serve first, and the output synchronizer takes care of the resource switching. This technique is called ARBITRATION. Since it is used quite often in parallel buses, it is described in detail in sections 5.2 and 5.3.

We can again use the example of a human discussion to illustrate the various exclusive access techniques. In a meeting, the right to speak could be routed to all participants in a sequence according to their position around the table. This describes the TOKEN PASSING technique; it would not work in a large assembly, however, because most of the time would be spent just asking people if they had something to say. Another possibility is to allow people to start talking in an autonomous way, when the current speaker has finished. In this case many people may start to talk at the same time; but as soon as one senses that others are active too (COLLISION DETECTION), one stops, waits, and starts again. A more efficient way of communicating in a large group could be to require people to raise their hands if they wished to speak (this is a REQUEST), and then to have a higher authority (the ARBITER) select the next speaker.

### 5.1.3 Sequential token passing

The simplest allocation technique is an a priori assignment of the resource: a unique "right to use" is granted in turn to each unit, without considering if it actually made a resource request or not. This right can be seen as a TOKEN; only the user that owns the token has the grant and can thus access the resource. Since only one token can circulate in the system, the resource is automatically granted to only one requester at a time. No contention can arise, and this SEQUENTIAL TOKEN PASSING technique guarantees that collisions are avoided. A sequential token passing allocator does not need to know if any request is pending. We can model it as shown in figure 5.4; the resource requests are always active and the input synchronizer is not needed.

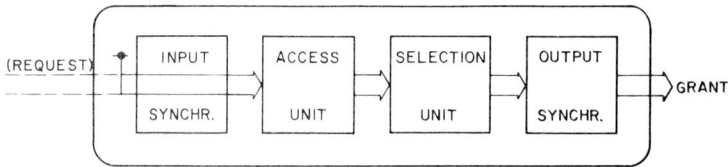

Fig. 5.4 Model of sequential token passing allocator

# 5 Multiple-master Buses

The token passing operation can be handled by a centralized controller which sends the token to all potential users sequentially. This process requires the selection of the specific unit which will next receive the token. It is therefore similar to an addressing operation and can be performed using the protocols already described in Chapter 4.

Another possibility is to handle the token in a fully distributed way: each master module passes the token directly to another without going through the centralized control unit. In serial buses, for example, the token is carried in the form of a message, sent by the controller to all the masters sequentially (centralized allocation), or by the current master to the next potential master (distributed allocation). This is called an EXPLICIT MASTERSHIP TRANSFER. The message is sometimes transmitted in a "piggy-back" configuration with the last useful piece of information. In some cases, the message is transmitted by default, e.g. each device keeps track of the activity on the bus to see whether a master has used its time slot or not.

Using distributed token passing, a procedure must guarantee the presence of one and only one token in the system. If the token were lost, for example, no unit could use the resource, while if it were duplicated, two users might be granted the bus at the same time and a collision would occur. Therefore, in order to avoid multiple tokens or none at all, all distributed token passing structures also include an arbitration or a collision detection system, which is used to generate a single token at startup or in the case of a fault.

A fixed time-slot bus can be seen as an example of a centralized token-passing bus control. The bus is sequentially assigned to each unit for a pre-defined time interval, as shown in figure 5.5.

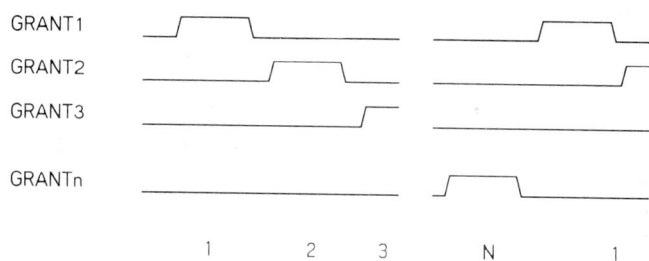

Fig. 5.5 Assignment of the bus to N users in fixed time slots

The token is generally passed in the same order as that of the device identifier, that is, it follows a ROUND ROBIN scheme, but it could also be passed in a random order. The round robin technique guarantees each device a maximum access time which is equal to the sum of all of the participants' maximum resource use time.

Since the worst-case wait time may be too long for some users, the access unit may follow another policy called STRICT PRIORITY. A rank (priority) is assigned to each device, and the token is always returned after use to the device with the highest priority, or is passed along according to a scheme which favours higher priority units. Some examples are shown in figure 5.6.

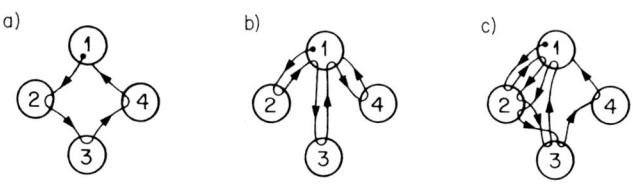

*Fig. 5.6 Token passing schemes and service sequences*
  *a) Round robin: 1,2,3,4,1,2,...*
  *b) Priority: 1,2,1,3,1,4,1,2,1,3,1,...*
  *c) Priority: 1,2,1,2,3,1,2,3,4,1,2,1,...*

### 5.1.4 Switch-on-demand token passing

In the example of figure 5.6, the allocator passes the token in a fixed sequence. The granted user has no control of the token itself, that is, it cannot "send" the token back if no request is pending. A handshake structure as shown in figure 5.7a may be used to improve the efficiency of the system. In this case, the unit that receives the token without having requested the resource would return the token by activating the GRANTACK signal, while a unit which has a pending request would receive and use the resource, then release it, activating the GRANTACK signal.

Another improvement of the token passing technique calls for a procedure which does not pass along the token until there is a request for it. Thus, a device which repeatedly requests the resource, which would be probable in parallel buses, can use the resource without giving back the token and waiting for it to return again; it keeps the token as long as no other device requests the resource. In this case, the allocator must know that a request is pending through a generalized request signal. In parallel buses, this BUSREQUEST signal is the OR of all individual user requests, and is usually implemented with a wired-OR line. This technique is called RELEASE ON DEMAND; it reduces the average waiting time, not the maximum wait time. An example of release on demand token passing is shown in figure 5.7b.

## 5 Multiple-master Buses

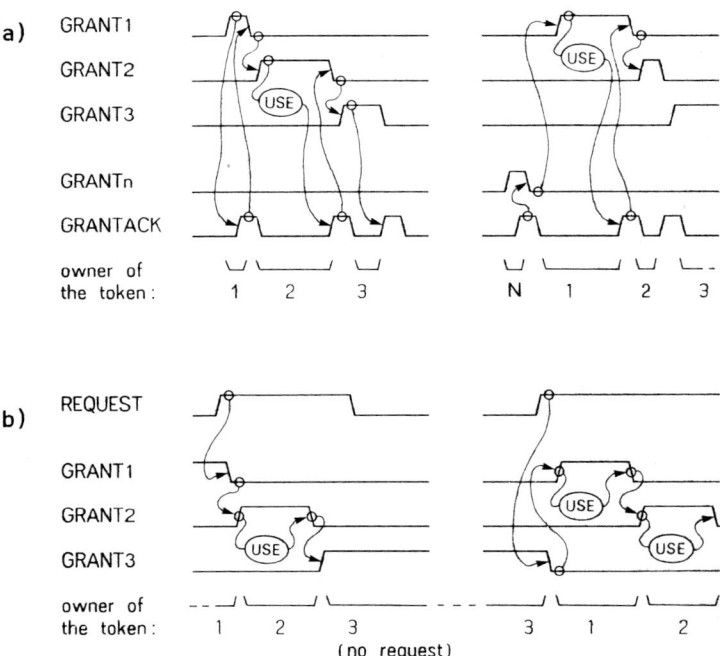

*Fig. 5.7 Modified token passing schemes*
  *a) Handshaken grant*
  *b) Release on demand*

The necessary allocator to implement release on demand token passing is shown in figure 5.8. The access unit is informed that one or more requests are pending, but does not know the identity of the requesters.

A combination of the release on demand procedure and the priority operation can reduce the average access time of some units

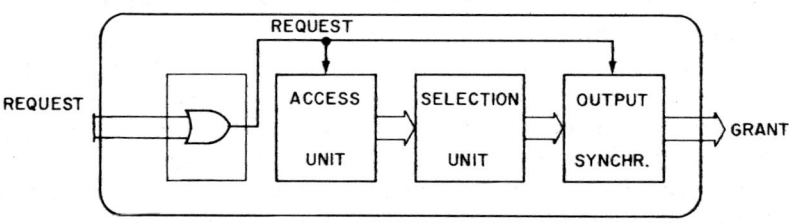

*Fig. 5.8 Release on demand allocator*

even further: the token would be stationed at the device with the highest priority and would only be circulated upon request.

In all priority schemes, the priority of each user is internally known to the allocator. Note that the priority is not a property of the requester; for instance, if a device is allowed to change its priority, then this mechanism must be handled as part of the allocator itself, since this change would influence all users. Priority by itself is not a goal; it is introduced as a means to achieve an access policy: devices whose functions are time-critical, for example, receive a higher priority in order to reduce their waiting time.

### 5.1.5  Multiple access by collision detection

With the collision detection technique, requests are directly mapped into WIN signals and synchronized only with resource activity, as shown in figure 5.9.

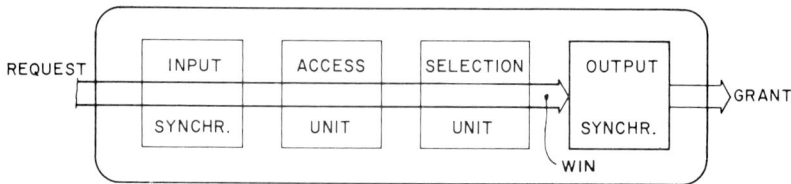

*Fig. 5.9  Collision detection allocator*

Each requesting unit is therefore able to use the resource as soon as it becomes available. Due to the propagation delay and the finite amount of time required to make a decision (see Chapter 8), a requester may see the resource as being available even if another one has already started to use it. This may cause a collision which would be detected by the users which, in turn, would release the resource. In order to avoid a loss of information caused by these collisions, the most recent transfers would be repeated. The simplified sequence of elementary operations for collision detection is the following:

- a requester checks if the resource is in use (busy), for instance, by means of carrier sense circuitry;
- if busy, the requester waits; if free, it starts to use the resource and monitors possible collisions;
- if a collision is detected, the access is aborted; the user frees the resource and retries after some time;
- if no collision is detected, the requester continues to use the resource until the end of the operation.

# 5 Multiple-master Buses 137

An example is shown in figure 5.10: due to the delay from "sense free" (action 1 and 2) to "signal busy" (actions 3 and 4), the two requesters both find the resource free and start to use it. This collision is detected (5), and both users abort the operations. Then requester 1 tries again (6) to use the resource and receives it (7); the other requester tries a little later (8), sees that the resource is busy, and waits.

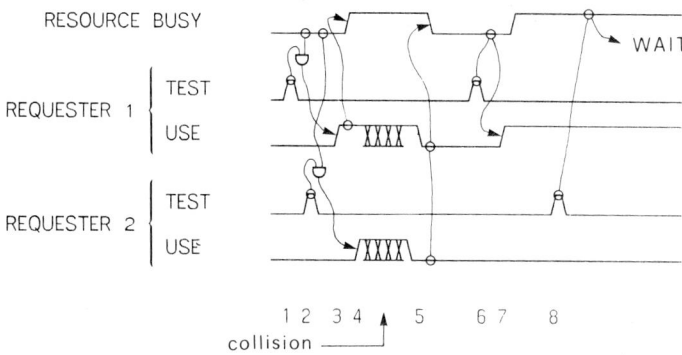

*Fig. 5.10 Collision between two requesters*

A collision may therefore occur only at the beginning of an operation, when a user tries to OCCUPY the bus. The duration of this OCCUPATION PHASE thus defines a COLLISION WINDOW which depends on the maximum propagation delay of the system and on the speed of the interfaces. A late collision is not part of the allocation scheme, and would thus be considered an error. In some cases, the occupation phase may contain part of, or be all of, the message.

Since the collision detection procedure involves an abort-and-retry process, the interfaces of the communicating units must be able to handle operations such as message buffering and trial count, and must also be able to manage recovery procedures. For these reasons, collision detection is mainly used on serial communication systems, where each unit owns a link controller and a processor which takes care of higher protocol layers, in order to guarantee information integrity. The busy logic is fully distributed in this case; each unit is able to detect the status of the resource and the collision conditions by looking at the information channel.

On the lower level, collision detection is sometimes used inside the bus arbitration mechanism itself. An example of a collision-based arbitration technique is described in section 5.3.5.

## 5.2 EXCLUSIVE ACCESS BY ARBITRATION

Another way to handle multiple accesses is to avoid collisions by assigning the resource to only one of the requesters. In this case, the allocator must be able to detect pending requests and, in addition, the identities of the requesters. This technique, called *ARBITRATION*, is widely used in parallel buses, because it can be implemented very easily and quickly : no protocol overhead for abort-and-retry is required, nor is any time wasted giving the token to non-requesting units or aborting the transfer. The actual difference between the token passing method and arbitration technique is that in the former, the identities of the requesters are not known.

### 5.2.1 FIFO resource handling

Since the identities of the requesters are known, a possible access policy would serve first the request which arrived first and queue the others in the sequence that they arrive. After the first user has released the resource, it is granted to the requester which arrived second, and so on. This strategy is called *FCFS (First Come First Served)* or *FIFO (First In First Out)*. The sequence of operations in a FIFO allocator is shown in figure 5.11 : the arrival and service sequences are the same (2, 4, 3, 1).

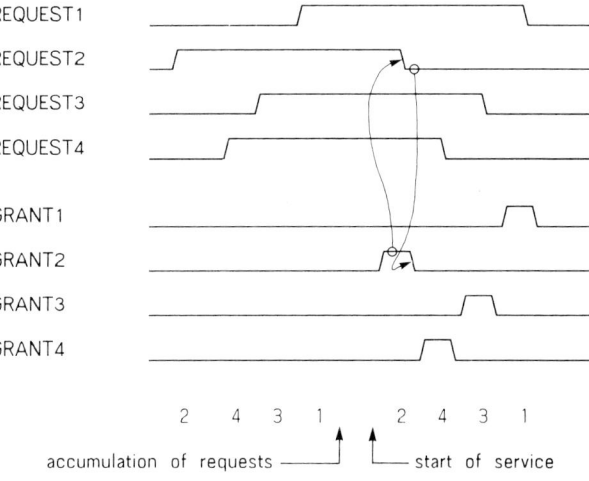

*Fig. 5.11 Example of FIFO resource handling with 4 requests*

# 5 Multiple-master Buses

In principle, this scheme would give all participants an equal opportunity to use the bus, but no maximum access time can be guaranteed if a device can keep the resource continuously.

## 5.2.2 Fixed priority arbiters

An allocator is not concerned with time, as long as it can distingush the order of the requests. But if the requests are spaced too closely together, the input synchronizer might not be able to distinguish which one comes first. Time could always be sliced sufficiently small so that there will always be a time difference between two events, if not, for example, by 1 $\mu s$, then by 1 ns or by 1 ps, but real systems have a finite time resolution called a *SLOT TIME*. In asynchronous (non-clocked) systems, the slot time depends on the speed of the logic devices and on the physical size of the system. In synchronous systems, it is related to the clock rate, because the sequence of events within the same clock period cannot be distinguished. Thus, any signals that are spaced together too closely could not be ordered by this system.

When information on the arrival time is not available, we must use other techniques to produce the service sequence. Any such ordering process introduces a hierarchy among the requests: when two or more of them are active, the highest ranked one is granted first, and the others will follow in sequence of decreasing rank. This is the same *PRIORITY* concept already mentioned in section 5.1.3, and the structure becomes a *PRIORITY ARBITER*.

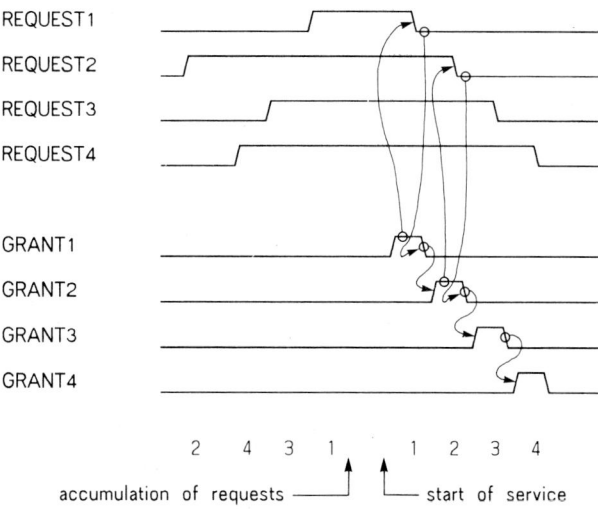

*Fig. 5.12 Example of priority resource handling with 4 requests*

The access policy defines the ordering rule, that is, the way the access unit gives a priority code to a request. The sequence of operations with a priority allocator is shown in figure 5.12. The arrival sequence is the same as that of figure 5.11, but the service sequence is 1, 2, 3, 4 (1 corresponds to the highest priority).

A priority ranking mechanism is not required in a FIFO arbiter as long as the requests can be assigned to different time slots. If the requests are filtered or synchronized before the allocator in such a way as to guarantee the above-mentioned condition, the access unit would become a pure FIFO queue handler. A more detailed analysis (see section 5.4.1) shows, however, that this is only possible if part of the allocator (at least the input synchronizer) is distributed to the users.

On the other hand, we can use the priority arbitration method even when requests cannot be separated in time. This is actually the case in the example of figure 5.12: the states of the requests are sampled just before the selection of the next user. Any information on the arrival sequence is thus lost, and the only criterion in selecting the service sequence is priority.

### 5.2.3 Variable-priority arbiters

A strict priority scheme leads to the problem of STARVATION: the low priority requesters may be excluded from using the resource if high priority devices alternate with their control of it. An example of

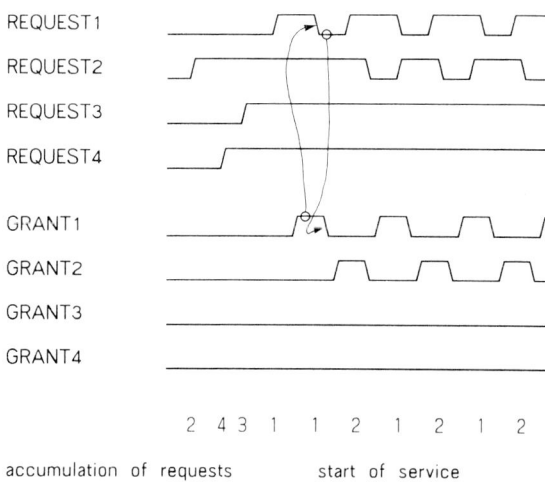

*Fig. 5.13 Example of starvation*

starvation is given in figure 5.13: requests from units 3 and 4 are never served, because higher priority units (1 and 2) continue to make new requests.

Because of these possible occurrences, it is impossible to guarantee an upper limit to the service time of any request. This constraint is not acceptable in real-time systems, which must complete some activities within pre-defined time delays. This problem did not exist for the token passing schemes discussed in sections 5.1.3 and 5.1.4, because of the fixed service sequence, even if it gave more opportunities to some devices, it would guarantee every unit a finite service time.

A starvation-free allocator is *FAIR*, that is, its access unit follows some *FAIRNESS* rule, such as to:
- raise the priority of the requesters which have been waiting too long;
- lower the priority of the requesters which have already been served;
- redistribute all priorities at every service, either randomly or in a regular way;
- inhibit new requests until all pending requests are served.

Some examples of these techniques are shown in figure 5.14. At the start of the service, REQUEST1 has the highest priority and is honoured. In order to show the effects of the various strategies, we assume that new requests are continuously being made by users 1 and 2.

Figure 5.14a illustrates the *TIMEOUT* technique: the priority of REQUEST4, which has been waiting for a long time, is raised and will be served immediately; the same then happens for REQUEST3. In figure 5.14b, the requests of served users are ignored until there are no more pending requests; this is called *MASKING*. If the priority of the last-served user is lowered and, at the same time, all other requests are raised by one step, as shown in figure 5.14c, we get *CIRCULAR PRIORITY* or a *ROUND ROBIN* sequence.

All the techniques shown in figure 5.14 are fair, because they guarantee in any case an upper limit to the service time even for low-priority requests. There are, however, differences in the actual service sequence; the last two techniques provide the same sequence and may be considered only different implementations of the basic round-robin scheme.

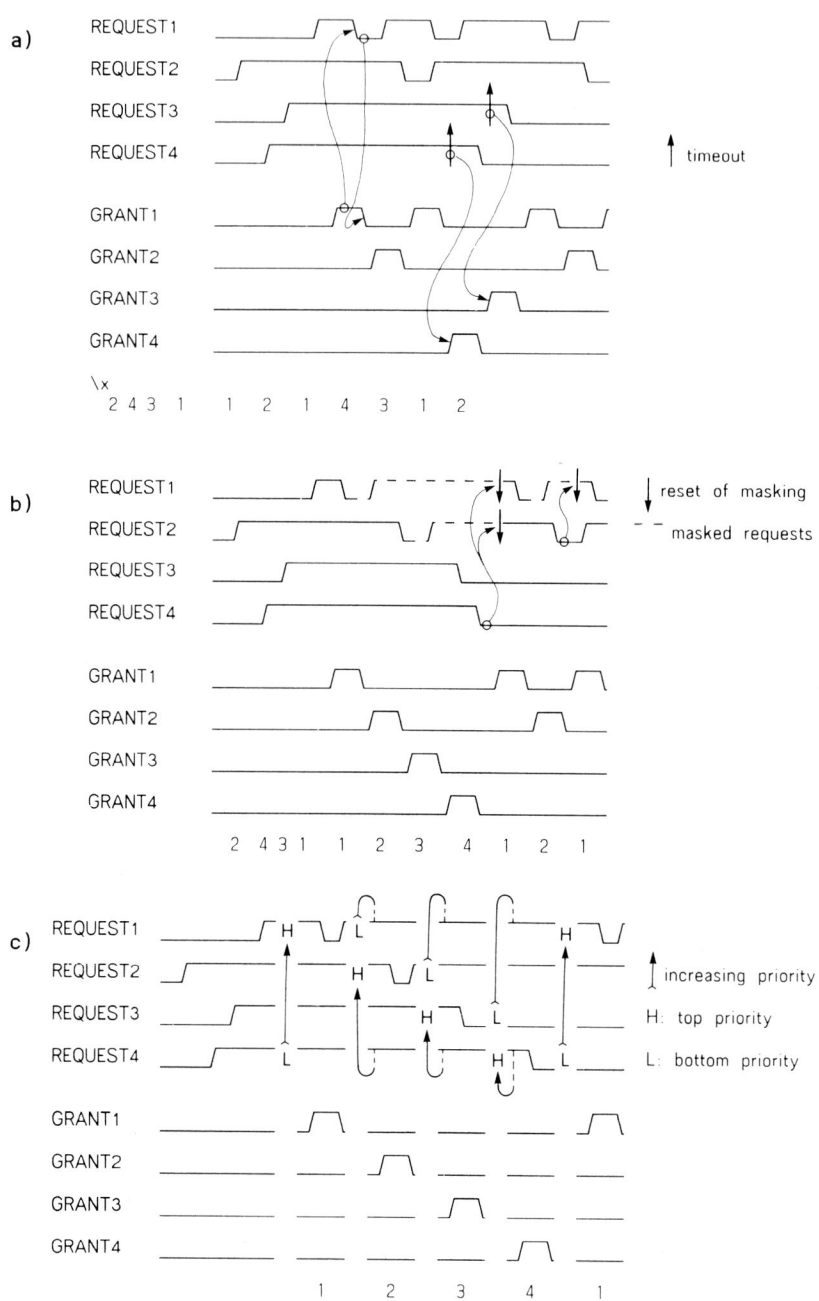

*Fig. 5.14 Service sequences with variable-priority allocation in the 4-user system*
  *a) time out: 1,2,1,4,3,1,2*
  *b) masking of served requests: 1,2,3,4,1,2,1*
  *c) round-robin redistribution: 1,2,3,4,1*

It must also be pointed out that any variable-priority approach has to guarantee that, at all times, each requester has a unique priority level. This is automatically achieved if priority is handled only by the access unit.

## 5.3 ARBITRATION CIRCUITS

Many different techniques are used to build the four parts of an allocator. Various choices exist for the allocation policy and for synchronization, while all selection circuits can be seen as different implementations of the same basic priority logic. The distinction centralized/distributed is mostly a matter of scale; if we looked inside a centralized arbiter closely, we would find the same logic as that of a distributed one. At a higher level, a distributed allocator is seen as a unique logic unit.

This section will give general classification criteria and examples of the most common circuits used inside a selection unit. Some of the arbitration circuits discussed here can be modelled as hardware implementations of token passing (daisy chain, section 5.3.2), or collision detection (self-selection, section 5.3.4).

### 5.3.1 Arbitration structures

A single allocator, and therefore a single arbiter, must be associated with each multiple access resource. The basic implementation choices are shown in figure 5.15; the usual terms CENTRALIZED, and DECENTRALIZED or DISTRIBUTED refer to fully centralized or fully distributed structures, although in some cases, for instance we might find distributed access logic tied to a centralized selection unit.

Centralized arbiters are selected mainly when the number of users is fixed or limited. Distributed arbiters use a set of identical units with modular connection structures, such as the bus, and are generally selected for more complex systems. Contrary to what is often written, the unreliability of a centralized structure is not a motivation for choosing a distributed one. In fact, a malfunctioning module connected to a single bus could do just as much harm, and in a distributed system there are several of them.

We shall now review the basic implementation techniques for arbitration systems. They are ordered according to the degree of centralization. The usable access policies are also discussed for each type.

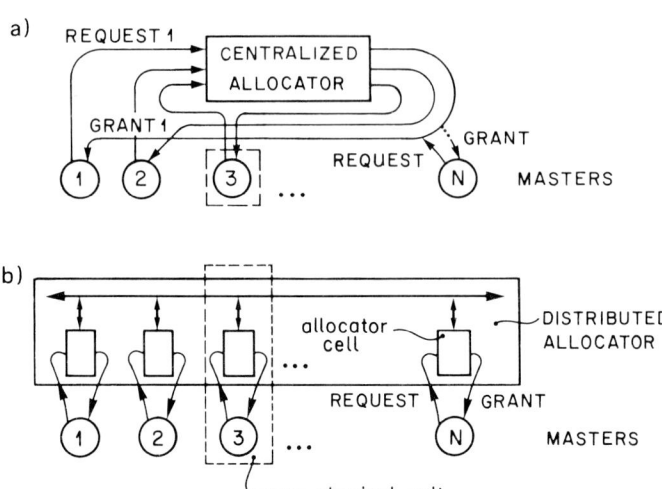

Fig. 5.15 Arbitration structures
a) Centralized
b) Distributed

## 5.3.2 Basic priority circuits

The selection logic of a centralized arbiter is a standard priority circuit. For other circuits (as for adders), we can choose between two implementation approaches: ripple or look-ahead, as shown in figure 5.16. The look-ahead logic is faster but requires different and more complex parts. The ripple logic has a regular structure but is slower.

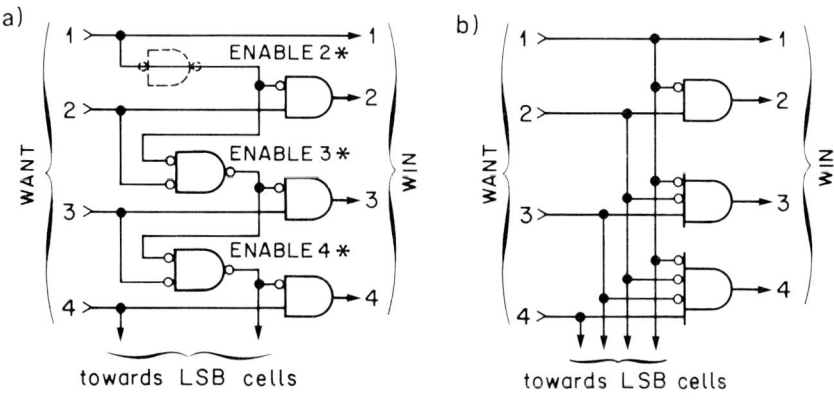

Fig. 5.16 Priority circuits
a) Ripple logic
b) Look-ahead logic

## 5 Multiple-master Buses

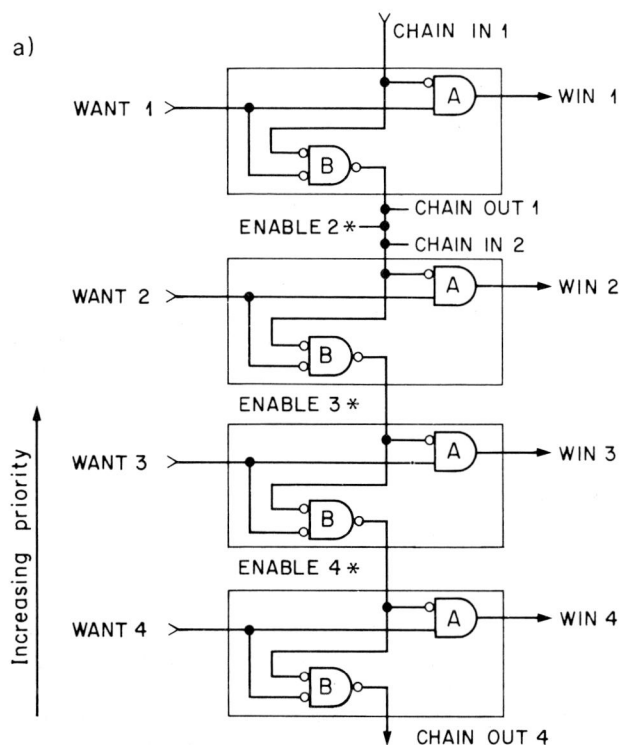

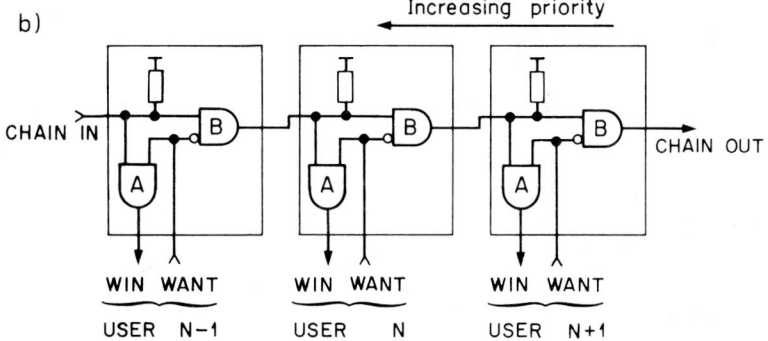

*Fig. 5.17 Daisy chain circuits*
  *a) Redrawing of the ripple priority logic as a modular chain*
  *b) Active high chain for TTL logic*

In order to achieve a variable-priority system, the access unit would simply be made to modify the mapping of a NEED into a WANT, according to a suitable priority change algorithm. The implementation of the selection logic into a centralized unit is not the most convenient choice for bussed systems, because in order to arbitrate and select N users, we must use $2 \cdot N$ point-to-point connections for the WANT/WIN pairs, organized with a star topology. This arbiter is often used, however, because of its simplicity and speed. A centralized access unit may guarantee the uniqueness of the priority levels, giving more freedom in the rules for changing a priority.

Some complete arbitration-based allocators for up to 8 requesters are available as single integrated devices. A centralized arbiter is used, for instance, in the MULTIBUS 1 (see Appendix). It is possible to reduce the number of lines used by a centralized arbiter by encoding the WIN outputs. A WINVALID signal would then be required to deskew the transmission of encoded WIN signals (see section 3.2.1). The same can be done with GRANT signals, while REQUESTs cannot be encoded because many of them may be active at the same time.

### 5.3.3 Daisy chain arbiters

If the ripple priority logic shown in figure 5.16b is divided into separate cells distributed among the users, as in figure 5.17a, we obtain the basic DAISY CHAIN arbitration structure. The daisy chain is an example of a distributed arbiter, obtained directly from the centralized one. The ENABLE* signal ripples from each unit to the next one; when it is deactivated by a requester, the lower priority grants are inhibited. When the chain is implemented using TTL logic, the polarity of the signals is usually reversed in order to allow the use of pull-up resistors at uncommited CHAIN IN inputs. A TTL daisy chain is shown in figure 5.17b.

The daisy chain does not use bussed lines, but a backplane can be organized easily to carry the chain signals properly. It is more

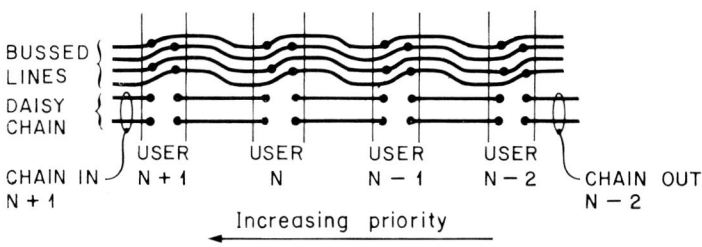

*Fig. 5.18 Example of backplane layout with two daisy chains*

# 5 Multiple-master Buses 147

difficult to obtain the chained wiring using flat cables. An example of a backplane layout with lines reserved for daisy chains is given in figure 5.18.

The chain must be continuous: in a broken chain, a requester in each trunk would receive the grant, as shown in figure 5.19. The boards which do not use the chain arbitration system must have a direct connection from CHAIN IN to CHAIN OUT, and dummy boards with the same direct connection must be inserted in the empty slots of the backplane in order to propagate the chain.

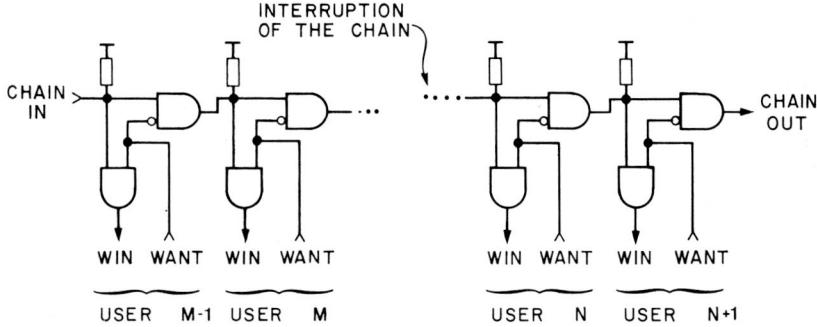

*Fig. 5.19 Broken daisy chain. If all requests are active, both users M and N are granted the resource*

In a daisy chain, the priority of each requester is fixed, because it depends on the physical position of the unit in the backplane. Starvation can be avoided by using closed loop chains with rotating priorities [ROET77], [CIVE82]. In this case, the access logic becomes a sequential machine in which the top priority level, that is the input of the chain, is routed sequentially to all requesters, for instance as shown in figure 5.20.

Another possibility is to use distributed fairness logic, that is, to mask new requests from served units until all pending requests are served, as discussed in section 5.4.2.

The arbitration speed of a daisy chain is proportional to the number of users. The daisy chain is slower than a centralized ripple priority arbiter for the same number of users, because the enable signals must propagate from board to board. A daisy-chain arbiter uses very few lines in the backplane, has simple circuitry, and is fully modular. New users can be added simply by inserting them into the chain in the position which corresponds to their priority.

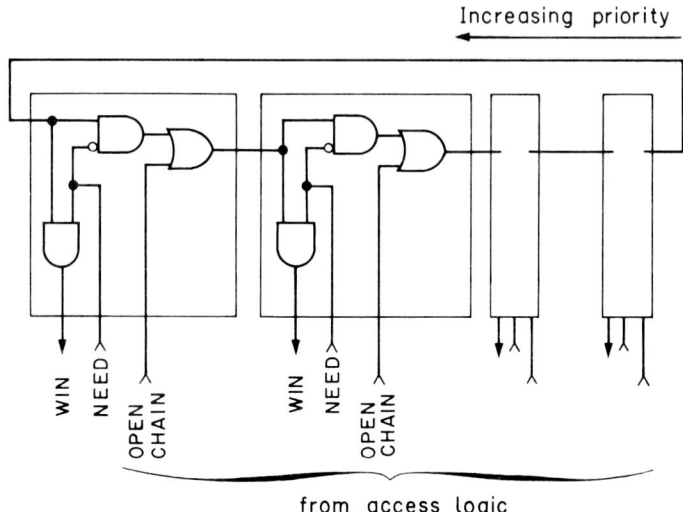

Fig. 5.20 Closed loop daisy chain with rotating priorities

On the other hand, the chain has a strictly fixed priority, requires continuity boards, and a special layout for at least one backplane line. Another drawback is that the identity of the commander is not visible: we cannot identify the winner of an arbitration by looking at the bus signals available at any slot.

Fixed priority daisy chain arbiters are used, for instance, in MULTIBUS 1, MUBUS, Unibus (see Appendix and [UNI75]), and in the Z80 family of devices.

### 5.3.4 The linear self-selection arbiter

A distributed self-selection arbiter can be obtained directly from the basic centralized arbiter by distributing the priority logic of figure 5.16 to the various users.

We shall call this structure a LINEAR DISTRIBUTED ARBITER. Since each unit decodes the grant with its own logic, this structure is also called a LINEAR SELF-SELECTION NETWORK. Figures 5.21a and 5.21b show the ripple and the look-ahead implementation, respectively, of the linear distributed arbiter. We can easily verify that the ripple self-selection arbiter is actually a daisy chain with a bus line assigned to each CHAIN-IN/CHAIN-OUT pair. Here, the access unit is the connection between the module requests and the bussed request lines. As for any arbitration scheme, a fairness structure can be used at this point.

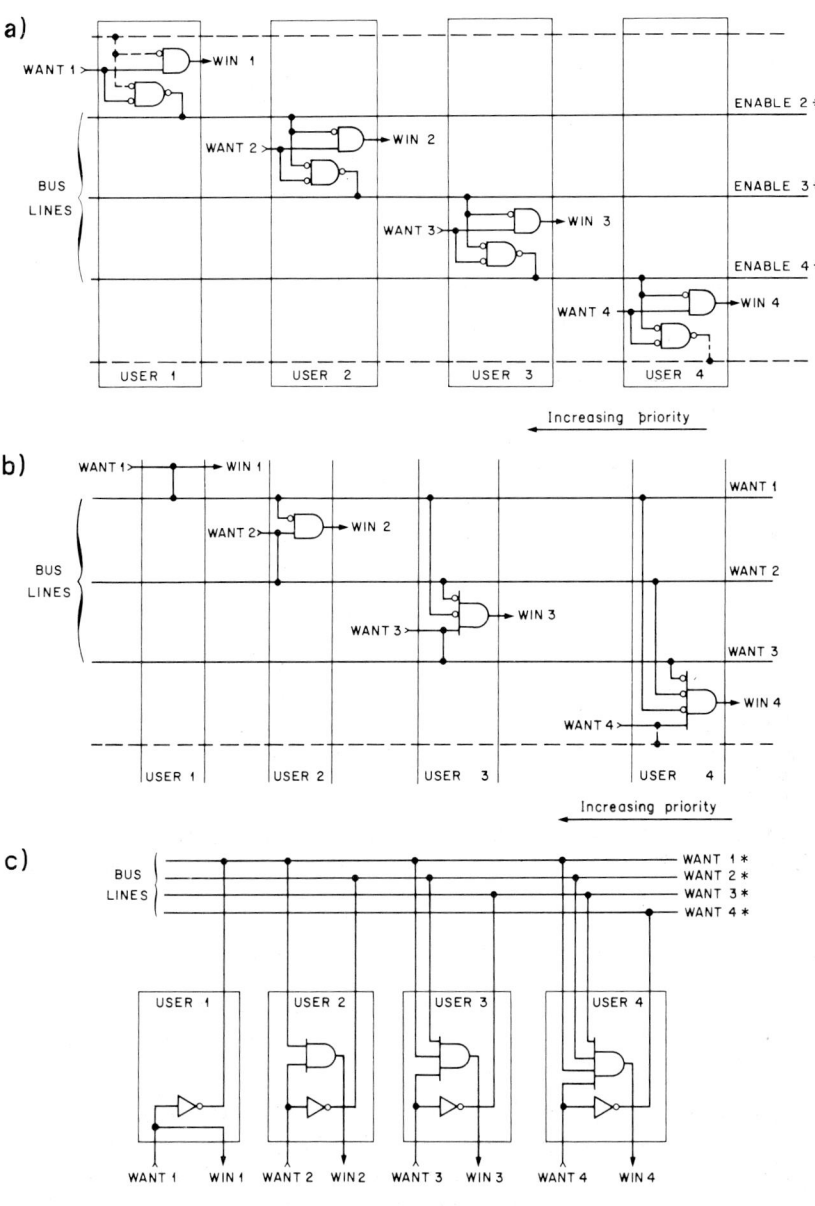

*Fig. 5.21 Linear self-selection distributed arbiters*
  *a) Ripple circuit*
  *b) Look-ahead circuit*
  *c) Inverted look-ahead (TTL implementation)*

Using TTL logic, the bus carries inverted requests, as shown in figure 5.21c, in order to mate the default level (high) with not-active requests. If we compare this linear distributed arbiter with the centralized one, we find that the local generation of grants cuts in half the number of bus lines used by the arbiter (N bus lines in figure 5.21 against 2 N in figure 5.16). For the same reason, this circuit is faster than the one using centralized units because only the requests must propagate on the backplane.

A linear self-selection allocation structure is used, for instance, in the DEC Synchronous Backplane Interconnect (SBI) [SBI78].

### 5.3.5 The coded self-selection arbiter

The number of bussed lines used by a self-selection arbiter can be reduced by encoding the requests: instead of assigning a reserved line to each user, we assign to it a binary code corresponding to its

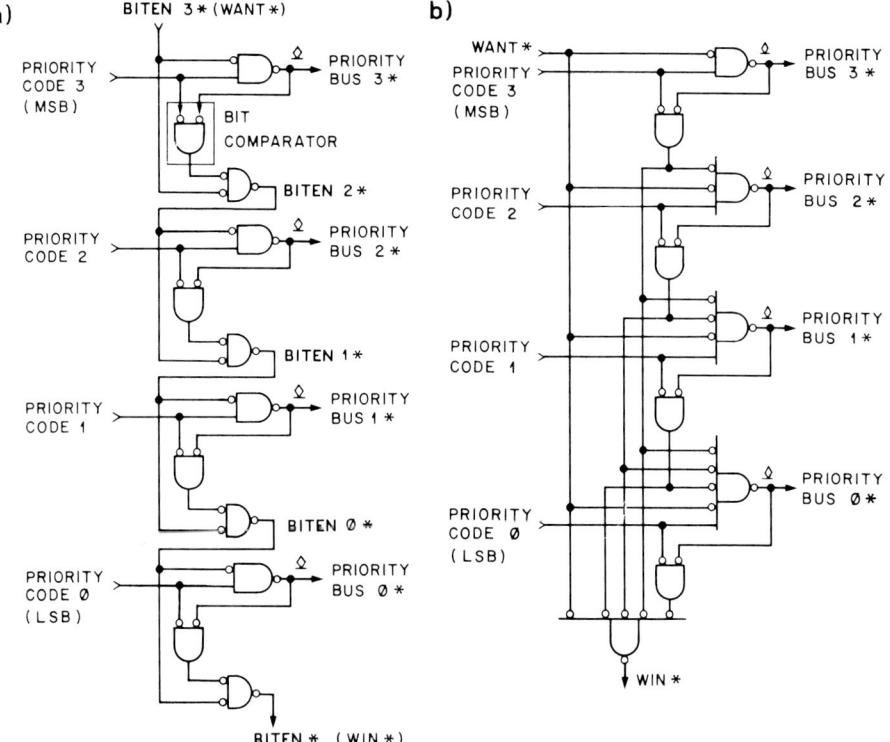

Fig. 5.22 Encoded self-selection distributed arbiters
 a) Ripple circuit
 b) Look ahead circuit

# 5 Multiple-master Buses 151

priority. With this approach, an N-bit code carried by N lines can distingush $2^N$ requesters, and we get an ENCODED DISTRIBUTED ARBITER [TAUB76]. The encoded distributed self-selection arbiter is composed of many identical units with different priority codes. These units drive, through open collector gates, a PRIORITY BUS (PRBUS), and compare the code read from this bus with their own PRIORITY CODE (PRCOD).

After a self-selection process, detailed in the following, the priority bus carries the code of the highest priority unit. This unit wins the arbitration and is allowed to become commander for the following operations. We shall discuss only the circuits that handle 4-bit codes here, but the same technique can be extended towards any number of lines. The diagram of a 4-bit ripple priority network for an encoded distributed arbiter is shown in figure 5.23a.

Let us now examine in more detail the behaviour of a self-selection network, looking at the circuit shown inf figure 5.22a. The priority code PRCOD is gated, with an inversion, to the priority bus PRBUS* only if the bit enable signals BITEN* are low for each bit. Since the PRBUS* lines are driven by open collector gates, we get on each of them the logic NOR of the corresponding bit of the enabled priority codes. That is, the PRBUS$_i$* line goes to the low level if at least one of the PRCOD$_i$ is high and is enabled by BITEN$_i$*. PRBUS$_i$* goes high only if all PRCOD$_i$ are low, or are disabled by BITEN$_i$*.

The logic level on each PRBUS* line is compared in each priority network to the corresponding bit of the vector PRCOD. The truth table of a comparison cell is shown in figure 5.23.

| PRCOD$_i$ | PRBUS*$_i$ | BITEN*$_i$ | BITEN*$_{i+1}$ |
|---|---|---|---|
| low | low | low | high |
| low | low | high | high |
| low | high | low | low |
| low | high | high | high |
| high | low | low | low |
| high | low | high | low |
| high | high | low | – |
| high | high | high | high |

*Fig. 5.23 Truth table of the coded self-selection logic*

When a disagreement on bit i is detected, the disable signal BITEN$_{i-1}$ is activated. Since this signal ripples towards the LSBs, all gates which drive lines $PRBUS_j*$ with $j<i$ are disabled. Due to the propagation of BITEN* from MSB to LSB, BITEN* from LSB is low only if all $BITEN_i*$ are low and if $PRBUS_0 = PRCOD_0$. This happens only if BITEN for MSB is high (BITEN* is low), and if the priority code PRCOD of the network is the complement of the code on PRBUS* lines. The BITEN from the LSB can therefore be used as a grant (not yet synchronized) to the highest priority requester. The BITEN to the MSB is made true when the unit wants to participate in the arbitration, and corresponds to the WANT input signal. The BITEN from the LSB is high when the unit has the highest priority among those arbitrating, and corresponds to the WIN output.

The encoded selection logic is obtained by adding a bit comparator gate to the centralized ripple priority circuit; this gate automatically disables LSBs whenever a collision is detected between the local priority code PRCOD and the priority bus PRBUS. Since the low level prevails on the open collector lines, and there is an inversion between PRCOD and PRBUS, the collision corresponds to a (low,low) condition, and the bit comparator may thus consist of a simple AND gate.

The arbitration delay of a self-selection system depends mainly on the time required to resolve the bit contention on the priority bus, and is therefore related to gate delays, settling and propagation time on bussed lines, and to the configuration of priority codes. It has been found that the worst-case delay is roughly proportional to the number of priority bits [TAUB82], [TAUB84], and can be reduced by using only a subset of codes [DELC84]. This last technique is applied in MULTIBUS 2 (see Appendix).

The priority network can be implemented using ripple logic, as already discussed, or using look-ahead logic, as in figure 5.22b. Since in most cases, gate delays are far lower than the propagation and settling times on the bus, there is no real speed benefit in the look-ahead circuit. It is also possible to serialize the self-selection process on a single line, without a significant increase in the selection time. This last technique is used with serial buses and will be discussed in Chapter 10.

The encoded self-selection arbiter requires more logic than the centralized one or than a daisy chain, but has some important benefits. For a given number of users, it needs fewer lines than the centralized logic, is faster than the daisy chain and, most importantly, the priority level of a user depends only on a code which can be easily changed at any time. Moreover, the identity of the arbitration winner can be read by any other unit from the bussed priority lines.

The access unit, in this case, selects the priority codes, and may implement a fair policy with the circuit described in section 5.4.2.

Distributed self-selection arbiters are used, for instance, in S100 [S10079], FASTBUS [FAST81], P896 [P89683], G96 [G9684] and M3 (see Appendix).

### 5.3.6 Mixed arbitration techniques

The arbitration techniques discussed in sections 5.3.1 to 5.3.4 can also be mixed, in order to gather the benefits and avoid the drawbacks of a single method. A widely used example of a mixed arbiter is the multi-level daisy chain, shown in figure 5.24. Instead of the single chain, which ripples through all units, we find here a set of independent chains which may bypass some units and which finally go into a centralized arbiter. Each chain is used only by a subset of users, and resolves the contention among them. The centralized allocator discriminates between requests from different chains.

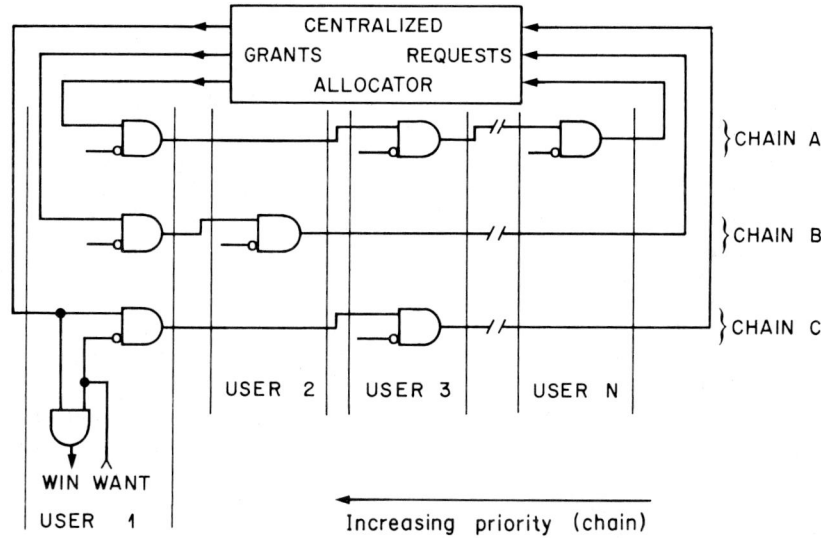

*Fig. 5.24 Multiple daisy chain*

This structure is more flexible than that of the single chain, because the priority of a user can be changed either by moving it to another chain, or by changing the priority of its chain in the central arbiter. The arbitration delay is shorter because fewer units are chained. This technique is used, for instance, in UNIBUS [UNI75] and in VME [VME82] (see Appendix).

Multiplexed self-selection schemes have been proposed, as a compromise between speed and the number of lines. Both linear and coded circuits can be used in each stage: for instance, a 4-line system allows arbitration in two time slots : either $4 \cdot 4 = 16$ requests with linear logic, or $2^4 \cdot 2^4 = 256$ requests with coded logic.

## 5.4 THE SYNCHRONIZATION PROBLEM

Let us now focus our attention on two units which are common to any exclusive access system, the synchronizers and the fairness logic. Synchronizers carry out the lowest exclusion operation; the selection logic only works if the inputs are properly synchronized. They are required because in the general case we must consider all signals as asynchronous, i.e. without any fixed timing relationship.

This section will also show that fairness can be implemented in any allocator, provided that information on pending requests (e.g. the BUSREQUEST signal) is available.

### 5.4.1 The basic exclusion mechanism

The arbiter must decide which input to select using a combinatorial circuit, such as a priority encoder. But since any logic circuit has a non-zero propagation time, what would happen if the inputs change state while the selection process was under way? The probability that such a situation could occur cannot be neglected. The outcome may be that several devices start using the resource at the same time, causing a collision.

The basic technique that prevents such a situation is called *INPUT SYNCHRONIZATION*. A participant should be prevented from intervening in a selection process which has started until it is finished. This is achieved by using a basic exclusion method which could be called "close behind you". The signal which initiates the selection process should freeze all the inputs, as implemented using the circuit shown in figure 5.25, for instance.

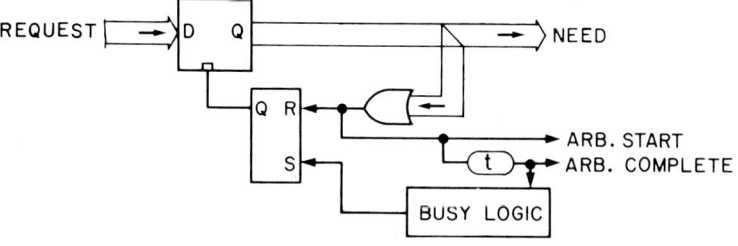

Fig. 5.25 Example of input synchronizer

# 5 Multiple-master Buses

In a centralized allocator, all requests are blocked in an input register when the selection is under way. In a distributed scheme the blocking signal is broadcast to all users, and prevents a device from participating if its request is not set before the start of the selection. A new selection can start when the previous one has been completed (and the identity of the next user stored in a GRANT register), or just before the end of the resource use. A technique to design fully asynchronous arbiters is presented in [COR75].

Synchronization is not an instantaneous process: it is subject to the metastable problem, discussed in section 2.1.9. Basically, due to the metastable problem, the selection cannot start immediately after the input synchronization. The selection logic must wait for a sufficient amount of time, which would make the probability of an input changing state spuriously after the synchronization acceptably low.

As an example of this problem, we can consider the basic two-way arbitration circuit, the R-S flip-flop, shown in figure 5.26.

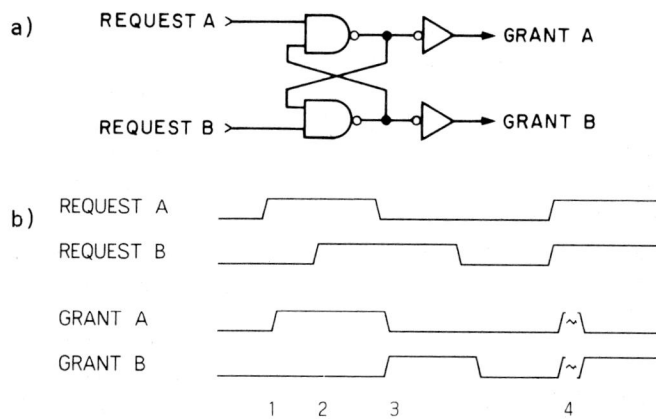

Fig. 5.26 Two-input arbiter
    a) Basic circuit
    b) Timing diagram

When no request is active, the flip-flop is in the "forbidden" condition (both inputs low), and the outputs are high (no grant active). If REQ A is raised first (step 1), it sets the flip-flop in the state which grants user A. If now, REQ B is also raised (2), the flip-flop goes to the "memory" input condition (both inputs high), and the outputs do not change. When request A becomes not-active (3), if REQ B is still active, the flip-flop toggles and B is granted.

This simple two-input queue handler fails if the delay between the two requests lies in the same range as the propagation delay of the flip-flop. In this case, the feedback loop does not have enough time to settle before the next input change, and the flip-flop may change state randomly for an undefined amount of time, or even go into a "fourth" state in which the two grant outputs may temporarily become active together, as shown in figure 5.26, case 4.

A possible solution is to mask the effects of false triggering of the arbitration flip-flop, as shown in figure 5.27: the delay $t_D$ decreases the probability of a false grant at the expense of an increased arbitration time. A similar technique is presented in [COR76].

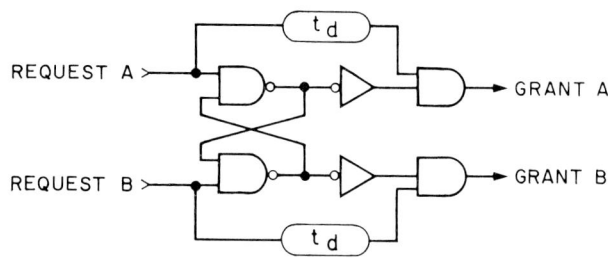

Fig. 5.27 Filtering of metastable states in the 2-input arbiter

In any case, the occurences of false synchronization can only be reduced by waiting, and a wrong triggering can never be excluded.

It is interesting to consider the "structure" that is influenced by the metastable-weakened basic synchronization. The elementary synchronization provides the basic selection, on which the bus arbitration is built. The bus allocation defines the sequence in time that is necessary for the basic lock operations, on which the semaphores are constructed. Semaphores are the basic tool for communication principles, on which process scheduling and communication is built. Process communication is required for data base locking, etc.

## 5.4.2 Fair access logic

As discussed in section 5.2.3, one of the possible solutions for avoiding starvation is to mask new requests from already-served users until all pending requests are served. In order to be able to support this policy, the allocator must know if at least one requester is still waiting. When this BUSREQUEST signal becomes active, the map of requests is frozen. Only when the last unit is being served, are all new requests again enabled. The block diagram of a circuit which implements fairness using this technique is shown in figure 5.28.

5 Multiple-master Buses                                                157

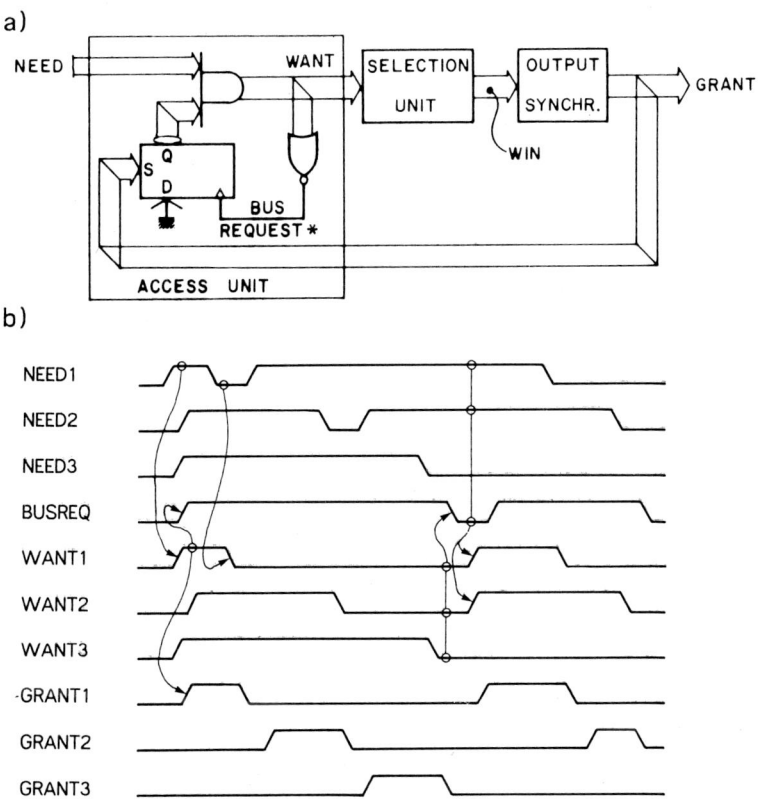

*Fig. 5.28 Fairness logic*
  *a) Block diagram*
  *b) Timing diagram*

This fairness scheme provides the two different levels of access needed for the selection logic: first, the NEED signals, which mean that a device needs the resource and has been allowed to participate in the current arbitration (by the input synchronizer); then, the permission to go on the service list, which corresponds to the WANT signal. This type of filtering of requests is handled by the access unit, which in this case consists of the fairness flip-flops and the bus request logic. In the example shown in figure 5.28 user 1, 2, and 3 are allowed to raise freely their first requests (NEED signals). As user 1 is granted, the corresponding fairness flip-flop is set, and NEED1 cannot generate WANT1. When user 2 has been served, the state of WANTs is still frozen because BUSREQ is active (WANT3 pending). The fairness flip-flop is reset (and NEED sampled) when all pending wants have been served, and BUSREQ goes to inactive level.

In a distributed allocator, the "user waiting" information is obtained by ORing the pending requests (BUSREQUEST*) from the various units on the line. An example of a distributed fairness circuit is shown in figure 5.29.

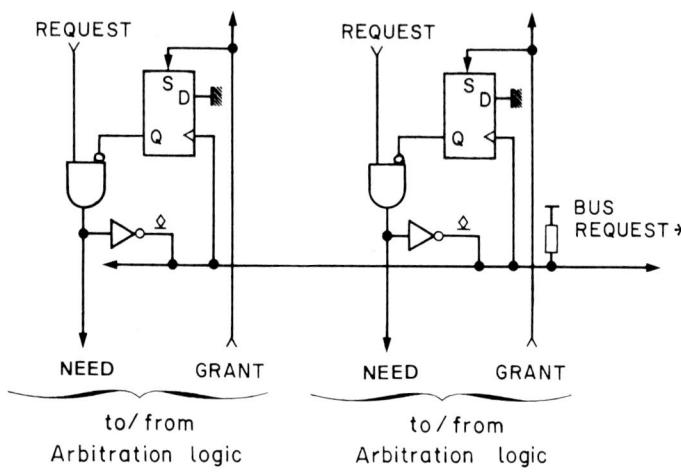

*Fig. 5.29 Distributed fairness logic*

To simplify these schemes, we assume here that the grant signal remains asserted as long as the request does. The fairness flip-flop is reset by the trailing edge of the grant, and set when BUSREQUEST becomes not asserted.

The fairness unit freezes the state of inputs to the selection logic when one user is granted. This is not input synchronization, because requests which come before the grant (that is during the selection process), are not blocked. The fairness unit and the input synchronizer have different functions; in some cases they are inverted: fairness masking is placed before the synchronizer.

## 5.4.3 Output synchronization

As already discussed in section 5.2.1, the bus can be assigned to a new requester only after the previous user has completed its operations. In other words, one cannot change the mastership of a bus while a transfer is being carried on: it is mandatory to wait until the transfer is completed and the transfer control signals return to the idle state.

# 5 Multiple-master Buses

The allocator must satisfy this requirement by sending a grant only at the correct time. Grants must therefore be synchronized with the activities performed on the resource. The basic synchronization technique is shown in figure 5.30: a BUSY signal indicates if someone (or no one) is using the resource, which can be reassigned only when no one is using it. The BUSY signal can be obtained by simply ORing all the grants. In a distributed allocator, this logic operation is performed using wired-ORs on a BUSBUSY* line.

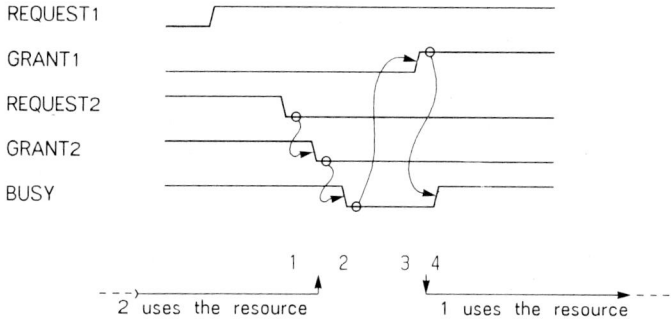

*Fig. 5.30 Bus exchange sequence*

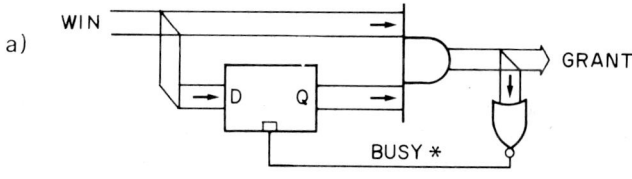

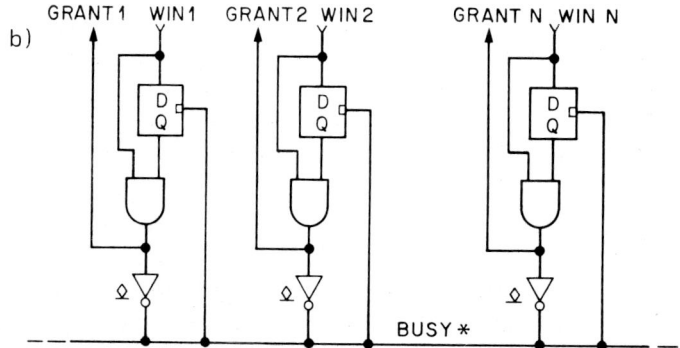

*Fig. 5.31 Grant synchronization in distributed arbiters*
    *a) Centralized synchronizer*
    *b) Distributed synchronizer*

This basic mechanism can be used with any allocation technique with only minor variations, using D flip-flops or other registers to switch the grants only at well-defined times, as shown in figure 5.32a. In most cases, these registers can be clocked directly by the BUSY signal. In a distributed arbiter, the synchronization logic is divided into single flip-flops placed on each unit, as shown in figure 5.32b.

### 5.4.4 Sequencing of allocation operations

For each transaction, the allocation of the communication channel must be performed before the addressing and data transfer operations. However, depending on the structure of the channel, allocation can be SEQUENTIAL or CONCURRENT with these operations, as shown in figure 5.32. Allocation operations are labelled by letters, (A,B,C); channel use (addressing and data transfers) by numbers.

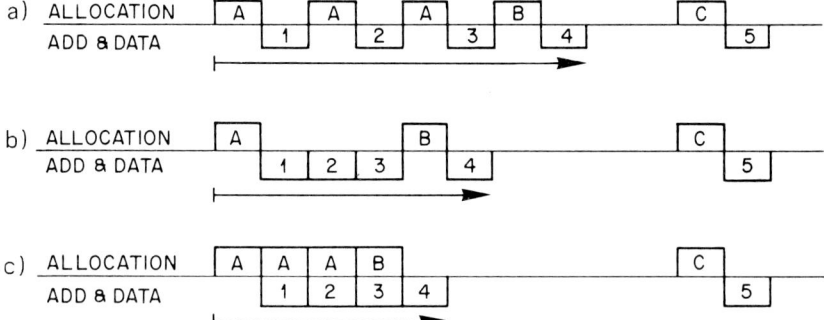

Fig. 5.32 Sequencing of allocation and transfer
 a) Sequential allocation
 b) Sequential, switch-on-demand
 c) Concurrent allocation

If the allocation is interleaved with the use of the resource, it is started at the end of each use as in figure 5.32a. This means that the resource cannot be allocated immediately, and service alternates with allocation, thus decreasing the system's performance. The throughput can be increased with switch-on-demand or default mastership policies, as shown in figure 5.32b, because in these cases allocation occurs only when actually required. Another possibility is to start allocation at a specified time inside the transaction itself [SBI78]. If allocation is done concurrently with resource use as shown in figure 5.32c, the resource can be allocated immediately after this use, but a separate communication channel is required. In figure 5.32 the arrows indicate the time used for 4 complete transactions.

# 5 Multiple-master Buses

Sequential allocation is less costly in hardware, although not as efficient, compared with the concurrent one; it is the only usable method when there is only one channel available, as in serial buses. Parallel buses use, in many cases, concurrent allocations, both because the extra channel is available, and because of higher speed.

Allocation, addressing and data transfer are inherently sequential for a single master, but in a multiple master bus, several of these operations can be concurrent, because they are being triggered by independent processors. If many channels are available, it is therefore possible to pipeline bus operations as shown in figure 5.33.

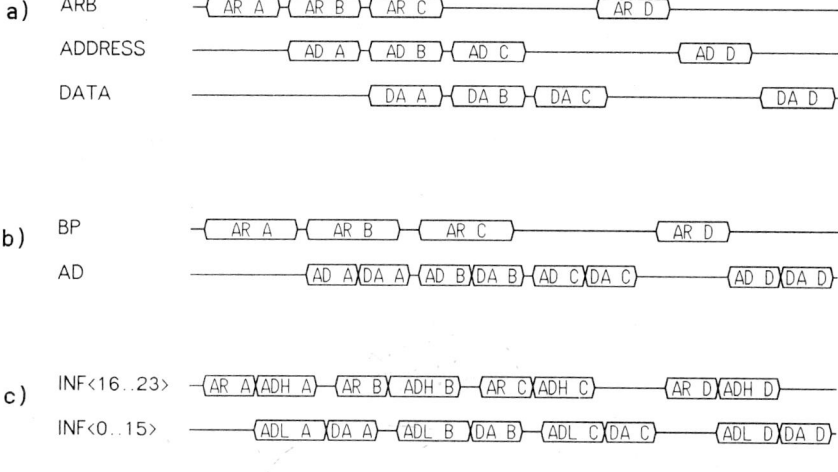

Fig. 5.33 Pipelining of bus operations
   a) Three-level pipelining
   b) Two-level pipelining (P896)
   c) Three-level pipelining with two buses (M3)

The degree of pipelining depends on the bus structure; to implement three-level pipelining, we need three independent buses, for arbitration, addressing and data transfer, as in figure 5.33a. Since the arbitration in many cases requires more time than the addressing and data transfer, a good compromise between the speed and the number of lines is the two-level pipeline shown in figure 5.33b; it is used, for instance, in P896. Figure 5.33c shows the technique of M3BUS: each transaction uses three time slots, but only two operations (arbitration and data transfer) are actually concurrent.

# 6 SPECIAL PROTOCOLS

Some information transfer operations differ from the usual arbitration-addressing-data transfer procedures. They are for instance the identification of an interrupting device, the transfer of streams of data on a multiplexed bus, or some special operations performed by a hardware debug unit.

These operations use the same fundamental protocols already presented in the previous sections, but also posess peculiar features which are discussed in this chapter.

## 6.1 INTERRUPTS

We shall not describe here the details of interruption mechanisms inside processors. Only this should be recalled: the *INTERRUPT* is an external event which changes the execution flow of a sequential machine. The interrupt can be viewed as a "hardware subroutine call". As shown in figure 6.1, it has the same effect as the execution of a "CALL XXX" instruction, where XXX is the starting address of a routine which executes the task requested by the interrupt. When interrupted a processor also performs other operations, e.g. saving the program counter on the stack, changing the current privilege level, etc. We shall not consider these operations here, because they are either internal to the processor or executed with protocol operations already examined in the previous chapters.

The operations triggered by an interrupt are not always the same, and some means to select them must be provided. This is equivalent to changing the "XXX" argument of the "hardware call" instruction. Some information to identify the starting address of the subroutine must be provided by the interrupting device, and transmitted over the bus; therefore we again need suitable protocols.

This section discusses interrupt mechanisms of various complexity, and shows how the different requirements can be fulfilled by a combination of the basic protocols already discussed.

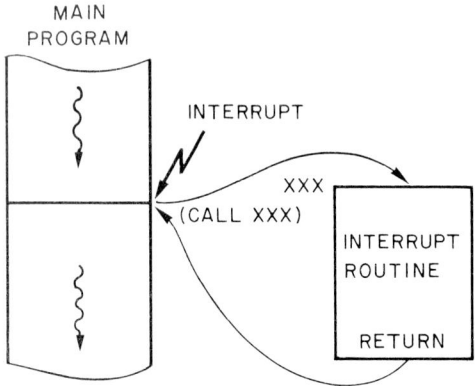

Fig. 6.1  The interrupt as a "hardware CALL"

The problem of handling multiple interrupts can be seen also from another point of view; let us consider the processor as a resource, which is shared by many users: the main program and the interrupting devices. The default user is the main program but, as soon as an interrupt becomes active, the resource PROCESSOR is granted to the requester in order to execute the service routine. When many requests become active at the same time, we must use a resource allocation mechanism, as discussed in Chapter 5, to handle the bus mastership. The designer has again the choices presented there: collision detection or avoidance, centralized or decentralized arbitration, etc. All the techniques described in Chapter 5 can be also used to grant the processor to one interrupt requester at a time. The only difference is that now the resource must know the identity of the granted user to start the execution of the proper service routine. For the bus this was not necessary, because it is a passive resource, used by all requesters in the same way.

### 6.1.1 Requirements of an interrupt system

Interrupts are external events which are asynchronous with processor activities. They must therefore be synchronized to interact properly with the program execution. The synchronization must occur in such a way as to avoid metastable states. We must also consider that, to guarantee the recoverability of the current program, the service routine may start only after the execution of the current instruction. Some processors also handle interrupt-like commands which can break the execution of an instruction and resume it later. This happens for

# 6 Special Protocols 165

instance with virtual memory systems [MAD84]: when data is not in the main memory, the instruction is aborted, the memory paged as required, and then execution can continue. In most cases all these operations are performed inside the processor, and do not involve the communication structure. For this reason we shall not discuss further the problem of interrupt/processor synchronization.

Processors may have one or more interrupt inputs. In this last case each input to the processor corresponds to a different default XXX argument in the hardware call; a different service routine is therefore directly executed in response to each different request. If the system contains a number of interrupt sources less or equal to the number of interrupt inputs of the processor, the interrupt communication subsystem consists only of a set of point-to-point lines, as shown in figure 6.2.

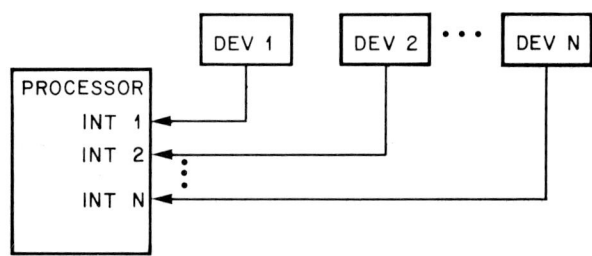

*Fig. 6.2 Multiple interrupt requests directly handled by the processor*

The interrupt request signal is usually acknowledged by the service routine, which resets a flag in the control register of the interrupt source using a write operation. This process uses the standard addressing and data transfer structure, and does not require additional signals. With this organization, if many requests become active at the same time, the service sequence is completely handled by the processor and requires selection logic in the communication structure or in the interfaces. All of the communication support and circuitry needed are shown in figure 6.2

This simple case is limited to very low complexity systems; in larger ones the number of interrupting devices is higher than the number of interrupt inputs of the processor and this makes the task more complex. In this last case we must design a circuit which reduces the number of interrupts to the processor and resolves possible contentions caused by the activation of many requests at the same time. The same logic must also allow identification of the requester, in order to start the correct service routine.

Some interrupt selection and identification logic exists also in the first case discussed in this section (as many direct interrupt inputs as many requesters), but it is completely hidden inside the processor.

### 6.1.2 Handling of multiple interrupts

Since we must only select the first request to be served, the same techniques discussed in Chapter 5 to handle the resource BUS can be used. The simplest solution, which does not need any dedicated hardware support in the communication system, and can be seen as a software token passing, is the POLLING. The interrupt requests are ORed to a single interrupt input of the processor, and the selection and identification are completely handled by the software: on any request a unique routine starts to read the status registers of the devices which can generate an interrupt. The first device with a request pending is served. A block diagram of a polling interrupt handling system is shown in figure 6.3.

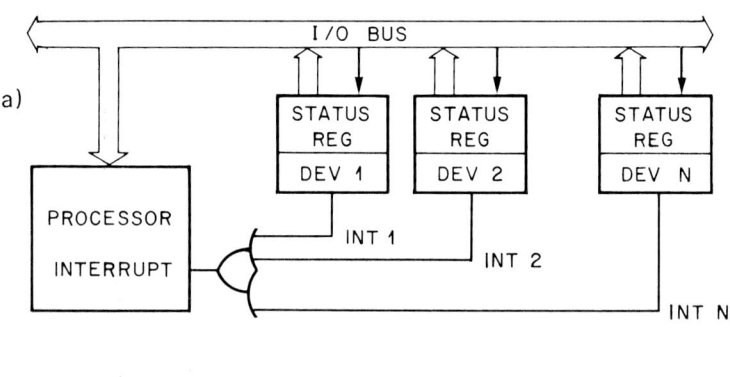

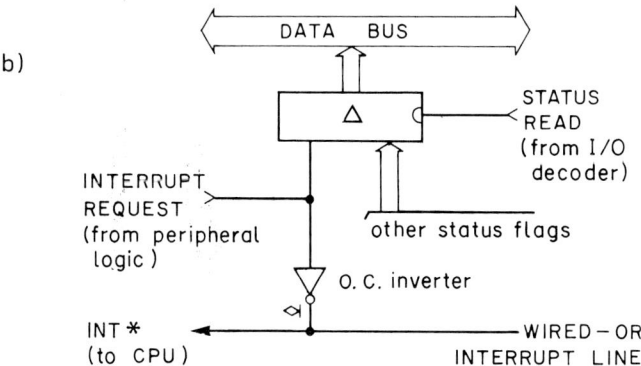

*Fig. 6.3 Multiple interrupt with status polling*
 *a) System block diagram*
 *b) Device logic block diagram*

The status is read using normal memory or I/O transfer operations, and the only hardware support required with this organization is the OR logic to generate the single interrupt request; in a bused system it may consist of wired-OR logic and a single bus line.

The software polling is slow; since interrupts are often used for fast servicing, the selection and identification mechanisms are in most cases built into the hardware. Owing to its good tradeoff between speed and complexity, the ARBITRATION technique is used for this purpose. The methods and the circuits described in sections 5.2 and 5.3 are still valid; the only difference is that now the GRANT signals do not go to requesters (interrupting units in this case), but are used by the resource (the processor) to identify which is the request to be served.

This information is usually transmitted as a word which is called *INTERRUPT VECTOR*. The communication structure must therefore support the protocol primitives to handle also this type of transfer, by providing two basic mechanisms:

- an arbitration system, to select the interrupt request to be served first;
- an identification system, that is a means to transfer the interrupt vector.

The vector can be accessed directly : the address of the service routine, an offset to find this address in a table, an instruction to jump to the subroutine, or even the first instruction of the subroutine itself. The exact use of the vector depends on the processor and is transparent to the information transfer system.

In multiple-interrupt systems, all requests are ORed to the processor INTERRUPT REQUEST. This input must be level-sensitive, to read multiple interrupts as the served requests are removed.

A variety of interrupt handling techniques can be obtained by combining the various possibilities for the implementation of arbiters with the various choices for information transfer protocols. In the following we shall discuss the more frequently used organization for multiple interrupt systems.

### 6.1.3 Centralized interrupt controller

When all interrupt requests are carried to a single unit which selects the next requester to be served and generates the corresponding interrupt vector for the processor, we speak of

CENTRALIZED INTERRUPT CONTROL. The organization of a centralized interrupt controller is shown in figure 6.4, and is similar to a centralized arbiter with grants encoded to build the interrupt vector.

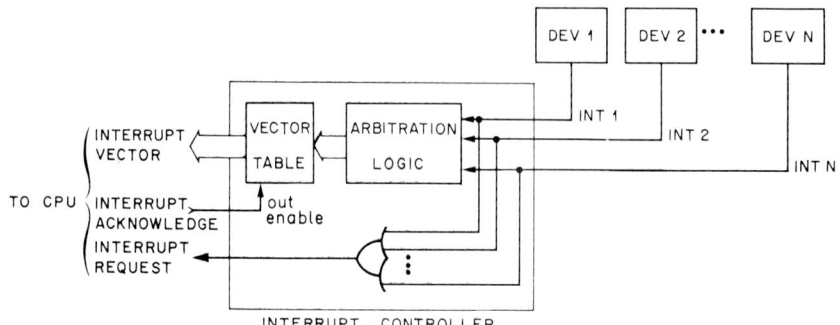

Fig. 6.4  Centralized control interrupt structure

The vector can be transferred on the data lines of the memory/I/O bus or on a set of reserved lines. In the last case the request can be processed concurrently with program execution; the response is faster and the same structure can be used for exceptions which must be accepted during the execution of instructions. This technique is used, for instance, in the Motorola MC68000. The processor activates an INTerrupt ACKnowledge signal (INTACK) to indicate that the interrupt has been received and to request the vector from the interrupt controller. INTACK can be a separate strobe or a static status signal strobed by a READPULSE. This transfer operation can use asynchronous, semisynchronous or synchronous protocols. Since a centralized interrupt controller is usually placed on the same board of the processor, the transfer of the vector is in many cases synchronous. If the vector is read through the data lines it is handled as a READ operation, qualified by the INTACK signal, and the same handshake of data transfers is used. Some examples of INTERRUPT VECTOR transfer are given in figure 6.5.

All of the features and the circuits discussed in section 5.3.1 are valid also for this type of interrupt handling technique. The main benefits of a centralized controller are speed, simplicity and freedom from priority algorithms. The drawbacks are the fixed number of inputs and the high number of bus lines used.

### 6.1.4  Daisy chain distributed interrupt controller

With the same procedure used for bus arbiters in figure 5.16, we can divide the ripple priority logic between the requesters to obtain

a)
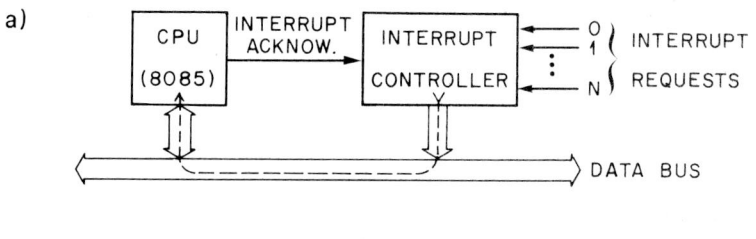

b)
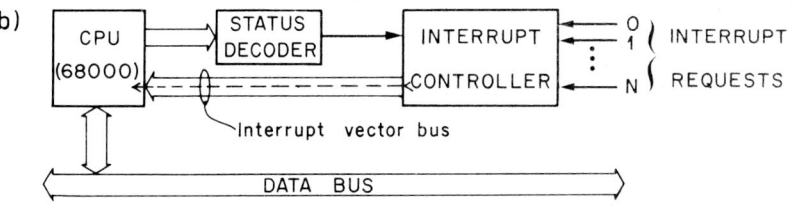

*Fig. 6.5  Structure to provide the INTERRUPT VECTOR to the processor*
*a) Using data lines (Intel 8085)*
*b) Using separate lines (Motorola MC68000)*

a distributed DAISY-CHAIN INTERRUPT handling structure. Since this organization is used in bus-based systems, the generalized interrupt request is obtained on a single bused line with wired-OR logic. The transfer of the interrupt vector is still synchronized using the INTACK signal, but this vector is now issued by the granted requester. Two examples of interrupt systems organized with these techniques are shown in figure 6.6a and 6.6b. In the first one the INTERRUPT ACKNOWLEDGE ripples through the chain; in the other it is used as a timing signal bused to all units.

With a daisy chain, the priority of each requester depends only on the physical position in the backplane. The arbitration time is proportional to the number of users; owing to the multiple propagation on bus lines, a daisy chain is slower than a centralized controller. From this point of view the circuit shown in figure 6.6b is faster, because the chain signals propagate and settle independently from transfer timing. The chain is fully modular, and new users are added by simply inserting the board in the backplane. As for arbitration, chain continuity must be guaranteed to avoid multiple grants. This technique is used for instance in the Zilog Z80 family of peripherals.

The structure shown in figure 6.6 is an allocator; therefore we must take care of input synchronization. New requests must not be raised while the selection logic is working, that is during the settling

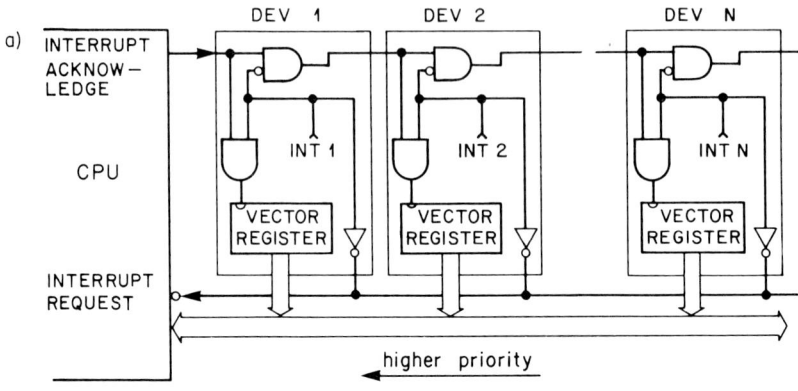

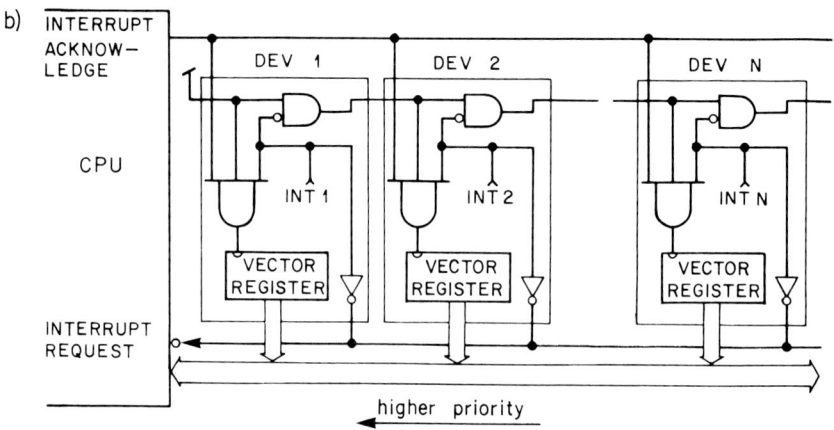

*Fig. 6.6  Daisy chain vectored interrupt structures*
  *a) Ripple INTACK*
  *b) Look ahead INTACK*

of the chain. This is accomplished by a synchronization Flip-flop on INT lines. This part is not shown in figure 6.6, because usually it is built inside peripheral interfaces. When using devices which belong to the same "family" as the processor, this synchronization is fully handled inside peripheral interfaces. The designer must verify the synchronization (and eventually add other components) only when mixing families.

The multi-level daisy chain shown in figure 5.24 can be used also to handle interrupts, giving some flexibility to priority level assignments.

## 6.1.5 Self-selection distributed interrupt controller

The interrupt arbitration system can be implemented also with the self-selection techniques presented in sections 5.3.3 (decoded) and 5.3.4 (encoded), using the structures shown in figure 6.7. In both cases the highest priority requester can be identified from the bus. The distributed decoded selection logic is seldom used because it requires the same number of bus lines as the centralized encoder, with more logic on requesters. With the encoded self-selection technique the vector can be read directly from the priority lines of the bus at the end of the self-selection process. The benefits of this technique are the same as the corresponding bus arbitration: modularity, speed, no chain, visibility of served unit with a higher complexity.

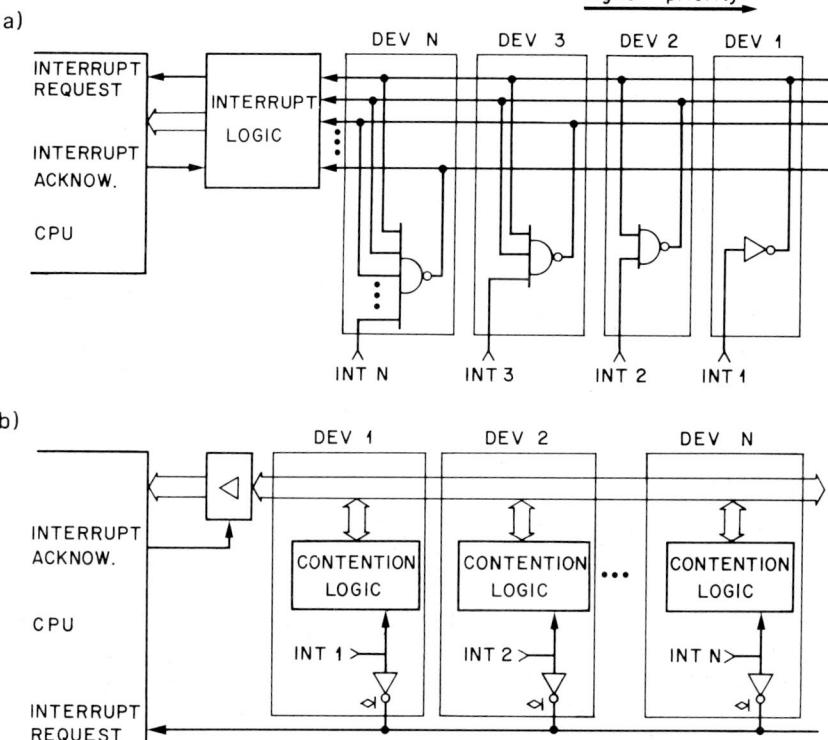

*Fig. 6.7 Self-selection distributed interrupt control*
  *a) Linear selection*
  *b) Encoded selection*

## 6.1.6 Mixed interrupt control systems

In more complex processing systems, where many interrupts must be handled in a fast and flexible way, the interrupt structure may combine some of the basic techniques discussed above. An example of such organization is given in figure 6.8.

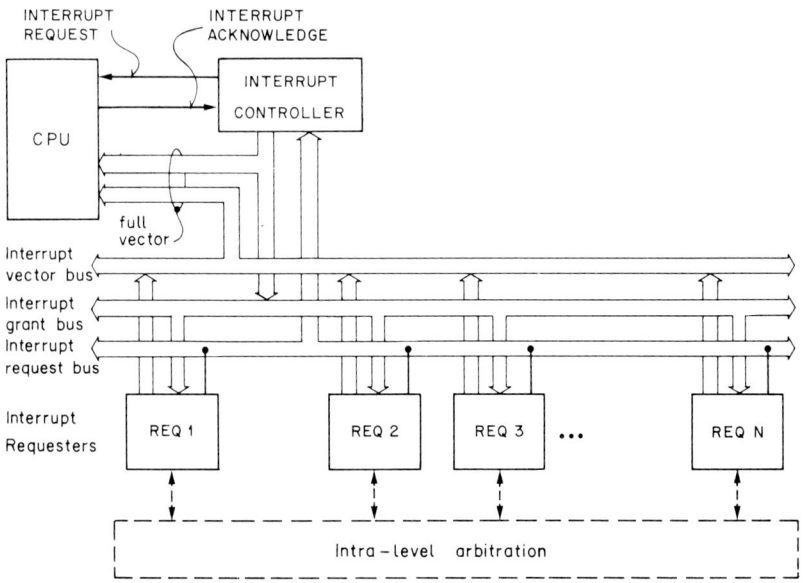

*Fig. 6.8 Example of complex interrupt system*

The requesters send interrupts to the controller on a set of INTREQ lines; the controller selects the highest priority request using the INTerrupt GRANT bus. The granted requester sends the vector on the INTerrupt VECTor bus. The processor can read the requester identifier from the controller and a device identifier from the requester. Each requester may contain many interrupt sources with internal arbitration. In some cases an arbitration structure allows many requesters to share the same INTREQ line. For instance, VME uses for this purpose a daisy chain.

The organization shown in figure 6.8 is used in MULTIBUS 1, VME, M3, with different allocations of the interrupt buses to the address/data lines. As shown in figure 6.9, M3 multiplexes all the interrupt signals with addresses; MULTIBUS 1 and VME use a separate set of INTREQ lines, and address/data respectively for grant/vector.

6 Special Protocols                                                     173

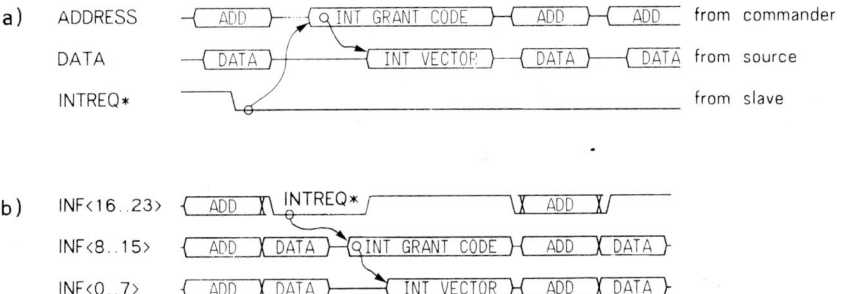

Fig. 6.9  Allocation of interrupt signals in the information
         transfer bus
         a) MULTIBUS and VME
         b) M3

## 6.2 SPECIAL TRANSFER CYCLES

Besides interrupt handling, there are other types of information transfer which cannot immediately lead to the basic cycles examined in Chapters 3 and 4. For instance, the usual sequence abitration-addressing-transfer is not always followed exactly, or can be interleaved with other operations. This section gives an example of these special cycles, and shows how they still rely on the elementary operations defined in Chapter 3.

### 6.2.1 Split cycles

In a SPLIT CYCLE the usual sequencing ADDRESSING-DATA-TRANSFER is broken; other masters can get access to the bus after the addressing and before the data transfer. This operation can be used, for instance, to read back data from slow peripherals without keeping the bus busy for the wait time. An example of a split cycle operation is given in figure 6.10.

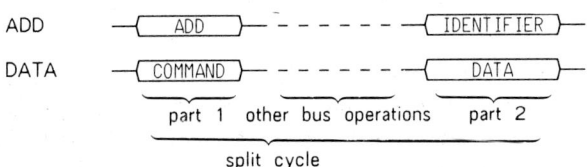

Fig. 6.10 Example of split cycle

Since the commander releases the bus after the first half of the cycle, the information sent back in the second half must also identify the destination (that is the requesting commander). A split cycle operation can be seen as a "write only" protocol: the commander writes an operation code to the responder which, later, becomes in turn commander and sends the data to the requester. The bus is used as a half-duplex link, that is, it acts independently in the two directions. This cycle saves time which would otherwise be lost by waiting for the results of a READ operation. Split cycles are used in some sophisticated structures, where each interface has enough intelligence to carry out the operations.

## 6.3 EXTENDED PROTOCOLS

Up to now we have only considered the exchange of information between two units. A more general case is the transfer between more than two units. Examples of these types of operations are transfers from one source to many destinations, which are called BROADCAST, or the collection of data from many sources, that is termed BROADCALL, or a mixing of both. These will be called N-PARTNER transfers, compared to the usual two-partner operations.

As long as one uses synchronous protocols without handshake, broadcast is obtained automatically by tying many destinations to the link or, in bused systems, by assigning the same address to many slaves. In the same way, to perform a broadcall one must select all the sources and connect them to the bus using suitable techniques to avoid damage of drivers caused by possible electrical collisions.

The modules involved in a broadcast or in a broadcall may have widely different response speeds, not only because of the different technologies, but, for instance, because the information comes through a bus window which is slowed down by the arbitration time of the next bus level. The control structures of the protocols discussed in Chapter 3 are not suitable for asynchronous fully handshaked N-partner transfers because they handle only a single acknowledge. We must therefore define new control techniques which allow us to detect when all the destinations acknowledge a broadcast, or when all sources have data ready for a broadcall. These operations are supported by the EXTENDED PROTOCOLS described in this section.

### 6.3.1 N-partner handshake

Let us consider as a first example a broadcast. In order to guarantee the handshake in a broadcast the source must be able to detect if all destinations have accepted the data. The logic structure of a handshaken broadcast is shown in figure 6.11.

# 6 Special Protocols

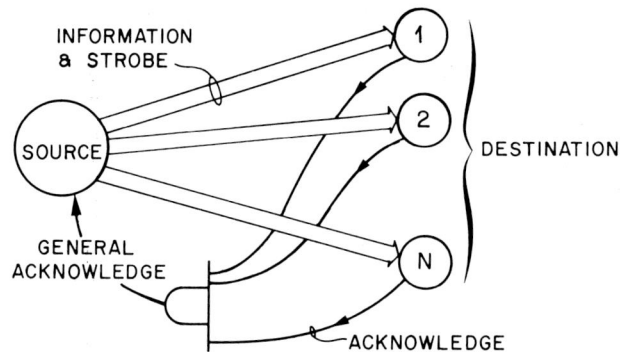

*Fig. 6.11 Logic structure of a broadcast operation*

In bus-based systems we cannot use a set of point-to-point lines and the AND gate to get the general acknowledge signal. These logic operations are better performed on the bus itself, as shown in figure 6.12, using the wired-logic technique. This approach matches the organization of bused systems and is modular, because to add one input to the AND logic function, one must only tie a new driver to the bus line.

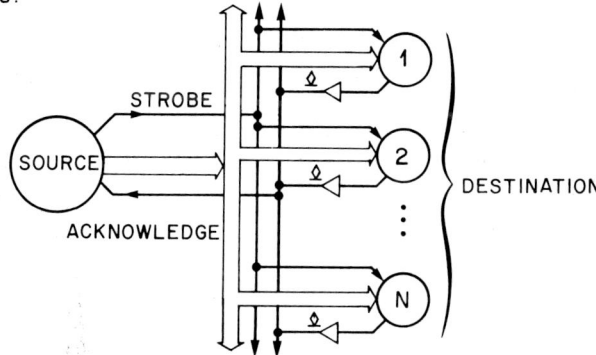

*Fig. 6.12 Protocol logic to support broadcast (wired-AND handshake)*

With TTL technology the wired logic uses open-collector gates, and the wired-AND is obtained using active-high signals on the bus lines. Figure 6.13a shows a protocol where the ACCEPT action is encoded into the rising edge of a READY signal; this signal is carried, without inversion, by a bused line driven by open collector gates. The non-active state of such a line corresponds to the high electrical level; therefore this line must be in the high state before and after each information transfer cycle. To keep the high default level and to encode the ACCEPT action in the rising edge, we must insert a dummy falling edge at the beginning of a cycle, as in figure 6.13b. This edge breaks the handshake and changes the synchronous protocol into a semisynchronous one.

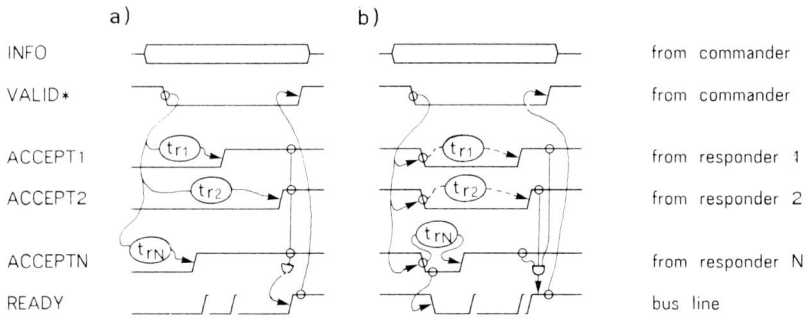

Fig. 6.13 N-partner broadcast
a) One-edge handshake
b) Semisynchronous handshake

As described in section 3.6.5, a semisynchronous protocol is dependant on the technology; the designer must make assumptions regarding the speed of communicating modules, and insert fixed delays in the sequence of actions. These constraints are extremely disappointing for the N-partner transactions, because the acknowledge delays may vary over a wide range owing to the many modules involved in the operations. Figure 6.14 shows an example of semisynchronous broadcast where one of the destinations, being far slower than the others, cannot store the correct information.

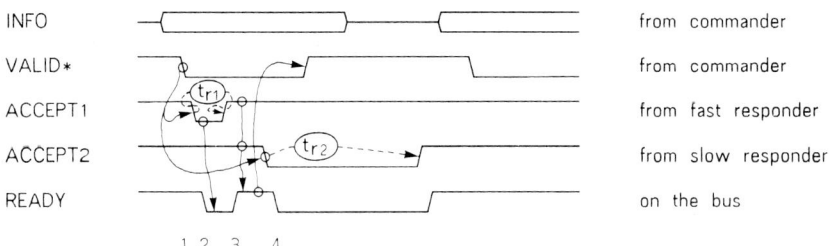

Fig. 6.14 Error in a semisynchronous broadcast: unit 2 is too slow and cannot receive the information

Another possibility is to keep the ACCEPT signal not active (low level) before the beginning of the cycle. This solution works for fixed connection topologies, but causes problems with master-slave bused structures. In this case, the ACCEPT signal should be handled only by the slaves which have been selected as responders in the current cycle. The units which are not selected will release the line which goes to the default level (high). So, if no slave unit has been selected, the master senses the ACCEPT signal active and will proceed at maximum speed.

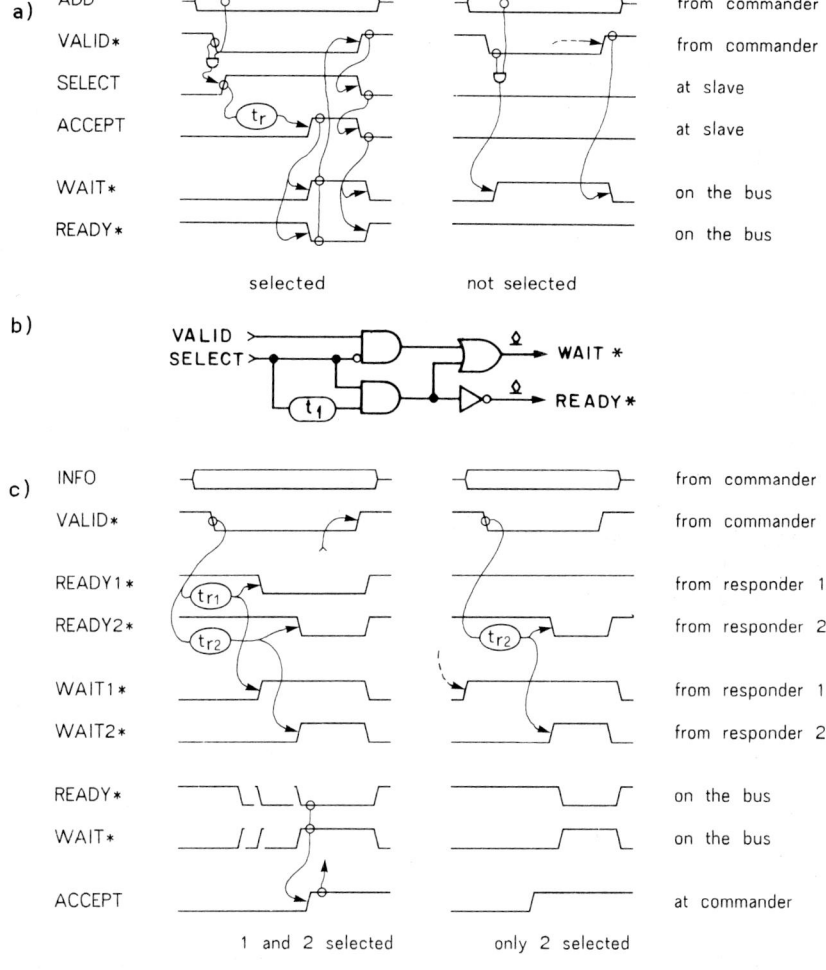

Fig. 6.15 Fully handshaken N-partner broadcast
    a) Timing diagram of responder logic
    b) Interface logic
    c) Timing diagram on the bus

To keep the fully asynchronous handshake we can also encode the ACCEPT action into the rising edge of another signal (WAIT*) and synchronize the protocol with a combination of READY and WAIT, as shown in figure 6.16. SELECT becomes true in all selected slaves (responders); they get control of the READY and WAIT signals. When a responder has used the information, it activates ACCEPT. If no slave is selected the WAIT signal stays active, and a master can detect the error condition. This technique is used for addressing and data broadcast/broadcall in the 896 bus.

### 6.3.2 An example of N-partner protocol: IEC 625

The IEC 625 (interface bus, also known as IEEE 488, see Appendix) uses a three-wire handshake for asynchronous N-partner transfers. This bus does not follow the usual master/slave organization; a CONTROLLER defines, with two addressing operations, the source and the destination of the following transfers. Each cycle is always initiated by the source, and all operations are either broadcast (for the source/destination selection cycles), or single-destination write. In the two-partner write protocols detailed in section 3.5 the actions READY and ACCEPT were encoded into a single signal. Here these actions are encoded into the high levels of Not Ready For Data (NRFD*) and Not Data ACcepted (NDAC*) lines respectively. These lines are driven by open collector gates, and implement a wired-AND on the READY and

a)

| ACTION | SIGNAL | STATE |
|--------|--------|-------|
| VALID  | DAV*<br>DAV* | low<br>high |
| ACCEPT | NDAC*  | low-to-high |
| READY  | NRFD*  | low-to-high |

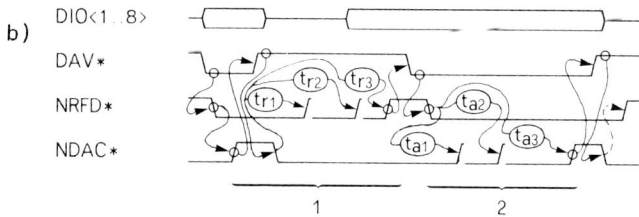

Fig. 6.16 The IEC 625 three-wire handshake
  a) Action encoding
  b) Timing diagram : during phase 1, NRFD* delays the READY action, during phase 2, NDAC* delays the ACCEPT action

ACCEPT conditions from all active modules. The use of separate wires allows a fully handshaked broadcast: the action sequence can only start when all destinations are ready, and data are removed only when all destinations have accepted the new information.

### 6.3.3 The Enable/Disable technique

The technique described in the previous section for the multiple acknowledge can be extended to any other protocol action, simply by encoding the action itself into a pair of bus signals. One signal is used to indicate that the action is enabled, and the other one to disable the same action; we shall call this technique ENABLE/DISABLE, and the two signals a ENABLE/DISABLE PAIR [DELC79b]. In the example of the previous section, the signals NRFD* and NDAC* can be seen as an Enable/Disable pair for the ACCEPT action. This section describes how this method can be exploited to add new primitives to information exchange protocols.

In a protocol using the Enable/Disable technique, the activation of an action ACT is triggered by a double condition:
- an ACT-Enable (ACT-EN) signal is active
- an ACT-Disable (ACT-DIS) signal is not active.

If the ENABLE/DISABLE signals are connected to the bus by with an open collector drivers, with the technique shown in figure 6.15, every unit can read from the bus:
- the first activation of an action, looking at the active low ACT-EN line. It becomes active (low level) when at least one module has activated the action
- the last activation of the same action, looking at the active low ACT-DIS line. It becomes not-active when all disable signals are not active.

The previous section showed how this method can be applied to the ACCEPT action, that is to the acknowledge signal, in order to get fully handshaken information transfers towards multiple destinations, but the same technique can be used to control other actions of the

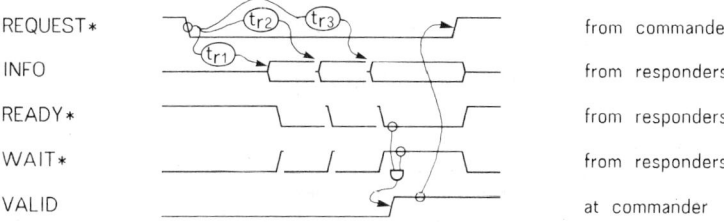

*Fig. 6.17 Broadcall handshaken cycle*

protocol. For instance, in the broadcall operation we must delay the VALID action until all sources have put the information on the bus. A broadcall protocol which uses the Enable/Disable technique is shown in figure 6.17.

It must be pointed out that if ACT-DIS is never activated, the action ACT is ruled by ACT-EN only. The modules which will never participate in N-partner operations simply do not handle ACT-DIS, and a system which supports a N-partner protocol works correctly also when all transactions use the two-wire handshake and involve only two modules.

### 6.3.4 Generalization of the Enable/Disable technique

The Enable/Disable technique can be used also with signals which are not brought to the bus. For instance, the memory disable signals INH1* and INH2* used in the Multibus for phantom memories can be included in Enable/Disable pair with the buffer enable generated inside memory boards. When either INH1* or INH2* is active, a standard memory, even if addressed, is not selected; an example of this operation is shown in figure 6.18. MRDC*/INH* act as an Enable/Disable pair for the SELECT action.

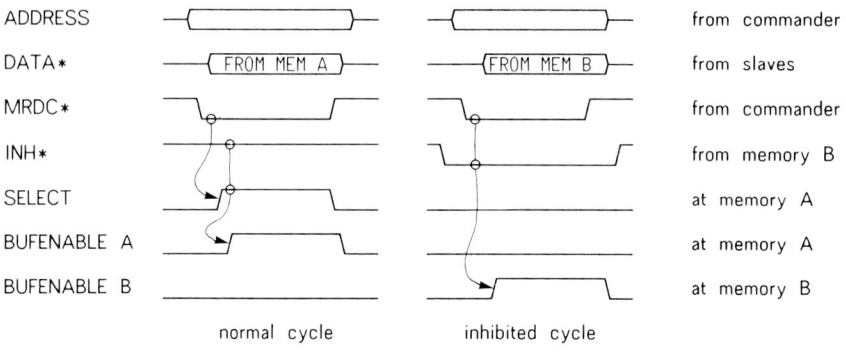

Fig. 6.18 MULTIBUS I memory read cycles without and with inhibition

The combination of the Enable/Disable pair for VALID action with an Enable/Disable pair for the INF buffer enable, shown in figure 6.19 allows one to replace the information put on the bus by the source with the information coming from another module. In this case the buffer enable action is controlled by the two signals:

- BUF-EN :internal to the source module, and
- BUF-DIS :from the bus; this signal is controlled by the unit that sources the new information.

# 6 Special Protocols

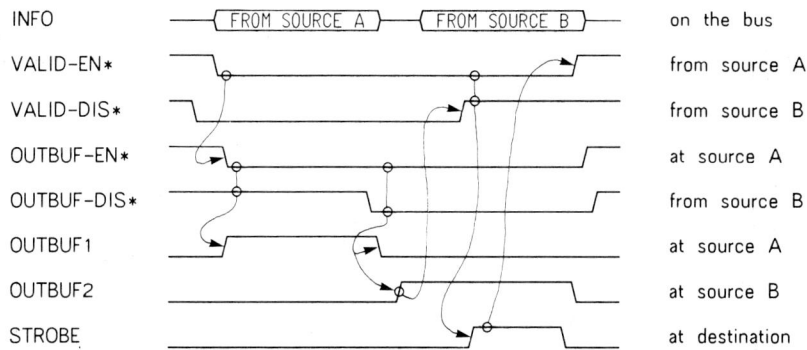

*Fig. 6.19 Information replacement by means of E/D pairs*

Similarly, a WRite-DISable signal WRDIS can inhibit write operations on memory or I/O registers, as shown in figure 6.20.

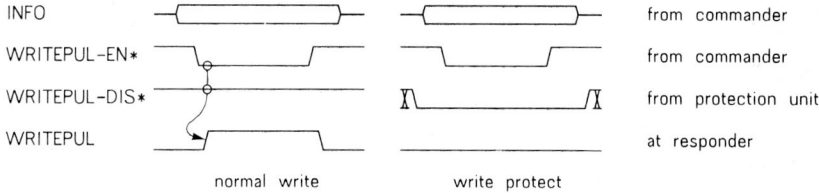

*Fig. 6.20 Write protection by means of E/D pairs*
  *a) Normal write cycle*
  *b) Write-protect cycle*

The edges in an Enable/Disable pair must be properly sequenced to avoid race conditions or spurious spikes. Only one signal should be responsible for the protocol timing; the other one must act only as a static enabling condition. Some examples are given in figure 6.21.

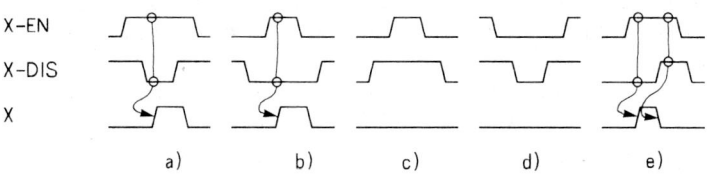

*Fig. 6.21 Timing of an E/D pair: cases a), b), c), d) are correct; e) is not correct*

## 6.3.5 Bus supervisors

The Enable/Disable primitives defined in the previous section can be combined to extend the functions supported by the communication structure of a system. The modules which use the the Enable/Disable technique to modify the operations carried out on the bus are here called SUPERVISORS [DELC82], [PLAT81].

The level of interaction of a supervisor unit with the bus spans a wide range. The lowest level is the simple observation, with the possibility of modifying the speed of the information transfer. A passive monitoring of information exchange allows one to trace the program execution and to insert breakpoints. These operations can be performed without affecting the real time behaviour of the observed system if the supervisor logic is fast enough. By means of an Enable/Disable pair with handshake a supervisor can delay and synchronize the observed process to perform more complex and time-consuming operations, such as multiple table search, symbolic tracing, etc.

A stronger interaction occurs when the information being transferred is replaced with other data, as already shown in figure 6.18. This feature can be used in the debug phase to switch memory banks of a development system into the memory of the target machine or to reallocate memory accesses for memory management.

Some of these features are also supported by In Circuit Emulators (ICE), but the use of a supervisor removes some problems that arise from the use of an ICE, such as those due to slight differences in timing and electrical characteristics between the emulator probe and the actual device. A supervisor, being connected to bus lines which are buffered and terminated, should not influence the electrical behaviour of the system. Moreover, the supervisor hardware is defined according to the system bus rather than from the CPU specifications, and the same module can support monitoring and intervention with different processors.

In the examples given above we used separate Enable/Disable pairs for each operation, but it must be pointed out that full duplication of control lines is not required. Since the type of operation is already specified by one of the Enable/Disable signals, the other one can be multiplexed. This technique is widely used in M3BUS [M3B82], [CON83], to get full Enable/Disable control of all operations using only two additional lines.

# 7 ERROR HANDLING

Although great care is taken to ensure a reliable transmission in links and buses, the probability of error cannot be reduced to zero. In parallel buses, crosstalk and external fields disturb the signals. In guided transmissions, perturbations are due mainly to electromagnetic interference (EMI) caused by power equipments, relays, microwave ovens, and ground currents. In atmospheric transmission, fading, lightning, sun bursts, rain, and obstacles are likely to corrupt transmission. Digital transmission is far more sensitive to transmission errors than the human ear is. What sounds like a click on a telephone line would barely disturb a conversation, but if the same line is transmitting data from a modem at 2400 b/s, some 100 or more bits are affected. In reality, as much information is lost for the speech signal, but human speech contains many redundancies and our ear is a very good decoder which reconstructs most lost information.

This chapter deals with the sources of error, the way to detect them and the way to correct them.

## 7.1 DEFINITIONS

### 7.1.1 Error sources and effects

A *FAILURE* is defined as a behaviour of a device which is contrary to the intention of its designer, or, to put it more formally, contrary to its specifications. An *ERROR* is a change of state, in particular a change in stored or transmitted data due to a failure. In computers, an error manifests itself as the unintended inversion of a bit of data. This inversion is the standard error type assumed in parallel buses. Serial communications often work with three states (e.g. 1,0, nothing) and, therefore, in addition to inversion, erasure may occur. Microwave links and some modems encode data in several levels and a value may be transformed into another one by noise, but these are rather special problems. We will consider here only binary data inversion as the standard error kind.

PERSISTENT ERRORS remain present until repaired. A persistent error is generally attributed to a physical damage, such as a stuck-at-high driver. VOLATILE ERRORS or TRANSIENT ERRORS are caused by a temporary malfunction, such as an external noise. Volatile errors leave the hardware intact, but they may remain memorized when they affect a storage element such as a RAM or a flip-flop.

Some authors use the terms "hard" errors and "soft" errors to tag persistent and volatile errors, respectively. We have avoided these terms because of the confusion with hardware vs. software errors. A HARDWARE ERROR is caused by the physical failure of an element, which results in a persistent error. If repaired, a hardware failure can occur again with a certain probability (given by the MTBF, Mean Time Between Failures, of that element). A SOFTWARE ERROR is due to a design or programming mistake. If corrected, it should not appear again (but maybe another error will show up because of the correction). The distinction between software and hardware errors cannot be clearly made, since most, if not all, hardware failures are due to design mistakes, like poor shielding, insufficient cooling, bad location or incorrect technology.

A FAULT is the physical or algorithmic cause of an error. Note that a fault does not necessarily cause an error. Most programs in use today have bugs in them, but these bugs will only produce errors in specific, rarely used cases. A hardware fault may remain lurking for weeks before been noticed by an error it produces. The distinction between fault and error has been introduced to express specifically this lurking error problem.

Within a computer, one can assume that something like 90% of the errors are of the volatile type, and this proportion rises to about 99.9% in a telecommunication link. These figures mean that it is possible in most cases to resume operation after an error without having to repair parts, since the hardware is not damaged, provided one can deal with the errors.

The type of error in transmission systems has a great impact on the methods used to deal with them. In general, one assumes that the errors are volatile and occur at random. In a digital transmission, the figure of merit is the ERROR RATE $E_r$, which is the relation of the erroneous data to the total transmitted data. Typical figures of error rate are $10^{-5}$ for a transmission over telephone lines, and $10^{-9}$ for a transmission over a coaxial cable.

The assumption that errors occur at random is not correct when considering equipment used in rough environments like industrial plants, atmospheric propagation (radio waves) or a telephone network. There, the errors tend to occur grouped in BURSTS, which affect several consecutive bits of information. Burst errors are caused by surges of current in neighbouring equipment, like starting of motors, relays closing, welding equipment, etc. Burst errors are more difficult to correct than random errors but, on the other hand, for the same error rate, burst errors affect a smaller percentage of the communication than random errors, since the errors concentrate on certain messages, instead of being scattered over all messages: typically, 90% of the burst errors can be found in only 10% of the messages.

The first care of the designer is FAULT AVOIDANCE, that is, the improvement of the quality of the equipment to achieve an acceptably low error rate. Careful design, use of reliable media such as coaxial cables with double shield or fibre optics reduce the error rate at the expense of soaring costs. Above a certain level, fault avoidance is not economical any more and one should deal with the errors instead of avoiding them. In fact, it makes no sense to try to build a completely error-free communication link where error correction is possible.

### 7.1.2  Fault tolerance

FAULT TOLERANCE is the ability of a system to operate in the presence of faults. This can only be achieved through the use of REDUNDANCY. Redundancy is any kind of resource which would not be needed in case the system were error-free. Redundancy comes in the form of additional hardware, additional time for computation or additional software, i.e. multiversion programming and diverse designs. The first step of fault tolerance is ERROR DETECTION. Practically all digital communication links which spread over more than a few metres transmit along with the useful data some redundant data for error detection.

To detect all errors in a computing system, it is in principle necessary to replicate completely the system. The redundant units can execute the same operations and errors will show up by comparison. This holds provided that the same error will not affect both redundant paths in the same manner, but the probability of such a case, called COMMON MODE ERROR, is usually ignored when the error rate of the units is low enough. The common mode error is a nightmare for the designer, since most common mode errors are due to design faults: if both redundant units run the same faulty program, no error will be detected by comparing them. Diverse designs can cope with this problem.

The second step of fault tolerance is *ERROR CORRECTION*. To correct an error, an additional redundancy is required besides the redundancy needed to detect errors.

A complete fault tolerant system requires therefore a threefold amount of resources (hardware, time, bandwidth): one resource to do the work, one redundancy to detect errors, another to correct them. In reality, more redundancy is required because fault-tolerance imposes a certain overhead.

As an example, consider a communication link which transmits files. If no error is expected, the file is transmitted and treated as correct. Now, if errors are expected, the file could be transmitted twice (by using time redundancy) so that the receiver can compare the two versions. Only the unlikely case of the same error in both transmissions would remain undetected (common mode error). In case of discrepancy, the receiver cannot yet tell which file is faulty. It will therefore request a third version of the file to decide (which hopefully will agree with one of the previous two). Therefore, correction needs a second redundancy. In reality, more redundancy is needed because of the error handling messages. The above may not seem to be a very efficient way to handle errors but, in reality, fault tolerance does require that many resources. We can only hope to reduce the amount of redundancy by proper assumptions on the nature of the errors and the type of information transmitted.

Error correction on a communication channel is simplified by the fact that, contrary to a memory, a transmission line does not memorize errors as long as there are no permanent failures. So correction can be easily made by retransmission if time is available for it and a two-way (duplex) communication exists. The destination which receives a faulty message may signal the fact by sending a *NEGATIVE ACKNOWLEDGE* (NACK) to the source to request a copy of the spoiled message. This scheme is rarely used alone: if the message is so damaged that the destination address is blurred, no destination reacts and there will be no negative acknowledge.

The usual scheme lets the destination send a *POSITIVE ACKNOWLEDGE* (PACK) message for each message it correctly received. If the positive acknowledge is missing, the source will attempt retransmission after a time-out elapsed. Here, however, some care is required where there is no upper bound to the delay across the link, such as in Ethernet. It is then possible that the acknowledge arrives after the source timed-out, with the result that the message is duplicated. Several protocols are used to prevent loss or duplication of messages, such as sequence numbering, time stamps, etc. In parallel buses, retransmission is seldom attempted at the interface level but, rather, an error triggers a bus error trap in the CPU, which attempts to retry the instruction using the same mechanisms as for virtual memory support.

When time is available and error rates are low, retransmission is an efficient way to correct errors. In this case, the transmissions require redundancy only to detect errors.

When time is critical, or when only one-way communication is feasible, for instance when the data is broadcast to a large number of stations like digital TV or transmitted from a space probe near Jupiter, it may not be possible to retransmit the data within an acceptable delay, especially if the transmission channel is shared among several masters. Here, redundant information for error detection as well as for error correction must be transmitted together with the useful data.

Similarly, in memory banks, especially in highly integrated dynamic memories, data cells have a non-negligible probability of losing information. Errors remain memorized, and reading the same corrupted memory location twice will not yield the correct information. Therefore, the storing of redundant information in the form of an error correcting code has become a common practice for large memory banks.

It is assumed that when fault tolerance is available, every detected error ceases to be dangerous, since there are methods to cope with it either by retransmission or by correction. The integrity is only jeopardized by undetected errors. The ratio of the number of undetected wrong messages to the total number of messages is called the RESIDUAL ERROR RATE, $R_{er}$ when estimated empirically or measured. When this figure is calculated analytically, one speaks of residual error probability. The $R_{er}$ depends of course on the error rate. Although the $R_{er}$ can be reduced substantially by proper redundancy, it cannot be made zero. In industrial environments where safety equipment is involved, a typical requirement asks for a residual error rate $R_{er}$ of at least $10^{-18}$ for an error rate of $10^{-6}$. The residual error rate dictates ultimatly the amount of redundant information that must be transmitted with the data to detect errors [FUNK83].

## 7.1.3 Coding theory

The detection of errors and the correction of data is based on the CODING THEORY, which is a branch of mathematics concerned with the representation and transformation of data. We expect from this theory efficient schemes to transmit redundant information, which make better use of the channel capacity than transmitting the data twice or threefold.

We recommend the classical book of Peterson [PET72] on this subject, which explains the mathematical background of the coding theory and describes numerous error detecting and correcting codes. We will not go into the details, but just explain in plain terms the most important coding schemes found in practice.

Let us consider that a message is transmitted piecewise, with each piece having a length of k bits. For instance, text files may be transmitted using 7-bit ASCII characters, with k = 7, which yield an ALPHABET of M = $2^k$ = 128 different signs or SYMBOLS. A BLOCK CODING consists of assigning to each of the $2^k$ combinations of the alphabet another combination of length n (n >= k), called a CODEWORD. One characterizes the coding scheme as (n, k) code.

For instance, when 7-bit ASCII characters are transmitted, a redundant eighth bit (called the parity bit, see next section) is often appended for error detection. Therefore, an 8-bit codeword corresponds to each 7-bit ASCII symbol; this is a (8,7) code.

In the simplest case, a secret code which assigns as a codeword the next symbol in the alphabet (A -> B, B -> C, ... Z -> A) is a (k, k) code. Only some scrambling is performed. The codeword has the same length as the original symbol (n = k) and therefore errors cannot be detected.

In most codes used for error detection, the original symbol is still present in the codeword, so we can consider that a block code is generated by appending a redundant information to a block of data. This is called a SYSTEMATIC CODE. Since the message bits appear in clear text, the message can be read directly from the data field if there is no error. In this case, both the block size and the redundant or check block have a fixed size as shown in figure 7.1.

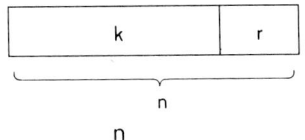

Fig. 7.1 Codeword consisting of k data and r check bits

The total length of the transmitted block is n, consisting of k data bits and r check bits. The redundant bits need not be appended to the data, they can be intertwined with it.

# 7 Error Handling

When there are more codewords than symbols, that is, when the codeword has more bits than the original data, then error detection becomes possible since, of the $2^n$ possible codewords, only $2^k$ correspond to a symbol of the original alphabet, and the presence of an unassigned codeword signals an error. Codewords which correspond to error-free symbols are called LEGAL or VALID codewords.

We define the HAMMING WEIGHT (HW) as the number of bits with value "1" in a codeword. For instance, the HW of 01001111 is 5. Note that an error which tilts one bit in a word increases or decreases its HW by one.

We define the HAMMING DISTANCE (HD) between two codewords of the same length as the number of bits in which they differ.

For instance, the HD between the two codewords 01100110 and 00101001 is 5. The HD can be computed by building a new word consisting of the bit-by-bit exclusive-OR (XOR) combination of the two compared words, and by counting the number of "1s" in the result :

```
      01100110
   +  00101001
      01001111   consisting of 5 "1s".
```

Note now that an error which changes one bit in a word creates a new word which is at a Hamming Distance of one from the original. Two errors will create a word which is at a distance of two from the original if they do not compensate, and in general n errors increase the Hamming Distance between the original and the incorrect word to n in the worst case.

We define the Hamming Distance (or distance) of a code as the minimum HD between two legal codewords. Even if most legal codewords are at HD=8 from each other, it is sufficient that there exist 2 valid codewords at HD=2 to bring the distance of the code down to 2.

If the Hamming Distance of a code is one, then a single error can change a valid codeword into another valid codeword and there is no guarantee that a single error can be detected. If the distance of the code is two, two errors are needed to transform a valid codeword into another valid codeword and any single error can be detected. Thus, the Hamming Distance of a code is a measure of the robustness of a code against errors.

We can illustrate geometrically the Hamming Distance for a transmitted codeword of 3 bits, which carries 2 bits of information. We can locate the 8 possible combinations at the 8 corners of a cube (figure 7.2).

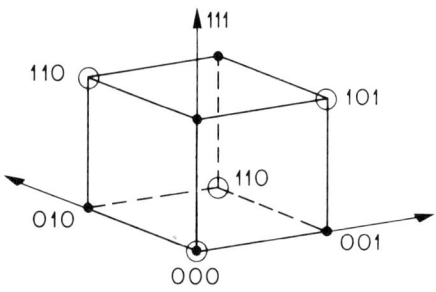

*Fig. 7.2 Code cube*

Since the useful information has only 4 combinations, we can distribute these 4 combinations on the 8 corners of the cube. It seems logical to put these legal combinations as far apart from each other as possible, so that there are at least 2 edges in between them (white spheres). The minimum number of edges between two legal combinations is the Hamming Distance of the code.

This result can now be generalized for an n-bit word to a n-dimensional lattice. The HD is still the number of edges between 2 combinations.

The problem of coding is to spread the valid codes over the set of all possible codes in such a way that one or several errors cannot turn a valid code into another valid codeword easily. Furthermore, the transformation which builds the codeword out of each data word and vice-versa should be simple to implement.

The aim of the error detecting codes is to reduce the number of redundant bits in proportion to the useful information for a given residual error rate. The *CODE EFFICIENCY* (or *RATE*) is defined as the ratio of the useful data to the total transported information (useful data plus checkbits):

$$CEF = \frac{k}{n}$$

## 7.2 ERROR DETECTION AND CORRECTION IN SMALL DATA ITEMS

### 7.2.1 Parity

The best known block code error detection is PARITY. The parity is a redundant information bit associated with a word of k bits which is transmitted as $(k+1)^{th}$ bit. The parity bit tells whether the number of "1s" in a codeword, i.e. its Hamming Weight, is odd or even. We define that an ODD PARITY BIT is chosen such that the Hamming Weight of the resulting codeword (including the parity bit) be ODD, i.e. the parity bit has the value "1" if the number of "1s" in the symbol (excluding the parity bit) is even and a "0" if that number is odd. Similarly, an EVEN PARITY BIT sets the number of ones in the codeword (including the parity bit) to an even number. The even parity bit is calculated as the exclusive OR (XOR) value of all symbol bits. Figure 7.3 shows the building of even parity for an 8-bit message word.

| Par | D7 | D6 | D5 | D4 | D3 | D2 | D1 | D0 |
|---|---|---|---|---|---|---|---|---|
| 1 | 0 | 1 | 1 | 0 | 0 | 0 | 0 | 1 |

Par = D7 $\oplus$ D6 $\oplus$ D5 $\oplus$ D4 $\oplus$ D3 $\oplus$ D2 $\oplus$ D1 $\oplus$ D0 = 1

*Fig. 7.3 Even parity (HW = 4)*

Unfortunately, the reverse definition of parity appears in the data sheets of some integrated circuits: "odd" means there that the sum of the "1s" excluding the parity bit is odd, which is just the opposite of the commonly accepted definition.

Note that the parity bit is generally considered as being the bit with the highest weight. This is because serial transmissions usually transmit the least significant bit first, and parity is then appended to the message.

In general, the parity kind is chosen so as to force a difference between transmission and the lack of transmission. If a transmission is binary, i.e. if it has only two distinct levels, the quiescent level (passive level) cannot be distinguished from one of the logical levels. Then the parity is chosen so that at least one bit is active when the word consists only of passive levels. For instance, if the passive level is "0", the parity should be odd. If the passive level is "1", the parity should be chosen as even if the number of bits in the transmitted word is even, or as odd if the number of bits is odd.

The parity bit does not provide a 100% error detection. In fact, if any 2 bits in the codeword containing the data and the parity bit are inverted, the parity is again correct, although a double error occurred. Therefore, the Hamming Distance of parity is only 2.

Obviously, it is not reasonable to protect a 512-block file with a single parity bit. The length of the word which a parity bit protects effectively depends on the acceptable residual error rate.

The residual error rate $R_{er}$ can be calculated as follows. Let $E_r$ be the probability that one bit is in error. The probability that a particular bit is not in error is $(1-E_r)$. The probability that any of the n bits is in error is equal to $E_r^n$, and that no bit is in error is $(1-E_r)^n$.

The probability that a given bit is in error and no other is $(1-E_r)^{n-1} \cdot E_r$ and, since there are n bits, the probability that exactly one bit is in error is $n \cdot (1-E_r)^{n-1} \cdot E_r$. Therefore, the probability that the word has either no error or exactly one error is:

$$R_{er} = 1 - \underbrace{(1-E_r)^n}_{\text{not no error}} - \underbrace{n \cdot E_r \cdot (1-E_r)^{n-1}}_{\text{exactly one error}}$$

This can be approximated to $R_{er} = n \cdot (n-1) \cdot E_r^2$ for Er << 1.

Suppose now that the error rate is $10^{-5}$; if the protected word size is 8 bits (n = 9), the residual error rate is $72 \cdot 10^{-10}$. But if the protected data block has a length of 512 bits, n = 513 and the $R_{er}$ approximates to $2.6 \cdot 10^{-5}$ which means that the probability that an undetected error takes place in the block is higher than the bit error rate, and makes parity quite useless. Therefore, parity is used to protect small data items, typically 7 or 8 bits wide.

In parallel buses, parity is now commonly used. DEC's SBI has one parity bit for all 32 lines of information. IEEE 896, MULTIBUS II, VERSABUS and NUBUS have one parity bit for every 8 information lines.

### 7.2.2 Longitudinal parity

We consider now the transmission of a sequence of words such as a file. In some transmission schemes it is not possible to transmit a $(k+1)^{th}$ bit for each word, since the channel is not wide enough. For instance, most asynchronous serial channels allow the transmission of an 8-bit wide word. If one uses the $8^{th}$ bit as parity, only 7 bits remain as useful information. This is what the ASCII transmission standard recommends. However, if one transmits a binary file consisting

# 7 Error Handling

of 8-bit words (for instance an object file), the chunking of 8-bit words into 7-bit units is not a good practice. One prefers then to transmit 8-bit words and to protect them additionally by a parity word every $M^{th}$ word. Then parity is built over all bits belonging to the same column (figure 7.4).

| | |
|---|---|
| word 1 | 0 0 0 1 1 1 0 0 |
| word 2 | 1 0 1 1 0 1 1 1 |
| word 3 | 0 0 1 0 0 1 1 0 |
| word 4 | 0 0 0 0 0 1 1 0 |
| word 5 | 1 1 0 0 0 1 0 1 |
| word 6 | 1 1 1 0 1 0 1 0 |
| word 7 | 0 1 0 0 0 1 0 0 |
| word 8 | 0 0 0 1 1 1 1 0 |
| parity word: | 1 1 1 1 1 1 1 0 |
| word 9... | . . . . . . . . |

*Fig. 7.4  Longitudinal even parity over 8 bytes*

The parity is built column-wise, hence the name "longitudinal parity". Note that longitudinal parity indicates in which column the error took place. In a parallel transmission which is as wide as the individual words, if a column is repeatedly in error, this suggests damage on a particular line. In a serial transmission, it is unlikely that the same column is repeatedly affected.

## 7.2.3  Single error correction

Longitudinal parity can be used to correct errors as well, when combined with horizontal parity. If a single error occurred, then one can detect precisely which bit is in error since its position is known in term of row and column. Then this bit can be inverted again and the error corrected.

The principle of error correction found in the combination of longitudinal with horizontal parity was extended by Hamming around 1950 [HAM50] to correct single errors. *ERROR CORRECTING CODES* (ECC) are often employed to increase the reliability of memories. Error correcting codes are not common in parallel buses although they become attractive in 32-bit or wider buses. The biggest advantage of error correcting codes is that the overhead of retransmission can be avoided.

The method used by Hamming for *SINGLE ERROR CORRECTION* (SEC) is quite simple. To a data word of k bits, r Hamming check bits are concatenated to form a n-bit codeword. Let´s suppose, to see how it works, that a method exists for correcting errors in that codeword. By applying a proper algorithm to this codeword, we should be able to generate an error report, called a SYNDROME, which indicates precisely the position of the erroneous bit so we can invert it (we expect only one error to be present). If, for instance, the syndrome length is 4 bits, we can check with it a codeword which is 16 - 1 = 15 bits in length, the missing combination being needed to tell that there is no error.

Now, let us put down this 15-bit codeword W1..W15, without caring which bits are data and which are check bits. Below each position 1..15, we write the binary value of the syndrome that should be generated in case of error in that position (figure 7.5).

| Bit position | W1 | 2 | 3 | 4 | 5 | 6 | 7 | 8 | 9 | 10 | 11 | 12 | 13 | 14 | W15 |
|---|---|---|---|---|---|---|---|---|---|---|---|---|---|---|---|
| S0 | · | 1 | · | 1 | · | 1 | · | 1 | · | 1 | · | 1 | · | 1 | · | 1 |
| S1 | · | · | 1 | 1 | · | · | 1 | 1 | · | · | 1 | 1 | · | · | 1 | 1 |
| S2 | · | · | · | · | 1 | 1 | 1 | 1 | · | · | · | · | 1 | 1 | 1 | 1 |
| S3 | · | · | · | · | · | · | · | · | 1 | 1 | 1 | 1 | 1 | 1 | 1 | 1 |

↑ no error

*Fig. 7.5 Syndrome S0..S3 and bit positions*

The zero position corresponds to "no error". To make things more apparent, the zeros have been changed to dots. Consider, for instance, that after the building of the syndrome, we find S = 0110. This means that the bit in position 6 is incorrect and should be inverted.

Conversely, if bit 6 of the codeword is in error, then this should produce a "1" in the syndrome bits S1 and S2 and a "0" in S0 and S3. Now let us see how to generate such a syndrome.

Consider the first row (S0) in figure 7.5. Suppose that the sender uses the check bits of the codeword as parity bits in such a way that the parity over all bits of the codeword which have a "1" in the first syndrome row is odd. That is, if we build the parity over all odd positions W1, W3, W5, W7...W15, S0 will be zero. Obviously, one of the odd positions, W1..W15 contains a parity bit; we will see which one later.

At the destination, we can recompute the parity over the odd positions and it should still be zero if no error occurred in them. But if the computed parity is one, we know that one of the bits in the odd positions is in error, but we do not know which one. If an even location is wrong, this will not affect S0.

# 7 Error Handling

Similarly, let us arrange that the parity over all bits which have a "1" in the second syndrome row S1 (W2, W3, W6, W7, W10, W11, W14, W15) be even. We do the same for all bit positions which have a "1" in the third row S2 (W4..W7, W12..W15) and for all bit positions which have a "1" in the fourth row S3 (W8..W15).

Consider that if bit 6 in figure 7.5 is in error, then this will affect the parity of the second and third row, S1 and S2, but not S0 and S3. Therefore, the vector S0..S3 is 0110 and points to position 6 where the error took place.

As explained above, there must be in the codeword one parity bit for each row which completes the parity of its row to "0". These parity bits are called the HAMMING BITS H0..H3. There are obvious positions for the Hamming bits: every time a Hamming bit is in error, it should point to its own position. Therefore, the positions for the parity bits is where there is only one "1" in the column, that is, at positions 1, 2, 4, and 8. The rest of the codeword is filled with the data bits, as shown by figure 7.6.

| Position | 1 | 2 | 3 | 4 | 5 | 6 | 7 | 8 | 9 | 10 | 11 | 12 | 13 | 14 | 15 |
|---|---|---|---|---|---|---|---|---|---|---|---|---|---|---|---|
| S0 | · | 1 | · | 1 | · | 1 | · | 1 | · | 1 | · | 1 | · | 1 | · | 1 |
| S1 | · | · | 1 | 1 | · | · | 1 | 1 | · | · | 1 | 1 | · | · | 1 | 1 |
| S2 | · | · | · | · | 1 | 1 | 1 | 1 | · | · | · | · | 1 | 1 | 1 | 1 |
| S3 | · | · | · | · | · | · | · | · | 1 | 1 | 1 | 1 | 1 | 1 | 1 | 1 |
| Content | H0 | H1 | D0 | H2 | D1 | D2 | D3 | H3 | D4 | D5 | D6 | D7 | D8 | D9 | D10 |

H0 = parity over D0, D1, D3, D4, D6, D8, D10
H1 = parity over D0, D2, D3, D5, D6, D9, D10
H2 = parity over D1, D2, D3, D7, D8, D9, D10
H3 = parity over D4, D5, D6, D7, D8, D9, D10

*Fig. 7.6 Single error correction*

When the information is received, the receiver builds the parities over all codeword bits including the Hamming bits (figure 7.7). The resulting values of S0..S3 yield as a syndrome the position of the faulty bit. The syndrome is then fed to a logic circuit which inverts the faulty bit. This logic consists simply of an XOR gate placed in each data line, which complements the corresponding bit, and an address decoder, which selects one of the XOR gates.

It is quite easy to find how many Hamming bits are required for a given data length. A syndrome of length r points to $2^r$ positions, one of which is needed to signal that there is no error, that is, the codeword has a length of $2^r -1$ bits, of which r bits are Hamming bits. Therefore, the number of data bits is $2^r - 1 - r$. The number of code and data bits is shown in figure 7.8.

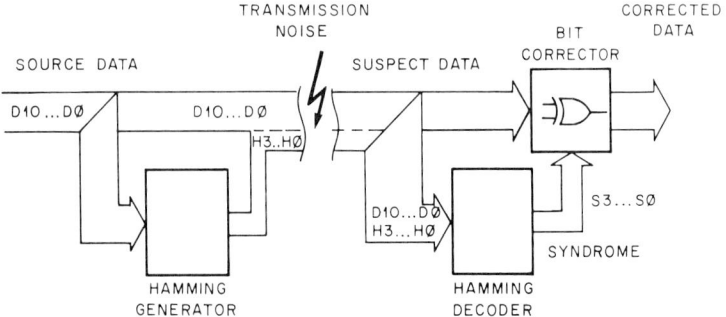

*Fig. 7.7   Single error correction (SEC) circuit*

| check bits r | codeword bits $n=2^r-1$ | data bits $k=n-r$ | Hamming code name (n, k) |
|---|---|---|---|
| 3 | 7 | 4 | (7,4) |
| 4 | 15 | 11 | (15,11) |
| 5 | 31 | 26 | (31,26) |
| 6 | 63 | 57 | (63,57) |
| 7 | 127 | 120 | (127,120) |
| 8 | 255 | 247 | (255,247) |

*Fig. 7.8   Codeword size for SEC*

The corresponding codes are known as HAMMING (n, k) CODES. Note that the efficiency of the code, i.e. the relation data bits/code bits, increases with the codeword length. Therefore, it is more efficient to protect a long word than a short one, but the limit is given by the acceptable residual error rate, like for parity.

The length of the data field (11, 26, 57, etc.) is unusual in the computer world, where word sizes are multiples of 4 or 8. This means that, in practice, some data positions are not used. If there is only an 8-bit data word to protect, then we can ignore the three positions D8..D10. If some positions are not exploited, we are able not only to correct all single errors, but also to detect some double errors: those which yield syndromes pointing to the unused positions. Except for this case, a double error will fool SEC, since it lets the logic correct the wrong bit.

Alternatively, the SEC Hamming codes can also be used to detect all double errors, but then they cannot correct them. Every time a syndrome appears which is different from 0, a single or double error occurred. Therefore, one should be careful since some manufacturers

# 7 Error Handling

advertise their circuits for "single error correction, double error detection" (SEC/DED), meaning that they can do either, but not both. The following section will show how both SEC and DED can be made.

## 7.2.4 Single error correction, double error detection

SEC codes can be used for SINGLE ERROR CORRECTION AND DOUBLE ERROR DETECTION (SEC+DED) at the expense of one additional check bit. With the previous SEC scheme a double error manifests itself as a seemingly correct syndrome which points to the wrong position.

Suppose that a first error is present, and the syndrome points (correctly) to location 6 (0110). A second error would change the syndrome into any of the following just by changing one bit: 1110, 0010, 0100, 0111. Note now, that an error which inverts one bit changes the number of "1s" in the word, that is its Hamming Weight. If the weight was even, an error makes it odd; if it was odd, it is made even.

So we now put the additional restriction on syndromes, that they all have the same Hamming Weight. A second error would then change the HW of the syndrome and this would be detected as a second (uncorrectable) error. To do so, we must sacrifice all bit positions which have an even Hamming Weight, as figure 7.9 shows.

| Bit position | 1 | 2 | 3 | 4 | 5 | 6 | 7 | 8 | 9 | 10 | 11 | 12 | 13 | 14 | 15 |
|---|---|---|---|---|---|---|---|---|---|---|---|---|---|---|---|
| S0 | · | 1 | · | 1 | · | 1 | · | 1 | · | 1 | · | 1 | · | 1 | · | 1 |
| S1 | · | · | 1 | 1 | · | · | 1 | 1 | · | · | 1 | 1 | · | · | 1 | 1 |
| S2 | · | · | · | · | 1 | 1 | 1 | 1 | · | · | · | · | 1 | 1 | 1 | 1 |
| S3 | · | · | · | · | · | · | · | · | 1 | 1 | 1 | 1 | 1 | 1 | 1 | 1 |
| Contents: | H0 | H1 | | H2 | | | D0 | H3 | | | D1 | | D2 | D3 | |

*Fig. 7.9 Valid syndromes for SEC+DED*

Only four data bit positions remain. (Of course, we choose to remove those bit positions which have an even weight so as not to remove the Hamming bits).

If the syndrome is now for instance 11 ( binary: 1011), inverting one of its four bits will yield one of the invalid bit positions (3, 9, 15 or 10), which will be flagged as a double error. However, a third error can fool SEC+DED. This means that 4 check bits are required to perform SEC+DED on a data word of 4 bits and, in general, the relation holds that $2^r \geqslant 2 \cdot n$.

We need therefore 3 check bits to protect one bit, 4 check bits for 4 bits, and so on as figure 7.10 shows.

| check bits r | codeword bits n | data bits k | Hamming code name (n, k) |
|---|---|---|---|
| 3 | 4 | 1 | (4,1) |
| 4 | 8 | 4 | (8,4) |
| 5 | 16 | 11 | (16,11) |
| 6 | 32 | 26 | (32,26) |
| 7 | 64 | 57 | (64,57) |
| 8 | 128 | 120 | (128,120) |

Fig. 7.10 Check, data and codeword size for SEC+DED

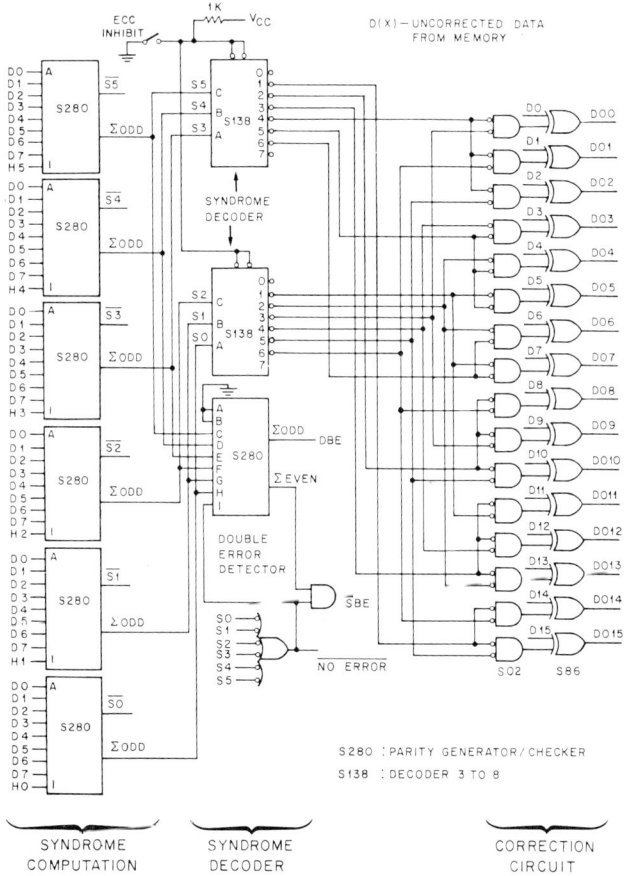

Fig. 7.11 SEC+DED circuit with integrated circuits

# 7 Error Handling

As for the above case of SEC, the data size of these codes is unusual in the computer world. Therefore, some positions remain unassigned. For instance, 5 bits are required to protect an 8-bit word with 3 unassigned positions, 6 bits are required for 16-bit words with 10 unassigned positions and 7 bits for 32-bit words with 25 unassigned positions. Most of the subtleties of the hardware design apply to the correct choice of unused combinations so as to minimize the logic.

Figure 7.11 shows a complete decoder circuit for SEC+DED built with standard TTL circuits [ALT79]. The data lines (D1..D16) and the Hamming bits (H0..H5) are applied at the input to the parity generators which build the syndrome bits S0..S5. The syndrome is decoded by the ´138 to select one of the 16 data complementers which form the correction circuit. Double errors are detected by building the parity over the syndrome word, which is even when there is no error or a double error.

Figure 7.12 shows the syndrome building matrix of the INTEL memory controller for SEC+DED on 16 bits [ALT79].

| Bit position | 1 | 2 | 3 | 4 | 5 | 6 | 7 | 8 | 9 | 10 | 11 | 12 | 13 | 14 | 15 | 16 | 17 | 18 | 19 | 20 | 21 | 22 |
|---|---|---|---|---|---|---|---|---|---|---|---|---|---|---|---|---|---|---|---|---|---|---|
| | H0 | H1 | H2 | D0 | H3 | D1 | D2 | D3 | H4 | D4 | D5 | D6 | D7 | D8 | D9 | H6 | D10 | D11 | D12 | D13 | D14 | D15 |
| | 1 | 2 | 4 | 7 | 8 | 11 | 13 | 14 | 16 | 19 | 21 | 22 | 25 | 26 | 28 | 32 | 35 | 37 | 38 | 41 | 42 | 44 |
| S0 | 1 |   |   | 1 |   | 1 | 1 |   |   | 1 | 1 |   | 1 |   |   |   | 1 | 1 |   | 1 |   |   |
| S1 |   | 1 |   | 1 |   | 1 |   |   | 1 |   | 1 |   | 1 |   |   | 1 |   | 1 |   | 1 |   |   |
| S2 |   |   | 1 | 1 |   |   | 1 | 1 |   |   | 1 | 1 |   | 1 |   |   | 1 | 1 |   |   |   | 1 |
| S3 |   |   |   |   | 1 | 1 | 1 | 1 |   |   |   | 1 | 1 | 1 |   |   |   |   | 1 | 1 | 1 |   |
| S4 |   |   |   |   |   |   |   |   | 1 | 1 | 1 | 1 | 1 | 1 | 1 |   |   |   |   |   |   |   |
| S5 |   |   |   |   |   |   |   |   |   |   |   |   |   |   |   | 1 | 1 | 1 | 1 | 1 | 1 | 1 |

*Fig. 7.12 Syndrome generator table for a 16-bit data word*

Note that positions 31 (011111), 47 (1001111), 55, 59, 61, and 62 are missing in figure 7.12. These positions have been dropped since their Hamming Weight is 5 and consequently these bits would need to be routed to 5 different parity generators instead of 3 for the other combinations. If only weight 1 (check bits) and weight 3 are considered, then a 20-bit word can be protected. The unassigned combinations are 49, 50, 52 and 56.

The manufacturers differ in which other combinations they drop to reduce the number of data bits to 16. Some, for instance, drop positions 21, 22, 41 and 42 and use combinations 49, 50, 52 and 56 instead. This is what the manufacturers call "modified Hamming Codes", and great care must be taken when interfacing the chips of different manufacturer that they have the same syndrome generator. Such errors tend not to appear to the designer, since most of the time, the circuit works error-free.

### 7.2.5 Efficiency of SEC and DED

One can calculate the maximum possible efficiency of a code without knowing whether such a code exists. For instance, we can calculate the theoretical efficiency of a code which is capable of single error detection, like the SEC Hamming Code.

Single Error Correction (or double error detection without correction) requires a Hamming Distance (HD) of 3 between any 2 legal codewords. Figure 7.13 shows the Hamming Distance between the valid codewords A, B and C as a linear distance, although one should keep in mind that it is a distance in an N-dimensional space. For instance, A and C could be at a distance of 3 from each other.

For each legal combination, the nearest neighbours at HD = 1 are assumed to be the original combination with one bit in error (A´, A", B´, B", C´, C"). It seems likely that if combination A´ is found, the original combination was A rather than B, since the distance HD to A is only 1 while the distance to B is 2. SEC can be fooled by a double error, for instance if the original A was transformed into B´. The combinations (A, B, C) which are at a distance of 3 are legal, that is, a 3-bit error can remain undetected.

```
--->------o------<------>------o------<------>------o------<---
  A'      A     A"    B'     B     B"    C'     C     C"
```

Fig. 7.13 Single Error Correction (HD = 3)

We calculate now how many bits are needed to implement a Hamming Distance of 3: A codeword consists of n bits, divided in r check bits and k data bits. With n bits, $2^n$ combinations exist, of which only $2^k$ are legal. Around each legal combination, there are n illegal combinations at a distance of 1, which we can find out by inverting, one after the other, all bits of the original word and the check bits. So, for each data word, we need (n + 1) combinations, n for the illegal combinations and 1 for the original legal one.

Since the maximum possible number of combinations is $2^n$, we can state that:

$2^k \cdot (n+1) \leq 2^n$  or, since n = k + r:  $(k + r + 1) \leq 2^r$

This relation means, for instance, that for an 8-bit word we need 3 check bits, for a 16-bit word 4 check bits and for a 32-bit word we need 5 check bits to achieve a Hamming Distance of 3 between 2 legal codes. PERFECT CODES are codes for which the above relation is an equality, that is, all possible combinations of the n code bits are used. The SEC code we have seen is a perfect code. This is not evident, since few perfect codes have been discovered.

Using the same method, one can calculate the theoretical number of check bits and the rate for SED+SEC codes (figure 7.14) and codes with higher Hamming Distances. However, although we can calculate the theoretical number of check bits, this does not give us the code. The fact is that mathematics can only tell us how good a known solution is; they are not capable of generating the solution. Numerous encoding schemes still remain to be discovered.

```
>------0------<------x------>------0------<------x------>------0------<
A'     A      A"     X      B'     B      B"     X      C'     C      C"
```

Fig. 7.14 SEC+DED (HD = 4)

## 7.3 ERROR DETECTION IN LONG MESSAGES

### 7.3.1 Checksum

The Hamming codes require that the data be divided into pieces of short length, e.g. 8, 16 or 32 bits, which are individually coded. When long messages are transmitted, this method becomes inefficient and error detection and retransmission is preferred. Furthermore, in some transmissions, the length of the data field is not known in advance. For these cases, other coding schemes are used which account for any block length and are relatively easy to implement.

We have already seen a code which is not dependent on the message length: longitudinal parity. Longitudinal parity suffers from the same problem as parity: any double error will fool it. This is not a problem as long as the error rate is low enough. CHECKSUM is another longitudinal check currently used to protect binary files. It consists of treating the data words as binary numbers, regardless of their actual meaning. Then, every $M^{th}$ word we insert the sum modulo n of all M prior n-bit words before it. For instance:

|          |       |                            |
|----------|-------|----------------------------|
| word 1   | H'12  | (hexadecimal representation) |
| word 2   | H'34  |                            |
| word 3   | H'03  |                            |
| word 4   | H'F0  |                            |
| Checksum: | H'39 | (modulo H'100)             |

A double error is sufficient to fool the checksum. But unlike parity, the 2 errors must compensate themselves arithmetically, and this is more unlikely. However, since this possibility exists, the Hamming Distance of a checksum scheme is only 2, like for parity.

### 7.3.2 Cyclic Redundancy Check

There are more efficient codes than checksum, which provide a higher minimum Hamming Distance with the same number of check bits. Most serial transmissions are protected today by the so-called CYCLIC REDUNDANCY CHECKS (CRC).

CRC are a class of error detecting codes which have been found by applying the theory of set algebra to the coding of data. This theory is rather complicated and lies outside of the scope of this book. The reader is referred to the literature for the details [PET72] and [BLA83]. We shall, however, explain how these codes are built and what they can do without explaining the whys.

The basic idea of the CRC is similar to the checksum principle. The data field is treated as a number, regardless of its actual meaning. A mathematical operation is performed on this number, and the result of that operation is transmitted along with the number as a redundancy check. Upon reception, the same operation is executed on the data field and the result is compared with the transmitted result. If they match, it is very likely that no error occurred (but never impossible).

To increase the code efficiency, the redundancy check should have a short length in relation to the data field length and preferably be of fixed length. Furthermore, the mathematical operation should be easy to perform, i.e. require little hardware or software and be independent of the data field's length.

Division is such a convenient mathematical operation. We can divide the data field by a fixed divisor and transmit the remainder of the division as a redundancy check. Since the remainder of the division is always smaller than the divisor, we can choose a short divisor. If, for instance, the divisor has 17 bits, the length of the checkword will always be 16 bits, independently of the length of the data field.

Let us take an example in the decimal system. Suppose the data is the number 9977788, possibly transmitted as BCD (Binary Coded Decimal) digits. Let us suppose we can afford only one digit for checking purposes. So we divide the data number by a divisor which is smaller than 10, such as 9. Dividing 9977788 by 9 yields a

# 7 Error Handling

remainder of 1, which is appended to the original number. The transmitted message will be 99777881. At the opposite end, we will also divide the first seven digits of the message and check if the remainder is really 1, like the eighth digit tells it should be.

Division is easily performed even on long messages because this operation only requires a shift-and-subtract operation. Remember how a division is done by hand: one starts with the most significant digits of the dividend and compares them to the divisor, working one's way down to the least significant digits. While operating on the most significant digits, the least significant digits of the dividend are not needed yet and could still be in transit; once digits of the dividend have been used in the operation, they are not needed any more and could be transmitted. The subtractor/comparison circuit is just as wide as the divisor (DR), independently of the size of the dividend (DD), which makes it convenient for a hardware implementation.

There remains one point to be cleared: what would be a good divisor? Obviously, using 1 as a divisor is useless, and 2 boils down to the same as parity. The divisor should generate as many different remainders as possible, yet it should not generate a predictable result. For instance, if the length of the check should be one decimal digit, a division by 10 would generate all digits from 0 to 9 as a remainder, but it would be of little use, since that digit would always be equal to the last digit of the data field and, therefore, errors on the other digits would remain undetected. Our above choice of 9 for a one-digit check seems to be convenient. It is however not casual, but stems from the following idea.

Appending the remainder to the original number creates a new number obtained by multiplying the original number by 10 and adding the remainder of the division to it. Now, a refinement consists in subtracting instead of adding the remainder. In the above example, instead of transmitting 9977788 · 10 + 1 = 99777881 we transmit 9977788 · 10 - 1 = 99777879. This last number is now divisible by 9 and would yield a remainder of 0 if no transmission error occurred. The decoding circuit is simplified (no comparison logic is required) and other desirable effects result from it. This scheme works only for a few divisors, which we may find by the following reasoning.

Let the transmitted word be TR = (DD · 10) - R, DD being the original data and R the remainder of the division by DR, the divisor. If DD · 10 has the same remainder as DD when divided by DR, then TR is divisible by DR. So we look for a divisor such that (x) MODULO DR = (10 · x) MODULO DR. Of all numbers below 10, only 3 and 9 have this prOperty (6 MOD 3 = 60 MOD 3 = 600 MOD 3, etc.).

Nine is the best choice since it generates 9 different remainders while 3 generates only 3.

Suppose that the transmitted number was TR = (DD · 10) - R, and that a transmission error added an arbitrary number ER to it. Dividing TR + ER by DR would only yield a remainder of 0 if ER is divisible by DR, that is, an undetectable error should add a multiple of 9 to the transmitted word, which is a rather unlikely event.

The method has however one drawback: subtraction is an operation which requires an operation on the whole data word, and not only on a few digits, like division. This means that the whole message should be stored before the remainder can be computed, and this is not tolerable when the message is long such as in file transmission.

In practice, the above integer arithmetic division is not used in binary transmission (although its principle is taught to children to check multiplications done by hand, under the name of the "proof by nine"). A much more powerful checking mechanism has been found for binary transmissions which obviates the above restrictions and which has emerged from coding algebra. Not only is the hardware required for encoding and decoding much simpler, but the method has been generalized so as to account for an arbitrary high number of errors, and optimized for special kinds of errors, like burst errors.

The data field is not treated any more as a number, but as a polynomial. The n individual bits are considered as the coefficients of a polynomial of degree n-1. For instance, if the data word is 110011, then the associated polynomial is:

$$1 \cdot x^5 + 1 \cdot x^4 + 0 \cdot x^3 + 0 \cdot x^2 + 1 \cdot x^1 + 1$$

If x happens to be equal to 2, then this polynomial yields the value of an integer number whose natural binary representation is the data word, but this is not relevant here. Once the data field is treated as a polynomial, we can apply the rules for polynomial arithmetic to it. Polynomials can be added, subtracted, multiplied and divided, like numbers. For instance, we will make use of polynomial division instead of number division.

Now, a great simplification is introduced by restricting the coefficients of the polynomials to the values 1 and 0, that is to binary values. One speaks then of a {0,1} number system, for which the arithmetic has very simple rules: addition or multiplication of digits is done by XORing, respectively ANDing the individual digits. For instance, the sum of 2 polynomials using {0,1} arithmetic is obtained by XORing the individual coefficients:

# 7 Error Handling

$$P1 = 1110011$$
$$P2 = 1001101$$
$$P1 + P2 = 0111110 = P1 - P2$$

and subtraction is equal to addition. This will take care of our former problem of having to subtract the remainder from the transmitted message. Polynomial division is simpler than number division. As an example, consider the polynomial division in the decimal number system in figure 7.15.

```
               Dividend                              Divisor

3 x⁴ + 2 x³ +   0 x² + 1.0  x + 10    │  2 x² + x + 1
3 x⁴ + 1.5 x³ + 1.5 x²                 │ ─────────────────────
      0.5 x³ - 1.5 x² + 1.0 x          │  1.5 x² + 0.25 x - 0.875
      0.5 x³ + 0.25 x² + 0.25 x        │
                                        │         Quotient
            - 1.75 x² + 0.75 x + 10
            - 1.75 x² - 0.875 x - 0.875
   Remainder polynomial 1.625 x + 10.875
```

*Fig. 7.15 Polynomial division in the decimal number system*

Let us see how polynomial division is done in the {0,1} number system (figure 7.16).

```
x¹⁰ x⁹ x⁸ x⁷ x⁶ x⁵ x⁴ x³ x² x 1

1 1 0 1 1 1 0 1 0 0 1     │  1 1 0 0 1    Divisor (x⁴ + x³ + 1)
1 1 0 0 1                 │ ──────────────
─────────                 │  1 0 0 1 1 0 0
    1 0 1 0 1             │
    1 1 0 0 1             │     Quotient (x⁶ + x³ + x²)
    ─────────
      1 1 0 0 0
      1 1 0 0 1
      ─────────
        0 0 0 0 1 0 1
      Remainder (x² + 1)
```

*Fig. 7.16 Polynomial division in the {0,1} number system*

In the binary system, polynomial division greatly simplifies the comparison logic: the circuit is no longer a full adder, but consists of half-adders, or XOR gates. No carry needs to be generated nor propagated, and therefore the encoding time is greatly reduced. Further, the polynomial division can be executed by a simple shift register with feed-back loops. The division circuit can now be made very fast. Indeed, it would be quite hard to generate the check bits by software at the 10 Mb/s rate (100 ns/bit) of common networks.

Again here, the choice of the divisor polynomial, or GENERATOR POLYNOMIAL is important. Similar considerations apply as above for our choice of 9. The degree of the divisor polynomial is equal to the number of digits in the remainder. For instance, a polynomial of degree 16 will yield 16 digits of remainder.

Numerous generator polynomials are in use and their coefficients are listed in every book on error control codes. Of these, several polynomials have been standardized (figure 7.17).

| | |
|---|---|
| CRC-12 | $x^{12} + x^{11} + x^3 + x^2 + x + 1$ |
| CRC-16 (BSC protocol) | $x^{16} + x^{15} + x^2 + 1$ |
| CRC-CCITT (HDLC protocol) | $x^{16} + x^{12} + x^5 + 1$ |
| CRC-32 (Ethernet) | $x^{32} + x^{26} + x^{23} + x^{22} + x^{16} + x^{12} + x^{11} + x^{10}$ $+ x^8 + x^7 + x^5 + x^4 + x^2 + x + 1$ |

Fig. 7.17 Standard generator polynomials

Note that there are several possible generator polynomials for a 16-bit CRC; in fact, this list is not exhaustive. The actual rules of use of these polynomials are, however, somewhat more complicated, to take care of initialization problems and particularities of the transmission. For instance, the CRC used for HDLC (see 10.3.12) is optimized to detect the corruption of the flag field at the beginning.

Although these polynomials seem quite complicated, the CRC is easily computed by a shift register and a few gates, as shown in figure 7.18. This is the beauty of this scheme. A CRC-16 is capable of detecting all single errors, all double errors for messages of reasonable length, all cases in which the number of errors is odd and all burst errors smaller than the size of the divisor.

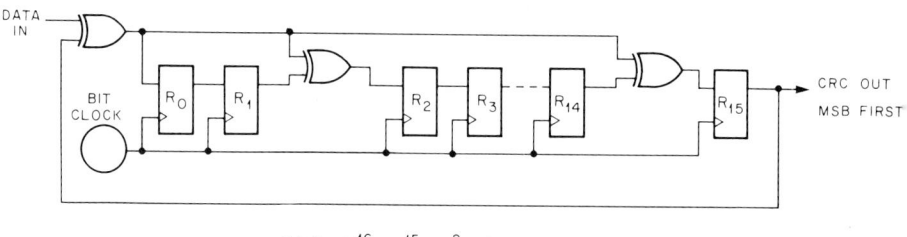

$G(x) = x^{16} + x^{15} + x^2 + 1$

Fig. 7.18 Computation circuit for CRC-16

# 8 CHARACTERISTICS OF BUS LINES

This chapter explains the theory of transmission lines applied to serial and backplane buses, including which effects of this theory are important and which design rules must be followed to make a bus work properly. The calculations, based on the wave equations, and two tools, the lattice diagram for simple cases and Bergerons´s diagram, which accounts for non-linear elements, will be described.

## 8.1 METHODS AND TOOLS

The timing diagrams in a bus specification show neat straight lines and neat sharp edges as shown in figure 8.1a.

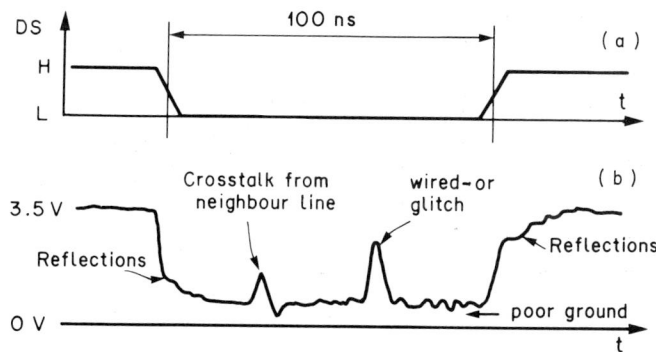

Fig. 8.1  A timing diagram and its representation on the scope

The signals in reality, viewed with an oscilloscope connected to the bus, look different: the edges become rounded, and strange pulses appear where there should be no transition, as shown in figure 8.1b. We therefore need an analytical model to predict the behaviour of a line as closely as possible. There are two different approaches, using either the CONCENTRATED or the DISTRIBUTED model.

If the line is short with respect to the wavelength of the signals, then a model consisting of discrete (concentrated) elements is sufficient. In such a concentrated model, the transmission line is modelled by an equivalent circuit consisting of a capacitance, an inductance and a resistance, to which the classical AC theory is applied. For instance, the "ringing" of a transmission line at switch-on can be modelled by treating the line as a resonant circuit with a centre frequency and a damping factor.

The concentrated model will not produce accurate results when the bus is long with respect to the wavelength of the signals involved. If we consider that current logic circuits produce signal edges in the order of 1 ns to 10 ns, the electromagnetic waves in printed circuits would travel some 16 cm to 160 cm during one edge. This wavelength is within the dimensions of a backplane bus or a large printed circuit board and the concentrated model ceases to be accurate. Serial buses, though, can extend in length from one metre to several km. The limitations due to the finite propagation speed of the waves will come fully into play for them and thus one cannot rely on the concentrated model any more to model their behaviour.

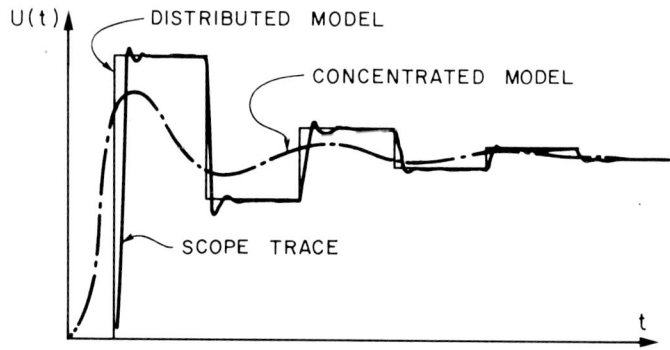

*Fig. 8.2  Behaviour of a line according to the concentrated model, the transmission line model, and the oscilloscope trace*

# 8 Characteristics of Bus Lines

The analysis of distributed systems is therefore carried out with the distributed model, applying the differential wave equations rather than their integral form as in the concentrated model. The distributed theory, also called the *TRANSMISSION LINE THEORY*, was originally developed to explain the behaviour of telegraph and telephone lines and hydraulic oscillations. This model is well suited to explain the behaviour of buses and links and we will use it throughout this chapter. Figure 8.2 shows a comparison of both models and an actual measurement.

## 8.2 IDEAL TRANSMISSION LINE BEHAVIOUR

This section will provide an intuitive view of the behaviour of a signal travelling on a transmission line, such as one single line of a bus. The theoretical bases and the equations that govern these waves are well described in mathematical literature, in particular in [BLO82] and [DWO79], which are recommended for a rigorous analysis. They will not be reproduced here. Instead, the models developed in the literature will be used without justification.

### 8.2.1 An experiment

Consider a single line, driven at one end by a transmitter, and having a receiver at the other end. This is a good model for a serial link. The end of the line near the transmitter is called the *NEAR END*, the opposite end of the line is the *FAR END*.

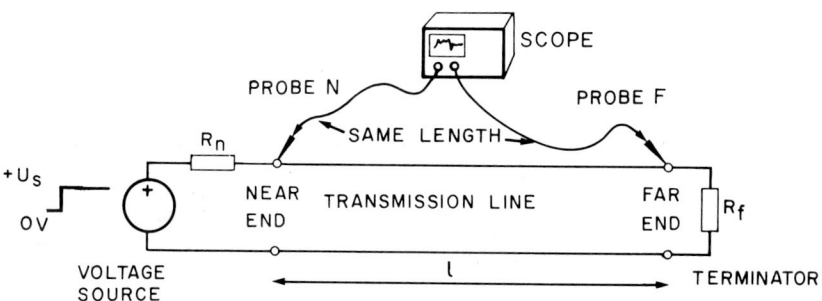

Fig. 8.3  *A transmission line*

The transmitter can be modelled as a voltage source with an internal resistance $R_n$ connected to the line. It is capable of generating a step of height $U_s$ with a sharp edge and of arbitrary duration. The receiver at the far end is modelled by a resistance $R_f$.

The behaviour of the bus is observed with the help of 2 probes, one attached to each end of the backplane. They measure the voltages at the locations n (for near) and f (for far) as a function of time, u(n,t) and u(f,t) respectively. These high-impedance probes do not disturb the signals on the bus, and since they are of equal length, we may pretend to observe both ends of the bus at the same time.

Initially, the line is at a quiescent voltage of zero. At time t = 0, the transmitter is turned on. After an infinite amount of time, assuming that the line has no resistance of its own, the voltage on the line will eventually reach the value:

$$U_\infty = U_s \cdot \frac{R_f}{(R_n + R_f)} = u(n,\infty) = u(f,\infty)$$

We will now examine what happens between switch-on and the quiescent state: The signal form registered by two probes appears in figure 8.4.

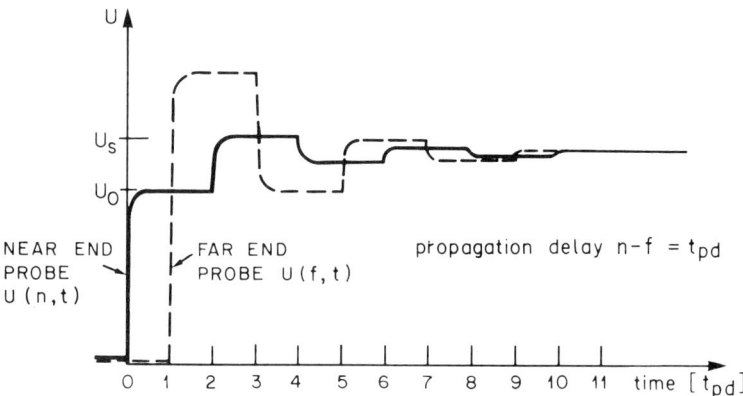

Fig. 8.4 Switching-on a transmitter on a transmission line

Such curves can be observed effectively on a standard 100 MHz oscilloscope if the transmission line is fairly long (> 30 m). Only a very fast (> 1 GHz) oscilloscope can show these same curves on a short (< 50 cm) backplane bus, because a slower oscilloscope would smooth out the waveform. The probes must be of the high impedance type and they must be carefully grounded.

### 8.2.2 Behaviour at switch-on (0 ⩽ t < $t_{pd}$)

At t = 0, the probe placed near the transmitter registers a voltage step. The probe placed at the far end of the line registers nothing yet, as figure 8.4 illustrates. This is because the change of voltage and current at the transmitter propagates as a wave toward the far end of the line, but has not yet arrived there.

# 6 Characteristics of Bus Lines

It is interesting to note that the voltage rise at the near probe is not equal to the amplitude of the step $U_s$. One could make some measurements varying the source resistance $R_n$, and find out that the line behaves as if it had a resistance of its own which is much larger than the ohmic resistance of the line (which can be measured with an ohmmeter). In fact, while the copper resistance of the line is a fraction of an $\Omega$, the apparent resistance $R_w$ of the line at switch-on is in the order of 100 $\Omega$. It thus seems as if the transmission line opposes a resistance to the wave that propagates.

In the first moment, the source only sees a network of the form shown in figure 8.5.

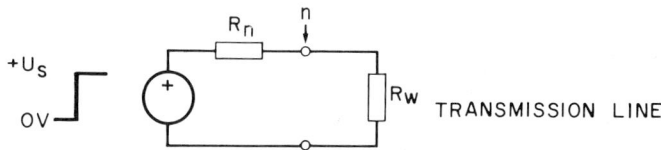

*Fig. 8.5   What the driver sees at turn-on*

And the first voltage step is given by the relation:

$$u(n,0) = U_s \cdot \frac{R_w}{(R_n + R_w)}$$

A wave $\tilde{U}_0$ with that amplitude propagates from near to far. The little arrow on top of the waves like $\tilde{U}_0$ is there to remind the reader that these are not instantaneous values but waves, characterized by a speed and a waveform (the shape which an observer travelling along at the same speed as the wave would see).

Note that this relation does not depend on $R_f$. This should be evident if one considers that no information can travel faster than light. At turn-on, the source just cannot "know" that a termination resistor exists. Indeed, while $t < t_{pd}$, $R_f$ need not even be connected !

The resistance to the wave, $R_w$, is called the CHARACTERISTIC IMPEDANCE $Z_w$ of the transmission line. The characteristic impedance is a constant of a transmission line. It is the ratio of the voltage to the current of the travelling wave, as we could compute by measuring the current of the wave. Indeed, although our scope only registers voltages, the wave has a current as well. Voltage and current wave are related by:

$$\tilde{I} = \frac{\tilde{U}}{Z_w}$$

$Z_w$ is a pure resistance if the medium is a perfect conductor (without losses). The characteristic impedance does not depend on the line's length, but only on its geometry and dielectric properties. This will be detailed further in section 8.4.2.

### 8.2.3 First reflection ($t = t_{pd}$)

During $0 < t < t_{pd}$, the signal wave travels from the transmitter to the termination of the line. We could see it pass by inserting probes at different places along the line.

At $t = t_{pd}$, the second probe registers a voltage rise, as figure 8.4 shows. Obviously, it took some time for the wave to travel along the line. This time is the *PROPAGATION TIME* $t_{pd}$. The distance between the probes divided by the propagation time $t_{pd}$ gives the *TRANSMISSION SPEED* $v_p$ of the signal. The measured propagation speed is somewhat lower than the speed of light, it is about half as much ($v_p$ = 16 cm/ns versus c = 30 cm/ns) for an epoxi backplane, as we will see in section 8.4.3.

Now, the amplitude of the voltage step registered at the far end of the line at $t = t_{pd}$ is different from the voltage of the incoming wave. The voltage rise is due to the fact that the original wave which travelled from left to right has been *REFLECTED* at the end of the

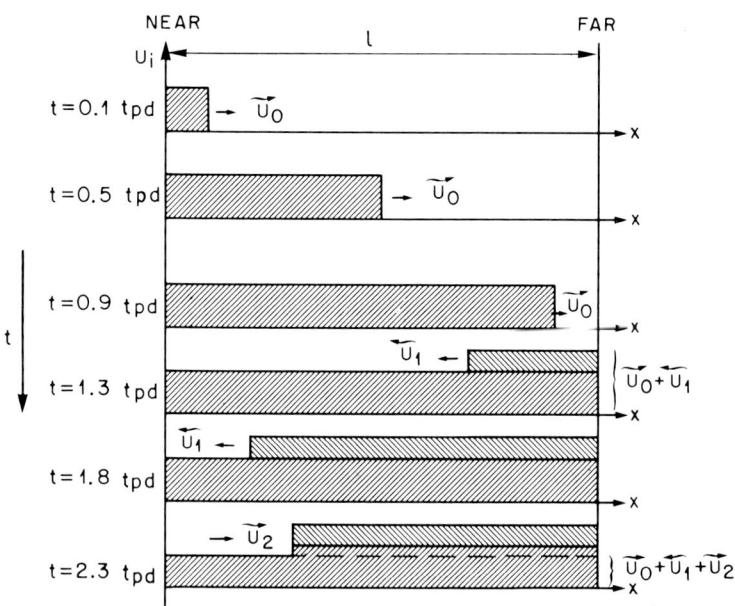

*Fig. 8.6 Reflection at the ends of the line*

# 8 Characteristics of Bus Lines

backplane. A new wave $\tilde{U}_1$ is created, which travels in the backward direction, from right to left, and superposes itself on the original wave $\tilde{U}_0$. What we observe at the termination is the sum of the forward and backward waves' amplitudes. Figure 8.6 shows a movie sequence of the state of the line's voltage.

The amplitude of this reflected wave depends exclusively on the relation between the termination resistor (figure 8.3) and the characteristic impedance. The ratio of the amplitude of the reflected wave to that of the original wave is called the REFLECTION COEFFICIENT r. The reflection coefficient at the far end, $r_f$, is given by the relation:

$$r_f = \frac{\tilde{U}_1}{\tilde{U}_0} = \frac{R_f - Z_w}{R_f + Z_w}$$

If the line is open ($R_f = \infty$), the incoming wave is completely reflected and the voltage $u(f, t_{pd})$ is exactly twice the amplitude of the incoming wave. The amplitude of the voltage of the reflected wave is equal to the amplitude of the original wave. The reflection coefficient is then $r_f = 1$. Since the sum of the currents of the forward and backward waves must be equal to zero (open circuit), the reflected wave's current is equal in value to the original wave's, but of opposite sign. And since the current is considered positive if it flows from left to right, the negative value of the current of the reflected wave is cancelled by the fact that the wave travels backwards, thus $r_f = 1$ holds for the current, too. No energy is lost in an open circuit.

If the line is short-circuited ($R_f = 0$), no voltage appears at the end of the line, but current flows. Here again, energy is conserved (no energy is lost in a short circuit). This means that the voltage of the reflected wave has the same amplitude as that of the incoming wave, but a negative sign ($r_f = -1$). The current of the reflected wave is identical in amplitude and sign to the current of the original wave, but since it travels backwards, the reflection coefficient for the current is also $r_f = -1$.

Thus we can see that the reflected wave can be either positive or negative, depending on the relation between $R_f$ and $Z_w$. As a rule of thumb, one could remember that the reflection coefficient is positive when the wave encounters a higher resistance.

The amplitude of the reflected wave can also be zero if $R_f = Z_w$, for which $r_f = 0$. The energy of the wave is totally transformed into heat by the termination resistance. This is called PERFECT MATCHING. Since perfect matching suppresses all reflections, it is the ideal case for a transmission line.

### 8.2.4 Return to sender ($t = 2 \cdot t_{pd}$)

Between $t = t_{pd}$ and $t = 2 \cdot t_{pd}$, the portion of the original wave that has been reflected returns toward the transmitter (figure 8.6). Of course, once several waves superpose, a probe at the site x along the line would only register the sum of the waves u(x,t). The previous relation:

$$\tilde{U} = Z_w \cdot \tilde{I}$$

applies only to the current and voltage of the same wave and not to the instantaneous values u(x,t) and i(x,t) which are the sum of all instantaneous wave values.

At $t = 2 \cdot t_{pd}$, the reflected wave reaches the transmitter. Only at this time can an observer at the transmitter probe know that a termination exists. Even then, if the line were perfectly matched ($R_f = Z_w$), no reflection would travel back, and a probe at the driver could not tell the difference between a finite, perfectly terminated line and an infinite line.

If the source impedance $R_n$ of the transmitter is different from the characteristic impedance, the backward wave $\tilde{U}_1$ is reflected and a new forward wave $\tilde{U}_2$ is created. Just as at the far end, the amplitude of the reflected wave is equal to the incoming wave's amplitude multiplied by the reflection coefficient at the near (transmitter) end, $r_n$:

$$r_n = \frac{R_n - Z_w}{R_n + Z_w}$$

In this example, we assume that the impedance of the transmitter is lower than the impedance of the line. Therefore, the second forward wave $\tilde{U}_2$ has a negative sign and the voltage at the near end drops.

The wave reflected at the transmitter travels back from right to left towards the far end, which it reaches at time $t = 3 \cdot t_{pd}$. Again, a reflected wave:

$$\tilde{U}_3 = r_f \cdot \tilde{U}_2$$

appears, which will reach the near end of the line at $t = 4 \cdot t_{pd}$, and so on. Since energy is lost with each reflection (if the line is not open or short circuited), the amplitude of the wave becomes smaller at every reflection, and after an infinite amount of time and numerous "ping-pongs", the amplitude at both the transmitter and the

# 8 Characteristics of Bus Lines

termination end will reach the stationary value that we calculated at the beginning of this section:

$$U_\infty = U_s \cdot \frac{R_f}{(R_n + R_f)}$$

## 8.2.5 Matching the line

The designer of high-speed circuits and transmission links is especially interested in matching the transmitter, the receiver and the

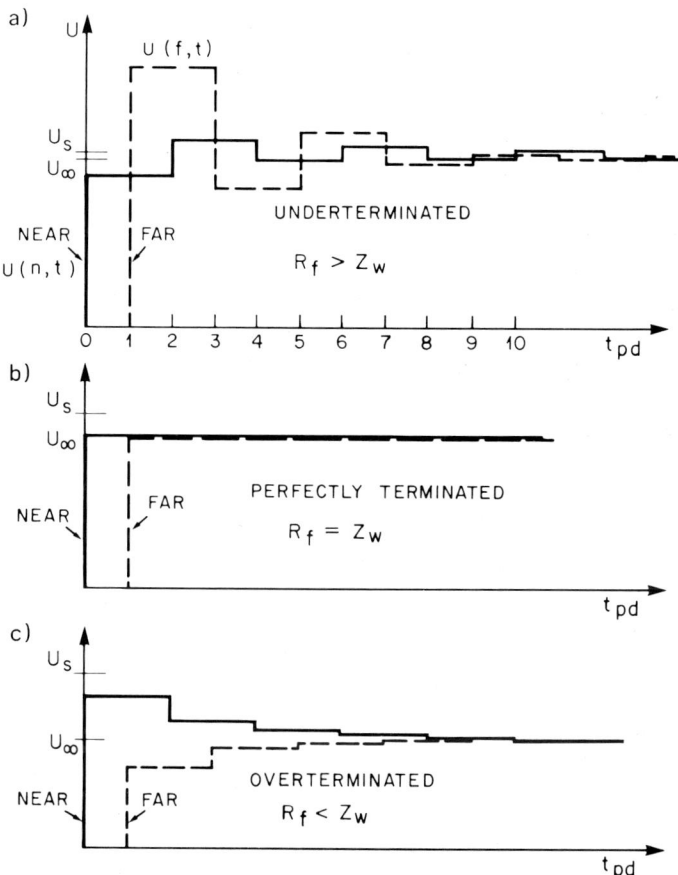

Fig. 8.7  Line ringing as a function of the termination
   a) Underterminated
   b) Perfectly terminated (matched)
   c) Overterminated line

transmission line. The parameters which are the easiest to modify are the values of the resistances at the ends of the line, while the characteristic impedance is a constant of the medium. The resistances modify the reflection coefficient and determine the ratio of the amplitude of the incident to the amplitude of the reflected wave.

In figure 8.7, we observe the instantaneous voltages at the near and at the far end corresponding to different reflection coefficients at the end.

Although a perfect termination is desirable for a good design, it may not always be feasible because of layout restrictions or power dissipation requirements, for instance. The terminator is usually a single resistor connected to the return conductor. We will see other kinds of terminators in section 8.8.

## 8.3 WAVE PROPERTIES

### 8.3.1 Linear model

The voltage and current changes are transmitted as waves through the transmission line. If the transmission medium has negligible losses, the wave shape and amplitude do not change down the line; for example, an observer travelling at the speed of the wave would always see the same shape. This is what we will assume in the following calculations, since the losses are negligible for all media that are relevant to us.

Even if the transmission medium has losses, it remains linear: the superposition principle holds, and the instantaneous voltage value u(x,t) is equal to the sum of the waves. If the losses are not frequency-dependent, the shape of a wave will not change down the line, but its amplitude may.

If the termination is a linear resistance, a reflected wave having the same shape as the original is generated. Figure 8.8 shows how two waves in opposite directions cross each other without disturbing their shape and how they are reflected at the ends.

In most of the subsequent calculations we assume that the signal has the form of a step wave which lasts for a large number of reflections. In reality, the output of a voltage source such as a transistor is not a step wave, but has at best the shape of a trapezoid.

This is not a severe restriction, since for all practical purposes, a transmission line is a linear system for which the law of superposition holds: for any calculations, an arbitrary waveform can be sliced into a

# 8 Characteristics of Bus Lines

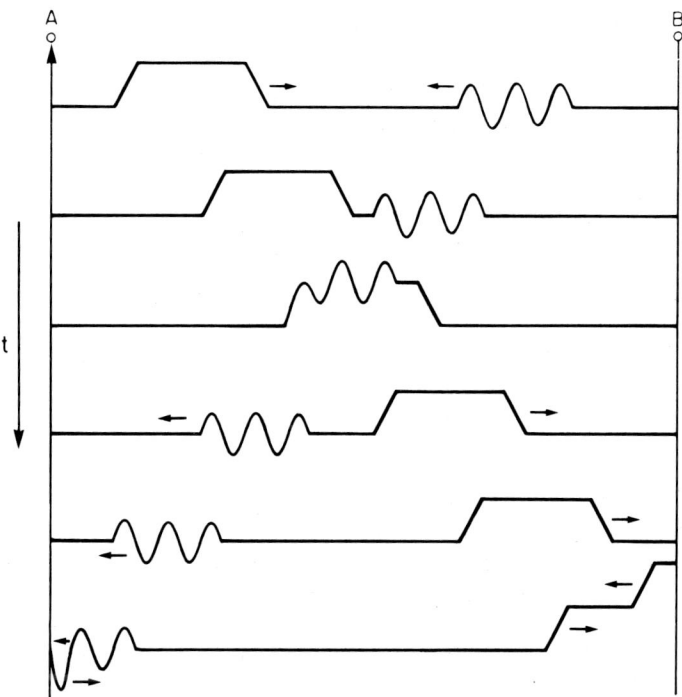

*Fig. 8.8  Two waves travelling in opposite directions*

series of rectangular waves. The instantaneous value of the line voltage is the sum of the instantaneous values of the existing waves. Furthermore, the square wave case will yield worst-case values for the reflected voltages.

## 8.3.2  Trapezoidal waves

When applying the superposition principle to a trapezoidal wave, the reflected waves are also trapezoidal and their slopes just add and subtract to the slope of the original wave. Figure 8.9 shows the case of an open far end and a short-circuited near end, considering only the (infinite) leading edge of a trapezoidal wave.

Note that the maximum amplitude of the deviation in figure 8.9 will remain constant and equal to the slope of the original wave multiplied by the propagation delay $t_{pd}$. The reader can verify that in

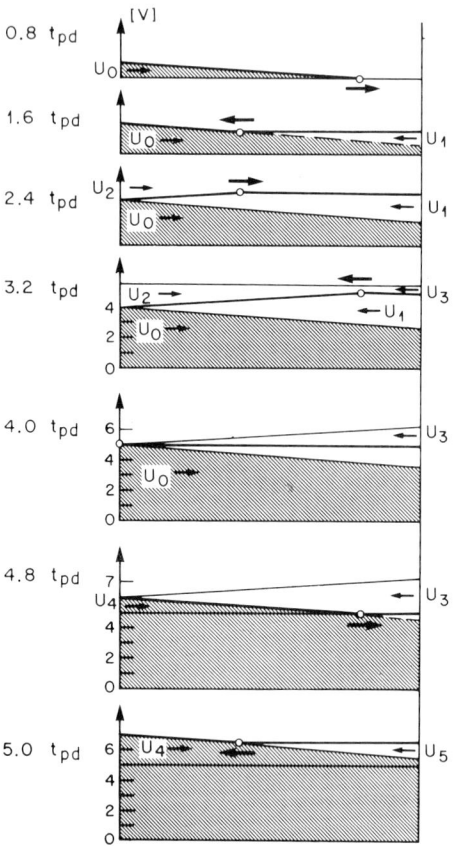

Fig. 8.9 Reflections on the leading edge of a trapezoidal wave

the example of figure 8.9, the maximum deviation will always remain equal to 1.25 V. Therefore, as time passes, the amplitude of the deviation relative to the amplitude of the original wave $\tilde{U}_0$ will decrease.

The reflections can therefore be neglected when the slope of the signal lasts longer than twice the propagation delay of the transmission line, even in the worst case of the open circuit at the far end. This result is of practical importance for a printed circuit board. For instance, the Schottky TTL has a rise time $t_r$ of about 3 ns. Therefore, no terminations will be required if the lines are shorter than 45 cm. On smaller distances, the circuit can be conveniently modelled by the concentrated model.

### 8.3.3 Frequency-dependent losses

The modelling will become more complicated as dielectric losses and the skin effect become appreciable. Both are frequency-dependent losses. DIELECTRIC LOSSES are due to the energy lost in changing the polarity of the dipoles in a dielectric material and they increase with frequency. Only a vacuum is free from dielectric losses, which are negligible when the dielectric is air or a gas.

The SKIN EFFECT is the displacement of the current path from the centre to the periphery of a conductor due to the field generated by the current itself. The net effect is that the resistance of the conductor increases with the frequency of the signal. For instance, at 10 MHz, a printed circuit line 1 mm wide and 35 $\mu$ thick will have about twice the ohmic resistance that it had at DC. The skin effect depends on the form of the conductor: at 10 MHz, a round conductor with the same section has twice the resistance of a flat one, which is the reason why some flat cable manufacturers advertise square conductors.

The skin effect and dielectric losses are proportional to the frequency. They cause the different frequency components of a signal to travel at different speeds and thus, DISPERSION will occur. Dispersion causes the filtering of the higher frequency components of the signal. Dispersion plays a role when the frequency of the signal is high, i.e. when the rising time of the signal is very short and distances are long. Dispersion limits the useful frequency range of a medium.

These effects will not be considered here, although they are responsible for a significant deviation from theory at the frequency of the fast logics. ECL circuits, for instance, exhibit 1 ns edges, which correspond to a limit frequency of 350 MHz. But other effects, including the reflections on all discontinuities of the backplane (such as connectors), the proximity of other lines, imperfections of the measuring equipment and even the operator's skill are more significant and less easy to deal with. A measurement accuracy of 10% is already good at these frequencies.

### 8.3.4 Non-linear elements

Although a transmission line is in general a linear element (even frequency-dependent losses do not change this fact), the transceivers and receivers at its ends are normally non-linear elements. Therefore, the shape of the reflected wave does not coincide with the shape of the original wave. We will see how to deal with these elements using Bergeron's method.

## 8.4 TRANSMISSION LINE PARAMETERS

### 8.4.1 Model of a transmission line

The behaviour of a transmission line can be approximated by the model of a DELAY LINE, consisting of infinitesimal inductances, capacitances, resistances and conductances, called the LUMPED MODEL. The value of the inductance per unit length is called the LINEAR INDUCTANCE L' which is measured in Henry per metre (H/m). Similarly, we define the LINEAR CAPACITANCE C', measured in Farad per metre (F/m), the LINEAR RESISTANCE R', measured in Ohm per metre ($\Omega$/m), and the LINEAR CONDUCTANCE G', measured in Siemens per metre (S/m).

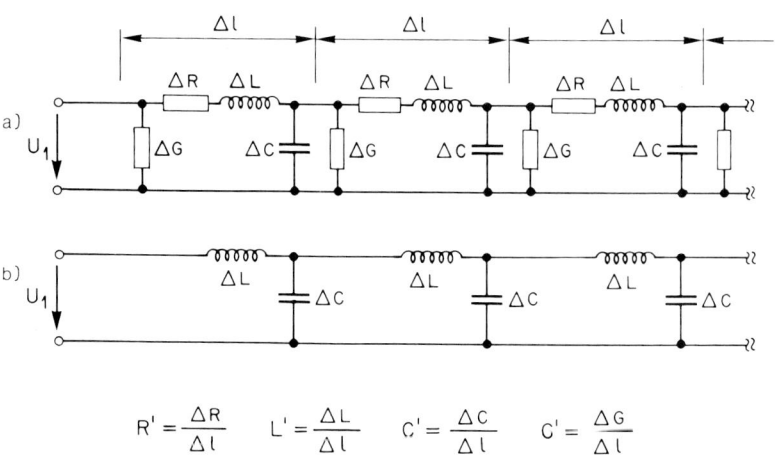

$$R' = \frac{\Delta R}{\Delta l} \quad L' = \frac{\Delta L}{\Delta l} \quad C' = \frac{\Delta C}{\Delta l} \quad G' = \frac{\Delta G}{\Delta l}$$

*Fig. 8.10 Delay line model of a transmission line*
  *a) Line with losses*
  *b) Line without losses*

In a perfectly conducting line (without losses), such as the one we will consider here, both the linear resistance R' and the linear conductance G' are zero (figure 8.10b).

# 8 Characteristics of Bus Lines

## 8.4.2 Characteristic impedance

The characteristic impedance $Z_w$ is a physical property of the transmission line. It does not depend either on the length of the line or on its termination, but only on the geometric and dielectric properties of the line. Although $Z_w$ is called an impedance, it is a pure resistance when the line has negligible losses: it has no capacitive or inductive components. And although it is a pure resistance, it dissipates no power (since the line has no losses). The characteristic impedance cannot be measured by an impedance bridge; it is calculated by measuring the reflections. The instrument which measures these reflections is called a time-domain reflectometer. It uses precisely the theory we are going to develop here.

The characteristic impedance is physically defined as the ratio of the voltage to the current of a wave:

$$Z_w = \frac{\tilde{U}}{\tilde{I}}$$

Remember that the voltage and the current of a wave are not identical to the measured voltage and current $u(x,t)$, $i(x,t)$ observed at the site x on the line, except when there is only one wave travelling (no superposition of waves). $Z_w$ does not depend on the shape of the wave.

The characteristic impedance is given by the relation:

$$Z_w = \sqrt{\frac{L'}{C'}}$$

where $L'$ and $C'$ are the inductance and capacitance per unit length of the line, respectively.

For simple geometries, the characteristic impedance can be calculated in closed form using Maxwell's equations. For complicated conductor forms, it is experimentally measured and made available in the form of a graph.

Even free space (vacuum) posseses a characteristic impedance $Z_0$, since waves travel through it have both a current and a voltage. $Z_0$ is calculated as

$$Z_0 = \sqrt{\frac{\mu_0}{\epsilon_0}} = 376 \; \Omega$$

where

$$\mu_0 = 4 \cdot \pi \cdot 10^{-7} \quad \text{H/m} \quad \text{(absolute permeability)}$$

$$\varepsilon_0 = 8.854 \cdot 10^{-12} \quad \text{F/m} \quad \text{(absolute permitivity)}$$

are the absolute permeability and permitivity of vacuum, respectively. In any other medium, the permeability $\mu$ and permitivity $\varepsilon$ are higher. We define :

$$\mu_r = \frac{\mu}{\mu_0} \quad \text{(relative permeability)}$$

$$\varepsilon_r = \frac{\varepsilon}{\varepsilon_0} \quad \text{(relative permitivity)}$$

Note that the characteristic impedance of a conductor can be higher than $Z_o$. There are standard 600 $\Omega$ telephone cables, for example.

### 8.4.3 Propagation speed

The propagation speed is also a property of the line. It is often indicated in the form of a propagation delay (inverse of the propagation speed).

The propagation speed can be deduced from the linear inductance and capacitance according to the relation:

$$v_p = \frac{1}{\sqrt{L'C'}}$$

When the medium is homogeneous (no discontinuities or concentrated elements are present) the propagation speed is equal to:

$$v_p = \frac{1}{\sqrt{\varepsilon \cdot \mu}}$$

The speed in an homogeneous medium does not depend on the geometry of the conductors, but only on the dielectric properties of the insulation. If $\varepsilon_r$ and $\mu_r = 1$, for example, then $v_p$ would be equal to the speed of light in a vacuum, c = 30 cm/ns.

The following table gives typical values of $\varepsilon$, $v_p$ and $C'$ for different media:

| $\mu = \mu_0$ | $\varepsilon_r$ | $v_p/c$ | $v_p$ (cm/ns) | $C'$ (pF/m) |
|---|---|---|---|---|
| Vacuum | 1 | 1 | 30 | 0 |
| Coaxial cable | 1.7 to 2.3 | 0.77 to 0.66 | 23 to 20 | 45 to 100 |
| Twisted pair | 2.3 | 0.65 | 20 | 120 to 300 |
| Flat cable | 1.8 | 0.7 | 22 | 42 to 95 |
| Epoxi PC board | 3.5 to 4.5 | 0.5 to 0.47 | 16 to 14 | 20 to 200 |

We note that the speed of electromagnetic waves along the surface of a PC board is generally only half the speed of light in a vacuum. To reduce losses and increase speed, coaxial cables are insulated by foam or use the dielectric only as a mechanical support in the form of a helix around the conductor in the centre.

### 8.4.4 Numerical values

The characteristic impedance and the propagation delay are deduced from the linear capacitance and inductance. These values depend on the geometrical arrangement of the conductors and of the dielectric. The starting point of all calculations is the knowledge that a wave requires two conductors to propagate, one which is considered the signal line and the other which is the reference or ground. This is the only way one can calculate a value for the linear capacitance and inductance. The characteristic impedance of a single line dangling in a circuit is not defined: it depends on the proximity of the line to the return conductor. Transmission lines which have a defined characteristic impedance are sometimes called "controlled impedance" lines.

It is interesting to note that any change in geometry which increases the line's capacitance will reduce its inductance and vice-versa. For instance, placing a conductor closer to its return path increases the capacitance, but reduces the inductance and the characteristic impedance, which tends to go in the same direction as the inductance, but the propagation delay changes very little. This is easily explained for a homogeneous medium, in which the propagation speed does not depend on $C'$ or $L'$, but only on their product, which is constant and equal to $\mu \cdot \varepsilon$ (above formula). Now, as long as the dielectric remains the same, the speed does not vary, and when $C'$ increases, $L'$ must decrease. This is also valid to a certain point in heterogeneous media.

Another interesting fact is that the characteristic impedance does not depend on the absolute dimensions of the conductors: shrinking all dimensions by any factor would yield the same characteristic impedance as long as the medium remains homogeneous.

The following tables show the characteristic impedance and the linear capacitance and inductance of the most important transmission line types: coaxial and (twisted) line pairs, flat cables, and micro-strip and striplines. Microstrip and striplines are good approximations of conductors in a printed circuit board.

The values for $Z_w$, $L'$, and $C'$ can be deduced analytically only for the simplest geometrical arrangements, such as coaxial cables and balanced twisted lines. In fact, all of the formulas that follow are only approximations, even for the mathematically "neat" case of the coaxial cable. The skin effect, for instance, has been neglected.

All the following figures assume that the relative magnetic permeability is equal to one (no magnetic materials are present). The term $Z_n$ is often introduced to normalize the results. $Z_n$ is called the nominal characteristic impedance. It has the value:

$$Z_n = \sqrt{\frac{\mu_0}{\epsilon_0}} \cdot \frac{1}{2\pi} = 60 \ \Omega$$

The values of 60 or 120 $\Omega$ in the tables below stem from this term. $Z_n$ should not be confused with the characteristic impedance of a vacuum, $Z_o$.

*COAXIAL CABLES* are used over long distances and have a high figure of merit (data rate per distance). The standard values for coaxial cables are 50, 75 and 93 $\Omega$ (figure 8.11).

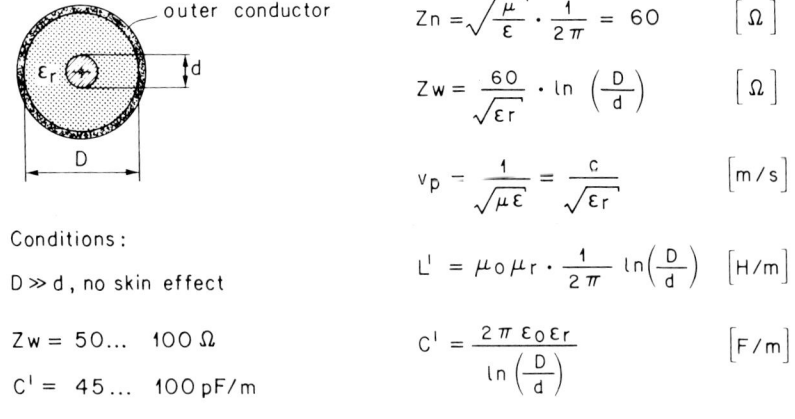

$$Zn = \sqrt{\frac{\mu}{\epsilon}} \cdot \frac{1}{2\pi} = 60 \quad [\Omega]$$

$$Zw = \frac{60}{\sqrt{\epsilon_r}} \cdot \ln\left(\frac{D}{d}\right) \quad [\Omega]$$

$$v_p = \frac{1}{\sqrt{\mu\epsilon}} = \frac{c}{\sqrt{\epsilon_r}} \quad [m/s]$$

Conditions:

$D \gg d$, no skin effect

$$L' = \mu_0 \mu_r \cdot \frac{1}{2\pi} \ln\left(\frac{D}{d}\right) \quad [H/m]$$

$Zw = 50... \ 100 \ \Omega$

$C' = 45... \ 100 \ pF/m$

$$C' = \frac{2\pi \epsilon_0 \epsilon_r}{\ln\left(\frac{D}{d}\right)} \quad [F/m]$$

*Fig. 8.11 Coaxial cable electrical characteristics*

# 8 Characteristics of Bus Lines

TWISTED WIRE pairs are cheaper than coaxial cable and widely used for low speed transmissions (figure 8.12).

$$Z_w = \frac{120}{\sqrt{\varepsilon_r}} \cdot \ln\left(\frac{2s}{d}\right) \quad [\Omega]$$

$$v_p = \frac{1}{\sqrt{\mu_0 \varepsilon_0 \varepsilon_r}} = \frac{c}{\sqrt{\varepsilon_r}} \quad [m/s]$$

$$L' = \mu_0 \cdot \frac{1}{\pi} \cdot \ln\left(\frac{2s}{d}\right) \quad [H/m]$$

$$C' = \varepsilon_0 \varepsilon_r \cdot \frac{\pi}{\ln\left(\frac{2s}{d}\right)} \quad [F/m]$$

Conditions: s >> d
h >> s

$Z_w$ = 50... 600 $\Omega$
$C'$ = 120... 300 pF/m

*Fig. 8.12 Twisted wire pair electrical characteristics*

The most common FLAT CABLES consist of an arrangement of parallel conductors. Flat cables made of several twisted pairs also exist.

The parameters of a flat cable can be deduced from the above wire-pair formulas. The characteristic impedance is always taken with respect to the return conductor. For instance, if a group of 10 lines have only one ground return at one edge of the cable, the line nearest to it has a characteristic impedance of some 100 $\Omega$ while the farthest can have an impedance of more than 1000 $\Omega$.

Several manufacturers offer flat cables with a controlled impedance by inserting ground lines between the signal lines (figure 8.13).

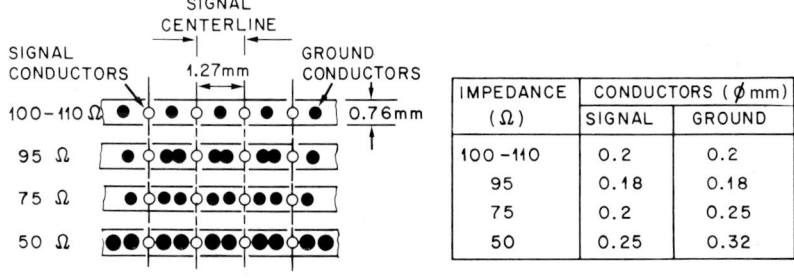

| IMPEDANCE ($\Omega$) | CONDUCTORS ($\phi$ mm) | |
|---|---|---|
| | SIGNAL | GROUND |
| 100-110 | 0.2 | 0.2 |
| 95 | 0.18 | 0.18 |
| 75 | 0.2 | 0.25 |
| 50 | 0.25 | 0.32 |

*Fig. 8.13 Section of different flat cables*

It is difficult to manufacture flat cables with an impedance lower than 50 $\Omega$. Current values are 50, 75, 93, 95, 100 and 140 $\Omega$.

The *SINGLE WIRE OVER GROUND* corresponds to a conductor running parallel to a ground plane. It is the base for the calculation of printed circuit lines, when one face of the printed circuit is a ground plane and the other a signal plane (figure 8.14).

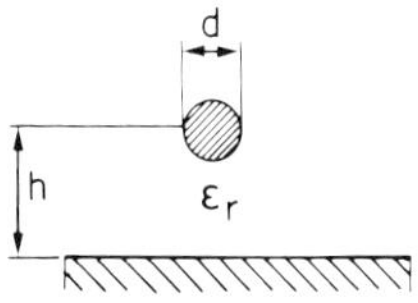

$$Z_w = \frac{60}{\sqrt{\varepsilon_r}} \cdot \ln\left(\frac{4h}{d}\right) \quad [\Omega]$$

$$v_p = \frac{1}{\sqrt{\mu_0 \varepsilon_0 \varepsilon_r}} = \frac{c}{\sqrt{\varepsilon_r}} \quad [m/s]$$

Conditions:
$h \gg d$

$$L' = \mu_0 \cdot \frac{1}{2\pi} \cdot \ln\left(\frac{4h}{d}\right) \quad [H/m]$$

$$C' = \frac{\varepsilon_0 \varepsilon_r \cdot 2 \cdot \pi}{\ln\left(\frac{4h}{d}\right)} \quad [F/m]$$

*Fig. 8.14 Single wire over ground*

The *MICROSTRIP* is a model for one etched line in a printed circuit with respect to a ground plane (figure 8.15). Conductors in PC boards without a parallel ground line or a ground plane have no defined characteristic impedance and can therefore only be used with predictable results over short distances. The microstrip has only one degree of freedom, which is the ratio of w/h. The thickness of the copper has little effect and cannot be changed easily in practice.

The microstrip and the following striplines formulas have been deduced by Cohn [COH54], by Kaupp [KAU67] and Wheeler [WHEE77] based on actual measurements. Composite dielectrics such as the

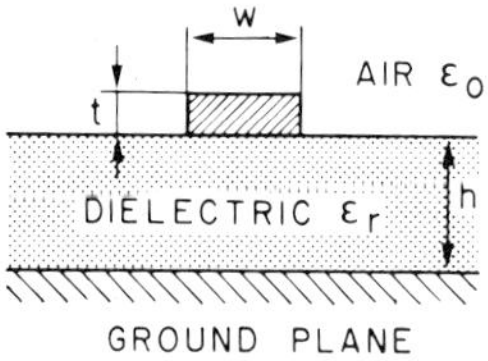

Effective epsilon: $\varepsilon_f = 0.475\, \varepsilon_r + 0.67$

$$Z_w = \frac{60}{\sqrt{\varepsilon_f}} \cdot \ln\left(\frac{4h}{0.535w + 0.669t}\right) \quad [\Omega]$$

effective diameter

$$v_p = \frac{c}{\sqrt{\varepsilon_f}} \quad [m/s]$$

Conditions:
$0.1 < \frac{w}{h} < 3,\ 1 < \varepsilon_r < 15$
$Z_w \approx 100\,\Omega$

$$L' = \frac{\mu_0}{2\pi} \cdot \ln\left(\frac{4h}{0.535w + 0.669t}\right) \quad [H/m]$$

$$C' = \frac{\varepsilon_0 \varepsilon_f \, 2\pi}{\ln\left(\frac{4h}{0.535w + 0.669t}\right)} \quad [F/m]$$

*Fig. 8.15 Microstrip geometry*

# 8 Characteristics of Bus Lines

printed circuit boards do not lend themselves to an accurate calculation: the fields are heterogeneous, since one half of the dielectric is air, while the other is epoxy. Therefore, the field lines are distorted and the wave does not even travel in the mode on which all the above theory is based (which is called the TEM or Transverse Electromagnetic Mode by the microwave engineers). Furthermore, the proximity of other transmission lines also has an influence. We use Kaupp's expressions here, which are accurate within 3% of actual measurements.

Printed circuit boards have an $\varepsilon_r$ in the range of 3.5 to 5. The industry standard board thickness is 1.6 mm. When the other face is used as a ground, the distance to ground is 1.6 mm. When a multilayer board is used, the distance is a fraction of 1.6, e.g. 0.8 mm in a 3-layer board when the ground plane is the middle layer, and 0.5 mm for a four-layer board. The thickness of the conductor does not have much effect on the impedance, since it is typically 0.038 mm. The width of the conductors are generally standard, ranging from 0.34 mm to 10 mm. Figure 8.16 shows the range of characteristic impedances for typical PC-boards used in backplanes. Two limits are visible: that of the thinnest line which can be reliably manufactured, and that of the thickest line, which is dictated by the connector pin distance on a backplane. Standard values of 100 Ω for a 2-layer backplane, resp. 50 Ω for a multilayer backplane, are derived from this figure.

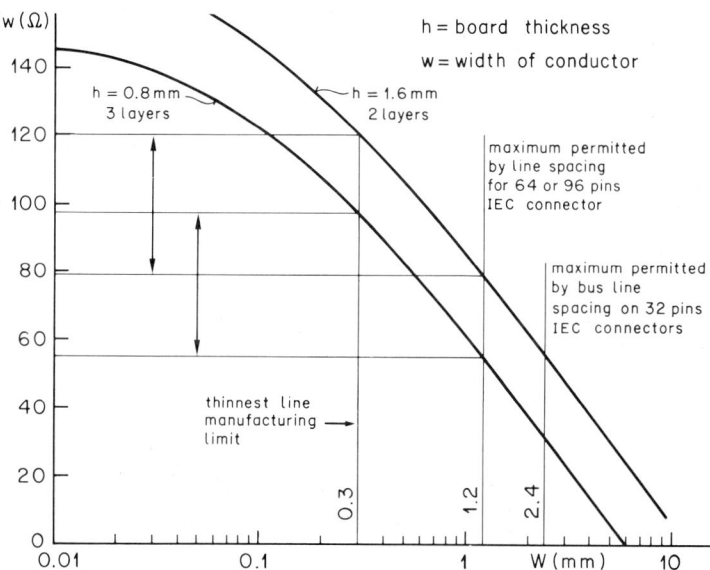

*Fig. 8.16 Printed circuit board characteristic impedances*

A *STRIPLINE* (figure 8.17) is an approximation for a printed circuit line running between two ground planes, as occurs in multilayer printed circuits. Since the wave travels in a homogeneous medium, the characteristics of the line are closely controlled.

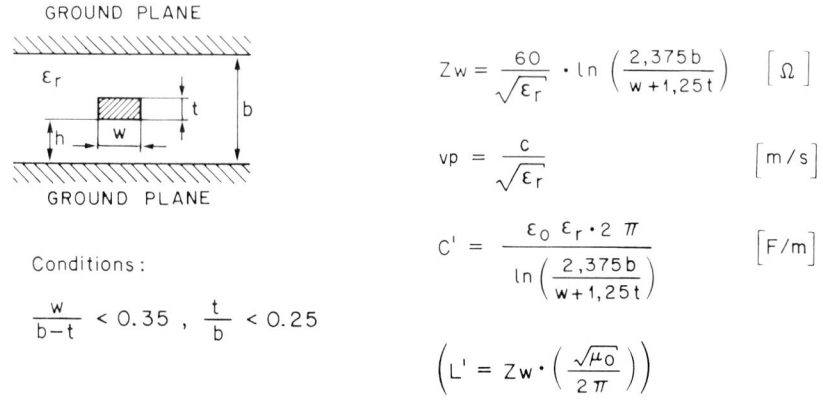

$$Zw = \frac{60}{\sqrt{\varepsilon_r}} \cdot \ln\left(\frac{2,375\,b}{w+1,25\,t}\right) \quad [\Omega]$$

$$vp = \frac{c}{\sqrt{\varepsilon_r}} \quad [m/s]$$

Conditions:

$$\frac{w}{b-t} < 0.35 \;,\; \frac{t}{b} < 0.25$$

$$C' = \frac{\varepsilon_0\,\varepsilon_r \cdot 2\,\pi}{\ln\left(\frac{2,375\,b}{w+1,25\,t}\right)} \quad [F/m]$$

$$\left(L' = Zw \cdot \left(\frac{\sqrt{\mu_0}}{2\,\pi}\right)\right)$$

*Fig. 8.17 Stripline geometry*

Striplines are used for very fast logic, such as ECL and microwave transmissions, for example.

## 8.4.5 Loading a line

A bus line is by definition a tapped line: each receiver and especially each transmitter introduces a capacitive load at the connection point (figure 8.18). Each connection also introduces a small inductive component, which is mainly due to the connector. It is neglected here but would compensate somewhat the following results.

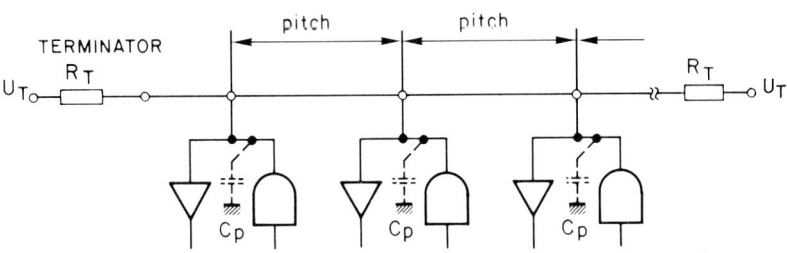

*Fig. 8.18 Loading a line*

# 8 Characteristics of Bus Lines

Since the discrete capacitors are inserted at a regular pitch, their effect can be considered as an additional linear capacitance:

$$Cl' = Cp / pitch$$

The resulting characteristic impedance is approximated by the formula:

$$Z_w = \sqrt{\frac{L'}{Co' + Cp/pitch}} = \frac{Z_w}{\sqrt{1 + Cl'/Co'}}$$

For instance, a bus line having a width of 0.34 mm and an $\varepsilon_r$ of 4.7, which is placed over a ground plane at a distance of 0.76 mm (middle layer), has the following characteristics, according to figure 8.16.

$$Co' = 60 \text{ pF/m} \quad Z_w = 93 \text{ } \Omega \quad v_p = 17 \text{ cm/ns}$$

If each board adds 15 pF, which corresponds to the loading by Schottky-TTL drivers, and the boards are inserted at a pitch of 2 cm, the total capacitive loading will be:

$$C' = 60 + 15/0.02 = 810 \text{ pF/m}$$

The net effect is a decrease in the characteristic impedance, which drops from 93 $\Omega$ to:

$$Z_w = \frac{93}{\sqrt{810/60}} = 25 \text{ } \Omega$$

Also, the propagation speed has been slowed down to:

$$v_p = \frac{17}{\sqrt{810/60}} = 4.6 \text{ cm/ns}$$

which is now equal to only one-sixth of the speed of light (30 cm/ns). A loaded line is truly a delay line. These figures are quite realistic: the measured values of commercial driver capacitance vary between 7 pF and 32 pF, with the most recent devices centering around 10 pF. Special low-capacitance drivers reduce the capacitive loading by separating the driver's output from the bus with the help of a Schottky diode, for example [BALA84], but must pay it with a 1V voltage drop over the diode.

In a filled backplane, the capacitive loading by the boards far outweigths the capacitive loading of the backplane itself.

All backplane buses are affected by the problem of capacitive loading. When the characteristic impedance is lowered, the voltage steps will be lower for the same current. Therefore, one has to either wait for additional reflections or increase the currents. The latter increases crosstalk (as we shall see) and power dissipation. The additional signal delay cannot be compensated for and will ultimately limit the useful bandwidth of the bus, since most parallel buses rely on some kind of handshake mechanism.

Furthermore, if an unloaded bus has been correctly terminated by its characteristic impedance, there will be a mismatch when the bus is loaded. Ideally, the termination resistance should change according to the number of boards inserted, but this is very impractical to achieve.

Serial buses are less affected by capacitive loading, since the taps are spaced at larger distances (most serial bus standards prohibit spacing closer than about one meter) and since the characteristic impedance of a coaxial cable is lower than that of a backplane bus. The reduction in speed must however be considered in the protocol.

## 8.5 LATTICE DIAGRAM

### 8.5.1 Homogeneous line with termination

The lattice diagram is a simple tool used to calculate the reflections on a line. Here, we consider both the current and the voltage amplitude of the wave.

We consider a line as in figure 8.19.

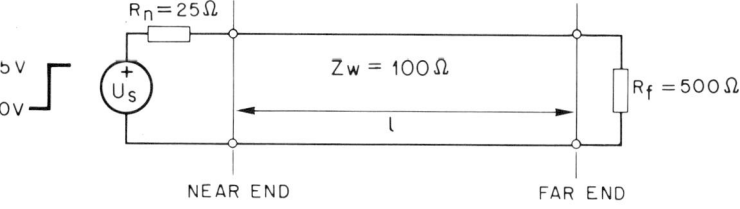

Fig. 8.19 A transmission line

With the values $R_n$ = 25 $\Omega$, $Z_w$ = 100 $\Omega$ and $R_f$ = 500 $\Omega$, the reflection coefficients at the ends compute to:

# 8 Characteristics of Bus Lines

$$r_n = \frac{R_n - Z_w}{R_n + Z_w} = -0.6 \qquad r_f = \frac{R_f - Z_w}{R_f + Z_w} = +0.6667$$

At first, the line is at 0 V. Then, at time t = 0, the transmitter is turned on from 0 V to a voltage of 5 V. The propagation delay through the line is $t_{pd}$.

Since in the first moment, the transmitter "sees" only the characteristic impedance, the first voltage step at the transmitter end is:

$$u(n,0) = U_s \cdot \frac{Z_w}{R_n + Z_w} = 0.8 \cdot 5 = 4 \text{ V}$$

A voltage wave $\tilde{U}_0 = 4$ V now travels toward the termination. The current wave has the amplitude:

$$\tilde{I}_0 = \frac{\tilde{U}_0}{Z_w} = 40 \text{ mA}$$

It is reflected at the far end at time $t = t_{pd}$ with a reflection coefficient $r_f$. The reflected wave $\tilde{U}_1$ has the value:

$$\tilde{U}_1 = \tilde{U}_0 \cdot r_f = 4 \cdot 0.6667 = 2.67 \text{ V}$$

$$\tilde{I}_1 = \frac{\tilde{U}_1}{Z_w} = 26.6 \text{ mA}$$

It adds to the value of the incoming wave to yield the voltage at the far end termination:

$$u(f, t_{pd}) = 4 + 2.67 = 6.67 \text{ V}$$

The backward wave $\tilde{U}_1$ returns to the transmitter, which it reaches at $t = 2 \cdot t_{pd}$. There it is reflected and generates a new forward wave (the reflection coefficient is negative):

$$\tilde{U}_2 = \tilde{U}_1 \cdot r_n = -1.60 \text{ V} \qquad \tilde{I}_2 = \frac{\tilde{U}_2}{Z_w} = -16 \text{ mA}$$

The new voltage at the transmitter is equal to the previous value $\tilde{U}_0$ plus the amplitude of the incoming backward wave $\tilde{U}_1$ plus the amplitude of the outgoing forward wave $\tilde{U}_2$:

$$u(n, 2 \cdot t_{pd}) = \tilde{U}_0 + \tilde{U}_1 + \tilde{U}_2 = 4 + 2.67 - 1.6 = 5.07 \text{ V}$$

This new forward wave will be reflected at $t = 3 \cdot t_{pd}$ at the termination, and so on. These results are summarized in the lattice diagram in figure 8.20.

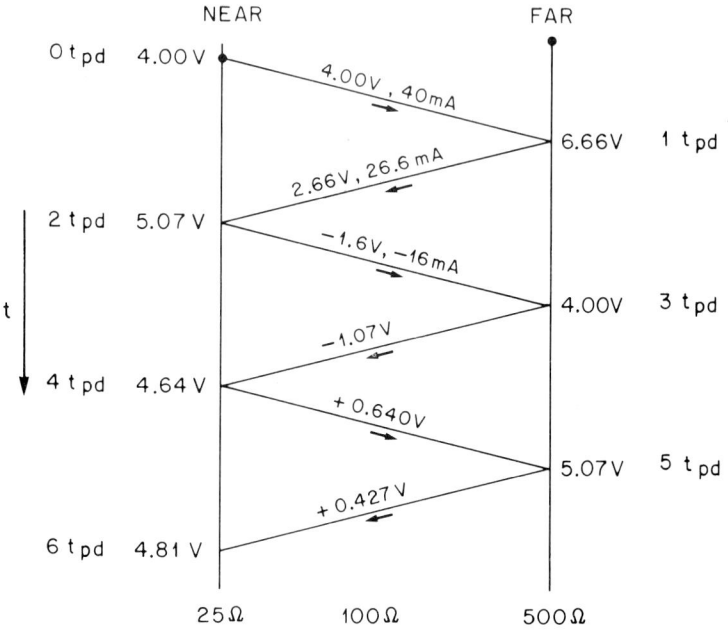

Fig. 8.20 Lattice diagram

Figure 8.21 shows the corresponding voltages observed by probes placed at each end of the line.

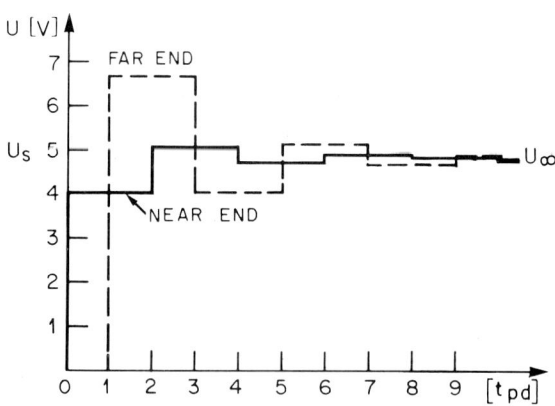

Fig. 8.21 Timing diagram corresponding to figure 8.20

## 8.5.2 Line with discontinuities

A transmission line seldom consists of only one homogeneous medium. Connectors, transitions to and from printed circuit boards, and even sharp bends in a cable or a PC line cause changes in the transmission line's geometry and in its characteristic impedance. When a wave reaches a discontinuity, a reflected back wave is created and a part of the original wave passes through, as shown in figure 8.22.

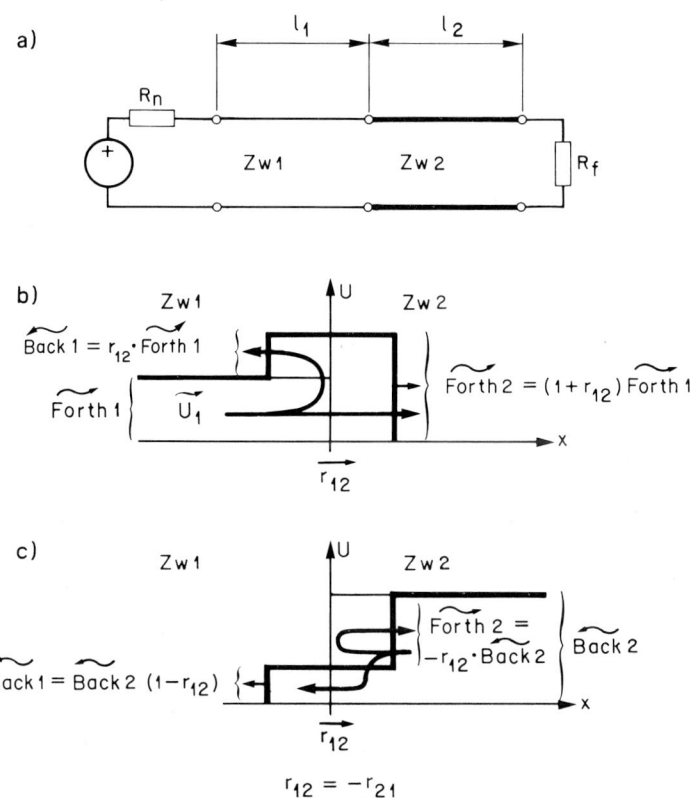

Fig. 8.22 Discontinuity

If $Zw_1$ and $Zw_2$ are the characteristic impedances of the sections of the line, then the reflection coefficient for a wave going from 1 to 2 has the value:

$$\frac{\widetilde{B}_1}{\widetilde{F}_1} = r_{12} = \frac{Zw_1 - Zw_2}{Zw_1 + Zw_2} = -r_{21}$$

The amplitude of the part of the wave that passes on down the line is equal to the amplitude of the original wave minus the reflected wave. The PENETRATION COEFFICIENT $p_{ij}$ is equal to:

$$\frac{\widetilde{F}_2}{\widetilde{F}_1} = p_{12} = 1 - r_{12} \quad \text{and} \quad \frac{\widetilde{B}_1}{\widetilde{B}_2}; = p_{21} = 1 - r_{21} = 1 + r_{12}$$

The penetration coefficient may be higher than one if the wave encounters a medium with a higher $Z_w$. Figure 8.23 shows the lattice diagram corresponding to a transmission line with only one discontinuity.

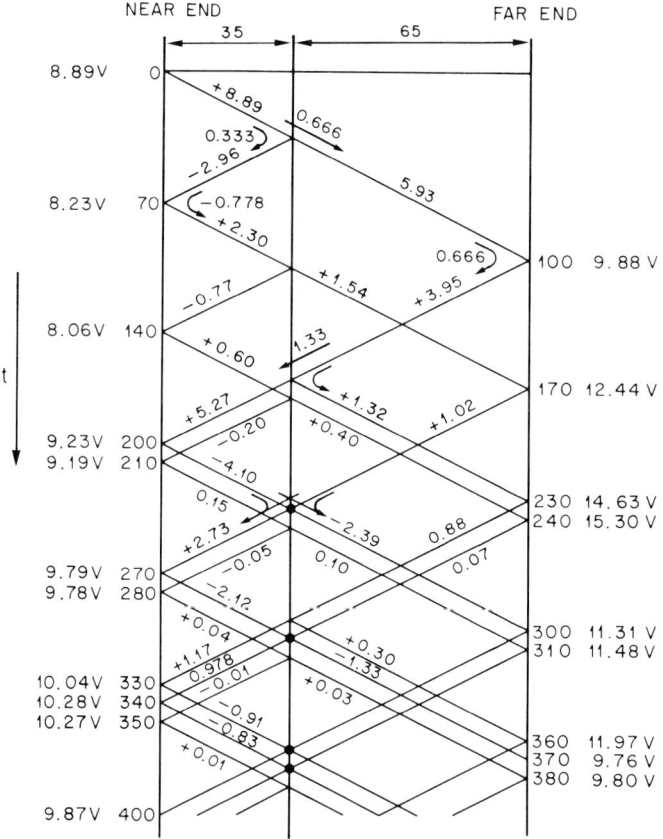

*Fig. 8.23 Lattice diagram of a transmission line with one discontinuity*

# 8 Characteristics of Bus Lines

The resulting voltages at the near and far ends are displayed in figure 8.24 along with the lattice diagram for comparison.

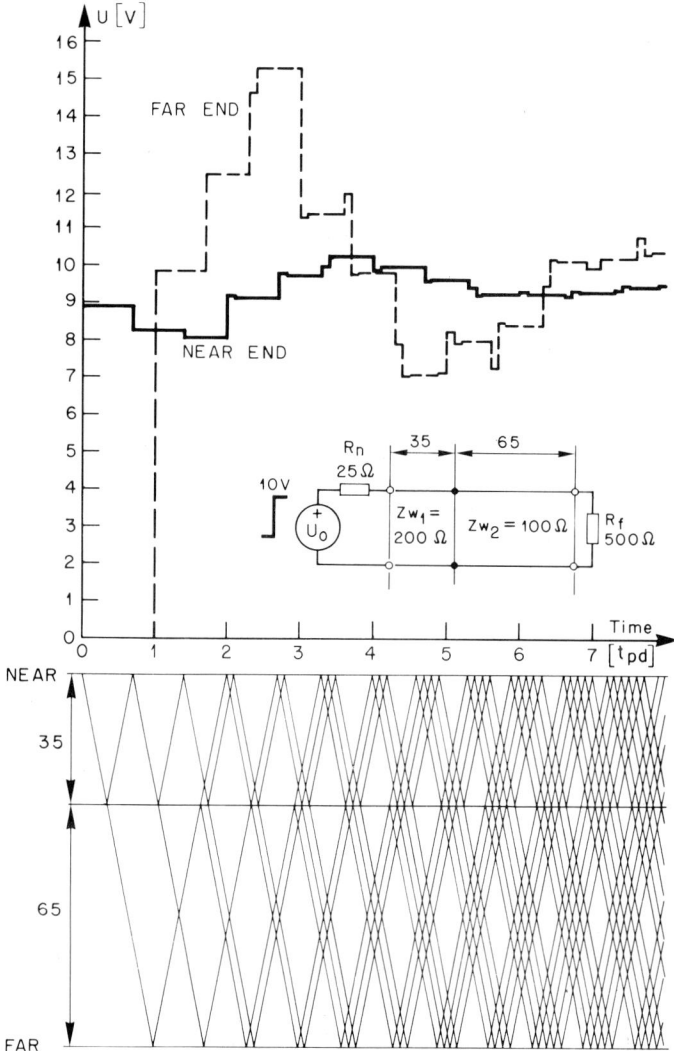

*Fig. 8.24 Voltages at the near and far end with a discontinuity*

The voltages in figure 8.24 are much more similar to the signals we saw on the oscilloscope described earlier in this chapter than the neat waveforms of the former examples. This shows what effect simple discontinuities, such as the connecting of oscilloscope probes, may have on the observed signals.

Of course, the calculation of the voltages at the different points can become quite tedious after the $10^{th}$ reflection. This task should be done using an algorithm such as that of Megill [MEG81], which will be explained here. The transmission line of length L is sliced into N segments with each a length of L/N. Each segment has a characteristic impedance which may or may not differ from its neigbour´s. Even if no reflection occurs at the boundary between two segments, we assume that a reflected wave and a propagated wave exist. Figure 8.25 shows the lattice used for the computations with N = 5 only.

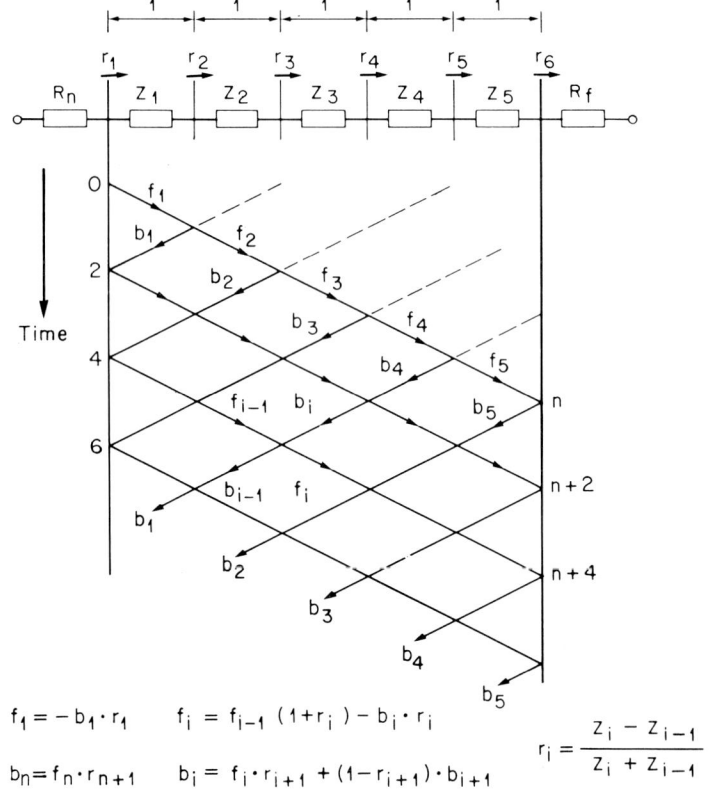

$$f_1 = -b_1 \cdot r_1 \qquad f_i = f_{i-1}(1+r_i) - b_i \cdot r_i$$

$$b_n = f_n \cdot r_{n+1} \qquad b_i = f_i \cdot r_{i+1} + (1-r_{i+1}) \cdot b_{i+1}$$

$$r_i = \frac{Z_i - Z_{i-1}}{Z_i + Z_{i-1}}$$

*Fig. 8.25 Algorithm for the lattice diagram*

In the first step, all forward waves are calculated, in the next, all backward waves, and so on. To initialize the calculations, all waves are set to zero except the first forward wave $f_1$.

### 8.5.3 Driving a line from the middle

A backplane bus is rarely driven at one end only. A transmitter can be located anywhere on the backplane. When a bus line is driven from the middle, the driver will behave as if it had to drive two transmission lines in parallel, and it will therefore "see" only half the characteristic impedance (figure 8.26).

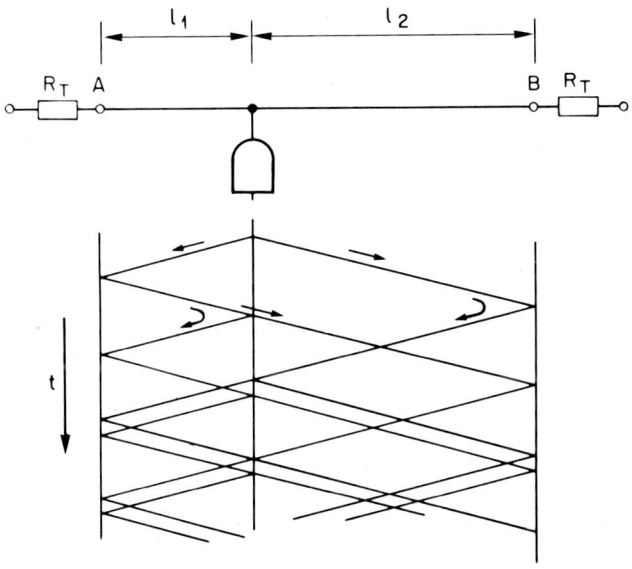

*Fig. 8.26 Driving a line from the middle*

This situation can occur for any bus, and in particular for backplane buses. The receivers will be subject to reflections coming from both line ends, and also from the driver, since it presents a low-impedance discontinuity in the middle of the backplane. The problem gets even more complicated when the impedance of the driver changes according to its state, as in open collector drivers.

The calculation can be done with the algorithm of figure 8.25. If the bus is fairly well terminated, the worst case will occur when the driver is at one end of the line and the receiver at the other end, which means that this problem is not so much annoying.

## 8.5.4 Wired-OR glitches

Some bus lines are driven by open collector drivers (figure 8.27).

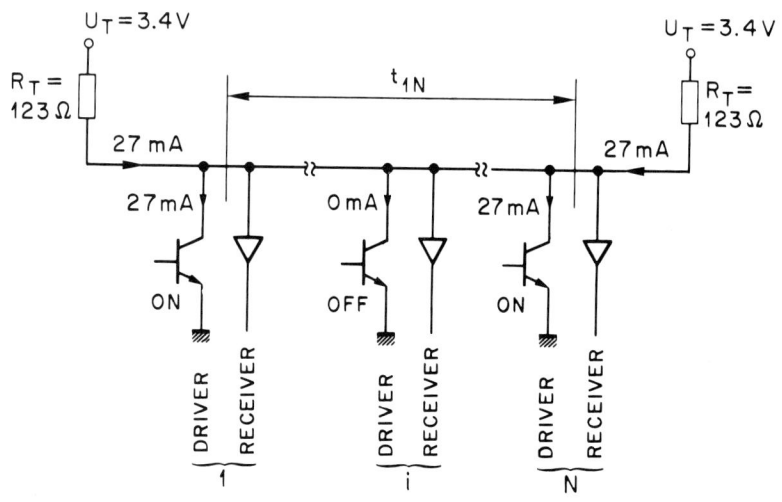

*Fig. 8.27 Bus line driven by open collector drivers*

These lines are often used as party-lines, i.e. any driver connected to it can drive it "low", for instance to signal an event such as an interrupt request or a bus request. The line goes "low" if any of the drivers are active, otherwise it is passively connected to a positive supply $U_T$ by a pull-up resistor $R_T$ and remains "high". The pull-up resistor acts at the same time as a bus termination. The resulting state of the line is the OR combination of the state of the drivers, hence the name wired-OR line.

At switch-off, a pulse appears when a driver releases the line (figure 8.28a). This pulse is called the WIRED-OR GLITCH [GUS83].

The origin of the wired-OR glitch is simple: when two drivers are simultaneously active, the current of the terminations is divided about evenly between the drivers. Thus, if two drivers are active, each sinks about half of the current supplied by the termination. For instance, if $U_T$ = 3.4 V and $R_T$ = 123 $\Omega$ at both ends, the termination current is 3.4/123 = 27 mA and the current sunk by each

8 Characteristics of Bus Lines 239

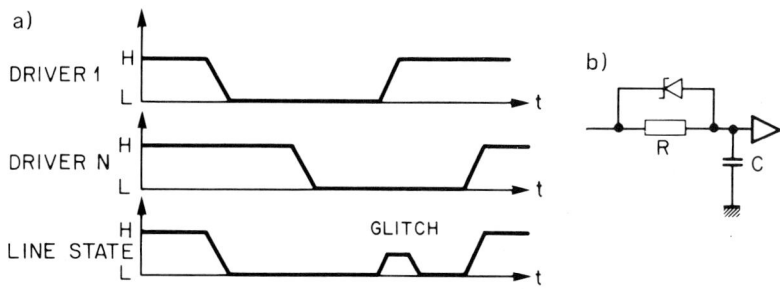

*Fig. 8.28 Wired-OR glitch*
  *a) Waveform*
  *b) Glitch filter*

driver is about 27 mA. If three drivers are active, each one sinks about a third of 54 mA, assuming that the drivers are approximately matched.

When an active driver releases the line, the current is cut and a wave propagates from this driver toward the ends of the bus. The height of the wave is equal to the current formerly sunk by the driver multiplied by half the characteristic impedance of the backplane (since we drive the bus in the middle). In our example, if $Z_w = 120\ \Omega$ and a driver sinks 27 mA, the amplitude of the wave is $0.027 \cdot 60 = 1.62$ V. This is sufficient to cause a false triggering of a receiver. If the driver 1 of figure 8.27 becomes inactive, then one half of the wave propagates to the left termination where it is absorbed. The other half travels to the right and passes by receiver i, for instance, until it reaches driver N which is active and presents a low impedance. Driver N immediately sinks the additional current, and a negative current wave propagates to the left which annuls the previous current wave. There is no propagation to the right of driver N (matched line). Nevertheless, it will take twice the propagation delay $t_{1N}$ between driver 1 and N for receiver 1 to register that there is another driver to its right which is also active. Until this time, receiver 1 assumes that the line went inactive, and this is sufficient to cause protocol errors.

The worst wired-OR glitch occurs when the two active drivers are located at opposite ends of the bus. Then the duration of the glitch is equal to twice the propagation delay of the bus. Furthermore, the amplitude can be higher than the calculated one if the drivers are unbalanced and the driver which carried most of the current is switched off first. If the bus is fully loaded, the glitch has a smaller amplitude, since $Z_w$ is lower, but a longer duration, since the propagation speed $v_p$ decreases and the propagation delay $t_{1N}$ increases.

The glitch cannot be suppressed. The usual protection against it is a filter connected between each receiver and the line (figure 8.28b). This filtering should be designed keeping in mind the fact that the glitch only occurs on the positive edge of the waveform. Furthermore, since the worst glitch occurs when the bus is unloaded and the drivers are at opposite ends, it is wise to fill a backplane cabinet starting from one end and not to plug boards in randomly.

## 8.6 BERGERON'S DIAGRAM

The reflected waves and the lattice diagram could be calculated from the characteristics of the line and its terminations. A very useful graphical construction method also exists, which gives the same results but in a more intuitive way. This method, called Bergeron's diagram, also accounts for non-linear elements.

This section will describe how this diagram is constructed but we will leave the burden of explaining the theory to the mathematics books. *BERGERON'S DIAGRAM* expresses the relations between voltage and current at the terminations and on the line itself. The diagram plots the voltages against the currents. The two relations shown in the diagram, the wave equations and the terminations, are explained in the following subsections.

### 8.6.1 The wave equations

The line voltage at any point in space or time is given by the superposition of a forward (travelling left-to-right) wave on a backward (travelling right-to-left) wave. The relation of the instantaneous current and voltage at a given point x on the line due to a forward wave is defined by the following equation [WEB68]:

$$u(x,t) + Z_w \cdot i(x,t) = 2 \cdot \tilde{U}_0$$

This equation is represented in Bergeron's diagram by a line with a slope of $-Z_w$ which crosses the axis at twice the value of the amplitude of the forward wave.

The drawing (and scaling) becomes much easier if the voltage is plotted against a normalized current $I \cdot Z_w$. A forward wave is drawn as a line with a slope of $-1$ ($-45°$), such as in figure 8.29.

# 8 Characteristics of Bus Lines

Similarly, a backward (travelling right-to-left) wave satisfies the relationship:

$$u(x,t) - Z_w \cdot i(x,t) = 2 \cdot \tilde{U}_1$$

A backward wave is plotted as a line with a slope of 1 (45°), which crosses the axes at twice the amplitude of the backward wave.

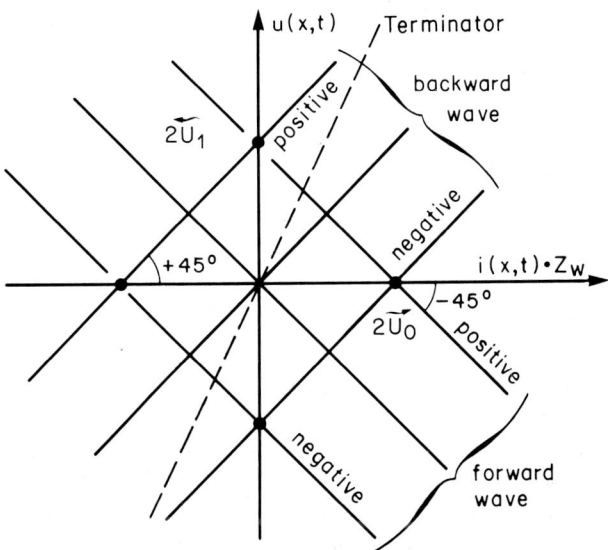

*Fig. 8.29 Wave equations in Bergeron's diagram*

## 8.6.2 The terminations

If the line is terminated at the far end by a resistor $R_f$, the relation holds:

$$u(f,t) = i(f,t) \cdot R_f \quad \text{or} \quad u(f,t) = [i(f,t) \cdot Z_w] \cdot \frac{R_f}{Z_w}$$

The terminator will be represented in figure 8.29 by a line with a slope of $R_f/Z_w$.

The U/I characteristic of the source is plotted similarly in the diagram.

Figure 8.30 shows a transmission line driven by a voltage source which generates the voltage $U_s$ (a step going from 0 V to 5 V), with an internal resistance $R_n$ of 25 Ω. The line has a characteristic impedance of 100 Ω which is a typical value for PC-board lines and the termination has an impedance of 500 Ω. For comparison purposes, these are the same numerical values as in figure 8.19.

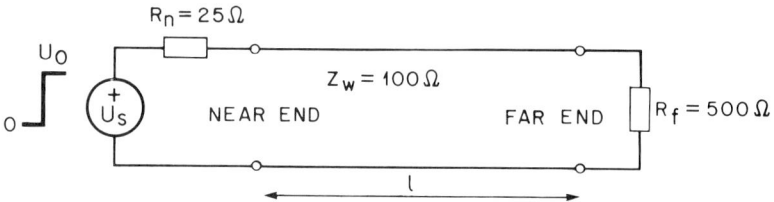

Fig. 8.30 Line driven by a voltage source

Figure 8.31 shows the corresponding Bergeron diagram.

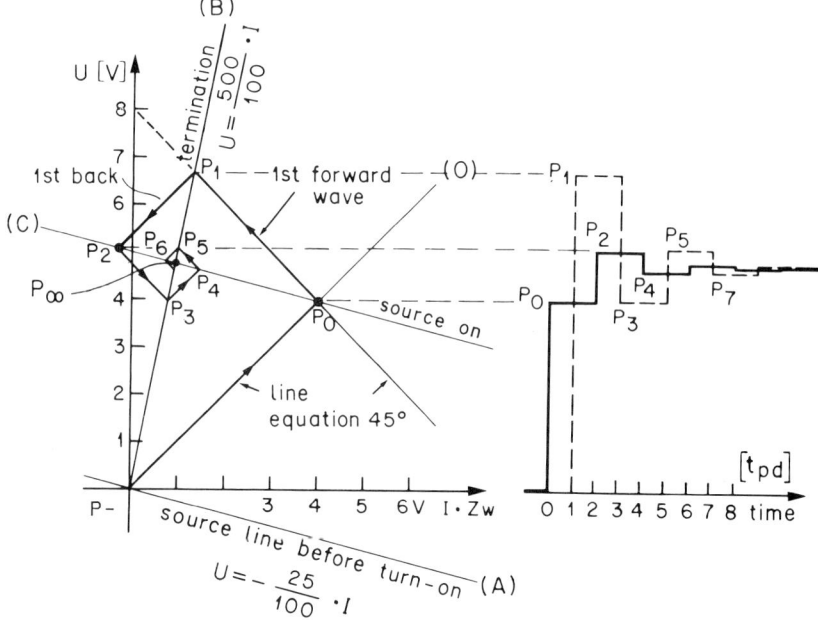

Fig. 8.31 Line at turn-ON (corresponding to previous figure)

One begins by drawing on the $\{U, I \cdot Z_w\}$ diagram the characteristics of the source in both states (before turn-on and after) and of the termination.

# 8 Characteristics of Bus Lines

## 8.6.3 Quiescent state

First, let us suppose that the source is at zero volts. The characteristic of the source is given by line (A). Since:

$$u(n,t) = Us - \frac{R_n}{Z_w} \cdot [i(n,t) \cdot Z_w]$$

the source's characteristic is a line with a slope of $-R_n/Z_w = -0.25$ passing through the origin. The U/I characteristic of the far end termination is (B): its slope is $R_f/Z_w = 5$. The point where the two lines intersect is the quiescent workpoint P-, which is at the origin in this particular case.

## 8.6.4 Turn-on

Now the source is turned on. The new U/I characteristic of the source is given by (C): its slope is still $-R_n/Z_w$, but this time, it crosses the y-axis at + 5 V.

The intersection of B and C determines the next quiescent point, which will be reached when the reflections will have died out ($P_\infty$), but let us see what happens in between.

When the source is first turned on, no wave is travelling from the right, but the backward wave equation must nevertheless be satisfied: the wave equation for a backward wave is the line (0) with slope of +1, which passes through the quiescent point, since the initial amplitude of the backward wave is zero.

The intersection $P_0$ of (0) and (C) defines the voltage and current at the beginning of the line at the first step. The first voltage step has the height:

$$\tilde{U}_0 = Us \cdot \frac{Z_w}{(R_n + Z_w)}$$

## 8.6.5 Forward and backward waves

The wave equation for the first wave travelling from right to left is represented by a line with a slope of $-1$ which crosses the x-axis at the value of twice the voltage step. Since the voltage step is given by $P_0$, and $P_0$ lies on the +1 slope, the forward wave line (1) passes through the point $P_0$.

This wave equation must be satisfied and at the same time the U/I characteristic of the termination must be respected. The intersection of both determines $P_1$, which is the height of the voltage step at the termination at the first reflection.

The returning wave is represented by a line with a slope of +1 which passes through the voltage value the wave had at the termination, here through $P_1$. This line intersects the source characteristic at $P_2$ and thus defines the value of the second step at the near end.

The same procedure is continued, now defining a forward wave which passes through $P_2$ and crosses the termination characteristic at $P_3$, and so on, until the quiescent point $P_\infty$ is reached. In practice, it is seldom necessary to plot more than six reflections. The reflections might form the typical pattern known as "Bergeron's snail", but the pattern may also be of the zig-zag form.

### 8.6.6 Timing diagram

On the right of the diagram are the corresponding voltages at the near and at the far end of the line plotted in function of time. Figure 8.32 shows the same line, but at turn-off.

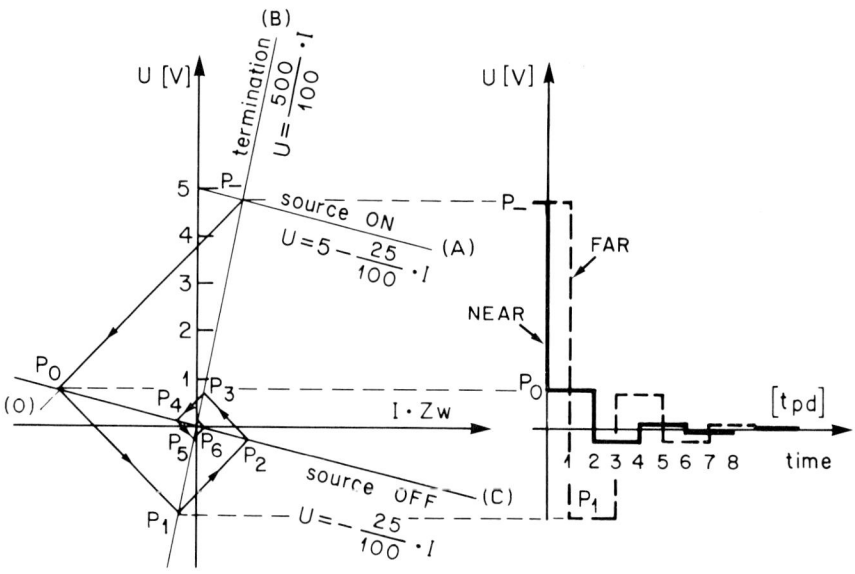

Fig. 8.32 Line at turn-off

Other examples of Bergerons's diagram will follow. There exist some alternative representations of Bergeron's diagram in other textbooks, some prefer to plot the current (vertically) against the voltage, others do not use a normalized current. But even if no normalized current is used, it is recommended to try to keep the

# 8 Characteristics of Bus Lines

slopes of the wave equations at about 45°, to obtain the maximum accuracy in the drawing. The drawback of using a normalized current is that changing $Z_w$ requires a rescaling of the x-axis. But in most cases, $Z_w$ is given and is not subject to change.

## 8.7 NON-LINEAR DRIVERS

### 8.7.1 Open collector driver

The above examples assumed a perfect, linear voltage source, meaning that its internal resistance does not change in function of the voltage. However, the real sources of voltage and the terminations are rarely linear.

The typical bus driver using totem-pole transistors for the output has a low impedance when in the "low" state (about 10 to 25 Ω), and a medium impedance when in the "high" state (about 50 Ω to 130 Ω). Open collector drivers are even more asymmetrical: they exhibit a low output impedance in the "low" state and a very high impedance when in the "high" state.

Therefore, the behaviour of the line must be calculated differently at turn-on and switch-off. Figure 8.33 shows a line driven at one end by an open collector driver. The driver is modelled by a switch and a resistor $R_n$ in series.

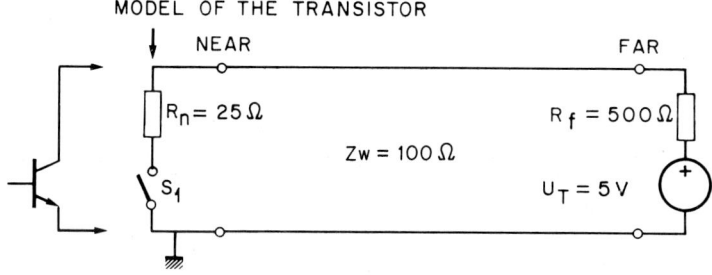

*Fig. 8.33 Line driven by an open collector driver*

The quiescent voltage is supplied by the termination, which is modelled by a resistor $R_f$ in series with an ideal voltage source $U_T$.

Let us first consider a low-to-high transition, assuming that the switch is closed at first. The initial voltage at the driver and at the termination are:

$$u(n,t-0) = U_T \cdot \frac{R_n}{(R_n+R_f)} = u(f,t-0)$$

The current flowing in the quiescent state is:

$$i(n,t-0) = \frac{U_T}{(R_n + R_f)}$$

At $t = 0$, the switch is opened (the transistor is blocked). The voltage at the driver immediately rises to the value:

$$u(n, 0) = u(n,t-0) + i(n,t-0) \cdot Z_w$$

A voltage step with a height of $\tilde{U}_0 = i(n,t-0) \cdot Z_w$ propagates to the right. When it reaches the end, it is reflected, as usual, with a reflection coefficient $r = (R_f-Z_w)/(R_f+Z_w)$. Figure 8.34 shows the corresponding Bergeron diagram.

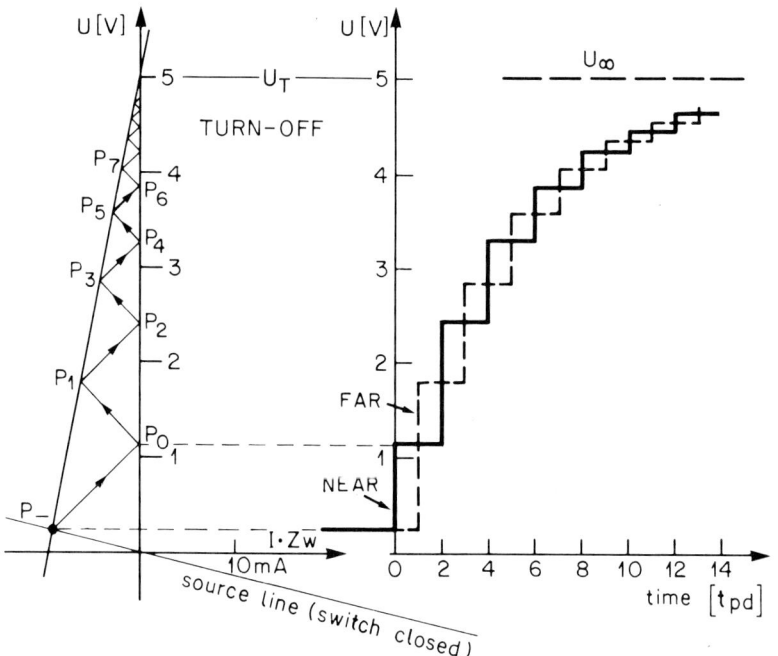

Fig. 8.34 Bergeron diagram of the open collector line when the transistor is turned off

# 8 Characteristics of Bus Lines

For a high to low transition, the line is at the quiescent voltage $U_T$. At turn-on, the switch is closed. The voltage at the driver immediately drops to the value:

$$u(n, 0) = U_T - U_T \cdot \frac{Z_w}{(R_n + Z_w)} = U_T \cdot \frac{R_n}{R_n + Z_w}$$

Figure 8.35 shows the corresponding Bergeron diagram.

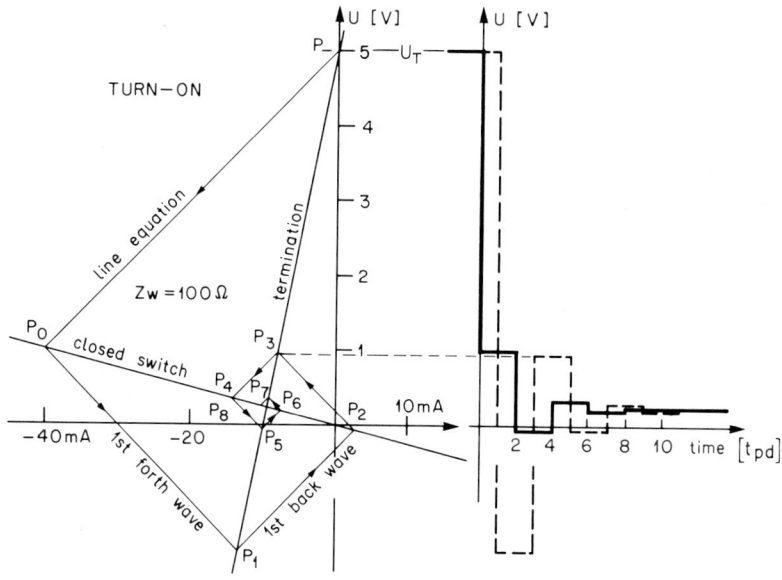

Fig. 8.35 *Line driven by an open collector driver when the transistor is turned on*

## 8.7.2 Three-state driver

A three-state driver behaves as a standard totem-pole TTL driver as long as it is enabled. The case of a three-state driver at enable or disable time is a little more complex but it can be treated by the same method.

The totem-pole output shown in figure 8.36 is modelled by a pair of resistances tied to ground and to a supply of 3.5 V respectively, and connected by a "make-after-break" type switch to the driven line.

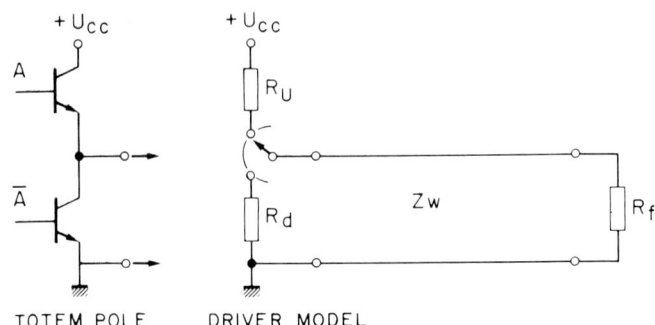

*Fig. 8.36 Driving a line with a totem-pole driver*

The line's $Z_w$ is again chosen as 100 Ω. The values of the resistors depend on the driver type. Typical three-state drivers have a pull-up resistance of about 50 Ω and a pull-down resistance of 10 Ω. Standard TTL has values of 120 Ω and 25 Ω, respectively, but these values are only approximations. It is better to draw the output characteristics of the driver in the "low" and in the "high" state directly in the diagram, as shown in figure 8.37.

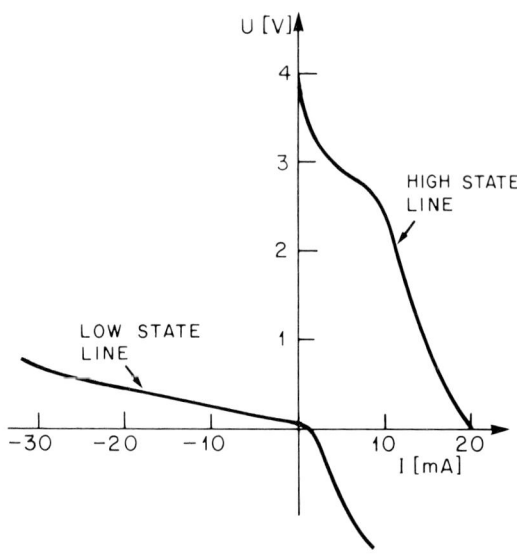

*Fig. 8.37 Three-state driver's characteristics in Bergeron's diagram*

8 Characteristics of Bus Lines                                            249

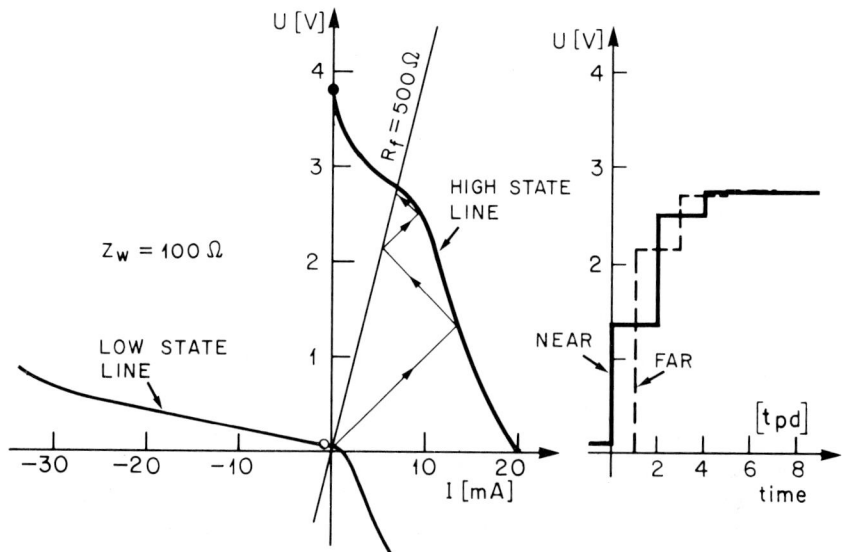

*Fig. 8.38 Three-state going from low to high*

Figure 8.38 shows the low-to-high transition of a line driven by a totem-pole driver. Since the upper transistor's resistance is about the same as the characteristic impedance of the line, few reflections occur.

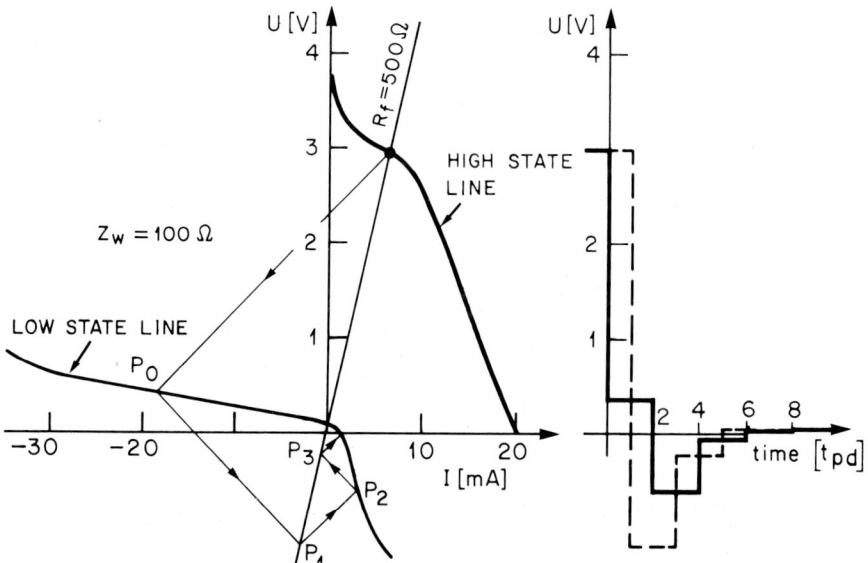

*Fig. 8.39 Three-state driver going from high to low*

During the low-to-high transition, the lower transistor ceases to conduct before the upper draws any current (this, of course, is necessary to prevent high transverse currents). The first voltage step on the line is therefore not due to the upper transistor, but to the current change through the lower transistor. Only some 2 ns afterwards does the upper transistor conduct, but this effect is not considered in figure 8.38.

The behaviour of a three-state driver during the high-to-low transition is similar to that of an open collector driver during the turn-on phase. The upper transistor ceases to conduct before the lower transistor is conducting, but again, this is not considered here. More reflections occur since the lower transistor's resistance is lower than the characteristic impedance.

### 8.7.3 Receiver characteristic

Until now, we assumed that the termination resistance $R_f$ was linear. In point-to-point links, the termination resistance is only a model for a receiver's input, such as a TTL gate. The U/I characteristics of the receivers are not linear functions. Few receivers exhibit an infinite impedance, especially when the voltages are outside of the normal operating range. A receiver built using TTL logic, for instance, exhibits a high impedance when the line is at the "high"

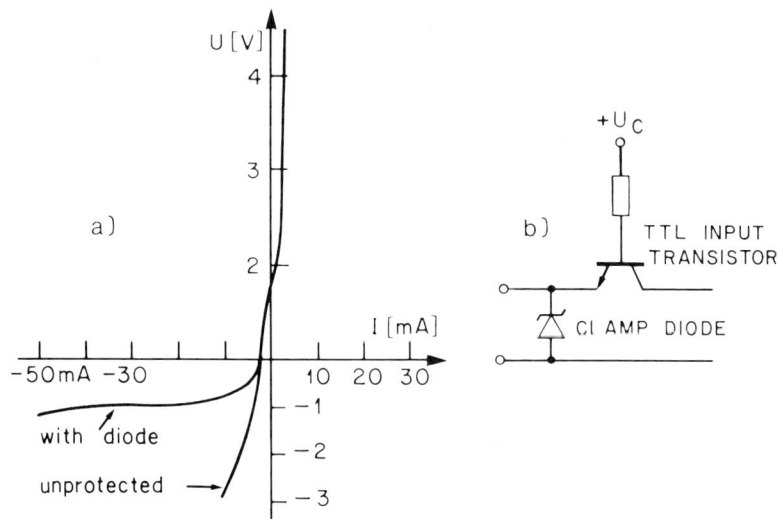

Fig. 8.40 Receiver input characteristics with and without a clamp diode
 a) Characteristic
 b) Circuit

8 Characteristics of Bus Lines                                   251

level, and a medium impedance when the line is at the "low" level. To reduce reflections, clamp diodes are integrated into all receivers today (see figure 8.40b). They exhibit a low impedance when negative voltages are applied. Figure 8.40a shows the input characteristics of a receiver with and without a clamp diode.

Bergeron's diagram in figure 8.41 shows the behaviour of the line when the receiver has no clamp diode: big reflections occur because the impedance of the receiver is very large, even if it may decrease a bit near the origin. These reflections could cause false switching, but they may also destroy the driver and the receiver. The driver will get back nearly twice its output voltage at the first reflection, and the receiver would be operated in the negative voltage region.

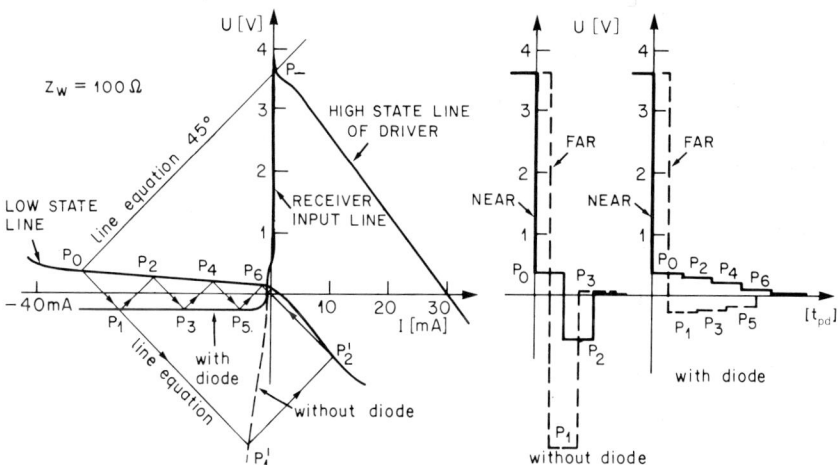

Fig. 8.41 Reflections with and without clamp diode

Figure 8.41 also shows the effects of the clamp diode, which begins to conduct when the input voltage becomes negative. We can see on Bergeron's diagram by how much the reflections can be reduced with a clamp diode.

### 8.7.4 Reflections and the operating region

Two important points of the above examples (open collector and three-state drivers) should be kept in mind:

1) The first voltage drop at the high-to-low transition is exclusively a function of the internal resistance of the driver toward ground $R_n$, of the quiescent voltage $U_q$ and of the characteristic

impedance $Z_w$. This holds equally for three-state and for open collector drivers. Hence, $U_q$ is the quiescent voltage in the "high" state :

$$\tilde{U}_\emptyset = Z_w \cdot \frac{U_q}{R_n + Z_w} \qquad U_{(t=\emptyset)} = U_q \cdot \frac{R_n}{R_n + Z_w}$$

2) The first voltage rise at the low-to-high transition is exclusively a function of the characteristic impedance of the line and of the current $I_q$ flowing in the quiescent ("low") state. This holds for a three-state driver also, as long as the upper transistor does not conduct. Thus, if $U_s$ is the quiescent voltage in the "low" state (saturation voltage) :

$$\tilde{U}_0 = Z_w \cdot I_q \qquad U_{(t=0)} = U_s + Z_w \cdot I_q$$

A receiver has two guaranteed voltage thresholds, $U_{IL}$ and $U_{IH}$. When the input voltage is below $U_{IL}$, the receiver is guaranteed to recognize a "low"; when the voltage is above $U_{IH}$, the receiver will see a "high"; however, when the receiver's input is in between, the output is undefined.

Two typical pulse forms are shown in figure 8.42: the upper one originates from a high current driver, the lower from a low current driver. To achieve the highest possible transmission speed, the signal must cross the transition region of the receiver at the very first swing. If the signal builds up to $U_{IH}$ only after several reflections, the receiver will be delayed by an integer number of bus reflections.

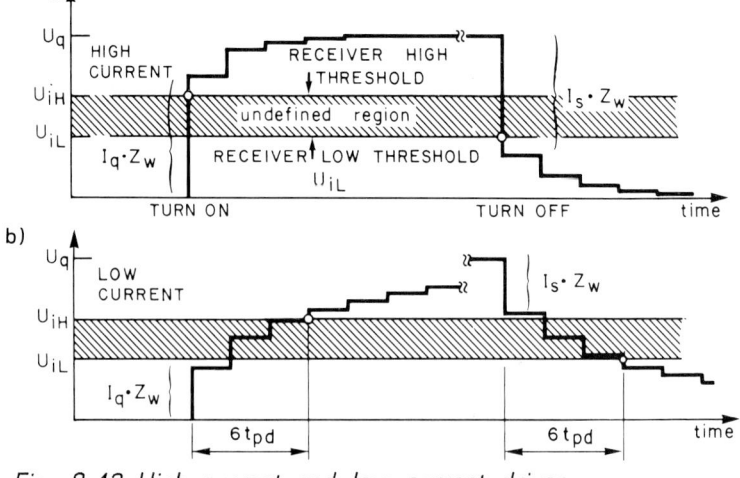

*Fig. 8.42 High current and low current driver*

# 8 Characteristics of Bus Lines

The fastest transmission is achieved if the quiescent current $I_q$ and the line impedance $Z_w$ are high enough so that the receiver's threshold is crossed on the first transition. To catch the first transition at turn-on, the relation:

$$I_q \cdot Z_w > U_{IH}$$

must hold.

Now, when considering buses, the characteristic impedance that the driver sees is only half that of the bus line itself, since it must drive two lines (right and left) at the same time. To achieve the same voltage step, twice the current as in case of the line is necessary. Furthermore, since the bus impedance decreases as the number of drivers (inserted boards) increases, loaded buses require still higher currents for a correct function. The following table shows an example with the specifications of a typical open collector driver, the 74LS241:

| | |
|---|---|
| Source impedance of the driver in the low state | 5 Ω |
| Saturation voltage at driver in the low state | 0.2 V |
| Rated $I_{OL}$ driver current: | 48 mA |
| Receiver's $U_{IL}$ | 0.8 V |
| Receiver's $U_{IH}$ | 2.0 V |
| Characteristic impedance of the bus: | 100 Ω |
| ($Z_w$ seen by the driver on the bus: | 50 Ω) |
| Termination resistor on each side: | 195 Ω |
| Quiescent voltage at the termination | 3 V |
| Quiescent current in the "low" state: | 2·15 mA = 30 mA |

The value of the first transition at switch-on (see 8.7.1) is:

$$3 \cdot \frac{5}{55} = 0.273 \text{ V}$$

This is sufficient for the signal to cross the receiver's threshold correctly. The current at that time would be 54.5 mA.

If the driver cannot supply that amount, but just its saturation current $I_s$, the first transition's value will be:

$$U = U_q - I_s \cdot Z_w$$

Assuming that $I_s$ is 48 mA (it is in reality better), the level reached at the first transition will be 0.6 V, which is still sufficient.

At switch-off, the first transition value is 0.2 + 50 · 0.030 = 1.7 V. This is not sufficient to cross the receiver's no-man's land, and an additional reflection must be waited for. The above figures hold for a lightly loaded bus. If the capacitive loading is increased, then the signal will need several reflections to reach $U_{IH}$.

### 8.7.5 Open collector vs. three-state drivers

All buses use open collector drivers for party lines like the Bus Request line, but for the remaining signal lines, most buses use three-state drivers, while a few prefer open collector. The choice is not casual, but depends on the speed, distance and reliability objectives of the designer.

We have seen in the preceding section that the bus speed depends on the duration of the signal edges, which themselves depend on how many reflections one must wait until the level $U_{OL}$ changes to $U_{OH}$. Therefore, we can compare three-state and open collector on the base of the number of reflections required to cross the no-man's land. If the bus is contained within a crate and loaded with a board in every slot, each reflection takes about 20 ns (back and forth). If the bus extends to some 5m as the Q-BUS does and the bus is operated up to the maximum load, each step takes some 50 ns. Therefore, the number of expected reflections is significant for the protocol speed.

Consider first the case at turn-on (high-to-low transition), as in figure 8.42. For both three-state and open collector drivers the behaviour is the same, since this transition is actively pulled low by the pull-down transistor on both kind of devices. If the current sink capability of the pull-down transistor is high enough, the $U_{OL}$ low level can be reached at the first transition. In fact, the (dynamic) current sink of the driver is often better than what the data sheet indicates for the steady current, and therefore the $U_{OL}$ level is normally crossed at the first reflection. For this transition, the termination resistors have no influence, since the value of this step depends only on the characteristic impedance and on the current that the pull-down transistor can sink. There is here no difference between three-state and open collector.

The difference between open collector and three-state shows up in the low-to-high transition. Here, the height of the first upward step is given by the current flowing through the pull-down transistor in the "low" state, which is determined by the termination resistors. The lower the termination, the higher the current and the higher the step. To reach the first transition on a loaded backplane ($Z_w \simeq 35$ Ohm), a

## 8 Characteristics of Bus Lines

terminator current of about 100mA is required (50 mA per termination). This is quite a high current, and normally open collector lines may wait for the second or the third reflection when the bus is loaded (low $Z_w$).

Three-state drivers, by contrast, can reach the $U_{OH}$ level much faster since the pull-up transistor conducts some 2ns after the lower transistor switches off. The current sourcing of that transistor should be high enough for the signal to cross the $U_{OH}$ level before the first reflection comes back. Therefore, three-state drivers provide the same speed at the rising edge of the signal as an open collector driver which uses a much higher terminator current. This is why open collector drivers for such buses as the Q-BUS are rated 100mA, while the three-state drivers of VME are rated only 48mA.

Three-state drivers have some problems, however. The advantage of the pull-up transistor is lost if the three-state driver is disabled (both transistors switched-off) while its output is in the LOW state. Then, the three-state driver behaves worse than open collector driver, since the terminator current has been reduced. The line can dangle for a long time until it reaches a defined level. Therefore, the protocol of a three-state bus should specify that the driver be returned to the quiescent state before it is disabled. This, in turn, delays the protocol.

Accidental turn-on of several three-state drivers may damage them due to the transverse current. Such a situation is not uncommon if transmission errors are expected (several destinations responding to the same address) or at turn-on of the power supply (some older three-state devices presented a low-impedance state at power-on). Open collector drivers are inherently immune to such a collision, since there is only one level active. This property allows them to implement party lines and arithmetic operations on the bus, such as the arbitration (see section 5.3.5). This and the fact that open collector drivers dissipate less power for the same current than three-state (since half is dissipated in the termination resistors) makes the open collector drivers somewhat more reliable than three-state and permits their easier integration in a bus controller chip. On the other hand, open collector drivers tend to work with higher currents, and therefore produce more noise (crosstalk, ground current and wired-or glitches) and this, in turn, reduces the reliability.

In general, it can be observed that most open collector buses spread over a distance of 50 cm to several meters. The reason is that a long bus should be correctly terminated by its (unloaded) characteristic impedance, or else the reflections are long enough to cause false triggering. If both ends are terminated with the matching impedance, then the terminator current flowing should be high enough to catch the first transition. Therefore, three-state brings little increase in speed.

The market seems to decide in favor of three-state, mostly because three-state devices are believed to use less power. There are few manufacturers of high-current open collector drivers, among them AMD and National Semiconductor. Their circuits have normally four transceivers in one package. Some Fast (Fairchild) and ALS (Texas Instruments) octal devices can be used as open collector transceivers. Most three-state devices are octal or nonal (for parity) devices. They are cheaper than open collector devices because of the larger shipping volumes.

We resume the arguments in the following table:

| OPEN COLLECTOR | THREE-STATE |
| --- | --- |
| higher terminator current at same speed | lower terminator current at same speed |
| more reliable | less reliable |
| allows wired-or | collision leads to damage |
| power dissipated at the termination | power dissipated at the driver and at termination |
| adapted for long buses | use for short buses (<50 cm) |
| mostly quad packages | octal and nonal packages |
| 4 manufacturers | 5 manufacturers |

Finally let's point out a dilemma common to both driver types: to increase the speed, the current flowing should also be increased (higher steps at each reflection). The current is usually increased by reducing the termination resistors, to the current limit that the drivers can tolerate.

On the other hand, the increase in current increases the noise level, especially in form of crosstalk (which is proportional to di/dt) and an increase in ground current through the return path which is common to all drivers. Consider a backplane bus with 32 information lines, 4 parity and 8 control lines driven by 48 mA drivers. If all lines switch at the same time, some 2 A will flow through the return conductor. This will lift-up the ground level by some 200 mV and reduce the noise margin, just when crosstalk is highest. It makes no sense to filter out such glitches, since this would slow the bus down more than a reduction in drive current would. To reduce the noise, costlier backplanes with buried tracks to reduce crosstalk and ground planes are required. Note also that a backplane is noisiest when unloaded, since the capacitances added by loading smooth the signal edges and reduce crosstalk - but they also slow down the bus.

## 8.8 TERMINATIONS

### 8.8.1 Parallel termination

A receiver used in a transmission line should ideally exhibit a resistance equal to the characteristic impedance of the line, but most receivers exhibit a high impedance, which gives rise to high reflections. To match the receiver, one can shunt with a resistor of the appropriate value (figure 8.43).

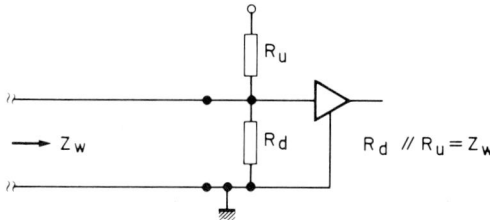

*Fig. 8.43 Parallel terminator at far end termination*

Note that the termination resistor will reduce the total voltage swing with respect to the high-impedance case. Therefore, this solution is not readily applicable to most logic designs, and especially not when there are several receivers on the same line.

In fact, the reflection does not really harm the receiver that much. On the contrary, the voltage swing at a high-impedance receiver would double and make the switching easier. The only cause for concern is the return wave, which will arrive $2 \cdot t_{pd}$ later, because the wave reflected at the driver has a negative sign.

### 8.8.2 Series termination

Therefore, another solution known as a series termination is used: the receiver has no termination, but the driver is terminated by a

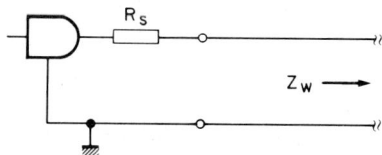

*Fig. 8.44 Series termination*

series resistor, which eliminates the difference between the driver's and the line's impedance (figure 8.44). But then, the voltage drop over the serie resistor must be considered in the calculation of the levels.

Both series and parallel terminations are only relevant with point-to-point links.

### 8.8.3 Bus termination

If several receivers are connected to the same line, the line itself can be terminated and the reflections can be damped by the termination.

With the methods described earlier in this chapter, we were able to calculate the value of the ideal termination resistance of a backplane bus. We have seen that since the characteristic impedance depends on the number of boards, it is not possible to have a perfect termination in all cases. Furthermore, the value of the perfect termination resistor is so low that common drivers would not be capable of driving a backplane bus in a way in which the signal would be able to cross the transition region on the first wavefront (this requires some 100 mA of driving capability). Thus, the value of the termination resistances will be dictated more by the driving current capability of the available drivers than by the backplane's characteristics. In fact, with the possible exception of FutureBus, no commercial backplane bus today is terminated by its characteristic impedance.

There is, however, one strong reason to terminate the bus correctly at least for the unloaded case: the electrical problems (glitches, crosstalk) are worst when the bus is unloaded. This is due to the fact that the capacitive loading smooths the effects of spikes

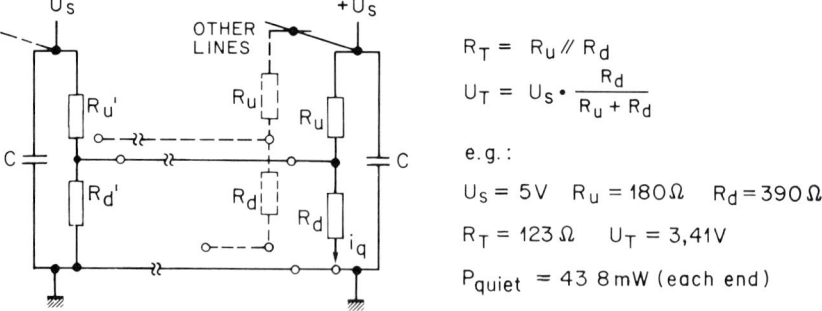

$R_T = R_u \mathbin{/\mkern-5mu/} R_d$

$U_T = U_S \cdot \dfrac{R_d}{R_u + R_d}$

e.g.:

$U_S = 5V \quad R_u = 180\,\Omega \quad R_d = 390\,\Omega$

$R_T = 123\,\Omega \quad U_T = 3{,}41V$

$P_{quiet} = 43{,}8\,mW$ (each end)

*Fig. 8.45 Thevenin termination*

and sharp edges. Furthermore, reflections are not really a nuisance in a backplane, since they generally add to the signal, if the first reflection does not coincide with the receiver's threshold (possible jitter). Schmitt-trigger inputs can take care of that case.

In most buses, the terminator must simultaneously supply the quiescent voltage, even with three-state drivers. There are three termination networks which are common. The first (figure 8.45) is a classical *THEVENIN CIRCUIT*. It requires only passive elements and a power source at the termination. Note the bridging capacitance, which is absolutely necessary (if it were not there, the bus lines would be coupled over the termination).

The second terminator (figure 8.46) is called the *VOLTAGE SOURCE TERMINATION*. It uses only one resistor per line, which means that it will end up with half as many passive components as for the Thevenin network. In addition, its power dissipation is lower, since there is no transverse current. By comparison, a Thevenin network, consisting of 2 resistors of 180 Ω and 390 Ω connected to +5 V and ground respectively, and operating with a 1:4 pulse ratio on the bus (most of the time the bus is idle), would consume more than twice the power of a single 123 Ω resistor fed by a 3.41 V voltage source to which it is electrically equivalent.

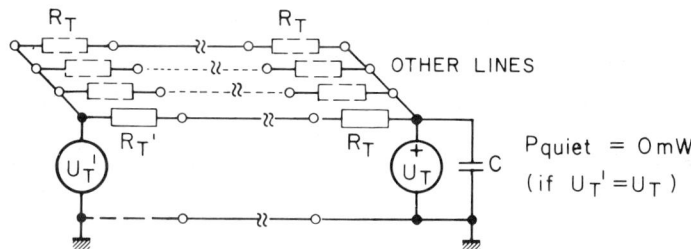

*Fig. 8.46 Voltage source termination*

The voltage source terminator has one small setback, however. If the bus were terminated at both ends, and 100 lines were terminated in parallel with 100 Ω of termination resistors each, the resistance between the sources would be less than 2 Ω and a strong transverse current would flow from one source to the other if they weren't at exactly the same voltage. Even a small unbalance would cause the regulator of one of the sources to shut down (since it would sense a voltage higher than there should be), and the other source would assume all the current. Then there would be no more termination at the end of the source which has shut down. Therefore, the best solution is to have only one common voltage source for both bus ends and a special conductor which brings the termination voltage to the other end of the backplane.

The third termination is used in low-power buses such as C-MOS buses. It is called an ACTIVE TERMINATION (figure 8.47). The active termination should eliminate the need for a quiescent current flow when all signals are static. When the terminator senses that the bus is at a "low" voltage, it switches the termination voltage to ground. When it senses a "high" voltage, it switches the termination voltage to that voltage. Therefore, no termination current flows when the lines are static. The problem is that this circuit requires a large number of active components, since each line requires its individual voltage sensor and switch. Power dissipation, however, is minimized.

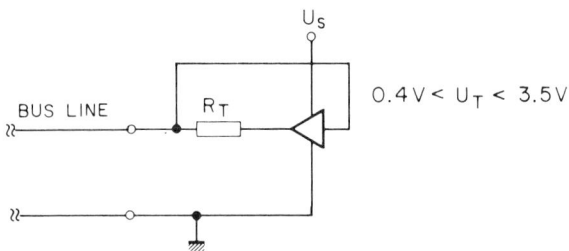

Fig. 8.47 Active termination

In short buses, it is permitted to terminate at one end only. Some constructors propose to terminate the bus lines with a termination resistor coupled to the bus line by a capacitor (Philips's CMOS bus, S-100). Such a coupling has the advantage of dissipating no power in the quiescent state. However, the voltage levels on the bus depend now on the pulse ratio of the signals, and there is no defined quiescent line voltage unless one introduces a DC coupling somewhere. This method requires a great care in the design and it is not recommended for general purposes.

Finally, some even pretend that backplane buses which do not extend over more than one crate need not be terminated at all if properly driven by three-state drivers, since the reflections cause less noise than the crosstalk due to the high terminator currents. In fact, the reflection at the open ends causes a duplication in voltage, which is absorbed at the driver when the wave comes back if the driver has a high enough internal impedance, or can be clamped at the terminator by a clipping diode. At least one manufacturer claims to have built a bus with a 125ns cycle time with CMOS-drivers and a very weak termination. The levels, however, are falsified and this solution remains to be field-proven in an industrial environment.

## 8.9 CROSSTALK

Until now, we have only considered a single transmission line and studied the reflections on that line. In many cases, several lines run in parallel and get reciprocally influenced. The general term for this mutual influence is CROSSTALK.

### 8.9.1 Definitions

Let us suppose that only one of several parallel lines is driven (figure 8.48).

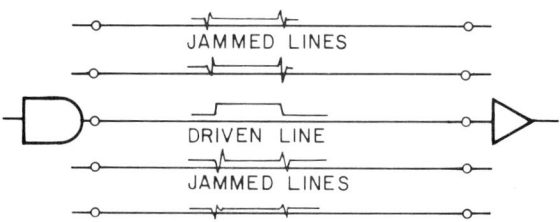

*Fig. 8.48 Several lines in parallel*

The driven line influences all other lines in several ways:
- there is a voltage induced on them by the magnetic field due to the current wave travelling down the driven line. This INDUCTIVE CROSSTALK is proportional to the di/dt of the driven line
- there is a current induced in them due to the change of difference in potential existing between the conductors. This CAPACITIVE CROSSTALK is proportional to the du/dt of the driven line
- there is a coupling when the lines use a common impedance, such as ground, for a return path, called COMMON PATH CROSSTALK. If the common impedance is purely resistive, this RESISTIVE CROSSTALK is proportional to the current flow.

Figure 8.49 summarizes the different crosstalk types.

Crosstalk is a common problem in parallel buses, because there exists a large number of lines running in parallel which carry relatively high currents. In backplane buses, it is difficult to shield the lines against one another. Even an intermediate shield line reduces considerably the signal line's width, making the bus manufacturing process difficult.

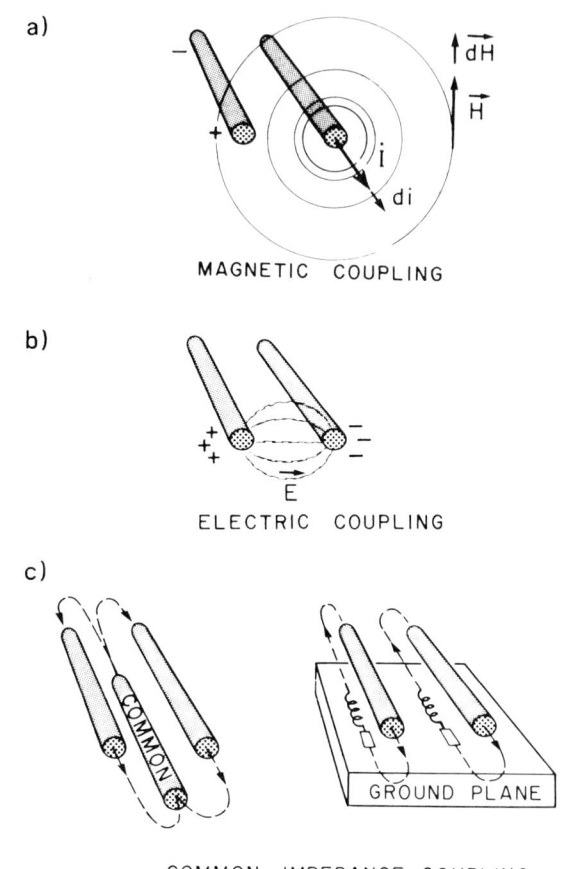

*Fig. 8.49 Magnetic, electric and common path coupling of parallel lines*

Furthermore, since there are normally many more signal lines than ground lines, crosstalk due to common return paths is also present. Serial buses are not so much affected by crosstalk since there is usually only one conductor. Interferences, however, do exist, originating not from the signal lines, but from the power lines that may run in parallel, from ground currents, and from external UHF sources that manage to leak through the shield.

Crosstalk can be neglected in coaxial cables and is completely eliminated in fiber optics.

## 8.9.2 Calculating crosstalk

A first approach to calculating crosstalk makes use of the lumped model. One considers both the driven and the jammed line as coils of a transformer with a common winding and common coupling capacitances. Then one can calculate the mutual inductance and capacitance and plot the amplitude of the resulting crosstalk as a function of frequency. The figures obtained are, however only applicable to low-frequency signals, such as the interference of a power line.

Measurements show that the amplitude of crosstalk with fast digital signals is higher than what the above theory predicts. This can be understood by considering figure 8.50.

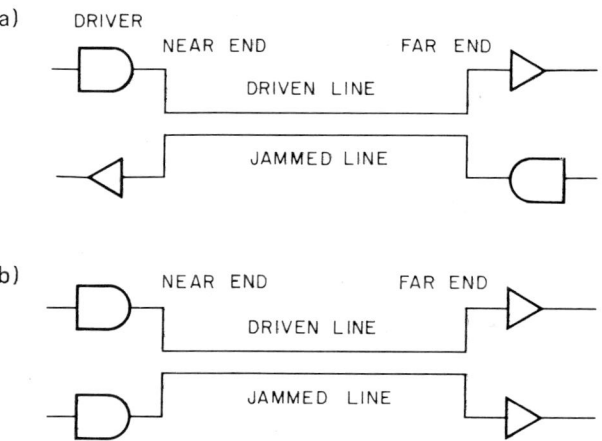

*Fig. 8.50 Lines in the opposite and same direction*

It turns out that when the receiver of the jammed line is near the transmitter of the driven line, the receiver is far more sensitive to crosstalk than when it is near the receiver of the driven line. In fact, the crosstalk does not have the same amplitude at the near end (close to the driver of the driven line) and at the far end (close to the receiver of the driven line).

Again, one must turn to the wave theory to explain this. When a wave travels down the driven line, the change of current at its front induces a voltage in the jammed line. Everything occurs as if a voltage source were connected to the jammed line, travelling down that line at the speed of the wave like an electric streetcar (figure 8.51).

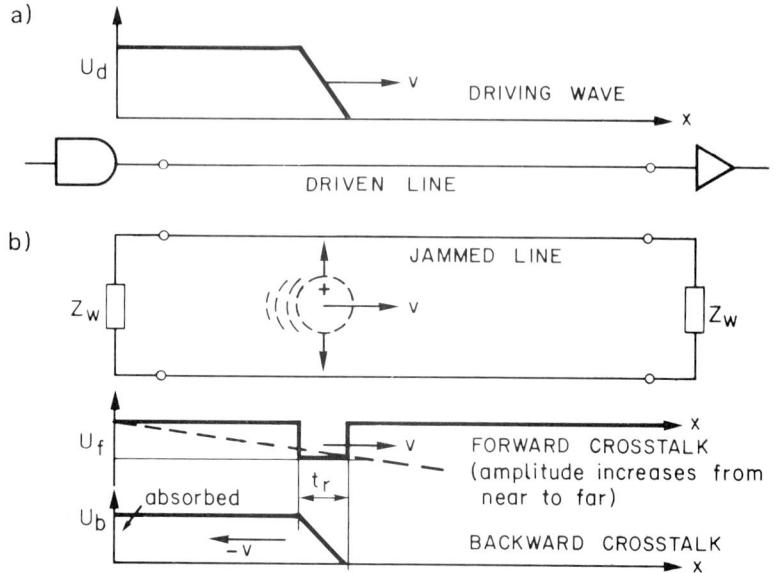

*Fig. 8.51 Forward and backward crosstalk*

This source causes two waves to appear: a backward wave, returning towards the near end, and a forward wave travelling towards the far end at the same speed as the source, i.e. the source is "riding the surf".

Let us assume that there are no reflections, neither on the driven nor on the jammed line, and that the driven wave has a trapezoidal form, with a leading slope duration of $t_r$. The FORWARD CROSSTALK will be a (normally negative) pulse of length $t_r$. Since this pulse rides the front of the driving wave, its energy increases with the distance travelled. The driving wave pushes the forward crosstalk somewhat like a snow plow handles snow. Therefore, the forward crosstalk's amplitude is proportional to the transmission line's length. Naturally, this increase in crosstalk cannot go on forever, so the amplitude of forward crosstalk stabilizes to a certain point, due to attenuation and dispersion, as figure 8.52 shows for a flat cable [SOU81].

In most backplane buses, the lines length is short enough so that forward crosstalk does not become an important factor. Even so, the duration of forward crosstalk is only equal to the rising time of the driving wave. If high-speed circuits are used, then the slopes of the signals are short and the duration of forward crosstalk would only be a few ns, which is usually not sufficient to switch the receiver. Some bus receivers are especially designed to ignore pulses which are shorter than the risetime of the logic.

# 8 Characteristics of Bus Lines

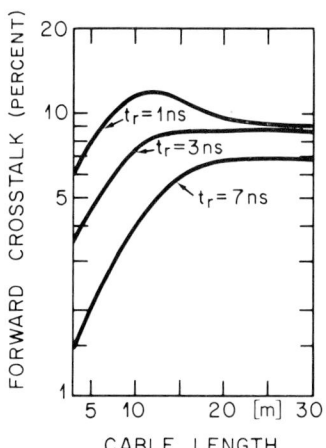

*Fig. 8.52 Forward crosstalk as a function of a line's length*

BACKWARD CROSSTALK is a pulse which is produced during the time equal to that needed for the hypothetical source to travel to the far end, i.e. during the line propagation time $t_{pd}$. However, since this source ceases to be produced at the far end of the line, it takes another $t_{pd}$ for its trailing edge to reach the near end of the line. Thus, the duration of backward crosstalk is equal to twice the bus propagation time (plus the rise time of the driving pulse).

Since the propagation time $t_{pd}$ in a 50 cm backplane bus is in the order of 3 ns, the duration of backward crosstalk could reach 6 ns, which is sufficiently long to trigger the logic. The amplitude of backward crosstalk is independent of the line's length, except when the signal rise-time is longer than twice the propagation time $t_{pd}$.

The amplitude of the crosstalk waves is approximated by the following formulas [REY74]:

$$U_f = \frac{1}{2} \cdot \left\{\frac{L_m}{L} - \frac{C_m}{C}\right\} \cdot t_{pd} \cdot \frac{U_d}{t_r}$$

$$U_b = \frac{1}{4} \cdot \left\{\frac{L_m}{L} + \frac{C_m}{C}\right\} \cdot U_d \quad (\text{for } t_r < 2t_{pd})$$

where C and L are the specific capacitance and inductance, while $C_m$ and $L_m$ are the mutual capacitance and inductance; $t_{pd}$ is the propagation delay of the signal down the line; $t_r$ is the rise-time of the driving wave.

Note that the amplitude of forward crosstalk increases with an increase in the propagation delay $t_{pd}$. Furthermore, the forward crosstalk's sign is given by the relation of the capacitive to the inductive coupling. Forward crosstalk could therefore be made zero by a proper line arrangement, such as striplines (buried conductors).

Interestingly, the amplitude of backward crosstalk does not depend on the slope of the signal, but it is increased by any coupling.

The value of crosstalk observed at the near end is called the *NEAR END CROSSTALK*. It is equal to the backward crosstalk when there are no reflections, i.e. when the line is terminated by its characteristic impedance; otherwise, it is composed of the superposition of the induced waves. Equally, the *FAR END CROSSTALK* is the value of the crosstalk observed at the far end of the line, and it is equal to the forward crosstalk when there are no reflections. Figure 8.53 shows the value of the near and of the far end crosstalk for the case of perfect termination.

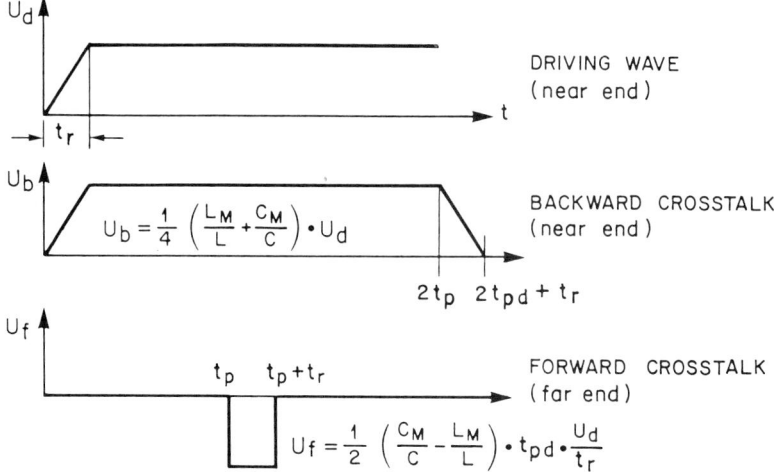

*Fig. 8.53 Near end and far end crosstalk for the case of perfect termination*

When reflections come into play, the superposition principle holds. The worst situation occurs when the line at the near end is open or a high impedance – this is unfortunately the case with standard receivers. Here, the backward crosstalk is reflected and the near end crosstalk voltage rises to twice its regular value. Even if the far end is short-circuited to ground, this will not reduce the duration of near end crosstalk.

# 8 Characteristics of Bus Lines

Numerous situations have been calculated by Kaupp [KAU66], to whom we refer. To reduce crosstalk, one can lower the slope of the signal edges. This can be easily done with an RC-filter. A somewhat faster method uses controlled slope drivers which deliver a trapezoidal wave [BALA83]. But slope influences only forward crosstalk, which can be reduced and even suppressed totally using buried tracks, so the two terms in figure 8.53 cancel each-other.

Since backward crosstalk is the major component of interference in backplane buses, and since the slope of the signal does not influence backward crosstalk, the utility of drivers with controlled slopes (trapezoidal drivers) is not evident. Additional factors may also cause interference, such as the fact that the jammed line itself influences the driven line, and that the lines tend to act as antennas, but it is impractical to consider these effects, since there is always a significant deviation in practice from the theoretical results.

## 8.9.3 Reducing crosstalk by line arrangement

The amplitude of backward crosstalk (which is the annoying one) is only a function of the relation between the mutual and the self-coupling characteristics of a conductor. We can deduce some general rules by considering two conductors on a backplane, as figure 8.54 shows.

a)
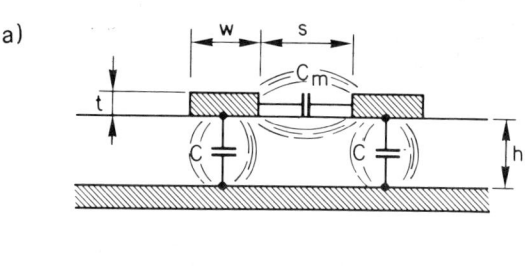

b)
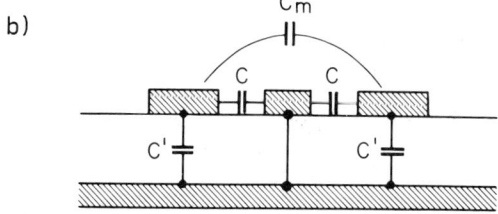

*Fig. 8.54 Coupling of 2 conductors*

First, as we have seen when studying the characteristic impedance (8.4.2), the coupling factors do not depend on the absolute dimensions of the conductors. If all dimensions were multiplied by a certain factor, the values for characteristic impedance or coupling factors would not change.

Then, to control crosstalk, there must be a common ground plane or conductor, or else C would be undefined and thus tend to be equal to $C_m$ (since the other conductor is now used by the wave to propagate).

Since only the relation of mutual to self coupling is important, we can reduce this coupling either by reducing $C_m$ or increasing C. Both methods have an influence on the characteristic impedance of the backplane and on the propagation delay. Possible solutions are hence:

- spacing the conductors further apart (larger s gives smaller $C_m$, no effect on $Z_w$, $t_{pd}$)
- reducing the thickness t (smaller $C_m$, C is also decreased, but less than $C_m$ ($Z_w$ is slightly increased, the resistance of the line increases). Since a copper lane is already very thin, little can be gained here
- increasing the conductors' sizes (larger w gives higher C, but decreases the characteristic impedance). But there are limitations here due to the conductor's spacing
- decreasing the distance of a conductor to ground (smaller h gives higher C, but decreases the characteristic impedance). Multi-layer boards behave therefore better than two-sided boards
- introducing a shield conductor between 2 signal conductors (increases C, but decreases the characteristic impedance). This is however limited by the connector spacing and reduces in any case the line's width

It may seem curious that most measures to reduce crosstalk decrease the characteristic impedance. This is because any change in geometry which increases the specific capacitance will decrease the specific inductance, and therefore decrease $Z_w$.

In flat cables, the need to control crosstalk and the characteristic impedance dictate a mixed arrangement of grounds and signal lines, as shown in figure 8.55.

For instance, the arrangement of figure 8.55a in which the left line GND is the common ground for several signal lines D7..D0 is poor: the characteristic impedance of the conductor D7 is about 100 Ω, but that of line D0 can exceed 1000 Ω. Since the capacitive

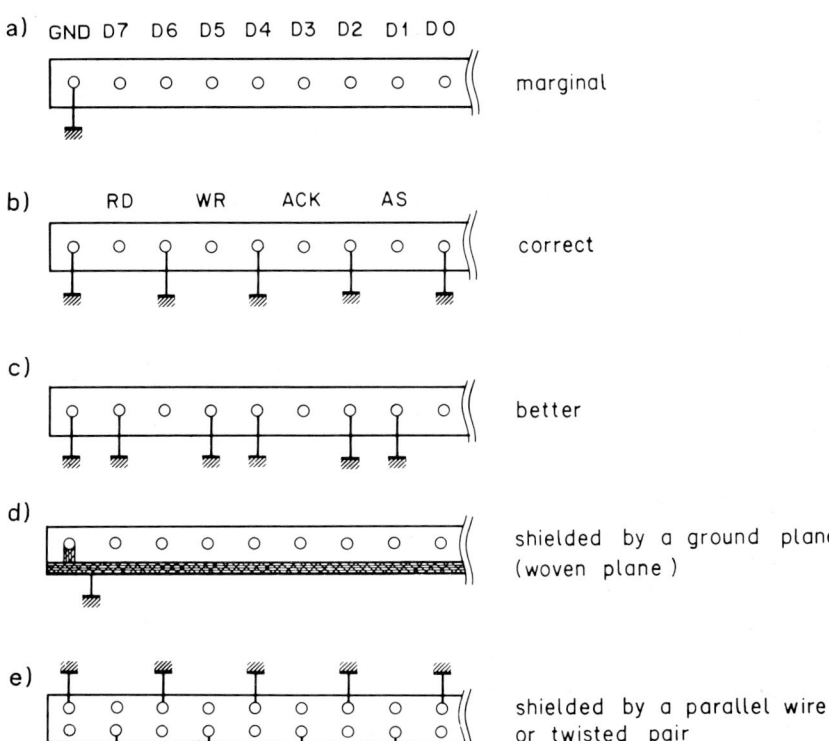

*Fig. 8.55 Arrangements of grounds and signals to reduce crosstalk in flat cables*

coupling between adjacent conductors remains the same, crosstalk increases as a function of the distance from line GND. The different characteristic impedances between the lines are also responsible for different delays, which cause an additional skew. Such an arrangement could be tolerated for signal lines which carry information in parallel, but not for control lines.

An improvement consists in placing the grounded line in the middle but even so, such a solution is only acceptable in low-speed circuits with adequate filtering and when all signal lines are synchronous, for instance when they all carry the different bits of a word and they all go in the same direction.

A better solution for control lines is shown in figure 8.55b, in which every second line is connected to ground. An even better shielding is provided by interleaving more grounds, as in figure 8.55c.

Some flat cables are shielded (figure 8.55d) by a woven ground plane. This not only controls the characteristic impedance, but also decreases crosstalk. Note that the outer conductors of the cable are normally connected to the shield for easier clipping at the connector.

Other flat cables have two rows with vertical columns of conductors (figure 8.55d), where one of them is the shield row with all its conductors connected to ground. Although it may seem that this type of shielding is less efficient than a woven plane, this is not the case, since the distance between the pairs can be kept smaller than the distance of the conductors to the woven shield. When conductors are assignable, it may be advantageous to alternate grounds.

Finally, there exist flat cables consisting of twisted wire pairs and even coaxial cables for harsh environments.

Similar considerations apply to the pin-out of connectors for backplane buses. In principle, there should be a ground line for every four signal lines or at least for every driver package (8 or 9 drivers), but one unfortunately needs every available pin for signals and ground lines are often sacrificed during the design phase. As a replacement rule, if the number of ground lines is insufficient to give each signal line group its own ground line, the grounds should be grouped around the asynchronous timing lines, so that at least these lines can be shielded properly, and scattered evenly between the synchronous lines, such as address and data lines.

The use of multi-layer boards with a ground plane in the middle is recommended in any case. The cost difference with respect to double-sided boards is not worth the gamble. Multi-layer boards allow the manufacture of buried tracks (striplines) which suppress forward crosstalk. The insertion of shield lines between signal lines is also a help. These lines should be connected to the ground shield at close intervals by plated-through holes. The loops formed by the shield lines/ground plane also reduce the inductive coupling [BLO82].

Finally, it should be noted that if the backplane is properly designed, then resistive crosstalk will be again the major source of noise. Resistive crosstalk can only be reduced by lowering the impedance of the common paths. This means that a large number of signal returns should be provided in any case and that great care must be taken in the layout to locate the drivers close to the bus and provide large ground planes close to the connector. The choice of the connector is also important. Recent connectors have been designed especially to meet these requirements.

# 9 INTERFACE DESIGN

A lot of knowledge and experience is required to design properly the hardware of a bus. One has to compromise with an incomplete and slowly expanding set of components, and cope with many timing constraints. When the length of the lines exceeds a few decimetres, it is necessary to take the wave nature of signals into consideration (see Chapter 8).

It is not possible here to provide a full study on how to design processor and interface cards for each standard or dedicated bus. The purpose of this chapter is only to describe an approach to the problem and emphasize the methodology. More detailed bus design presentations can be found in [CON83] and in the manufacturer's application notes.

This chapter is mostly based on Chapters 4 and 5; the few hardware notions given in Chapter 2 were intended to prepare the reader for this chapter. A great amount of additional knowledge, mostly provided by manufacturers in a dispersed way, is required to understand correctly or design bus interfaces.

## 9.1 SYSTEM DECOMPOSITION

The natural decomposition of a system into masters and slaves, in addition to the need for a modularly built system, leads to the usual set-up of a backplane bus and inserted cards. The size of these cards depends mostly on the complexity of the system. Simple 8-bit systems have settled on Eurocards (100 x 160mm). Recent 16-bit microprocessors need double-size Eurocards at least (230 x 160mm). Minicomputer systems use much larger boards. In general, the faster the bus, the more expensive and larger the bus interface. Therefore, designers tend to use larger boards in order to keep the relative cost of the bus interface reasonable.

## 9.1.1 Single processor bus system

Most microcomputer systems have a simple set-up, including a single processor card and several slave cards such as memory and I/O (figure 9.1). These cards plug into a backplane (figures 1.1, 1.2, 2.21 and 4.9), which enables the boards to communicate with each other, sometimes including the I/O boards and their devices.

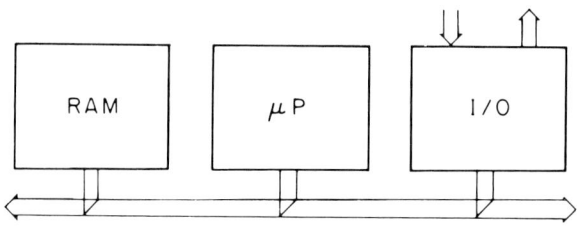

*Fig. 9.1 Single bus system*

A GENERAL PURPOSE BUS can support a great variety of memory and I/O devices, and hence is thus adequate for a number of applications. Most of these buses are processor dependent, that is some bus signals are easily obtained from a given processor, but it is much more difficult to generate them with the correct timing for other processors. Every manufacturer considers its bus as a standard; however, only a few of these buses have been accepted by Standards Organizations (see Appendix).

## 9.1.2 Dedicated buses

Dedicated buses are frequently used to increase a system's performance or to lower its cost. They provide the functionality required with no provision for future extension and other services (figure 9.2). The main memory is sometimes closely connected to the processor with a dedicated bus in order to lower the propagation time and to simplify the memory interface.

A simplified bus for I/O interfaces is also frequently useful. Only a portion of the usual number of bus signals is implemented (8-bit data, few address lines), and the timing may be adapted to allow cheaper components on such a bus. The GPIB IEEE488/IEC625 is a well known dedicated I/O bus for instrumentation.

Most general purpose microprocessor buses support in addition to the main bus a number of dedicated buses. For example, MULTIBUS systems (IEEE 796) include the iSBX or IEEE 959 dedicated I/O bus. MULTIBUS II has a fast memory bus named iLBX.

9 Interface Design 273

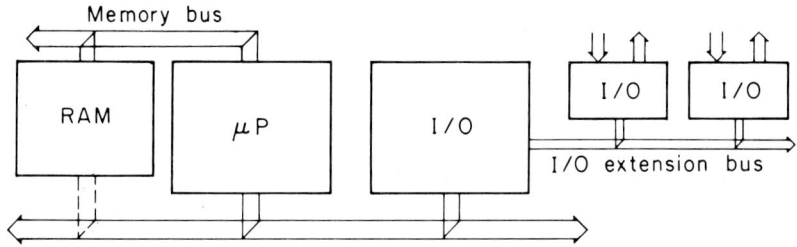

*Fig. 9.2 Dedicated memory and I/O bus*

## 9.1.3 Multiprocessor bus systems

It is possible to have a multiprocessor system which uses only a single bus (figure 9.3a); the arbitration lines would enable the mastership of one processor at a time. However, the bus would rapidly become a bottleneck for the processing units if they all used the bus for instruction fetches and data transfers.

The interface to the common bus for parallel bus systems is usually established in the form of a direct pathway via a BUS WINDOW set up by a BUS CONTROLLER. In the case of serial buses and local networks a GATEWAY, which stores and forwards the message (that is establishes a virtual circuit between the units at the expense of propagation time), is more frequently implemented, because it is not possible to wait for a low level acknowledge.

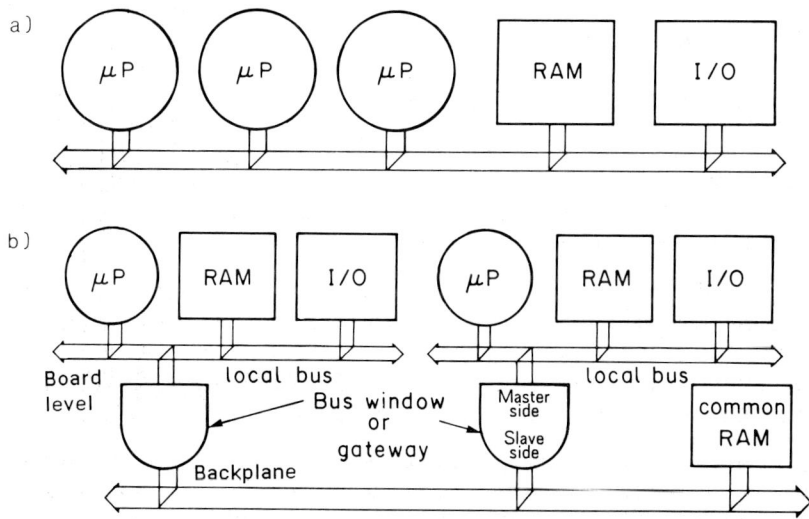

*Fig. 9.3 Single and multiple multiprocessor bus systems*

The bus window usually has only one master function, meaning that it cannot respond to a transfer request from the common bus to the local bus (figure 9.3b). When such a request is possible, special care must be taken to avoid deadlocks, since two processors may simultaneously request a resource on the local bus of the other processor, and be both stopped half-way by each other's request.

## 9.2 SYNCHRONIZATION TECHNIQUES

Each external device connected to the processor has its own time reference. Hence, simultaneous requests may occur and must be finally arbitrated at the level of a flip-flop, risking the emergence of metastable states (section 2.1.9). This major problem is frequently ignored by designers of simple systems, due to the rather low probability of errors when the requests are infrequent.

### 9.2.1 Asynchronous approach

A full handshake arrangement between all requests is possible. This causes numerous delays, however, due to the necessity of taking the propagation time of signals and the decision time of the concerned functions into account. The PDP-11 family and its UNIBUS is based on this asynchronous approach, where each operation occurs as soon as the preceding operation is finished.

The triggering of the next operation is gated with the conditions that enable that operation. The metastable problem occurs only when there are simultaneous requests for a non-shareable resource. The two-input filtered arbiter explained in section 5.4.1 (figure 5.27) has to be used to decrease the probability of these conflicts.

The asynchronous approach is not suited for the design of LSI controllers, due to the lack of regularity in the distributed handshake nodes, the difficulties of test and simulation, the problem of generating deskew delays (section 9.3.4) within a chip and the impossibility of encoding asynchronous signals using fewer lines.

### 9.2.2 Synchronous approach

Synchronous systems are easy to design, since a predictable state follows each clock transition (see section 2.1.8, figure 1.21). In a complex system, however, propagation delays complicate the design of a synchronous system: the propagation time must be less than the clock period minus the input set-up time and propagation delays of the logic functions; possible clock skew must also be taken into account. Frequent resynchronization is hence required. In some cases this can

# 9 Interface Design

increase the efficiency of a system due to the pipelining of operations. More frequently, however, time is just lost during the resynchronization process. In a synchronous world, all devices simultaneously decide to change. Simultaneity means that a fraction of the clock period is used for the propagation time of signals. This restricts the size of this world to a few boards. The problem of interconnection with the external worlds remains. All inputs to a synchronous world look asynchronous, even if they come from another synchronous world, and must thus be synchronized.

## 9.2.3 Synchronization of non-synchronous data

Metastable problems may occur each time external information has to be read by a synchronous system. Double synchronization at a low enough frequency, as shown in figure 2.15, is the only way substantially to lower the probability of error. The technology of the synchronizer and the architecture of the flip-flops influences the sampling frequency. The ECL (Emitter Coupled Logic), AS (Advanced Schottky) and F (Fast) family of devices are recommended; flip-flops inside PALs are very poor for this application. Flip-flops made of discrete gates are also very poor, due to the length of their connecting lines.

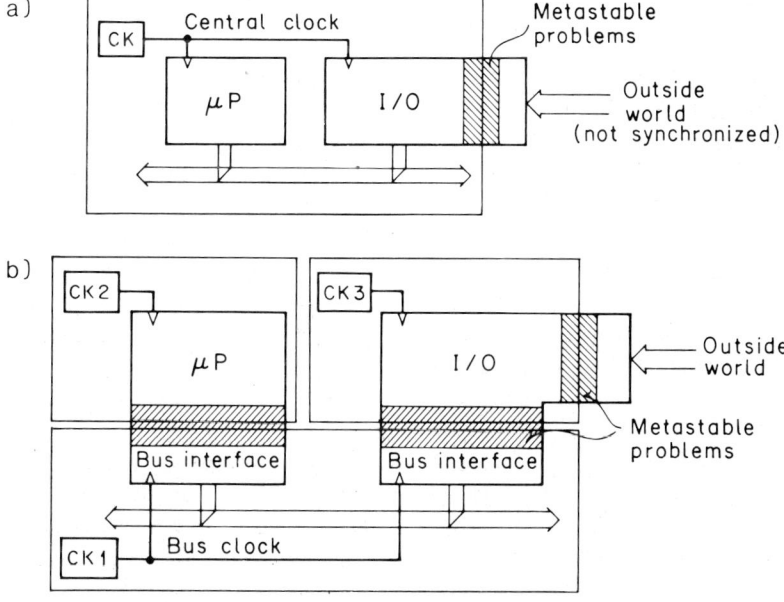

Fig. 9.4 Single clock and multiple clock systems

If the system is fully synchronous, as in figure 9.4a, only signals from the outside world must be synchronized. These signals are usually slow and data is frequently serialized, hence limiting the number of critical opportunities for a metastable problem to occur.

If the bus is synchronous with its own clock, and subsystems with their own clock are attached to it, synchronization must be performed between each synchronous block. For instance, figure 9.4b shows two processors having a different synchronizing clock, and a bus with its own clock. Special care has to be taken at the interface level, as shown in section 9.3.4. This situation is often found in multiprocessor systems, when microprocessors with different clock rates coexist.

### 9.2.4 Synchronization design

Logic and propagation delays must be considered when designing synchronized systems. The calculation of all timing is complicated even further by the propagation delays and the skew of the clock itself. The model of a processor and I/O board synchronized by the same system clock (as in figure 9.4a) is given in figure 9.5. This model shows how data and/or control information is sent from the processor to the I/O board where this information is processed and the return of data and/or control information is triggered. External events may be interleaved into the model after proper synchronization.

The maximum clock frequency that can be used depends on the maximum delay that can occur for a signal in traveling between consecutive registers. One can achieve multiples of this clock delay time by inserting a frequency divider which spaces the sampling periods, as shown on the right-hand-side of figure 9.5. This introduces an additional delay for the clock of this register, which must be taken into account in the next synchronization step.

Two types of delay exist. Unavoidable delays are due to the propagation times through gates and wires. Due to differences in these delays, the time relationship between signals are modified. Two signals which are transmitted close together but in a defined sequence, may arrive in an unpredictable sequence at the receiver. This is called *SKEW*, and in order to rebuilt the correct sequence with guarantied time margins, one must insert a *DESKEW DELAY* on the path of the signal which sould arrive later. Designed delays are inserted as a correction for unavoidable delays, to deskew the signals going in the same directions (that is add a deskew delay to one signal to rebuilt the correct ordering), and to compensate for component timing variations.

9 Interface Design 277

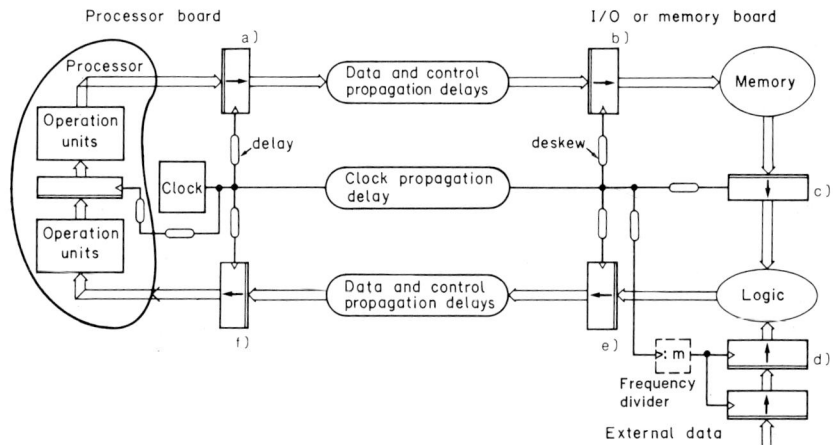

*Fig. 9.5 Delay model in a synchronous system*
*a) Processor interface output register*
*b) I/O input register*
*c) Resynchronization*
*d) Dual synchronization of external events*
*e) I/O output register*
*f) Processor interface input register*

## 9.3 BUS INTERFACE

Decomposition is helpful in the description and implementation of bus interfaces, just as it is in the writing of software. Layering (section 2.3) is however, difficult and costs propagation time.

### 9.3.1 Master and slave

A typical decomposition of a master and a slave bus interface is given in figure 9.6. Typically, the master is a processor and its interface includes the bus arbitration logic (not required in a single master system), the transfer and handshake logic, and the interrupt request logic. The slave is typically a memory or simple input/output device. Its bus interface includes the address selection, the transfer handshake logic, and the interrupt request logic. The electrical bus interface guarantees the correct propagation of signals.

A full transfer sequence commences with a request for the bus, followed by a selection of the partner and a data transfer. The implementation of the many types of transfers of the previous chapters

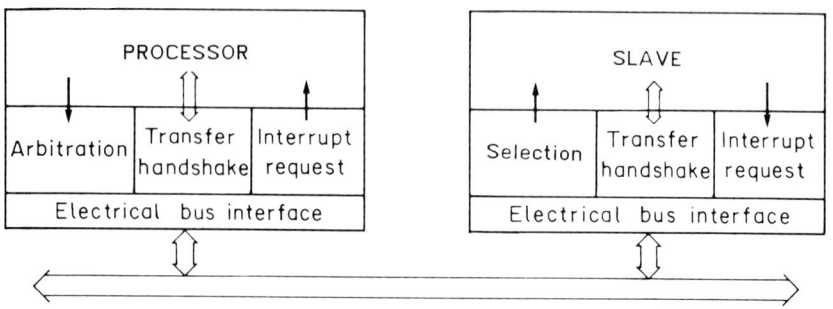

*Fig. 9.6 Master and slave decomposition*

will not be covered here. Only simple examples will be given to show the interface design methodology.

### 9.3.2 Transfer handshake

Let us take the rather simple example of a processor writing information to memory, both devices being connected to a general purpose bus. The processor itself is multiplexed and of the 8086 type; an ALE (address latch enable) pulse indicates the beginning of the cycle, which lasts as long as the WAIT input is active. The bus is non-multiplexed and has two full handshake signals, ST (strobe) and AK (acknowledge). All lines on the bus are inverted (active low), as is usual with open-collector or three-state buses. The inverted bus signals have a postfix inverting star instead of an overline bar. The memory responds to a group of addresses and accepts the written information by activating the signal ACCept shortly after the select input SEL is activated. Figure 9.7 provides a clear block diagram of both interfaces.

It is easy to follow the sequence of operations related to a transfer, as shown in figure 9.7, but more information is needed for a complete understanding of all the details. The cycle starts when the processor announces exactly what it intends to do, in this case at the end of the ALE pulse. The address lines indicate the selected device, and the mode lines determine the nature of the cycle. Since the selected device is on the bus, the bus arbiter must agree to put the data on the bus before a transfer may occur.

The master Strobe ST_M signal at the processor and bus interface is activated as soon as the arbiter grants the bus. The Bus Strobe ST* signal itself is delayed with respect to ST_M in order to deskew the propagation time on all the data lines. This delay is increased in some cases to include enough set-up time to avoid further delays at the slave logic.

# 9 Interface Design

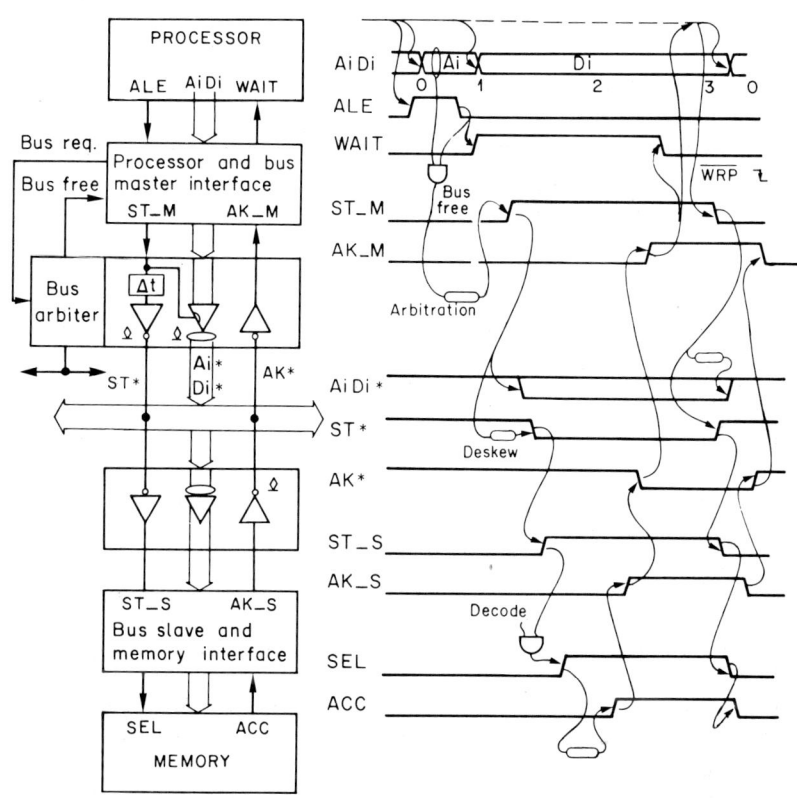

Fig. 9.7 *Transfer handshake : block decomposition and asynchronous timing*

The Slave Strobe ST_S is used at the bus slave interface to gate the decoder and generate the SEL signal; delays may have to be added according to the memory set-up time specifications. The ACC signal is generated when the memory has completed the requested operation, and goes back to the processor through the AK* bus line to clear the WAIT flip-flop. This flip-flop is required in the processor interface due to differences between the processor semi-synchronous handshake (section 3.6.5 and 3.7.6) and the bus full-handshake philosophy. The WAIT flip-flop is set by the ALE trailing edge, and cleared when AK_M is activated (figure 9.9). The processor continues its cycle as soon as WAIT becomes inactive; it deactivates ST_M (due to an end of cycle signal which is not shown) when the cycle is terminated.

Indeed, after a write cycle has been performed and after the memory has accepted the information, the bus could be released as soon as AK_M is activated. Many similar situations occur on real buses in order to eliminate useless delays, taking into account the expected delays of other elements. The bus slave and memory interface, for instance, assuming that the processor is slow and its memory fast enough, could return the AK_S immediately after the address has been recognized.

Similar technological assumptions are made at all levels, and thus complicate the understanding and the verification of a design. One of these technological assumptions has been made earlier in this section and we hope that the reader has noticed this simplification: the data information is provided by the processor following a delay after ALE has been deactivated. A $\overline{WRP}$ (write pulse) signal is provided by the processor to signal when the data is stable. In our design, ALE triggers only the ST* signal; a delay between ALE and ST* that is too short will cause the storing of unstable data in the memory. Figure 9.8 explains this in more detail, and shows that one has to use the $\overline{WRP}$ signal available on the processor in order to ensure that the ST* signal will not be activated as long as the data on the bus is not valid.

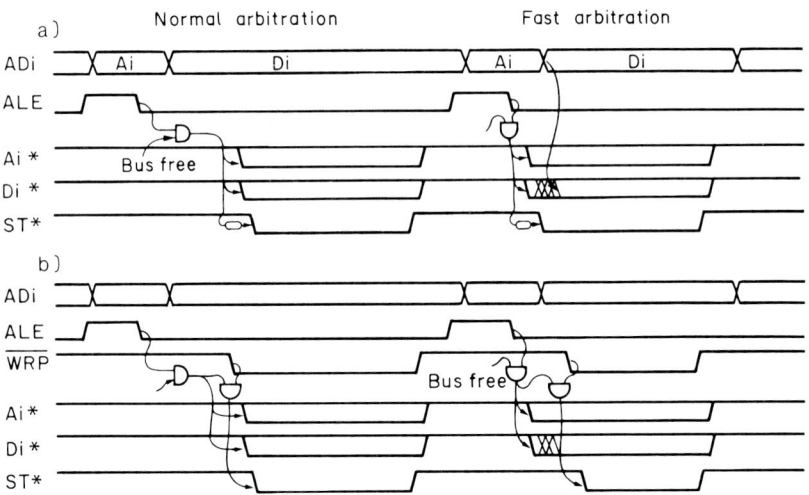

Fig. 9.8 Bus cycle with slow and fast arbitration
 a) ALE-only control
 b) ALE and $\overline{WRP}$ control

Also notice in figure 9.8 that when ST* is delayed due to the data information not yet being valid, the selection is also delayed. Since the selection takes time, a more efficient scheme would be to

# 9 Interface Design

separate the ST* signal into an address strobe (the ST* of figure 9.8a) and a data strobe (the ST* of figure 9.8b). Only the data strobe is delayed in this case, and the response time is better.

The representation of the sequencing with timing diagrams is rather clear and emphasizes the many timing dependencies and propagation delays. This representation is, however, based on the intuitive understanding of the interface, and is prone to oversight and errors. A representation using a state diagram is also recommended but this does not show the many sub-states of an asynchronous system. The processor and bus interface, in this simple example, may be considered as having four states, as shown in figure 9.9. The bus itself can be considered as having two states (data not valid and data valid when ST* active), or four states, if AK* is taken into account.

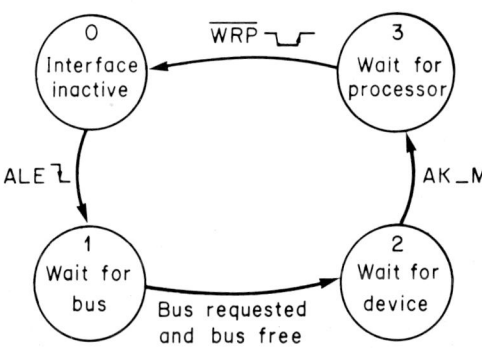

*Fig. 9.9 State diagram for the processor and bus interface*

A hardware descriptive language may in the future provide a better way of describing the specifications and the proposed implementations of interfaces, and provide design verification programs [BAR85].

## 9.3.3 Asynchronous implementation

The timing implementation diagram of figure 9.7 suggests an asynchronous implementation of this handshaken transfer, which is easy to design from the timing or the state diagram.

Figure 9.10 shows a possible scheme using functional elements. The next step is the selection of real gates and flip-flops, the verification of the loads of each output and the calculation of all timing.

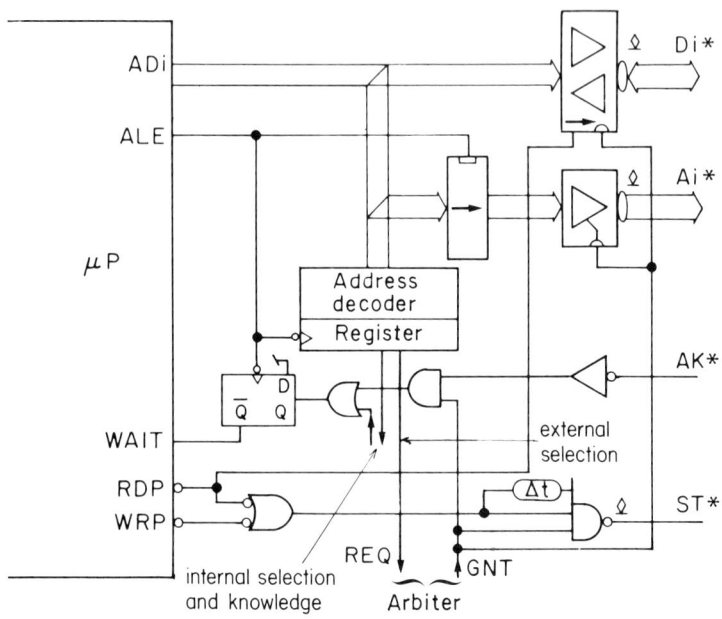

*Fig. 9.10 Typical simplified bus interface schematic (master)*

The proposed circuit does not implement functions which are not required by present-day technology and would be too expensive. For instance, the ST* to Ai* and Di* deskew are delayed with the beginning of the ST signal. But at the end of the cycle, the signals, ST*, Ai* and Di* are deactivated together, assuming that the decoding logic on each slave will not be triggered by these signals in transition (see section 9.3.7).

### 9.3.4 Synchronous implementation

A strictly synchronous implementation of a system occurs when each signal of the system is sampled with a clock edge. A high frequency clock of 20 MHz or more is required at the bus level, since propagation and decoding times are in the range of 5 to 40 ns. Such a high sampling rate is a problem for the processor and memory, since propagation time differences of present VLSI processors may easily reach more than 50 ns (between min and max specified values). If too slow a clock is used, the efficiency of the bus decreases, since only multiples of the clock periods are resolved. The major advantage of a synchronous implementation is the possibility of a systematic description based on state diagrams, with exhaustive lists of conditions and future states, thus allowing an easier program verification. Clock

# 9 Interface Design

delays and timings have to be very carefully verified, as shown in figure 9.5.

The asynchronous timing introduced in figure 9.7 has a typical synchronous variant, as shown in figure 9.11. All the interface signals are synchronized to a high frequency clock, the speed of which depends on the maximum logic and propagation delays of the propagated signals. Double synchronization is required since master and slave clocks differ from the bus clock. Synchonization is required at each step if the clock is supposed to be at a maximum frequency defined by the elementary propagation delays.

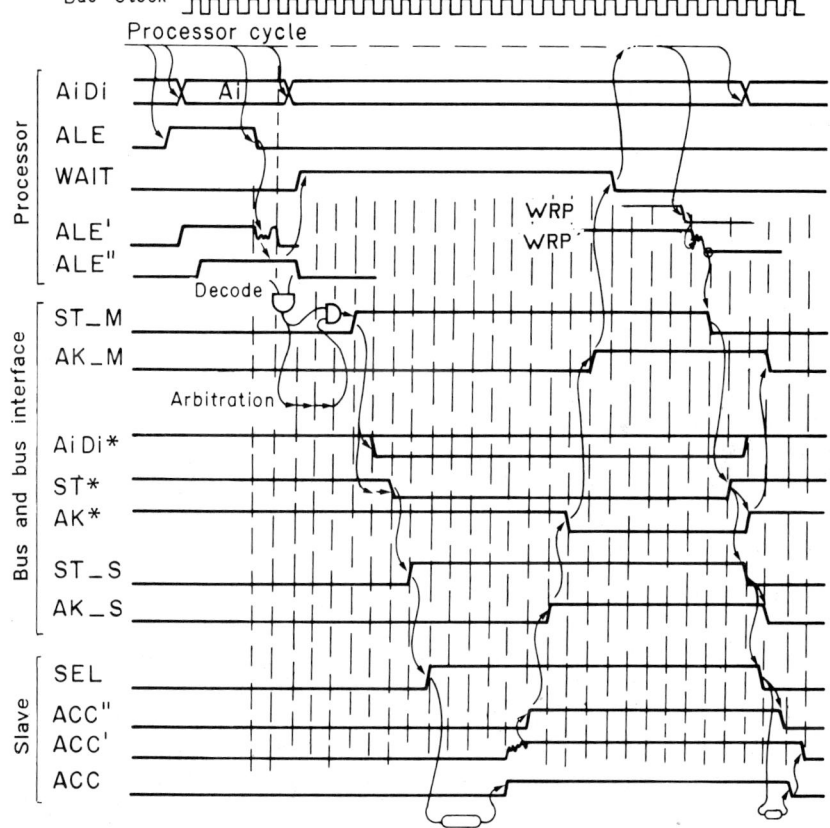

*Fig. 9.11 Timing diagram with a synchronous transfer*

From figure 9.11 it can be seen that three signals have to be double-synchronized due to possible metastable states: ALE, WRP (from the processor), and ACC (from the memory or I/O), and that the resynchronization process at each interface level significantly slows down the transfer operation (the slave response time is the same as in figure 9.7). In order to save a little bit of time, the return to inactive condition of the AK signal is not propagated through the bus, but instead deactivation occurs at each level of the interface: as soon as the strobe signal is deactivated, the cycle is terminated.

Microprocessor buses using a synchronous design are Nubus and Multibus II (see Appendix). High performance minicomputers frequently use a synchronous bus, especially when split cycles (section 6.2.1) are implemented. All transfers on the bus are pipelined, and use the bus for only one or two bus clock cycles to write the address and data.

The synchronous approach for systems will be more frequently used in the future. Bus interfaces built with VLSI require synchronous logic, and faster processors will allow higher clock sampling signals.

Most present designs use a semi-synchronous approach, similar to the previous example of figure 9.7. The WAIT signal is in this case sampled synchronously by the processor. The double-synchronization, which avoids metastable states, is performed inside the processor, although in some cases the manufacturer may require an external synchronization (e.g. Intel 8080, 8086).

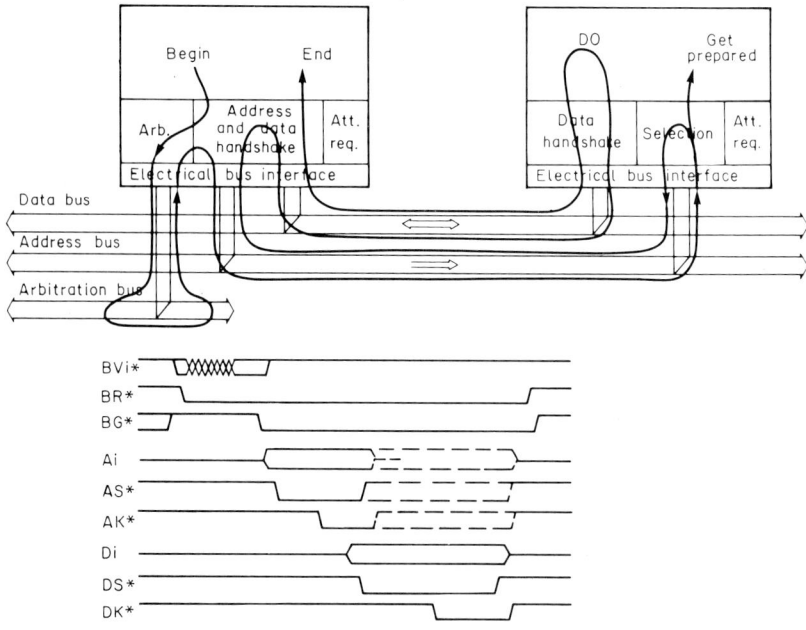

*Fig. 9.12 Complete handshaken transfer sequence*

## 9.3.5 Complete transfer sequence

A transfer sequence from a commander to a responder first implies an arbitration and a certain amount of waiting time for the bus. The selection of the responder can take place as soon as the data and address buses are free. The selection is implicitly or sometimes explicitly acknowledged before the data transfer may take place. Many steps are required for a complete transfer sequence (figure 9.12). Each step can be analysed as for the data transfer of figure 9.7.

A complete handshaken protocol guarantees technology independence, since propagation and handshake delays can be modified in each part of the system separately and independently. The IEEE-896 bus follows this philosophy.

Most buses are designed to use some implicit timing according to current processor and memory technology. Most present buses do not separately acknowledge the address and then the data. The termination of the cycle depends on the acceptance of the address, and on the time required to store or provide the particular data (figure 9.13). The block and timing diagrams of this figure correspond to the simple transfer scheme of section 9.3.2. Other variations are given in section 4.2.

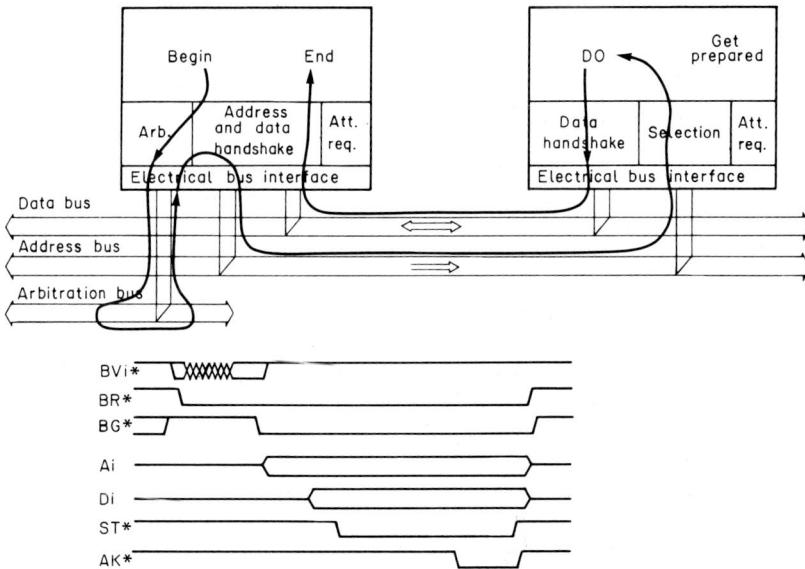

*Fig. 9.13 Simplified handshaken transfer sequence*

## 9.3.6 Arbitration

Arbitration techniques have been comprehensively studied in Chapter 5. A careful design of the arbitration part must be made in order to avoid multiple allocation of the bus following a metastable state.

As an example of a bus arbiter interface, let us consider the VME [VME82] daisy chain arbiter, limiting ourselves to only one of its three modes, named "ONE" due to the fact that it uses only one of its four daisy chains. The block diagram and signal names are given in figure 9.14, together with a typical timing diagram. The situation depicted corresponds to one inactive master in slot A1 and two potential masters in slots A2 and A3. Our objective is to design the arbiter interface for the two potential masters.

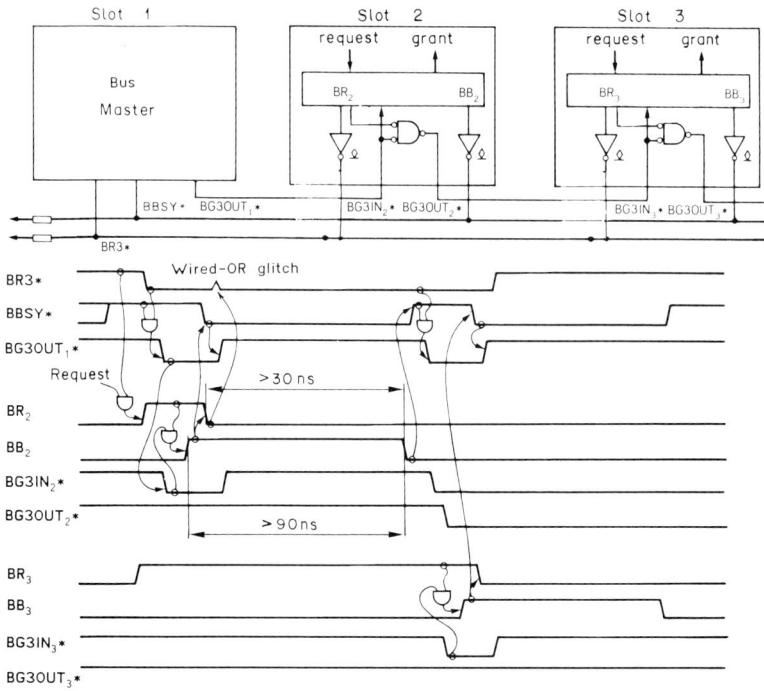

*Fig. 9.14 Block diagram and signals for the VME "ONE" arbiter mode*

# 9 Interface Design

Each I/O device requests the bus resource and is granted its use by the interface; two logic signals are sufficient for this. On the bus, VME defines four signals:

- BR3*  Bus Request low (wired-or)
- BBSY* Bus Busy low (wired-or)
- $BG3IN_i*$  Bus Grant chained intput at slot i
- $BG3OUT_i*$ Bus Grant chained output at slot i

The timing diagram shows the case of two simultaneous requests from devices in slots 2 and 3 (same request level). The requests are transmitted to the master through the BR3* line, which activates the $BG3OUT_1*$ signal as soon as the bus is free (BBSY* inactive). The device in slot 2 receives this signal as $BG3IN_2*$, takes the bus, and releases its bus request. This may create a wired-or glitch (section 8.5.4) which briefly asserts BR3*; further checking will be required to verify that this is acceptable. As soon as device in slot 2 releases the bus by deactivating BBSY, the master again activates $BG3OUT_1*$. Now, the device in slot 3 takes control. There is some probability that the device in slot 2 asks for the bus when $BG3IN_2$ is active. That request must be deferred, otherwise the two devices in slot 2 and 3 could get the bus together. If there simultaneity between $BR_2$ and $BG3IN_2$, the $BR_2$ latch may go into a metastable state and it is necessary to delay significantly the $BG3OUT_2$ signal. VME specifications recommend not to go over 70 ns, for performance reasons. This metastable problem must be considered very carefully; Problems have been reported on several multiprocessor systems.

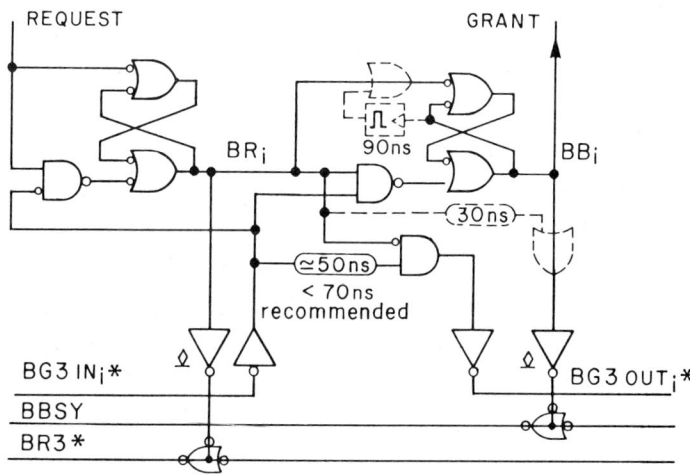

*Fig. 9.15 Bus arbiter interface for VME (mode "ONE")*

The untested schematic of figure 9.15 seems to meet all the VME requirements. The request at level i is latched when $BG3IN_i$ is not active. $BG3OUT_i$ is delayed by the propagation time of this latch, plus some time to minimize metastability. Fast logic and short interconnecting wires are required for this latch.

VME specifies 30 ns from the end of BR3* to the end of BBSY*. This delay is usually much lower than the duration of the bus transfer. If not, the delay shown in dotted lines must be inserted. The VME requirement for a larger than 90 ns BBSY* pulse, if not implied by the device, can be garanteed by a one-shot, also shown in dotted lines. There are no other timing constraints, due to the asynchronous nature of the handshake.

### 9.3.7 Selection

The selection of the responder is most frequently performed by specifying its address, and thus we shall only consider this case. An encoded address is validated by a signal edge or a selection pulse; in the first case the condition is loaded into a dynamic register; in the second case, a latch is adequate. The decoding logic is frequently split into three parts :

- the commander decoder, which decides if the resource is external to the board and if the bus has to be requested
- the responder decoder, which decides which local device must be selected
- the responder device decoder, which selects a specific I/O or memory register.

Each of these decoders must provide clean selection pulses. Due to the propagation time within the decoder and a small set-up and hold time of the address with respect to the strobe signal, there is a risk of glitches as shown in figure 9.16. Adequate additional delays must be introduced in this case, but these delays may be undesirable for some other operations, which may in turn have to be delayed.

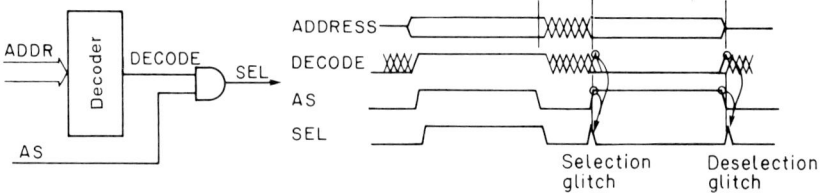

*Fig. 9.16 Decoder selection and glitches*

# 9 Interface Design

Latches or edge-triggered registers may be a solution to prevent false selection glitches. If the bus is multiplexed, they are required to store the selection condition; this can be done according to one of the three solutions of figure 9.17.

The solution of figure 9.17a disables the decoder when the address changes. The following solution of figure 9.17b is dangerous if differences of propagation time occur inside the decoder, generating false selection pulses. The last solution of figure 9.17c is preferred.

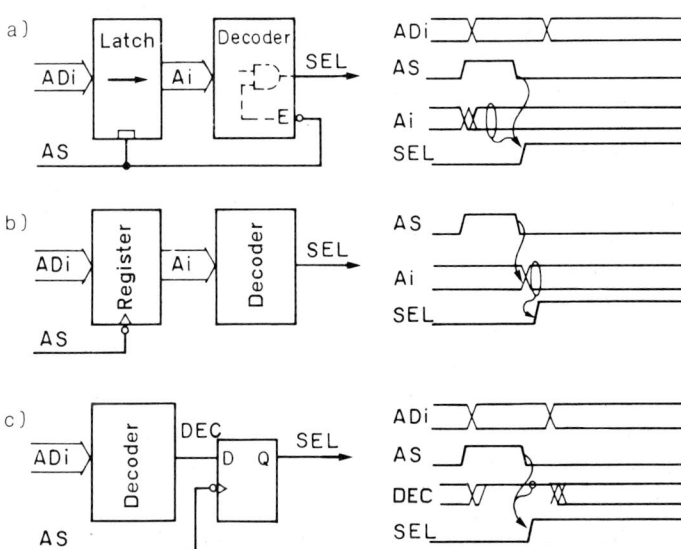

Fig. 9.17 Selection principles for a multiplexed bus

## 9.3.8 Interrupt request

Interrupts and exception requests are broadcast by the slaves towards one or several masters. No specific problems occur with these requests, since the corresponding lines are sampled and serviced by one of the previously described mechanisms, such as the arbitration of requesting devices and their selection.

## 9.4 DATA MULTIPLEXING AND ALIGNMENT

The process of putting address and data on a set of lines is far from being standardized. Due to the cost of lines and the power dissipation of drivers, the multiplexing of address and data is frequently practiced.

The arrangement of the data bytes on the bus is subject to many solutions, and prevents, in many cases, the mixture of processors and co-processors of different makes on the same bus.

### 9.4.1 Multiplexing

The multiplexing of the arbitration vector, the address, and the data information on the same lines is possible without losing too much time (figure 9.12).

The principle of address/data multiplexing has been explained in section 4.3 and a specific example appears in figure 9.18. On a multiplexed bus, the master activates the address driver while sending an address strobe pulse AS, which latches the address in a slave address latch. The data transfer follows and is synchronized by a data strobe pulse DS. The arbitration is shown here as using the same lines, but frequently special lines are provided, in order to be able to arbitrate the next transfer in parallel with a data transfer (section 5.4.4).

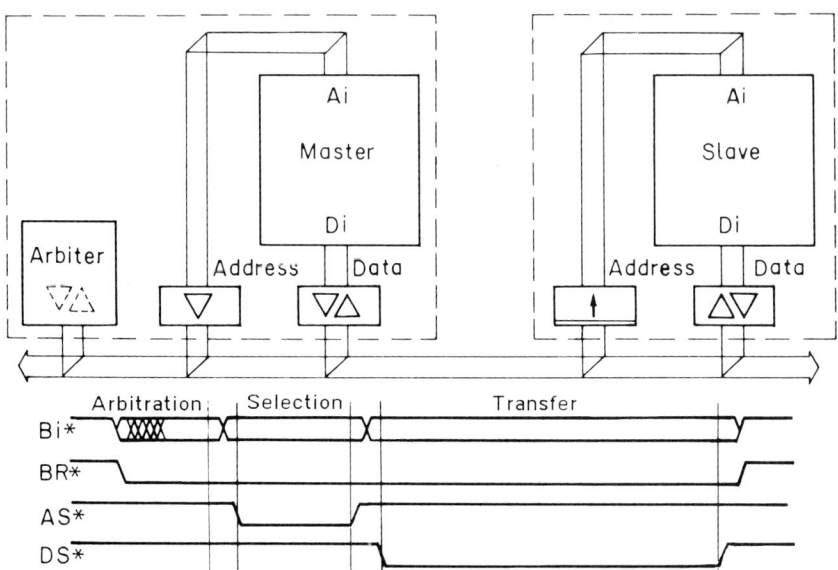

Fig. 9.18 Multiplexed bus interface

## 9.4.2 Driver arrangement

To minimize the load on the bus (connection of circuit boards) the schematic of figure 9.18 is usually replaced by the interface of figure 9.19. This interface is more complex and slower when transferring addresses due to the additional layer of drivers.

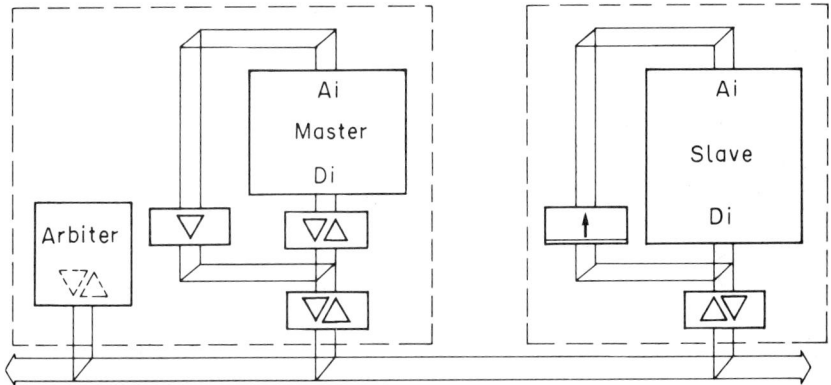

*Fig. 9.19 Recommended driver location on a multiplexed bus*

If the arbitration lines are multiplexed on the same bus lines, they usually do not go through the address/data driver, due to the special wired-or function which is performed by the distributed arbiters (see section 5.3.5).

## 9.4.3 Address space

Most processors use byte-addressing of memory elements. Physical memories are organized with 8-, 16- and 32-bit data paths and sometimes local addresses are considered as 16-bit or 32-bit word addresses. The processor handles various data types of 8-, 16-, 32-, 64-, 80-bits. The bus may be 8-, 16- or 32-bit wide, but on a large bus, only part of it may be used for a transfer. A clear understanding of the correspondence of address elements and alignment possibilities is important. Figure 9.20 shows the alignment problem for data items of different sizes.

## 9.4.4 Straight and justified buses

Even on a wide bus, it is necessary to connect 8- or 16-bit devices; for instance, most programmable interfaces are 8 bits wide. Let us take the example of a 32-bit bus, from which it is easy to generalize to 64 bits or more, or to simplify down to 16 bits. The connected devices are 32-, 16- or 8-bit wide, that work with

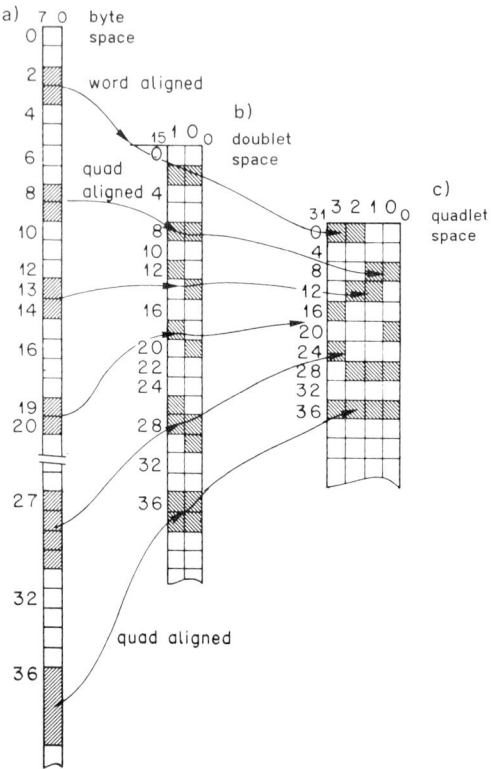

*Fig. 9.20 Byte, doublet and quadlet space*

quadlet, doublet or byte addresses internally (figure 9.20). The case of more complex devices able to handle several sizes will be considered later.

The two basic ways of connecting 8- and 16-bit devices are to use a STRAIGHT BUS or a JUSTIFIED BUS. With a straight bus (figure 9.21a), a 16-bit device may be attached to either half of the 32-bit bus, but will get only half of the addresses. A more complex interface, including a 32- to 16-bit multiplexer, will allow the access of all even addresses, as shown in dotted lines on figure 9.21. An 8-bit device may be connected to any one of the four groups of 8 lines, but it will be selected by only one out of every four addresses. An 8- to 32-bit multiplexer, shown with dotted lines, is required to access all addresses. With the justified bus, 16- and 8-bit devices are aligned on the low byte and can be selected by all addresses (figure 9.21b).

9 Interface Design                                                    293

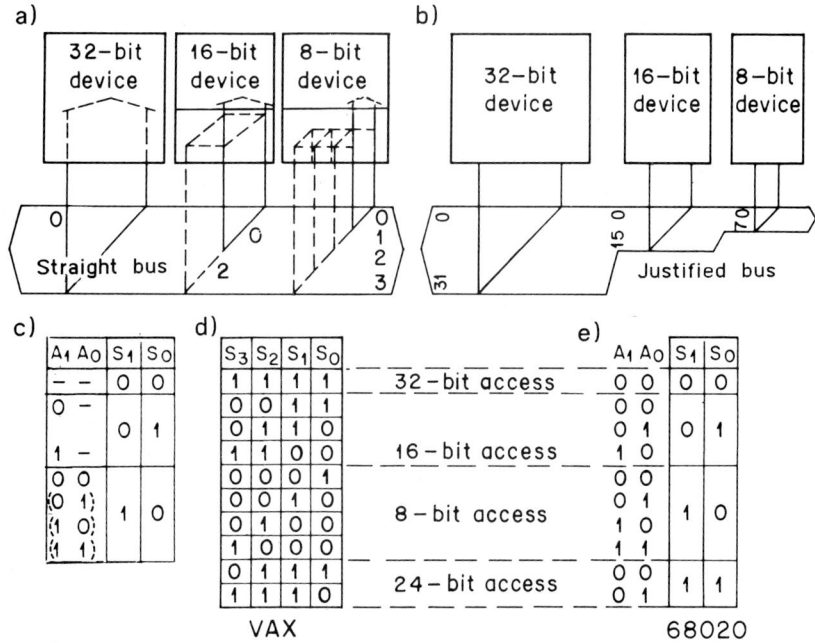

Fig. 9.21 Addressing with a straight and a justified bus

Two bits of status information are required in addition to the address to define whether the transfer is 32-, 16- or 8-bits wide (figure 9.21c). That information may be encoded together with the 2 low bits of the address, in the case of a straight bus. Four data strobes can define which groups of 8 lines are used for the data transfer. That solution is used on the VAX SBI and BI buses (figure 9.21d). The solution used on the IEEE-P896 is very similar.

The justified bus is encoded according to the size of the transferred word and its address. Two status bits are replaced by the two lowest address bits, as in figure 9.21e. The processor 68020 uses this encoding. Mixed solutions are possible, as for the VME bus which is justified for 16-bit transfers and straight (inside 16-bit words) for 8-bit transfers.

## 9.4.5 Complex devices and bus drivers

The choice between a straight and a justified bus depends on hardware complexity and speed [KIRR83]. The devices do not usually follow the simplification given earlier; a 32-bit wide memory must be accessed by byte, doublet or quadlet. The processor has instructions to access bytes, doublet, quadlets. Processor, memory and I/O devices can be built to look like, and be directly compatible with, a straight or justified bus. Internally, the 32-bit memory chips form a straight bus, but the processor registers are viewed by the programmer as carrying justified data. The conversion from the processor format to the memory format can be performed inside the processor, on the processor interface or on the memory board. There may be situations where non useful conversions will have to be done, for compatibility reasons.

Let us limit ourselves to the case of straight devices, which accept smaller size data items, that is 8- and 16-bit transfers can occur for a 32-bit device, and 8-bit transfers for a 16-bit device. Figure 9.22 shows the bus drivers required for interfacing to a straight bus. The drivers are easy to control with the 4-line status encoding proposed in figure 9.21d.

A 32-bit processor addresses a 16-bit or 8-bit device through a 32-bit word (quadlet) address and a status word, which specifies on which lines it has put the information. As said earlier, if there are addressing limitations, e.g. if an 8-bit peripheral can only respond to an address multiple of 4, some drivers may be saved.

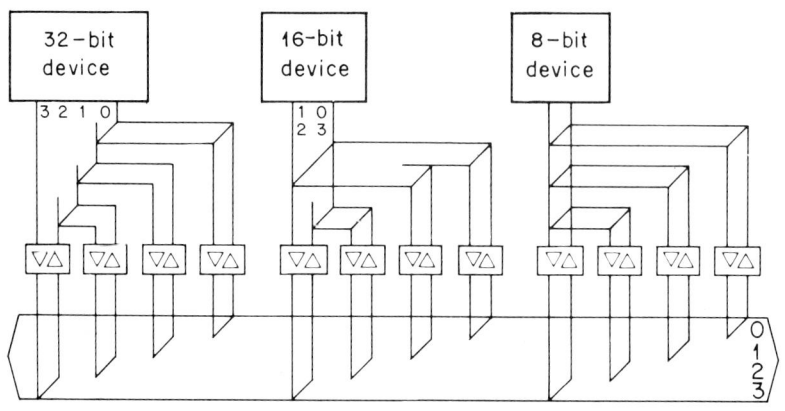

*Fig. 9.22 Drivers on a straight bus*

The interface for a justified bus is more complex, except for 8-bit devices. For 16-bit devices which can be byte accessed, it may be necessary to access the more significant byte of the device using an odd address. The 32-bit interface has similar requirements for bytes and doublets.

9 Interface Design 295

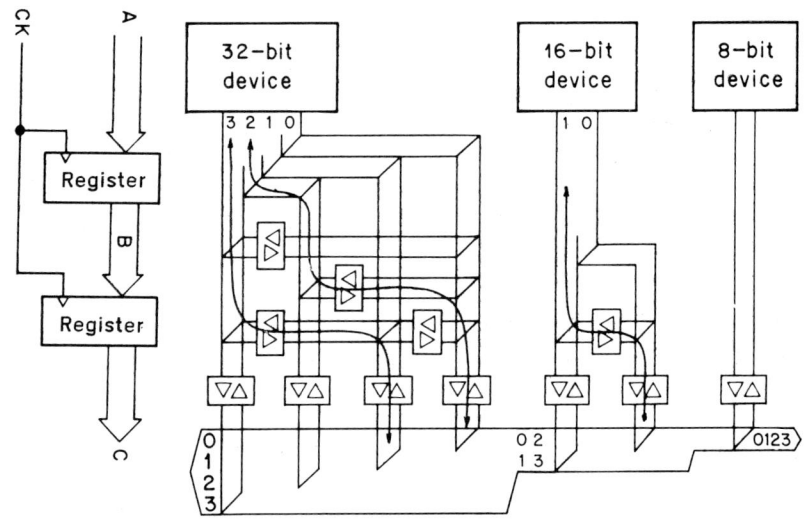

*Fig. 9.23 Bus drivers on a justified bus*

The situation depicted in figure 9.20, where there are no power-of-two boundaries, is even more complex, due to the necessity of performing multiple transfers.

Note that even with a straight bus, as with the 68020 microprocessor, the internal access to registers when byte and doublet access are specified implies the logic of figure 9.23. But this is done inside the processor. No justified bus exists for sizes larger than 16 bits, due to the high cost of memory boards if byte access must be supported.

### 9.4.6 Big endian and little endian

Bit and byte numbering in computers is in terrible disarray. One option concerns the numbering of the bits in a word. A few computer manufacturers assign the value 0 (sometimes 1) to the most significant bit. Happily, all microprocessor manufacturers now agree that bits should be numbered from right to left (least significant bit towards most significant bit), starting with bit 0, as for the binary weights.

There is no hope, however, of settling the fight between the *LITTLE ENDIAN* and the *BIG ENDIAN*, as defined by the amusing paper of Professor Cohen [COH81] : some manufacturers prefer, in a multiple-byte word, to number bytes from left to right, as with bits (the "little" byte end on the LSB side), while others have decided to number bytes in the other direction, that is with the "big" byte on the LSB side (figure 9.24).

```
MSB   31        24 23        16 15        8 7        1 0  LSB
little  ┌─────────┬──────────┬───────────┬──────────┐
endian  │    3    │    2     │     1     │    0     │
big     ├─────────┼──────────┼───────────┼──────────┤       "end"
endian  │    0    │    1     │     2     │    3     │
        └─────────┴──────────┴───────────┴──────────┘
```

*Fig. 9.24 Byte ordering*

The address spaces and buses described earlier (figure 9.21) were of the "little endian" type; Among manufacturers, Motorola promotes the big endian type while Intel and DEC are staunch supporters of the little endian cause. Figure 9.25 shows how to connect 8- and 16-bit devices to the big-endian bus of the M68020 microprocessor.

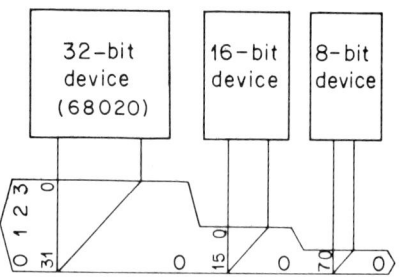

*Fig. 9.25 Big-endian justified bus*

There are major difficulties when one tries to put a big endian and a little endian processor on the same bus. They cannot work on the same data structure in memory unless some limitations are accepted or more complex interfaces are designed [KIRR83].

## 9.5 LOGIC DESIGN AND IMPLEMENTATION

Logic design is an art which implies a vast knowledge of a fast-moving technology. The designer learns from manufacturers' documentation and by looking at other people's schematics. Few books dare to take the description of the implementation of the few simple components mentioned in section 2.1 [FLET80] [PEAT80] [ROBI79] [WINK80]. No real methodology exists to handle complex designs and the new CAD tools allow more formal approaches to the design; it is hence not possible in this book to provide more than several warnings and hints.

## 9.5.1 Component selection

A good knowledge of the existing components, with their real availability, is the first requirement for logic designers. TTL, CMOS and ECL families continually evolve with new devices and redesigned circuits using an improved technology. Few MOS circuits are used in the bus interface itself, but the purpose of the interface is to connect several complex MOS circuits, and the characteristics of that technology must thus also be known.

Three technologies are used at the bus interface level. The HC-MOS technology looks promising for low-speed applications; the family of HC-MOS devices is now complete enough, and fully HC-MOS systems can be designed, with a very low power consumption.

TTL technology is still the most frequently used family of logic, with a mixing of -LS, -S, -AS and -F subfamilies, according to the speed requirements and the availability of devices. Power dissipation may be important, which implies the necessity of good ventilation.

ECL technology is required for the high speed applications; the level of integration is lower within this family, that is more devices are required for the same functions. This in part helps to solve the heat dissipation problem, although one version of Fastbus still has to use watercooled boards.

A very important component is the bus driver, for which a large, but incomplete set of devices exists. The four major features of a bus transciever are :

- its output and input current
- its polarity (direct or inverted)
- its organization (mono- or bidirectional, separate selection or direction control, latches or registers)
- its size (4-, 6-, 8-, 9- or 10-bit wide)
- its pin-out (crossed or aligned).

Hence with these five orthogonal parameters, for each technology and driving current, many different drivers should exist to provide a sufficient amount of freedom for the designer. As shown in figure 9.26, this is not the case, and thus a lot of thought must be spent on managing with the available devices. Fast buses require low-impedance high-current drivers (section 8.7). The best signal shape is trapezoidal, as for the DS 3896/3897 [BALA84].

| Sink current | Fct | Three-state ▽ | O. C. ◇ | Inv. three-state o▽ | Inv. O. C. o◇ | $T_{pd}$ ns | Power mW | Pins |
|---|---|---|---|---|---|---|---|---|
| 24 mA @ 0.5V | a | HC241 HC244 | | HC240 | | 60 | 0.2 | 20 |
| | a' | HC541 | | HC540 | | 60 | 0.2 | 20 |
| | b | HC623 | | HC620 | | 60 | 0.2 | 20 |
| | b' | HC245 HC645 | | HC640 | | 60 | 0.2 | 20 |
| | b'ʀ | HC658 | | HC659 | | - | 0.5 | 24 |
| 24 mA @ 0.5V | a | LS241 LS244 | | LS240 | | 18 | 150 | 20 |
| | a' | LS541 | | LS540 | | 18 | 150 | 20 |
| | b | LS623 Am2949 | LS622 | LS620 Am2948 | LS621 | 25 | 450 | 20 |
| | b' | LS245 LS645 | LS641 | LS640 | LS644 | 25 | 450 | 20 |
| | b' | | LS638 | | LS639 | 25 | 450 | 20 |
| | c | LS646 | LS647 | LS648 | LS649 | 30 | 800 | 24 |
| | c' | LS652 Am2952 | LS654 | LS651 Am2953 | LS653 | - | 500 | 24 |
| | d | LS442 | LS440 | LS443 | LS441 | 30 | 400 | 20 |
| 48 mA @ 0.5V | a | | | 25LS240 | | 18 | 150 | 20 |
| | b' | LS645-1 | | LS640-1 | | 18 | 320 | 20 |
| 64 mA @ 0.5V | a | S244 F244 | | S240 F240 | | 18 | 500 | 20 |
| | b | 29863₁, 29861₁₀ | | 29864 29862 | | 10 | 750 | 24 |
| | bʀ | 29833 29853 | | 29834 29854 | | 12 | - | 24 |
| 100 mA @ 0.8V | b' | | | DS3896 | | | | |
| | e | | | 26S10,11 | | 20 | 320 | 16 |
| | e | | | DS3897 | | 20 | 250 | 16 |
| | f | | | 2905,06, | | 20 | 340 | 24w |
| | f | | | 2907,08, | | 20 | 360 | 24w |

8 devices in a package unless 4,9,10 specified. ʀ means a parity generator is included.

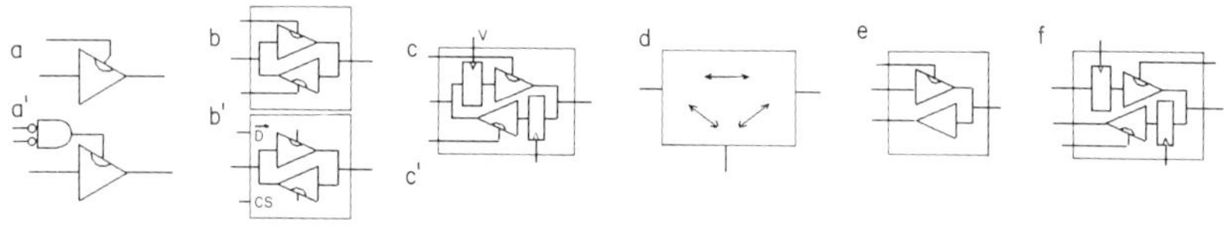

Fig. 9.26 Open-collector and three-state drivers

## 9.5.2 Timing analysis

The designer must compare the timing specifications of the bus, the processor, the memory, and the other components he must interface with. These provide the constraints of the interface and several iterations are frequently required until the best solution is found. One solution of providing more time for the propagation of signals is by adding processor wait states, although the penalty will be a decrease in performance.

Several examples of timing diagrams have been given earlier. Their purpose was primarily to show the functions performed and their sequencing. Timing diagrams are also used to verify the worst case delay specifications. Computer programs are a great help in this respect, and design systems that incorporate the drawing of schematic diagrams, the verification of electrical parameters, the logical simulation and the timing verification are becoming essential for designers.

### 9.5.3 Board layout

The design of a board for a standard bus is strongly influenced by the size of the board and the placement of the connectors. Major changes in the block diagram and the initial specifications may occur when the final components are selected and the layout undertaken. A good layout must guarantee short connections and adequate heat distribution. The different component sizes provide an additional challenge, and the recent trend in surface mounting brings about difficulties by the need to mix two types of components with different soldering technologies, or to simply accept the constraint of having to reject components having inadequate packages.

Printed circuit boards inevitably consist of four layers in most commercial designs. The two middle layers are for the power supply and ground. More than two layers are frequently used for logic signals, but the debugging becomes difficult when design errors are found. Unless really high density components are used, the use of many layers reveals a poor layout or an inefficient routing algorithm.

### 9.5.4 Backplane and connectors

The backplane is a very important part of the system, and a careful impedance analysis following the recommendations of Chapter 8 must control its design. The terminating resistors are located at the end of the backplane, optionally on connectors.

The location of the bus drivers close to the connector is important. The connector pin layout influences the ease of connection with the drivers, that is it allows short connections which are required for a good bus performance. Endless discussion occurs among designers when this pin-out has to be defined, since it depends on the implementation of the drivers next to the connector. Some connector pin-outs have been very poorly designed: they randomly interleave the address, data and control signals, and do not provide enough ground lines for power return and decoupling.

### 9.5.5 Conclusion

The design of modern bus interfaces for any new 32-bit bus is a task for experienced professionals; it necessitates understanding all the issues of computer-aided design tools and a good control of printed board technology and component placement. Hardware description languages will be of an increasing help in the future [BAR85].

The interfacing of personal computer buses and old 8-bit buses is much simpler but requires careful work if one wants a reliable and manufacturable design. The decision to develop an original interface instead of buying it must be taken after a detailed evaluation and prediction of the work involved for designing, debugging and writing the software, and for going into production. Existing cards on the market are rarely perfect, and a similarly complete evaluation ought to be carried out before any purchasing.

| | |
|---|---|
| 10 | SERIAL LINKS |

A serial link transfers information one bit at a time, usually over much longer distances than a parallel link. It may use several lines for the control of the transfer, but in most cases a single electrical line (plus current return and optional shield) is preferred. Other transfer media like optical fibers or radiowaves are frequently used. Serial information is also stored on and read from moving magnetic or optical media.

Serial lines are used for long distance transmissions. The important propagation time over the lines does not allow the use of bidirectional lines with frequent changes of direction. Special care must also be taken due to the lower reliability of transmission. Hence, serial links rely more on software protocols than parallel links. This software aspect has been partly covered in Chapter 7; it will not be covered in this book with the same level of detail as the hardware.

## 10.1 SERIALIZATION OF INFORMATION

As shown in previous chapters, parallel links use separate groups of lines for
- data (Chapter 2)
- handshake (Chapter 3)
- address (Chapter 4)
- arbitration (Chapter 5)
- interrupt (Chapter 6)
- power, inititialization.

On a serial link, the functions performed by these lines are encoded, implemented by the protocol, or suppressed (e.g. the reset line). Information is considered as a stream of bits grouped in words or characters and forming messages in which control, address and actual data can be found.

Similarly to parallel transfers, synchronization and flow control (handshake) are related issues. Mechanisms must be provided for the synchronization of bits and characters, and flow control may be applied at different levels: bit, character and/or message.

### 10.1.1 Bit transfers and synchronization

If a word is transferred bit by bit, an adequate synchronization must be provided for each bit. Each bit can be considered as a one-bit word, and the synchronization techniques described in Chapters 2 and 3 for n-bit word transfers are applicable for this 1-bit word. The problem of transferring only one bit is however somewhat different, since there is no skew (section 3.2.1) between data bits, and since read cycles are usually not supported (section 10.1.4).

The possible schemes either combine a previously encountered synchronization technique with one data line, or are specifically designed for single bit transmission. One line is always used to carry information (this is the analog to the INFO path in parallel buses, see Chapters 2, 3, 4), and additional lines may be present for the control structure. Hence, one can consider :

- 3+1 lines n-partner 1-bit transfer (section 6.3.1)
- 2+1 lines 1-bit transfer full-handshake (section 3.3)
- 1+1 lines with handshake (sections 3.6.7 and 10.3.7)
- 1+1 lines synchronous 1-bit transfer (sections 3.6.3 and 3.6.6)
- 2 lines encoded synchronous transfer (figure 10.1).
- 1 line transfer (section 10.2)

The first four solutions are derived from parallel transfer schemes limited to 1-bit width and are not used for long transmission lines. Specific 2-line solutions exist. Figure 10.1 shows for instance a possible encoding on two lines, sometimes used on low cost magnetic tapes using a stereo head.

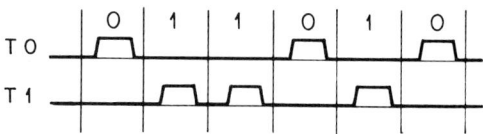

Fig. 10.1 2-line data transfer

One-line bit transfer is the one most frequently used on magnetic media. Synchronization is accomplished using special modulation of the signal or data formatting. This will be covered in section 10.2. For a one-line transfer, the clock required to synchronize the data bits may be extracted from the modulation of each data bit cell or once every several bits, taking care of the maximum phase errors between synchronization.

The trend for parallel buses is to provide better handshakink for increased performance. For a serial bus, bit handshaking is performed in the case of the 4, 3 and 2 line transfers previously mentioned; it may be done on one line using a trick, but one should realize that correct operation of any handshaking scheme implies taking care of the propagation time. For instance, at the typical speed of 20 cm/ns, a 100 m line requires 500 ns for the propagation time of the signal. If handshaking is performed for each bit, this restricts the transmitted bit frequency to 1 MHz. An example of bit handshaking (the one used on $I^2C$ bus) will be explained in section 10.3.8.

### 10.1.2 Character transfer and synchronization

Word or character transfers have been covered in Chapters 2 and 3 and may be solved for serial transfer using the same mechanisms (see section 10.3). Specific solutions exist for saving lines and taking care of the longer propagation time over the lines. An exhaustive study of all the possible solutions is not realistic and we shall limit ourselves to the major aspects.

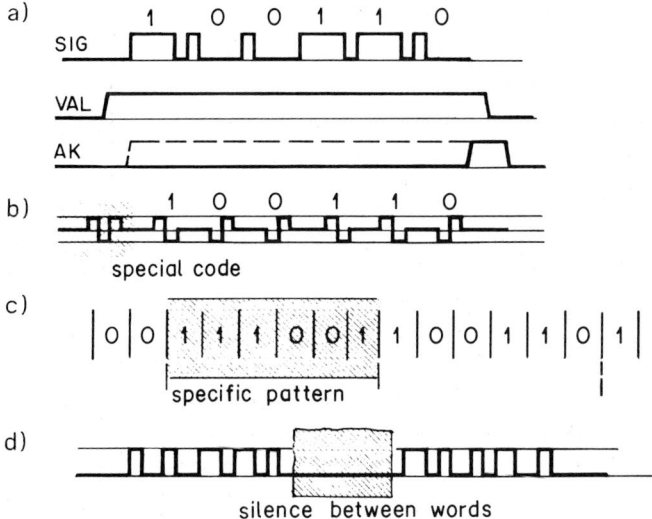

*Fig. 10.2 Character synchronization*

There are four basic schemes which can be used to synchronize characters; these schemes are illustrated in figure 10.2 and require :
- special hardware lines (e.g. figure 10.2a)
- special bit encoding (e.g. figure 10.2b)
- special bit sequencing (e.g. figure 10.2c)
- special bit duration or spacing (e.g. figure 10.2d).

The Morse code is a good example of the last case.

Character handshaking can be provided by a special hardware line (figure 10.2a) or by acknowledge information coming back on the same line. That information may be a pulse, a bit or a character. For instance, figure 10.3 shows the possible transmission of an 8-bit character at 10 MHz over 100 m with a handshake pulse. Maximum speed may reach 400 k characters per second which is an average of 3.2 Mb/s.

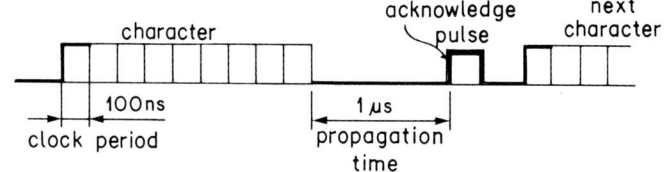

Fig. 10.3 Character handshake using a feedback pulse

Bit and word synchronization may be provided by the same mechanism. For instance, if the beginning of a transmitted character is well defined, and if the bits are transferred at a fixed known speed, the bit synchronization is implicitly provided for some time. This will be found in the well known start-stop scheme described in section 10.3.9, in which a start bit preceded by a space provides both the bit and character synchronization.

### 10.1.3 Message transfer and synchronization

At the higher level of messages, that is for complete transactions with arbitration, specific techniques are used for the serial transfer of address and data information.

Message synchronization and handshaking usually do not use hardware mechanisms, even if they could be done using the same principle as for characters. A special symbol or character or set of characters may indicate the beginning and the end of messages. Another symbol (a bit, a character or a full message) returned on the same line can acknowledge the correct reception of the message.

Addresses on a serial link are usually multiplexed on the same line as the data. Usually, an address is provided for blocks of data, as for a block transfer (section 4.3) and corresponds to the address of the station which must receive the data. Precise formating of the address, data and control is part of the protocol and may vary according to the application. Arbitration will be considered in section 10.5.

### 10.1.4 System organization

Bidirectionnal transfers are usually not supported for a serial bus in the same way as for a parallel bus, where a control line defines the direction of the transfer. The latter usually does not exist, due to the cost of the additional line. Some buses support read operations by encoding the direction of the transfer in the control field of the message. The concept of master and slaves (section 1.1.7) is replaced by a CALLER and RESPONDER concept. At a given instant of time, a TRANSMITTER sends its information to a RECEIVER, when it believes it is able to do so, and not under direct control of some direct signal issued by a commander.

Two major cases have to be considered :
- unidirectional or broadcast transfers
- bidirectional or bussed transfers.

Associated topologies have been mentioned in section 1.1.5. It is important to distinguish the logical and the physical topologies. A physical star may simulate a logical bus, e.g. if the central point handles only one transfer at a time; a physical bus may just emulate a star or a ring logic structure. Bidirectional transfers have all the problems of contention and arbitration explained in Chapter 5 and section 10.6. Token passing avoids the arbitration problems as long as the token is alive and unique.

## 10.2 MODULATIONS TECHNIQUES

Saving connections with a serial transfer can only be done at the expense of time. Few simply shaped signals, such as a byte stream from a keyboard, can be replaced by a single signal of a more complex shape. That shape can be analysed at reception to regenerate the original signal. As shown in figure 10.4, one can distinguish a digital transformation, named CODING and DECODING, and an analog transformation, named MODULATION and DEMODULATION. The transmission media is called a CHANNEL and may not be fully protected against external perturbations.

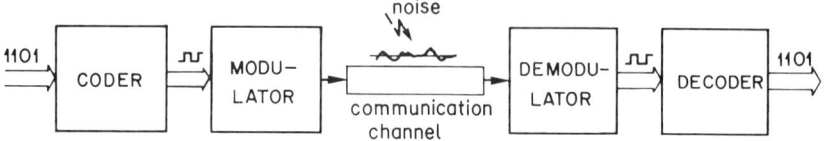

*Fig. 10.4 Digital coding and analog modulation*

Frequently, the coder and modulator on one side, and the demodulator and decoder on the other side will be considered as a single device, and the modulated signal is just a digital signal. This section applies both to data transmission over any type of lines (telephone, coax, optical fibers), and to data recorded on magnetic or optical media. People working in these two fields have introduced a terminology which has some useless differences (figure 10.40).

More on modulation techniques can be found in [SEV80], [FON83], [PIOT83], [KOB79] and [SAL77].

## 10.2.1 Principles of modulation/demodulation

A typical serially modulated transfer is depicted in figure 10.5. The input stream is a sequence of bits synchronized by a clock. The data bit cells, when the data changes, are delimited by the negative edge of the clock. Data is characterized by the bit value 0 and 1, or by the equivalent timing diagram. Logical 1 is frequently named *MARK* and logical 0 *SPACE*.

The *MODULATOR* converts the input stream into a modulated signal. The shape of the signal used in figure 10.5 is purely

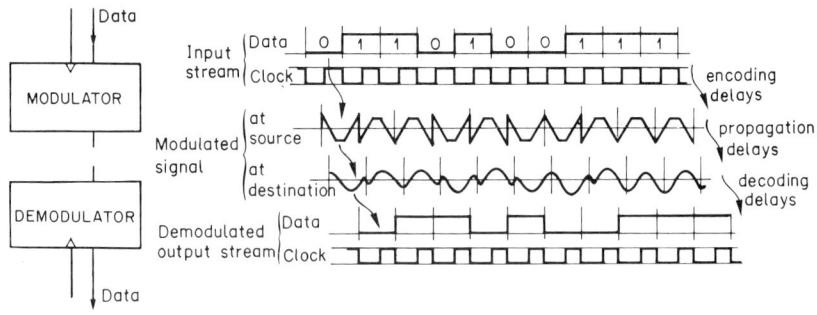

*Fig. 10.5 Modulation and demodulation mechanism*

indicative. The channel delays, attenuates and filters the signal, and adds noise. In some cases, the wave is deformed, owing to different types of distortion. The role of the DEMODULATOR is then to restore the original data bit cells and sometimes also to recover the data rate.

In some cases (e.g. for magnetic recording or multipath radio links), the data bit cell period of the demodulated signal is not necessarily regular and identical to the input period. This is of no importance as long as the data bit cells are well specified (minimum and maximum values, signal levels) and correctly synchronized by a clock.

The encoded signal may or may not have a shape which allows to the recognition of the bit boundaries. When this is the case, the signal is said to be SELF-CLOCKING; when a clock cannot be generated by the demodulator, two signals have to be considered or other special solutions, described in the next sections, have to be used.

Decoding a signal implies both analog and digital techniques. The EYE DIAGRAM (figure 10.6), which shows the superposition of the received signals correctly synchronized is a good way to estimate the quality of a signal.

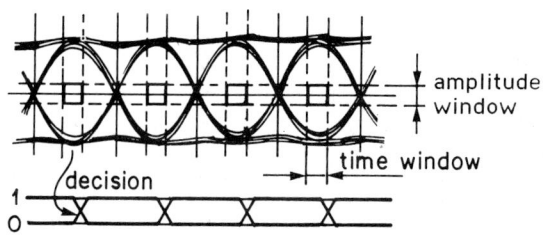

*Fig. 10.6 Eye diagram for a simply encoded signal*

Handling of analog signals will not be described in this book. In the example of figure 10.6, the analog circuitry will provide a digital signal from the decision taken in the sampling window. This signal is further decoded to recognize the information and the associated clock.

## 10.2.2 Capacity and bandwidth

The CAPACITY of a line is the rate at which bits can be transmitted over the line without errors. It is expressed in BITS/SECOND (b/s). The line has a given BANDWIDTH (W) (that is a range of correctly transmitted frequencies) which allows one to use a maximum *MODULATION SPEED (B)* or *SYMBOL RATE* expressed in *BAUDs (Bd)*. The inverse of the Baud rate is the *SYMBOL PERIOD*, each symbol representing elements of information which may correspond to many bits. Another important characteristic of a channel is its *SIGNAL TO NOISE (S/N)* ratio.

Shannon has shown [SHA49] that the capacity C of an information channel is linked to the bandwidth W and the signal to noise ratio S/N by the formula:

$$C = W \log_2 (1 + S/N)$$

To make this intuitively understandable, let us consider the example of figure 10.7 which encodes groups of two bits by different signal amplitudes. The bit rate here is twice the speed of modulation; this shows that the bit rate and Baud rate are not the same, even if the mistake is frequently made by microcomputer specialists. If the encoding can be improved thanks to a good signal to noise ratio, the bit rate can be increased. For instance, on a telephone line with a bandwidth of 3000 Hz and an rather good signal to noise ratio of 20 dB, the bit rate could theoretically reach 20 000 bits per second. Modems do exist up to 19 200 bits per second.

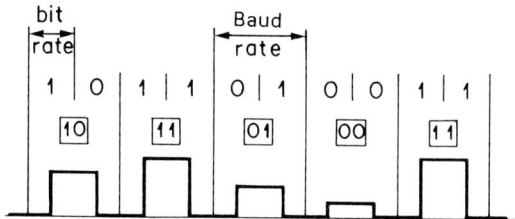

*Fig. 10.7 Difference between bit rate and Baud rate*

### 10.2.3 Encoding/decoding schemes

The sequence of bits transmitted on a serial line must be synchronized by an explicit, implicit or encoded clock. Whith an *EXPLICIT CLOCK*, an independent line is used to transfer the clock; this clock may be issued by the transmitter (figure 10.8a) or by the receiver (figure 10.8b). This corresponds to synchronous write and read operations (section 3.1.3). A third technique for an explicit clock uses two self-synchronized clocks which keep exactly the same frequency (figure 10.8c). An explicit clock is rather unusual for long distances, and will be considered again in section 10.3.

The *IMPLICIT CLOCK* scheme assumes that a clock of the same frequency is used at both ends to allow the decoding of the serial stream (figure 10.8d). This is frequently named asynchronous encoding; the resynchronization occurs at the character or frame level.

With an ENCODED CLOCK (self-clocking scheme), the clock is decoded at the receiver (figure 10.8e). Clock precision depends on encoding schemes and clock decoding techniques.

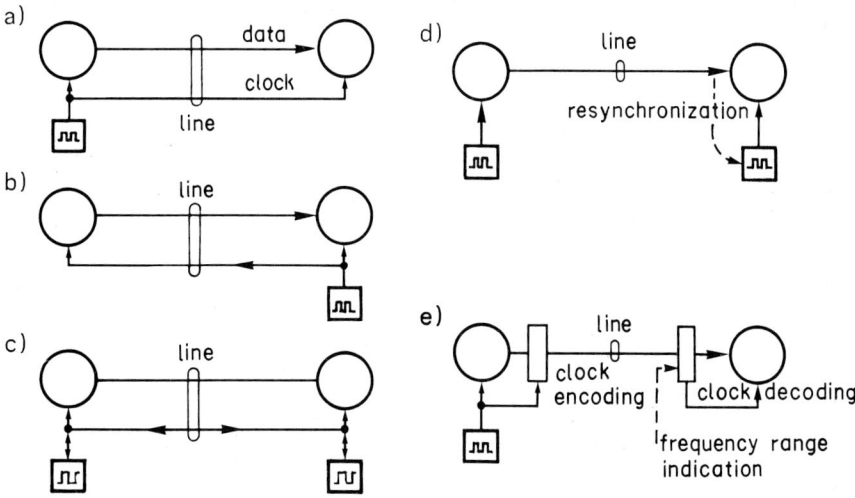

Fig. 10.8 Synchronization of serial transfers
    a) Explicit clock from transmitter (write)
    b) Explicit clock from receiver (read)
    c) Self-synchronized explicit clock
    d) Implicit clock
    e) Encoded clock (self-clocking)

## 10.2.4 Implicit clock schemes

In the implicit clock scheme, the clock generator of the receiver is synchronized from time to time by incoming symbols. Between each synchronization, the decoding of data relies on the matching (precision, stability) of transmitter and receiver clock generators. Several encoding/decoding schemes are possible; they are more or less dependant on the precision of the receiver clock in relation to the transmitter clock. Most codes are given a name of a few letters.

The NRZ-L (Non Return to Zero - Level) code is the most simple since it corresponds to the encoding of the data bit cells 0 and 1 by two adequate voltage levels. In the example of figure 10.9, the modulator is a voltage converter which assigns to bit 0 a line voltage close to +12V and to bit 1 a line voltage close to -12V. Using higher voltages usually provides a better S/N ratio. NRZ-L is used for RS-232 (section 10.4); states 0/1 are called respectively ON/OFF or MARK/SPACE.

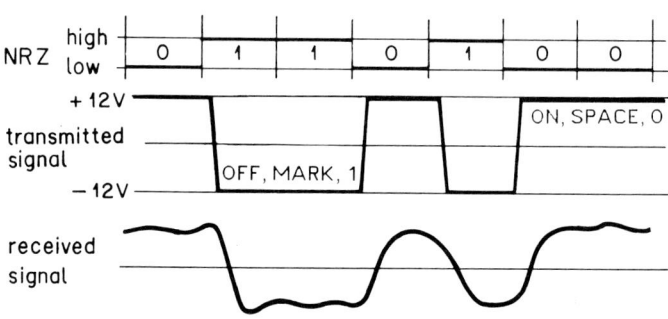

Fig. 10.9  NRZ-L signals

The RZ (Return to Zero) encoding is characterized by a return to zero between bit cells. The signal may have the two shapes, as shown in figure 10.10, depending if it is unipolar or bipolar. One can notice that bipolar RZ is self-clocking and belongs indeed to the next section.

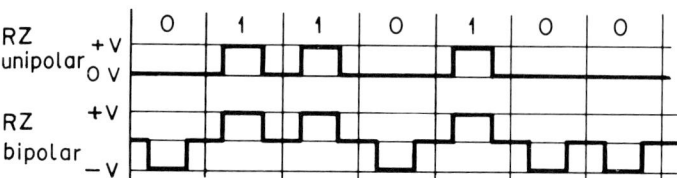

Fig. 10.10  RZ signals

Instead of directly copying the state of the data input cell, the encoder can change its output according to the input value. With NRZ-S (Non Return to Zero - Space), the output changes from one cell to the next one when the input is inactive (0 or Space). The output does not change at the midpoint of the bit period when the input is active (1 or Mark). Figure 10.11a shows this scheme, also named NRZI (Non Return to Zero Inverted).

The NRZ-M (Non Return to Zero - Mark) encoding is just the reverse; the output changes for each 1 (figure 10.11b).

# 10 Serial Links

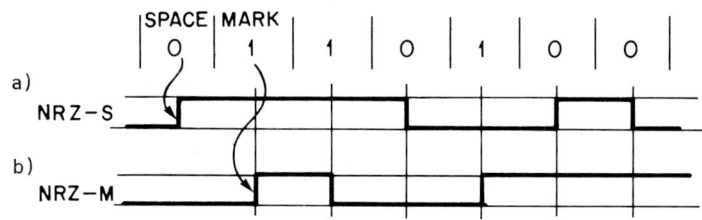

*Fig. 10.11 NRZ-S and NRZ-M code*

One can notice that if one of the two signals of figure 10.11 is transmitted on a channel which does not transmit DC current (e.g. a capacitively coupled line or a magnetic media), it is not possible to rebuild the data and its clock from long strings of zeros or ones. If both NRZ-S and NRZ-M are recorded, the clock is easy to decode, and the scheme is more efficient than the one proposed in figure 10.1.

The previous codes are biased, that is the signal average value depends on the message. The *AMI (Alternative Mark Inversion)* code provides a polarity changing signal for each 1 (figure 10.12). As a result, the mean value of the signal is null; this is for instance important in telephony, due to the long lines and isolation transformers.

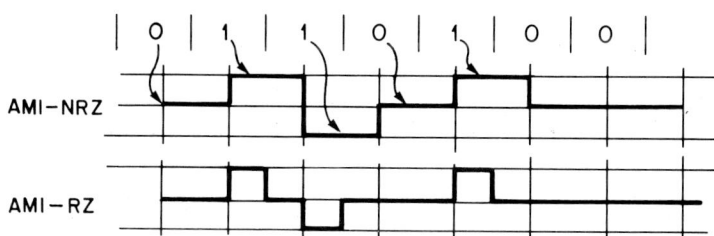

*Fig. 10.12 AMI code*

Strings of consecutive zeros cause the decoder of the previous codes to lose its synchronization. The *HDB3 (High Density Bipolar with max 3 consecutive zeros)* code modifies the code of any fourth zero in a string. This zero is coded as a one, but with a violation of the AMI "alternation" rule, which makes it possible to recognize it. In addition, if two strings of four zeros are separated by an even number of ones, the first zero of the second string gets an inverted pulse, in order to maintain a zero mean value of the signal (figure 10.13). Again, this self-clocking code really belongs to the next section, but is left here due to its association with the AMI code.

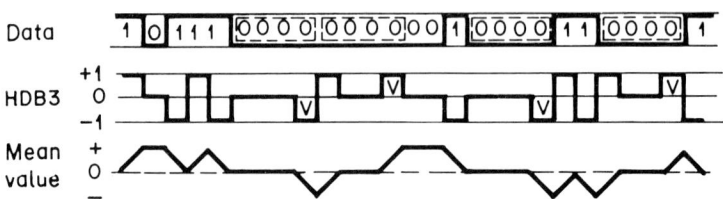

Fig. 10.13 HDB3 code

## 10.2.5 Self-clocking schemes

A simple self-clocked modulation scheme, used on single density floppy disks and for low speed modems, is the FM (Frequency Modulation) or FSK (Frequency Shift Keying) scheme. A signal of different frequency is sent depending if the data cell is zero or one. Maximum speed for a fixed bandwidth is reached when the period of the signals associated with the 0 and 1 is respectively equal to, and double of the data cell period (figure 10.14a). A greater reliability is obtained if higher frequency signals are transmitted (figure 10.14b).

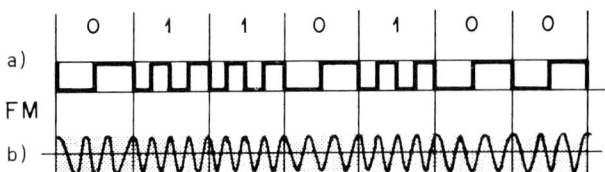

Fig. 10.14 FM encoding
 a) As used on single density floppy disks
 b) As used on low speed modems

New encoding possibilities occur when the encoder can create a mid-cell positive or negative transition depending on one or two consecutive data input cells. The MANCHESTER code or Biφ-L (Biphase-Level) creates a LOW to HIGH transition in response to a 0, and a HIGH to LOW transition in response to a 1 (figure 10.15a). A similar code with different level encodings providing a zero mean value is the TOP HAT code (figure 10.15b).

One can see that the Manchester code is self-clocked. However, the same stream of Manchester bits can be interpreted in different ways, as shown in figure 10.16a and 10.16b, if the frequency or the bit cell limits are not known in advance. Hence some synchronization must precede a data transfer. This is typically performed by sending 8 zeros followed by a 3-bit cell command synchronization pulse which violates the code and fixes the bit cell size, as in figure 10.16c.

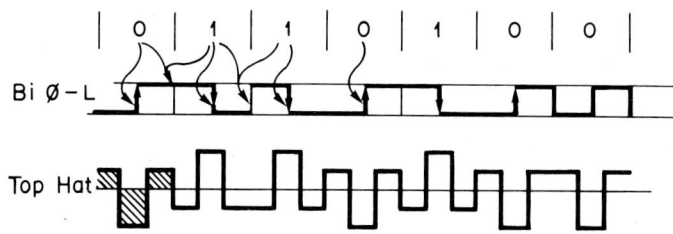

Fig. 10.15 Manchester or Biφ-L code and Top Hat code

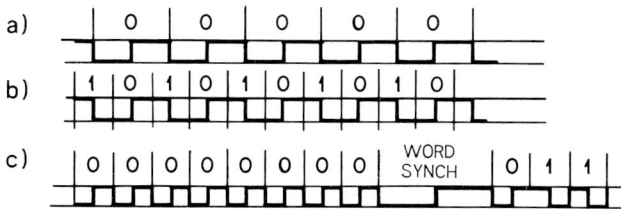

Fig. 10.16 Synchronization of Manchester sequences
 a) Decoded as a string of zeros
 b) Decoded as a string of alternating zeros and ones
 c) Code violation as a synchronization mark

Similar in performance to the Manchester codes, the Biφ-S (Biphase-Space) and the Biφ-M (Biphase-Mark) codes are self-clocked and highly suitable for data transmission and recording (figure 10.17. They are slightly more difficult to encode and decode, since the signal shape takes account of two consecutive bits.

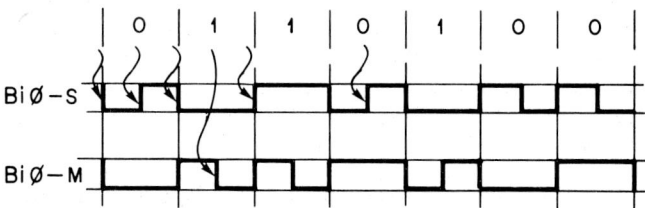

Fig. 10.17 Biphase encoding

An efficient modulation scheme must use little bandwidth. Biphase codes are better than FM with this respect. *MILLER* or *DM-NRZ-M* (*Delay Modulation - Non Return to Zero - Mark*), also named MFM (*Modified Frequency Modulation*) codes, are as efficient as NRZ codes, with the additional advantage of self-clocking.

The principle of the Miller code (-Mark) is to change the output at the middle of a bit period for each "one", and at the end of the bit period for each "zero". But when a "one" bit cell follows a "zero" bit cell, there is no transition at the end of the "zero" cell, in order to avoid a half period pulse (figure 10.18a). *DM-NRZ-S* (*Delay Modulation - Non Return to Zero - Space*) inverts the role of Mark and Space. Notice that Miller codes are easily derived from Biφ codes using a simple divide by two flip-flop.

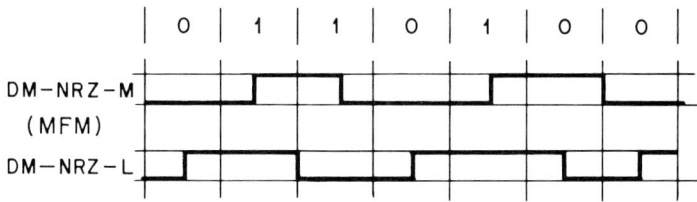

*Fig. 10.18 Miller codes*

The $M^2FM$ (*Modified twice Frequency Modulation*) or $M^2$ (*Modified Miller*) code, as shown in figure 10.19, saves a few transitions but requires the same bandwidth as simpler Miller codes. A transition is produced in the middle of a data bit cell for each "one"; an isolated "zero" produces no transition, subsequent "zeros" produce a transition at the beginning of the data cell.

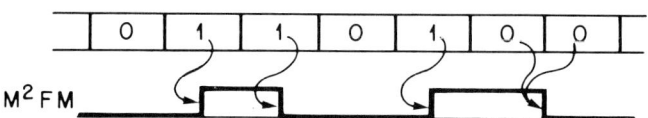

*Fig. 10.19 $M^2FM$ code*

## 10.2.6 Special encodings

GCR (*Group Code Recording*) is used for magnetic and optical disks to decrease the number of transitions by replacing certain successions of bits by others. The result is, for instance, that 5 data bits are encoded into 7-bit cells with an increased time between transitions.

# 10 Serial Links

Used on low cost magnetic media, PULSE RATIO codes are self-clocked. They encode bits by a short pulse (1/3 of the period for a zero) or a long pulse (2/3 for a one), as shown in figure 10.20. The decoding can be easily done with an up/down counter which is sampled by positive edges and then reset. The counter counts up when the input signal is active and down when inactive. Positive or negative values, when the next bit starts, decode the bit.

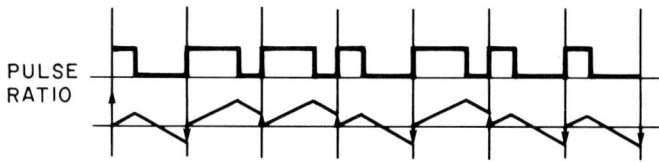

*Fig. 10.20 Pulse ratio code*

As a last example, let us consider the encoding used in the HP-IL (Hewlett Packard Interface Loop), which is a ring for connecting small calculators and personal computers with their peripherals [LAND83]. Each point-to-point connection uses a shielded twisted pair. Synchronization bit cells have been defined in addition to the "zeros" and the "ones", as shown in figure 10.21a. Each frame consists of one synchronization bit followed by ten bits (2 control, 8 data).

The actual scheme of an HP-IL interface is shown in figure 10.21b. One can see that even in a case which has to be

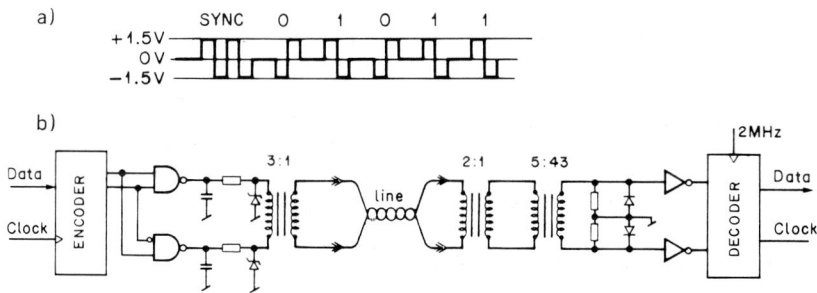

*Fig. 10.21 HP-IL code and detailed modulator/demodulator logic*

small and low cost, the correct implementation taking care of electrostatic and electromagnetic interferences is not so simple. Transformers are used for galvanic insulation, and various devices (resistors, capacitors, zener diodes), are required to protect the equipment and reduce noise.

### 10.2.7 Comparison

The usefulness of a code depends on its efficiency and its ability to be transmitted over long distances and then reliably decoded. The POWER SPECTRUM of randomly transmitted bits is a good measure of the code efficiency for what concerns the bandwidth usage. Figure 10.22 gives the power spectrum for several interesting codes [PIOT83].

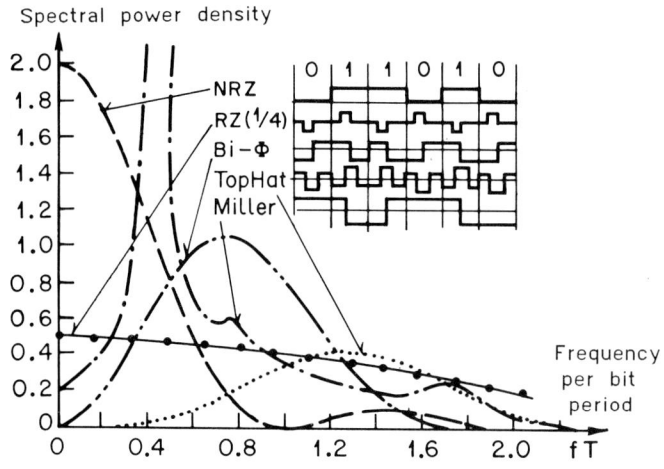

Fig. 10.22 Power spectrum of several codes

A good encoding scheme must have a spectrum with no steady current component and have a narrow frequency spectrum. The Miller code may look good, but small high and low frequency components degrade long distance transmission, as it can be seen in figure 10.23.

Signals transmitted over long distances are deformed by the difference in propagation speed with respect to the frequency (section 8.4.3), which introduces a phase distortion. An amplitude distortion is added to this, low frequencies being less attenuated than high frequencies. The eye diagram is a good way to visualize the

# 10 Serial Links 317

effect of transmission lines. Figure 10.23 shows the same signal after propagation over 1 km and 4 km of twisted-pair line without repeaters.

In the case of a magnetic media, the deformation of the waves is due to different problems (dipole repulsion, brownian movement). The major change is due to the speed variation between the recording time and the playback time.

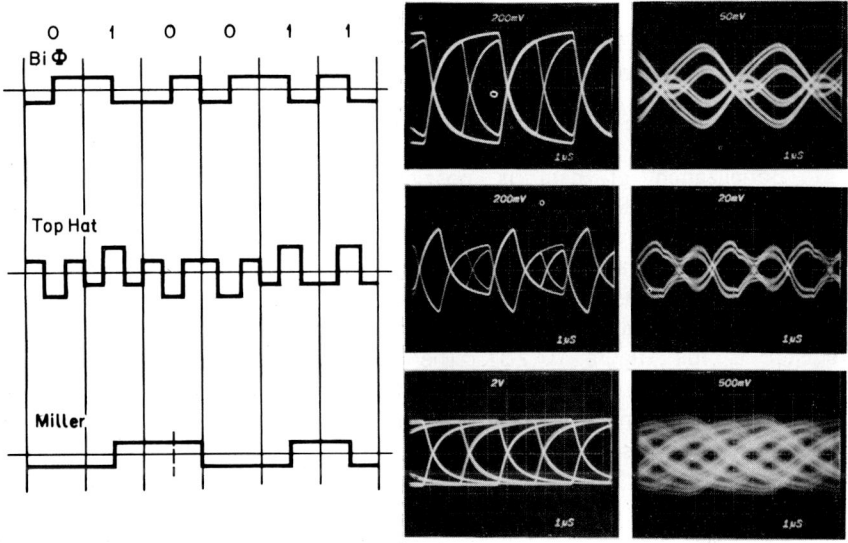

*Fig. 10.23 Eye diagram for three codes*

## 10.3 IMPLEMENTATION OF SERIAL SCHEMES

The many possibilities for serial transfers have been reviewed in section 10.1 from a general point of view. A more practical aspect similar to the scope of Chapter 9 is taken here.

### 10.3.1 Transfer of parallel data

For the purpose of comparizon, the most general scheme using 2-lines with full handshake (section 3.6.1) is repeated in figure 10.24. Functional signals (section 1.2.7) are used in the following schematic and timing diagram.

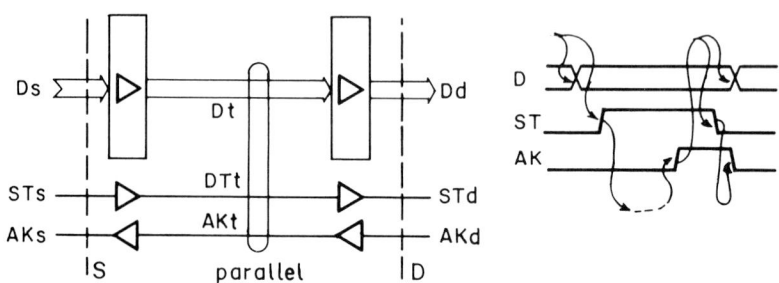

Fig. 10.24 Parallel transfer with full handshake

## 10.3.2 Source controlled full serial transfer

Serialization of data is possible using a Parallel-In-Serial-Out (PISO) shift register (section 2.1.8). The $ST_s$ (source strobe) edge loads the register with the data and triggers a clock pulse train which shifts both the transmitter and the receiver register. The transmitted strobe $ST_t$ is delayed until the end of the shift, so that the destination gets it when the receiver Serial-In-Parallel-Out (SIPO) register is full (figure 10.25). The acknowledge signal AK is direct, but of course one could imagine more sophisticated logic that would, when possible, anticipate the AK as soon as the first register is loaded (if the transfer of the previous word is finished).

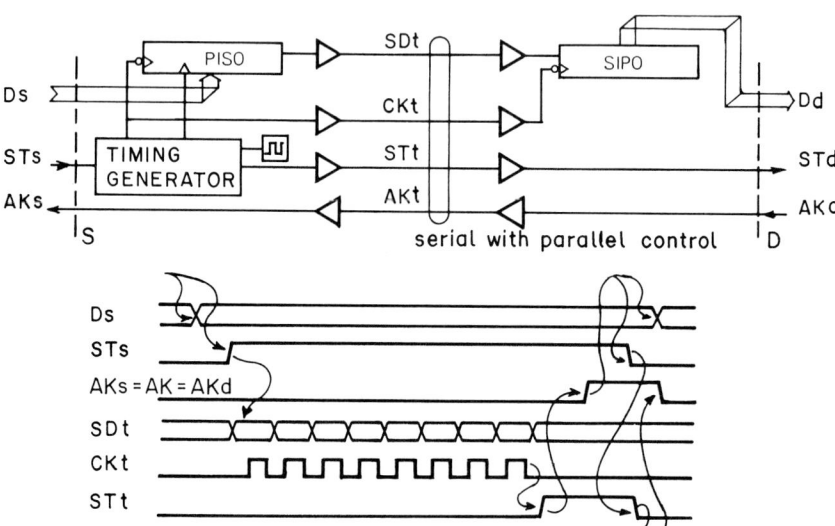

Fig. 10.25 Serial transfer controlled by the source

The phase difference between data and clock is important in relation to the clock and data relative skew due to propagation time. A deskew delay must be inserted on the data line, as shown in figure 10.26a. Maximum shift frequency depends on the set-up and hold time of the flip-flop, on the skew value and on the deskew delay. A half period deskew delay is frequently convenient, even if it lowers considerably the maximum frequency. It can be achieved by inverting the clock at the receiver, as shown in figure 10.26b.

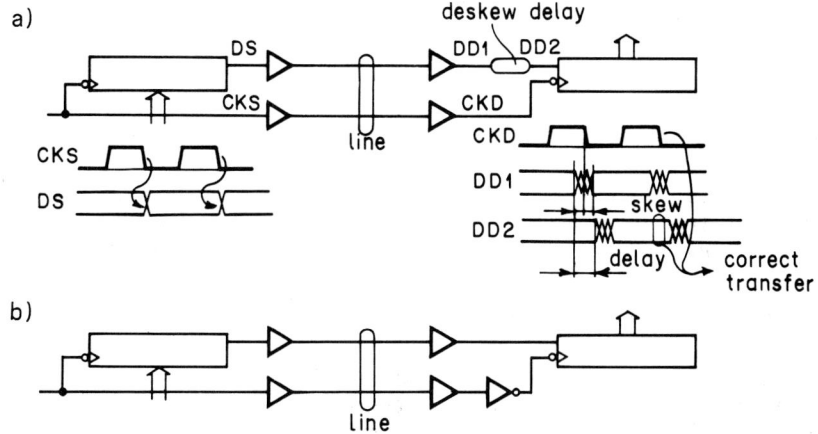

*Fig. 10.26 Deskew of serial transfer*

## 10.3.3 Destination controlled full serial transfer

A scheme very similar to the previous one consists in putting the clock generator and counter in the receiver rather than in the transmitter. The skew problem is avoided, but the maximum transfer speed is reduced, due to the clock "handshake" with data bits. In figure 10.26, the speed is limited by the skew, while in figure 10.27, it is limited by the propagation time.

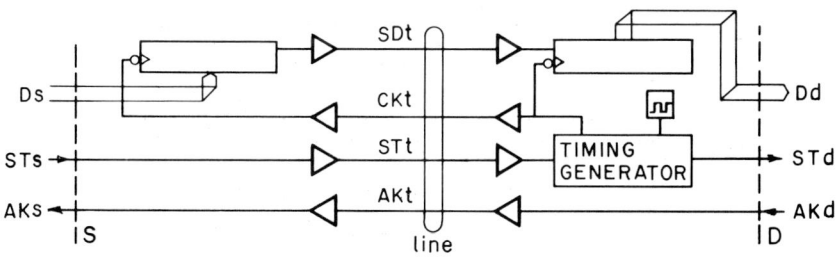

*Fig. 10.27 Serial transfer controlled by the destination*

## 10.3.4 Distributed clock

The clock required at both ends of the line may be duplicated and connected together, as shown previously in figure 10.8c. A possible clock schematic is given in figure 10.28, which allows one to have as many synchronized clocks as required. This scheme implies an open-collector line and the maximum frequency (1 or 2 MHz) decreases as the number of oscillators increases. This scheme allows the handshaking of the transmission on a bit per bit basis, since the clock can be stopped by both units.

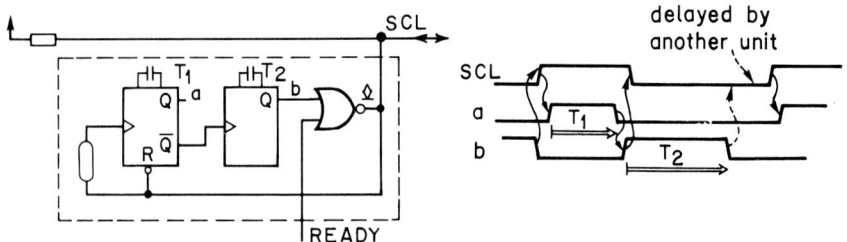

Fig. 10.28 Scheme for a distributed clock

## 10.3.5 Bidirectional transfers

Several solutions are possible for bidirectional transfers. We consider here the use of a "read/write" line, which implies a master/slave relationship and is never employed for buses longer than a few decimeters. Two registers may be used with a common or a separate clock. A single register and a single data line allow only half

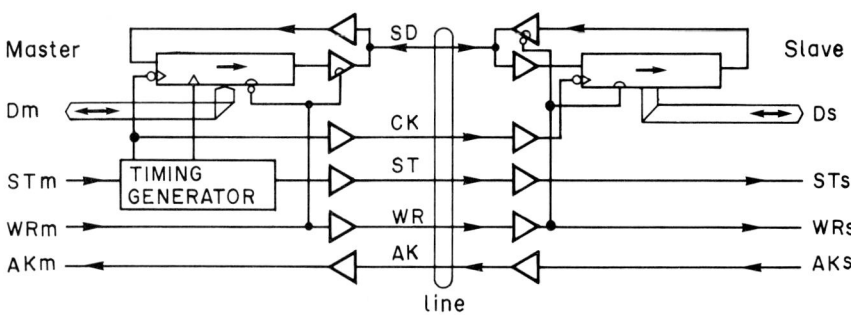

Fig. 10.29 Bidirectional serial transfer

duplex transfers, which correspond to the way parallel transfers are usually performed. A possible block diagram is given in figure 10.29. The implementation may have many solutions, according to the components used; a serial-in, serial-out, and parallel register (e.g. 74LS299) solves elegantly the problem.

### 10.3.6 Example : NOVRAM circuit control

Many integrated circuits use serial schemes at the board level, for saving lines and pins when the speed is not critical. For instance the non-volatile memories NOVRAM may include a memory of any size using only four communication pins (minimum is two) and two power pins.

The block diagram of the NOVRAM is given in figure 10.30. Separate shift registers receive the address, control, data in and data out information. A transfer sequence starts with an address and a control part transferred toward the NOVRAM, and is followed by the transfer of the data in one direction or the other.

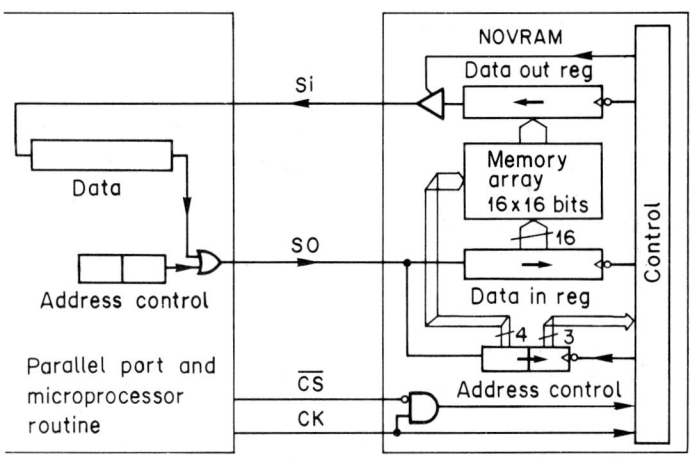

*Fig. 10.30 NOVRAM circuit and interface*

The interface for a NOVRAM circuit consists functionally of two shift registers and a clock pulse generator. The parallel port of a programmable interface is used for the four signal lines and a simple program using standard instructions like MOVE, SHIFT, SETBIT, etc., generates the clock and the data signals.

## 10.3.7 Two-line transfers

A straightforward two-line serial scheme uses NRZ encoding, as provided by the output of a shift register, and the associated clock. The clock provides the bit synchronization, and special solutions have to be found for byte synchronization and block synchronization.

A first solution is to send bursts of information and recognize the steady states between bursts as byte or block separators (figure 10.31a). Retriggerable delays are used for this purpose. Signal M1 with a short delay recognizes the bytes, and M2 with a longer delay, the data blocks.

Another solution is to have a special synchronization character at the beginning of each transmission. The synchronization character may be followed by the block size indication, by the data and by some error checking information (figure 10.31b). If the next character is not

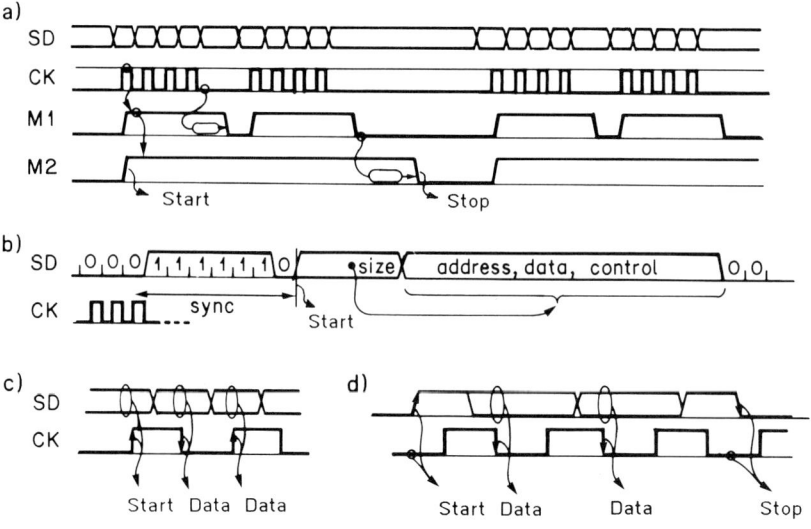

Fig. 10.31 Two-line transfer and word/block synchronization
a) Delays for character and block separation
b) Synchronization character
c) All clock edges active
d) Data and clock edges active

available for transmission, it is necessary to send a neutral synchronization character, otherwise the bit or byte synchronization could be lost. This is not required when the modulation technique is self-clocking or differenciates "zeros", "ones" and no information, as for instance the HP-IL (section 10.2.6).

A different approach consists of using both edges of the clock for sampling data and control information as in figure 10.31c. It is also possible to use the clock and data edge relationship (figure 10.31d); this has been proposed by Philips/Valvo [PHIL83] for the $I^2C$ (Inter Integrated Circuits) network (see section 10.6.10).

## 10.3.8 One-line transfers

A single line transfer (figure 10.32) implies the encoding of the clock, according to one of the several self-clocking schemes seen in section 10.2.

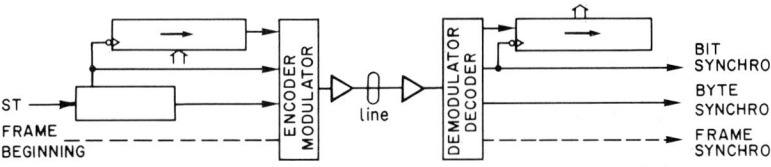

*Fig. 10.32 Serial transfer over a single line*

Once bit synchronization is solved, word and block synchronization may use the same techniques as for two-line transfers (figure 10.28). The self-clocking code used may provide additional facilities for word synchronization; for instance phase violation (section 10.2.5) or special synchronization symbols (section 10.2.6).

## 10.3.9 Asynchronous transfers

The widely used *ASYNCHRONOUS* scheme is based on the NRZ code. It uses a combination of the delays and the synchronization techniques shown in figure 10.28. As depicted in figure 10.33, a *START BIT* is followed by a known number of data and parity bits. At least one *STOP BIT* of opposite polarity of the start bits is put at the end of each character to guarantee a transition for clock resynchronization. The decoding at reception is simple since the start bit triggers a sequential system which samples the data bits at about the middle of the data bit slots. The error between the time reference

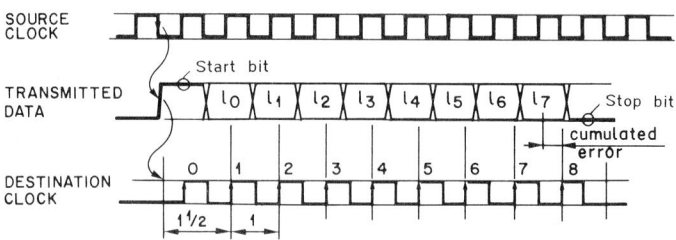

*Fig. 10.33 Asynchronous transfers*

at source and at destination depends on word length. For usual 8-bit characters, it may be of a few percent without any problem (figure 10.34).

A typical scheme for decoding an asynchronous data stream is given in figure 10.34. A clock frequency multiple of the expected bit rate (typically 16 times higher) is used to synchronize the decoding logic. The start bit sets the flip-flop ENR which enables the divide by 16 counter. The output of this counter is hence in phase with the incoming data stream. An increasing skew will result from the lack of precision of the clock frequency. The divide by 9 counter counts the bits and generates an ENDCNT pulse at the beginning of the stop bit. The parallel transfer of the register to another register must occur before the next start bit. This schematic could be improved to check the validity of the stop bit and to signal parity errors.

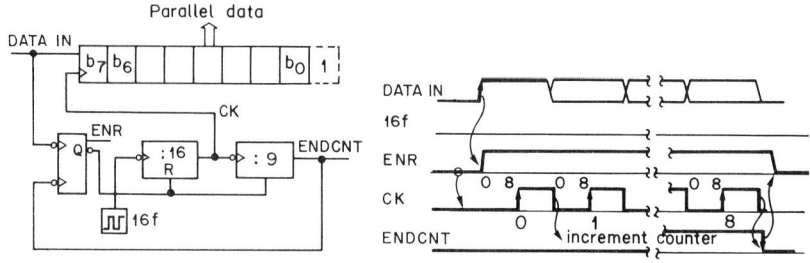

*Fig. 10.34 Logic and timing diagram for an asynchronous input interface*

Asynchronous transfers are abundantly used; their applications will be described in section 10.4.

## 10.3.10 Example : SIMSER transfers

For communication over short distances (<50 m) between computers and peripherals, *SIMSER (Simple Serial)* has proven to be a very convenient and efficient scheme [NIC76]. Compared to the RS-232-like schemes which will be described in section 10.4, SIMSER has the advantage of full handshaking, and does not require a precise clock at both ends of the link. It is adapted to the low cost serial circuits developed for RS-232 applications and is easy to implement.

The basic idea of SIMSER has been partly shown in figure 10.27. Figure 10.35 shows that the clock is provided by the destination. This costs a line to transmit the clock back, but no ST/AK line is required for full handshaking, as was the case in figure 10.27. The destination unit just stops the clock when not ready to receive. Hence no data will be lost as is frequently the case with RS-232 when the receiver is too slow or has a too small FIFO. In addition, clock does not need to be precise, since it is the same for both the transmitter and the receiver. As long as the connection is not established, there is no clock, and data waits.

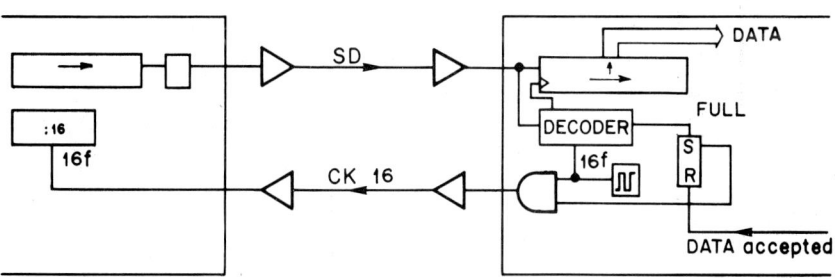

*Fig. 10.35 SIMSER link*

## 10.3.11 Character oriented protocols

Serial transmissions are sometimes not very reliable and some procedures must be defined in order to guarantee the correct transfer of blocks of information. Each block consists of several frames having an adequate structure. Error detection is performed at the frame level in order to allow the repetition of bad frames of data.

BYTE PROTOCOLS or COPs (Character Oriented Protocols) suppose that the transfer of characters is reliable, and reserve a few control characters for specifying the nature of the frames. The BSC (Byte Synchronous Communication) procedure, the DDCMP (Digital Data Communication Message Protocol) [MCNA77] and similar procedures defined by ANSI and ISO, have frames bracketed with special communication control characters.

Characters transferred follow the ASCII code, also named by European telecommunication people the IA5 (International Alphabet no 5)[ISO77]. For instance, ten communication characters are reserved for the BSC protocol [FOLT82]:

SOH = H'01  Start of Heading (address and control characters)

STX = H'02  Start of Text (and terminate heading)

ETX = H'03  End of Text

EOT = H'04  End of transmission (abort normal transmission)

ETB = H'17  End of transmission block

ENQ = H'05  Enquiry (request for a response)

ACK = H'06  Acknowledge (affirmative reply, ready to receive)

NAK = H'15  Negative acknowledge (negative response)

SYN = H'16  Synchronous idle (used in the absence of valid characters for maintaining the synchronization)

DLE = H'10  Data Link Escape prefix to more ASCII characters in order to extend the control code.

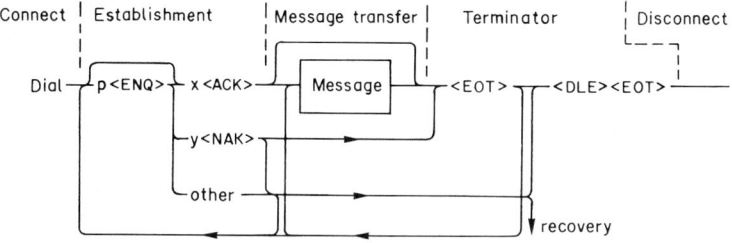

Fig. 10.36 Example of a simple BSC procedure

A typical protocol sequence, as documented in ANSI X2.28 [FOLT82] is given in figure 10.36. It shows the establishment of a communication. To ensure a proper circuit connection, the station goes through an identification procedure. Messages are transferred until the master station sends a disconnect sequence and then initiates termination of the circuit connection.

### 10.3.12 Bit oriented protocols

The principle of a *BIT PROTOCOL* or *BOP (Bit Oriented Protocol)* has already been shown in figure 10.31b. Each frame consists of a synchronization character followed by any number of bits, specified as an advance information. The three most frequently used protocols are ADCCP *(Advanced Data Communication Control Procedure)* (ANSI-X3.66 and ISO equivalents), HDLC *(High-level Data Link Control)* (CCITT-X25, ANSI-X3.66 and ISO equivalents) [FOLT82] and SDLC *(Synchronous Data Link Control)* used by IBM [DOLL78].

These procedures are very similar. Data is viewed as a continuous stream of bits. Each time five consecutive "ones" appear at the encoder input, a "zero" is automatically inserted. It will be removed by the decoder and guarantees a good synchronization if a code like AMI-S or NRZ-S is used. This is called *BIT STUFFING* or *ZERO INSERTION*.

This also allows one to force the transmission of six consecutive "ones" for synchronizing the messages. This *FLAG* correspond to the binary word 01111110. It is inserted at the beginning and the end of each frame (figure 10.37), and is easily decoded at reception as a code violation.

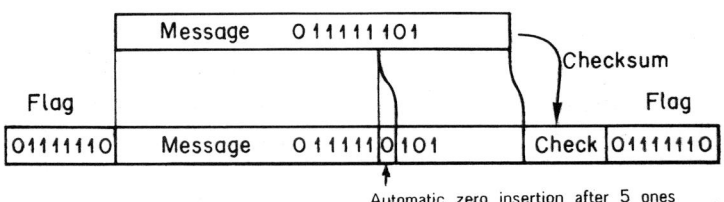

*Fig. 10.37 Example of HDLC frame*

The details of the formats of the frames, which belong to the ISO/OSI layer 2, do not fit within the scope of this chapter.

## 10.3.13 Protocol conversion

The multiplicity of communication protocols implies protocol conversion done by controllers named *PAD* *(Packet Assembly Disassembly)*. These PADs have enough processor and buffering power to control several lines at a time. Since BSC, HDLC, and similar protocols include a source and destination address, PADs may multiplex the information received from several simple ports on a single high speed port.

## 10.4 RS-232-LIKE LINKS

Within the microcomputer industry, EIA-RS-232 or its equivalent CCITT-V24/V28 pair is considered as the universal standard which can solve most of the data transfer problems. Unhappily, the complete specifications of RS-232 standard are not followed by most designers, and not understood by most users. The reason is that RS-232, designed for modem interface, is not suited for microcomputer to peripheral transfers. Simplifications hence occur, causing incompatibilities and making the interconnection of RS-232-"guaranteed" and RS-232-"like" equipment difficult [WIT83].

Due to the importance of solving this problem, this chapter explains RS-232 and similar standards in the realm of microcomputer users and not telecommunication specialists. RS-232 is an old standard which has to be correctly used until it dies. New standards have to be encouraged, but their number must be kept under control. The slowness of standardization organizations does not help in this respect.

For microcomputer people, RS-232 means asynchronous communication (but this is not specified by the standard), a 25-pin connector (but the subminiature D25 connector is not specified), and electrical specs with good noise margin (which are not followed by the widely-used RS-232 circuits like the 1489). Connector polarity is well defined, but seldom respected on peripherals. In such a difficult situation, one should keep a strict compatibility with the RS-232 only when there are good reasons to still use it (with old modems), and replace it with something more appropriate for the microcomputer world (see section 10.5).

### 10.4.1 DTE and DCE

For people concerned with communications, the telephone line or its replacement is the centre of the world. A communication equipment is attached to it, and the user is at the end of the equipment chain (figure 10.38).

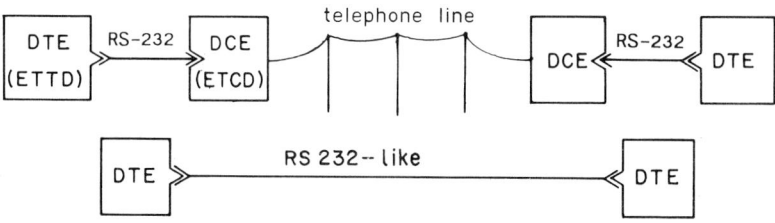

*Fig. 10.38 Communication over telephone lines*

The terminal, peripheral or computer, in front of the user is named a *DTE (Data Terminal Equipment)*. At each end of the communication line, a *DCE (Data Communication Equipment)* is required. "Official RS-232" and other derived standards provide a solution for the DTE-DCE Communication, taking care of the problem of controlling a DCE (usually a modem). Formerly, the DTE at one end was a computer and the other DTE was a terminal or some peripheral. Hence RS-232 has been kept for direct computer-peripheral connections; in this case modem control signals are not required, and they were partially removed for simplicity. These "RS-232-like" standards propose simplified solutions for direct DTE to DTE connection, solving partly the problems of computer to peripheral control. These solutions are always improperly named "RS-232".

### 10.4.2 Modem control

On a telephone line, three transmission modes are possible, as shown in figure 10.39. A *SIMPLEX* line transmits information in one direction only. A *FULL DUPLEX* line uses two SIMPLEX lines, one in each direction. A *DUPLEX* line provides on the same line simultaneous two-way independant transmission in both direction, using the proprieties of electrical waves, which may overlap (figure 8.8). *HALF DUPLEX* alternates the direction of transmission in order to provide all the bandwidth of the line in the selected direction.

Between the DCE and DTE, the distance is of only a few metres and there is no real need for limiting the number of wires. Therefore, full duplex mode is always used and many control lines are added between the DTE and DCE.

Hardware handshake on a bit per bit basis, or on a byte per byte basis, is not possible over telephone lines. Echo after each character is possible, but is terribly slow. The dataflow control is performed either on a frame basis, or on a buffer size basis.

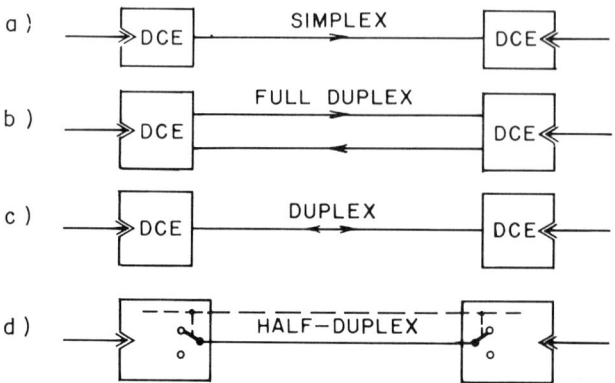

*Fig. 10.39 Transmission modes*

When the data is not structured, there is a risk of overflow of the input buffer. The receiver sends an XOFF character to tell the transmitter to stop the data stream. An XON character restarts the sender. The reaction cannot be instantaneous and communication buffers must be large enough to accommodate the worst case, which can easily reach 20 characters with well known systems.

Higher level protocols as mentioned for BSC, HDLC, etc., guarantee the integrity of the data transfer even in the case of data errors. RS-232-like transfers are not concerned about this level, and even the XON/XOFF protocol is not documented in the RS-232 standard [DOLL78][NGH79].

### 10.4.3 RS-232 connectors and conventions

RS-232 uses a "subminiature" 25 pin connector, male on the DTE and female on the DCE. The RS-232-like interface generally uses the same connector, but in most cases with the wrong polarity and an incorrect pinout, as explained later. RS-232 lines can be classified in 5 groups :

- Signal return and shield (2 lines)
- Data transfer (2 lines)
- Simple modem control (6 lines)
- Additional modem control
- Spare.

We will consider only the first three groups and explain them in the following sections. In order to understand the RS-232 philosophy, only data transfers will be considered as a first step.

|     | 0 | 1 |
|-----|---|---|
| V1  | SPACE<br>START<br>Travail<br>Tone-off<br>High frequency<br>Opposite phase<br>No phase inversion<br>No perforation | MARK<br>STOP<br>Repos<br>Tone-on<br>Low frequency<br>Reference phase<br>Phase inversion<br>Perforation |
| V28 | ON<br>>+3 V | OFF<br><-3 V |
| V31 | OFF<br>Open contact<br>(>250kΩ) | ON<br>Closed contact<br>(<10 Ω) |

*Fig. 10.40 Equivalent names for the two states of a line*

The RS-232 and similar standard terminology is very rich and sometimes confusing. Data bits 0 and 1 are used in their correct sense, but the active / not-active meaning may refer to the function or to the state of the line. New terms which correspond to historical names or are related to the modulation technique are sometimes used, as shown in figure 10.40.

### 10.4.4 RS-232-like data transfers

RS-232-like data transfers are usually asynchronous (section 10.3.9) with a start bit (SPACE) and one or two stop bits (MARK). Microprocessor controllers called UART (*Universal Asynchronous Receiver-Transmitter*) serialize the information. They work between 0 and +5V; interface circuits which invert the electrical levels create the RS-232 +12V and -12V voltages (figure 10.41).

The two data transfer lines are called *TxD* (*Transmit Data*) and *RxD* (*Receive Data*). There is an inconsistency associated with the mnemonic names of these two lines; since the data bit values on the lines are inverted (logical 0 is +12V), these mnemonices should be inverted and an inverting circle shown on the side of the line. Due to the fact that the stop bit is a "one" level, and the start bit is a low state, the line looks like an active high line with a steady state at "zero".

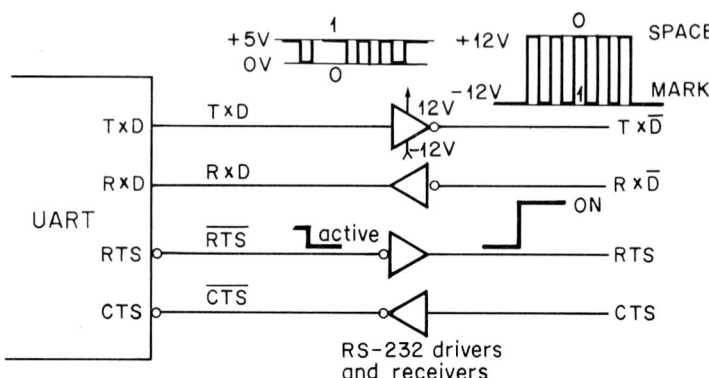

*Fig. 10.41 Typical interface between a UART and the RS-232 line*

The start bit is usually considered as an active signal and nothing in the notation shows that the data bits are inverted on the line. We will be more precise in our own documentation and write $\overline{TxD}$, $\overline{RxD}$ to show that the data signals on the line are considered as non-inverted signals, but transfer inverted data information. On the serial interface chip, the data is called, as all manufacturer's do, TxD and RxD. The control signals RTS and CTS (see section 10.4.6) generally use correct naming conventions; they are inverted on the UART pins (active low), and usually shown as such.

The bit rate is the same for the start, the data and each stop bit. Frequently improperly named Baud rate (see section 10.2.2), the bit rate has one of many standard values : (50), 75, (110), (200), 300, (600), 1200, 2400, 4800, 9600 or 19200 bits per second. Values between brackets should not be considered for new designs.

The number of transmitted bits may vary between 5 and 8, and an odd or even parity bit may be added. Programmable serial interface circuits (UARTs) provide for a lot of modes, but the RS-232 associated standards (CCITT-X4, ISO-1177) recommendations are rather clear : seven data bits (ASCII code) are followed by an even parity bit (the sum of the 8 bits is even). It should be stated that RS-232 does not specify start-stop asynchronous transfers, as always understood in the microcomputer industry. For synchronous transmissions, the ISO-1177 recommends use of an odd parity bit. All the encountered solutions for ASCII code transfers are depicted in figure 10.42.

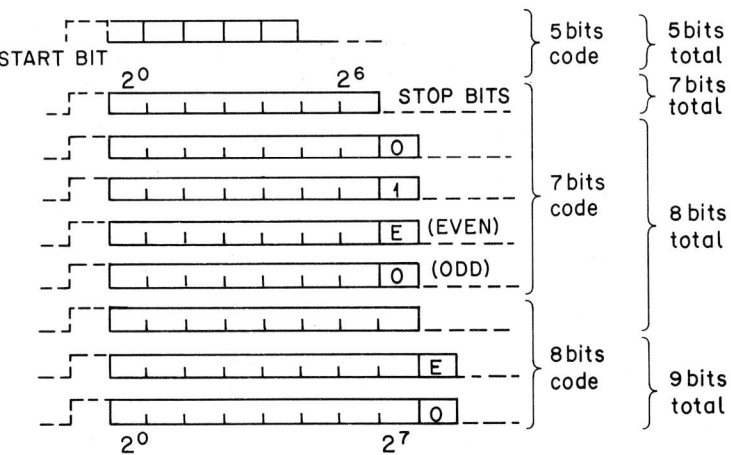

*Fig. 10.42 RS-232 words*

The mode of the receiver must match the mode of the transmitter. A "no parity" mode which just ignores the parity bit is the most tolerant. One stop bit is recommended above 200 bits/sec. If a SPACE state occurs when STOP bits are expected, serial interface circuits signal a FRAMING ERROR. A line maintained at the SPACE level for more than about 20 periods is considered as a BREAK SIGNAL. In most systems it aborts the transmission task. A BREAK KEY is sometimes provided to a user to generate this special signal.

## 10.4.5 DTE to DTE direct transfers

DTEs are not supposed to be directly connected. RS-232 supports only DTE to DCE connections, which are made with a direct extension cable (pin n to pin n). Figure 10.43a shows the simplified wiring with the two data transfer lines only. The polarity of the connector and pin number on the 25-pin connector are clearly depicted. As a mnemonic trick, pin 2 has a shape specifying the direction of the information transmitted by that pin (on a DTE, connector is male and data is outputted on pin 2).

If a direct connection must be performed between two DTEs, the only correct solution is to insert a NULL-MODEM which simulates the missing transmission line and its associated modems (figure 10.43b). A less expensive (but confusing) solution consists of hiding the null-modem inside one of the plugs of the extension cable (figure 10.43c).

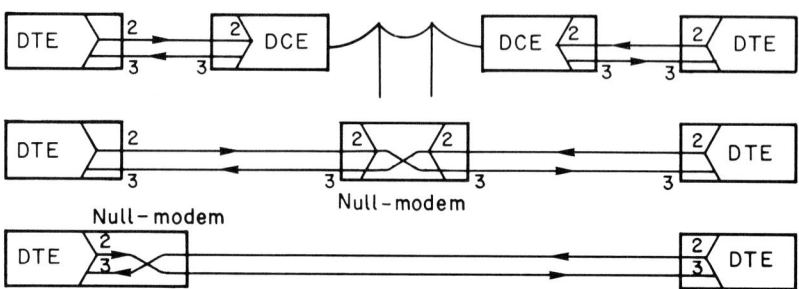

Fig. 10.43 DTE to DTE connections
a) Link through two modems
b) Link with a null-modem
c) Link with a special null-modem cable

Unfortunately, what occurs in many sets of equipment is that the null modem is hidden inside the equipment and the same DB25 connector is provided. This sometimes lowers the cost of connecting cables between the equipment of a given manufacturer; the usage of flat cables unhappily encourages this trend.

A first, incorrect solution exchanges pin 2 and pin 3 (figure 10.44a) of one of the DTE, and allows one to use a simpler cable (if the permutation has not been done on both DTEs). A second solution uses a female connector, and considers that the DTE is a DCE (figure 10.44b). This may seem correct for data signals, but will not be so for the control signals considered later. Since there is the possibility to have two DTEs with a female connector, a last permutation may have been decided by some confused engineer (figure 10.44c). Mixing two of these incorrect DTEs may require cables with pin 2 connected to pin 3. In brief, 4 kinds of DTE, claimed in all cases to be RS-232 "compatible", may be connected with 6 kinds of cables. And this without considering the control lines!

The only way to improve the connection consistency when equipment does not strictly follow the DTE rules is to use an adapting cable which corrects the situation. The increased cost of the additional connector and the need for a null-modem cable is small compared to the time lost by highly qualified software or system people not concerned by polarity of connectors and not specialists of RS-232 anomalies. The only acceptable solution is to have a pseudo-DCE plug on a DTE, as shown in figure 10.43c, with an associated labelling specifying the role of the control signals.

Happily, a DCE is always correct, since RS-232 has been designed for modems by modem people, and these people know the rules.

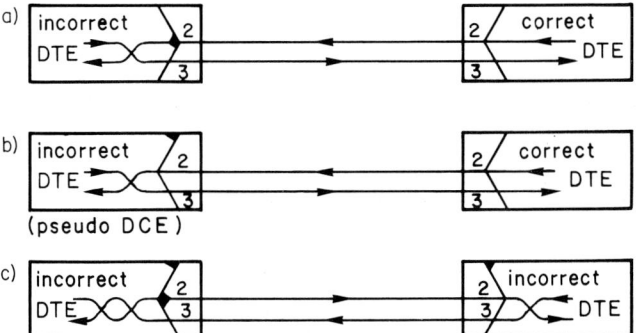

*Fig. 10.44 Incorrect DTE to DTE connections (dark triangle shows incorrect pin or polarity)*
  *a) Data should get out the DTE at pin 2*
  *b) Polarity of DTE connector are wrong*
  *c) Polarity and pinout is wrong*

## 10.4.6 RS-232 control signals

RS-232 control signals help the establishment of communications over telephone lines through a modem (figure 10.45). Two lines

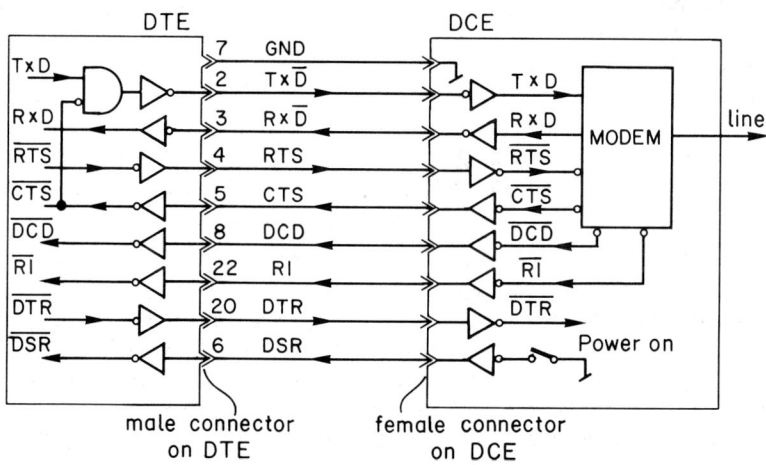

*Fig. 10.45 Control signals of a DTE/DCE interface*

(DTR and DSR) check the readiness of the DTE-DCE connection. Two lines from the modem (RI and DCD) are related to the establishment of the communication and the presence of the modulation. Two lines (RTS and CTS) control the transfer of the information. Data transfer is possible in the two directions only if RTS, CTS, DTR and DSR are active. It should be remembered that pins 2, 4 and 20 have a polarity which shows the direction of the related information.

The description of these signals is given in figure 10.46, together with the pin number on a 25-pin connector and the circuit name or number of EIA-RS-232 and CCITT-V24 documents.

| Pin | Abbreviation | RS-232 | V24 | |
|---|---|---|---|---|
| 1 | Chassis | AA | 101 | Protective ground |
| 7 | GND | AB | 102 | Common return of all DTE and DCE signals |
| 2 | Tx$\overline{\text{D}}$ | BA | 103 | Transmitted Data from DTE to DCE |
| 3 | Rx$\overline{\text{D}}$ | BB | 104 | Received Data from DCE to DTE |
| 4 | RTS | CA | 105 | Request of the DTE to the DCE to be ready To Send on the line the data supplied on Tx$\overline{\text{D}}$ |
| 5 | CTS | CB | 106 | Indication of the DCE to the DTE that DCE is ready (Clear) To Send data to the line |
| 20 | DTR | CD | 108 | Indication of the DTE to the DCE that the Data Terminal equipment is Ready (power up, not in test mode) |
| 6 | DSR | CC | 107 | Indication of the DCE to the DTE that the Data Set equipment (modem) is Ready (connected). It does not mean that communication is established |
| 8 | DCD | CF | 109 | Indication of the DCE to the DTE that Data Carrier is Detected |
| 22 | RI | CE | 125 | Indication of the DCE to the DTE that a Ring Indicator signal is received |

*Fig. 10.46 Major RS-232 signals*

A typical communication is established according to figure 10.47. The case of a duplex transmission, when RTS and CTS are both active, is shown in figure 10.47a. For a half duplex communication, data is send alternately in one direction and then in the other. A higher level protocol decides the direction and the unit which is able to transmit activates RTS and waits for CTS active before carrying out the transfer (figure 10.47b).

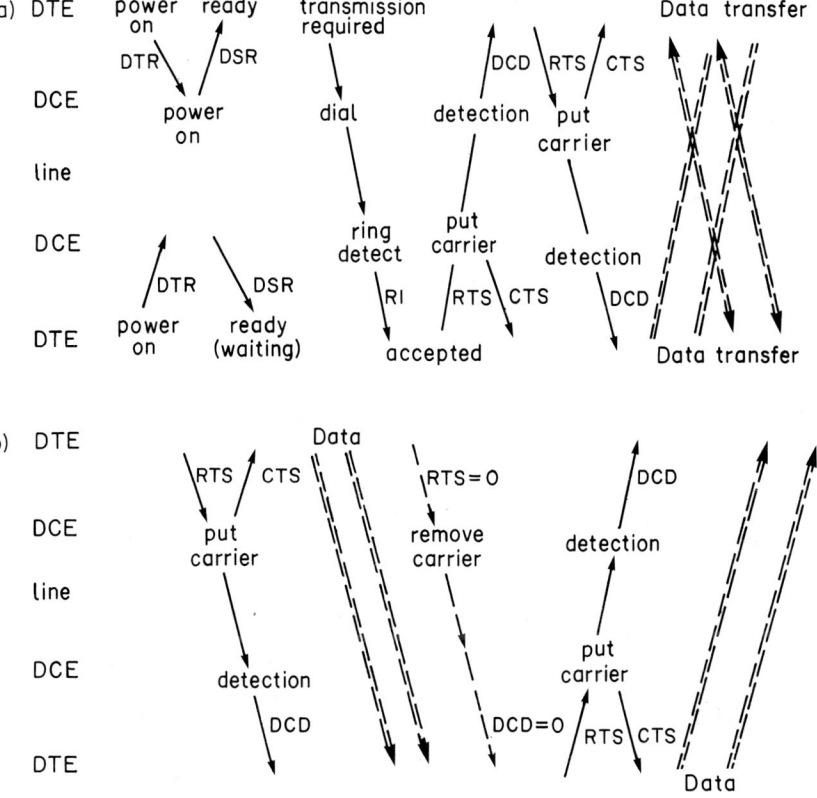

Fig. 10.47 Sequence for establishing a communication between two DTEs
  a) Establishment of the communication and full duplex transfer
  b) Half-duplex transfer

## 10.4.7 Null-modems and Null-DTE

When the modems are suppressed in order to establish a direct DTE to DTE connection a null-modem must be inserted on both sides; this null-modem should look like a perfect modem pair ready to transmit instantaneously. A three-line null-modem (figure 10.48a) corresponds to this.

Usually, one tries to have some sort of handshake performed between the two DTEs. For this hardware handshake, not part of the RS-232 specification, one should have DTR/DSR and not RTS/CTS reserved for half-duplex control. The null-modem of figure 10.48b is preferred for this. Digital Equipment recommends the null-modem of figure 10.48c.

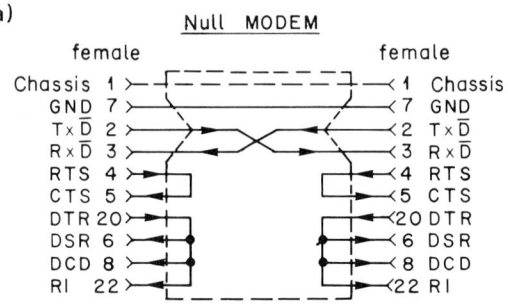

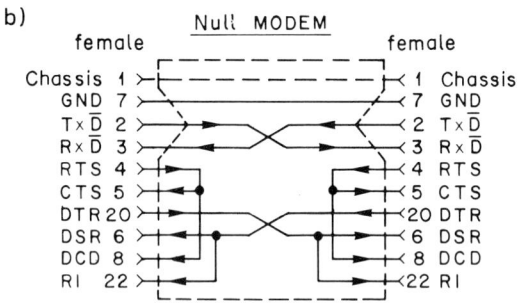

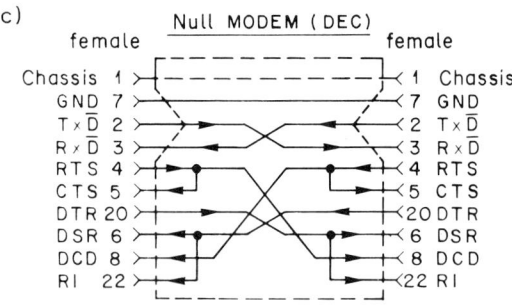

*Fig. 10.48 Null-modems*

A NULL-DTE is very seldom used but is required if two modems of the same speed are to be connected together. The null-DTE simulates a pair of terminals that are always ready. The schematic is given in figure 10.49.

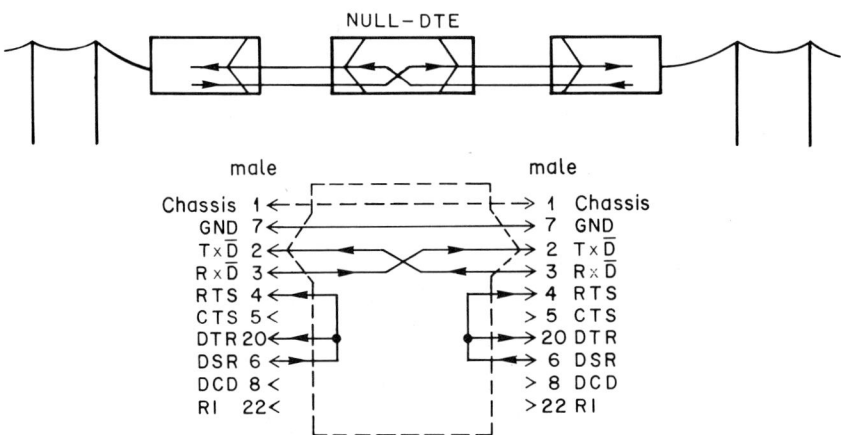

*Fig. 10.49 Null-DTE*

## 10.4.8 Extension cables

RS-232 extension cables may include all 25 wires. Generally this is not required and the 10 previously defined lines are sufficient. Even three lines (plus chassis) are satisfactory in most cases, since only a few microcomputer systems correctly handle the control lines, due to the differences between RS-232-like systems. A 3-line extension cable results directly from the 3-line null-modem and the 3-line null-DTE; it

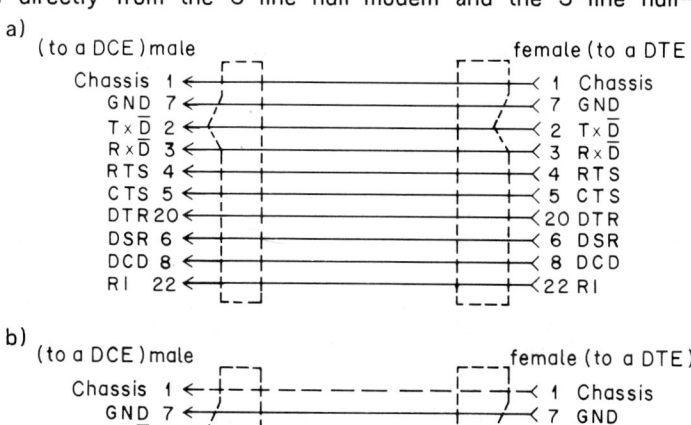

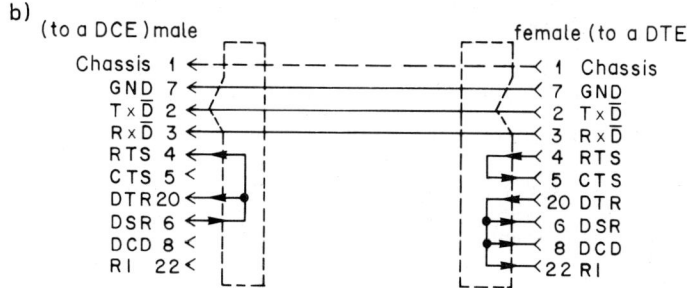

*Fig. 10.50 RS-232 extension cable*

establishes direct connections between unused pins (figure 10.50). No simpler extension cable should exist. As mentioned earlier, an adapter behind the DTE should take care of the design flaw of the computer or peripheral.

### 10.4.9 Not connected lines

A DTE or a DCE that is not connected to some other equipment should not be activated. On the DTE, input signals DSR, DCD and CTS should be inactive, that is, since they are inverted, they should be maintained at a voltage lower than −3 V with a resistor connected to the −12 V. However, if one wants to be tolerant to users who do not correctly wire a simplified cable and try to make it work with only pins 2, 3 and 7 connected, it is better to have DSR, DCD and CTS active (>+3 V). Data should be inactive (voltage lower than −3 V), but in some cases, this input line is active by default and a BREAK character is transmitted as long as the line is not connected.

## 10.5 OTHER SERIAL STANDARDS

Due to the weakpoints of RS-232, several other serial standards exist and continue to be proposed. They tend to improve RS-232, but due to the omnipresence of this standard and a search for compatibility, only part of the RS-232 usual features are changed.

The electrical specifications are improved with RS-423, RS-422, current-loop, S 5/8 (section 10.5.2) or fiber optic transmissions. Handshake philosophy is revised with X20, X21, SIMSER and S 5/8. The huge "subminiature" 25-pin RS-232 connector is replaced by a smaller one in ISO-4093 and S 5/8, and by all kinds of low cost connectors in personal computers.

The hardware DTE-DCE protocol, complicated in a first step with the RS449 standard not covered here, is replaced by software protocols with X20, X21 and S 5/8. The direct DTE to DTE communications aspects are still ignored by the communication people defining the international standards. S 5/8 is the only proposal optimizing this aspect.

In such a jungle of "standards", more or less understood and followed, it is difficult to be exhaustive and clear. This field will continue to change over the next few years, and new proposals may appear [SCHU83].

## 10.5.1 RS-423/V10 electrical specifications

The RS-232 standard mixes the functional and electrical specifications, which have been separated in the CCITT standards and in more recent EIA standards. *V28* corresponds to the electrical specification part of RS-232. These specifications have been upgraded, still being partly compatible, with the *RS-423/V10/X26* standards [FOLT82]. New equipment should be made compatible with these, and adequate integrated circuits exist to make the designer's work easy.

A brief summary of the RS-232/V28 electrical specifications is given in figure 10.51a. Distances up to 50 metres are possible. For short distances (5 metres), voltages of ±5V may be used with appropriate circuits. RS-423/V10 is adequate up to 1 km at 10 kbits/sec, due to the adapting resistor on the receiver side (figure 10.51b). The output is compatible with RS-232/V28.

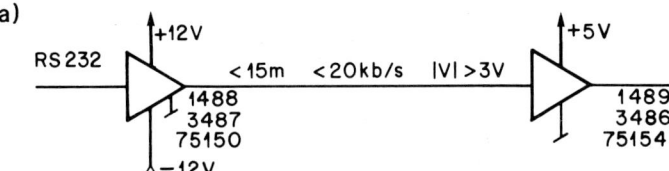

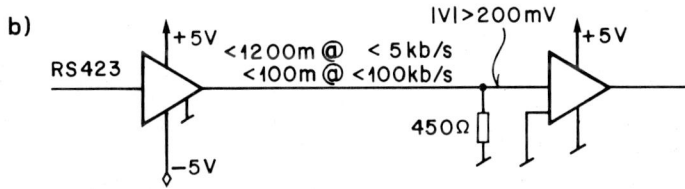

*Fig. 10.51 Electrical characteristics*
  *a) RS-232/V28/X26*
  *b) RS-423/V10*

## 10.5.2 RS-422/V11 electrical specifications

Using balanced twisted pairs, the *RS-422/V11/X27* standard allows much better speed and distance. The RS-232 connector does not

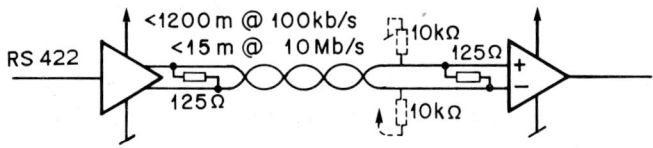

*Fig. 10.52 RS-422 electrical characteristics*

support balanced pairs, but X21 connectors do (see Appendix). The major electrical specifications of RS-422 are given in figure 10.52. One of the advantages of RS-422, besides its far better performance, is to work with a single +5 V supply [WIT83].

The two 10 kΩ resistors are not part of the standard. They are required only for asynchronous transmissions.

The RS-485/V12 standard is very similar to RS-422. Its specifications allows multipoint connections with up to 32 connected stations.

### 10.5.3 Current loop

Current loop interfaces, frequently named 20 mA loops (or 60 mA loops), were developed 100 years ago for the first teletypes. They are as confusing to use as RS-232, but for other reasons. The ambiguity resides in which of the two connected units supplies the current and in what direction the current goes.

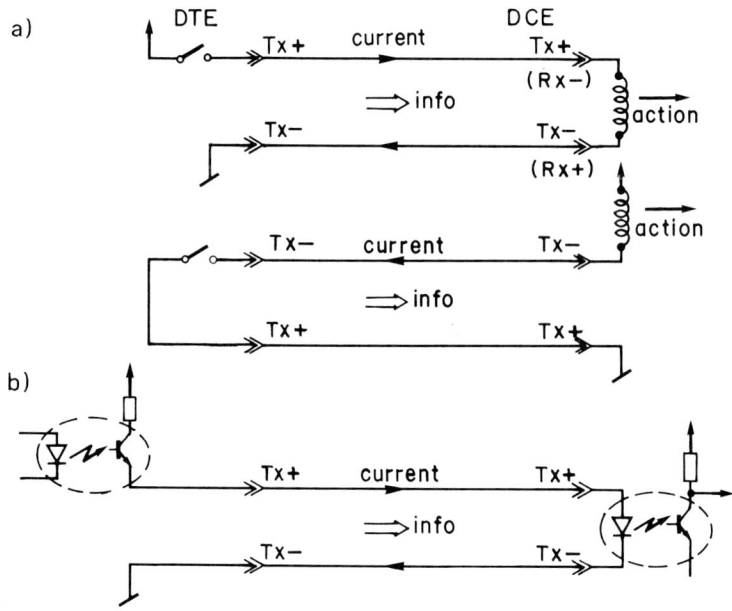

Fig. 10.53 Current loop interface
 a) Active source
 b) Active destination
 c) Optically coupled active source

The pins should be clearly labelled Tx+, Tx-, Rx+, Rx- to show the direction of the current in (-) and out (+) with respect to the DTE. Possible schematics are given in figure 10.54. Optocouplers are recommended, since their usage is very simple. Current flow corresponds to a "one" (Mark), as specified in V31. Hence, a break of the line generates a break character.

Current loop is normalized by DIN 66258/66348 and is preferred to RS-232 by several industries, due to its better noise immunity and longer lines (up to 400 m). No Modem exists with a 20 mA loop interface, due to the fact the DTE/DCE philosophy is not clear.

Connectors for 20 mA-loop are standardized by DIN (see Appendix). Several RS-232 connectors include the four required signals on unused pins. This should be absolutely avoided.

### 10.5.4 X20 and X21 recommendations

The CCITT X20 and X21 [FOLT82][DEB84] had been proposed in 1976 for asynchronous and synchronous operations respectively, for usage on public data networks, but they have never been promoted within the microcomputer industry. They use a 15-pin connector (see Appendix), but implementations are proposed by DIN for 9-pin connectors. The electrical associated standard is RS-422/V11/X27. The DTE/DCE concept is kept, but the names of signals have been changed.

The X20 standard gets rid of all control lines and uses only two active lines:

T (Transmit)   Transmitted data from the DTE to the DCE

R (Receive)    Received data from the DCE to the DTE

G Ga Gb        Ground and signal returns

On X20, data is asynchronous and the "break" condition is used to encode the information "line ready for a transaction". A *TRANSACTION* is typically

- calling another device through a DCE (a modem or a network port)
- transferring data blocks
- releasing the line.

A typical sequence for a calling a DTE and transfering some data is given in figure 10.54.

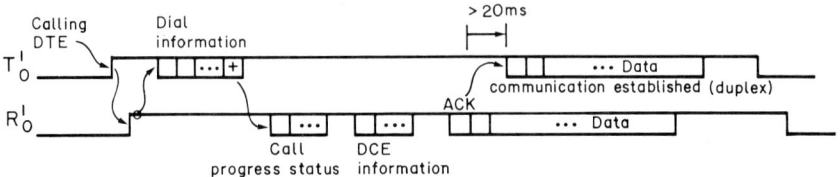

*Fig. 10.54 X20 typical data transfer*

The X21 uses synchronous protocols only. Four more signals are added to the connector: two control and status lines, and two synchronization signals generated by the modem.

C (Control)    Control information from the DTE

I (Indication) Status information from the DCE

S (Signal)    Bit timing indication (clock) from the DCE

B (Byte)      Optional byte timing indication from the DCE

### 10.5.5  Serial interface S5/8

There is a clear need for a simple serial link between microcomputers and peripherals, which supports XON-XOFF protocols and has very few or no control lines. Preferably, a single supply of +5V should be used and the connector should be shielded for correct electromagnetic protection.

One good solution has been originated by the Central Computer and Telecommunication Agency [CCTA85] and will be submitted to the British Standard Institution. The application is for portable personal computers and it is named *S5/8 (Serial 5V on 8 pins)*. It uses a DIN 8 pin connector, but most devices are connected with easy to find cables having 5- or 3-pin DIN connectors.

Six active signals are available on S5/8. They go by pairs and have clear names. Ground (signal return) and +5V power supply are the two remaining signals. Shield is available through the connector case. On D-type devices, power is provided on pin 8 only for adaptors like converter boxes, opto-isolators, and for S-type devices (e.g. a keyboard) which do not need more than 20 mA. These devices must have a 8-way captive cable with a male connector.

The S5/8 signals are the followings:

| | | | |
|---|---|---|---|
| 1 | DINP | Data Input |
| 3 | DOUT | Data Output |

|   |      |                    |
|---|------|--------------------|
| 4 | HINP | Handshake Input    |
| 5 | HOUT | Handshake Output   |
| 6 | SINP | Status Input       |
| 7 | SOUT | Status Output      |
| 2 | GND  | Ground             |
| 8 | +5V  | Power supply +5 V  |
| Shield | | Shield          |

Data is transferred at 9600 bits/sec, with 8 data bits and one stop bit. Other formats are possible, but should be used only for compatibility with existing equipments which cannot support the recommended values. The two data lines and the ground are the minimum required to transmit data, if an XON/XOFF protocol is used. As mentioned in section 10.5.4, the data line carries inverted data bits. But since the start bit is positive, the signal is not considered inverted (DINP corresponds to $\overline{RxD}$).

The handshake lines control directly and immediately the data transfer. HINP inactive stops the DOUT flow at the end of a character, like CTS. HOUT can be deactivated in response to an input buffer full.

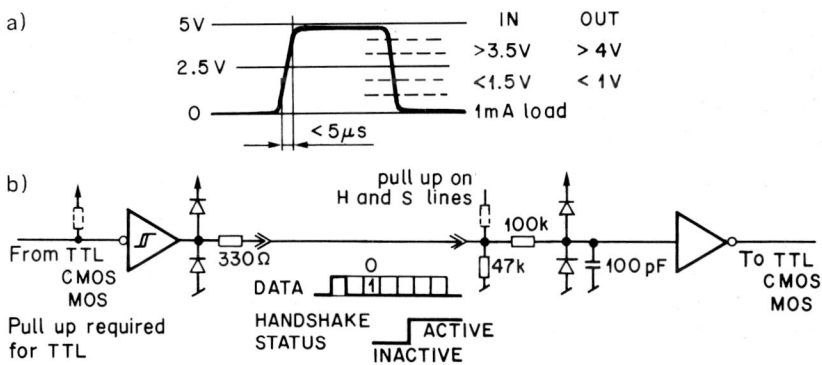

*Fig. 10.55 S5/8 electrical specifications and typical interface*
  *a) Major electrical specifications*
  *b) Typical receiver and transmitter section*

The status lines are general purpose signals which depend on the application. On a modem, SOUT (SINP on the modem side) can be a data/control indication or SOUT can be used for half-duplex control like RTS. The interface signal specification is given in figure 10.55a and a typical schematic is given in figure 10.55b. CMOS gates are very suitable for this application, and connections can be established over several metres without any problems. Input resistor, capacitor and protective diodes provide a good noise immunity and voltage transient suppression.

The proposed connector is an 8-pin DIN 45329 female plug on the equipment (see Appendix). Cables have 7, 5 or 3 wires and may use 5-pin or 3-pin connectors if the software allows it. Connecting cables are mirrored, as shown in figure 10.56, even in the case of a personal computer to modem connection. All units are considered as smart devices having to transfer data. An extension chord with a male and a female connector is not mirrored.

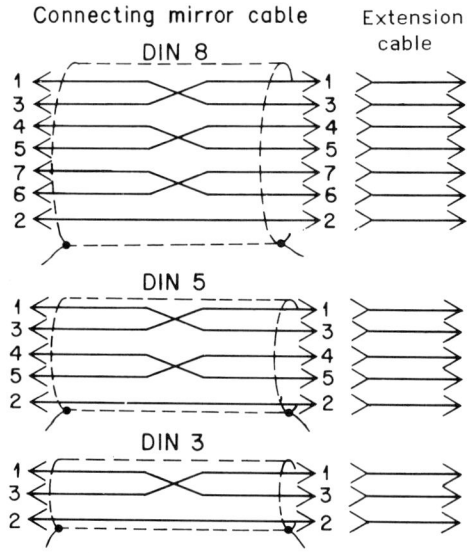

*Fig. 10.56 S5/8 cables*

Interfacing S5/8 electrically with RS-232 does not require an active adapter in most cases. S5/8 has not the negative voltage required by RS-232, but since most RS-232 devices use a line receiver chip of the "1489" type as input circuit; a direct connection is acceptable over short distances. These interface circuits change state at +0.8 V (they are powered by +5 V only) and will accept the <0.3 V/>3.5 V levels of S5/8 instead of the <-3 V/>+3 V levels of RS-232. When receiving a +/- 15 V maximum amplitude RS-232 signal, the input resistor and diodes protect the S5/8 inputs (see Appendix).

The interface of S5/8 toward RS-422 or RS-485 implies to use the corresponding drivers and receivers, which have to be powered by an external device, due to their important power needs.

Interfacing S5/8 to RS-232 and respecting the RS-232 philosophy is more difficult, since S5/8 does not follow the DCE/DTE concept. All stations are just transmitters/receivers. If an S5/8 is viewed as a DCE, in order to connect it to an RS-232 DTE device (male connector on the equipment), the following connections are recommended:

- DINP (input) with $\overline{\text{TxD}}$ (pin 2, output)
- HINP (output) with CTS (pin 5, input)

- DOUT (output) with $\overline{\text{RxD}}$ (pin 3, input)
- HOUT (input) with DSR (pin 20, input)

- SINP (input) with RTS (pin 4, output)
- SOUT (output with DSR and/or DCD (pins 6 and 8, inputs)

According to the RS-232 specifications, and the usual behaviour of UART circuits, CTS stops the transmission before the next character, but DSR inactive does not mean that the input buffer is full and the transmission must be stopped; that function may be programmed by software, taking care of the response time of the routine.

## 10.6 MULTIPLE ACCESS SERIAL BUSES

Multipoint links introduce the problem of exclusive access. Serial buses are not basically different in this respect to parallel buses, and the considerations of Chapter 5 are still applicable. The distance to be covered is however a few hundreds metres or more and not of few decimetres. Specific solutions of no interest with parallel buses are used for serial buses.

The major differences between serial and parallel buses are due to the propagation times of information. At 200'000 km/s, one bit at 10 Mb/s spans a distance of 20 m and covers 1 km in 5 µs. A 256-bit block spans 5 km. At 500 kb/s, a single bit spans 400 m. Serial protocols are strongly influenced by this. Handshaking is usually too slow on a bit or character basis (see figure 10.3). Hence data is grouped into *PACKETS* of up to 1kB and packets are exchanged between stations.

This section is greatly simplified and presents only a few concepts specifically for hardware engineers. A more detailed, easy to read and well structured description of computer networks can be found in [TAN81].

### 10.6.1 Access mechanism

On a multipoint line or through ether, for a given bandwidth, a single data transfer may occur at a given time. If the media is not correctly granted to the transmitter, collision will occur and the information may not be recognizable. On the media itself, waves may overlap; collisions are referenced to at the receiving point. Collisions may also be detected at the transmitting point, if the sender reads back the data line.

Arbitration problems have been explained in Chapter 5. Serial buses have two distinctive features in comparison with parallel buses: only one line is used (and the same line is also used for data transfers), and propagation delays are several orders of magnitude higher. Hence, three basic mechanisms are possible for reliable commmunications between several simultaneously active stations sharing a multipoint line:

- a single master polls the other stations which are just slaves (section 10.6.2)
- a token is passed by the current master to a next master, so that it is clear at any time who controls the bus (section 10.6.3)
- all units are masters and can transmit at any time; messages may collide and are retransmitted until correctly received (section 10.6.4).

The collision of messages has to be detected as soon as possible to improve the efficiency of the last scheme. For this purpose:

- a unit does not start if traffic is detected (section 10.6.5)
- a unit stops transmitting if simultaneous traffic is detected on the bus (section 10.6.6)
- an immediate acknowledge is provided when it is efficient to do so (section 10.6.7)
- an arbitration phase precedes the transmission of the data information (section 10.6.8).

These schemes are illustrated in the next sections.

### 10.6.2 Polling

The *POLLING* of the slaves by a single master allows one to transmit information between any two devices, under the control of the master. This technique is not very efficient and not reliable (a single point controls all the traffic), but it is simple.

### 10.6.3 Token passing

The right to access the bus may depend on a *TOKEN* which is passed from one unit to another. Only a unit that has the token can transmit. The token passing scheme avoids collisions and applies to rings as well as to buses; it has been explained in section 5.1.2. The token consists of a short message. It may be lost by one station, and adequate procedures must detect the loss and recreate a single token.

A major advantage of token schemes is that they are deterministic. Any station is sure to get the token after a given amount of time. The efficiency when the traffic is heavy is much better than with collision schemes, but of course the response time for light traffic is not as good, due to the token delay time.

### 10.6.4 Pure broadcast (Aloha)

In 1970, the University of Hawaii installed a network based on radio transmitters and receivers all tuned to the same frequency and all having the right to send messages at any time. This system was named *ALOHA* [ABR70] [BIN75] and has been abundantly studied as a broadcast system.

After transmitting a packet, the station waits for a given amount of time for an acknowledgement. If none is received, the packet is retransmitted. The receiving station accepts packets if their checksum is correct; no action is taken if the packet is incorrect. A typical exchange is shown in figure 10.57, assuming 500 kbit/sec speed, 256 byte packets and three aligned stations 400 km apart. These distances are much longer than the real ones at Hawaii in order to illustrate the collision process.

It is clear that with such a mechanism, saturation is quickly reached. Statistical analysis shows that the transfer capacity is at best 18% of the channel capacity. One can increase the utilization of the Aloha channel capacity to a theoretical 37% by having a central clock define time slots in which messages can start. This is called *SLOTTED ALOHA*. For the example of figure 10.57, a time slot of 3 ms would apparently be very favourable; only messages directed to close by stations would overlap.

### 10.6.5 Carrier sense

If the distances are much shorter than in the Aloha network, e.g. if a coaxial cable is used as the transmission media, then only a small fraction of the message is transmitted before it begins to be received at the other places. It is hence efficient not to start sending a message if it is recognized that some other message is being received. With human discussion, this is an elementary courtesy.

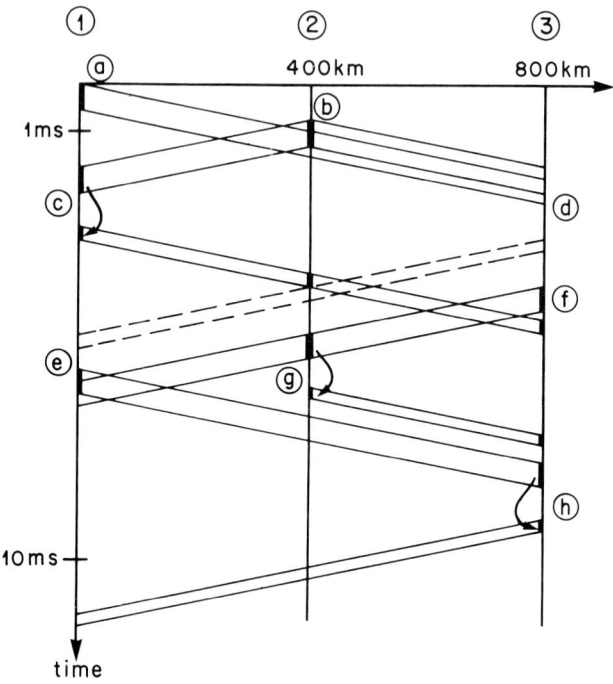

Fig. 10.57 Example of Aloha transmissions
　　a) (1) transmits to (3)
　　b) (2) transmits to (1)
　　c) (1) responds to (2)
　　d) (3) sees a jammed message and does nothing
　　e) (1) does not get the expected acknowledge and retransmit to (3)
　　f) (3) transmits to (2)
　　g) (2) transmits to (3)
　　h) (3) responds to (1)

This rule of "listen before talk" is usually named CSMA (Carrier Sense Multiple Access) due to the carrier detection circuits which allow one to recognize another transmission [MET76]. If several stations are waiting to transmit a packet due to traffic on the line, they should, when the line is recognized as free, wait for a random time in order to avoid collision as much as possible and prevent deadlock conditions, as for example when two stations always try to send their messages simultaneously. NON-PERSISTENT CSMA is the name given to this protocol. A simpler algorithm called p-PERSISTENT CSMA samples the line during fixed time slots and, if the line is found free, it is then taken with a probability of p [KURO84].

### 10.6.6 Collision detection

A transmitter can detect when a collision occurs by mean of modulation errors before the end of the packet occurs, so there is no need to continue. This is named CD (Collision Detection) and is always associated with CSMA. As shown in figure 10.58 the saving of time is significant for long packets.

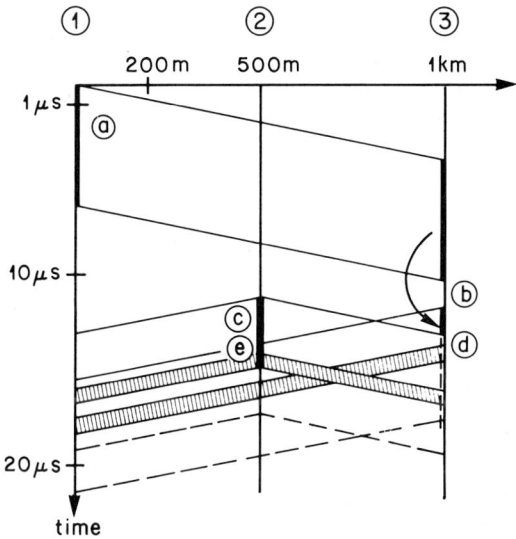

Fig. 10.58 CSMA and CSMA/CD transmission
    a) (1) transmits a short packet to (3)
    b) (3) acknowledges
    c) (2) transmits a packet to (1)
    d) (3) sees that its acknowledge is jammed and puts more jammed data
    e) (2) sees also that its packet is jammed

### 10.6.7 Immediate acknowledge

Messages can be broadcasted on a bus toward stations that do not exist. If no acknowledge signal is received, the message must be retransmitted several times before it becomes clear that the destination is not in operation. In order to reduce such nonproductive line usage, an immediate acknowledgement, following the transmission of the address and control part, is generated on some systems [BURR83]. Due to the carrier-sense delay, no other message is allowed while waiting for the acknowledge. This scheme is named *IA (Immediate Acknowledge)* and is more efficient than the preceding long messages with short control packets; it allows one to check at the beginning of each message if the destination unit is ready to receive it (figure 10.59).

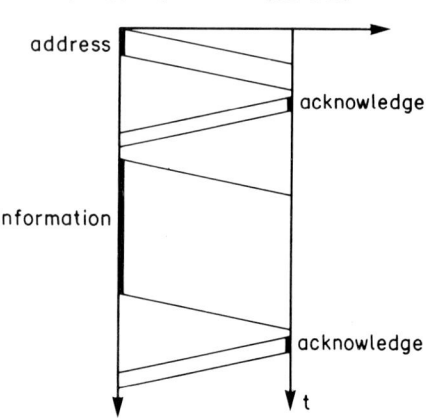

Fig. 10.59 *Immediate acknowledge on the identification packet*

### 10.6.8 Collision arbitration

There is a possibility of arbitrating collisions and to have a single winner at the end of the colliding part; this is only possible if both units start "together", that is within a time depending on the propagation delay over the line and the device logic. This is named *CA (Collision Arbitration)* and is applicable only for rather short buses.

The modulation scheme used must allow a "wired-OR" function on the line, and provide the time to perform it on a bit per bit basis. Hence if an active and a not active signal collide, the active signal will dominate and the station trying to set a "zero" will recognize it and remove itself. An open collector line and NRZ-encoding is adequate, but implies that the line length is small in relation to the distance covered by one bit cell.

### 10.6.9 Example : the COBUS network

The *COBUS (Coaxial Bus)* network was designed at EPFL and has been in use since 1977 [SOMM76][NIC76][SOMM81]. Optimized for short distances (200-300 m), it implements CSMA/CD/CA/IA. The line is electrically equivalent to a wired-OR gate. Output transistors force a +10 V for an active level.

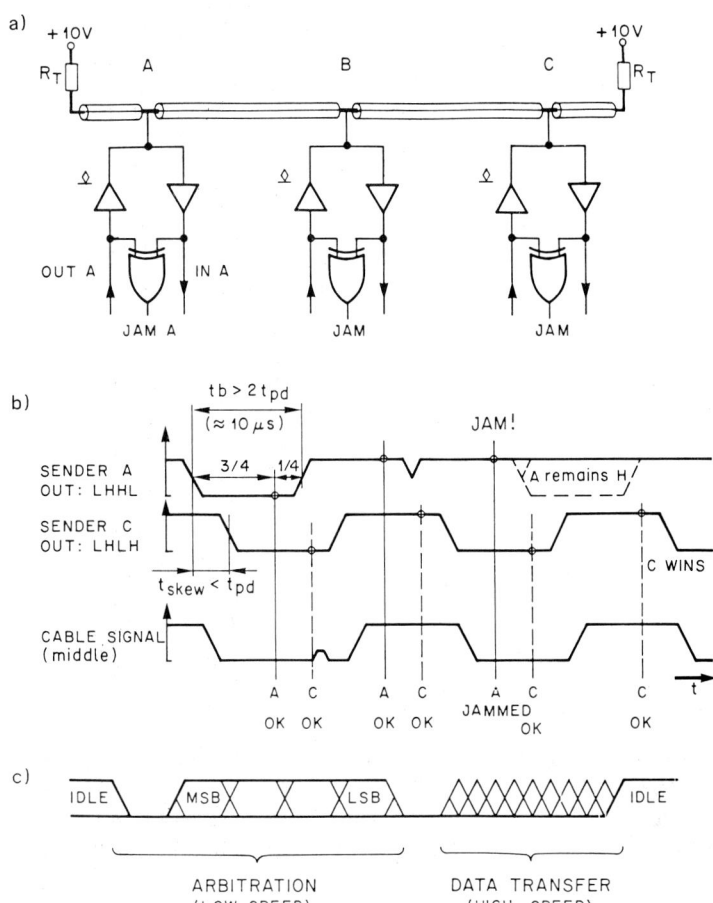

Fig. 10.60 Cobus main features
  a) Bus interface
  b) Arbitration example
  c) Packet format

Bytes are sent as NRZ asynchronous characters (start bit, 8 data bit, parity bit, one stop bit). Any bit written on the line is read back at the 3/4 period point (figure 10.60a). A "high" on the line, when a "low" is output, indicates a simultaneously started transmission by a higher priority. For instance, in figure 10.60b, "A" starts simultaneously with "C" but aborts at the third byte, when the conflict is recognized.

After the transmission of the destination address byte and the source address byte (maximum 256 stations), it is certain that only one station is on the line. The selected destination unit immediatly sends back an acknowledge character. A point-to-point connection is then established and the transfer speed changes in order to go as fast as the interface will permit (figure 10.60c).

A new transmission can start very soon after the end of a message. The delay is slightly longer than the maximum acknowledge delay and, due to the arbitration, all units can have the same delay. Of course, the address of each unit defines a fixed priority scheme, and the low priority devices are slowed down by the traffic of high priority devices.

### 10.6.10 Example : the I$^2$C network

The Philips I$^2$C *(Inter Integrated Circuits)* bus [PHIL83] is designed for short buses of up to 10 metres. It uses one clock line and one data line, as explained in section 10.3.6. Both are WIRED OR lines. Hence the clock line is used for handshaking on a bit per bit basis (see section 10.3.4) and the data line is used for arbitration (as for COBUS). An immediate acknowledge is provided at the end of a byte (figure 10.61a).

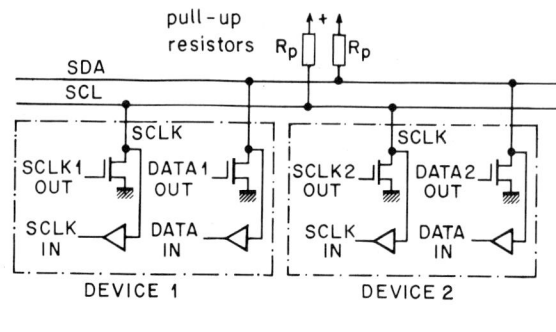

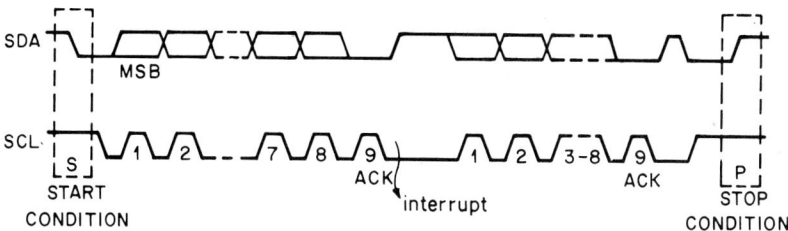

*Fig. 10.61 Major I$^2$C features*
  *a) Bus interface logic*
  *b) Message format*

10 Serial Links                                                355

The $I^2C$ interface is used in the 8400 processor, a processor of the 8048 family similar to the Intel 8022. Unhappily, both the bus clock and data lines are connected directly to the chip, and do not allow the insertion of the line drivers required for distances greater than a few metres (figure 10.61b).

## 10.6.11 Efficiency comparison

The access mechanism and packet size influence the efficiency of a serial bus. For a given bandwidth, the total throughput depends on the traffic. The important parameters refer to how well a loaded network behaves globally for a given user. Most networks have "foldback" characteristics, that is the throughput decreases when the load increases. Figure 10.62 shows typical characteristic curves and indicates that the token passing method is better when the response time must be predictable, e.g. due to a real-time application such as voice transfers. CSMA/CD is excellent for low to middle traffic on short buses. Short and slow buses have an evident advantage due to the arbitration, but suffer also from non-deterministic response times, if the priority between stations is fixed [STU83][TOB79].

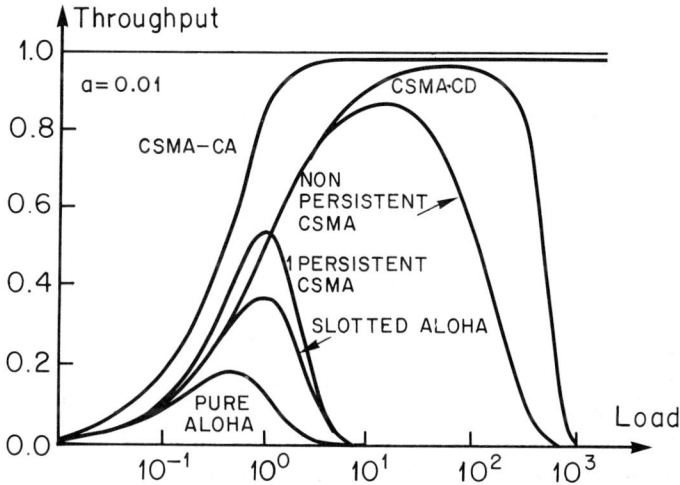

Fig. 10.62 Efficiency of bus access mechanism

## 10.7 NETWORK

Network considerations, with their hardware, software and applications aspects can fill books. The purpose of this section is to briefly list and characterize the present solutions. A rapid evolution is expected over the next few years, and only the principles explained in the previous sections will stay relevant as the level of hardware integration and software complexity increases.

### 10.7.1 Topology and technology

The topology of a network is either a star, a ring, a bus or a tree (figure 10.63). More complex meshed topologies have been proposed for improving the performance, but it seems for the moment, at least for the many small networks built around personal computers, that the limitation is more frequently due to the operating system and disk accesses than to transmission bottlenecks [STAL84] [KOT82] [SCHW77] [TRO81].

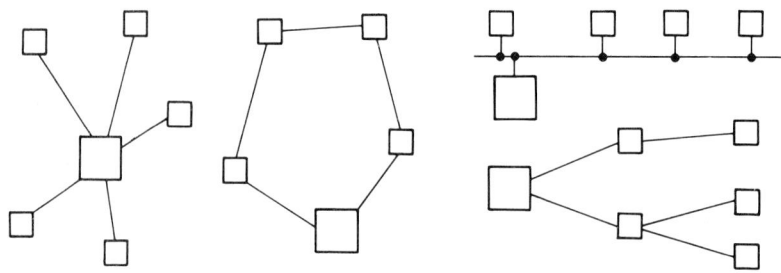

*Fig. 10.63 Network topologies: star, ring, bus, tree*

It is important to distinguish between the logical and the physical topologies. A physical star may simulate a logical bus, e.g. if the central point handles only one transfer at a time, and a physical bus may just be used to emulate a star or a ring logic structure. A bus may also be wired as a star, in order to simplify the extensions and maintenance.

The technology used for transmitting data influence the topology; solutions are:

- electrical signals on lines (Chapter 8)
- optical signals on fibers
- modulated broadband signals
- broadcasted waves

## 10.7.2 PABX and ISDN

Local networks may be implemented using the telephone lines, already available in each office, instead of specially installed cables. Transmission speed is low (48 or 64 kilobits/sec), but the star architecture allows one to have several simultaneous transmissions. Mixing of voice and data is easy due to the fact that voice is digitalized using PCM (Pulse Code Modulation) techniques and transmitted at 64 Kbits/second using an AMI or HDB3 code (see section 10.2).

Integrated circuit technology will favour future low cost implementations of this scheme. The traffic control is performed by PABX (Private Automatic Branch eXchange) equipment, which can handle a few hundred telephones or terminals. Similar services will be offered in a few years on a public basis under the name of ISDN (Integrated Services Digital Network), but the high investment in telephone cables and telephone exchanges will slow down the evolution.

## 10.7.3 Metropolitan networks

Data transmission over distances of 10 to 1000 km must use the telephone network which provide speeds of 1200 b/s to 1 Mb/s over leased lines. Multiple routing of the information is required in order to increase the reliability and equalize the load. This requires adequate addressing capabilities. The X25 scheme includes these and provides all the facilities for building a network of any size. The SNA (Standard Network Architecture) used by IBM is based on SDLC and competes with X25 [IBM83].

## 10.7.4 Ring architectures

Each station in a ring architecture must transmit messages for other stations and intercept its own messages when they pass by. The transmission of a message can be started only after a token has been received. Several messages can follow the same token [FOR77].

A mechanism must exist for inserting and removing packets. This can be done by software, with each station processing the data received in its input FIFO before retransmitting it (figure 10.64a). A hardware shift register is more efficient, allowing the insertion or removal of a packet in real time (figure 10.64b).

The weak point of a ring is its sensitivity to the non functioning of a single node. Mechanical relays should shorten the line as long as a node is not correctly powered and fully software operational.

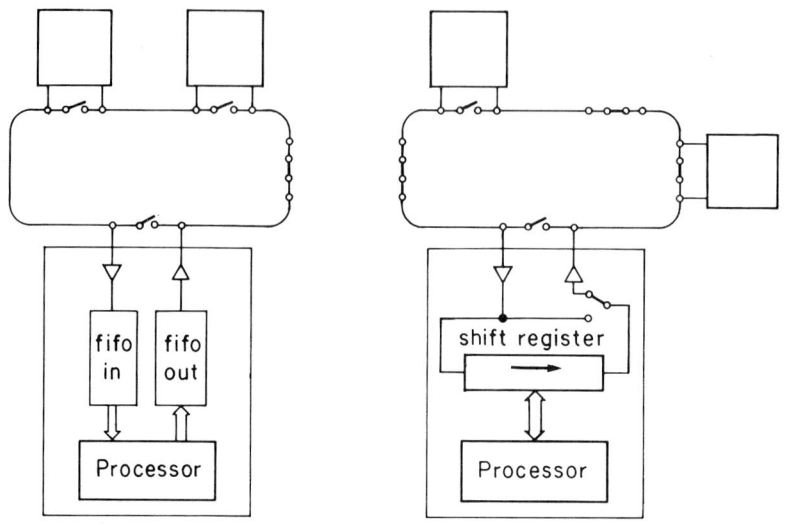

*Fig. 10.64 Ring interface*

### 10.7.5 Twisted pair buses

Twisted pairs are an efficient and low cost media for distances up to a few kilometres. They have been abundantly used for commercial [EIS82] [SAAL83] and industrial networks such as PROWAY [PRO83] and the PDV-Bus standardized as DIN 19241-1. Most of these buses use a simple polling scheme, guarantee the integrity of data (fault recovery), and use rather high voltages and galvanic insulation.

### 10.7.6 Coaxial cable buses

Coaxial cable is fast, reliable and easy to implement. Many commercially proposed networks use it, but Ethernet and its future lower cost solutions are clear commercial winners.

Ethernet was developed at Xerox Parc as a CSMA/CD local network using a 10 Mbit/sec transfer rate over coaxial cable. In 1979, three companies decided to support Ethernet and published the *DIX (Digital, Intel, Xerox)* proposal [DIX80]. This specification has served as the basis for the IEEE-802 Standard Committee, which is now extending Ethernet (see section 10.7.10).

The address of an 802 station is either a 16-bit address or a 48-bit address. The short 16-bit address is used for small networks; the first bit defines individual or group accesses. The second bit of the 48-bit address format distinguishes the addresses assigned by Xerox to users licensing the network. Other addressing modes are possible. The broadcast mode sends the same information to all stations; the spy mode allows a host to receive all packets.

Speed and detailed implementation are the object of the 802 standard. Speeds from 1 Mb/s to 150 Mb/s are being considered. The 802.3 specification corresponds to the original Ethernet mode, only slightly modified by the Committee, as for instance concerning the addressing. Packet length is up to 1518 bytes.

Electrically, 802.3 uses a baseband Manchester encoding. Modulation, carrier and collision detection are performed in a small box named *MAU (Medium Attachement Unit)* placed directly against the cable, in order to minimize the degradation effect of T-shaped lines. A 15-wire cable connects that box to the main controller, for distances up to 25 metres.

Ethernet controller chips or chip sets are available from several manufacturers. They implement most of the second OSI layer. Coupled with a DMA controller, they unload the processor of most of the low level network control tasks.

The cost of an Ethernet MAU is a significant part of the cost of an Ethernet interface. The 10 MHz speed implies also a TTL or ECL technology for the serialization and modulation part, thus not allowing a single chip design with the present state of technology. Hence, a proposal named *CHEAPERNET* accepts only a speed of 1 Mbit/sec and total bus length of 300 metres, in order to lower the cost of interface.

### 10.7.7 Broadband networks

The *CATV (Community Antenna Television)* is a widely used technology providing a high bandwidth (500 MHz) and long distances (several km) on 12 mm or larger coaxial cables. For local network applications, the bandwidth is split into several channels. More than one local network may exist on the same cable. Voice, video, and fast point-to-point data transfers may also exist for different frequency bands. Thousands of terminals may be connected to a broadband network. The major trunk cable of 12.5 mm diameter is followed by feeder lines of 10 mm diameter and user drops using a cable of 7 mm diameter. A modem must be used for each terminal and repeaters-amplifiers must be distributed along the cable [DINE81] [HOPK82].

Data cannot be transmitted and received on the same frequency. SINGLE-TRUNK systems perform two-way transmissions using two frequency bands. At the head of the cable, a device called the REMODULATOR shifts the frequency of the upstream data and reflects them backstream (figure 10.65a).

Dual cable systems use two parallel cables. The INBOUND CABLE collects the data to be sent. The OUTBOUND CABLE distributes the data (figure 10.65b). No frequency shift is required in this case.

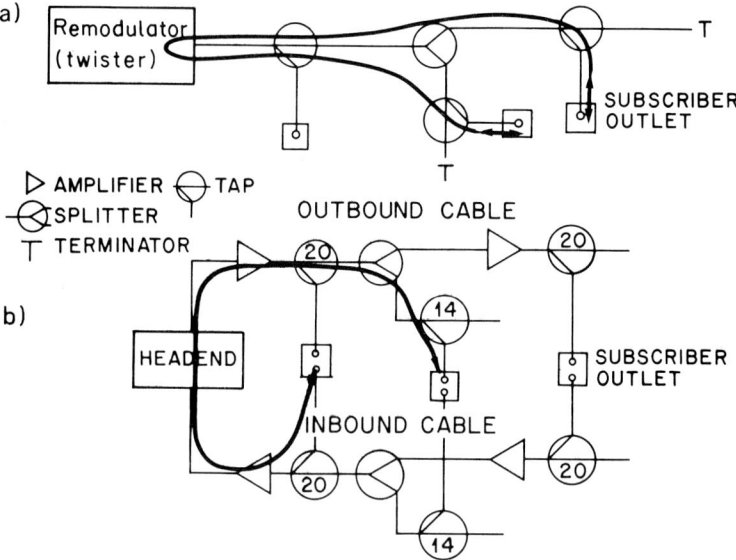

Fig. 10.65 Broadband network
  a) Single cable with remodulator
  b) Dual cable system

### 10.7.8 Fiber optic networks

Fiber optic is a difficult technology for buses. Solutions are not possible without substantial losses. The few demonstrated solutions (e.g. Fibernet at Xerox PARC) use a star coupler which is rather easy to build (figure 10.66). All units have to be connected to the coupler (local bus, physical star), and they follow a CSMA/CD access mechanism. Other access methods would be usable as well [DOOR83].

### 10.7.9 Radio waves

Radio waves can be directive, and hence simulate point-to-point connections, in particular with satellite relays. Broadcast radiowave

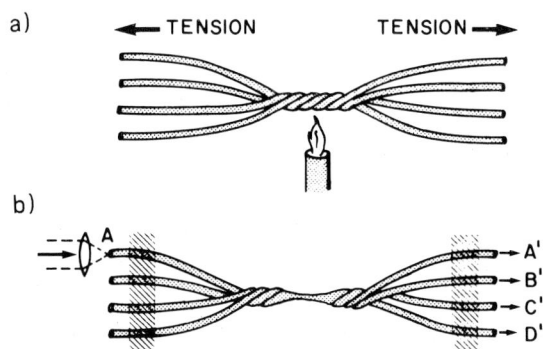

*Fig. 10.66 Fiber optic star coupler*
  *a) Preparation of a coupler*
  *b) Operational coupler*

networks require efficient protection against perturbations. An interesting solution is to built networks in which each station repeats the incoming information. Adequate algorithms help to keep control of the inundation created by a single message. The advantage is the replacement of a few central points with high power transmitters by many low power ones. A higher reliability also results from the redundancy of information paths.

### 10.7.10 The 802 family of standards

In February 1980, the IEEE Standard Committee started project P802 for a local network [GRAU84]. It used the Ethernet specification as a starting point, but the committee was quickly split into other groups proposing token passing schemes (for ring or buses), and other technologies. Layer 3 and above are common, with only layer 3 being specified (figure 10.67).

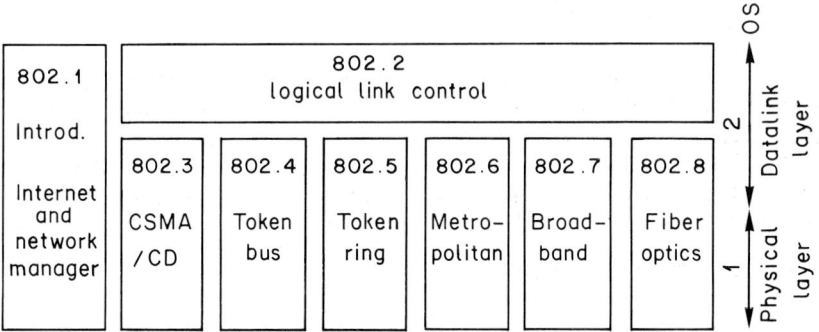

*Fig. 10.67 IEEE 802 standards*

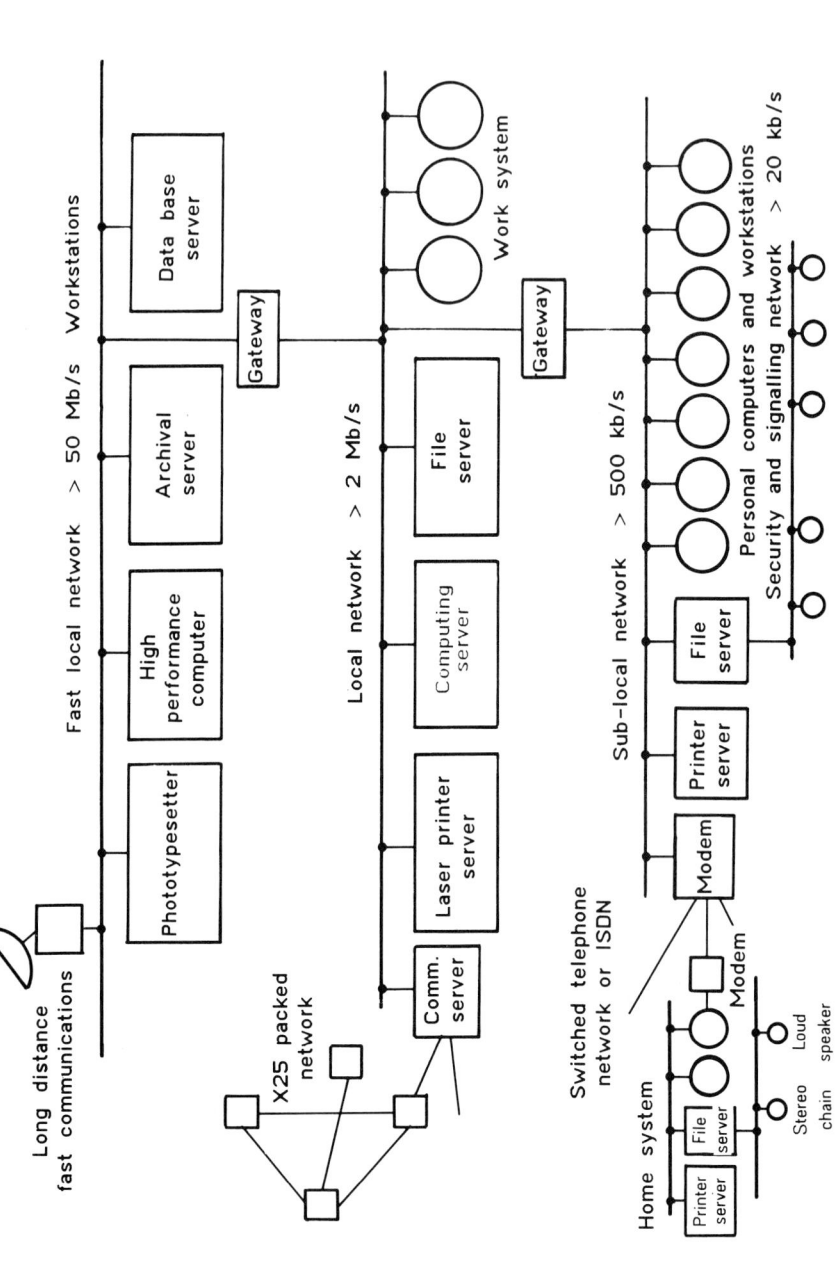

Fig. 10.68 Local network hierarchy

The work has been split into several working groups:
- 802.1-A   Introduction to 802 Family of Standards
- 802.1-B   Inter-networking and Network Management
- 802.2     Logical Link Control
- 802.3     Carrier Sense Multiple Access/Collision Detection
- 802.4     Token bus
- 802.5     Token ring
- 802.6     Metropolitan Area Network
- 802.7     Broadband Technical Advisory Group
- 802.8     Fiber Optics Technical Advisory Group

Several of these working groups have only come into being recently. The 802.2, 802.3 and 802.4 drafts are the closest to official acceptance.

### 10.7.11 Hierarchy

A complete spectrum of transmission facilities exists from simple multidrop configurations to nationwide networks. The distance to be covered strongly influences the transmission media, the speed and the protocol. A proposed terminology and associated examples are given below :

```
< 5 cm          Component network
< 50 cm         Backplane network       (P896)
< 5 m           Device network          ($I^2C$)
< 100 m         Office network          (Cobus)
< 800 m         Small area network      (Cheapernet, Omninet)
< 4 km          Local network           (Ethernet)
< 100 km        Metropolitan network
no limitation   Long haul network       (Arpa, Telenet)
```

Local network technology will expand considerably in the coming years. A few standard solutions will dominate the market, but many other solutions will be found, due to the different applications. As shown in figure 10.68, a hierarchy of networks should coexist in any environment. A GATEWAY allows transparent communication between the different networks. The 64 kb/s of ISDN may decrease the need of local networks for communications between individuals, but graphics and a large database will imply fast transfers over coaxial cable and fiber optic.

The comparison of buses depends on many more parameters. The required span and the interface cost are major selection criteria. Availability of hardware and software, and the reputation of the manufacturer will lead to the final decision [MYE82].

# 11 APPENDIX

This appendix provides a survey of the hardware associated with a number of major serial and parallel links and backplane buses.

Each survey does not of course provide enough information to design an interface or even to understand it completely. But the pinout information and the standard presentation format will be of help in a comparison of the selected links and buses.

The selection has been based on what the authors feel to be most important from a market acceptance and potential interest point of view. Many other links and buses have not been included due to space limitations. However, future editions of this book will be updated to include the devices in accordance with new trends.

## 11.1.1 Centronics-Epson

| | | | |
|---|---|---|---|
| DESCRIPTOR | 8-bit parallel, monodirectionnal De facto standard for printers, but tend to be replaced by RS 232 | CONNECTOR | 36-pin Amphenol 57-40360-12-D56 Male connector on equipment chassis Female to female connecting straight cable <br><br> $\overline{STB}$ 1■ ■19 Gnd <br> DA0 2■ ■20 Gnd <br> DA1 3■ ■21 Gnd <br> DA2 4■ ■22 Gnd <br> DA3 5■ ■23 Gnd <br> DA4 6■ ■24 Gnd <br> DA5 7■ ■25 Gnd <br> DA6 8■ ■26 Gnd <br> DA7 9■ ■27 Gnd <br> $\overline{ACK}$ 10■ ■28 Gnd <br> BUSY 11■ ■29 Gnd <br> Paper Error 12■ ■30 Gnd <br> Selected 13■ ■31 $\overline{Reset}$ <br> 0 V 14■ ■32 $\overline{Fault}$ <br> nc 15■ ■33 Gnd <br> 0 V 16■ ■34 nc <br> Chassis 17■ ■35 nc <br> +5 V 18■ ■36 (Demand) <br><br> Sometimes, a 25-pin subminiature D-type connector is used with an unpredictable pinout |
| SPONSOR | Centronics ≃1975 | | |
| STANDARD | None | | |
| ADDRESS SPACE | not applicable | | |
| DATA FORMAT | 8-bit | | |
| TRANSFER TYPE | Write only | | |
| | | BUS LENGTH | 5m |
| TIMING | Handshake with an ACK pulse at the end of the cycle, a BUSY signal is provided for inhibiting transfer of all characters but DC1 | DRIVER | Outputs: 7406 or equivalent Inputs: 7414 or equivalent with 1 kΩ pull-up (RC filter on STB) |
| ARBITRATION | – | | |
| | | SPEED | 100 kB/s |
| INTERRUPTS | – | OPTIONS | – |
| | | REFERENCES | EPSON and most other manufacturers |
| ERROR HANDLING | – | | |
| OTHER FUNCTIONS | Paper Error (printer output) Selected (printer output) Fault (printer output) Reset (printer input) | REMARKS | Initially used in several printers from Centronics, the interface has been better defined by EPSON |

# 11 Appendix

## 11.1.2 HP-IB, IEEE 488 or IEC 625

| | | | |
|---|---|---|---|
| DESCRIPTOR | 8-bit parallel, monodirectionnal, multi-master (token-passing) One controller, one talker, several listeners | CONNECTOR | 24-pin Amphenol 57-40360-12-D56 Female connector on equipment chassis Male to Male connecting straight cable, hermaphroditic plugs for piggy back connections |
| SPONSOR | Hewlett-Packard ≈1972 | | DIO1  1■ ■$^{13}$DIO5<br>DIO2  2■ ■$^{14}$DIO6<br>DIO3  3■ ■$^{15}$DIO7<br>DIO4  4■ ■$^{16}$DIO8<br>EOI   5■ ■$^{17}$REN<br>DAV   6■ ■$^{18}$Gnd<br>NRFD  7■ ■$^{19}$Gnd<br>NDAC  8■ ■$^{20}$Gnd<br>IFC   9■ ■$^{21}$Gnd<br>SRQ  10■ ■$^{22}$Gnd<br>ATN  11■ ■$^{23}$Gnd<br>Shield 12■ ■$^{24}$Isolated Gnd |
| STANDARD | IEEE 488, IEC 625 | | |
| ADDRESS SPACE | 31 devices | | |
| DATA FORMAT | 8-bit parallel | | |
| TRANSFER TYPE | Write only Talker toward listener(s) or commander toward all others | BUS LENGTH | 15 m |
| | | DRIVER | Special 24 mA drivers |
| TIMING | Handshaken 3-wires broadcast transfer DAV Data Valid NDAC Not Data Accepted NRFD Not Ready For Data | SPEED | 1 MByte/s |
| ARBITRATION | Token passing: the controller addresses the next controller SRQ Service Request when the controller assigns modes | OPTIONS | – |
| INTERRUPTS | ATN Attention (polled or vectored protocols) EOI End of Input (abort transfers) REN Remote Enable (removes control from instrument panel) | REFERENCES | IEEE Computer Society Order Dep. Box 80452, Worldway Postal Center Los Angeles, CA 90080, USA IEC 625, Rue de Varembé 3, CH-1200 Geneva, Switzerland |
| ERROR HANDLING | Parity bit DIO7 when 7-bit ASCII characters | REMARKS | The 488 is mostly used for data acquisition and connection of Hewlett-Packard peripherals Programmable interfaces and drivers exist and simplify the development of microprocessor interfaces |
| OTHER FUNCTIONS | – | | |

## 11.1.3 SCSI

| | | | |
|---|---|---|---|
| DESCRIPTOR | 8-bit parallel bus, up to 8 masters. There are 8 operational bus phases: bus free, arbitration, selection, reselection, command, data, status, message | CONNECTOR | 50-pin flat cable. Male connector on equipment chassis. Female to female connecting flat cable |
| SPONSOR | Shugart Associates ≈1982 | | Single-ended: Gnd 1● ●2 DB0, Gnd 3● ●4 DB1, Gnd 5● ●6 DB2, Gnd 7● ●8 DB3, Gnd 9● ●10 DB4, Gnd 11● ●12 DB5, Gnd 13● ●14 DB6, Gnd 15● ●16 DB7, Gnd 17● ●18 DBpar, Gnd 19● ●20 Gnd, Gnd 21● ●22 Gnd, Gnd 23● ●24 Gnd, nc 25● ●26 Termp, Gnd 27● ●28 Gnd, Gnd 29● ●30 Gnd, Gnd 31● ●32 ATN*, Gnd 33● ●34 Gnd, Gnd 35● ●36 BSY*, Gnd 37● ●38 ACK*, Gnd 39● ●40 RST*, Gnd 41● ●42 MSG*, Gnd 43● ●44 SEL*, Gnd 45● ●46 C/D*, Gnd 47● ●48 REQ*, Gnd 49● ●50 I/O*.  Differential: Shield 1● ●2 Gnd, +DB0 3● ●4 -DB0, +DB1 5● ●5 -DB1, +DB2 7● ●8 -DB2, +DB3 9● ●10 -DB3, +DB4 11● ●12 -DB4, +DB5 13● ●14 -DB5, +DB6 15● ●16 -DB6, +DB7 17● ●18 -DB7, +DBpar 19● ●20 -DBpar, Diffsen 21● ●22 Gnd, Gnd 23● ●24 Gnd, Termp 25● ●26 Termp, Gnd 27● ●28 Gnd, +ATN 29● ●30 -ATN, Gnd 31● ●32 Gnd, +BSY 33● ●34 -BSY, +ACK 35● ●36 -ACK, +RST 37● ●38 -RST, +MSG 39● ●40 -MSG, +SEL 41● ●42 -SEL, +C/D 43● ●44 -C/D, +REQ 45● ●46 -REQ, +I/O 47● ●48 -I/O, Gnd 49● ●50 Gnd |
| STANDARD | ANSI X3T9.2, ECMA, ISO TC97 | | |
| ADDRESS SPACE | Each of the 8 data lines are assigned as target's or initiator's SCSI device ID | | |
| DATA FORMAT | 8-bit parallel | | |
| TRANSFER TYPE | Target-driven phases: command, data, status, message | | |
| TIMING | Handshaken (asynchronous) transfer or synchronous transfer | | |
| ARBITRATION | This phase is set by initiator or target. Highest priority given to devices that are not fully buffered | BUS LENGTH | 6 m (single-ended) 25 m (differential) |
| | | DRIVER | 48 mA drivers or differential pair drivers |
| INTERRUPTS | ATN line activated by an initiator to tell a target a message is pending. RST line immediately clear all the devices from SCSI bus | SPEED | 1.5 MByte/s for handshaken transfers. 4 MByte/s for synchronous transfers |
| ERROR HANDLING | 9th parity bit | OPTIONS | - |
| OTHER FUNCTIONS | Up to 64 k blocks of data can be transfered with a single host command; each block is 256, 512 or 1024 bytes long | REFERENCES | Most manufacturers (NCR, Adaptec, Sysgen, Thompson CSF, etc.) |
| | | REMARKS | SCSI is the successor of SASI, a single master bus with similar features. The standard is hampered by many vendor-dependant commands and implementations. |

# 11 Appendix

## 11.1.4 Floppy interface

| | | | |
|---|---|---|---|
| DESCRIPTOR | 8-bit serial, monodirectionnal<br><br>De facto standard for 5" and 3$1/2$" floppy disks | CONNECTOR | 34-pin flat cable<br>Male connector on floppy<br>Female to female connecting flat cable<br><br>Gnd $^1\bullet$ $\bullet^2$ nc<br>Gnd $^3\bullet$ $\bullet^4$ InUse or HeadLoad<br>Gnd $^5\bullet$ $\bullet^6$ Sel3<br>Gnd $^7\bullet$ $\bullet^8$ Index<br>Gnd $^9\bullet$ $\bullet^{10}$ Sel0<br>Gnd $^{11}\bullet$ $\bullet^{12}$ Sel1<br>Gnd $^{13}\bullet$ $\bullet^{14}$ Sel2<br>Gnd $^{15}\bullet$ $\bullet^{16}$ MotorOn<br>Gnd $^{17}\bullet$ $\bullet^{18}$ Dir(out)<br>Gnd $^{19}\bullet$ $\bullet^{20}$ Step<br>Gnd $^{21}\bullet$ $\bullet^{22}$ WriteData<br>Gnd $^{23}\bullet$ $\bullet^{24}$ WriteGate<br>Gnd $^{25}\bullet$ $\bullet^{26}$ Track00<br>Gnd $^{27}\bullet$ $\bullet^{28}$ WriteProt<br>Gnd $^{29}\bullet$ $\bullet^{30}$ ReadData<br>Gnd $^{31}\bullet$ $\bullet^{32}$ SideSel<br>Gnd $^{33}\bullet$ $\bullet^{34}$ Ready |
| SPONSOR | Shugart and all other floppy disk manufacturers $\simeq$1976 | | |
| STANDARD | None | | |
| ADDRESS SPACE | -<br>- | | |
| DATA FORMAT | Serial | | |
| TRANSFER TYPE | 256 bytes per sector | | |
| | | BUS LENGTH | 5m |
| TIMING | MFM or M$^2$FM encoding | | |
| | | DRIVER | Output: 7438 or equivalent<br>Input: 7414 or equivalent with 470 $\Omega$ pull-up resistor |
| ARBITRATION | - | | |
| | | SPEED | 250 kb/s (M$^2$FM)<br>125 kb/s (FM) |
| INTERRUPTS | - | OPTIONS | - |
| | | REFERENCES | Most floppy manufacturers |
| ERROR HANDLING | - | | |
| OTHER FUNCTIONS | - | REMARKS | Future generations of floppies will need a faster interface. SCSI may be the replacement solution |

## 11.1.5 Disk interface ST506/412

| | | | |
|---|---|---|---|
| DESCRIPTOR | 8-bit serial, monodirectionnal<br>De facto standard for 5" and $3^{1/2}$" winchester disks | CONNECTOR | 34-pin and 20-pin flat cable<br>Male connector on disk<br>Female to female connecting flat cable<br><br>J1 (bussed)<br>Gnd 1• •2 Head $2^3$<br>Gnd 3• •4 Head $2^2$<br>Gnd 5• •6 Wr Gate<br>Gnd 7• •8 Seek Complete<br>Gnd 9• •10 Track 0<br>Gnd 11• •12 Wr Fault<br>Gnd 13• •14 Head $2^0$<br>Gnd 15• •16 –<br>Gnd 17• •18 Head $2^1$<br>Gnd 19• •20 Index<br>Gnd 21• •22 Ready<br>Gnd 23• •24 Step<br>Gnd 25• •26 Drive Sel 1<br>Gnd 27• •28 Drive Sel 2<br>Gnd 29• •30 Drive Sel 3<br>Gnd 31• •32 Drive Sel 4<br>Gnd 33• •34 Dir In<br><br>J2 (one per drive)<br>Drive Selecte 1• •2 Gnd<br>Res 3• •4 Res<br>Wr Desabled 5• •6 Gnd<br>Res 7• •8 Res<br>Gnd 9• •10 Gnd<br>Gnd 11• •12 Gnd<br>+MFM Write 13• •14 –MFM Write<br>Gnd 15• •16 Gnd<br>+MFM Read 17• •18 –MFM Read<br>Gnd 19• •20 Gnd |
| SPONSOR | Seagate and all other disk manufacturers<br>≃1981 | | |
| STANDARD | None | | |
| ADDRESS SPACE | – | | |
| DATA FORMAT | 8-bit serial | | |
| TRANSFER TYPE | 256 byte per sector | | |
| TIMING | $M^2FM$ encoding | | |
| ARBITRATION | – | BUS LENGTH | 6m |
| INTERRUPTS | – | DRIVER | J1 outputs: 7438 or equivalent<br>J1 inputs: 7414 or equivalent with 220/330 Ω resistors<br>J2 outputs: 26LS32 differential pair<br>J2 inputs: 26LS32 with 100 Ω res. |
| | | SPEED | 5 Mb/s |
| ERROR HANDLING | – | OPTIONS | – |
| OTHER FUNCTIONS | – | REFERENCES | Most small winchester disk manufacturers |
| | | REMARKS | Future generations of disks will need a faster interface. SCSI may be the replacement solution. |

# 11 Appendix

## 11.2.1 RS 232 or V 24 / V 28

| | | | |
|---|---|---|---|
| DESCRIPTOR | Serial link for connecting a DTE (data terminating equipment) to a DCE (data communication equipment) Usually asynchronous and implemented with a 25-pin connector (ISO-2210) | CONNECTOR | 25-pin female connector on DCE 25-pin male connector on DTE Female to male connecting flat cable <br><br> CCITT  EIA  Usual name <br> 101  AA  Shield     1 — 14 <br> 103  BA  $Tx\overline{D}$   2 — 15 <br> 104  BB  $Rx\overline{D}$   3 — 16 <br> 105  CA  RTS        4 — 17 <br> 106  CB  CTS        5 — 18 <br> 107  CC  DSR        6 — 19 <br> 102  AB  Gnd        7 — 20  DTR  CD 109 <br> 109  CF  CD         8 — 21 <br>                        9 — 22  RI   CE 125 <br>                       10 — 23 <br>                       11 — 24 <br>                       12 — 25 <br>                       13 |
| SPONSOR | EIA (Electronic Industries Association) ≃1969 | | |
| STANDARD | EIA, CCITT, ISO | | |
| ADDRESS SPACE | – | | |
| DATA FORMAT | 5- to 8-bit serial | | |
| | | BUS LENGTH | 20m |
| TRANSFER TYPE | Asynchronous (start-stop transmission) (not part of the standard) | DRIVER | RS 232/V24 drivers <br>       Input level            Output level <br> 0,SPACE,ON: >+3V, <+25V    >+12V <br> 1,MARK,OFF: <-3V, >-25V    <-12V |
| TIMING | Predefined bit-rate | SPEED | 20 kb/s |
| | | OPTIONS | – |
| ARBITRATION | – | | |
| | | REFERENCES | Electronic Industries Association, Standard Sales 2001 Eye Street NW, Washington, DC 20 006, USA or CCITT, CH-1211 Genève 20, Switzerland |
| INTERRUPTS | – | | |
| | | REMARKS | RS232 is used in the microcomputer world for communications between two DTEs. The null-modem is unhappily included into one or both connected devices, and/or into the connecting cable; this is seldomly well documented. As a result, establishing an RS232 connection between two DTEs is frequently a time consuming task. |
| ERROR HANDLING | Optional parity bit | | |
| OTHER FUNCTIONS | – | | |

## 11.2.2 X 20 with DIN-66 258 connectors

| | | | |
|---|---|---|---|
| DESCRIPTOR | Serial asynchronous link | CONNECTOR | 9-pin female connector on DCE<br>9-pin male connector on DTE<br>Female to male connecting cable<br>X20 on DIN 66258 (ISO 4902)<br><br>RS422/V11<br>Shield 1● ●6 -T transmit<br>+T 2● ●7 Gnd<br>Gnd 3● ●8 -R receive<br>+R 4● ●9 nc<br>Gnd 5● <br><br>RS423/V10<br>Shield 1● ●6 T transmit<br>nc 2● ●7 Gnd<br>nc 3● ●8 R receive<br>nc 4● ●9 nc<br>nc 5● |
| SPONSOR | ≃1978 | | |
| STANDARD | CCITT, ISO | | |
| ADDRESS SPACE | – | | |
| DATA FORMAT | 8-bit serial | | |
| TRANSFER TYPE | Asynchronous (start-stop transmission)<br>CCITT alphabet No5 (ASCII) | BUS LENGTH | RS422: 15 m @ 10 Mb/s<br>(V11) 1200 m @ 100 kb/s<br>RS423: 100 m @ 100 kb/s |
| | | DRIVER | RS422/V11 drivers, 100 Ω adapting resistor<br>RS423/V10 drivers, 450 Ω adapting resistor |
| TIMING | Predefined bit-rate | | |
| | | SPEED | According to distance, see above |
| ARBITRATION | – | OPTIONS | – |
| INTERRUPTS | – | REFERENCES | CCITT, Place des Nations<br>CH-1211 Genève 20, Switzerland<br>or<br>US Dept of Commerce, 5285 Port Royal Rd, Springfield, VA 22 161, USA |
| ERROR HANDLING | Optional parity bit | REMARKS | X20 is not well known in the microcomputer world, due to the attachement to RS-232 and lack of supporting ICs. |
| OTHER FUNCTIONS | – | | |

## 11.2.3 X 21 with ISO-4903 connectors

| | | | |
|---|---|---|---|
| DESCRIPTOR | Serial synchronous link | CONNECTOR | 15-pin female connector on DCE<br>15-pin male connector on DTE<br>Female to male connecting cable<br>ISO-4903, RS422/V11<br>Shield 1 — 9 -T<br>transmit T 2 — 10 -C<br>control C 3 — 11 -R<br>receive R 4 — 12 -I<br>indicator I 5 — 13 -S<br>signal timing S 6 — 14 -B<br>byte timing B 7 — 15 reseved<br>Gnd 8 |
| SPONSOR | CCITT<br>≈1978 | | |
| STANDARD | CCITT, ISO | | |
| ADDRESS SPACE | – | | |
| DATA FORMAT | 8-bit serial<br>CCITT alphabet No5 (ASCII) | | |
| TRANSFER TYPE | Synchronous | BUS LENGTH | RS422: 15 m @ 10 Mb/s<br>(V11) 1200 m @ 100 kb/s |
| | | DRIVER | RS422/V11 drivers |
| TIMING | Predefined bit-rate | | |
| | | SPEED | According to distance |
| ARBITRATION | – | | |
| | | OPTIONS | – |
| INTERRUPTS | – | REFERENCES | CCITT, Place des Nations, CH 1211 Genève 20, Switzerland<br>or<br>US Dept of Commerce, 5285 Port Royal Rd, Springfield, VA 22 161, USA |
| ERROR HANDLING | Optional parity bit | REMARKS | X21 is ideally suited for modems. It is however not well supported by microcomputer manufacturers. |
| OTHER FUNCTIONS | – | | |

## 11.2.4 S5/8

| | | | |
|---|---|---|---|
| DESCRIPTOR | Serial link 5V<br>D-devices are self-powered and have an 8-pin female socket<br>S-devices are powered by the D-devices they are connected to, using an attached cable with an 8-pin male plug | CONNECTOR | 8-pin female DIN 45326 connector on self-powered D-devices<br>5-pin male to male (DIN 41524) mirror cable between D-devices<br>8-pin male plug on an attached cable for unpowered S-devices |
| SPONSOR | British Standard Association<br>Central Computer and Telecommunications Agency | | 1● Dinp (Rx$\overline{D}$)<br>2● Gnd<br>3● Dout (Tx$\overline{D}$)<br>4● Hinp (DTR)<br>5● Hout (CTS,Busy)<br>6● Sinp (reserved)<br>7● Soutp (reserved)<br>8● +5V, 20mA |
| STANDARD | Submitted to BSI | | |
| ADDRESS SPACE | – | | |
| DATA FORMAT | 8-bit serial | | |
| | | BUS LENGTH | 10 m (100 m with good cables) |
| TRANSFER TYPE | Asynchronous (start-stop transmission)<br>No parity bit<br>1 stop bit | DRIVER | HCMOS drivers, 5 V<br>Load capacitance < 2500 pF |
| TIMING | 9600 b/s unless a converter box to an old equipment is used | SPEED | 9600 b/s |
| | | OPTIONS | – |
| ARBITRATION | – | | |
| | | REFERENCES | CCTA, Room 213, River Walk House, 157-161 Millbank,<br>London SW1P 4RT, UK |
| INTERRUPTS | – | | |
| ERROR HANDLING | – | REMARKS | S5/8 has been recently proposed and related products using it are still in early production phase (1985).<br>There is a great need for a simple and easy to implement serial link like S5/8 in order to connect personal and lap-top computers with their peripherals.<br>Additional S5/8 standards are planned, to cover software line flow, character coding, escape sequences and possibly document interchange. |
| OTHER FUNCTIONS | Full compatibility to RS-232 requires an active circuit, but in most cases, a passive cable is adequate | | |

# 11 Appendix

## Notes associated with the descriptions of backplane buses

Note 1: The descriptor indicates the address size followed by the data size. Address and data size are separated by a slash (/) if the bus is multiplexed or by a plus (+) if the bus is simplex.
The bus type then follows: a P indicates if the bus is intended for single processor systems (with a permanent master and possibly some DMA temporary masters). A G denotes a global bus for multiprocessors.
The last character pair denotes the main protocol type (see note 4)

Note 2: An OR separates two mutually exclusive options (e.g. the board size is: $23 \times 20$ cm$^2$ OR $10 \times 20$ cm$^2$).

Note 3: LITTLE ENDIAN: the least significant byte of an integer or an address should be stored at the lowest memory address (e.g. INTEL 8086, PDP11).
BIG ENDIAN: the most significant byte is stored at the lowest address (e.g. MOTOROLA 68000, IBM).
NON-JUSTIFIED means that a single byte may be transmitted on either byte lane DA<7..0> or DA<15..8>, etc... depending on the byte's address.
JUSTIFIED means that a single item (byte, doublet) is always transfered on the same lanes, regardless of its address. Some 16-bit buses are byte justified (single byte always on D<7..0>, some 32-bit buses like Multibus II are 16-bit justified.

Note 4: Convention for timing:
Synchronization type:
- HS: 2- or 3-wire handshake (e.g. P1000, MULTIBUS 1, Q-BUS, VME)
- SW: semi-synchronous with wait (e.g. STD, MUBUS)
- CW: clocked by master clock with wait (e.g. STD-88, S-100)
- SY: synchronous with respect to bus clock (e.g. NuBus, Multibus II)

Select mode: (at data time)
- RP-WP: separate read and write pulses (e.g. Multibus 1)
- AW-DS: advanced write and same data strobe for read and write (e.g. VME)
- PAK: positive acknowledge, always present in HS (e.g. VME, QBUS)
- NAK: negative acknowledge - the slave reports transfer problems (e.g. VME)
- MP-PP: separate address strobes for memory + I/O (e.g. Multibus 1)

Note 5: The duration of a single read transfer has been chosen as representative for the bus's speed, admitting that most transfers are reads. This calculation advantages somewhat multiplexed buses and disadvantages somewhat buses capable of sequential transfers. This speed figure considers only bus and protocol delays, but no logic or memory delays. It does not include the arbitration time (which can be zero if the system has only one master or if the default master uses the bus).

Note 6: An OPTION is an alternate specification for a compatible unit. OPTIONS are either COMPATIBLE, UPWARDS COMPATIBLE or INCOMPATIBLE.
"Compatible" options assumes that units which support the alternate options are capable of auto-adapting to the difference between them. Typical of compatible options are the multi-standard TV sets, which recognize the format of the signal and adapt to it, or the "hunt" mode in serial links). Compatible options are seldom.
"Upward compatible" means that if 2 units implement alternate options, only the common part of the functionality is retained, generally the weakest.
"Incompatible" or "conflicting" options are in reality different standards under the same name. Some intermediate unit is necessary to let the incompatible units interwork.

Note 7: In the pin list, lines with alternate definition are enclosed in parenthesis (). In the second column, the origin of the signals is given according to the following key:
- A: arbiter (centralized module or permanent master in single processor systems)
- B: backplane, power supply supervisor
- C: centralized controller, e.g. clock generator (normally in one reserved slot)
- D: daisy chains (one end is a centralized controller, e.g. an arbiter)
- I: interrupter (normally a peripheral, can also be a master)
- M: current bus master or interrupted master in vector fetch, interrupt destination
- R: requester, bidding master in arbitration
- S: slave in transfers
- panel: operator panel
- ser: serial bus, different specification

Note 8: * (asterisk) means inverted signals; signal names in lower cases instead upper cases are used for typographic reasons.

## 11.3.1 IEEE P961 (STD)

| | | | |
|---|---|---|---|
| DESCRIPTOR (notes 1) (note 2) | 16+8 P SW (STD-88: 20/8 P CW) simple, cheap 8-bit processor bus | MULTIPROC. SUPPORT | Single master bus, two-master proposed for standardization centralized multiprocessor possible |
| | | BOARD AREA | 115 mm * 165 mm = 190 cm$^2$ |
| SPONSOR | PRO-LOG, MOSTEK (USA) 1976 | CONNECTOR | Edge, 2*28 contacts |
| STANDARD | IEEE Project 961 STD Manufacturers Group | BUS LENGTH | 16 slots |
| ADDRESS SPACE | MEM: A16 16-bit address A17 possible with MEMEXP (A20 in STD-88) I/O: P8 assumed (separate MEM and I/O strobes) | DRIVER | TTL-LS 3S, 24 mA OC, 24 mA |
| DATA FORMAT (note 3) | D8 8-bit (D16 in evaluation) | SPEED (note 5) | 500 ns/8-bit |
| | | OPTIONS (note 6) | The asynchronous timing depends on the processor The STD-88 (20 bit address multiplexed) is not compatible with some older boards The unique daisy chain may be used for interrupts or for arbitration |
| TRANSFER TYPE | Read + write, refresh, vector (separate read and write strobes) | | |
| TIMING (note 4) | Semisynchronous with wait (SW) (STD-88: clocked semisynchronous with wait) RP-WP | AUXILIARY BUSES | Second connector with iSBX Front panel bus for second daisy chain or interrupt requests |
| ARBITRATION | Central arbiter; daisy chain possible only if not needed by interrupt | REFERENCES | IEEE P961 Commitee Matt Biewer Pro-Log Corp., 2411 Garden Road Monterey, CA 93940, USA |
| INTERRUPTS | Non-maskable interrupt Vectored 8-bit transfers possible if daisy chain is not needed by arbitration 2 interrupt levels | REMARKS | The most popular 8-bit bus in the market. Originally designed for cheap I/O, it has been used in medium performance systems. Mostly used for industrial control and instrumentation. The address extension to 20 bit by multiplexing the data lines (8088 mode) has been done recently by the STD Manufacturer's group: Bert Forbes Ziatech Corporation, 3433 Roberto Court, San Luis Obispo, CA 93401, USA The numerous options make interworking of products of different firms problematic To enhance this standard, the IEEE developped the P1000 bus. |
| ERROR HANDLING | None | | |
| OTHER FUNCTIONS | Refresh, system. clock, cpu clock, status1..0 for logic analyzer | | |

# 11 Appendix

## IEEE P961 (STD)

| Line name | Source | Description | Driver | #Lines |
|---|---|---|---|---|
| Information: | (note 7) | | | |
| A<15..0> | M | byte address | 3S24 | 16 |
| D<7..0> | M/S | data | 3S24 | 8 |
| | | (multiplexed with A<23..16> in STD-88) | | |
| Command & Status: | | | | |
| MEMRQ* | M | MEM address | 3S24 | 1 |
| IOREQ* | M | I/O address | 3S24 | 1 |
| MEMEXP | M/C | memory expansion or overlay | 3S24 | 1 |
| IOEXP | M/C | I/O substitution | 3S24 | 1 |
| REFRESH* | M/C | refresh cycle | 3S24 | 1 |
| STATUS<1..0> | M | instruction fetch / operation type | 3S24 | 2 |
| Control & Timing: | | | | |
| CLOCK* | M | processor clock (especially STD-88) | TP24 | 1 |
| MCSYNC* | M | address latch enable (demultiplexing) | 3S24 | 1 |
| CNTRL* | M | auxiliary timing | 3S24 | 1 |
| RD* | M | read strobe | 3S24 | 1 |
| WR* | M | write strobe | 3S24 | 1 |
| WAITRQ* | S | wait request | OC24 | 1 |
| Arbitration: | | | | |
| BUSRQ* | R | bus requested by bidding master | OC24 | 1 |
| BUSAK* | A | bus grant from permanent master | TP24 | 1 |
| PCI/PCO | D | daisy chain (arbitration OR interrupt) | TP24 | 2 |
| Interrupt: | | | | |
| INTRQ* | I | interrupt requested | OC24 | 1 |
| INTAK* | M | interrupt vector read strobe | 3S24 | 1 |
| NMIRQ* | I | non maskable interrupt requested | OC24 | 1 |
| Others: | | | | |
| SYSRESET* | M | reset | OC24 | 1 |
| PBRESET* | panel | push-button reset | OC24 | 1 |
| (DCPOWOK* | B | dc power OK (STD-88 instead of VBB#2) | OC24 | 1) |
| Power: | | | | |
| GND (0V) | | logic ground | | 2 |
| +5 V | | main power supply | | 2 |
| VBB#1 | | −5 V OR standby supply VBAT in STD-88 | | 1 |
| VBB#2 | | −5 V supply OR DCPOWOK* in STD-88 | | 1 |
| AUX GND | | auxiliary ground | | 2 |
| AUX +12 V | | +12 Vdc auxiliary supply | | 1 |
| AUX −12 V | | −12 Vdc auxiliary supply | | 1 |
| | | | TOTAL: | 56 |

3S24: three-state, 24 mA, terminated by 4.7 kΩ to +5 V at PM slot
TP24: TTL totem pole, 24 mA, not terminated (except CLOCK as 3S24)
OC24: open-collector, 24 mA, terminated by 511 Ω to +5V at PM slot
                                10 kΩ pullup at each driver.

Recommended termination for all bus lines is a 100 Ω resistor to ground decoupled by a 100 pF capacitor at the end of the backplane.

Connector pinout:

| Component side | Solder side |
|---|---|
| +5 V — 1 | 2 — +5 V |
| Gnd — 3 | 4 — Gnd |
| VBB #1 — 5 | 6 — VBB #2 |
| D3 — 7 | 8 — D7 |
| D2 — 9 | 10 — D6 |
| D1 — 11 | 12 — D5 |
| D0 — 13 | 14 — D4 |
| A7 — 15 | 16 — A15 |
| A6 — 17 | 18 — A14 |
| A5 — 19 | 20 — A13 |
| A4 — 21 | 22 — A12 |
| A3 — 23 | 24 — A11 |
| A2 — 25 | 26 — A10 |
| A1 — 27 | 28 — A9 |
| A0 — 29 | 30 — A8 |
| WR* — 31 | 32 — RD* |
| IORQ* — 33 | 34 — MEMRQ* |
| IOEXP — 35 | 36 — MEMEX |
| Refresh — 37 | 38 — Mcsynch* |
| Status1 — 39 | 40 — Status0* |
| BusAK* — 41 | 42 — BusRQ* |
| IntAK* — 43 | 44 — IntRQ* |
| WaitRQ* — 45 | 46 — NMIrq* |
| Sysreset* — 47 | 48 — Pbreset* |
| Clock* — 49 | 50 — Cntrl* |
| PCo — 51 | 52 — PCi |
| Aux Gnd — 53 | 54 — Aux Gnd |
| Aux +V — 55 | 56 — Aux −V |

## 11.3.2 MUBUS

| | | | |
|---|---|---|---|
| DESCRIPTOR (notes 1) (note 2) | 16+16 P SW 8-bit processor bus. | MULTIPROC. SUPPORT | Centralized multiprocessor only: single interrupt destination, decentralized arbitration |
| | | BOARD AREA | Single euroboard 100 mm * 160 mm = 160 cm$^2$ |
| SPONSOR | Swiss Federal Institute of Technology and Politecnico Torino, Italy, 1976 | CONNECTOR | Edge, 2*37 contacts |
| STANDARD | EPFL, user's group GESO | BUS LENGTH | 50 cm, 21 slots |
| ADDRESS SPACE | MEM: A16 16-bit address I/O: P8 8-bit assumed (P16 unofficial) (separate strobe for MEM & I/O) | DRIVER | TTL-LS 3S, 24 mA OC, 24 mA |
| DATA FORMAT (note 3) | D16 OR D8 no single byte select in D16 | SPEED (note 5) | 200 ns/16-bit |
| TRANSFER TYPE | Read, write, refresh , vector (advanced R/W indicator) | OPTIONS (note 6) | Many versions exist on different connectors, in particular DIN or BERG. Some add an "Enable" line to be compatible with motorola's 6809. Numerous obsolete lines are used for other purposes like Phantom lines (substitution of destination); extreme contacts (0 and 38) are sometimes used for EPROM programming voltages. |
| TIMING (note 4) | Semi-synchronous with Wait and Nodata lines: AW-DS (MEM & I/O address strobe are data strobes) | AUXILIARY BUSES | none |
| ARBITRATION | Daisy chain, fair recommended, two arbitration levels | REFERENCES | MICROSCOPE Special issue on MuBus Standard Vol.1 No 8. April 1977 P.O.Box 141, CH-1000 Lausanne 13, Switzerland |
| INTERRUPTS | Vectored 8-bit transfers (daisy chain), non-maskable interrupt | REMARKS | The Mubus was originally designed as standard bus of the Laboratoire de Microinformatique of the Swiss Federal Institute of Technology, Lausanne. It is popular in Western Switzerland and Northern Italy, It is probably the cheapest 8-bit bus available. There is a small timing delay with processors such as Z-80 which do not announce in advance the kind of transfer (Read/Write), but it is quite easy to interface and unproblematic in timing. |
| ERROR HANDLING | None | | |
| OTHER FUNCTIONS | Refresh, system clock, 50 Hz/1 Hz clock. | | |

# 11 Appendix

| | | MUBUS | | |
|---|---|---|---|---|
| Line name | Source | Description | Driver | #Lines |
| Information: | (note 7) | | | |
| A<15..0> | M | address | 3S24 | 16 |
| D<15..0> | M/S | data | 3S24 | 16 |
| Command & Status: | | | | |
| WRITE* | M | advanced write | 3S24 | 1 |
| Control & Timing: | | | | |
| ADMEM* | M | address & write data valid | 3S24 | 1 |
| ADPER* | M | peripheral & write data valid | 3S24 | 1 |
| REFRESH* | M | refresh cycle (7 address bits out) | 3S24 | 1 |
| NOTYET* | S | wait signal from slave | OC24 | 1 |
| NODA* | C | disables drivers for data substitution | 3S24 | 1 |
| Arbitration: | | | | |
| HOLDREQ* | R | bus requested | OC24 | 1 |
| PROCREQ* | R | bus requested by high-priority master | OC24 | 1 |
| HOLDACK* | A | bus acknowledge (bus free) | 3S24 | 1 |
| HOLDin | D | bus grant in (pull-up) | TP5 | 1 |
| HOLDout | D | bus grant out | TP5 | 1 |
| Interrupt: | | | | |
| INTREQ* | I | interrupt requested | OC24 | 1 |
| INTACK* | M | interrupt read vector | 3S24 | 1 |
| INTin | D | interrupt vector grant in (pull-up) | TP5 | 1 |
| INTout | D | interrupt vector grant out | TP5 | 1 |
| NMI* | I | non-maskable interrupt requested | OC24 | 1 |
| Miscellaneous: | | | | |
| RESET* | panel | system reset pulse | OC24 | 1 |
| SYSTEMCLOCK | B | unspecified system clock | TP24 | 1 |
| USERSCLOCK | B | 1 Hz or 50 Hz clock | TP24 | 1 |
| coding slots | | | | 2 |
| Power: | | | | |
| GND (0V) | | logic ground | | 4 |
| +5 V | | main power supply | | 4 |
| -5 V | | auxiliary power supplies | | 2 |
| +12 V | | | | 2 |
| -12 V | | | | 2 |
| GND (A) | | analog ground and +/-15 V supplies | | 2 |
| +15 V (A) | | | | 1 |
| -15 V (A) | | | | 1 |
| GND(X), | | special supply for back-up or isolated parts | | 2 |
| +5V(X) | | | | 1 |
| | | | TOTAL: | 74 |

3S24: three-state,   24 mA,   terminated by 1 kΩ to +5 V at each end
OC24: open-collector, 24 mA,  terminated by 511 Ω to +5 V at PM slot
TP24: TTL totem pole, 24 mA,  terminated by 1 kΩ to +5 V at each end
TP5 : TTL totem pole,  5 mA,  not terminated (daisy chain not bused)

Connector pinout:

| # | a | b |
|---|---|---|
| 1 | +15 V (A) | -15 V (A) |
| 2 | Gnd (A) | Gnd (A) |
| 3 | Gnd (X) | Gnd (X) |
| 4 | +12 V | +12 V |
| 5 | -12 V | -12 V |
| 6 | 50 Hz/1 Hz | +5 V (X) |
| 7 | (key) | (key) |
| 8 | AD0 | AD8 |
| 9 | AD1 | AD9 |
| 10 | AD2 | AD10 |
| 11 | AD3 | AD11 |
| 12 | AD4 | AD12 |
| 13 | AD5 | AD13 |
| 14 | AD6 | AD14 |
| 15 | AD7 | AD15 |
| 16 | Refresh* | (SystClock) |
| 17 | NMI* | Procreq* |
| 18 | Intreq* | Intack* |
| 19 | Holdreq* | Holdack* |
| 20 | Reset* | Noda* |
| 21 | Write* | Admem* |
| 22 | Notyet* | Adper* |
| 23 | DA0 | (DA8) |
| 24 | DA1 | (DA9) |
| 25 | DA2 | (DA10) |
| 26 | DA3 | (DA11) |
| 27 | DA4 | (DA12) |
| 28 | DA5 | (DA13) |
| 29 | DA6 | (DA14) |
| 30 | DA7 | (DA15) |
| 31 | Intout | Intin |
| 32 | Holdout | Holdin |
| 33 | -5 V | -5 V |
| 34 | +5 V | +5 V |
| 35 | +5 V | +5 V |
| 36 | Gnd | Gnd |
| 37 | Gnd | Gnd |

### 11.3.3 IEEE P1000 (STE)

| | | | |
|---|---|---|---|
| DESCRIPTOR (notes 1) (note 2) | 20+8 P HS 8-bit processor bus. | MULTIPROC. SUPPORT | Centralized interrupt, decentralized arbitration, multiprocessor possible up to three masters |
| | | BOARD AREA | Single euroboard 100 mm * 160 mm = 160 cm$^2$ |
| SPONSOR | IEEE-Computer Society 1982 | CONNECTOR | Two-piece 64 pin DIN 41612-C64 |
| STANDARD | IEEE project 1000 | BUS LENGTH | 50 cm, 21 slots (14 at minimal spacing 15 mm) |
| ADDRESS SPACE | MEM: A20 (20-bit) I/O: P12 (12-bit) (MEM/IO encoded in command) | DRIVER | TTL-LS 3S, 24 mA OC, 24 mA |
| DATA FORMAT (note 3) | D8 (8-bit only) | SPEED (note 5) | 200 ns/ 8 bit |
| | | OPTIONS (note 6) | none |
| TRANSFER TYPE | Read, write, read-modify-write, interrupt vector fetch, sequential (R/W encoded in command, RMW, SEQ not announced) | | |
| TIMING (note 4) | Handshake on data, (DATSTB, DATACK) (separate address and data strobe) HS, AW-DS, PAK | AUXILIARY BUSES | None |
| ARBITRATION | Central arbiter on backplane | REFERENCES | IEEE P1000 working group W. Shield, chairman 4901 Morena Blvd, Suite 804 San Diego, CA 92117, USA |
| INTERRUPTS | 8 attention lines, implicit response or explicit vector transfer | REMARKS | The P1000 (originally named STE) follows the objective of the STD bus but with european board format and extension of the address to 20 bits. It resulted in a completely different bus which is quite streamlined today. Its market share is still insignificant, but expected to grow. It could become a standard for 8-bit devices used in process control. The vector fetch interrupt mode is quite complicated for a simple processor bus. |
| ERROR HANDLING | SYSERR line | | |
| OTHER FUNCTIONS | Clock | | |

# 11 Appendix

## IEEE P1000 (STE)

| Line name | Source | Description | Driver | #Lines |
|---|---|---|---|---|
| Information: | (note 7) | | | |
| A<19..00> | M | address | 3S24 | 20 |
| D<7..0> | M/S | data | 3S24 | 8 |
| Command & Status: | | | | |
| CM<2..0> | M | (command clocked by DATSTB !) | 3S24 | 3 |
| | | CODES: | | |
| | | 000 reserved     100 I/O Write | | |
| | | 001 reserved     101 I/O Read | | |
| | | 010 reserved     110 memory Write | | |
| | | 011 vector fetch 111 memory Read | | |
| Control & Timing: | | | | |
| ADRSTB* | M | address strobe | 3S24 | 1 |
| DATSTB* | M | data strobe | 3S24 | 1 |
| DATACK* | S | data positive acknowledge | 0C24 | 1 |
| TFRERR* | S | transfer error (negative acknowledge) | 0C24 | 1 |
| Arbitration: | | | | |
| BUSRQ<1..0>* | R | bus request (not bussed, to arbiter) | 0C24 | 2 |
| BUSAK<1..0>* | A | bus grant (from arbiter, no daisy) | TP24 | 2 |
| Interrupt: | | | | |
| ATNRQ<7..0>* | I | Attention (Interrupt) Request | 0C24 | 8 |
| | | 0 highest priority | | |
| Others: | | | | |
| SYSRST* | A | system reset | 0C24 | 1 |
| SYSCLK | C | system clock | TP24 | 1 |
| Power: | | | | |
| GND (0V) | | logic ground | | 8 |
| +5 V | | main power supply | | 4 |
| +12 V | | auxiliary supply (previously reserved) | | 1 |
| -12 V | | | | 1 |
| +VSTBY | | standby voltage (+5 V) | | 1 |
| | | | TOTAL: | 64 |

3S24: three-state, 24 mA, terminated by 270 Ω to +2.8 V at each end
0C24: open-collector, 24 mA, terminated by 270 Ω to +2.8 V at each end
TP24: TTL totem pole, 24 mA, terminated by 270 Ω to +2.8 V at each end
(except BUSAK*, pull-up to +5 V on board)

Connector pinout:

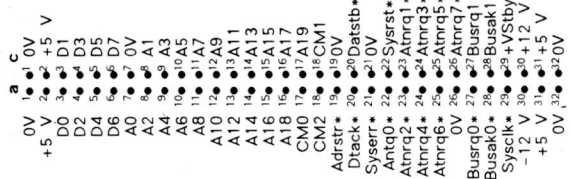

## 11.3.4 IEEE 696 (S100)

| | | | |
|---|---|---|---|
| DESCRIPTOR (notes 1) (note 2) | 24+16 P CW<br>Hobby computer bus | MULTIPROC. SUPPORT | Not well suited for multiprocessor, difficult master transfer sequence, centralized interrupts. |
| | | BOARD AREA | 255 mm * 130 mm = 331 cm$^2$ |
| SPONSOR | MITS, IEEE<br>1975 (1983) | CONNECTOR | Edge, 100 contacts |
| STANDARD | IEEE 696 | BUS LENGTH | ≃20 boards spaced 2 cm |
| ADDRESS SPACE | MEM:<br>   A24 (A16 bit obsolete)<br>I/O:<br>   P8<br>(command selects MEM or I/O at address time but additionally MWRT is issued at data write time for front panel compatibility) | DRIVER | TTL-LS<br>3S,   24 mA<br>OC,  24 mA |
| DATA FORMAT (note 3) | D8 uses D<15..8> for read, D<7..0> for write (justified)<br>D16 needs request/ack negotiation, D<7..0> is even address (uncommited data format, formerly big endian) | SPEED (note 5) | 1000 ns/ 16 bit |
| | | OPTIONS (note 6) | Old designs (8bit) should be upward compatible (no option) but numerous variants exist (e.g. 16-bit or 24 bit address). |
| TRANSFER TYPE | Read, write, vector fetch | | |
| TIMING (note 4) | Clock-synchronized halfsynchronous with WAIT by RDY or XRDY;<br>CW | AUXILIARY BUSES | None. |
| ARBITRATION | Self-selection 4 lines, one permanent master, explicitly disabled during master transfer (4 lines + 2 transfers required) | REFERENCES | IEEE Std 696-1983<br>IEEE Computer Society Order Department<br>PO Box 80452<br>Worldway Postal Center,<br>Los Angeles, CA 90080, USA |
| INTERRUPTS | 7 prioritized interrupt levels, no daisy chain, single destination. | REMARKS | Originally designed for the ALTAIR microcomputer, the S100 (surplus 100 pin bus) had a 16-bit address and separate 8-bit data paths for read and write (due to the lack of bidirectional transceivers at that time) and reflected the 8080 bus structure. Mechanisms such as disable lines and other phantoms were required at a time many functions were centralized in a front-panel. The S100 was very popular for personal computers. It was completely respecified during the standardization by the IEEE (696). There are now in reality two standards: the S100-8 and the 696. Today S-100 is superseded by the IEEE 796 (Multibus). It is still one of the cheapest buses in industry. |
| ERROR HANDLING | ERROR* signals slave problems | | |
| OTHER FUNCTIONS | System clock different from timing clock φ<br>push-button reset | | |

# 11 Appendix

## IEEE 696 (S100)

| Line name | Source | Description | Driver | #Lines |
|---|---|---|---|---|
| **Information:** | (note 7) | | | |
| A<23..00> | M | byte address | 3S24 | 24 |
| D<15..00> | M/S | data lanes | 3S24 | 16 |
| | | in older designs, D<7..0> are master data in write cycles, D<15..8> are slave data in read cycles | | |
| **Command & Status:** | | | | |
| sMEMR | M | memory read (no interrupt) | 3S24 | 1 |
| sM1 | M | instruction fetch | 3S24 | 1 |
| sINP | M | read from peripheral | 3S24 | 1 |
| sOUT | M | write to peripheral | 3S24 | 1 |
| sWO* | M | write transfer | 3S24 | 1 |
| sINTA | M | interrupt cycle | 3S24 | 1 |
| sHLTA | M | acknowledges a halt | 3S24 | 1 |
| sXTRQ* | M | 16-bit transfer requested | 3S24 | 1 |
| **Control & Timing** | | | | |
| φ | M | central clock | TP24 | 1 |
| pSYNC* | M | identifies first bus cycle | 3S24 | 1 |
| pSTVAL* | M | status valid | 3S24 | 1 |
| pWR* | M | write pulse | 3S24 | 1 |
| pDBIN* | M | read pulse | 3S24 | 1 |
| MWRT* | panel | front panel generated write signal | TP24 | 1 |
| PHANTOM* | C | substitutes the current slave | OC24 | 1 |
| RDY | S | first of two ready signals | OC24 | 1 |
| XRDY | S | second of two ready signals | | 1 |
| SIXTN* | S | slave accepts 16-bit mode | OC24 | 1 |
| ERROR* | S | slave detected error | OC24 | 1 |
| **Arbitration:** | | | | |
| pHLDA* | A | permanent master releases bus | TP24 | 1 |
| DMA<3..0>* | R | master ID lines for self-selection | OC24 | 4 |
| HOLD* | M | asserted by the new master | OC24 | 1 |
| SDSB* | M | disables the 8 status signals | OC24 | 1 |
| CDSB* | M | disables the 5 control signals | OC24 | 1 |
| ADSB* | M | disables the A<15..00> address lines | OC24 | 1 |
| DODSB* | M | disables the D<7..0> master data lines | OC24 | 1 |
| **Interrupt:** | | | | |
| INT* | I | interrupt requested | OC24 | 1 |
| VI<7..0> | I | vectored interrupt request | OC24 | 8 |
| NMI* | I | non-maskable interrupt | OC24 | 1 |
| **Others:** | | | | |
| RESET* | panel | reset pulse | OC24 | 1 |
| SLAVE CLR* | C | clears all slaves | OC24 | 1 |
| POC* | B | power-on clear | OC24 | 1 |
| PWRFAIL* | B | power fail pending | OC24 | 1 |
| CLOCK | C | 2 MHz clock | | 1 |
| NDEF | | not defined | | 3 |
| RFU | | reserved for future use | | 4 |
| **Power:** | | | | |
| GND (0V) | | logic ground | | 5 |
| +8 V | | unregulated main power supply | | 2 |
| +16 V | | unregulated auxiliary supply | | 1 |
| -16 V | | unregulated auxiliary supply | | 1 |
| | | | TOTAL: | 100 |

3S24: three-state, 24 mA, terminated by 180 Ω to 2.6 V at one end
OC24: open-collector, 24 mA, terminated by 180 Ω to 2.6 V and 1.5 kΩ to +5 V at one end
TP24: TTL totem pole, 24 mA, terminated by 180 Ω to 2.6 V at one end (except daisy chain)

Connector pinout:

| Pin | Signal | Pin | Signal | Pin | Signal | Pin | Signal | Pin | Signal |
|---|---|---|---|---|---|---|---|---|---|
| 1 | +8V | 11 | A20 | 21 | nc | 31 | A2 | 41 | D12 |
| 2 | +16V | 12 | A21 | 22 | ADSB* | 32 | A6 | 42 | D13 |
| 3 | XRDY | 13 | A22 | 23 | DODSB* | 33 | A7 | 43 | D16 |
| 4 | V10* | 14 | A23 | 24 | φ | 34 | A8 | 44 | D08 |
| 5 | V12* | 15 | nc | 25 | pSTVAL* | 35 | A13 | 45 | sINP |
| 6 | V13* | 16 | nc | 26 | pHLDA* | 36 | A14 | 46 | sINTA |
| 7 | V14* | 17 | nc | 27 | Res | 37 | A11 | 47 | sWO* |
| 8 | V15* | 18 | pSYNC* | 28 | Res | 38 | D02 | 48 | ERROR* |
| 9 | V16* | 19 | pWR* | 29 | A5 | 39 | D03 | 49 | POC* |
| 10 | V17* | 20 | Gnd | 30 | A4 | 40 | D07 | 50 | Gnd |
| 51 | +8V | 61 | A20 | 71 | nc | 81 | A1 | 91 | D11 |
| 52 | -16V | 62 | A21 | 72 | RDY | 82 | A3 | 92 | D13 |
| 53 | Gnd | 63 | A22 | 73 | INT* | 83 | A4 | 93 | D15 |
| 54 | SlaveClr* | 64 | A23 | 74 | HOLD* | 84 | A9 | 94 | D09 |
| 55 | DMA0* | 65 | nc | 75 | Reset* | 85 | A12 | 95 | sOUT |
| 56 | DMA1* | 66 | nc | 76 | pSYNC* | 86 | A0 | 96 | sMEMR |
| 57 | DMA2* | 67 | Phantom* | 77 | pWR* | 87 | A10 | 97 | sHLTA |
| 58 | sXTRQ* | 68 | MWRT | 78 | pDBIN | 88 | D00 | 98 | CLOCK |
| 59 | A19 | 69 | Res | 79 | A0 | 89 | D04 | 99 | POC* |
| 60 | SIXTN* | 70 | Gnd | 80 | A1 | 90 | D05 | 100 | Gnd |

## 11.3.5 IEEE 796 (MULTIBUS) and AMS-M

| | | | |
|---|---|---|---|
| DESCRIPTOR (notes 1) (note 2) | MUL: Intel Multibus 1, IEEE 796 (AMS: Siemens AMS-M Multibus on eurocard) 20+16 P HS (24+16 P HS) 16-bit non-multiplexed processor bus, extended to 24-bit address and eurocards by Siemens as "AMS-M" | MULTIPROC. SUPPORT | Multi-master arbitration, bus locking Up to 8 possible interrupt destinations (without vector) Several products exist |
| | | BOARD AREA | MUL: 305 mm * 170 mm = 522 cm$^2$ (AMS: 233 mm * 160 mm = 373 cm$^2$) |
| SPONSOR | INTEL, (Siemens) 1976 | CONNECTOR | MUL: edge P1 86 pins (ASM: two-piece 96 pins DIN 41612-C96) |
| STANDARD | MUL: IEEE 796, IEC (AMS: IEC, DIN) | BUS LENGTH | 45.7 cm, 16 slots (20 slots) |
| ADDRESS SPACE | MEM:     A16:   16-bit     A20:   20-bit     A24:   24-bit (AMS) I/O:     P8:    8-bit     P16:  16-bit | DRIVER | TTL-LS MUL: 3S,OC 16 mA (AMS: 3S,OC 48 mA) |
| | | SPEED (note 5) | 200 ns / 16 bit |
| DATA FORMAT (note 3) | D8:    8-bit D16:  16-bit (8-bit justified select by ADR+ Byte High Enable BHE) little endian | OPTIONS (note 6) | Data path: D8 OR D16 Memory address: M16 OR M20 (OR M24) I/O address: P8 OR P16 Interrupt cycles: V0 OR V2 OR V3 Interrupt triggering: edge OR level OR both Arbiter: centralized OR serial |
| TRANSFER TYPE | Read, write, vectored interrupt with 2 cycles (V2) and 3 cycles (V3) | | |
| TIMING (note 4) | Handshaken with RP-WP, RP-WP also serve as address strobes. XACK is slave handshake (PAK) | AUXILIARY BUSES | iLBX: memory execution bus on P2 iSBX: piggy-back I/O expansion Multichannel: on front connector |
| ARBITRATION | All boards configurable for both DAI: daisy chain BPRI/BPRO and CEN: centralized arbitration with individual BREQ/Grant Default mastership (CBRQ) Pipeline with data transfer (BUSY) Synchronous sampling (BCLK) | REFERENCES | IEEE Std 796 (Multibus) IEEE Computer Society Order Department POBox 80452 Worldway Postal Center Los Angeles, CA 90080, USA |
| INTERRUPTS | 8 request lines, either without bus vector (= V0 mode) or with vector fetch over the bus in 8085 ( 3 INTA pulses = V3) or 8086 (2 INTA = V2) mode; triggering is either edge (obsolete) or level | REMARKS | The most popular microprocessor bus in industry. Supported by more than 200 vendors and offering some 2500 boards in 1985, its share of the market is today about 50% in the US. Although the use of the second connector P2 is not specified in the standard, Intel and others use P2 to extend the address to 24 bits and perform additional functions (see Application Note AP-28A of Intel). Intel persists in numbering the lines in hexadecimal notation. |
| ERROR HANDLING | None, second connector P2 has some error report lines (not 796) if not used by iLBX | | |
| OTHER FUNCTIONS | Inhibit functions for selective addressing of RAM or PROM (obsolete use) | | |

# 11 Appendix

## IEEE 796 (MULTIBUS) and AMS-M

AMS-M specific features are noted between { }. The DIN 64-pin connector is not documented below

| Line Name | Source | Description | Driver | #Lines |
|---|---|---|---|---|
| **Information:** (note 7) | | | | |
| ADR<19..00> | M | byte address (IEEE 796) | 3S16 | 20 |
| {ADR<23..00> | M | byte address (AMS-M) | 3S24 | (4)} |
| DAT<15..00> | M/S | data | 3S16 | 16 |
| **Command & Status:** | | | | |
| BHEN* | M | select byte on DAT< 7..0> if ADR0 is 0 or DAT<15..8> if ADR0 is 1 | 3S16 | 1 |
| LOCK* | M | lock operation over several transfers | 3S16 | 1 |
| INH<2..1>* | C | inhibit lines for slave substitution (prioritized) | OC16 | 2 |
| **Control & Timing:** | | | | |
| MWTC* | M | memory write pulse | 3S32 | 1 |
| MRDC* | M | memory read pulse | 3S32 | 1 |
| IOWC* | M | peripheral write pulse | 3S32 | 1 |
| IORC* | M | peripheral read pulse | 3S32 | 1 |
| XACK* | M | slave positive acknowledge | 3S32 | 1 |
| **Arbitration:** | | | | |
| BCLK* | A | arbitration clock <10 MHz | TP48 | 1 |
| BPRN* | A/D | bus grant of centralized arbiter OR daisy chain in for serial arbitration | TP5 | 1 |
| BPRO* | D | daisy chain out for serial arbitration | TP5 | 1 |
| BUSY* | M | bus busy | OC20 | 1 |
| CBRQ* | R | bus requested by at least one device | OC20 | 1 |
| BREQ* | R | bus request by a master device (not bussed, used for parallel arbitration) | TP5 | 1 |
| **Interrupt:** | | | | |
| INT<7..0>* | I | interrupt requested (prioritized) | OC16 | 8 |
| INTA* | M | interrupt acknowledge (vector fetch) | 3S32 | 1 |
| **Others:** | | | | |
| INIT* | panel | reset pulse | OC32 | 1 |
| CCLK* | C | constant clock <10 MHz, unspecified | TP48 | 1 |
| reserved | | MUL: 4 lines (former -5V are now reserved) {AMS: 8 lines | | 4 (4)} |
| **Power:** | | | | |
| GND (0V) | | logic ground | | 8 |
| +5 V | | main power supply | | 8 |
| +12 V | | +12 Vdc auxiliary supply | | 2 |
| (-5 V | | -5 V dc auxiliary supply (from reserved lines) | | (2) |
| -12 V | | -12 V dc auxiliary supply | | 2 |
| | | | TOTAL: | 86 {96} |

**Connector pinout:**

3S32: three-state, 32 mA, terminated by 1 kΩ to +5 V (one end), except XACK, terminated by 510 Ω to +5 V)

3S16: three-state, 16 mA, terminated by 2.2 kΩ to +5 V (one end)

OC16: open collector, 16 mA, terminated by 1 kΩ to +5 V (one end)

OC20: open collector, 20 mA, terminated by 1 kΩ to +5 V (one end)

OC32: open collector, 32 mA, terminated by 2.2 kΩ to +5 V (one end)

TP5: TTL totem pole, 5 mA, terminated by pull-up 1 kΩ at arbiter (fac.)

TP48: TTL totem pole, 48 mA, terminated by 220//330 Ω to +5 V on backplane.

(P2) Comp. side / Solder side:
2 Gnd / 1 Gnd
4 +5 V / 3 +5 V
6 +5 Vbat / 5 Vbat
8 Res / 7 Res
10 Res / 9 E²PROMpower
12 Vbat / 11 Vbat
14 Res / 13 +12 Vbat
16 -12 Vbat / 15 -5 Vbat
18 ACLow / 17 Res
20 MPRO* / 19 Res
22 Gnd / 21 Res
24 +15 V / 23 -15 V
26 -15 V / 25 +15 V
28 Halt* / 27 Par1*
30 Wait* / 29 PLC*
32 ALE / 31 Par2*
34 Res / 33 Res
36 Res / 35 Res
38 Res / 37 Res
40 Res / 39 Res
42 Res / 41 Res
44 Res / 43 Res
46 Res / 45 Res
48 Res / 47 Res
50 Res / 49 Res
52 Res / 51 Res
54 Res / 53 Res
56 Res / 55 Res
58 adr23* / 57 Res
60 Res / 59 adr20*,adr21*

(P1) Comp. side / Solder side:
2 Gnd / 1 Gnd
4 +5 V / 3 +5 V
6 +5 V / 5 +5 V
8 +12 V / 7 +12 V
10 Res / 9 Res
12 Gnd / 11 Gnd
14 INIT* / 13 BClk*
16 BPRO* / 15 BPRN*
18 BREQ* / 17 BUSY*
20 MWTC* / 19 MRDC*
22 IOWC* / 21 IORC*
24 INH1* / 23 XACK*
26 INH2* / 25 LOCK*
28 AD16* / 27 BHEN*
30 AD17* / 29 CBRQ*
32 AD18* / 31 CCLK*
34 AD19* / 33 INTA*
36 INT6* / 35 INT7*
38 INT4* / 37 INT5*
40 INT2* / 39 INT3*
42 INT0* / 41 INT1*
44 ADR14* / 43 ADR15*
46 ADR12* / 45 ADR13*
48 ADR10* / 47 ADR11*
50 ADR8* / 49 ADR9*
52 ADR6* / 51 ADR7*
54 ADR4* / 53 ADR5*
56 ADR2* / 55 ADR3*
58 ADR0* / 57 ADR1*
60 DAT14* / 59 DAT15*
62 DAT12* / 61 DAT13*
64 DAT10* / 63 DAT11*
66 DAT8* / 65 DAT9*
68 DAT6* / 67 DAT7*
70 DAT4* / 69 DAT5*
72 DAT2* / 71 DAT3*
74 DAT0* / 73 DAT1*
76 Gnd / 75 Gnd
78 Res / 77 Res
80 -12 V / 79 -12 V
82 +5 V / 81 +5 V
84 +5 V / 83 +5 V
86 Gnd / 85 Gnd

## 11.3.6 G-64 and G-96

| | | | |
|---|---|---|---|
| DESCRIPTOR (notes 1) (note 2) | G-64: 16 + 16 .P, (SW OR HS) {G-96: 24 + 16 P, (SW OR HS)} processor bus, industrial applications | MULTIPROC. SUPPORT | G-96 supports up to 32 masters (distributed arbitration) |
| | | BOARD AREA | Single euroboard 160 mm * 100 mm = 160 cm$^2$ |
| SPONSOR | GESPAC 1981 | CONNECTOR | Two-piece DIN-41612C-96 G-64: uses rows a + b {G-96: uses rows a, b + c} |
| STANDARD | None | BUS LENGTH | 20 slots, 47.5 cm |
| ADDRESS SPACE | MEM: G-64: A16 (A17 with page) {G-96: A24} I/O: P10 separate address strobes for MEM and I/O. | DRIVER | TTL-LS 3S, 48 mA OC, 48 mA |
| DATA FORMAT (note 3) | D16: big-endian like 68000 non-justified (separate byte lane strobes) | SPEED (note 5) | CW: 1000 ns/16 bit HS: 200 ns/16 bit |
| | | OPTIONS (note 6) | G-96 OR G-64 (see remarks) Synchronous OR handshake operating mode MCLOCK OR SYSCLOCK Interrupt lines definition |
| TRANSFER TYPE | Read, write, read-modify-write Vector fetch | | |
| TIMING (note 4) | Dual timing protocol: SW: synchronous/wait mode (6809) HS: handshake mode (68000), PAK,AW | AUXILIARY BUSES | None. |
| ARBITRATION | G-64 uses daisy chain (if interrupt does not use it) G-96 uses self-selection with 6 ID lines | REFERENCES | GESPAC 3, chemin des Aulx CH-1228 Geneva, Switzerland or 550 E. Grandview Mesa, AZ 85203, USA |
| INTERRUPTS | Non-vectored (NMI) Two-level vectored interrupts arbitrate by daisy chain, if not used for bus arbitration Prioritized interrupts as alternate line definition | REMARKS | G-64 has a double timing protocol: either synchronous (similar 6809) or either 2-wire handshaken (like the 68000); Data are active low, but addresses are not, which is rather seldom. The G-96 option is in fact a different bus which adds 32 lines ( 8 address, 8 reserved, 2 interrupt request, 7 arbitration lines, 2 utilities and 5 power lines). Its self-select arbitration is completely different from G-64. |
| ERROR HANDLING | Negative acknowledge (BERR*) OR parity error report | | |
| OTHER FUNCTIONS | Halt, Memory Clock OR System Clock | | |

# 11 Appendix

## G-64 and G-96

| Line Name | Source | Description | Driver | #Lines |
|---|---|---|---|---|

Signals used for handshaken mode (double-defined lines) are between parenthesis
Signals specific to G-96 (c-row of connector) are between brackets

Information:  (note 7)
```
  A<15..00>      M       byte address                               3S48    16
 {A<23..16>     M       byte address (G96)                         3S48    { 8}
  D<15..00>*    M/S     data                                       3S48    16
Command & Status:
  R/W*           M       write cycle (low is write)                 3S48     1
  Page*          M       additional address select                  3S48     1
Control & Timing:
  Enable         M       master clock                               3S48     1
  VMA*           M       memory data strobe (address strobe)        3S48     1
  VPA*           M       peripheral address strobe                  3S48     1
  RDY            S       slave wait                                 0C48     1
  Parity err*    S       memory parity error                        0C48     1
 {DTACK*         S       slave positive acknowledge                 0C48    1}
 {DS<1..0>*      M       data strobes (resp. odd and even byte)     3S48    2}
 {BERR*          S       bus error, negative acknowledge.           0C48    1}
  MCLK           C       memory clock for refresh controller        TS48     1
Arbitration:
  BRQ*           R       bus requested by at least one device       0C48     1
  BGACK*         M       bus busy                                   0C48     1
  Chain in       D       daisy chain in                             TP5      1
  Chain out      D       daisy chain out                            TP5      1
  BGRT           A       bus granted                                TP48     1
 {ARBCL          A       arbiter clock for self-selection           TP48    1}
 {P<5..0>*       R       priority of bidder (self-selection)        0C48    6}
Interrupt:
  IRQ*  {INT2*}  I       interrupt requested                        0C16     1
  FIRQ* {INT6*}  I       high-priority interrupt requested          0C48     1
  NMI*  {INT7*}  I       non-vectored interrupt                     0C48     1
 {IRQ5,3         I       interrupt requested levels 3, 5            0C48    2}
 {SYSFAIL        any     system failure                             0C48    1}
  IACK           M       vector fetch cycle                         3S48     1
Others:
  RES*          panel    reset pulse                                0C48     1
  HALT*         panel    halt CPU (permanent master)                0C48     1
 {VED*            C      Valid Event Data                           0C48    1}
 {reserved                                                                  8}

Power:
  GND (0V)              logic ground                                        4 {4}
  +5 V                  main power supply                                   2 {1}
  +12 V                 +12 V dc auxiliary supply                           1
  -12 V                 -12 V dc auxiliary supply                           1
  -5 V                  -5 V dc auxiliary supply                            1
  +5 V bat              battery power supply                                1
                                                                           --
                                                         TOTAL:           64 {96}
```

Connector pinout:

```
c: 1●Gnd  2●A16  3●A17  4●A18  5●A19  6●A20  7●A21  8●A22  9●A23  10●Res  11●Res  12●Res  13●Gnd  14●Res  15●Res  16●IRQ3*  17●IRQ5*  18●VED*  19●Gnd  20●P5*  21●P4  22●P3*  23●P2*  24●P1*  25●P0*  26●Res  27●SYSFAIL*  28●ARBCK  29●Res  30●Res  31●+5 V  32●Gnd

b: 1●Gnd  2●A8   3●A9   4●A10  5●A11  6●A12  7●A13  8●A14  9●A15  10●BRQ*  11●DS1*  12●BGACK*¹  13●Enable  14●Reset*  15●NMI*  16●IRQ1*  17●IRQ2*  18●IACK  19●D12*  20●D13*  21●D14*  22●D15*  23●D4*  24●D5*  25●D6*  26●D7*  27●BERR*  28●ChainIn  29●+5 V bat  30●-12 V  31●+5 V  32●Gnd

a: 1●Gnd  2●A0   3●A1   4●A2   5●A3   6●A4   7●A5   8●A6   9●A7   10●BGRT*  11●DS0*  12●HALT*  13●SYSCK  14●VPA*  15●DTACK*²  16●VMA*  17●R/W*  18●IRQ4*  19●D8*  20●D9*  21●D10*  22●D11*  23●D0*  24●D1*  25●D2*  26●D3*  27●Page*  28●ChainOut  29●PWF*  30●+12 V  31●+5 V  32●Gnd

¹ also named BBUSY*
² also named RDY
```

3S48:
three-state, 48 mA,
terminated by
330//470Ω to
+5 V/Gnd (each end)

0C48:
open collector, 48 mA,
terminated by
330//470Ω to
+5 V//Gnd (each end)

TP5:
TTL totem pole, 5 mA,
not terminated (daisy
chain)

## 1.3.7 Q-BUS

| | | | |
|---|---|---|---|
| DESCRIPTOR (notes 1) (note 2) | 22/16 P HS<br>Processor bus of DEC's LSI-11 family | MULTIPROC. SUPPORT | Centralized interrupts and arbitration<br>Indivisible RMW transfer<br>Centralized multiprocessor only |
| | | BOARD AREA | Double: 132 mm * 214 mm = 282 cm$^2$<br>Quad: 265 mm * 214 mm = 567 cm$^2$ |
| SPONSOR | Digital Equipment Corporation 1973 | CONNECTOR | Edge, 2 * 36 contacts |
| STANDARD | None (broad user's group) | BUS LENGTH | 5 m, up to 40 loads |
| ADDRESS SPACE | MEM:<br>  A22 (Q-22 bus)<br>  A18 (Q-18 bus)<br>I/O:<br>  P11<br>(space selected at address time) | DRIVER | OC, 70 mA, 123 Ω termination |
| DATA FORMAT (note 3) | 16 & 8 bit non-justified little endian<br>(lane selected by address + size) | SPEED (note 5) | 300 ns / 16 bit |
| | | OPTIONS (note 6) | Q-16, Q-18, Q-22 (upward compatible)<br>Older memories do not implement sequential transfer |
| TRANSFER TYPE | Read, write, read-modify-write (RMW)<br>Interrupt vector fetch<br>Sequential SEQ (Q-22 only) (RMW, SEQ not announced) | | |
| TIMING (note 4) | Handshaken, RP-WP, PAK | AUXILIARY BUSES | None |
| ARBITRATION | Daisy chain 1 level<br>Round robin and position fixed priority | REFERENCES | Digital Equipment Corporation<br>PDP11 BUS HANDBOOK<br>Digital Press, 1979<br><br>Microcomputer and Memories,<br>Digital Press, 1983 |
| INTERRUPTS | 4 interrupt request lines, vectored interrupt<br>Event and powerfail interrupt<br>Daisy chain within one interrupt level | REMARKS | The Q-BUS was developed for the LSI-11, originally with a 16-bit address. It was successively extended to 18- and to 22-bit addresses by using spare lines, which were sometimes used by older boards for maintenance.<br>The Q-22 has the ability to perform sequential transfers, such as the LSI-11/23+ supports. Q-BUS holds about 1/3 of the board market in the USA, especially for high performance peripherals, workstations and scientific applications |
| ERROR HANDLING | Memory errors reported<br>AC and DC powerfail detect | | |
| OTHER FUNCTIONS | Refresh (obsolete) | | |

## 11 Appendix

### Q-BUS

| Line Name | Source | Description | Driver | #Lines |
|---|---|---|---|---|
| Information: | (note 7) | | | |
| DAL<15..00>* | M/S | multiplexed data & address | OC70 | 16 |
| DAL<17..16>* | M/S | A17, A16 and slave error report | OC70 | 2 |
| DAL<21..18>* | M | higher address bits | OC70 | 4 |
| Command & Status: | | | | |
| WTBT* | M | advanced write and byte transfer | OC70 | 1 |
| BS7* | M | bank 7 Select (I/O page) | OC70 | 1 |
| REF* | M | refresh (obsolete) | OC70 | 1 |
| Control & Timing | | | | |
| SYNC* | M | bus sync (address latch) | OC70 | 1 |
| DOUT* | M | bus data OUT (write strobe) | OC70 | 1 |
| DIN* | M | bus data IN (read strobe) | OC70 | 1 |
| RPLY* | S | bus reply (slave positive ack) | OC70 | 1 |
| Arbitration: | | | | |
| DMR* | R | bus DMA requested | OC70 | 1 |
| DMGi* | D | bus DMA grant In (token in) | OC70 | 1 |
| DMGo* | D | bus DMA grant out (token out) | OC70 | 1 |
| SACK* | A | bus DMA granted | OC70 | 1 |
| Interrupt: | | | | |
| EVNT* | I | event (non-maskable interrupt) | OC70 | 1 |
| IRQ<7..4>* | I | interrupt requested (prioritized) | OC70 | 4 |
| IAKI* | D | interrupt acknowledge in (daisy) | OC70 | 1 |
| IAKO* | D | interrupt acknowledge out (daisy) (DIN without SYNC is vector fetch) | OC70 | 1 |
| Others: | | | | |
| INIT* | panel | initialize | OC70 | 1 |
| HALT* | panel | processor halt | OC70 | 1 |
| DCOK* | B | DC power OK | OC70 | 1 |
| POK* | B | AC Power OK | OC70 | 1 |
| spares | | (S, M and P spares, some not bussed) | | 9 |
| Power: | | | | |
| GND (0V) | | logic ground | | 8 |
| +5 V | | power supply | | 3 |
| +12 V | | +12 V power supply | | 2 |
| -12 V | | -12 V power supply | | 2 |
| +12 V bat | | +12 V battery power supply | | 2 |
| +5 V bat | | +5 V battery power supply | | 2 |
| | | | TOTAL: | 72 |

OC70: open collector, 70 mA, terminated by 123 Ω to +3.4 V except daisy chains (levels are similar to TTL-LS, but special 100mA drivers like AMD2908 or 26S12 recommended)

Connector pinout:

| | Ax1 | Ax2 | | | Bx1 | Bx2 | |
|---|---|---|---|---|---|---|---|
| BIRQ5* | A | +5 V | BDOUT | BDCOK* | A | +5 V | BDAL2 |
| BIRQ6* | B | -12 V | BRPLY | BPOK* | B | -12 V | BDAL3 |
| BDAL16 | C | Gnd | BDIN | BC2 | C | Gnd | BDAL4 |
| BDAL17 | D | +12 V | BSYNC | BAD19* | D | +12 V | BDAL5 |
| SSPARE1 | E | | BWTBT* | BAD20* | E | | BDAL6 |
| SSPARE2 | F | | BIRQ4 | BAD21* | F | | BDAL7 |
| SRUN* | H | | BIAKi | SSPARE8 | H | | BDAL8 |
| | J | Gnd | BIAKo | | J | Gnd | BDAL9 |
| MSPAREA | K | | BBS7 | MSPAREB | K | | BDAL10 |
| MSPAREB | L | | BDMGi | MSPAREB | L | | BDAL11 |
| | M | Gnd | BDMGo | | M | Gnd | BDAL12 |
| BDMR* | N | | BINIT | BSACK* | N | | BDAL13 |
| BHALT* | P | | BDAL0 | BIRQ7* | P | | BDAL14 |
| BREF* | R | | BDAL1 | BEVNT* | R | | BDAL15 |
| +12 V bat | S | | | PSPARE4 | S | | |
| | T | Gnd | | | T | Gnd | |
| PSPARE1 | U | | | PSPARE2 | U | | |
| +5 V bat | V | | | +5 V | V | | |

## 11.3.8 M3-BUS

| | | | |
|---|---|---|---|
| DESCRIPTOR (notes 1) (note 2) | 24/16 G 3HS Processor and global bus for 16-bit micros with protocol extensions Multiplexed & pipelined arbitration, address, data and interrupt | MULTIPROC. SUPPORT | 64 master arbitration, bus locking, broadcast, interrupt; tailored for multiprocessor systems with local bus. |
| | | BOARD AREA | Double long euroboard 233 mm * 220 mm = 512 cm$^2$ |
| SPONSOR | National Research Council (CNR), Italy 1981 | CONNECTOR | 96-pin two-piece DIN 41612-C96 |
| STANDARD | User's group | | |
| | | BUS LENGTH | 47.5 cm, 20 slots |
| ADDRESS SPACE | MEM:     A24 I/O:     P16 | DRIVER | TTL-LS 3S,   48 mA (information) OC,   48 mA (control) |
| DATA FORMAT (note 3) | D16 (no 8-bit subset) 16-bit little endian 8-bit select with separate strobes (not justified) | SPEED (note 5) | 270 ns / 16 bit |
| | | OPTIONS (note 6) | Supervisor module Sequence transfers |
| TRANSFER TYPE | Read, write, interrupt, sequence | | |
| TIMING (note 4) | Semisynchronous address, 3-wire handshake data | AUXILIARY BUSES | Serial bus, local bus. |
| ARBITRATION | Self-selection 64 priorities with fairness | REFERENCES | Prof. D. Del Corso Dipartimento di Elettronica Politecnico di Torino I-10129 Torino, Italy |
| INTERRUPTS | Use 8 multiplexed lines during data transfer NMI, PWFAIL, PROCFAIL | REMARKS | The M3 (modular multi-micro) was designed as the backbone of a multiprocessor system (project TOMP 80). It includes many features of P896 Futurebus, as defined in the 1980 draft. It can be extended to 32 bits using central row. Used principally by manufacturers of industrial control systems. |
| ERROR HANDLING | Byte parity on all information lines | | |
| OTHER FUNCTIONS | Supervisor signals for access protection and address/data substitution Serial bus | | |

# 11 Appendix

## M3-BUS

| Line Name | Source | Description | Driver | #Lines |
|---|---|---|---|---|
| Information: (note 7) | | | | |
| INF<23..00> | M/S | multiplexed data, address and events | 3S48 | 24 |
| PAR<2..0> | M/S | parity on INF<23..00> | 3S48 | 3 |
| Command & Status: | | | | |
| ADDREN* | M | address phase | 3S48 | 1 |
| WRITE* | M | write operation | 3S48 | 1 |
| PAR3 | M | parity on INF<29..24> | 3S48 | 1 |
| INF<29..24> | M | operation type: | 3S48 | 5 |
| | | INF29: normal MEM or I/O / indivisible | | |
| | | INF28: normal/system | | |
| | | INF27: I/O or interrupt / memory | | |
| | | INF26: DMA / permanent master | | |
| Control & Timing | | | | |
| CYCLE* | M | validates the address and command | 3S48 | 1 |
| PROCINT* | M | processor interrupt (event cycle) | 3S48 | 1 |
| LODAVAL* | M | even byte select | 3S48 | 1 |
| HIDAVAL* | M | odd byte select | 3S48 | 1 |
| TRACK* | S | transfer acknowledge | 0C48 | 1 |
| BRACK* | S | broadcast acknowledge | 0C48 | 1 |
| SUPON* | C | supervisor enable | 0C48 | 1 |
| INHIB* | C | inhibit for data substitution | 0C48 | 1 |
| PAREN* | M/S | parity enable | 0C48 | 1 |
| DAER* | S | data parity error on write | 3S48 | 1 |
| Arbitration: | | | | |
| SCK | C | system clock 4MHz | 3S48 | 1 |
| BREQ* | R | bus requested | 0C48 | 1 |
| BBUSY* | M | bus busy | 0C48 | 1 |
| | | (INF<24..27> used for self-selection) | | |
| Interrupt: | | | | |
| NMI* | I | non-maskable interrupt | 0C48 | 1 |
| PWFAIL* | B | power fail | 0C48 | 1 |
| | | (INF<16..23> used as interrupt requests) | | |
| Others: | | | | |
| RESET* | panel | initialize | 0C48 | 1 |
| PROCDW* | M | processor down | 0C48 | 1 |
| SERCK | all | serial bus clock | 0C48 | 1 |
| SERDAT | ser | serial bus data / arbitration | 0C48 | 1 |
| reserved | | | | 21 |
| Power: | | | | |
| GND (0V) | | logic ground | | 12 |
| +5 V | | power supply | | 5 |
| +15 V | | +15 V power supply | | 1 |
| -15 V | | -15 V power supply | | 1 |
| +5 V bat | | +5 V battery power supply | | 1 |
| | | | TOTAL: | 96 |

3S48: three-state, 48 mA, terminated by 400 Ω to 3.3 V at both ends
0C48: open-collector, 48 mA, terminated by 400 Ω to 3.3 V at both ends

Connector pinout:

c: 1●Gnd 2●+5V 3●INF1 4●INF3 5●INF5 6●INF7 7●INF9 8●INF11 9●INF13 10●INF15 11●INF17 12●INF19 13●INF21 14●INF23 15●INF25 16●INF27 17●INF29 18●DAER* 19●CYCLE* 20●HIDAVAL* 21●TRACK* 22●BRACK* 23●PAR3 24●SERCK 25●INHIB* 26●BBUSY* 27●SERDAT 28●Reset* 29●-15V 30●SCK 31●+5V backup 32●Gnd

b: 1●Gnd 2●+5V 3●Res 4●Res 5●Res 6●Res 7●Res 8●Res 9●Res 10●Res 11●Res 12●Res 13●Res 14●Res 15●Res 16●Res 17●Res 18●Res 19●Gnd 20●Gnd 21●Res 22●Res 23●Res 24●Res 25●Res 26●Gnd 27●Gnd 28●Res 29●Res 30●PROCINT* 31●+5V 32●Gnd

a: 1●Gnd 2●+5V 3●INF0 4●INF2 5●INF4 6●INF6 7●INF8 8●INF10 9●INF12 10●INF14 11●INF16 12●INF18 13●INF20 14●INF22 15●INF24 16●INF26 17●INF28 18●PAREN* 19●WRITE* 20●LODAVAL* 21●ADDREN* 22●PAR0 23●PAR1 24●PAR2 25●SUPON* 26●BREQ* 27●PWFAIL* 28●NMI* 29●PROCDW* 30●-15V 31●+5V 32●Gnd

## 11.3.9 IEEE P1014 (VME)

| | | | |
|---|---|---|---|
| DESCRIPTOR (notes 1) (note 2) | EXP: 32+32 G 2HS OR NEXP: 24+16 G 2HS Global multiprocessor bus 2 major options: NEXP (1 connector), EXP (2 connectors) | MULTIPROC. SUPPORT | 20 masters, multi-destination interrupt, read-modify-write |
| | | BOARD AREA | Single and double euroboard DOUBLE: 233 mm * 160 mm = 373 cm$^2$ SINGLE: 100 mm * 160 mm = 160 cm$^2$ |
| SPONSOR | MOTOROLA, PHILIPS SIGNETICS 1980 | CONNECTOR | Two-piece 96 pins EXP: 2 * DIN 41612-C96 OR NEXP: 1 * DIN 41612-C96 |
| STANDARD | IEEE P1014 | | |
| | | BUS LENGTH | 42.6 cm, 20 slots |
| ADDRESS SPACE | A32: 32-bit (implies EXP) OR A24: 24-bit OR A16: 16-bit 6 address modifier bits for access control (supervisory, program, data, peripherals) Peripherals are memory-mapped | DRIVER | TTL, 3S 48 mA (info) TTL, 3S 64 mA (timing) TTL, OC 48 mA (control) TTL, TP 8 mA (daisy chain) |
| DATA FORMAT (note 3) | D32 = (32, 16, 8) implies EXP. 16-bit-justified big endian, no 24-bit transfer D16 = (16, 8) non-justified big endian, 2 individual byte strobes | SPEED (note 5) | 210 ns / 32 bit (EXP) |
| | | OPTIONS (note 6) | Modules: master, slave, interrupter interrupt handler, clock Board size: DOUBLE OR SINGLE Connector: EXP (implies DOUBLE) OR NEXP Address size: A32 (implies EXP), A24 (A16)) Data size: D32 (implies EXP), D16, D8 Interrupt: line activated I(x) Serial messages: YES OR NO |
| TRANSFER TYPE | Read, write, read-modify-write Interrupt vector BT: block transfer read + write, not announced | | |
| TIMING (note 4) | Handshaken: separate address + data strobes, acknowledge, buserr HS, AW-DS, PAK, NAK | AUXILIARY BUSES | local bus VMX or MVMX (2nd connector) serial bus VMS (1st connector) |
| ARBITRATION | 4 daisy chains (prioritized) PRI: fixed priority OR RRS: round robin OR ONE: single level RWD: (release when done) OR ROR: (release on request) | REFERENCES | VME Bus Specification Manual Motorola document M68KVMEB(D1) User's group REV. B (AUG 82) |
| INTERRUPTS | 1 daisy chain, 4 levels I(x) option: uses one of 7 interrupt request lines R(x) option: level soft-configurable | REMARKS | VME evolved in 1981 in Munich from a redesign of Motorola's Versabus on a european board format and DIN connectors. Adopted by a consortium of firms (Motorola, Signetics, Mostek, Philips, Thomson-CSF) and a large user's group to support the 68000 processor family. Numerous options difficult configuration. Although claimed to be processor-independent, it is optimized for 680x0 processors. Second connector reserved for I/O OR VMX extension bus. However, since VMX is not well adapted for the MC68020, Motorola supports the MVMX instead. VME is a compromise between a global bus and a local bus. |
| ERROR HANDLING | Bus error, system failure, AC power fail, time out | | |
| OTHER FUNCTIONS | System reset, bus error, system clock AC power fail, system failure | | |

# 11 Appendix

## IEEE P1014 (VME)

| Line Name | Source | Description | Driver | #Lines |
|---|---|---|---|---|
| Information: | (note 7) | | | |
| A<23..01> | M | word address | 3S48 | 23 |
| (A<31..24> | M | address on J2 connector for VME-32) | 3S48 | 8) |
| D<15..00> | M/S | data | 3S48 | 16 |
| (D<31..16> | M/S | data J2 connector for VME-32 | 3S48 | 16) |
| Command & Status: | | | | |
| AM<5..0> | M | address modifiers (clocked by AS) | 3S48 | 6 |
| LWORD* | M | long (32-bit)-word (clocked by AS) | 3S48 | 1 |
| WRITE* | M | advanced write (clocked by DS) | 3S48 | 1 |
| Control & Timing: | | | | |
| AS* | M | address strobe | 3S64 | 1 |
| DS1* | M | data strobe for D<15..8> | 3S64 | 1 |
| DS0* | M | data strobe for D< 7..0> | 3S64 | 1 |
| DTACK* | S | slave positive acknowledge | 0C48 | 1 |
| BERR* | S | transmission error | 0C48 | 1 |
| Arbitration: | | | | |
| BR<3..0>* | R | bus request | 0C48 | 4 |
| BG<3..0>in* | D | bus grant input | TP8 | 4 |
| BG<3..0>out* | D | bus grant output | TP8 | 4 |
| BBSY* | M | bus busy | 0C48 | 1 |
| BCLR* | A | bus arbitration clear | TP64 | 1 |
| Interrupt: | | | | |
| IRQ<7..1>* | I | interrupt requested | 0C48 | 7 |
| IACKin* | D | vector grant input | TP8 | 1 |
| IACKout* | D | vector grant output | TP8 | 1 |
| IACK* | M | interrupt acknowledge | 3S48 | 1 |
| Others: | | | | |
| SYSRESET* | panel | system reset | 0C48 | 1 |
| SYSCLK* | C | system clock | TP64 | 1 |
| ACFAIL* | B | AC power fail | 0C48 | 1 |
| SYSFAIL* | any | system failure | 0C48 | 1 |
| reserved | | | | { 1} |
| SERCLK* | all | serial bus clock (VMS specification) | | 1 |
| SERDAT* | ser | serial bus data (VMS specification) | | 1 |
| Power: | | | | |
| GND (0V) | | logic ground | | 8 { 4} |
| +5 V | | main power supply | | 3 { 3} |
| +5 V stdby | | standby power supply | | 1 |
| +12 V | | +12 V auxiliary supply | | 1 |
| -12 V | | -12 V auxiliary supply | | 1 |
| | | | TOTAL: | 96 {32} |

```
3S48: three-state,   48 mA,  terminated by 330/470 Ω to +5 V at each end
3S64: three-state,   64 mA,  terminated by 330/470 Ω to +5 V at each end
0C48: open-collector, 48 mA, terminated by 330/470 Ω to +5 V at each end
TP64: totem pole,    64 mA,  terminated by 330/470 Ω to +5 V at each end
TP8:  totem pole,     8 mA,  not terminated (daisy chain)
```

Connector pinout:

```
c row: 1•D08  2•D09  3•D10  4•D11  5•D12  6•D13  7•D14  8•D15  9•Gnd  10•SYSfail*  11•BERR*  12•SYSreset*  13•LWORD*  14•AM5  15•A23  16•A22  17•A21  18•A20  19•A19  20•A18  21•A17  22•A16  23•A15  24•A14  25•A13  26•A12  27•A11  28•A10  29•A09  30•A08  31•+12 V  32•+5 V

b row: 1•BBSY*  2•BCLR*  3•ACfail*  4•BG0in*  5•BG0out*  6•BG1in*  7•BG1out*  8•BG2in*  9•BG2out*  10•BG3in*  11•BG3out*  12•BR0*  13•BR1*  14•BR2*  15•BR3*  16•AM0  17•AM1  18•AM2  19•AM3  20•Gnd  21•SERclk  22•SERdat  23•Gnd  24•IRQ7*  25•IRQ6*  26•IRQ5*  27•IRQ4*  28•IRQ3*  29•IRQ2*  30•IRQ1*  31•+5 Vstdby  32•+5 V

a row: 1•D00  2•D01  3•D02  4•D03  5•D04  6•D05  7•D06  8•D07  9•Gnd  10•SYSCLK  11•Gnd  12•DS1*  13•DS0*  14•WRITE*  15•Gnd  16•DTACK*  17•Gnd  18•AS*  19•Gnd  20•IACK*  21•IACKin*  22•IACKout*  23•AM4  24•A07  25•A06  26•A05  27•A04  28•A03  29•A02  30•A01  31•-12 V  32•+5 V
```

## 11.3.10 NuBus

| | | | |
|---|---|---|---|
| DESCRIPTOR (notes 1) (note 2) | 32/32 G SY<br>Global bus for 32-bit Multiprocessors | MULTIPROC. SUPPORT | 16 masters, multi-destination interrupt, arbitration locking |
| | | BOARD AREA | Triple extended euroboard<br>366 mm * 280 mm = 1024 cm$^2$ |
| SPONSOR | Texas Instruments, Western Digital, M.I.T. 1980 | CONNECTOR | Two-piece 96 pin<br>(1 * DIN 41612-C96) |
| STANDARD | Submitted to the IEEE User's group | BUS LENGTH | 47.5 cm, 16 slots |
| ADDRESS SPACE | MEM:<br>   M32 (32-bit)<br>I/O:<br>   Not specified. interrupts, configuration and I/O are included into 32-bit memory address space (slot space) | DRIVER | TTL, 3S 60mA ( 72 Ω) clock<br>TTL, 3S 48mA (171 Ω) info<br>TTL, 3S 48mA (171 Ω) control<br>TTL, OC 60mA (130 Ω) arbiter |
| DATA FORMAT (note 3) | 32, 16, 8 (no 24)<br>Non-justified, little endian (select by address + width at address time) | SPEED (note 5) | 300 ns/32-bit (single read)<br>150 ns/32-bit (sequential) |
| | | AUXILIARY BUSES | 2 unassigned additional connectors; large board size should make local memory bus unnecessary. |
| TRANSFER TYPE | Read, write, sequential transfer (only 32-bit items) defined by command field at address time | OPTIONS (note 6) | Master (all devices have the slave function)<br>Clock generation<br>Block transfer:YES OR NO<br>Parity (compatible option) |
| TIMING (note 4) | Synchronous, asymmetric 10 MHz clock | | |
| ARBITRATION | Self-selection, 16 fixed priorities, default mastership, locking, fairness | REFERENCES | NuBus Specification<br>Texas Instruments<br>TI-2242825-0001<br>Irvine, Ca 92714, USA |
| INTERRUPTS | Uses write transfer to slot space of any master, otherwise unspecified | REMARKS | Evolved from the asynchronous version of M.I.T. to a synchronous bus. Streamlined for simplicity, but slightly restricted by its inability to perform 24-bit transfers, by its prescribed alignment and by the fact that it must announce block transfers in advance. No higher level protocols defined.<br>Some improvements are discussed in the IEEE, such as smaller boards, an interrupt for simple slaves (IRQ* = a31), power-on and improvements in block transfers, which would permit its use in personal workstations. |
| ERROR HANDLING | Parity on information, timeout, slave status | | |
| OTHER FUNCTIONS | System reset, system clock (10 MHz), 4-bit geographical addressing (position on backplane) | | |

# 11 Appendix

| NuBus | | | | |
|---|---|---|---|---|
| Line Name | Source | Description | Driver | #Lines |
| Information: (note 7) | | | | |
| AD<32..00>* | M/S | multiplexed address + data | 3S48 | 32 |
| SP<3..0>* | M/S | parity on AD<32..00> | 3S48 | 1 |
| Command & Status: | | | | |
| TM<1..0>* | M | transfer mode | 3S48 | 2 |
| | | TM1: read / write* | | |
| | | TM0: 16,32 or block / byte* | | |
| | | (together with AD1 & AD0) | | |
| START* | M | address/command cycle | 3S48 | 1 |
| ACK* | S | slave acknowledge | 3S48 | 1 |
| SPV* | M/S | parity valid | 3S48 | 1 |
| Control & Timing: | | | | |
| CLK* | C | asymmetric 10 MHz bus clock | TP60 | 1 |
| Arbitration: | | | | |
| ARB<3..0>* | R | bidder ID (ARB3* = high priority) | OC60 | 4 |
| RQST* | R | bus requested | OC60 | 1 |
| Interrupt: | | | | |
| none | | (uses message transfer) | | |
| Others: | | | | |
| RESET* | C | reset | OC60 | 1 |
| ID<3..0>* | B | geographical address | wired | 4 |
| PWF* | B | power fail warning (coupled with reset) | OC60 | 1 |
| Power: | | | | |
| GND (0V) | | logic ground | | 23 |
| +5 V | | main power supply | | 11 |
| -5 V | | auxiliary power | | 8 |
| +12 V | | +12 V auxiliary supply | | 2 |
| -12 V | | -12 V auxiliary supply | | 2 |
| | | | TOTAL: | 96 |

3S48: three-state, 48 mA, terminated by 270/470 Ω to +5 V both ends
OC60: open-collector, 60 mA, terminated by 180/330 Ω to +5 V both ends
TP60: TTL totem pole, 60 mA, terminated by 120/180 Ω to +5 V far end

Connector pinout:

c: 1 Reset*, 2 Gnd, 3 +5 V, 4 TM0*, 5 AD0*, 6 AD2*, 7 AD4*, 8 AD6*, 9 AD8*, 10 AD10*, 11 AD12*, 12 AD14*, 13 AD16*, 14 AD18*, 15 AD20*, 16 AD22*, 17 AD24*, 18 AD26*, 19 AD28*, 20 AD30*, 21 PFW*, 22 ARB0*, 23 ARB2*, 24 ID0*, 25 ID2*, 26 START*, 27 +5 V, 28 +5 V, 29 Gnd, 30 Gnd, 31 CLK*

b: 1 -12 V, 2 Gnd, 3 Gnd, 4 +5 V, 5 +5 V, 6 +5 V, 7 -5.2 V, 8 -5.2 V, 9 -5.2 V, 10 Gnd, 11 Gnd, 12 Gnd, 13 Gnd, 14 Gnd, 15 Gnd, 16 Gnd, 17 Gnd, 18 Gnd, 19 Gnd, 20 Gnd, 21 Gnd, 22 Gnd, 23 -5.2 V, 24 -5.2 V, 25 -5.2 V, 26 +5 V, 27 +5 V, 28 +5 V, 29 Gnd, 30 Gnd, 31 +12 V

a: 1 -12 V, 2 Gnd, 3 SPV*, 4 SP*, 5 TM1*, 6 AD1*, 7 AD3*, 8 AD5*, 9 AD7*, 10 AD9*, 11 AD11*, 12 AD13*, 13 AD15*, 14 AD17*, 15 AD19*, 16 AD21*, 17 AD23*, 18 AD25*, 19 AD27*, 20 AD29*, 21 AD31*, 22 Gnd, 23 ARB1*, 24 ARB3*, 25 ID1*, 26 ID3*, 27 ACK*, 28 +5 V, 29 RQST*, 30 Gnd, 31 +12 V

## 11.3.11 MULTIBUS II iPSB

| | | | |
|---|---|---|---|
| DESCRIPTOR (notes 1) (note 2) | 32/32 G SY<br>Global bus for 32-bit multiprocessors<br>Part of a family of 5 buses. | MULTIPROC. SUPPORT | 20 masters, multi-destination interrupt, transfer locking, Reset-Not-Complete |
| | | BOARD AREA | Long euroboard<br>DOUBLE: 233 mm * 220 mm = 512 cm$^2$<br>SINGLE: 100 mm * 220 mm = 220 cm$^2$ |
| SPONSOR | INTEL Corporation. 1983 | CONNECTOR | 1 * two-piece, 96 pins<br>DIN 41612-C96 |
| STANDARD | Submitted to IEEE & IEC | | |
| | | BUS LENGTH | 47.5 cm, 20 slots |
| ADDRESS SPACE | MEM:<br>    A32    (32-bit)<br>I/O:<br>    P24    (24-bit)<br>Messages:<br>    M16    (16-bit)<br>Interconnect:<br>    C8    ( 8-bit) | DRIVER | TTL, 3S 48 mA (info)<br>TTL, 3S 64 mA (command)<br>TTL, OC 60 mA (requests) |
| DATA FORMAT (note 3) | D32 = (32, 24, 16, 8) OR<br>D16 = (16, 8)<br>16-bit-justified little endian (select by address + width during address phase) | SPEED (note 5) | 300 ns/32-bit single read<br>150 ns/32-bit sequential transfer |
| | | AUXILIARY BUSES | iLBX memory bus (2$^{nd}$ connector), iSBX processor bus (piggy back) iSSB serial bus, Multichannel I/O Bus |
| TRANSFER TYPE | Read, write, sequential R/W, locked (mode indicated at address time) | OPTIONS (note 6) | RQA: Master (all devices have the slave function).<br>CSM: Command and Service Module (one module must be CSM).<br>Data size: D32 OR D16<br>Block transfer: BT OR NoBT<br>SINGLE OR DOUBLE Eurocard. |
| TIMING (note 4) | Synchronous 10 MHz | | |
| ARBITRATION | Selfselection, 5-bit<br>20 priorities and arbitration ID distributed at initialization time<br>ROUND (fair) OR FIXED PRIORITY | REFERENCES | Order number 146077 C<br>INTEL Corporation<br>5200 NE Elam Young Parkway<br>Hilsboro, Or 97123, USA |
| INTERRUPTS | Message passing system: uses 32-bit write transfers to message space of any master or/and uses serial bus | REMARKS | Multiprocessor bus for high-performance applications. Synchronous operation allows easy design, but limits speed in future designs. Single eurocard of little interest, since large portion of real estate taken by bus interface. Support chips exist or are under development. Optimized for message passing communication "backplane area network". |
| ERROR HANDLING | Parity on AD<32..00> + SC<7..0>, bus error, powerfail, timeout | | |
| OTHER FUNCTIONS | Geographical address<br>Aux. system clock (20 MHz)<br>Reset, protect, slot address<br>Clock feeder | | |

# 11 Appendix

## MULTIBUS-II iPSB

| Line Name | Source | Description | Driver | #Lines |
|---|---|---|---|---|
| Information: | (note 7) | | | |
| AD<32..00> | M/S | multiplexed address + data | 3S48 | 32 |
| PAR<3..0> | M/S | even parity per byte lane | 3S48 | 4 |
| Command & Status: | | | | |
| SC<3..0> | M | master command ADDRESS CYCLE: (address/data, lock, data size) DATA CYCLE: (address/data, lock, end-of-transfer, master ready) | 3S64 | 4 |
| SC9 | M | even parity for SC<3..0> | 3S64 | 1 |
| SC<7..4> | M/S | master command and slave status ADDRESS CYCLE: (address space, read/write) DATA CYCLE: (slave ready, slave error report) | 3S64 | 4 |
| SC8 | M/S | even parity for SC<7..4> | 3S64 | 1 |
| Control & Timing: | | | | |
| BCLK* | C | bus clock 10 MHz (each clock line drives half backplane) | TP60 | 2 |
| BUSERR* | M/S | bus error | OC60 | 1 |
| TIMOUT* | C | timeout | TP48 | 1 |
| Arbitration: | | | | |
| ARB<5..0> | R/C | bidder ID (ARB5* = high priority) | OC60 | 6 |
| BREQ* | R | bus requested | OC60 | 1 |
| Interrupt: | | | | |
| none | | (uses message transfer) | | |
| Others: | | | | |
| RST* | C | reset | TP48 | 1 |
| RSTN* | any | reset not completed | OC60 | 1 |
| DCLOW* | C | DC power low | TP48 | 1 |
| PROT* | C | power fail protection | TP48 | 1 |
| CCLK* | C | constant clock at 20 MHz | TP60 | 1 |
| LACHn* | C | latch ID for initialization (connected to ADxx* lines) | wired | 1 |
| reserved | | | | 1 |
| SDA, SDB | ser | serial bus (iSSB specifications) | | 2 |
| Power: | | | | |
| Gnd (0V) | | logic ground | | 15 |
| +5 V | | main power supply | | 9 |
| +5 V bat | | standby power supply | | 2 |
| +12 V | | +12 V auxiliary supply | | 2 |
| -12 V | | -12 V auxiliary supply | | 2 |
| | | | TOTAL: | 96 |

Connector pinout:

```
  c                                                                              
  1 •Gnd       5 •Gnd       9 •PAR0*    13•AD10*   17•PAR2*   21•PAR3*   25•SC5*    29•SC2*    
  2 •+5V       6 •CCLK*     10•PAR0*    14•AD15*   18•AD25*   22•Resv    26•Arb0*   30•-12V    
  3 •+12V      7 •Gnd       11•AD06*    15•AD16*   19•AD28*   23•Buserr* 27•SC7*    31•+5V     
  4 •BCLK*     8 •AD03*     12•AD12*    16•AD21*   20•AD30*   24•Arb4*   28•SC8*    32•Gnd     

  b                                                                              
  1 •PROT*     5 •SDB       9 •AD05*    13•AD14*   17•AD23*   21•Resv    25•Rstnc*  29•SC3*    
  2 •DClow*    6 •AD01*     10•+5V      14•Gnd     18•Gnd     22•+5V     26•Gnd     30•+5Vbat  
  3 •+5V Bat   7 •Gnd       11•AD09*    15•AD18*   19•AD27*   23•RST*    27•SC8*    31•SC1*    
  4 •SDA       8 •AD05*     12•+5V      16•AD18*   20•Gnd     24•+5V     28•Gnd     32•SC0*    

  a                                                                              
  1 •Gnd       5 •Timout*   9 •AD04*    13•AD13*   17•AD22*   21•AD31*   25•Arb3*   29•SC4*    
  2 •+5V       6 •LACHn*    10•AD07*    14•PAR1*   18•AD24*   22•+5V     26•Arb1*   30•-12V    
  3 •+12V      7 •AD00*     11•AD08*    15•AD17*   19•AD26*   23•Busreq* 27•SC6*    31•+5V     
  4 •Resv      8 •AD02*     12•AD11*    16•AD20*   20•AD29*   24•Arb5*   28•SC4*    32•Gnd     
```

3S48:
three-state, 48 mA, terminated by 330/470 Ω to +5 V

3S60:
three-state, 60 mA, terminated by 220/330 Ω to +5 V

OC60:
open-collector, 60 mA, terminated by 220/330 Ω to +5 V

TP48:
TTL totem pole, 48 mA, terminated by 330/470 Ω to +5 V

TP60:
TTL totem pole, 60 mA, terminated by 110/120 Ω to +5 V

## 11.3.12 IEEE P896 (FutureBus)

| | | | |
|---|---|---|---|
| DESCRIPTOR (notes 1) (note 2) | 32/32 G HS multiprocessor bus, workstation and graphic applications | MULTIPROC. SUPPORT | Conceived as backbone for multiprocessor systems; supports distributed arbitration and interrupt, replicated caches |
| | | BOARD AREA | Preferred: triple long euroboard 280 mm * 366 mm = 1024 cm$^2$ |
| SPONSOR | IEEE Computer Society Microprocessor Standard Commitee | CONNECTOR | One 96-pin two-part DIN 41612-C96 2 DIN connectors unassigned |
| STANDARD | IEEE 896 (expected in 1986) | BUS LENGTH | 32 slots, 50 cm |
| ADDRESS SPACE | MEM: A32: 32-bit address I/O and other spaces are mapped into the 32-bit address space, the definitions of these spaces is not part of the P896 document | DRIVER | O.C. 50 mA trapezoidal drivers, not TTL (voltage swing : 1 V..2 V, Schottky diode decoupling to reduce capacitive loading) |
| DATA FORMAT (note 3) | 32-bit transfers, ordering not specified, not justified, (separate mask bit for each byte lane) | SPEED (note 5) | Single read: 160 ns / 32 bit Sequential read/write: 80 ns / 32 bit |
| | | AUXILIARY BUSES | Large boards make local execution bus unnecessary Serial bus (inter-processor messages) |
| TRANSFER TYPE | Read, write, read-modify-write, sequential | OPTIONS (note 6) | None |
| TIMING (note 4) | Handshaken, 2 modes: broadcast or single destination; sequential transfers use both edges of the timing signals to double rate | | |
| ARBITRATION | Self-selection mechanism with 7 priority lines Arbitration handshaken with 3 lines | REFERENCES | IEEE Computer Society Order Department POBox 80452 Worldway Postal Center Los Angeles, CA 90080, USA |
| INTERRUPTS | Done by write transfer to interrupt memory space | REMARKS | Probably the best multiprocessor bus available in 1986: It is very fast, optimized for sequential transfers, supports broadcast and replicated caches. The abscence of options makes it a true standard. It is currently backed by a few firms like Textronix, Ferranti, Radar Signal Establishment. It has not been developed by a firm, but by volunteer members of the IEEE CS as a manufacturer independent bus. |
| ERROR HANDLING | Parity on all information and arbitration lines, bus error report; all single errors believed to be detectable | | |
| OTHER FUNCTIONS | 5-bit geographical address, reset, error detection valid, reserved | | |

# 11 Appendix

## IEEE P896 (Futurebus)

| Line Name | Source | Description | Driver | #Lines |
|---|---|---|---|---|
| **Information:** (note 7) | | | | |
| AD<32..00>* | M/S | multiplexed address and data | TD50 | 32 |
| ED<3..0>* | M/S | error detection for AD field (byte parity) | TD50 | 4 |
| **Command & Status:** | | | | |
| CM<4..0>* | M | master command<br>ADDRESS CYCLE:<br>(read, lock, block transfer, broadcast, extended command)<br>DATA CYCLE:<br>(read, byte lane selection) | TD50 | 5 |
| CP* | M | command parity | TD50 | 1 |
| EV* | M | error detection valid | TD50 | 1 |
| ST<2..0>* | S | slave status reply<br>(illegal, valid, busy, access error, end-of-data, reserved parity error, illegal) | TD50 | 3 |
| **Control & Timing** | | | | |
| AS* | M | address strobe | TD50 | 1 |
| AK* | S | address positive acknowledge | TD50 | 1 |
| AI* | S | address inverse acknowledge (broadcast) | TD50 | 1 |
| DS* | M | data strobe | TD50 | 1 |
| DK* | S | data positive acknowledge | TD50 | 1 |
| DI* | S | data inverse acknowledge (broadcast) | TD50 | 1 |
| **Arbitration:** | | | | |
| AN<6..0>* | R | arbitration number (self-selection) | TD50 | 7 |
| AP*,AQ*,AR* | R | arbitration 3-way handshake P,Q,R | TD50 | 3 |
| AC* | R | arbitration condition | TD50 | 1 |
| GA<4..0>* | B | geographical slot address (not bussed) | wired | 5 |
| **Interrupt:** | | | | |
| none: | | interrupt done by write transfers to synapses | | 0 |
| **Others:** | | | | |
| RE* | C | reset | TD50 | 1 |
| SB0*,SB1* | ser | serial bus clock and data | TD50 | 2 |
| RFU<2..0> | | reserved for future use | | 3 |
| **Power:** | | | | |
| Gnd (0V) | | logic ground | | 10 |
| 0 Vdc | | 0 V power return | | 6 |
| +5 V | | power supply | | 6 |
| | | | TOTAL: | 96 |

TD50: open collector, 50 mA, trapezoidal drivers with UoL = 1 V and UoH = 2 V low capacitive load through Schottky diode. Terminated by 39 Ω to +2 V on both sides.

Connector pinout:

**c:** 1•0Vdc  2•+5V  3•AD2*  4•AD4*  5•AD7*  6•AD8*  7•Gnd  8•AD13*  9•AD15*  10•AD17*  11•AD19*  12•Gnd  13•ED2*  14•AD25*  15•AD28*  16•AD30*  17•Gnd  18•CM2*  19•CM4*  20•ST0*  21•ST2*  22•DK*  23•AP*  24•AC*  25•AN1*  26•AN6*  27•Gnd  28•SB1  29•RE*  30•RFU2  31•+5V  32•0Vdc

**b:** 1•0Vdc  2•+5V  3•AD1*  4•AD6*  5•ED0*  6•AD10*  7•AD12*  8•GA1*  9•AD16*  10•AD18*  11•AD21*  12•AD23*  13•GA2*  14•AD27*  15•AD29*  16•ED3*  17•CM1*  18•GA3*  19•EV*  20•ST1*  21•AK*  22•DS*  23•GA4*  24•AN0*  25•AN5*  26•AN4*  27•RE*  28•RFU1  29•+5V  30•0Vdc

(Note: columns reproduced from image — a column shown last reads 1•0Vdc  2•+5V  3•AD0*  4•AD3*  5•Gnd  6•AD9*  7•AD11*  8•AD14*  9•ED1*  10•Gnd  11•AD20*  12•AD22*  13•AD24*  14•AD26*  15•Gnd  16•AD31*  17•CM0*  18•CM3*  19•Gnd  20•CP*  21•AS*  22•AI*  23•AR*  24•AQ*  25•Gnd  26•AN2*  27•AN3*  28•AN4*  29•SB0  30•RFU0  31•+5V  32•0Vdc)

# 1 REFERENCES

[ABR70]  N. Abramson, *The Aloha System, Another Alternative for Computer Communication Networks,* Proc. FJCC, 1970, pp. 281-285

[ALT79]  J. Altnether, *Error Detecting and Correcting Codes, part 1,* Memory Components Handbook, 1979, INTEL Corp, Santa Clara

[BALA83]  R.V. Balakrishnan, *Cut Bus Reflections, Crosstalk with a Trapezoidal Transceiver,* EDN, August 1983, pp. 151-156

[BALA84]  R.V. Balakrishnan, *The Proposed IEEE 896 Futurebus - A Solution to the Bus Driving Problem,* IEEE Micro, August 1984, pp. 23-27

[BAR85]  M.R. Barbacci, T. Uehara, *Computer Hardware Description Languages : the Bridge between Software and Hardware,* IEEE Computer, Vol. 18, No. 2, February 1985, pp. 6-8

[BIN75]  R. Binder, et al., *Aloha Packet Broadcasting - A Retrospect,* NCC, May 1975, pp. 215-220

[BLA83]  R. Blahut, *Theory and Practice of Error Control Codes,* 1983, Addison Wesley, Reading

[BLO82]  W.R. Blood Jr, et al., *MECL System Design Handbook,* May 1982, Motorola Semiconductor Products Inc., Phoenix

[BOR80]  P. Borrill, *Microprocessor Bus Structures and Standards,* Proceedings Euromicro 1980, pp. 285-296

[BOR84]  P. Borrill, J. Theus, *An Advanced Communication Protocol for the Proposed IEEE 896 Futurebus,* IEEE Micro, August 1984, pp. 42-56

[BUR79]  W. Burr, et al., *A Bus System for the Military Computer Family,* IEEE Computer, April 1979, pp. 11-23

[BURR83]  *Shared Terminal Interface Chip (STI),* Preliminary Data Sheet, January 1983, Burroughs Corporation

[CCTA85]  *S5/8 Unipolar Serial Interface for Data Transfer between Computers and Peripherals,* September 1985, CCTA, London

[CHAN72]   T.J. Chaney, et al., Beware the Synchronizer, Compcon, 1972, pp. 317-319

[CIV80]   B. Civera, D. del Corso, Indivisible Test and Set Operation for Microprocessor, Alta Frequenza, Vol. 49, No. 3, 1980, pp. 254-255

[CIV82]   P. Civera, et al., The μ* Project : an Experience with a Multiprocessor System, IEEE Micro, May 1982pp. 38-55

[COH54]   S.B. Cohn, Characteristic Impedance of the Shielded-Strip Transmission Line, Transactions IRE, Vol MTT-2, 1954, pp. 52-57

[COH81]   D. Cohen, On Holy Wars and a Plea for Peace, IEEE Computer, Vol. 14, No. 10, October 1981, pp. 48-54

[CON83]   G. Conte, et al., Multiprocessors: M3 Bus Systems and TOMP Architectures, 1983, 199 p., Ufficio MUMICRO, Bologna

[COR75]   P. Corsini, Self-Synchronizing Asynchronous Arbiter, Digital Processes, Vol. 1, 1975, pp. 67-73

[COR76]   P. Corsini, Asynchronous Interlock Units for Speed-Independent Multiprocessor Systems, Informatik-Fachberichte, September 1976, pp. 457-464

[DAY83]   J.D. Day, H. Zimmermann, The OSI Reference Model, Proceedings of the IEEE, Vol. 71, No. 12, December 1983, pp. 1334-1340

[DEB84]   P. Debesson, Y. Choi, Tests et particularités du protocole de communication X.21 : difficultés et solutions, Minis et Micros, No. 217, Septembre 1984, pp. 65-71

[DELC79]   D. Del Corso, Description and Classification of Processor/Peripheral Interfaces, International Conference on Measure Systems and Distributed Processing, Pavia, October 15-16, 1979, pp. 111-120

[DELC79b]   D. Del Corso, A Test Technique for Microprocessor Based Machines, Alta Frequenza, Vol. XLVIII N. 2, February 1979, pp. 63-67

[DELC81]   D. Del Corso, G. Duchi, M3Bus: System Specification for High Performance Multimicroprocessor Machines, BIAS 1981 Proceedings, Milano, October 1981

[DELC82]   D. Del Corso, F. Maddaleno, Extension of Bus Protocols : A Technique for Modular Upgrade of Processing Systems, Proceedings Euromicro, 1982, pp. 169-179

[DELC84]   D. Del Corso, L. Verrua, Contention Delay in Distributed Priority Networks, Microprocessing and Microprogramming, Vol. 13, 1984, pp. 21-29

[DIJK65]   E.W. Dijkstra, Solution of a Problem in Concurrent Programming Control, CACM, Vol. 8 No. 9, September 1965

# References

[DINE81] M.A. Dineson, *Broadband Local Networks Enhance Communication Design*, EDN, March 1981, pp. 77-86

[DIX80] Digital, Intel, Xerox, *The Ethernet, a Local Aera Network*, 1980

[DOLL78] D.R. Doll, *Data Communications*, 1978, J. Wiley & Sons, New York

[DOOR83] J.P. Van Dooren, *Local Area Networks on Optical Fiber*, 4th Telecommunications Forum, Genève, November 1983

[DWO79] L.N. Dworsky, *Modern Transmission Line Theory and Applications*, 1979, John Wiley and Sons, New York

[EIS82] B. Eisenhard, *OMNINET : A Low Cost CSMA Network for Microcomputers*, Proceedings of the Compcon, Spring 1982, pp. 174-181

[FAST81] *Fastbus Tentative Specification*, August 1981, US NIM Committee

[FLET80] W.I. Fletcher, *An Engineering Approach to Digital Design*, 1980, Prentice-Hall, Englewood Cliffs

[FOLT82] H.C. Folts, *McGraw-Hill Compilation of Data Standards*, 1982, McGraw-Hill, New York

[FOLT83] H.C. Folts, et al., Special issue on *"Open Systems Interconnection (OSI) - New International Standards Architecture and Protocols for Distributed Information Systems"*, Proceedings of the IEEE, December 1983

[FON83] P.G. Fontolliet, *Systèmes de Télécommunications*, Traité d'Electricité, Vol. XVIII, 1983 Presses Polytechniques, Lausanne

[FOR77] B. Forss, and al., *Distribution of Logical Process in Telephone Systems*, Proceedings of the National Telecommunications Conference NTC'77, Los Angeles, December 5-7, 1977

[FUNK83] G. Funk, *Frame transmission with specified data integrity*, NTZ-Archiv, Bd 5, Vol. 11, 1983

[G9684] *G64 and G96 Specifications Manual*, November 1984, Gespac Geneva

[GRAU84] M. Graube, *Local Area Networks*, IEEE Computer, October 1984, pp. 242-247

[GUS83] D.B. Gustavson, J. Theus, *Wire-OR Logic on Transmission Lines*, IEEE Micro, June 1983, pp. 51-55

[GUS84] D.B. Gustavson, *Computer Buses - a Tutorial*, IEEE Micro, August 1984, pp. 7-22

[HAM50] B.W. Hamming, *Error Detecting and Error Correcting Codes*, The Bell System Technical Journal, Vol. 26 No. 2, April 1950

[HOPK82] G.T. Hopkins, N.B. Meisner, *Data Communications Choosing between Broadband and Baseband Local Networks*, Mini-Micro Systems, June 1982, pp. 265-274

[IBM83] *Special Issue on "Systems Network Architecture"*, IBM Systems Journal, Vol. 22 No. 4, 1983, pp. 296-463

[ISO177] *Transfert de l'information, Recueil de Normes*, 1977, ISO, Genève

[JEN76] E.D. Jensen, et al., *A Review of Systematic Methods in Distributed Processor Interconnection*, Proc. ICC, 1976, pp. 18-23

[KAU66] H.R. Kaupp, *Pulse Crosstalk between Microstrip Transmission Lines*, Proceedings of Wescon 1966, August 1966

[KAU67] H.R. Kaupp, *Characteristics of Microstrip Transmission Lines*, IEEE Transactions on Electronic Computers, Vol. EC-16, No. 2, 1967, pp. 185-193

[KIRR83] H. Kirrmann, *Data Format and Bus Compatibility in Multiprocessors*, IEEE Micro, August 1983, pp. 32-47

[KOB79] H. Kobayshi, *A Survey of Coding Schemes for Transmission or Recording of Digital Data*, IEEE Transactions on Communication Technology, Vol. 19, No. 6, December 1979, pp. 1087-1100

[KOT82] G. Kotelly, *Local-area Networks Technology*, EDN, February 1982, pp. 109-150

[KURO84] F. Kurose, and al., *Multiple-Access Protocols and Time-Constrained Communication*, ACM Computing Surveys, Vol. 16, March 1984, pp. 43-70

[LAND83] C.J. Landsness, *The Electronics Interface for the Hewlett-Packard Interface Loop*, Hewlett-Packard Journal, January 1983, pp. 11-17

[LANG81] Glen Langdon, *IEEE Subcommittee on Definitions for Interface Buses*, 1981, IBM Research Lab, San José

[LEVY78] J.V. Levy, *Buses, the Skeleton of Computer Structures*, in Computer Engineering, pp. 421-451, 1978 Digital Press, Maynard

[MARI81] L.R. Marino, *General Theory of Metastable Operation*, IEEE Transactions on Computers, Vol. C-30 No. 2, February 1981, pp. 107-115

[MCNA77] J.E. McNamara, *Technical Aspects of Data Communication*, 1977, Digital Press, Maynard

[MEAD80] C. Mead, L. Conway, *Introduction to VLSI Systems*, 1980, Addison-Wesley, Reading

[MEG81] N.D. Megill, *TDRs Profile Impedances of Backplanes and PC Boards*, Electronics, July 14, 1981, pp. 113-117

[MET76] R.M. Metcalf, D.R. Boggs, *Ethernet: Distributed Packet Switching for Local Computer Networks*, Communications of the ACM, Vol. 19 No. 7, July 1976, pp. 395-404

# References

[MMI84] *PAL Programmable Array Logic Handbook*, third edition, 1984, Monolithic Memories Inc., Santa Clara

[MU283] *Multibus II Bus Architecture Specification Handbook*, 1983, Intel Corporation, Santa Clara

[MYE82] W. Myers, *Toward a Local Network Standard*, IEEE Micro, pp. 28-45, August 1982

[NGH79] P.T. Nghiem, *Transmission des données*, 1979, Infoprax, Pontoise

[NIC76a] J.D. Nicoud, *Peripheral Interface Standards for Microprocessors*, Proceedings of the IEEE, Vol. 64, No. 6, June 1976, pp. 896-903

[NIC83] J.D. Nicoud, *Microinformatique: architecture, interfaces et logiciel*, 1983, Dunod, Paris

[P89683] P896 Working Group, *Specifications for Advanced Microcomputer Backplane Buses*, Draft 7.1b, , IEEE Computer Society, November 1985

[PATZ80] R. Patzelt, *Digital Measurement Systems, Standards and Future Developments*, Euromicro Journal Vol. 6, 1980, pp. 283-287

[PEAT80] J.B. Peatman, *Digital Hardware Design*, 1980, McGraw-Hill, Auckland

[PET72] W. Peterson, E.J. Weldon, *Error Correcting Codes*, 1972, MIT Press, Cambridge, Mass

[PHIL83] *I2C bus specification*, January 1983 Philips, Eindhoven

[PIOT83] J. PIOT, *Comparaison de quelques modes de transmission binaires*, AGEN Mitteilungen, No. 37, Novembre 1983

[PLAT81] B. Plattner, J. Nievergelt, *Monitoring Program Execution: A Survey*, IEEE Computer, November 1981, pp. 76-93

[PRO83] *Proway Lan Study Document*, Submitted to TC65C/WG 6, Revision B, October 1983, US National Committee

[REY74] E.M. Reyner II, *Crosstalk Analysis of Digital Interconnection Systems*, Appl. Note, 1974, pp. 133-143, AMP Inc.

[ROBI79] M. Robin, Maurin T., *Interfaçage des microprocesseurs*, 1979, Bordas, Paris

[ROET77] H. Röthlisberger, *A Standard Bus for Multiprocessor Architecture*, Proceedings Euromicro, 1977, pp. 23-34, North Holland, Amsterdam

[S10079] K.A. Elmquist, et al., *Standard Specification for S-100 Bus Interface Devices*, IEEE Computer, July 1979

[SAAL83] H. Saal, *Local Area Networks, An Update on Microcomputers in the Office*, Byte, May 1983, pp. 60-76

[SAL77] H.W. Sallet, *Magnetic Tape: a High Performer*, IEEE Spectrum, July 1977, pp. 26-31

[SAM82]   M. Samet, et al., *Metastable Phenomenon in Sequential Circuits: Simulation and Prediction*, Proceedings AMSE, Modelling and Simulation, Vol. 3-4, 1982, pp. 70-73

[SBI78]   *The Synchronous Backplane Interconnect*, Vax 11/780 Architecture handbook, 1978, 23p., Digital Equipment, Maynard

[SCHU83]  H. Schumny, *Anforderungen der Physikalisch-Technischen Bundesanstalt an die Ausführung von digitalen Schnittstellen für serielle Punkt-zu-Punkt-Verbindung bei Start-Stop-Uebertragung*, PTB-Mitteilungen, 93, May 1983, pp. 189-192

[SCHW77]  M. Schwarz, *Computer-Communication Network Design and Analysis*, 1977, Prentice-Hall, Englewood Cliffs

[SEV80]   R.H. Severt, *Encoding Schemes Support High Density Digital Data Recording*, Computer Design, Vol. 19, No. 5, May 1980

[SHA49]   C. Shannon, *The Mathematical Theory of Communication*, 1949, The University of Illinois Press, Urbana

[SOMM76]  R. Sommer, *Cobus, a Firmware Controlled Data Transmission System*, Proceedings Euromicro, 1976, pp. 299-304, North-Holland, Amsterdam

[SOMM81]  R. Sommer, *A Real-time Protocol for a Sub-local Network*, Local Networks & Distributed Office Systems, London, May 1981

[SOU81]   R.K. Southard, *Interconnection System Approaches for Minimizing Data Transmission Problems*, Computer Design, March 1981, pp. 107-116

[STAL84]  W. Stallings, *Local Networks*, ACM Computing Surveys, Vol. 16, No. 1, March 1984, pp. 3-42

[STO82]   P.A. Stoll, *How to Avoid Synchronization Problems*, VLSI Design, November/December 1982, pp. 56-59

[STU83]   B. Stuck, *Calculating the Maximum Mean Data Rate in Local Area Networks*, IEEE Computer, May 1983, pp. 72-76

[TAN81]   A.S. Tanenbaum, *Computer Networks*, 1981, Prentice-Hall Int. Editions, Englewood Cliffs

[TAUB76]  D.M. Taub, *Contention Resolving Circuits for Computer Interrupt Systems*, Proceeding IEE, No. 9, September 1976

[TAUB82]  D.M. Taub, *Worst-Case Arbitration Time in S100-Type Computer BUS system*, Electronics Letters, No. 18, September 1982

[TAUB84]  D.M. Taub, *Arbitration and Control Acquisition in the Proposed IEEE 896 Futurebus*, IEEE Micro, August 1984, pp. 28-41

[THUR79]  K. Thurber, J. Masson, *Distributed Processor Communication Architecture*, 1979, Lexington Books, Lexington

[THUR81]  K.J. Thurber, H.A. Freeman, *Local Computer Networks*, 1981, IEEE Society, New York

| | |
|---|---|
| [TOB79] | F.A. Tobagi, V.B. Hunt, *Performance Analysis of Carrier Sense Multiple Access with Collision Detection*, Local Area Communications Network Symposium, Boston, May 1979 |
| [TOR77] | H.C. Torng, *The Optimal Interconnection of Circuit Modules in Microprocessor and Digital System Design*, IEEE Transactions on Computers, Vol. C.25 No. 5, May 1977, pp. 450-457 |
| [TRO81] | C. Tropper, *Local Computer Network Technologies*, 1981, Academic Press, New York |
| [TTL84] | *The TTL Data Book for Design Engineers*, 1984, Texas Instruments |
| [UNI75] | *Unibus theory and operation*, PDP11 Peripherals Handbook, 1975, Unibus |
| [VME82] | *VMEbus Specification Manual*, 1982, Motorola Phoenix |
| [WAR81a] | C. Warren, *Understanding Bus Basics helps resolve Design Conflicts*, EDN, May 27, 1981, pp. 159-173 |
| [WAR81b] | C. Warren, *Compare Microcomputer-bus Specs to find the Bus you need*, EDN, June 10, 1981, pp. 141-153 |
| [WAR81c] | C. Warren, *High-Performance Buses clear a Path for Future Microcomputers*, EDN, June 24, 1981, pp. 157-162 |
| [WEB68] | H. Weber, *Leitungs theorie*, 1968, AMIV-Verlag, ETH Zürich |
| [WHEE77] | H.A. Wheeler, *Transmission Lines Properties of a Strip on a Dielectric Sheet on a Plane*, IEEE Transactions on Microwave Theory and Technique, Vol. MTT-25, No. 8, August 1977 |
| [WINK80] | D. Winkel, Prosser F., *The Art of Digital Design*, 1980, Prentice-Hall, Englewood Cliffs |
| [WIT83] | I.H. Witten, *Welcome to the Standards Jungle*, Byte, February 1983, pp. 146-178 |

# 1 INDEX

| | | | |
|---|---|---|---|
| ACCESS | 43 | ATTENUATION | 27 |
| ACCESS DATA | 47 | | |
| ACCESS POLICY | 131 | BACKPLANE BUS | 33 |
| ACCESS PROCEDURES | 44 | BACKWARD CROSSTALK | 265 |
| ACCESS UNIT | 131 | BALANCED | 29 |
| ACKNOWLEDGE | 2, 73 | BANDWIDTH | 27, 307 |
| ACTION | 52, 57 | BASEBAND | 30 |
| ACTIVE | 15 | BAUD (Bd) | 308 |
| ACTIVE LOW | 16, 19 | BERGERON'S DIAGRAM | 240 |
| ACTIVE TERMINATION | 260 | BIDIRECTIONAL | 72 |
| ACTIVE/NOT ACTIVE | 59 | BIG ENDIAN | 295 |
| ADCCP (Advanced Data Communication Control Procedure) | 327 | BINARY | 37 |
| | | BINARY NUMBER | 14 |
| | | BIQUAD | 14 |
| ADDRESS | 102 | BIT (b) | 14 |
| ADDRESSING | 9, 100 | BIT PROTOCOL | 327 |
| ADVANCED READ | 74 | BIT STUFFING | 327 |
| ADVANCED WRITE | 74 | BITS/SECOND (b/s) | 307 |
| AFNOR (Association Française de NORmalisation) | 54 | BLOCK CODING | 188 |
| | | BLOCK DIAGRAM | 26 |
| ALLOCATOR | 128 | BLOCK OF DATA | 14 |
| ALOHA | 349 | BLOCK TRANSFER | 125 |
| ALPHABET | 188 | BOOLEAN VARIABLES | 15 |
| ALU (Arithmetic and Logic Unit) | 20 | BOP (Bit Oriented Protocol) | 327 |
| | | BREAK KEY | 333 |
| AMI (Alternative Mark Inversion) | 311 | BREAK SIGNAL | 333 |
| | | BROADBAND | 30 |
| AND | 18 | BROADCALL | 9, 27, 174 |
| ANSI (American National Standards Institute) | 54 | BROADCAST | 9, 27, 174 |
| | | BSC (Byte Synchronous Communication) | 326 |
| APPLICATION | 52 | | |
| APPLICATION LAYER | 50 | BSO (British Standard Organization) | 54 |
| ARBITER | 131 | | |
| ARBITRATION | 10, 132, 138 | BUFFER | 20 |
| ASSERTED | 15 | BUS | 7 |
| ASYMMETRIC | 36 | BURSTS | 185 |
| ASYNCHRONOUS | 63, 323 | BUS CONTROLLER | 273 |

| | | | |
|---|---|---|---|
| BUS SIGNAL | 59 | CONTENTION | 128 |
| BUS SIGNAL LINES | 16 | CONTROL | 42 |
| BUS WINDOW | 273 | CONTROL PATH | 58 |
| BUSED | 7 | CONTROLLER | 178 |
| BYTE (B) | 14 | COP (Character Oriented | |
| BYTE PROTOCOLS | 326 | Protocols) | 326 |
| Biφ-L (Biphase-Level) | 312 | CPU (Central Processing Unit) | 2 |
| Biφ-M (Biphase-Mark) | 313 | CROSSTALK | 28, 261 |
| Biφ-S (Biphase-Space) | 313 | CSMA (Carrier Sense | |
| | | Multiple Access) | 350 |
| CA (Collision Arbitration) | 352 | CYCLE | 59 |
| CALLER | 305 | CYCLE level | 52 |
| CAPACITIVE CROSSTALK | 261 | CYCLIC REDUNDANCY | |
| CAPACITY | 307 | CHECKS | 202 |
| CATV (Community Antenna | | | |
| Television) | 359 | D FLIP-FLOP | 22 |
| CCITT (Comité Consultatif | | DAISY CHAIN | 146 |
| International des Télégraphes | | DAISY-CHAIN INTERRUPT | 169 |
| et Téléphones) | 54 | DATA ENCAPSULATION | 51 |
| CD | 28 | **DATA LINK LAYER** | **49** |
| CD (Collision Detection) | 351 | DCE (Data Communication | |
| CEI (Comitado Eletrotecnico | | Equipment) | 329 |
| Italiano) | 54 | DDCMP (Digital Data | |
| CENTRALIZED | 143 | Communication Message | |
| CENTRALIZED INTERRUPT | | Protocol) | 326 |
| CONTROL | 168 | DECENTRALIZED | 143 |
| CHANNEL | 305 | DECIMAL | 15 |
| CHARACTERISTIC IMPEDANCE | 211 | DECODED | 100 |
| CHEAPERNET | 359 | DECODER | 20 |
| CHECKSUM | 201 | DECODING | 305 |
| CIRCULAR PRIORITY | 141 | DECUPLET | 14 |
| CLOCKED INTERFACES | 90 | DEFAULT ASSIGNMENT | 129 |
| CLOCKED PROTOCOL | 90 | DELAY LINE | 220 |
| COAXIAL CABLE | 29, 224 | DEMODULATION | 305 |
| COBUS (Coaxial Bus) | 352 | DEMODULATOR | 307 |
| CODE EFFICIENCY | 190 | DEPTH | 54 |
| CODED (or ENCODED) | | DESCRIPTION | 55 |
| ADDRESSING | 102 | DESKEW DELAY | 276 |
| CODEWORD | 188 | DESTINATION | 58 |
| CODING | 305 | DESTINATION-ACTIVATED | 64 |
| CODING THEORY | 187 | DIELECTRIC LOSSES | 219 |
| COLLISION | 129 | DIFFERENTIAL | 29 |
| COLLISION DETECTION | 131 | DIGITAL SYSTEM | 18 |
| COLLISION WINDOW | 137 | DIN (Deutsche Industrie | |
| COMMANDER | 69 | Normen) | 54 |
| COMMON MODE ERROR | 185 | DIRECT CONNECTORS | 34 |
| COMMON PATH CROSSTALK | 261 | DIRECTIONAL | 28 |
| COMPARATOR | 20 | DISCONTINUITIES | 28 |
| CONCENTRATED | 208 | DISPERSION | 219 |
| CONCURRENT | 160 | DISTRIBUTED | 143, 208 |

| | | | |
|---|---|---|---|
| DIX (Digital, Intel, Xerox) | 358 | FALSE | 15, 59 |
| DM-NRZ-M (Delay Modulation - Non Return to Zero - Mark) | 314 | FAR END | 209 |
| | | FAR END CROSSTALK | 266 |
| | | FAULT | 184 |
| | | FAULT AVOIDANCE | 185 |
| DM-NRZ-S (Delay Modulation - Non Return to Zero - Space) | 314 | FAULT TOLERANCE | 185 |
| | | FCFS (First Come First Served) | 138 |
| | | FIFO (First In First Out) | 138 |
| DOUBLET | 14 | FLAG | 327 |
| DOWNWARD COMPATIBILITY | 54 | FLAT CABLES | 32, 225 |
| DRIVER | 36 | FLIP-FLOPS | 21 |
| DTE (Data Terminal Equipment) | 329 | FLOW | 42 |
| | | FM (Frequency Modulation) | 312 |
| DUAL FLIP-FLOP | 22 | FORMAL SPECIFICATION | 55 |
| DUPLEX | 329 | FORWARD CROSSTALK | 264 |
| DYNAMIC FLIP-FLOPS | 21 | FRAMING ERROR | 333 |
| | | FREE-SPACE | 27 |
| EARTH | 28 | FREQUENCY MULTIPLEX | 30 |
| ECL (Emitter Coupled Logic) | 16 | FSK (Frequency Shift Keying) | 312 |
| ECMA (European Computer Manufacturers Association) | 54 | FULL DUPLEX | 329 |
| | | FULL INTERLOCK | 64 |
| EDGE CONNECTORS | 34 | FULLY HANDSHAKEN | 64 |
| EDGE-TRIGGERED | 21, 22 | FUNCTIONAL DECOMPOSITION | 40 |
| EIA (Electronic Industry Association) | 54 | GATE | 18 |
| ELECTRICAL | 52 | GATEWAY | 273, 363 |
| EMI (Electro-Magnetic Interferences) | 28 | GCR (Group Code Recording) | 314 |
| | | GENERAL PURPOSE BUS | 272 |
| ENABLE/DISABLE | 179 | GENERATOR POLYNOMIAL | 206 |
| ENABLE/DISABLE PAIR | 179 | GEOGRAPHICAL | 106 |
| ENCODED CLOCK | 309 | GEOMETRIC | 105 |
| ENCODED DISTRIBUTED ARBITER | 151 | GRANT | 129 |
| | | GRANTED | 129 |
| ERROR | 183 | GROUND | 28 |
| ERROR CONTROL | 42 | GROUNDING | 28 |
| ERROR CORRECTING CODES | 193 | GUIDED TRANSMISSIONS | 27 |
| ERROR CORRECTION | 186 | | |
| ERROR DETECTION | 185 | HALF DUPLEX | 329 |
| ERROR RATE | 184 | HAMMING (n, k) CODES | 196 |
| EVEN PARITY BIT | 191 | HAMMING BITS | 195 |
| EXCLUSIVE ACCESS | 128 | HAMMING DISTANCE | 189 |
| EXPLICIT CLOCK | 308 | HAMMING WEIGHT | 189 |
| EXPLICIT MASTERSHIP TRANSFER | 133 | HANDSHAKE | 2, 63 |
| | | HANDSHAKEN | 63 |
| EXTENDED PROTOCOLS | 174 | HANDSHAKEN CYCLES | 63 |
| EYE DIAGRAM | 307 | HARDWARE ERROR | 184 |
| | | HDB3 (High Density Bipolar) | 311 |
| FAILURE | 183 | HDLC (High-level Data Link Control) | 327 |
| FAIR | 141 | | |
| FAIRNESS | 141 | HEXADECIMAL | 14 |

| | |
|---|---|
| HIGH | 5, 16, 59 |
| HORIZONTAL COMMUNICATION | 43 |
| HYSTERESIS | 38 |
| | |
| IA (Immediate Acknowledge) | 352 |
| IA5 (International Alphabet no 5) | 326 |
| ICs (Integrated Circuits) | 3 |
| IDU (Interface Data Units) | 47 |
| IEC (International Electrotechnical Committee) | 54 |
| IEEE (Institute of Electrical and Electronics Engineers) | 54 |
| IMPLEMENTATION SPECIFICATION | 55 |
| IMPLICIT CLOCK | 308 |
| INBOUND CABLE | 360 |
| INCOMPLETE | 105 |
| INDIRECT CONNECTORS | 34 |
| INDIVISIBLE | 123 |
| INDUCTIVE CROSSTALK | 261 |
| INFORMATION PATH | 58 |
| INPUT SYNCHRONIZATION | 154 |
| INPUT SYNCHRONIZER | 130 |
| INSTABLE STATE | 25 |
| INTERFACE | 43 |
| INTERFACE CONTROL | 43 |
| INTERFACE DATA | 43, 47 |
| INTERFERENCES | 28 |
| INTERRUPT | 2, 163 |
| INTERRUPT VECTOR | 167 |
| ISDN (Integrated Services Digital Network) | 357 |
| ISO (International Organization for Standardization) | 54 |
| $I^2C$ (Inter Integrated Circuits) | 323, 354 |
| | |
| J-K FLIP-FLOP | 22 |
| JUSTIFIED BUS | 292 |
| | |
| KILO (K) | 14 |
| | |
| LATCH | 21, 22 |
| LEGAL | 189 |
| LEVEL OF ABSTRACTION | 40 |
| LINEAR | 100 |
| LINEAR CAPACITANCE C' | 220 |
| LINEAR CONDUCTANCE G' | 220 |
| LINEAR DISTRIBUTED ARBITER | 148 |
| LINEAR INDUCTANCE L' | 220 |
| LINEAR RESISTANCE R' | 220 |
| LINEAR SELF-SELECTION NETWORK | 148 |
| LINES | 16, 59 |
| LINK | 58 |
| LITTLE ENDIAN | 295 |
| LOCKVARIABLE | 123 |
| LOGICAL SIGNALS | 15 |
| LOGICAL VARIABLES | 15 |
| LOSSES | 27 |
| LOW | 5, 16, 59 |
| LSB (Least Significant Bit) | 14 |
| LUMPED MODEL | 220 |
| | |
| MANCHESTER | 312 |
| MARK | 306 |
| MARK/SPACE | 310 |
| MASKING | 141 |
| MASTER | 10, 71 |
| MAU (Medium Attachement Unit) | 359 |
| MEGA (M) | 14 |
| MEMORY LOCATION | 14 |
| MERGED | 113 |
| MESSAGE | 14, 49 |
| METASTABLE STATE | 25 |
| MFM (Modified Frequency Modulation) | 314 |
| MICROCYCLE | 110 |
| MICROSTRIP | 226 |
| MILLER | 314 |
| MIXED ADDRESSING | 104 |
| MODULAR DECOMPOSITION | 40 |
| MODULATION | 305 |
| MODULATION SPEED (B) | 308 |
| MODULATOR | 306 |
| MOS (Metal Oxide Semiconductor) | 3 |
| MSB (Most Significant Bit) | 14 |
| MULTIDROP | 7 |
| MULTIPLE-MASTER BUS | 127 |
| MULTIPLEXED BUS | 117 |
| MULTIPLEXER | 20 |
| MULTIPOINT | 7 |
| $M^2$ (Modified Miller) | 314 |
| $M^2FM$ (Modified twice Frequency Modulation) | 314 |
| | |
| N-PARTNER | 174 |

# Index 413

| | | | |
|---|---|---|---|
| NEAR END | 209 | PEER ENTITIES | 42 |
| NEAR END CROSSTALK | 266 | PENETRATION COEFFICIENT | 234 |
| NEGATED | 15 | PERFECT CODES | 201 |
| NEGATIVE ACKNOWLEDGE | 186 | PERFECT MATCHING | 213 |
| NEGOTIATION | 42 | PERSISTENT ERRORS | 184 |
| NETWORK LAYER | 50 | PHYSICAL | 52 |
| NIBBLE | 14 | PHYSICAL LAYER | 48 |
| NON-PERSISTENT CSMA | 351 | PIPELINED | 123 |
| NOT | 18 | PIPO (Parallel-in Parallel-Out) | 24 |
| NOT ACTIVE | 15 | PISO (Parallel-In Serial-Out) | 24 |
| NRZ-L (Non Return to Zero - Level) | 309 | PLAs (Programmable Logic Arrays) | 17 |
| NRZ-M (Non Return to Zero - Mark) | 310 | POINT-TO-POINT | 7, 57 |
| | | POLLING | 166, 348 |
| NRZ-S (Non Return to Zero - Space) | 310 | POSITIVE ACKNOWLEDGE | 186 |
| | | POWER SPECTRUM | 316 |
| NRZI (Non Return to Zero Inverted) | 310 | p-PERSISTENT CSMA | 351 |
| | | PRESENTATION LAYER | 50 |
| NULL-DTE | 338 | PRIORITY | 139 |
| NULL-MODEM | 333 | PRIORITY ARBITER | 139 |
| | | PRIORITY ENCODER | 21 |
| OCCUPATION PHASE | 137 | PROMs (Programmable Read Only Memory) | 17 |
| OCCUPY | 137 | PROPAGATION DELAY | 27 |
| OCTUPLET | 14 | PROPAGATION TIME | 212 |
| ODD PARITY BIT | 191 | PROTOCOL | 3, 42, 46, 58 |
| OMNIDIRECTIONAL | 28 | PROTOCOL INFORMATION | 42 |
| ON/OFF | 310 | PULSE RATIO | 315 |
| OPEN COLLECTOR | 19 | | |
| OR | 18 | QUAD | 14 |
| OSI-RM (Open System Interconnection Reference Model) | 46 | QUADLET | 14 |
| | | QUADQUAD | 14 |
| OUTBOUND CABLE | 360 | | |
| OUTPUT SYNCHRONIZER | 131 | R-S FLIP-FLOP | 21 |
| | | RATE | 190 |
| PABX (Private Automatic Branch eXchange) | 357 | READ | 2, 69 |
| | | READ-AFTER-WRITE | 124 |
| PACKETS | 347 | READ-MODIFY-WRITE | 123 |
| PAD (Packet Assembly Disassembly) | 328 | READ-WRITE PROTOCOLS | 70 |
| | | READPULSE | 73 |
| PALs (Programmable Array Logic) | 17 | RECEIVER | 38, 305 |
| | | REDUNDANCY | 185 |
| PARALLEL BUS | 117 | REFLECTED | 212 |
| PARALLEL LINK | 6 | REFLECTION | 28 |
| PARALLEL REGISTERS | 22 | REFLECTION COEFFICIENT | 213 |
| PARALLEL TRANSFER | 117 | REGISTER | 14, 17 |
| PARITY | 191 | RELEASE ON DEMAND | 134 |
| PCM (Pulse Code Modulation) | 357 | REMODULATOR | 360 |
| PDU (Protocol Data Units) | 46 | REQUEST | 67, 129 |
| PEER DATA | 43 | REQUIREMENT SPECIFICATION | 55 |

| | |
|---|---|
| RESIDUAL ERROR RATE | 187 |
| RESISTIVE CROSSTALK | 261 |
| RESPONDER | 69, 305 |
| ROLEs | 69 |
| ROUND ROBIN | 133, 141 |
| RS-422/V11/X27 | 341 |
| RS-423/V10/X26 | 341 |
| RS-485/V12 | 342 |
| RZ (Return to Zero) | 310 |
| RxD (Receive Data) | 331 |
| SAP (Service Access Points) | 48 |
| SDLC (Synchronous Data Link Control) | 327 |
| SDU (Service Data Units) | 48 |
| SELECTION | 131 |
| SELF-CLOCKING | 307 |
| SEMI-SYNCHRONOUS | 85 |
| SEQUENTIAL | 160 |
| SEQUENTIAL TOKEN PASSING | 132 |
| SERIAL BUS | 117 |
| SERIAL LINKS | 6 |
| SERIAL TRANSFER | 117 |
| SERVICE | 42, 44 |
| SESSION ESTABLISHMENT | 42 |
| SESSION LAYER | 50 |
| SESSION TERMINATION | 42 |
| SEV (Schweizerischer Elektrotechniker Verein) | 54 |
| SHIELD | 28 |
| SHIFT REGISTERS | 23 |
| SIG | 16 |
| SIGNAL | 15, 58 |
| SIGNAL RETURN LINE | 28 |
| SIGNAL TO NOISE (S/N) | 308 |
| SIMPLEX | 329 |
| SIMSER (Simple Serial) | 325 |
| SINGLE ERROR CORRECTION | 193 |
| SINGLE ERROR CORRECTION AND DOUBLE ERROR DETECTION | 197 |
| SINGLE WIRE OVER GROUND | 226 |
| SINGLE-TRUNK | 360 |
| SIPO (Serial-In Parallel-Out) | 24 |
| SKEW | 276 |
| SKEWING | 61 |
| SKIN EFFECT | 219 |
| SLAVES | 10, 71 |
| SLOT TIME | 139 |
| SLOTTED ALOHA | 349 |
| SNA (Standard Network Architecture) | 357 |
| SOFTWARE ERROR | 184 |
| SOURCE | 58 |
| SOURCE-ACTIVATED | 64 |
| SOURCE DESKEWING | 61 |
| SPACE | 306 |
| SPECIFICATION | 55 |
| SPEED BY DISTANCE | 28 |
| SPLIT CYCLE | 173 |
| STANDARD | 56 |
| START BIT | 323 |
| STARVATION | 140 |
| STATE | 15, 17 |
| STATE DIAGRAM | 17 |
| STATE MACHINE | 24 |
| STATIC FLIP-FLOPS | 21 |
| STOP BIT | 323 |
| STRAIGHT BUS | 292 |
| STRICT PRIORITY | 134 |
| STRIPLINE | 228 |
| SUPERVISORS | 182 |
| SYMBOL | 188 |
| SYMBOL PERIOD | 308 |
| SYMBOL RATE | 308 |
| SYMMETRIC | 29 |
| SYNCHRONOUS | 63, 81 |
| SYNDROME | 194 |
| SYSTEM BUS | 2 |
| SYSTEMATIC CODE | 188 |
| S 5/8 (Serial 5V on 8 pins) | 344 |
| TAP | 27 |
| TERMINATOR | 36 |
| TERNARY | 37 |
| THEVENIN CIRCUIT | 259 |
| THREE-STATE | 20 |
| TIMEOUT | 141 |
| TIMING DIAGRAM | 17 |
| TOKEN | 131, 132, 349 |
| TOKEN PASSING | 131 |
| TOP HAT | 312 |
| TOPOLOGY | 8 |
| TRANSACTION | 49, 52, 343 |
| TRANSCEIVERS | 39 |
| TRANSIENT ERRORS | 184 |
| TRANSMISSION LINE | 35 |
| TRANSMISSION LINE THEORY | 209 |
| TRANSMISSION SPEED | 212 |
| TRANSMITTER | 36, 305 |

# Index

| | | | | |
|---|---|---|---|---|
| TRANSPORT LAYER | 50 | VALIDATION | 55 |
| TRANSPORT SERVICE | 42 | VERIFICATION | 55 |
| TRIPLET | 14 | VERTICAL COMMUNICATION | 43 |
| TRUE | 15, 59 | VOLATILE ERRORS | 184 |
| TTL (Transistor Transistor Logic) | 16 | VOLTAGE SOURCE TERMINATION | 259 |
| TWISTED PAIR | 29 | $V_{IH}$ (Voltage In High) | 16 |
| TWISTED WIRE | 225 | $V_{IL}$ (Voltage In Low) | 16 |
| TWO-PART CONNECTORS | 34 | | |
| TYPE | 69 | WIRED AND | 20 |
| TxD (Transmit Data) | 331 | WIRED OR | 20 |
| | | WIRED-OR GLITCH | 238 |
| | | WORD | 14 |
| UART (Universal Asynchronous Receiver-Transmitter) | 331 | WRAPPED | 50 |
| | | WRITE | 2, 69 |
| UPWARD COMPATIBILITY | 54 | WRITEPULSE | 73 |
| USER DATA | 42 | | |
| | | XOR | 18 |
| V28 | 341 | | |
| VALID | 189 | ZERO INSERTION | 327 |